Fodor's 96
The South

" "When it comes to information on regional history, what to see and do, and shopping, these guides are exhaustive."

—*USAir Magazine*

"Usable, sophisticated restaurant coverage, with an emphasis on good value."

—Andy Birsh, *Gourmet Magazine* columnist

"Valuable because of their comprehensiveness."

—*Minneapolis Star-Tribune*

"Fodor's always delivers high quality...thoughtfully presented...thorough."

—*Houston Post*

"An excellent choice for those who want everything under one cover."

—*Washington Post* **"**

Fodor's Travel Publications, Inc.
New York • Toronto • London • Sydney • Auckland

Fodor's The South

Editor: Melissa Rivers

Editorial Contributors: Steven K. Amsterdam, Janet Clark, Andrew Collins, Suzanne DeGalan, Mitzi Gammon, Kevin Garrett, Wayne Greenhaw, Sylvia Higginbotham, Ann Hughes, Susan Ladd, Bevin McLaughlin, Honey Naylor, William Schemmel, Mary Ellen Schultz, Carol L. Timblin

Creative Director: Fabrizio La Rocca

Cartographer: David Lindroth

Cover Photograph: Everett Johnson/Southern Stock

Text Design: Between the Covers

Copyright

Special Sales

Fodor's Travel Publications are available at special discounts for bulk purchases for sales promotions or premiums. Special editions, including personalized covers, excerpts of existing guides, and corporate imprints, can be created in large quantities for special needs. For more information, contact your local bookseller or write to Special Markets, Fodor's Travel Publications, 201 East 50th Street, New York, NY 10022. Inquiries from Canada should be directed to your local Canadian bookseller or sent to Random House of Canada, Ltd., Marketing Department, 1265 Aerowood Drive, Mississauga, Ontario L4W 1B9. Inquiries from the United Kingdom should be sent to Fodor's Travel Publications, 20 Vauxhall Bridge Road, London SW1V 2SA, England.

PRINTED IN THE UNITED STATES OF AMERICA

10 9 8 7 6 5 4 3 2 1

CONTENTS

Maps

ON THE ROAD WITH FODOR'S

A GOOD TRAVEL GUIDE is like a wonderful traveling companion. It's charming, it's brimming with sound recommendations and solid ideas, it pulls no punches in describing lodging and dining establishments, and it's consistently full of fascinating facts that make you view what you've traveled to see in a new light. In the creation of *The South '96,* we at Fodor's have gone to great lengths to provide you with the very best of all possible traveling companions— and, by extension, to make your trip the best of all possible vacations.

About Our Writers

The information in these pages is a collaboration of a whole roster of extraordinary writers.

Mark Beffart has experienced the enormous growth of Atlanta firsthand, having moved here from Alabama in February 1978. Self-employed as a writer since 1979, he is the author of *France on the TGV, Paris for Free (Or Extremely Cheap), Walking Tours of France, Citypack Atlanta,* and over 200 feature magazine articles about art, business, health, and travel topics.

Since 1992, **Jane Schneider** has been chasing the ideal food-and-wine match for readers of the *Atlanta Journal-Constitution,* for whom she writes a column on the subject. She has coauthored a residents' guide to Atlanta, a city in which she has nibbled and sipped for more than 25 years. A former magazine editor and college professor, she now enjoys travel, reading, and writing about Georgia history, hiking, white-water rafting, and a host of other salubrious pursuits.

Born to a Creole–Acadian mother with an affinity for cooking, it's no surprise that **Gene Bourg** maintains an acute interest in the unique cuisines of New Orleans. "Eating Out" columnist for the *Times-Picayune* from 1985–94, he is currently a freelance food writer and host of *News You Can Eat,* a weekly program on New Orleans radio station WBYU. He adds his insight to our New Orleans dining reviews.

South Carolina is the bailiwick of **Patricia Cheatham,** who also contributes to Fodor's USA guide. In her fantasy of fantasies, she tells us, she reclines on a Pawleys Island hammock on the veranda of her 14,000-acre Georgetown County rice plantation, proving her theory that re-introduction of indigo cultivation bodes well for the cure of the common cold.

Susan Ladd, a lifetime resident of North Carolina, covers travel for the *News & Record* in Greensboro, North Carolina, and has updated the North Carolina chapters of this and other Fodor's guides. She travels regularly to far-flung locales like Micronesia, but like Dorothy, believes that there's no place like home.

The introduction to *The South* and the Louisiana chapter were written by gregarious **Honey Naylor,** a Louisiana native whose checkered past includes her own piano/accordion radio show at age 15; a stint teaching ballroom dancing; and an array of entertainment jobs (acting, dancing, and playing piano in a piano bar). This longtime resident of New York began her writing career 10 years ago after returning to live in New Orleans . . . she just couldn't keep her enlightened observations bottled up, so we gave her an outlet back then and have been thoroughly entertained by her lively writing ever since.

Patti Nickell was born and raised in the South and considers herself a "New Age southern belle," as knowledgeable about Alabama football and Kentucky basketball as she is about the antebellum architecture of Natchez and the Creole cuisine of New Orleans. A freelance writer based in Louisiana, she updated the Mississippi and Tennessee chapters of this book.

Dick Pivetz, a Montgomery-based travel columnist, is a familiar figure throughout the Heart of Dixie, pounding his beat in search of intriguing places; hidden gems; and tasty grits, corn bread, and barbecue to focus on in his weekly column in the *Montgomery Advertiser.* He updated the Alabama chapter, so you're in good hands.

Editing this book brought back fond memories of all the glorious food **Melissa Rivers** indulged in as a teenager growing up in the South (specifically Memphis, Tennessee). She fine-toothed the dining sections, expanding and defining as needed, working with local critics to bring you the latest "in" places . . . just reading the reviews should make you salivate.

What's New

A New Design

If this is not the first Fodor's guide you've purchased, you'll immediately notice our new look. More readable and easier to use than ever? We think so—and we hope you do, too.

Let Us Do Your Booking

Our writers have scoured the South to come up with an extensive and well-balanced list of the best B&Bs, inns, and hotels, both small and large, new and old. But you don't have to beat the bushes to come up with a reservation. Now we've teamed up with an established hotel-booking service to make it easy for you to secure a room at the property of your choice. It's fast, it's free, and confirmation is guaranteed. If your first choice is booked, the operators can line up your second right away. Just call 800/FODORS–1 (or 800/363–6771 (0800/89–1030 when in Great Britain; 800/55–9101 when in Ireland; and 0014/800-12-8271 when in Australia).

Travel Updates

In addition, just before your trip, you may want to order a Fodor's Worldview Travel Update. From local publications all over the South, the lively, cosmopolitan editors at Worldview gather information on concerts, plays, opera, dance performances, gallery and museum shows, sports competitions, and other special events that coincide with your visit. See the order blank at the back of this book, call 800/799–9609, or fax 800/799–9619.

And In The South

Last year was the 25th anniversary of the **U.S. Space and Rocket Center** in Huntsville, Alabama, and as a result of the celebration, new additions like "Journey to Jupiter" (a 20-minute ride in a cargo pod) join other interactive exhibits including a space station mock-up and simulated space walk.

Atlanta, Georgia, hosts the **1996 Olympic Games** and, after spending several hundred million dollars, the city is fully geared up to be inundated by visitors this year. Around 11 million tickets went on sale for the various events, so things should really be jumping in Atlanta. Many of the new facilities built for the games—the 85,000 seat Olympic Stadium, the Velodrome and Oympic Village on the Georgia Tech campus—will become venues for sports and other entertainment options following the games.

In Louisiana, work finally began on **Harrah's Casino New Orleans**, an $800 million, 250,000 square-foot facility slated to be the "world's largest casino." There are also plans for additional riverboat casinos to join the ranks already afloat, making New Orleans the land of plenty for gambling enthusiasts. Spurred by the convention center expansion project, 18 new hotel developments were open, underway, or announced in 1995, so the number of rooms available in New Orleans continues to grow. The U.S. Congress has approved legislation for the **Cane River Heritage Park** in the Natchitoches area. Details on the $14 million project have not yet been announced, but the park will probably encompass all of Oakland Plantation and the outbuildings of Magnolia Plantation.

In Winston-Salem, North Carolina, the **Museum of Early Southern Decorative Arts** plans to open a new discovery center this year. Big things are also expected at the **North Carolina Zoological Park** in Asheboro, which should complete its large North American exhibit this year; polar bears, grizzly bears, and a large stream-side exhibit are just a few of the new attractions planned. With a new convention center, two pro sports teams and new attractions underway, Charlotte's reputation is soaring. The Carolina Panthers, the state's new NFL team, should move into its new stadium in downtown Charlotte in 1996, while the Charlotte Hornets, one of the newest NBA franchises, continue to create a buzz throughout the state.

The 350-acre, $250 million **Broadway at the Beach,** South Carolina's newest entertainment complex at Myrtle Beach, got underway in the summer of 1995 with the opening of the Carolina Place Theater.

Other theaters, restaurants, shops, and entertainment options—a nightclub district, an amusement area, a miniature golf course, and the Coastal Aquarium of the Carolinas—are planned.

How To Use This Book

Organization

Up front is the **Gold Guide,** comprising two sections on gold paper that are chock-full of information about traveling within your destination and traveling in general. Both are in alphabetical order by topic. **Important Contacts A to Z** gives addresses and telephone numbers of organizations and companies that offer destination-related services and detailed information or publications. Here's where you'll find information about how to to get to the South from wherever you are. **Smart Travel Tips A to Z,** the Gold Guide's second section, gives specific tips on how to get the most out of your travels, as well as information on how to accomplish what you need to in the South.

Chapters in *The South* are arranged alphabetically. Each chapter covers exploring, shopping, sports, dining, lodging, and arts and nightlife and ends with a section called Essentials, which tells you how to get there and get around and gives you important local addresses and telephone numbers.

Stars

Stars in the margin are used to denote highly recommended sights, attractions, hotels, and restaurants.

Restaurant and Hotel Criteria and Price Categories

Restaurants and lodging places are chosen with a view to giving you the cream of the crop in each location and in each price range.

In all restaurant price charts, costs are per person, excluding drinks, tip, and tax. In hotel price charts, rates are for standard double rooms, excluding city and state sales taxes.

Hotel Facilities

Note that in general you incur charges when you use many hotel facilities. We wanted to let you know what facilities a hotel has to offer, but we don't always specify whether or not there's a charge, so when planning a vacation that entails a stay of several days, it's wise to ask what's included in the rate.

Dress Code in Restaurants

In general, we note a dress code only when men are required to wear a jacket or a jacket and tie.

Credit Cards

Thee following abreviations are used: **AE,** American Express; **D,** Discover; **DC,** Diners Club; **MC,** MasterCard; and **V,** Visa.

Please Write to Us

Everyone who has contributed to *The South '96* has worked hard to make the text accurate. All prices and opening times are based on information supplied to us at press time, and the publisher cannot accept responsibility for any errors that may have occurred. The passage of time will bring changes, so it's always a good idea to call ahead and confirm information when it matters—particularly if you're making a detour to visit specific sights or attractions. When making reservations at a hotel or inn, be sure to speak up if you have a disability or are traveling with children, if you prefer a private bath or a certain type of bed, or if you have specific dietary needs or any other concerns.

Were the restaurants we recommended as described? Did our hotel picks exceed your expectations? Did you find a museum we recommended a waste of time? We would love your feedback, positive and negative. If you have complaints, we'll look into them and revise our entries when the facts warrant it. If you've happened upon a special place that we haven't included, we'll pass the information along to the writers so they can check it out. So please send us a letter or postcard (we're at 201 East 50th Street, New York, NY 10022). We'll look forward to hearing from you. And in the meantime, have a wonderful trip!

Karen Cure
Editorial Director

The South

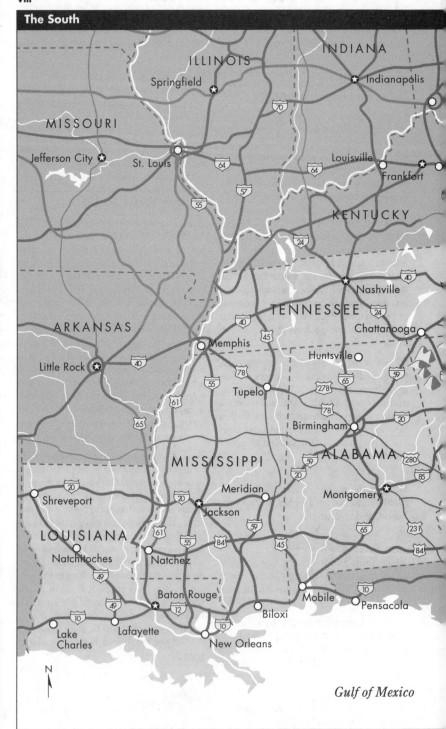

Gulf of Mexico

The United States

World Time Zones

Numbers below vertical bands relate each zone to Greenwich Mean Time (0 hrs.).
Local times frequently differ from these general indications,
as indicated by light-face numbers on map.

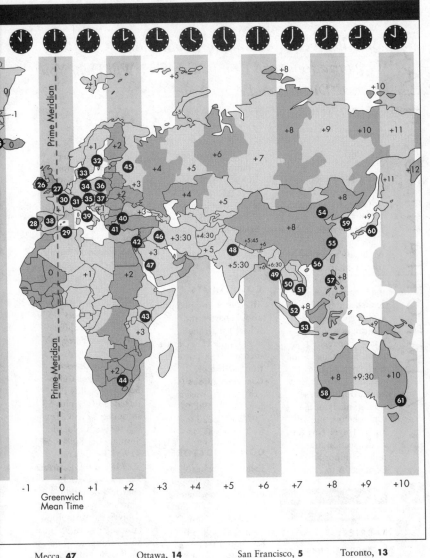

THE GOLD GUIDE / IMPORTANT CONTACTS

IMPORTANT CONTACTS A TO Z

An Alphabetical Listing of Publications, Organizations, and Companies That Will Help You Before, During, and After Your Trip

No single travel resource can give you every detail about every topic that might interest or concern you at the various stages of your journey—when you're planning your trip, while you're on the road, and after you get back home. The following organizations, books, and brochures will supplement the information in *The South.* For related information, including both basic tips on visiting the South and background information on many of the topics below, study Smart Travel Tips A to Z, the section that follows Important Contacts A to Z.

A

AIR TRAVEL

CARRIERS

For information on airports and major airlines serving the South, *see* individual state chapters.

For inexpensive, no-frills flights, contact **Branson Airlines** (☎ 800/422–4247), **Southwest Airlines** (☎ 800/444–5660), and **ValuJet** (☎ 404/994–8258 or 800/825–8538).

Major airlines fly from the United Kingdom to most Southern cities,

including **American Airlines** (☎ 0345/789789), **British Airways** (☎ 0181/897–4000), **Continental Airlines** (☎ 0800/776464), **Delta Airlines** (☎ 0800/414767), and **TWA** (☎ 0800/222–222).

COMPLAINTS

To register complaints about charter and scheduled airlines, contact the U.S. Department of Transportation's **Office of Consumer Affairs** (400 7th St. NW, Washington, DC 20590, ☎ 202/366–2220 or 800/322–7873).

CONSOLIDATORS

Established consolidators selling to the public include **Euram Tours** (1522 K St. NW, Suite 430, Washington, DC 20005, ☎ 800/848–6789) and **TFI Tours International** (34 W. 32nd St., New York, NY 10001, ☎ 212/736–1140 or 800/745–8000).

PUBLICATIONS

For general information about charter carriers, ask for the Office of Consumer Affairs' brochure **"Plane Talk: Public Charter Flights."** The Department of Transportation also publishes a 58-page booklet, **"Fly Rights"**

($1.75; Consumer Information Center, Dept. 133B, Pueblo, CO 81009).

For other tips and hints, consult the Consumers Union's monthly **"Consumer Reports Travel Letter"** ($39 a year; Box 53629, Boulder, CO 80322, ☎ 800/234–1970) and the newsletter **"Travel Smart"** ($37 a year; 40 Beechdale Rd., Dobbs Ferry, NY 10522, ☎ 800/327–3633); *The Official Frequent Flyer Guidebook,* by Randy Petersen ($14.99 plus $3 shipping; 4715-C Town Center Dr., Colorado Springs, CO 80916, ☎ 719/597–8899 or 800/487–8893); *Airfare Secrets Exposed,* by Sharon Tyler and Matthew Wonder (Universal Information Publishing; $16.95 plus $3.75 shipping from Sandcastle Publishing, Box 3070-A, South Pasadena, CA 91031, ☎ 213/255–3616 or 800/655–0053); and *202 Tips Even the Best Business Travelers May Not Know,* by Christopher McGinnis ($10 plus $3.00 shipping; Irwin Professional Publishing, Box 52927, Atlanta, GA 30355, ☎ 708/789–4000 or 800/634–3966).

B

BETTER BUSINESS BUREAU

For local contacts, consult the **Council of Better Business Bureaus** (4200 Wilson Blvd., Arlington, VA 22203, ☎ 703/276–0100).

C

CAR RENTAL

Major car-rental companies represented in the South include **Alamo** (☎ 800/327–9633, 0800/272–2000 in the U.K.), **Avis** (☎ 800/331–1212, 800/879–2847 in Canada), **Budget** (☎ 800/527–0700, 0800/181–181 in the U.K.), **Hertz** (☎ 800/654–3131, 800/263–0600 in Canada, 0181/679–1799 in the U.K.), and **National** (☎ 800/227–7368, 0181/950–5050 in the U.K., where it is known as Europcar).

CHILDREN AND TRAVEL

FLYING

Look into **"Flying With Baby"** ($5.95 plus $1 shipping; Third Street Press, Box 261250, Littleton, CO 80126, ☎ 303/595–5959), cowritten by a flight attendant. **"Kids and Teens in Flight,"** free from the U.S. Department of Transportation's Office of Consumer Affairs, offers tips for children flying alone. Every two years the February issue of *Family Travel Times* (*see* Know-How, *below*) details children's services on three dozen airlines.

KNOW-HOW

Family Travel Times, published 10 times a year by Travel With Your Children (TWYCH, 45 W. 18th St., New York, NY 10011, ☎ 212/206–0688; annual subscription $55), covers destinations, types of vacations, and modes of travel.

The *Family Travel Guides* catalogue ($1 postage; ☎ 510/527–5849) lists about 200 books and articles on family travel. Also check *Take Your Baby and Go! A Guide for Traveling with Babies, Toddlers and Young Children,* by Sheri Andrews, Judy Bordeaux, and Vivian Vasquez ($5.95 plus $1.50 shipping; Bear Creek Publications, 2507 Minor Ave., Seattle, WA 98102, ☎ 206/322–7604 or 800/326–6566). *The 100 Best Family Resorts in North America,* by Jane Wilford with Janet Tice ($12.95), and the two-volume *50 Great Family Vacations in North America* ($18.95 per volume), both from Globe Pequot Press (plus $3 shipping; Box 833, 6 Business Park Rd., Old Saybrook, CT 06475, ☎ 203/395–0440 or 800/243–0495, 800/962–0973 in CT) help plan your trip with children, from toddlers to teens.

LOCAL INFORMATION

Publications filled with events listings, resources, and advice for parents include *Atlanta Parent* (4330 Georgetown Sq., Suite 506, Atlanta, GA 30338, ☎ 404/454–7599), which regularly features a "Family Calendar" of events that's especially for visiting families. It's available free at area libraries, supermarkets, and museums, or by mail for a small fee.

CUSTOMS

CANADIANS

Contact **Revenue Canada** (2265 St. Laurent Blvd. S, Ottawa, Ontario K1G 4K3, ☎ 613/993–0534) for a copy of the free brochure **"I Declare/Je Déclare"** and for details on duties that exceed the standard duty-free limit.

U.K. CITIZENS

HM Customs and Excise (Dorset House, Stamford St., London SE1 9NG, ☎ 0171/202–4227) can answer questions about U.K. customs regulations and publishes **"A Guide for Travellers,"** detailing standard procedures and import rules.

D

FOR TRAVELERS WITH DISABILITIES

COMPLAINTS

To register complaints under the provisions of the Americans With Disabilities Act, contact the U.S. Department of Justice's **Public Access Section** (Box 66738, Washington, DC 20035, ☎ 202/514–0301, FAX 202/307–1198, TDD 202/514–0383).

ORGANIZATIONS

FOR TRAVELERS WITH HEARING

IMPAIRMENTS➤ Contact the **American Academy of Otolaryngology** (1 Prince St., Alexandria, VA 22314, ☎ 703/836–4444, FAX 703/683–5100, TTY 703/519–1585).

FOR TRAVELERS WITH MOBILITY PROBLEMS➤ Contact the **Information Center for Individuals with Disabilities** (Fort Point Pl., 27–43 Wormwood St., Boston, MA 02210, ☎ 617/727–5540, 800/462–5015 in MA, TTY 617/345–9743); **Mobility International USA** (Box 10767, Eugene, OR 97440, ☎ and TTY 503/343–1284, FAX 503/343–6812), the U.S. branch of an international organization headquartered in Belgium (*see below*) that has affiliates in 30 countries; **MossRehab Hospital Travel Information Service** (1200 W. Tabor Rd., Philadelphia, PA 19141, ☎ 215/456–9603, TTY 215/456–9602); the **Society for the Advancement of Travel for the Handicapped** (347 5th Ave., Suite 610, New York, NY 10016, ☎ 212/447–7284, FAX 212/725–8253); the **Travel Industry and Disabled Exchange** (TIDE, 5435 Donna Ave., Tarzana, CA 91356, ☎ 818/344–3640, FAX 818/344–0078); and **Travelin' Talk** (Box 3534, Clarksville, TN 37043, ☎ 615/552–6670, FAX 615/552–1182).

FOR TRAVELERS WITH VISION IMPAIRMENTS➤ Contact the **American Council of the Blind** (1155 15th St. NW,

Suite 720, Washington, DC 20005, ☎ 202/467–5081, FAX 202/467–5085) or the **American Foundation for the Blind** (15 W. 16th St., New York, NY 10011, ☎ 212/620–2000, TTY 212/620–2158).

IN THE U.K.

Contact the **Royal Association for Disability and Rehabilitation** (RADAR, 12 City Forum, 250 City Rd., London EC1V 8AF, ☎ 0171/250–3222) or **Mobility International** (Rue de Manchester 25, B1070 Brussels, Belgium, ☎ 00–322–410–6297), an international clearinghouse of travel information for people with disabilities.

PUBLICATIONS

Several free publications are available from the U.S. Information Center (Box 100, Pueblo, CO 81009, ☎ 719/948–3334): **"New Horizons for the Air Traveler with a Disability"** (address to Dept. 355A), describing legally mandated changes; the pocket-size **"Fly Smart"** (Dept. 575B), good on flight safety; and the Airport Operators Council's worldwide **"Access Travel: Airports"** (Dept. 575A).

Fodor's *Great American Vacations for Travelers with Disabilities* ($18; available in bookstores, or call 800/533–6478) details accessible attractions, restaurants, and hotels in U.S. destinations. The 500-page *Travelin' Talk Directory* ($35; Box 3534, Clarksville, TN 37043,

☎ 615/552–6670) lists people and organizations who help travelers with disabilities. For specialist travel agents worldwide, consult the *Directory of Travel Agencies for the Disabled* ($19.95 plus $2 shipping; Twin Peaks Press, Box 129, Vancouver, WA 98666, ☎ 206/694–2462 or 800/637–2256). The Sierra Club publishes *Easy Access to National Parks* ($16 plus $3 shipping; 730 Polk St., San Francisco, CA 94109, ☎ 415/776–2211 or 800/935–1056).

TRAVEL AGENCIES AND TOUR OPERATORS

The Americans with Disabilities Act requires that travel firms serve the needs of all travelers. However, some agencies and operators specialize in making group and individual arrangements for travelers with disabilities, among them **Access Adventures** (206 Chestnut Ridge Rd., Rochester, NY 14624, ☎ 716/889–9096), run by a former physical-rehab counselor. In addition, many general-interest operators and agencies (*see* Tour Operators, *below*) can also arrange vacations for travelers with disabilities.

FOR TRAVELERS WITH HEARING IMPAIRMENTS➤ One agency is **International Express** (7319-B Baltimore Ave., College Park, MD 20740, ☎ and TDD 301/699–8836, FAX 301/699–8836), which arranges group and independent trips.

FOR TRAVELERS WITH MOBILITY IMPAIRMENTS➤ A number of operators specialize in working with travelers with mobility impairments: **Hinsdale Travel Service** (201 E. Ogden Ave., Suite 100, Hinsdale, IL 60521, ☎ 708/325–1335 or 800/303–5521), a travel agency that will give you access to the services of wheelchair traveler Janice Perkins, and **Wheelchair Journeys** (16979 Redmond Way, Redmond, WA 98052, ☎ 206/885–2210), which can handle arrangements worldwide.

FOR TRAVELERS WITH DEVELOPMENTAL DISABILITIES➤ Contact the nonprofit **New Directions** (5276 Hollister Ave., Suite 207, Santa Barbara, CA 93111, ☎ 805/967–2841).

DISCOUNTS

Options include **Entertainment Travel Editions** (fee $28–$53, depending on destination; Box 1068, Trumbull, CT 06611, ☎ 800/445–4137), **Great American Traveler** ($49.95 annually; Box 27965, Salt Lake City, UT 84127, ☎ 800/548–2812), **Moment's Notice Discount Travel Club** ($25 annually, single or family; 163 Amsterdam Ave., Suite 137, New York, NY 10023, ☎ 212/486–0500), **Privilege Card** ($74.95 annually; 3391 Peachtree Rd. NE, Suite 110, Atlanta, GA 30326, ☎ 404/262–0222 or 800/236-9732), **Travelers**

Advantage ($49 annually, single or family; CUC Travel Service, 49 Music Sq. W, Nashville, TN 37203, ☎ 800/548–1116 or 800/648–4037), and **Worldwide Discount Travel Club** ($50 annually for family, $40 single; 1674 Meridian Ave., Miami Beach, FL 33139, ☎ 305/534–2082).

G

GAY AND LESBIAN TRAVEL

ORGANIZATION

The **International Gay Travel Association** (Box 4974, Key West, FL 33041, ☎ 800/448–8550), a consortium of 800 businesses, can supply names of travel agents and tour operators.

PUBLICATIONS

The premier international travel magazine for gays and lesbians is **Our World** ($35 for 10 issues; 1104 N. Nova Rd., Suite 251, Daytona Beach, FL 32117, ☎ 904/441–5367). The 16-page monthly **"Out & About"** ($49 for 10 issues; ☎ 212/645–6922 or 800/929–2268), covers gay-friendly resorts, hotels, cruise lines, and airlines.

TOUR OPERATORS

Toto Tours (1326 W. Albion, Suite 3W, Chicago, IL 60626, ☎ 312/274–8686 or 800/565–1241) has group tours worldwide.

TRAVEL AGENCIES

The largest agencies serving gay travelers are **Advance Travel** (10700

Northwest Freeway, Suite 160, Houston, TX 77092, ☎ 713/682–2002 or 800/695–0880), **Islanders/Kennedy Travel** (183 W. 10th St., New York, NY 10014, ☎ 212/242–3222 or 800/988–1181), **Now Voyager** (4406 18th St., San Francisco, CA 94114, ☎ 415/626–1169 or 800/255–6951), and **Yellowbrick Road** (1500 W. Balmoral Ave., Chicago, IL 60640, ☎ 312/561–1800 or 800/642–2488). **Skylink Women's Travel** (746 Ashland Ave., Santa Monica, CA 90405, ☎ 310/452–0506 or 800/225-5759) works with lesbians.

I

INSURANCE

Travel insurance covering baggage, health, and trip cancellation or interruptions is available from **Access America** (Box 90315, Richmond, VA 23286, ☎ 804/285–3300 or 800/284–8300), **Carefree Travel Insurance** (Box 9366, 100 Garden City Plaza, Garden City, NY 11530, ☎ 516/294–0220 or 800/323–3149), **Near Travel Services** (Box 1339, Calumet City, IL 60409, ☎ 708/868–6700 or 800/654–6700), **Tele-Trip** (Mutual of Omaha Plaza, Box 31716, Omaha, NE 68131, ☎ 800/228–9792), **Travel Insured International** (Box 280568, East Hartford, CT 06128-0568, ☎ 203/528–7663 or 800/243–3174), **Travel Guard International** (1145 Clark St., Stevens

THE GOLD GUIDE / IMPORTANT CONTACTS

Point, WI 54481, ☎ 715/345–0505 or 800/826–1300), and **Wallach & Company** (107 W. Federal St., Box 480, Middleburg, VA 22117, ☎ 703/687–3166 or 800/237–6615).

IN THE U.K.

The **Association of British Insurers** (51 Gresham St., London EC2V 7HQ, ☎ 0171/600–3333; 30 Gordon St., Glasgow G1 3PU, ☎ 0141/226–3905; Scottish Provident Bldg., Donegall Sq. W., Belfast BT1 6JE, ☎ 01232/249176; call for other locations) gives advice by phone and publishes the free **"Holiday Insurance,"** which sets out typical policy provisions and costs.

L
LODGING

APARTMENT AND VILLA RENTAL

Members of the travel club **Hideaways International** ($99 annually; 767 Islington St., Portsmouth, NH 03801, ☎ 603/430–4433 or 800/843–4433) receive two annual guides plus quarterly newsletters, and arrange rentals among themselves.

HOME EXCHANGE

Principal clearinghouses include **Intervac International** ($65 annually; Box 590504, San Francisco, CA 94159, ☎ 415/435–3497), which has three annual directories; and **Loan-a-Home** ($35–$45 annually; 2 Park La., Apt. 6E, Mount Vernon, NY 10552-3443, ☎ 914/664–7640),

which specializes in long-term exchanges.

M
MONEY MATTERS

ATMS

For specific **Cirrus** locations in the United States and Canada, call 800/424–7787. For U.S. **Plus** locations, call 800/843–7587 and enter the area code and first three digits of the number you're calling from (or of the calling area where you want an ATM).

WIRING FUNDS

Funds can be wired via **American Express MoneyGram**^{SM} (☎ 800/926–9400 from the U.S. and Canada for locations and information) or **Western Union** (☎ 800/325–6000 for agent locations or to send using MasterCard or Visa, 800/321–2923 in Canada).

O
THE OLYMPIC GAMES

The Olympic Games will be held in Atlanta, Georgia, July 19–August 4, 1996. Tickets for Olympic events went on sale by mail order in spring 1995. They range in price from $6 to $250 for sporting events, but about 95% of them will sell for less than $75; tickets for opening and closing ceremonies will run between $200–$600. All tickets include local transit on bus and rapid rail. Phone orders will be accepted starting February 1, 1996; however, the telephone numbers had not been

released at press time. For further information, dial 404/744–1996 for automated ticket information or contact the **Atlanta Committee for the Olympic Games** (ACOG, Box 1996, Atlanta, GA 30301, ☎ 404/224–1996, FAX 404/224–1993).

P
PASSPORTS AND VISAS

U.K. CITIZENS

For fees, documentation requirements, and to get an emergency passport, call the **London passport office** (☎ 0171/271–3000). For visa information, call the **U.S. Embassy Visa Information Line** (☎ 0891/200–290; calls cost 49p per minute or 39p per minute cheap rate) or write the **U.S. Embassy Visa Branch** (5 Upper Grosvenor St., London W1A 2JB). If you live in Northern Ireland, write the **U.S. Consulate General** (Queen's House, Queen St., Belfast BTI 6EQ). In Scotland, apply to the consulate at 3 Regent Terrace, Edinburgh EH7 5BW.

PHOTO HELP

The **Kodak Information Center** (☎ 800/242–2424) answers consumer questions about film and photography.

S
SENIOR CITIZENS

EDUCATIONAL TRAVEL

The nonprofit **Elderhostel** (75 Federal St., 3rd Floor, Boston, MA 02110, ☎ 617/426–7788), for people 60 and older, has offered inexpensive study programs since 1975. The nearly 2,000 courses cover everything from marine science to Greek myths and cowboy poetry. Fees for programs in the United States and Canada, which usually last one week, run about $300, not including transportation.

ORGANIZATIONS

Contact the **American Association of Retired Persons** (AARP, 601 E St. NW, Washington, DC 20049, ☎ 202/434–2277; $8 per person or couple annually). Its Purchase Privilege Program gets members discounts on lodging, car rentals, and sightseeing, and the AARP Motoring Plan furnishes domestic trip-routing information and emergency road-service aid for an annual fee of $39.95 per person or couple ($59.95 for a premium version).

For other discounts on lodgings, car rentals, and other travel products, along with magazines and newsletters, contact the **National Council of Senior Citizens** (membership $12 annually; 1331 F St. NW, Washington, DC 20004, ☎ 202/347–8800) and **Mature Outlook** (subscription $9.95 annually; 6001 N. Clark St., Chicago, IL 60660, ☎ 312/465–6466 or 800/336–6330).

PUBLICATIONS

The 50+ Traveler's Guidebook: Where to Go, Where to Stay, What to Do, by Anita Williams and Merrimac Dillon ($12.95; St. Martin's Press, 175 5th Ave., New York, NY 10010, ☎ 212/674–5151 or 800/288–2131), offers many useful tips. **"The Mature Traveler"** ($29.95; Box 50400, Reno, NV 89513, ☎ 702/786-7419), a monthly newsletter, covers travel deals.

STUDENTS

GROUPS

Major tour operators include **Contiki Holidays** (300 Plaza Alicante, Suite 900, Garden Grove, CA 92640, ☎ 714/740–0808 or 800/466–0610).

HOSTELING

Contact **Hostelling International–American Youth Hostels** (733 15th St. NW, Suite 840, Washington, DC 20005, ☎ 202/783–6161) in the United States, **Hostelling International–Canada** (205 Catherine St., Suite 400, Ottawa, Ontario K2P 1C3, ☎ 613/237–7884) in Canada, and the **Youth Hostel Association of England and Wales** (Trevelyan House, 8 St. Stephen's Hill, St. Albans, Hertfordshire AL1 2DY, ☎ 01727/855215 and 01727/845047) in the United Kingdom. Membership ($25 in the U.S., C$26.75 in Canada, and £9 in the U.K.) gets you access to 5,000 hostels worldwide that charge $7–$20 nightly per person.

I.D. CARDS

To get discounts on transportation and admissions, get the International Student Identity Card (ISIC) if you're a bona fide student or the **International Youth Card** (IYC) if you're under 26. In the United States, the ISIC and IYC cards cost $16 each and include basic travel accident and illness coverage, plus a toll-free travel hot line. Apply through the Council on International Educational Exchange (*see* Organizations, *below*). Cards are available for $15 each in Canada from Travel Cuts (187 College St., Toronto, Ontario M5T 1P7, ☎ 416/979–2406 or 800/667–2887) and in the United Kingdom for £5 each at student unions and student travel companies.

ORGANIZATIONS

A major contact is the **Council on International Educational Exchange** (CIEE, 205 E. 42nd St., 16th Floor, New York, NY 10017, ☎ 212/661–1450) with locations in Boston (729 Boylston St., Boston, MA 02116, ☎ 617/266–1926), Miami (9100 S. Dadeland Blvd., Miami, FL 33156, ☎ 305/670–9261), Los Angeles (1093 Broxton Ave., Los Angeles, CA 90024, ☎ 310/208–3551), 43 college towns nationwide, and the United Kingdom (28A Poland St., London W1V 3DB, ☎ 0171/437–7767). Twice a year, it publishes *Student Travels* magazine. The CIEE's Council Travel Service offers domestic air passes for bargain travel within the United States and is the exclusive U.S.

agent for several student-discount cards.

Campus Connections (325 Chestnut St., Suite 1101, Philadelphia, PA 19106, ☎ 215/625–8585 or 800/428–3235) specializes in discounted accommodations and airfares for students. The **Educational Travel Centre** (438 N. Frances St., Madison, WI 53703, ☎ 608/256–5551) offers rail passes and low-cost airline tickets, mostly for flights departing from Chicago.

In Canada, also contact **Travel Cuts** (*see above*).

T
TOUR OPERATORS

Among the companies selling tours and packages to the South, the following have a proven reputation, are nationally known, and have plenty of options to choose from.

GROUP TOURS

For deluxe escorted tours of the South, contact **Maupintour** (Box 807, Lawrence, KS 66044, ☎ 800/255–4266 or 913/843–1211) and **Tauck Tours** (11 Wilton Rd., Westport, CT 06880, ☎ 800/468–2825 or 203/226–6911). Another operator falling between deluxe and first class is **Globus** (5301 South Federal Circle, Littleton, CO 80123, ☎ 800/221–0090 or 303/797–2800). In the first-class and tourist range, try **Collette Tours** (162 Middle Street, Pawtucket, RI 02860, ☎ 800/832–4656 or 401/728–3805), and

Mayflower Tours (1225 Warren Ave., Downers Grove, IL 60515, ☎ 708/960–3430 or 800/323–7604). For budget and tourist class programs, contact **Cosmos** (*see* Globus, *above*).

PACKAGES

Independent vacation packages are available from major tour operators and airlines. Contact **American Airlines Fly AAway Vacations** (☎ 800/321–2121), **Globetrotters** (139 Main St., Cambridge, MA 02142, ☎ 800/999–9696 or 617/621–9911), **Continental Airlines' Grand Destinations** (☎ 800/634–5555), **Delta Dream Vacations** (☎ 800/872–7786), **Certified Vacations** (Box 1525, Fort Lauderdale, FL 33302, ☎ 305/522–1414 or 800/233–7260), **United Vacations** (☎ 800/328–6877), **Kingdom Tours** (300 Market St., Kingston, PA 18704, ☎ 717/283–4241 or 800/872–8857), and **USAir Vacations** (☎ 800/455–0123). **Funjet Vacations,** based in Milwaukee, Wisconsin, and **Gogo Tours** in Ramsey, New Jersey, sell packages to the South only through travel agents.

FROM THE U.K.➤ Tour operators offering packages to the Southern states include **Jetsave** (Sussex House, London Rd., East Grinstead, West Sussex RH19 1LD, ☎ 01342/312033), **Key to America** (1–3 Station Rd., Ashford Middlesex, TW15 2UW, ☎ 01784/248777), **Pre-**

mier Holidays (Premier Travel Center, Westbrook, Milton Rd., Cambridge CB4 1YG, ☎ 01223/516–688), and **Trailfinders** (42–50 Earl's Court Rd., London W8 6FT, ☎ 0171/937–5400; 58 Deansgate, Manchester M3 2FF, ☎ 0161/839–6969).

ORGANIZATIONS

The **National Tour Association** (546 E. Main St., Lexington, KY 40508, ☎ 606/226–4444 or 800/682–8886) and **United States Tour Operators Association** (USTOA, 211 E. 51st St., Suite 12B, New York, NY 10022, ☎ 212/750–7371) can provide lists of member operators and information on booking tours.

PUBLICATIONS

Consult the brochure *"Worldwide Tour & Vacation Package Finder"* from the National Tour Association (*see above*) and the Better Business Bureau's **"Tips on Travel Packages"** (publication No. 24-195, $2; 4200 Wilson Blvd., Arlington, VA 22203).

TRAVEL AGENCIES

For names of reputable agencies in your area, contact the **American Society of Travel Agents** (1101 King St., Suite 200, Alexandria, VA 22314, ☎ 703/739–2782).

V

VISITOR

INFORMATION

Contact the **Alabama Bureau of Tourism and Travel** (401 Adams Ave., Box 4309, Montgomery, AL 36103, ☎ 334/242–4169 or 800/252–2262, FAX 334/264–7060), the **Georgia Department of Industry, Trade and Tourism** (Box 1776, Atlanta, GA 30301, ☎ 404/656–3590 or 800/847–4842, FAX 404/651–9063), the **Louisiana Office of Tourism** (Box 94291, Baton Rouge, LA 70804-9291, ☎ 504/342–8100 or 800/334–8626), the

Mississippi Division of Tourism (Box 1705, Ocean Springs, MS 39566, ☎ 601/359–3297 or 800/927–6378), the **North Carolina Division of Travel and Tourism** (430 N. Salisbury St., Raleigh, NC 27611, ☎ 919/733–4171 or 800/847–4862, FAX 919/733–8582), the **South Carolina Division of Tourism** (1205 Pendleton St., Box 71, Columbia, SC 29202, ☎ 803/734–0122, FAX 803/734–0133), and the **Tennessee Department of Tourism** (Box 23170, Nashville, TN 37202, ☎ 615/741–9001, FAX 615/741–7225).

IN THE U.K.

Contact the **United States Travel and Tourism Administration** (Box 1EN, London W1A 1EN, ☎ 0171/495–4466). For a free USA pack, write the USTTA at Box 170, Ashford, Kent TN24 0ZX. Enclose stamps worth £1.50.

W

WEATHER

For current conditions and forecasts, plus the local time and helpful travel tips, call the **Weather Channel Connection** (☎ 900/932–8437; 95¢ per minute) from a touch-tone phone.

THE GOLD GUIDE / IMPORTANT CONTACTS

SMART TRAVEL TIPS A TO Z

Basic Information on Traveling in the South and Savvy Tips to Make Your Trip a Breeze

The more you travel, the more you know about how to make trips run like clockwork. To help make your travels hassle-free, Fodor's editors have rounded up dozens of tips from our contributors and travel experts all over the world, as well as basic information on visiting the South. For names of organizations to contact and publications that can give you more information, *see* Important Contacts A to Z, *above.*

A
AIR TRAVEL

If time is an issue, **always look for nonstop flights,** which require no change of plane and make no stops. If possible, **avoid connecting flights,** which stop at least once and can involve a change of plane, although the flight number remains the same; if the first leg is late, the second waits.

CUTTING COSTS

The Sunday travel section of most newspapers is a good source of deals.

MAJOR AIRLINES➤ The least-expensive airfares from the major airlines are priced for round-trip travel and are subject to restrictions.

You must usually **book in advance and buy the ticket within 24 hours** to get cheaper fares, and you may have to **stay over a Saturday night.** The lowest fare is subject to availability, and only a small percentage of the plane's total seats are sold at that price. It's good to **call a number of airlines—and when you are quoted a good price, book it on the spot**—the same fare on the same flight may not be available the next day. Airlines generally allow you to change your return date for a $25 to $50 fee, but most low-fare tickets are nonrefundable. However, if you don't use it, you can apply the cost toward the purchase price of a new ticket, again for a small charge.

CONSOLIDATORS➤ Consolidators, who buy tickets at reduced rates from scheduled airlines, sell them at prices below the lowest available from the airlines directly—usually without advance restrictions. Sometimes you can even get your money back if you need to return the ticket. Carefully read the fine print detailing penalties for changes and cancellations. If you doubt the reliability of a consol-

idator, **confirm your reservation with the airline.**

ALOFT

AIRLINE FOOD➤ If you hate airline food, **ask for special meals when booking.** These can be vegetarian, low cholesterol, or kosher, for example; commonly prepared to order in smaller quantities than standard catered fare, they can be tastier.

SMOKING➤ Smoking is banned on all flights within the United States of less than six hours' duration and on all Canadian flights; the ban also applies to domestic segments of international flights aboard U.S. and foreign carriers. Delta has banned smoking system-wide.

C
CAMERAS, CAMCORDERS, AND COMPUTERS

LAPTOPS

Before you depart, **check your portable computer's battery,** because you may be asked at security to turn on the computer to prove that it is what it appears to be. At the airport, you may prefer to **request a manual inspection,** although security X-rays do not harm hard-disk or floppy-disk storage.

PHOTOGRAPHY

If your camera is new or if you haven't used it for a while, **shoot and develop a few rolls of film** before you leave. Always **store film in a cool, dry place**—never in the car's glove compartment or on the shelf under the rear window.

Every pass through an X-ray machine increases film's chance of clouding. To protect it, carry it in a clear plastic bag and **ask for hand inspection at security.** Such requests are virtually always honored at U.S. airports. Don't depend on a lead-lined bag to protect film in checked luggage—the airline may increase the radiation to see what's inside.

VIDEO

Before your trip, **test your camcorder, invest in a skylight filter to protect the lens, and charge the batteries.** (Airport security personnel may ask you to turn on the camcorder to prove that it's what it appears to be.)

Videotape is not damaged by X-rays, but it may be harmed by the magnetic field of a walk-through metal detector, so **ask that videotapes be hand-checked.**

CHILDREN AND
TRAVEL

BABY-SITTING

For recommended local sitters, **check with your hotel desk.**

DRIVING

If you are renting a car, **arrange for a car seat when you reserve.** Sometimes they're free.

FLYING

On domestic flights, children under two not occupying a seat travel free, and older children currently travel on the "lowest applicable" adult fare.

BAGGAGE➤ In general, the adult baggage allowance applies for children paying half or more of the adult fare.

SAFETY SEATS➤ According to the Federal Aviation Administration (FAA), it's a good idea to **use safety seats aloft.** Airline policy varies. U.S. carriers allow FAA-approved models, but airlines usually require that you buy a ticket, even if your child would otherwise ride free, because the seats must be strapped into regular passenger seats.

FACILITIES➤ When making your reservation, **ask for children's meals or a freestanding bassinet** if you need them; the latter are available only to those with seats at the bulkhead, where there's enough legroom. If you don't need the bassinet, **think twice before requesting bulkhead seats**—the only storage for in-flight necessities is in the inconveniently distant overhead bins.

LODGING

Most hotels allow children under a certain age to stay in their parents' room at no extra charge, while others charge them as

extra adults; be sure to **ask about the cut-off age.**

CUSTOMS AND
DUTIES

IN THE SOUTH

British visitors age 21 or over may import the following into the United States: 200 cigarettes or 50 cigars or 2 kilograms of tobacco; 1 U.S. liter of alcohol; gifts to the value of $100. Restricted items include meat products, seeds, plants, and fruits. Never carry illegal drugs.

BACK HOME

IN CANADA➤ Once per calendar year, when you've been out of Canada for at least seven days, you may bring in C$300 worth of goods duty-free. If you've been away less than seven days but more than 48 hours, the duty-free exemption drops to C$100 but can be claimed any number of times (as can a C$20 duty-free exemption for absences of 24 hours or more). You cannot combine the yearly and 48-hour exemptions, use the C$300 exemption only partially (to save the balance for a later trip), or pool exemptions with family members. Goods claimed under the C$300 exemption may follow you by mail; those claimed under the lesser exemptions must accompany you.

Alcohol and tobacco products may be included in the yearly and 48-hour exemptions but not in the 24-hour exemption. If you meet the age requirements of the province through which you reenter Canada, you may bring in, duty-free, 1.14 liters (40 imperial ounces) of wine or liquor *or* 24 12-ounce cans or bottles of beer or ale. If you are 16 or older, you may bring in, duty-free, 200 cigarettes, 50 cigars or cigarillos, and 400 tobacco sticks or 400 grams of manufactured tobacco. Alcohol and tobacco must accompany you on your return.

An unlimited number of gifts valued up to C$60 each may be mailed to Canada duty-free. These do not count as part of your exemption. Label the package "Unsolicited Gift— Value under $60." Alcohol and tobacco are excluded.

IN THE U.K.➤ From countries outside the EU, including the United States, you may import duty-free 200 cigarettes, 100 cigarillos, 50 cigars or 250 grams of tobacco; 1 liter of spirits or 2 liters of fortified or sparkling wine; 2 liters of still table wine; 60 milliliters of perfume; 250 milliliters of toilet water; plus £136 worth of other goods, including gifts and souvenirs.

D

FOR TRAVELERS
WITH DISABILITIES

When discussing accessibility with an operator or reservationist, **ask hard questions.** Are there any stairs, inside *or* out? Are there grab bars next to the toilet *and* in the shower/tub? How wide is the doorway to the room? To the bathroom? For the most extensive facilities, meeting the latest legal specifications, **opt for newer facilities,** which more often have been designed with access in mind. Older properties must usually be retrofitted and may offer more limited facilities as a result. Be sure to **discuss your needs before booking.**

DISCOUNT CLUBS

Travel clubs offer members unsold space on airplanes, cruise ships, and package tours at as much as 50% below regular prices. Membership may include a regular bulletin or access to a toll-free hot line giving details of available trips departing from three or four days to several months in the future. Most also offer 50% discounts off hotel rack rates. Before booking with a club, **make sure the hotel or other supplier isn't offering a better deal.**

I

INSURANCE

Travel insurance can protect your investment, replace your luggage and its contents, or provide for medical coverage should you fall ill during your trip. Most tour operators, travel agents, and insurance agents sell specialized health-and-accident, flight, trip-cancellation, and luggage insurance as well as comprehensive policies with some or all of these features.

Before you make any purchase, **review your existing health and home-owner policies** to find out whether they cover expenses incurred while traveling.

BAGGAGE

Airline liability for your baggage is limited to $1,250 per person on domestic flights. On international flights, the airlines' liability is $9.07 per pound or $20 per kilogram for checked baggage (roughly $640 per 70-pound bag) and $400 per person for unchecked baggage. However, this excludes valuable items such as jewelry and cameras that are listed in your ticket's fine print. Insurance for losses exceeding the terms of your airline ticket be bought directly from the airline at check-in for about $10 per $1,000 of coverage, but first **see if your home-owner's policy covers lost luggage.**

FLIGHT

You should **think twice before buying flight insurance.** Often purchased as a last-minute impulse at the airport, it pays a lump sum when a plane crashes, either to a beneficiary if the insured dies or sometimes to a surviving passenger who loses eyesight or a limb. Supplementing the airlines' coverage described in the limits-of-liability paragraphs on your ticket, it's expensive and basically unnecessary. Charging an airline ticket to a major credit card often automatically entitles you to coverage and may also embrace travel by bus, train, and ship.

FOR U.K. TRAVELERS➤ According to the Association of British Insurers, a trade association representing 450 insurance companies, it's wise to **buy extra medical coverage when you visit the United States.** You can buy an annual travel-insurance policy valid for most vacations during the year in which it's purchased. If you go this route, make sure it covers you if you have a preexisting medical condition or are pregnant.

TRIP

Without insurance, you will lose all or most of your money if you must cancel your trip due to illness or any other reason. Especially if your airline ticket, cruise, or package tour is nonrefundable and cannot be changed, it's essential that you **buy trip-cancellation-and-interruption insurance.** When considering how much coverage you need, look for a policy that will cover the cost of your trip plus the nondiscounted price of a one-way airline ticket should you need to return home early. Read the fine print carefully, especially sections defining "family member" and "preexisting medical conditions." Also **consider default or bankruptcy insurance,** which protects you against a supplier's failure to deliver. However, such policies often do not cover default by a travel agency, tour operator, airline, or cruise line if you bought your tour and the coverage directly from the firm in question.

L
LODGING

APARTMENT AND VILLA RENTALS

If you want a home base that's roomy enough for a family and comes with cooking facilities, **consider a furnished rental.** It's generally cost-wise, too, although not always—some rentals are luxury properties (economical only when your party is large). Home-exchange directories do list rentals—often second homes owned by prospective house swappers—and some services search for a house or apartment for you (even a castle if that's your fancy) and handle the paperwork. Some send an illustrated catalogue and others send photographs of specific properties, sometimes at a charge; up-front registration fees may apply.

HOME EXCHANGE

If you would like to find a house, an apartment, or other vacation property to exchange for your own while on vacation, **become a member of a home-exchange organization,** which will send you its annual directories listing available exchanges and will include your own listing in at least one of them. Arrangements for the actual exchange are made by the two parties to it, not by the organization.

M
MONEY AND EXPENSES

ATMS

Chances are that you can **use your bank card at ATMs** to withdraw money from an account and get cash advances on a credit-card account if your card has been programmed with a personal identification number, or PIN. Before leaving home, **check in on frequency limits** for withdrawals and cash advances.

On cash advances you are charged interest from the day you receive the money from ATMs as well as from tellers. Transaction fees for ATM withdrawals outside your home turf may be higher than for withdrawals at home.

TRAVELER'S CHECKS

Whether or not to buy traveler's checks depends on where you are headed; **take cash to rural areas and small towns, traveler's checks to cities.** The most widely recognized are American Express, Citicorp, Thomas Cook, and Visa, which are sold by major commercial banks for 1% to 3% of the checks' face value—it pays to **shop around.** Both American Express and Thomas Cook issue checks that can be countersigned and used by you or your traveling companion. Record the numbers of the checks, cross them off as you spend them, and keep this information separate from your checks.

WIRING MONEY

You don't have to be a cardholder to send or receive funds through MoneyGram^{SM} from American Express. Just go to a MoneyGram agent, located in retail and convenience stores and in American Express Travel Offices. Pay up to $1,000 with cash or a credit card, anything over that in cash. The money can be picked up within 10 minutes in cash or check at the nearest MoneyGram agent. There's no limit, and the recipient need only present photo identification. The cost, which includes a free long-distance phone call, runs from 3% to 10%, depending on the amount sent, the destination, and how you pay.

You can also send money using Western Union. Money sent from the United States or Canada will be available for pickup at agent locations in 100 countries within 15 minutes. Once the money is in the system, it can be picked up at any one of 25,000 locations. Fees range from 4% to 10%, depending on the amount you send.

P
PACKAGES AND
TOURS

A package or tour to the South can make your vacation less expensive and more convenient. Firms that sell tours and packages purchase airline seats, hotel rooms, and rental cars in bulk and pass some of the savings on to you. In addition, the best operators have local representatives to help you out at your destination.

A GOOD DEAL?

The more your package or tour includes, the better you can predict the ultimate cost of your vacation. Make sure you know exactly what is included, and **beware of hidden costs.** Are taxes, tips, and service charges included? Transfers and baggage handling? Entertainment and excursions? These can add up.

Most packages and tours are rated deluxe, first-class superior, first class, tourist, and budget. The key difference is usually accommodations. If the package or tour you are considering is priced lower than in your wildest dreams, **be skeptical.** Also, **make sure your travel agent knows the hotels** and other services. Ask about location, room size, beds, and whether it has a pool, room service, or programs for children, if you care about these. Has your agent been there or sent others you can contact?

BUYER BEWARE

Each year consumers are stranded or lose their money when operators go out of business—even very large ones with excellent reputations. If you can't afford a loss, take the time to **check out** **the operator**—find out how long the company has been in business, and ask several agents about its reputation. Next, **don't book unless the firm has a consumer-protection program.** Members of the United States Tour Operators Association and the National Tour Association are required to set aside funds exclusively to cover your payments and travel arrangements in case of default. Nonmember operators may instead carry insurance; look for the details in the operator's brochure—and the name of an underwriter with a solid reputation. Note: When it comes to tour operators, **don't trust escrow accounts.** Although there are laws governing those of charter-flight operators, no governmental body prevents tour operators from raiding the till.

Next, **contact your local Better Business Bureau and the attorney general's office** in both your own state and the operator's; have any complaints been filed? Last, **pay with a major credit card.** Then you can cancel payment, provided that you can document your complaint. Always **consider trip-cancellation insurance** (*see* Insurance, *above*).

BIG VS. SMALL▷ An operator that handles several hundred thousand travelers annually can use its purchasing power to give you a good price. Its high volume may also indicate financial stability.

But some small companies provide more personalized service; because they tend to specialize, they may also be experts on an area.

USING AN AGENT

Travel agents are an excellent resource. In fact, large operators accept bookings only through travel agents. But it's good to **collect brochures from several agencies,** because some agents' suggestions may be skewed by promotional relationships with tour and package firms that reward them for volume sales. If you have a special interest, **find an agent with expertise in that area;** the American Society of Travel Agents can give you leads in the United States. (Don't rely solely on your agent, though; agents may be unaware of small niche operators, and some special-interest travel companies only sell direct.)

SINGLE TRAVELERS

Prices are usually quoted per person, based on two sharing a room. If traveling solo, you may be required to pay the full double-occupancy rate. Some operators eliminate this surcharge if you agree to be matched up with a roommate of the same sex, even if one is not found by departure time.

Much of the South has hot, humid summers and sunny, mild winters. For colder months,

pack a lightweight coat, slacks, and sweaters; you'll need heavier clothing in the more northern states, where cold, damp weather prevails and snow is not unusual. Keeping summer's humidity in mind, **pack absorbent natural fabrics that breathe;** bring an umbrella, but leave the plastic raincoat at home. You'll want a jacket or sweater for summer evenings and for too-cool air-conditioning. And **don't forget insect repellent.**

Bring an extra pair of eyeglasses or contact lenses in your carry-on luggage, and if you have a health problem, **pack enough medication** to last the trip. In case your bags go astray, **don't put prescription drugs or valuables in luggage to be checked.**

LUGGAGE

Free airline baggage allowances depend on the airline, the route, and the class of your ticket; ask in advance. In general, on domestic flights you are entitled to check two bags—neither exceeding 62 inches, or 158 centimeters (length + width + height), or weighing more than 70 pounds (32 kilograms). A third piece may be brought aboard; its total dimensions are generally limited to less than 45 inches (114 centimeters), so it will fit easily under the seat in front of you or in the overhead compartment. In the United States, the FAA gives airlines broad latitude to limit carry-on allowances

and tailor them to different aircraft and operational conditions. Charges for excess, oversize, or overweight pieces vary.

SAFEGUARDING YOUR LUGGAGE➤ Before leaving home, **itemize your bags' contents** and their worth, and label them with your name, address, and phone number. (If you use your home address, cover it so that potential thieves can't see it.) Inside your bag, **pack a copy of your itinerary.** At check-in, **make sure that your bag is correctly tagged** with the airport's three-letter destination code. If your bags arrive damaged or not at all, file a written report with the airline before leaving the airport.

U.K. CITIZENS

British citizens need a valid passport. If you are staying fewer than 90 days and traveling on a vacation, with a return or onward ticket, you will probably not need a visa. However, you will need to fill out the Visa Waiver Form, 1-94W, supplied by the airline.

While traveling, **keep one photocopy of the data page** separate from your wallet and leave another copy with someone at home. If you lose your passport, promptly call the nearest embassy or consulate, and the local police; having the data page can speed replacement.

R
RENTING A CAR

CUTTING COSTS

To get the best deal, **book through a travel agent and shop around.** When pricing cars, **ask where the rental lot is located.** Some off-airport locations offer lower rates—even though their lots are only minutes away from the terminal via complimentary shuttle. You may also want to **price local car-rental companies,** whose rates may be lower still, although service and maintenance standards may not be up to those of a national firm. Also **ask your travel agent about a company's customer-service record.** How has it responded to late plane arrivals and vehicle mishaps? Are there often lines at the rental counter, and, if you're traveling during a holiday period, does a confirmed reservation guarantee you a car?

INSURANCE

When you drive a rented car, you are generally responsible for any damage or personal injury that you cause as well as damage to the vehicle. Before you rent, **see what coverage you already have** by means of your personal auto-insurance policy and credit cards. For about $14 a day, rental companies sell insurance, known as a collision damage waiver (CDW), that eliminates your liability for damage to the car; it's always optional and should never be auto-

matically added to your bill.

SURCHARGES

Before picking up the car in one city and leaving it in another, **ask about drop-off charges or one-way service fees,** which can be substantial. Note, too, that some rental agencies charge extra if you return the car before the time specified on your contract. To avoid a hefty refueling fee, **fill the tank just before you turn in the car.**

FOR U.K. CITIZENS

In the United States you must be 21 to rent a car; rates may be higher for those under 25. Extra costs cover child seats, compulsory for children under five (about $3 per day), and additional drivers (about $1.50 per day). To pick up your reserved car you will need the reservation voucher, a passport, a U.K. driver's license, and a travel policy covering each driver.

S
SENIOR-CITIZEN DISCOUNTS

To qualify for age-related discounts, **mention your senior-citizen status up front** when booking hotel reservations, not when checking out, and before you're seated in restaurants, not when paying your bill. Note that discounts may be limited to certain menus, days, or hours. When renting a car, **ask about promotional car-rental discounts**—they

can net lower costs than your senior-citizen discount.

STUDENTS ON THE ROAD

To save money, **look into deals available through student-oriented travel agencies.** To qualify, you'll need to have a bona fide student I.D. card. Members of international student groups also are eligible. *See* Students *in* Important Contacts A to Z, *above.*

T
TELEPHONES

LONG-DISTANCE

The long-distance services of AT&T, MCI, and Sprint make calling home relatively convenient and let you avoid hotel surcharges; typically, you dial an 800 number in the United States and a local number abroad.

W
WHEN TO GO

Spring is probably the most attractive season in this part of the United States. Cherry blossoms are followed throughout the region by azaleas, dogwood, and camellias from April into May, and by apple blossoms in May. Folk, craft, art, and music festivals tend to take place in summer, as do sports events. State and local fairs are held mainly in August and September, though there are a few in early July and into October.

CLIMATE

In winter, temperatures generally average in the

low 40s inland, in the 60s by the shore. Summer temperatures, modified by mountains in some areas, by water in others, range from the high 70s to the mid-80s, now and then the low 90s. The following are average daily maximum and minimum temperatures for key Southern cities.

Climate in the South

BIRMINGHAM, ALABAMA

Jan.	56F	13C	May	82F	28C	Sept.	86F	30C
	35	2		58	14		63	17
Feb.	58F	14C	June	89F	32C	Oct.	77F	25C
	37	3		66	19		51	11
Mar.	65F	18C	July	90F	32C	Nov.	64F	18C
	42	6		69	21		40	4
Apr.	74F	23C	Aug.	90F	32C	Dec.	56F	13C
	50	10		65	20		35	2

ATLANTA, GEORGIA

Jan.	52F	11C	May	79F	26C	Sept.	83F	28C
	36	2		61	16		65	18
Feb.	54F	12C	June	86F	30C	Oct.	72F	22C
	38	3		67	19		54	12
Mar.	63F	17C	July	88F	31C	Nov.	61F	16C
	43	6		70	21		43	6
Apr.	72F	22C	Aug.	86F	30C	Dec.	52F	11C
	52	11		70	21		38	3

NEW ORLEANS, LOUISIANA

Jan.	63F	17C	May	83F	28C	Sept.	86F	30C
	47	8		68	20		74	23
Feb.	65F	18C	June	88F	31C	Oct.	79F	26C
	50	10		74	23		65	18
Mar.	72F	22C	July	90F	32C	Nov.	70F	21C
	56	13		76	24		56	13
Apr.	77F	25C	Aug.	90F	32C	Dec.	65F	18C
	61	16		76	24		49	9

JACKSON, MISSISSIPPI

Jan.	59F	15C	May	85F	29C	Sept.	88F	31C
	38	3		63	17		65	18
Feb.	63F	17C	June	92F	33C	Oct.	81F	27C
	41	5		70	21		54	12
Mar.	68F	20C	July	94F	34C	Nov.	67F	19C
	47	8		72	22		43	6
Apr.	76F	24C	Aug.	94F	34C	Dec.	61F	16C
	54	12		70	21		40	4

RALEIGH, NORTH CAROLINA

Jan.	50F	10C	May	78F	26C	Sept.	81F	27C
	29	− 2		55	13		60	16
Feb.	52F	11C	June	85F	29C	Oct.	71F	22C
	30	− 1		62	17		47	8
Mar.	61F	16C	July	88F	31C	Nov.	61F	16C
	37	3		67	19		38	3
Apr.	72F	22C	Aug.	87F	31C	Dec.	52F	11C
	46	8		66	18		52	11

CHARLESTON, SOUTH CAROLINA

Jan.	59F	15C	May	81F	27C	Sept.	84F	29C
	41	6		64	18		69	21
Feb.	60F	16C	June	86F	30C	Oct.	76F	24C
	43	7		71	22		59	15
Mar.	66F	19C	July	88F	31C	Nov.	67F	19C
	49	9		74	23		49	9
Apr.	73F	23C	Aug.	88F	31C	Dec.	59F	11C
	56	13		73	23		42	6

NASHVILLE, TENNESSEE

Jan.	46F	8C	May	79F	26C	Sept.	83F	28C
	28	− 2		57	14		61	16
Feb.	51F	11C	June	87F	31C	Oct.	72F	22C
	30	− 1		65	18		48	9
Mar.	60F	16C	July	90F	32C	Nov.	59F	15C
	38	3		69	21		32	3
Apr.	71F	22C	Aug.	89F	32C	Dec.	50F	10C
	48	9		68	20		31	− 1

1 Destination: The South

SOUTHERN SUPERLATIVES

By Honey
Naylor

IF YOU HEAR a Southern farmhand threaten to cut off one of his arms and eat it, don't scream and call for help. That's just his way of saying that he is hungry—or, as he is also likely to put it, "so hungry my stomach thinks my throat's been cut." A Southern man is not just tired or ill-used. He feels "like I've been rode hard and put up wet" (the reference being to letting a hard-ridden horse unlather before stabling it). A Southern woman in the midst of a tizzy is "running around setting my hair on fire." And if things don't work out right, she may "have to go to bed with a cold rag on my head"; in an extreme case, she may "go completely to pieces."

A proclivity to exaggerate is at the very core of every Southerner's soul, and he will take any opportunity to exercise it—for all Southerners simply *love* to talk. A Southerner setting out to make a transaction, whether it's buying a Coke or a condo, is viscerally aware that in the South the first order of business is almost never business. It's "visiting"—passing the time of day.

Out of these two tendencies—to talk and to talk big—has sprung the age-old Southern tradition of spinning colorfully embroidered stories, which in turn has spawned some great American storytellers. The original version of Thomas Wolfe's novel *Of Time and the River* was about the length of 12 average novels, or twice the length of *War and Peace*. Simply unable to stem the flow of words, he stopped writing only after his editor told him that the novel was finished.

Thomas Wolfe was a Southerner, a native of Asheville, North Carolina, which means that he was born with a bad case of logorrhea.

Other notable Southern storytellers are Mississippi's two Pulitzer Prize winners, Tennessee Williams and Eudora Welty, and its

Nobel Prize winner, William Faulkner. All three wrote of eccentric, complex, and occasionally bizarre characters caught up in Byzantine plots, as did Savannah-born Flannery O'Connor, author of *Wise Blood*.

Faulkner wrote his first novel in an apartment overlooking Pirates Alley in New Orleans—a city that gave the world Truman Capote and Lillian Hellman, and which Tennessee Williams called "my spiritual home." A Pulitzer was awarded posthumously to New Orleanian John Kennedy Toole, who wrote the wildly funny *A Confederacy of Dunces*. Frances Parkinson Keyes bought a historic home in the French Quarter of New Orleans, where she wrote *Dinner at Antoine's* and *Steamboat Gothic*. The brilliant Walker Percy, a native of Birmingham, won the National Book Award for his first novel, *The Moviegoer*, and continued to turn out literary gems from his home in Covington, Louisiana.

In Flat Rock, North Carolina, the home of Pulitzer Prize–winning poet and biographer Carl Sandburg, is a National Historic Site. Tom Wolfe, author of *Bonfire of the Vanities*, was born in Richmond, and Pat Conroy, who write *Prince of Tides*, lives in Atlanta. Margaret Mitchell, also of Atlanta, wrote only one book in her life, but that book was *Gone With the Wind*—the biggest-selling novel of all time.

For other Southerners, the words soar off the page and into the air. The Southland gave birth to the blues, to jazz, and to songwriters and singers of every stripe. The King—Elvis—grew up in Tupelo, Mississippi, and launched his astonishing career in a Memphis recording studio. Each year millions of Presley fans make the pilgrimage to Graceland, his showy home and final resting place in Memphis. Florence, Alabama, gave us W. C. Handy, who first played his "St. Louis Blues" in a Memphis saloon, and Savannah produced Johnny Mercer, a songwriter of considerable notes. The versatile Wynton Marsalis, the late Louis Armstrong, and the lively Pete Fountain are among the scores of great jazzmen from New Orleans, where jazz itself was born. Leontyne Price of Laurel, Mississippi, sang the role of Bess on Broadway in *Porgy and Bess* before giving voice to opera on a grand scale.

Speaking of which, opera lovers the world over flock to the annual Spoleto Festival USA in Charleston, which also features theater, ballet, and jazz. In the spring, musicians from as far away as Australia and Finland turn up for the Jazz and Heritage Festival in New Orleans, a city that is not exactly jazzless the rest of the year. Out in the bayous of South Louisiana, contagious Cajun music has virtually the whole world two-stepping; and up in the Blue Ridge Mountains of North Carolina, the hills sing with bluegrass music. Tennessee has produced more country-music songwriters, singers, and musicians than you can shake a mike at, and Nashville, the "Country Music Capital of the World," is the foot-stomping ground of the Grand Ole Opry.

"Dixie," incidentally, penned in 1859 by Yankee Dan Emmett, was a marching song originally played by bands of both the North and the South as they paraded into the Recent Unpleasantness—a period of time known to everyone but Southerners as the Civil War.

The Civil War, with a few exceptions, notably Gettysburg, was fought on Southern soil. South Carolina, inflamed by the rhetoric of firebrand John C. Calhoun, was the first state to secede, causing a Union loyalist to snap, "South Carolina is too small for a republic and too big for a lunatic asylum." But the first shots rang out over Charleston Harbor, and the bloody war began. Virtually every Southern city, country crossroad, and sleepy creek was touched by the war, and even now the memories linger on, preserved for all time in yet more colorful stories, passed along from generation to generation in the rooms of antebellum mansions throughout the South.

Today, south of the Mason-Dixon Line (surveyed in the 1700s by British astronomers Charles Mason and Jeremiah Dixon to settle a territorial dispute between Pennsylvania and Maryland), there are almost as many Civil War commemorative plaques as there are black-eyed peas. A slew of the South's most famous sights were once the scenes of hideous battles. Glitzy, modern Atlanta literally grew up out of the ashes Sherman left behind. Lookout Mountain, Tennessee, with its stunning view, was a vantage point that both sides fought for pretty keenly, and down in Mississippi, Vicksburg held Grant off for 47 days and nights before surrendering. New Orleans fell not long after Farragut shouted, "Damn the torpedoes, full speed ahead!"

The region is also fertile territory for aficionados of earlier American history. Fort Moultrie, South Carolina, is the site of the fledgling nation's first decisive victory over the British during the Revolutionary War.

NATCHITOCHES, LOUISIANA, was the first permanent settlement in the territory comprising the Louisiana Purchase, and the town has a small but beautifully restored historic district. (Holding title to the "oldest" or "first in this country" is dear to the hearts of tradition-cherishing Southerners, and visitors may find themselves deluged with the latter adjectives.) New Orleans's French Quarter, famed for Bourbon Street jazz haunts and exquisite Creole cuisine, is the original colony founded by French Creoles, and there are important historic districts in Savannah, Charleston, and Mobile.

But the South is much more than time-honored historic sites. It is a vast sports arena for snow-skiers and water-skiers, scuba divers and horseback riders, spelunkers and hunters, shrimpers and saltwater anglers, hikers, bikers, tennis buffs, golfers, and beachcombers.

Lush carpets of white sand roll down the Atlantic Coast and sweep along the Gulf of Mexico. Seekers of sun and fun head for such resorts as Sea Island, Georgia, and, in the Carolinas, Cape Hatteras, Hilton Head Island, and Myrtle Beach. Alabama barely sticks its big toe in the Gulf, but Mobile Bay's swank resorts and colorful artists' colonies are among the state's most popular attractions. Twenty-six miles of sun-kissed beaches stretch along the Mississippi coast, dotted with resorts such as Pascagoula, Pass Christian, and Biloxi.

If beaches bore you, there are plenty of hills to head for. The breathtakingly beautiful Blue Ridge Mountains roll through the Carolinas and northern Georgia, and the Great Smokies soar over the North Carolina–Tennessee border. Playgrounds abound in "them thar hills," such as Gatlinburg, Tennessee, and Blowing Rock, North Carolina.

One last note before you go: If you expect to hear the Hollywood version of a Southern accent, you're likely to be surprised. About the only generalization that can be made is that the Southern voice is gentle and soft—except at football games and hog-calling contests. You *will* hear drawls and "y'alls." ("Y'all," incidentally, is a contraction of "you all." It's the equivalent of "you guys," something you will almost never hear a Southerner say.) In south Louisiana, the language isn't even English—it's Cajun French. And in New Orleans you'll hear an accent that is soft, slightly slurred, but decidedly Brooklynese.

The truth is, the voices of the South are as rich and varied as the land itself. In its shops, restaurants, and homes you can be sure you'll hear those melodic Southern voices say, "Y'all come back."

And that's not just whistling Dixie.

WHAT'S WHERE

Alabama

From archaeological sites occupied by the prehistoric Native Americans for 8,000 years before the arrival of European settlers, to forts occupied during French colonial settlement in the 1700s and the American Revolution in the 1800s, to antebellum mansions that survived the civil war, to more modern events such as the birth of the Civil Rights movement in Montgomery and the design of the Saturn rocket at Huntsville's Space and Rocket Center, Alabama is a state rife with historical sights. It's also brimming with physical beauty—wooded hills and vast caves in the northeast, expansive lakes and broad rivers in the interior, and snow-white beaches along the Gulf Coast—and thriving cities like Birmingham, Montgomery, and Mobile.

Georgia

Georgia is notable for its contrasting landscapes and varied cities and towns, each reflecting its own special Southern charm. The northern part of the state has the Appalachian Mountains and their waterfalls; Dahlonega, the site of the nation's first gold rush; and Alpine Helen, a re-created Bavarian village in the Blue Ridge Mountains. Also in the north is Atlanta, a fast-growing city that serves as a banking center and the host for the 1996 Summer Olympics; and Macon, an antebellum town with thousands of cherry trees. If you drive some five hours southeast from Atlanta, you'll reach Savannah, which has the nation's largest historic district, filled with restored Colonial buildings. From Savannah, the state's 100-mile Atlantic coast runs from the Savannah River south to the mouth of St. Mary's near the Florida border. Along this coast is a string of lush, subtropical barrier islands, the Golden Isles, which include the elegant seaside communities of Jekyll, Sea, and St. Simons islands. Further south is Cumberland Island National Seashore, a sanctuary of marshes, beaches, forests, lakes, and ponds. Southern Georgia consists of black, gator-infested swampland, including the mysterious rivers and lakes of Okefenokee Swamp.

Louisiana

Louisiana is a state divided, both physically and philosophically, around mid-state in Alexandria. North Lousiana, with its rolling hills and piney woods, is strongly southern in flavor and appeal, while flatter, marshy Southern Louisiana is considered Cajun Country, with sharp differences in food, music, and even language. Riverboats ply the mighty Mississippi and antebellum homes line the wayside in both regions, but it's New Orleans, home of the famous Mardis Gras festivities, that garners the lions' share of attention, drawing most visitors to Southern Louisiana.

Mississippi

Steeped in Civil War battlegrounds and slightly partisan tales of ancestors who fought valiantly for the Confederacy, Mississippi is a gold mine for history buffs, and offers some of the best preserved examples of antebellum architecture in the South. The Natchez Trace, a beautiful string of magnolias and hilltop vistas, cuts across the heart of Dixie passing through Tupelo (Elvis Presley's birthplace), Jackson (the capital), and antebellum Natchez. The mighty Mississippi provides the natural western border of the state, winding slowly through the delta past the port towns of Greenville and Vicksburg. Even the riverboat casinos along the Gulf Coast evoke a sense of the past.

North Carolina

Historic sights and natural wonders galore accentuate North Carolina, from Old Salem, where the 1700s spring to life today, to the Great Smoky and Blue Ridge Mountains, where waterfalls cascade over high cliffs into gorges thick with evergreens, to the Cape Hatteras and Cape Lookout national seashores, where tides wash over the wooden skeletons of ancient shipwrecks and lighthouses stand as they have for 200 years. Here, too, you'll find sophisticated cities like Charlotte, world-class golf in the Pinehurst Sandhills, and fields of tobacco in the rich farmland of the gently rolling Piedmont.

South Carolina

South Carolina's scenic Low Country shoreline is punctuated by the lively port city of Charleston, decked out with fine museums (several in restored antebellum homes), and the recreational resorts of Myrtle Beach and Hilton Head at each end of the coast. The state capital of Columbia is set in the fertile interior of the state, which stretches toward the Blue Ridge Mountains, providing the western border of the state. Also to the west are the rolling fields of Thoroughbred country (noted for top race horses and sprawling mansions) and Upcountry South Carolina, at the northwestern tip of the state (noted for incredible mountain scenery and whitewater rafting).

Tennessee

Tennessee's dominating characteristics are her music—the blues, which were born in Memphis; rock, which came into popularity with the rise of Elvis Presley (also in Memphis); and country music, which claims Nashville as it's capital—and her scenic geographical features, the Great Smoky Mountains forming the eastern border and the Mississippi River forming the western border. Here, too, are forests, fields, and streams for the nature lover, out-

let malls for the die-hard shopper, and an array of entertainment parks to keep the whole family happy.

FODOR'S CHOICE

Special Moments

★ **Birmingham Civil Rights Institute, Alabama.** Observing the multimedia exhibits covering the movement from the 1920s to today, you can't help but reflect on the civil rights struggle of decades past.

★ **The King Center, Atlanta, Georgia.** Memories of the civil rights movement in '50s and '60s America come alive as you view the eternal flame burning at Martin Luther King, Jr.'s tomb in front of the downtown center.

★ **The top the Westin Peachtree Plaza Hotel, Atlanta, Georgia.** For the best views of the city, have a relaxing drink or meal in the revolving, multilevel Sun Dial Restaurant and Lounge.

★ **Historic District, Savannah, Georgia.** Architecture buffs will have a field day strolling by the hundreds of Colonial buildings that have been lovingly restored downtown within a 2½-mile-square area.

★ **Pirate's Alley, New Orleans, Louisiana.** Romance comes alive in this section of town, redolent of Old New Orleans, especially when viewed through the early morning mists.

★ **French Quarter, New Orleans, Louisiana.** Colors and shapes draw the eye to this section of the shoreline, a great view of the city from the deck of a riverboat.

★ **Waking up in the Madewood plantation house, Napoleonville, Louisiana.** When café au lait and croissants are delivered while you're slowly waking in your antique bed, you'll gain true understanding of the word "luxuriate."

★ **Elvis's birthplace, Tupelo, Mississippi.** This tiny, two-room cabin, built by his father and furnished as it was when the Presley family lived there, is a clear demonstration of the meager, humble beginnings of the King of Rock and Roll.

★ **Plantation dinner, Monmouth, Mississippi.** Diners step back 150 years in time to experience the graciousness and grandeur of a formal soiree at this beautiful plantation in Natchez. An unforgettable experience in living history.

★ **Old Salem, North Carolina.** A 1700s village of brick and wood structures peopled by tradesmen and gentlewomen in period costume provide a slice of living history, a close-up of life for early immigrants who came to America in search of religious freedom.

★ **Exploring the Cape Hatteras National Seashore, North Carolina.** Stretching from Oregon Inlet to Ocracoke Island, this scenic coastline is dotted with charming beach communities, historic lifesaving stations, wildlife refuges, and undeveloped beaches cluttered only by wild sea oats.

★ **Cypress Gardens, South Carolina.** A boat tour among the spring blossoms reflecting in the black waters of the gardens is a visual dazzler.

★ **Shelling on Kiawah Island, South Carolina.** This island is a convergence area, so the beach is one of the best places on the east coast to collect shells and sand dollars. Go early in the morning before others have picked over the finds.

★ **Graceland during Elvis week, Tennessee.** Mecca to fans of the King, Graceland is absolutely inundated during this anniversary in August. Go if you're a people-watcher, otherwise pick another time to visit to avoid the crowds.

★ **Viewing the Great Smokies from Lookout Tower at Clingmans Dome, East Tennessee.** Here you'll see what the Cherokees, and their predecessors, saw—forested mountains capped by a grey haze of clouds as the early morning mists melt into midday. The drive up is more difficult in the morning mists, but those mists impart the true Smokies feel.

★ **Rhododendron Gardens in spring atop Roan Mountain, East Tennessee.** It's not often you'll find a natural garden on top of a mountain as you will here. In spring it's a burst of color amid a verdant forest.

Dining

★ **Highlands: A Bar and Grill, Birmingham, Alabama.** Located in an area known as Spanish Stores (so named for its stucco walls and tiled roofs), this sophisticated eatery, has garnered national attention. $$$

★ **Roussos, Mobile, Alabama.** You'll find that the crab claws, baked oysters, and seafood gumbo draw a crowd of locals here. $$

★ **Sahara Restaurant, Montgomery, Alabama.** Hands down one of the state's finest dining options, this place fairly oozes old South charm. $$$

★ **Dining Room in the Ritz-Carlton Buckhead, Atlanta, Georgia.** Sample the freshest regional products and haute cuisine at its finest at one of the best restaurants not only in town but in the country. $$$$

★ **Elizabeth on 37th, Savannah, Georgia.** In an elegant turn-of-the-century mansion in the city's Victorian district, the emphasis is on seafood enhanced by delicate sauces. $$$

★ **Ciboulette, Atlanta, Georgia.** Hot smoked salmon, Lyonnaise sausage, and game dishes are inventively prepared at this popular French bistro. $$$

★ **Buckhead Diner, Atlanta, Georgia.** American food with an elegant twist is served in a shimmering faux-diner wrapped in luscious neon hues. $$–$$$

★ **Mrs. Wilkes Dining Room, Savannah, Georgia.** Expect long lines waiting to devour the reasonably priced, well-prepared Southern food, served family-style at big tables. $

★ **Commander's Palace, New Orleans, Louisiana.** New Orleans's gastronomic heritage and celebratory spirit are perfectly captured in the creatively prepared Creole dishes served in a stately Garden District mansion. $$$$

★ **Lafitte's Landing, Donaldsonville, Louisiana.** Celebrity chef John Folse (of PBS fame) serves his regional fare in this charming Acadian cottage. $$$

★ **Joe's "Dreyfus Store," Livonia, Louisiana.** The old general store is still outfitted with polished wood cabinets and other period memorabilia, an interesting, relaxed setting for the southern Louisiana cuisine featured here. $$

★ **Prudhomme's Cajun Café, Carencro, Louisiana.** This rustic Acadian cottage is center stage for the marvelous Cajun cuisine of Inola Prudhomme, sister of celeb Paul Prudhomme, and a master chef and cookbook author in her own right. $$

★ **City Grocery Store, Oxford, Mississippi.** Spic-and-span decor, attentive service, and inventive southern cuisine are your reward for visiting this favorite. $$$–$$$$

★ **Nick's, Jackson, Mississippi.** As any local who comes here frequently to dine on the tasty seafood will tell you, Nick's is an institution, and no visit to Jackson is complete without a meal here. $$$

★ **Lamplighter, Charlotte, North Carolina.** Fine gourmet cuisine served in the softly lit interior of an old Dilworth home is the hallmark of this favorite. $$$$

★ **Gabrielle's at Richmond Hill, Asheville, North Carolina.** You'll find it under lodging in our reviews, but the fabulous dinners at this Victorian inn are not to be missed—held by some to be the most imaginative (wild boar sausage and grilled antelope medallions) and delicious food in the state. $$$$

★ **Pewter Rose Bistro, Charlotte, North Carolina.** Drawn by the fresh seafood, inventive pasta dishes, and smart setting, Charlotte's young movers and shakers hang out in this renovated textile mill. $$

★ **Louis's Charleston Grill, Charleston, South Carolina.** Highly personalized service, attention to detail, and an intimate setting make this the choice for that romantic dinner. $$$

★ **82 Queen, Charleston, South Carolina.** Locals and visitors to Charleston flock to this laid-back eatery for the top-quality Low Country cuisine. $$

★ **Sea Captain's House, Myrtle Beach, South Carolina.** The seafood is fresh, simply prepared, and affordable at this casual restaurant—a good choice for a family meal. $$

★ **Magnolias–Uptown/Down South, Charleston, South Carolina.** Lots of Low Country dishes and a magnolia theme infuse this refurbished warehouse with southern charm. $

★ **Chez Philippe, Memphis, Tennessee.** The ornate, art deco setting is incredible, and the food never fails to measure up to the surroundings. $$$$

★ **Burning Bush Restaurant, Gatlinburg, Tennessee.** The atmosphere is Colonial, the menu Continental at this pleaser. $$–$$$

★ **212 Market, Chattanooga, Tennessee.** Light, healthy cuisine—poached salmon in ginger-lime sauce or vegetable terrine—served in a colorful, contemporary setting draws a crowd at 212 Market. $$–$$$

Lodging

★ **Perdido Beach Resort, Orange Beach, Alabama.** Fantastic views, a splendid beach location and lovely Mediterranean style set this one apart. $$$$

★ **The Tutwiler, Birmingham, Alabama.** Marble floors, chandeliers, and period reproduction furnishings are fitting in this elegant National Historic Landmark. $$$$

★ **Riverfront Inn, Montgomery, Alabama.** This converted historic railway depot retains many of its original elements. $$

★ **Malaga Inn, Mobile, Alabama.** Two antique furnished town houses built by a wealthy landowner in 1862 house this romantic retreat, and the intimate restaurant in the former carriage house is an added bonus. $–$$

★ **Cloister Hotel, Sea Island, Georgia.** This famed resort with spacious rooms in a Spanish Mediterranean building has a superb spa and outdoor activities galore—golf, tennis, swimming, skeet shooting, sailing, biking, and fishing. $$$$

★ **Gastonian, Savannah, Georgia.** At this superior B&B in a 19th-century mansion, the sumptuous suites have working fireplaces and antiques from the Georgian and Regency periods. $$$$

★ **Ritz-Carlton, Atlanta, Georgia.** Marble writing tables, plump sofas, four-poster beds, and white marble bedrooms create a luxurious ambience in the large guest rooms of this efficiently run, European-flavored hotel. $$$$

★ **Ritz-Carlton, Buckhead, Georgia.** The Ritz's signature 18th- and 19th-century furnishings grace this discreetly elegant gem close to Lenox Mall and Phipps Plaza shopping. $$$$

★ **Mulberry Inn, Savannah, Georgia.** This traditional dependable lodging features a number of artistic treasures in its public rooms, including valuable Chinese vases and 18th-century oil paintings. $$$

★ **Windsor Court Hotel, New Orleans, Louisiana.** New Orleans's only five star hotel, the elegant Windsor is built around a $7 million collection of private English art. $$$$

★ **Loyd Hall Plantation, Cheneyville, Louisiana.** This quiet country retreat features surprisingly upscale accommodations furnished in grand 19th-century-Louisiana antiques. $$

★ **Marriott's Residence Inn, Baton Rouge, Louisiana.** All suites, affordable rates and a great location make this one a favorite. $$

★ **Cedar Grove, Vicksburg, Mississippi.** Civil War cannon balls are still visible in the walls of this enormous 1840s mansion set near the river in Vicksburg. $$$$

★ **Millsaps-Buie House, Jackson, Mississippi.** This 1888 Queen Anne Victorian, complete with turret and columned porch, was restored and opened as a bed-and-breakfast in 1987. $$$–$$$$

★ **Fearrington House, Chapel Hill, North Carolina.** This French-style country inn was once a working farm and looks like an English country village. Top-notch service in a genteel atmosphere. $$$$

★ **Grove Park Inn, Asheville, North Carolina.** Asheville's premier resort, Grove Park Inn has been the haunt of guests like Thomas Edison, Henry Ford, and F. Scott Fitzgerald since its opening in 1913. $$$$

★ **First Colony Inn, Nags Head, North Carolina.** Four-poster beds, English antiques, and Jacuzzis lend an air of romance to this inn by the ocean, reminiscent of the beach hotels of years past. $$$–$$$$

★ **John Rutledge House Inn, Charleston, South Carolina.** One of the newer inns in Charleston, the elegant John Rutledge House is impeccably furnished and maintained. $$$$

★ **Kingston Plantation: A Radisson Resort, Myrtle Beach, South Carolina.** This self-contained resort, loaded with facilities like a full-service spa and a marina, has a great location on a broad beach

well removed from the bustle of the pavilion area. $$$$

★ **Westin Resort, Hilton Head Island, South Carolina.** Top of the line for Hilton Head, the Westin concentrates on luxury and service. $$$$

★ **Omni Hotel at Charleston Place, Charleston, South Carolina.** The upscale address for Charleston, the Omni is conveniently located in the historic district. $$$

★ **Buckhorn Inn, Gatlinburg, Tennessee.** This unassuming country inn set on 40 secluded acres has been a celebrity hideaway for decades. $$$$

★ **Hyatt Regency Knoxville, Tennessee.** Stunning architecturally, and the best accommodations central Knoxville has to offer. $$$$

★ **Opryland Hotel, Nashville, Tennessee.** Of the multitudes close to Opryland, this resort hotel is top flight. $$$$

★ **The Peabody, Memphis, Tennessee.** Legendary in the Delta, this grand dame was the locale for movie scenes in *The Firm.* Observing the Peabody ducks on parade is a unique part of the experience here. $$$$

Scenic Drives

★ **Creole Nature Trail, Louisiana.** Trees draped in Spanish moss and exotic southern Louisiana wildlife are readily visible along this 105-mile scenic loop.

★ **Natchez Trace Parkway, Mississippi.** Originally a footpath of early American Indians and later used by outlaws, soldiers, and settlers, this scenic drive lined by magnolias, cypresses, and pines winds from one breathtaking vista to another as it crosses Mississippi.

★ **Blue Ridge Parkway, North Carolina.** This 469-mile scenic corridor meanders through breathtaking mountains and meadows, stretching from North Carolina into Virginia.

Nightlife

★ **Dancing at Mulate's, Breaux Bridge, Louisiana.** Devote at least one night to the foot stompin' fun at Mulate's.

★ **New Orleans funk at Tipitina's, New Orleans, Louisiana.** This music blends R&B and Afro-Caribbean rhythms to create a sound entirely unique to New Orleans. This is the music the locals prefer.

★ **Traditional jazz at Preservation Hall, New Orleans, Louisiana.** When most people think of the New Orleans sound, traditional jazz comes to mind, and there's no better showcase than Preservation Hall.

GREAT ITINERARIES

The following recommended itineraries, arranged by both theme and area, are offered as a guide to planning individual travel.

Prominent Sites of African-American History

ALABAMA TOUR➤ Alabama's historic Civil Rights sites provide a close look at a 200-year struggle for racial equality, culminating in the changes undergone during the 1960s.

Duration: Six or seven days

The Main Route: One day: In Mobile, see the antebellum State Street A.M.E. (African Methodist Episcopal) Zion Church, the St. Louis Street Missionary Baptist Church, and the Slave Market Site, where the last cargo of slaves to enter the country arrived in 1859 aboard the Clotilde.

Two or three days: Travel to Montgomery and visit the Dexter Avenue King Memorial Baptist Church, considered by many the birthplace of the civil-rights movement, and the World Heritage Museum (by appointment only, ☎ 334/263–7229), showcasing Montgomery's civil-rights movement. Then move on to Selma and see the Edmund Pettus Bridge, famous during the '60s for clashes between civil-rights marchers and police, and First Baptist Church, the scene of meetings and protests in the 1960s. Make an excursion east from Montgomery to the Tuskegee Institute National Historic Site, which consists of Booker T. Washington's home, The Oaks; the George Washington Carver Museum; and Tuskegee University.

One or two days: From Montgomery, go north to Birmingham and visit its Civil Rights District—the location of Kelly-Ingram Park, which served as a rallying place in the rights movement, and the Sixteenth Street Baptist Church. Then take in the Alabama Sports Hall of Fame; it pays tribute to many of the state's great African-American athletes.

One day: Travel north to Decatur and visit the Old Courthouse, noted for the 1933 retrial of the Scottsboro Boys. Northwest is Florence, site of the W. C. Handy Home and Museum.

Information: See Chapter 2.

Tennessee/Mississippi Tour

For a glimpse of African-American life in the Deep South, visit the cotton country of the Mississippi Delta.

Duration: Six or seven days

The Main Route: One day: Begin in Memphis with a stop at the National Civil Rights Museum, on the site of Martin Luther King Jr.'s 1968 assassination. Then walk through the shops and blues clubs in the Beale Street Historic District. About 45 miles northeast is Henning, hometown of the late Alex Haley and setting for his novel *Roots*.

Two days: Head to Oxford and the Ole Miss campus where an African-American was first graduated in 1963; see the Center for the Study of Southern Culture, which focuses on southern music and folklore. Then go 62 miles southwest to Clarksdale and tour the Delta Blues Museum, which pays tribute to famous blues musicians.

One or two days: Next stop is Jackson to get an overview of the civil-rights movement's history in Mississippi. See the Old Capitol Historical Museum, Jackson State University (☎ 601/968–2272), and the outstanding collection of art at Tougaloo College (☎ 601/977–7842).

Two or three days: Drive along the Natchez Trace Parkway 50 miles to Port Gibson to visit the African-American quilters' workshop. In Natchez, 25 miles away, shop at the "Mostly African Market," and see the historic churches and houses built by prominent free men of color before the Civil War.

Information: See Chapters 5 and 8.

Low Country Tour

Blacks and whites in South Carolina's Low Country have always lived side by side, though, as evidenced by the 1739 Stono Plantation Rebellion and the 1822 Denmark Vesey plot to take over Charleston, not always peaceably. This natural distrust also motivated blacks to develop a lilting dialect called Gullah to communicate exclusively with one another. Historic sites in the Lowcountry recall this unique black experience.

Duration: One or two days

The Main Route: One day: In Charleston, begin with a walking tour of Cabbage Row, home of DuBose Heyward and setting for his novel Porgy. Then see the Emmanuel A.M.E. Church—the place of worship of the South's oldest A.M.E. congregation. Also here is the Old Exchange and Provost Dungeon, site of the city's busiest slave market. The Avery Research Center in the historic district has an archives and museum that document the heritage of Lowcountry blacks.

One day: Travel on to Beaufort, where you'll see the Penn School Historic District and York W. Bailey Cultural Museum on St. Helena Island. This community center consists of 17 buildings on the campus of a school that was established in 1862 for freed slaves. Also in Beaufort County is the self-sufficient Daufuskie Island, until recently inhabited exclusively by descendants of slaves.

Information: *See* Chapter 7.

Prominent Civil War Sites

THE SOUTHEASTERN TOUR➤ South Carolina seceded from the Union on December 20, 1860, and the first shot of the war was fired the following April. The war was fought for the most part on Southern soil, and there are more commemorative plaques in the South than there are black-eyed peas. The following itineraries take in the major sites and sights.

Duration: Seven to 10 days

The Main Route: One day: Begin in Charleston, South Carolina, and visit the Ft. Sumter National Monument. On April 12, 1861, Confederate General P.G.T. Beauregard ordered the first shot fired, and the bloody four-year struggle began.

Two or three days: Drive the 300 miles south to Atlanta. See the Eternal Flame of the Confederacy, and visit the Cyclorama, depicting the 1864 Battle of Atlanta. Explore 3,200-acre Stone Mountain Park, where there's a Confederate Memorial—the world's largest monument—and the Kennesaw Mountain National Battlefield.

Two days: From Atlanta, drive 160 miles southwest to Montgomery, the Cradle of the Confederacy. Visit the State Capitol, which was the first capitol of the Confederacy, and the First White House of the Confederacy, which was occupied by President Jefferson Davis and his family.

Two or three days: From Montgomery head southwest toward Mobile. Next stop is Fort Morgan, about 20 miles from Gulf Shores. A museum in Fort Morgan describes the dramatic 1864 Battle of Mobile Bay, during which Admiral David Farragut shouted, "Damn the torpedoes! Full speed ahead!"

Information: *See* Chapters 2, 3, and 7.

THE SOUTH CENTRAL TOUR➤ The long, colorful trek through Mississippi, Louisiana, and Tennessee offers Civil War–history buffs a wealth of well-preserved battle sites.

Duration: 10 to 14 days

The Main Route: Two or three days: From Mobile, head west toward New Orleans (146 miles). Overlooking the Gulf of Mexico between Gulfport and Biloxi, Mississippi, is Beauvoir, the home of Confederate president Jefferson Davis. At the Louisiana–Mississippi border, turn off to Baton Rouge (bypassing New Orleans, which fell to the Union in 1862) and then north to the Port Hudson State Commemorative Area, a 650-acre area on the site of the lengthiest uninterrupted siege in American military history. In 1863, 6,800 Confederates held off 30,000 to 40,000 Federals from May 23 till July 9. Continue north to Vicksburg, an important Mississippi River city that withstood Grant's siege for 47 days and nights before falling. Here, visit the Vicksburg National Military Park.

Three days: From Vicksburg, make the 242-mile trip to Jackson then north to Memphis. Another 100 miles east of there is the Shiloh National Military Park and Cemetery, commemorating those who died in the April 1862 battle, one of the bloodiest of the Civil War.

Three days: After Shiloh, journey to Murfreesboro, where the 351-acre Stones River National Battlefield recalls the bloodiest battle west of the Appalachians. It was fought in the winter of 1862–63, and 25,000 men lost their lives.

Three to four days: From Murfreesboro, go south to Chattanooga. See the Confederama, touted as the world's largest battlefield display of its kind, and visit the eight locations of the Chickamauga–Chattanooga National Military Park, whose headquarters is 10 miles south of the city. This is one of the nation's largest and oldest national military parks.

Information: *See* Chapters 4, 5, and 8.

FESTIVALS AND SEASONAL EVENTS

Starting with Mardi Gras in New Orleans and ending with Christmas in Natchez, Mississippi, the Southern states hold a wide variety of festivals and special events throughout the year.

WINTER

DECEMBER➤ Christmas is celebrated all over the South, with events in almost every city. Highlights include Colonial Williamsburg's Christmas Special, where the holiday is celebrated the old-fashioned way with hot cider, cookies, and gifts, Creole Christmas in the French Quarter of New Orleans, and Old Salem Christmas, which recreates a Moravian Christmas in Winston-Salem, North Carolina. Tennessee holiday events of note are Christmas in the City in Knoxville, Smoky Mountain Christmas in Gatlinburg, and Nashville's Trees of Christmas. New Year's events include the Peach Bowl, played in Atlanta, and the First Night Charlotte festival, held on the Town Square in Charlotte, North Carolina.

JANUARY➤ The year begins with two major college football competitions, the Senior Bowl in Mobile, Alabama, and the Sugar Bowl, played in New Orleans. In South Carolina, Orangeburg invites the country's finest coon dogs to compete in the Grand American Coon Hunt. The Savannah Marathon and Half Marathon in Savannah, Georgia; and the Charlotte Observer Marathon and Runner's Expo in Charlotte, North Carolina, attract the region's runners. Martin Luther King Jr., Week is celebrated in Atlanta, and the New Orleans Classical Music Festival takes place late in the month.

FEBRUARY➤ The big event of the month is Mardi Gras in New Orleans— the South's biggest parade and party; the week is also celebrated in Mobile and Gulf Shores, Alabama; and Biloxi and Natchez, Mississippi. Black History Month is observed throughout the South, with special events at Tuskegee University in Tuskegee, Alabama, and the W. C. Handy home in Florence, Alabama. In North Carolina, Asheville welcomes visitors to its annual Winterfest Arts and Crafts Show, and Wilmington stages the North Carolina Jazz Festival. In Jackson, Mississippi, the Dixie National Livestock Show runs most of the month in conjunction with the Dixie National Rodeo and the Dixie National Western Festival.

SPRING

MARCH➤ The Old South comes alive: Antebellum mansion and garden tours are given in Natchez, Port Gibson, Vicksburg, and Columbus, Mississippi; and in Charleston and Beaufort, South Carolina. A Revolutionary War battle is reenacted on the anniversary of the Battle of Guilford Courthouse in Greensboro, North Carolina. The Grand Village of the Natchez Indians in Mississippi hosts the Natchez Pow-Wow. Spring is celebrated with a Cherry Blossom Festival in Macon, Georgia; the Spring Flower Show in Montgomery, Alabama; Springfest on Hilton Head Island, South Carolina; and the Great Smoky Arts and Crafts Community Spring Show in Gatlinburg, Tennessee. In Louisiana, Ville Platte hosts the Boggy Bayou Festival, and New Orleans celebrates its Tennessee Williams/New Orleans Literary Festival.

APRIL➤ In Alabama, a Civil War reenactment draws thousands to Selma in late April, and Eufaula stages its annual Pilgrimage and Antique Show. Spring festivals abound, including Dogwood Festivals in Atlanta; Fayetteville, North Carolina; and Knoxville, Tennessee. Also consider the Okefenokee Spring Fling in Waycross, Georgia; the Strawberry Festival in Ponchatoula, Louisiana; and the Spring Wildflower Pilgrimage in Gatlinburg, Tennessee. Fish and shellfish lovers should take note of the World Catfish Festival in Belzoni, Mississippi; the World's Biggest Fish Fry in Paris, Tennessee; and the Louisiana Crawfish Festival in St. Bernard, Louisiana. Music festivals include the New Orleans Jazz and Heritage Festival and, in Wilkesboro, North Carolina, the Merle Watson Memorial Festival, featuring Doc Watson's renowned bluegrass picking.

MAY➤ Festivals take to the air this month with the Alabama Jubilee Hot Air Balloon Classic in Decatur and the annual Hang Gliding Spectacular in Nags Head, North Carolina. Spoleto Festival USA in Charleston, South Carolina, is one of the world's biggest arts festivals; Piccolo Spoleto, running concurrently, showcases local and regional talent. Mississippi hosts two music festivals, the Atwood Music Festival in Monticello and the Jimmie Rodgers Country Music Festival in Meridian. In South Carolina, Beaufort's Gullah Festival highlights the fine arts, customs, language, and dress of Low Country blacks.

SUMMER

JUNE➤ June is food month in Louisiana, with the Okra Festival in Kenner, the Jambalaya Festival in Gonzales, the Great French Market Tomato Festival in New Orleans, the Louisiana Blueberry Festival in Mansfield, the Feliciana Peach Festival in Clinton, and the famed Louisiana Catfish Festival in Des

Allemands. Alabama hosts the Gehart Chamber Music Festival in Guntersville and June Jam—featuring the music group ALABAMA—in Fort Payne, as well as a Seafood Festival in Bayou la Batre. Mississippi hosts Biloxi's colorful Black Heritage and Culture Juneteenth Celebration and Monticello's Pioneer Pilgrimage of Lawrence County, celebrating Southern pioneer life. Summer gets underway at the Sun Fun Festival on Myrtle Beach's Grand Strand on the South Carolina coast. The International Country Music Fan Fair is held in Nashville, and the Carnival Music Festival is held in Memphis.

JULY➤ Independence Day celebrations are annual traditions around the South, including in Atlanta, Savannah, and Columbus, Georgia; and in Greenville, South Carolina, which hosts Freedom Weekend Aloft, the second-largest balloon rally in the country. Deep Sea Fishing Rodeos take place at both Dauphin Island, Alabama, and Gulfport, Mississippi; the latter is one of the largest fishing contests in the South. Cajun Bastille Day is celebrated in Baton Rouge for three days and both Franklinton, Louisiana, and Mize, Mississippi, host Watermelon Festivals. In North Carolina, clog and figure dancing are part of the Shindig-on-the-Green in Asheville, and the annual Highland Games & Gathering of the Scottish Clans is held on Grandfather Mountain near Linville.

AUGUST➤ Memphis, Tennessee, is home to the biggest event this month, Elvis International Tribute Week. Smaller happenings around the South include the Roscoe Turner Hot Air Balloon Race in Corinth, Mississippi; North Carolina's Apple Festival in Hendersonville; and the Louisiana Shrimp and Petroleum Festival in Morgan City. August music festivals include a Beach Music Festival in Jekyll Island, Georgia, and the annual Mountain Dance and Folk Festival in Asheville, North Carolina.

AUTUMN

SEPTEMBER➤ Truly a festival month, September welcomes local events throughout the South. In Alabama, Greensboro stages the Alabama Catfish Festival and Gulf Shores hosts the annual Orange Beach Fishing Rodeo. In Georgia, Atlanta's Fine Arts and Crafts Festival is held in Piedmont Park, and the Hot Air Balloon Festival floats over Helen. In Louisiana, some of the best festivals are the Zydeco Music Festival in Plaisance, the Frog Festival in Rayne, Festival Acadiens in Lafayette, and the Louisiana Sugar Cane Festival in New Iberia. In Mississippi, Columbus has the Possum Town Pig Fest, Indianola the Indian Bayou Arts and Crafts Festival, Biloxi the Seafood Festival, and Greenville the Delta Blues Festival. The annual

Woolly Worm Festival takes place in Banner Elk, North Carolina. Nashville hosts the Tennessee State Fair.

OCTOBER➤ Autumn brings more celebrations of food, including Alabama's National Shrimp Festival in Gulf Shores, the National Peanut Festival in Dothan, and the Chitlin' Jamboree in Clio. The National Pecan Festival is held in Albany, Georgia. A barbecue and parade of pigs guarantee fun at the Lexington Barbecue Festival in North Carolina. Oktoberfest is celebrated in Savannah, Georgia; in Myrtle Beach and Walhalla, South Carolina; and in Memphis and Clarkville, Tennessee. The "Ghost Capital of the World"— Georgetown, South Carolina—stages a Ghost Tour. In Mississippi, the Scottish Highland Games are held in Biloxi; Natchez stages the Fall Pilgrimage, highlighted by the prestigious Antiques Forum; and in Canton, the Canton Flea Market features antiques and objets d'art on the Courthouse Square.

NOVEMBER➤ Thanksgiving celebrations take place all over: The Creek Indian Thanksgiving Day Homecoming and Pow Wow is held in Poarch, Alabama, and the Richland Pumpkin Festival is held in Richland, Mississippi. Christmas preparations include Mistletoe Markets in both Albany, Georgia, and Jackson, Mississippi, and the start of Christmas in Roseland in Shreveport, Louisiana. Autumn food festivals include the Taste of Montgomery in Montgomery, Alabama, and the Pecan Festivals in Theodore, Alabama, and Colfax, Louisiana. The Catfish Festival takes place in Society Hill, South Carolina, and the Chitlin' Strut in Salley, South Carolina.

2 Alabama

Alabama is a state rife with historical sights. It's also brimming with physical beauty—wooded hills and vast caves in the northeast, expansive lakes and broad rivers in the interior, and snow-white beaches along the Gulf Coast— and thriving cities like Birmingham, Montgomery, and Mobile.

...idw
Updated by
Dick Pivetz

ALABAMA IS INDEED A STATE OF SURPRISES. Visitors are surprised by the physical beauty: from the dramatic rocky, wooded hills and vast caves of the northeast to the expansive lakes and broad rivers of the interior and the snow-white beaches of the Gulf Coast. At the high-tech world of Huntsville's Space and Rocket Center, near Redstone Arsenal, the Saturn rocket was designed. The state's largest city, Birmingham, is one of the South's major medical centers, with 22 institutions, including the University of Alabama at Birmingham Medical Center, ranked among the nation's highest in quality of health care. In 1992 the institution opened the new $125 million Kirklin Medical Center.

The traveler who ventures off the four-lane interstates will find something surprising at almost every turn—a cascading waterfall or showy stand of wildflowers, an archaeological excavation or a Colonial fort, perhaps one of Alabama's 12 covered bridges. At Florence, in 1873, William Christopher Handy, son of a Methodist minister descended from slaves, was born. A teacher, band leader, and author, the Father of the Blues is best remembered for the "Memphis Blues" and "St. Louis Blues." In nearby Tuscumbia, the tiny frame cottage where Helen Keller overcame the loss of hearing and sight sits as a monument to her inspirational life. A few miles south, tucked away on a wooded hillside, is a cemetery for coon hounds, begun in 1937 by the devoted master of Troop, its first resident. A few more miles south is a sunken park (called the Dismals) where junglelike plants, some of which are found nowhere else in this hemisphere, grow in profusion. Tuskegee Institute, founded in 1881 by the distinguished black educator, Booker T. Washington, was where the young botanist, George Washington Carver, headed the agricultural department and did his seminal work in plant derivatives and crop diversification.

Each spring, several Alabama towns hold "pilgrimages"—tours of historic homes (including many private residences not otherwise open to the public), mansions, plantations, churches, gardens, even cemeteries. Hosts and hostesses in period costume greet visitors and tell tales of life in bygone days. It's a lovely time to visit, with the gardens decked out in dogwood, azalea, magnolia, and many other blossoms. Candlelight tours add a romantic touch.

THE HIGHLANDS, INCLUDING BIRMINGHAM

Birmingham, set in a valley below the foothills of the Appalachians, first blossomed around the coal mines and the iron industry in the latter part of the 19th century. In the 1970s, after plastics became commonplace in auto manufacturing, the steel making plants that had polluted the valley air virtually vanished. The air cleared of soot and dust, and the University of Alabama at Birmingham, with its fast-growing medical center, became the city's largest employer.

Birmingham's image as a backward civil rights territory was reinforced during the '60s, when the notorious Eugene "Bull" Conner served as police commissioner and when Dr. Martin Luther King Jr. was put in jail for fighting racial inequality. When the turmoil had finally settled, however, a new city began to emerge. In 1979, Richard Arrington, a successful black businessman, was elected mayor. The racial climate

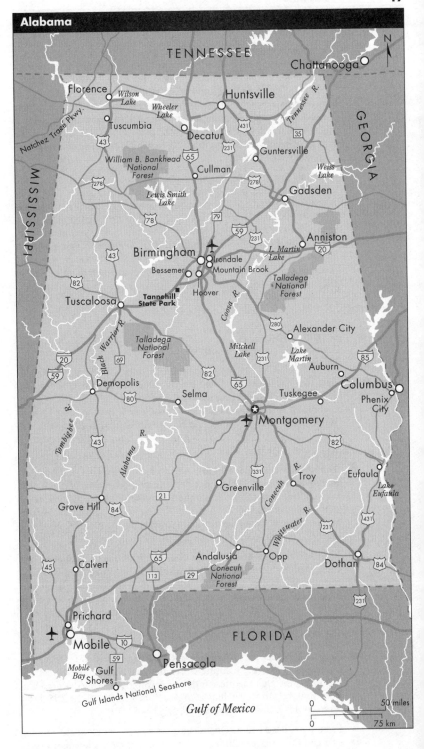

Alabama

TENNESSEE

Chattanooga

Florence
Wilson Lake
Wheeler Lake
Huntsville
Tuscumbia
Natchez Trace Pkwy.
43
231
Decatur
431
35
Guntersville
Tennessee R.
65
William B. Bankhead National Forest
Cullman
278
278
Weiss Lake
Gadsden
278
Lewis Smith Lake
78
79
59
231
Anniston
20
Birmingham
Irondale
Mountain Brook
Bessemer
L. Martin Lake
Talladega National Forest
Hoover
Tannehill State Park
43
82
Tuscaloosa
Coosa R.
Talladega National Forest
Alexander City
280
20
59
69
Black Warrior R.
Mitchell Lake
Lake Martin
231
Auburn
85
Demopolis
82
65
Columbus
80
Selma
Tuskegee
Phenix City
Tombigbee R.
43
Alabama R.
★ Montgomery
82
21
331
Conecuh R.
Troy
Eufaula
Greenville
Lake Eufaula
Grove Hill
84
Whitewater R.
231
431
45
Calvert
65
Andalusia
Opp
Dothan
84
113
29
Conecuh National Forest
231
Prichard
10
Mobile
59
Pensacola
FLORIDA
Mobile Bay
Gulf Shores
Gulf Islands National Seashore
Gulf of Mexico

MISSISSIPPI

GEORGIA

N

0   50 miles
0   75 km

now having improved considerably, the city dedicated the Birmingham Civil Rights Institute in November 1992.

Birmingham today is a glimmering, hospitable, thriving metropolis. Several 19th-century houses and commercial buildings have been restored to create a lively shopping and dining area called Five Points South. The city's last remaining antebellum mansion has been restored and functions as a museum. There's also a large zoo and a 67-acre Japanese and botanic garden. Looking down on it all from high atop Red Mountain—so named for the iron ore within it—looms a reminder of the source of an earlier prosperity: a 55-foot-high cast-iron statue of Vulcan, god of the forge.

North of Birmingham, Alabama's Highlands is a scenic area of small towns, mountains, lakes, national forests, and historic sites. The Highlands' largest and most cosmopolitan town is Huntsville, which has 160,000 residents and the U.S. Space and Rocket Center. The area's charm is in its natural beauty, slow pace, and lack of commercialism. Even when the region is at its busiest, you can always find a quiet spot to dangle a fishing line, swim, or boat. And if you've ever wondered where cotton comes from, visit in October, when white bolls blanket the landscape like a fresh snowfall.

Exploring

Birmingham

Numbers in the margin correspond to points of interest on the Birmingham map.

★ ❶ Alabama has long been noted for its excellence in sports, and the **Alabama Sports Hall of Fame Museum,** in the Civic Center, displays memorabilia of such Alabama heroes as coach Bear Bryant, Jesse Owens, Willie Mays, Billy Williams, and Hank Aaron. *Corner 22nd St. N and Civic Center Blvd.,* ☎ *205/323–6665.* ☛ *$5 adults, $4 senior citizens, $3 children.* ☼ *Mon.–Sat. 9–5, Sun. 1–5.*

❷ The **Birmingham Museum of Art,** two blocks south, has one of the world's largest collections of Wedgwood, the largest collection of contemporary Chinese paintings outside the People's Republic of China, some extraordinary examples of Western American art, plus Italian Renaissance and pre-Columbian art. *2000 Eighth Ave. N,* ☎ *205/254–2565.* ☛ *Free.* ☼ *Tues.–Sat. 10–5 (until 9 on Thurs.), Sun. 1–5.*

❸ Nearby is the **16th Street Baptist Church,** site of one of the saddest and most memorable occurrences of the civil rights movement. Here, on the morning of September 15, 1963, a bomb exploded and killed four little black girls who were attending Sunday school in the basement. A plaque erected to their memory bears this legend: *May Men Learn to Replace Bitterness and Violence with Love and Understanding. 6th Ave. N and 16th St. N,* ☎ *205/251–9402.*

❹ Across the street is the **Birmingham Civil Rights Institute.** Opened in November 1992, the institute traces the civil rights movement from the 1920s through the present day via exhibits, multimedia presentations, music, and storytelling. *6th Ave. and 16th St. N,* ☎ *205/328–9696.* ☛ *Free.* ☼ *Tues.–Sat. 10–6, Sun. 1–5.*

❺ From here, head south. One block past First Avenue North, running east and west between 20th and 24th streets, is **Morris Avenue,** a turn-of-the-century brick roadway lined with brick buildings of the period.

19

Alabama Sports Hall of Fame Museum, **1**

Arlington, **7**

Birmingham Civil Rights Institute, **4**

Birmingham Museum of Art, **2**

Birmingham Zoo, **19**

Botanical and Japanese Gardens, **20**

Discovery 2000, Red Mountain Museum, **17**

Five Points South, **8**

Five Points Theatre, **14**

Highlands United Methodist Church, **11**

Morris Avenue, **5**

Nabob Hill, **12**

Pickwick Hotel, **15**

Pickwick Place, **9**

Rube Burrows Food and Spirits, **16**

16th St. Baptist Church, **3**

Sloss Furnaces, **6**

Southside Baptist Church, **13**

Statue of Brother Bryan, **10**

Vulcan Park, **18**

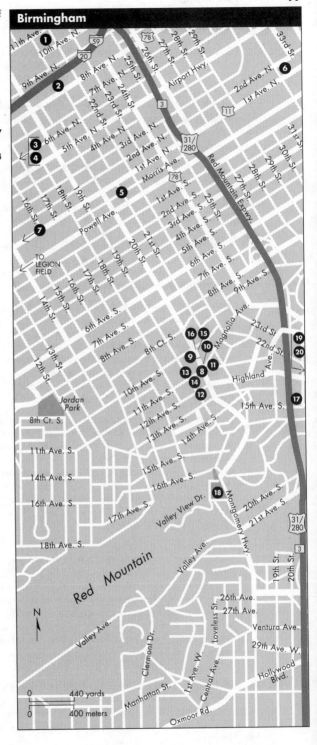

Birmingham

Many of these buildings have been renovated and are now used as professional offices. Gaslights add to the old-fashioned atmosphere.

6 Driving east on First Avenue North, over the Red Mountain Expressway, you'll see signs for **Sloss Furnaces,** a National Historic Landmark. The massive ironworks produced pig iron from ore dug from the hills surrounding Birmingham between 1882 and 1971. Retired blast-furnace workers who knew the heat of the flowing molten metal firsthand conduct guided tours through the plant, spicing the narrations with tales of their own experiences. *First Ave. N and 32nd St.,* ☎ *205/324– 1911.* ☛ *Free.* ☉ *Tues.–Sat. 10–4, Sun. noon–4.*

7 Return west on First Avenue North to reach **Arlington,** Birmingham's only remaining antebellum mansion. It was used as headquarters by Union General James H. Wilson in March 1865, as he and his raiders swept south through Alabama to Selma, destroying iron furnaces along the way. In the 1950s the city purchased the classic Greek Revival structure, and 50 prominent citizens donated funds for its renovation. Today it houses Civil War memorabilia, some prime examples of 19th-century furniture, and a museum dedicated to the women of Alabama. *331 Cotton Ave. SW,* ☎ *205/780–5656.* ☛ *$3 adults, $2 children 6– 18, under 6 free.* ☉ *Tues.–Sat. 10–4, Sun. 1–4.*

Heading east again on First Avenue North, turn right onto 20th Street and continue south for about 12 blocks to reach Magnolia Avenue and **8** **Five Points South,** an outdoor museum of turn-of-the-century architecture. **9** Start with the **Pickwick Place,** a miniature open-air shopping mall between 20th Street South and Magnolia Avenue. On this site the Pickwick Ballroom once stood. Big bands played swing tunes while the belles and their beaux danced the nights away beneath the large mirrored ball that now hangs in the mall's entranceway.

10 Outside CAPS Restaurant and Lounge at Five Points is the kneeling **11** stone **statue of Brother Bryan,** Birmingham's good-Samaritan minister. Across Magnolia, in front of the **Highlands United Methodist Church,** is a concrete Art Deco fountain. The church, built in 1909 in the Spanish Renaissance Revival style, was designed by the same architect responsible for Atlanta's Fox Theatre. In the first block of 11th Avenue, in what is called the Spanish Stores for its stucco walls and tiled roofs, is Highlands: A Bar and Grill (*see* Dining, *below*), which has won national awards.

If you're lucky, you'll arrive on a "special weekend" (occurring in spring and fall, most are unannounced, with the exception of Halloween). As soon as the sun falls, the locals come out. Street bands play. Teenagers mimic denizens of London's Soho with their multihued hair and loose-fitting, wildly colored costumes. And men in drag dance in the streets. Is it any wonder local pundits have named Five Points "Bourbon Street without the sleaze"? With all the street people out, it is comforting to know that the Five Points South owners have their own security patrol, which immediately alerts the police department in case of a crime. You can walk these streets without fear.

TIME OUT Behind 20th Street Antiques, through a narrow walkway, is Cobb Lane, where the **Back Alley Restaurant** has dining indoors and on an oak-shaded patio. The fare is soups, salads, sandwiches, quiche, and one or two Continental entrées each day. ☎ *205/933–6211. Closed Nov.–Feb.*

12 Walking north on 19th Street, you'll see a ridge on your left at 12th Avenue. Once called **Nabob Hill,** it was the site of five mansions in which the families of high-ranking Confederate officers lived. Today there's only a playground. A block beyond (at 1016 19th St. S) stands the large, columned **Southside Baptist Church.** Built in 1911, it is a prime example of Classical Revival architecture, resembling a Roman Ionic temple.

Turning right and back toward the center of Five Points, you come to the Art Deco facade of multicolored Carrara glass that was once the **Five Points Theatre** (1914 11th Ave. S, ☎ 205/251–0278), a popular movie house in the 1920s and '30s.

Back on 20th Street is the **Pickwick Hotel** (1123 20th St. S), built in 1931 as the Medical Arts Building, with offices for physicians, surgeons, and pharmacists. Today it retains the original polished-marble lobby, but renovations have created roomy suites and a cozy little lounge with an etched-glass mirror showing Pickwick dancers in their finest formals (*see* Lodging, *below*).

Half a block down 20th Street, near where the walking tour of Five Points began, is **Rube Burrows Food and Spirits** (1005 20th St. S, ☎ 205/933–5570), a watering hole and hamburger oasis named for Alabama's infamous 19th-century train robber.

After leaving the area, you can head south on U.S. 31 a short way until you come to the **Discovery 2000, Red Mountain Museum,** which showcases rocks, fossils, and minerals of the many types found in the area. Also here is the only solar telescope in North America open to the public; don't miss this chance to get a look at the sun's surface. *1421 22nd St. S, ☎ 205/939–1176. ☛ $2 adults, $1.50 children; includes admission to adjacent Discovery 2000, Discovery Place (see What to See and Do with Children, below). ☉ Tues.–Fri. 9–3, Sat. 10–4, Sun. 1–4.*

A pleasant way to end a day is to wend your way up Red Mountain to visit the **Vulcan Park** and the statue of Vulcan. From the enclosed observation deck at the base of the world's tallest cast-iron statue, there's a panoramic view of the city. There's also a circular stairway inside for the hardy. *Valley Ave. at Old Montgomery Hwy., ☎ 205/328–6198. ☛ $1 (under 6 free). ☉ Daily 8 AM–10:30 PM.*

The next part of the tour, a day in itself, takes you to Mountain Brook. This elegant suburb is a place for wandering along tree-shaded country roads, driving past great old and new Southern mansions. Here, too, nestled beneath a hammock of huge oaks, is the **Birmingham Zoo.** A miniature train snakes through the wooded acreage, or you may walk the paths at a leisurely pace. The zoo is known for the breeding of Siberian tigers, a number of which live here, along with the world's only self-sustaining breeding colony of golden spider monkeys in captivity. *2630 Cahaba Rd., ☎ 205/879–0409. ☛ $4 adults, $1.50 senior citizens and children 2–17, under 2 free. ☉ Daily 9–5.*

At the nearby **Botanical and Japanese Gardens,** under a great glass dome, waterfalls cascade into pools with plants of every shade of green and flowers of every color imaginable. Outside, there is a quiet Japanese garden with small bridges over bubbling brooks and an authentic teahouse set amid Japanese ferns, mosses, and trees. For visitors who are blind, there is a touch-and-see nature trail. *2612 Lane Park Rd., ☎ 205/879–1227. ☛ Free. ☉ Daily sunrise to sunset.*

Cullman
Numbers in the margin correspond to points of interest on the Alabama Highlands map.

Take I–65 north from Birmingham for 50 miles to the small town of Cullman. In the course of a leisurely stroll through the hillside garden **❶ Ave Maria Grotto,** you'll see nearly 150 miniature churches, buildings, and shrines, painstakingly created from originals in the United States and Europe by a Benedictine monk over the course of 50 years. Standing only a few feet in height, these tiny buildings were constructed from rare materials, such as marble and semiprecious stones, gathered from around the world. *Take I–65N to U.S. 278E, St. Bernard's Abbey, Cullman,* ☎ *205/734–4110.* ☛ *$3.50 adults, $3 senior citizens, $2 children 6–12, under 6 free.* ☼ *Daily 7* AM*–sunset.*

Decatur

It's another 30 miles north on I–65 and U.S. 31 to Decatur. This is ter- **❷** rific territory for outdoors enthusiasts: **Point Mallard Park** is a 749-acre spread with a swimming pool, a wave pool, and a water slide (summer only); plus an ice rink (mid-Nov.–mid-Mar.), campgrounds, an 18-hole championship golf course, miniature golf, a duck pond, and a 4-mile hiking and biking trail. *1800 Point Mallard Dr.,* ☎ *205/350–3000 or 800/669–9283.* ☛ *$7 adults, $5 children 3–11. Fees for activities range from $1 to $13.* ☼ *Aquatic Center 10–6, daily Tues.–Thurs. 6–9* PM *mid-May–Labor Day.* ☼ *Ice rink mid-Nov.–mid-Mar.*

★ Just east of Decatur, the **Wheeler Wildlife Refuge** is a safe haven for more than 300 species of waterfowl and other birds. There aren't too many places in the world where visitors can sit comfortably in a building overlooking the lake watching thousands of ducks and geese descend upon the water. Special one-way glass and spotting scopes allow viewing without disturbing the birds. *AL 67, 2 mi west of I–65,* ☎ *205/350–6639.* ☛ *Free.* ☼ *Daily dawn–dusk.*

Florence

Fifty miles west of Decatur via Alt. U.S. 72 is Florence. Blues fans flock every year to this city on the banks of the Tennessee River to see the **❸ W. C. Handy Home and Museum.** The birthplace of the internationally acclaimed Father of the Blues has been furnished with items typical of the period when he grew up. In the museum behind the cabin, a treasure trove of his memorabilia has been preserved. Here you'll see his piano and famous golden trumpet, original manuscripts, and testimonials to his genius by such contemporaries as George Gershwin and Louis Armstrong. The annual W. C. Handy Music Festival (☎ 205/766–7642), held during the first full week in August, draws thousands. *620 College St.,* ☎ *205/760–6434.* ☛ *$2 adults, 50¢ children 6–18, under 6 free.* ☼ *Tues.–Sat. 9–noon, 1–4.*

Tuscumbia

Just across the Tennessee River (south) from Florence, Tuscumbia is ★ **❹** home to **Ivy Green,** the childhood home of Helen Keller. At the carriage house, behind the simple white frame main house, Annie Sullivan taught her the meaning of language. *The Miracle Worker* is performed on the grounds Friday and Saturday nights in June and July. *300 W. North Commons,* ☎ *205/383–4066.* ☛ *$3 adults, $1 children 6–11, under 6 free.* ☛ *To The Miracle Worker: $5 general admission, $8 box seats.* ☼ *Mon.–Sat. 8:30–4, Sun. 1–4.*

Located outside of town on U.S. 72, 2 miles west of the intersection ★ of U.S. 72 and U.S. 43, is the **Alabama Music Hall of Fame,** where you can wander through the history of Alabama's musical heritage—seeing the original contracts of Elvis Presley's deal with Sun Records, the actual touring bus of southern rock band Alabama, and further exhibits

The Alabama Highlands

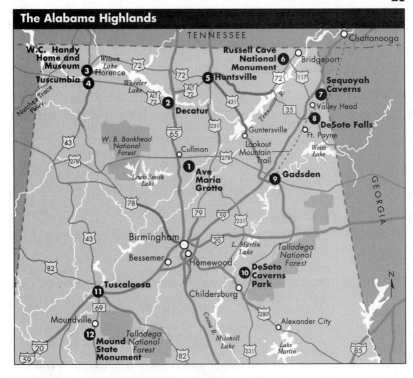

on the likes of Hank Williams, Lionel Richie, and Nat "King" Cole. *U.S. 72,* ☎ *205/381–4417 or 800/239–2643.* ☛ *$6 adults, $5 senior citizens, $3 children 6–12, under 6 free.* ☉ *Mon.–Sat. 9–5, Sun. 1–5.*

Huntsville

★ ❺ Drive 75 miles east on U.S. 72 to reach Huntsville. The **U.S. Space and Rocket Center** here is home to the U.S. Space Camp, where you can learn about space exploration and experience some of the training that real astronauts must undergo. The center offers a bus tour of the NASA labs and shuttle test sites; hands-on exhibits in the museum; a 33-minute Omnimax film, *Speed,* which describes every type of conveyance from the bicycle to the rocketship; and an outdoor park filled with spacecraft, including a full-size model of the Space Shuttle. *1 Tranquility Base, Huntsville,* ☎ *205/837–3400 or 800/637–7223.* ☛ *$11.95 adults, $9.95 over 60, $7.95 children 3–12, under 3 free; includes museum, film, NASA tour.* ☉ *Memorial Day–Labor Day, daily 9–6; Labor Day–Memorial Day, daily 9–5.*

Bridgeport

❻ Now that you've experienced the Space Age, travel back to the Stone Age with a visit to **Russell Cave National Monument,** in Bridgeport, 72 miles northeast via U.S. 72. This archaeological site was occupied by the Native Americans' prehistoric ancestors for 8,000 years before the arrival of European settlers. Visitors today can tour the cave shelter—the entrance to more than 7 miles of cavernous passages—and view museum exhibits of prehistoric artifacts and a Native American burial ground. There are also tool and cooking demonstrations, a slide program, a nature trail, a garden, a hiking trail, and picnic grounds. *Co. Rd. 75,* ☎ *205/495–2672.* ☛ *Free.* ☉ *Daily 9–5.*

Valley Head

❼ Continue your underground explorations at **Sequoyah Caverns,** at Valley Head, 25 miles southeast on AL 117. A half-mile guided tour through the caverns in Sand Mountain brings visitors past rock formations mirrored in lakes. In the 1930s, dances were held in the largest room, now called the Ballroom. Outside, there's a picnic area, a campground, a small zoo, a swimming pool, a playground, and hiking trails. *Sequoyah Rd.,* ☎ *205/635–0024.* ☛ *$6 adults, $4.50 senior citizens, $4 children under 12.* ☉ *Memorial Day–Labor Day, daily 8:30–4; Labor Day–Memorial Day, weekends 8:30–5.*

Fort Payne

❽ Ten miles south on U.S. 11 is Fort Payne and **DeSoto Falls.** This 100-foot waterfall is one of the loveliest attractions in the 5,000-acre De-Soto State Resort Park. Unsupervised swimming is allowed in the lake, and there is a supervised pool, picnic area, and campgrounds nearby. **Little River Canyon,** the deepest canyon east of the Rocky Mountains, is also in the park. The scenery is breathtaking at this 600-foot-deep and 16-mile-wide canyon. *Co. Rd. 89,* ☎ *205/845–0051 or 800/252–7275.* ☛ *Free, picnicking 50¢.* ☉ *Daily 7 AM–dusk.*

Gadsden

❾ In Gadsden, 35 miles south of Fort Payne on I–59, **Noccalula Falls** and Park is a 100-acre woodland area, with a 90-foot waterfall, miniature golf, train rides, a small zoo, a botanic garden, a covered bridge, and a 1776 pioneer homestead—four log cabins were moved here from the backwoods of Tennessee. There are also campgrounds and picnic areas. *1500 Noccalula Rd., Gadsden,* ☎ *205/549–4663.* ☛ *To homestead and garden: $1.50 adults, $1 senior citizens and children under 12; train ride 50¢.* ☉ *Daily 9–sunset.*

Stretching northeast from Gadsden, Alabama, to Chattanooga, Tennessee, the **Lookout Mountain Trail** runs along a mountain ridge and offers 100 miles of the prettiest scenery in the state for the adventurous hiker's delight. In Alabama the trail begins at Route 89 at the Georgia state line, travels into Mentone, Alabama, and continues via Route 89 to Dogtown and Routes 89 and 175 into Noccalula Falls at Gadsden. *Trail maps are available at the Welcome Center on I–59 at Valley Head,* ☎ *205/635–6522, or the Alabama Bureau of Tourism and Travel,* ☎ *800/272–2262.*

Childersburg

From Gadsden, take U.S. 411/231 south for 72 miles to Childersburg
❿ and **DeSoto Caverns Park.** The site of a 2,000-year-old Native American burial ground, these vast onyx caves were rediscovered in 1540 by Hernando DeSoto and later served as a Confederate gunpowder mining center and a Prohibition speakeasy. Curious rock formations created by stalagmites and stalactites allow the imagination free rein. During the tour, the largest cave (more than 12 stories high) hosts a sound, laser, light, and water show. *5185 DeSoto Caverns Pkwy.,* ☎ *205/378–7252 or 800/933–2283.* ☛ *$10.25 adults, $6.50 children 4–11, under 4 free. (FunPac includes Tour, maze, and gemstone mining tickets: $13.75 adults, $10 children.)* ☉ *Mon.–Sat. 9–5:30, Sun. 12:30–5:30.*

Tuscaloosa

Drive the 33 miles back to Birmingham on I–231/280 and pick up I–20/59 west to Tuscaloosa, another 57 miles. If you choose not to follow the complete Highlands tour, it's worth taking a day trip here from Birmingham. Although the city's leading export may well be football, its wealth of cultural offerings cannot be overlooked. History and ar-
11 chitecture aficionados can take a tour with the **Tuscaloosa County Preservation Society** (located at the Battle–Friedman House, ☎ 205/758–2256), music lovers can stop in to hear the estimable **Tuscaloosa Symphony Orchestra** (for schedule and box-office information, ☎ 205/752–5515), crafts collectors can enjoy October's outstanding **Kentuck Festival of the Arts** (in nearby Northport, ☎ 205/333–1252), and further information on the area can be obtained from the **Tuscaloosa Convention and Visitors Bureau.** *1305 Greensboro Ave., ☎ 800/538–8696. ⏲ Weekdays 8–5.*

If you are in town for a game, make it a point to see the **Paul W. "Bear" Bryant Museum,** which follows the University of Alabama's 100-year tradition of football preeminence. *323 Paul W. Bryant Dr., ☎ 205/348–4668. ☛ $2 adults, $1 children under 18. ⏲ Daily 9–4.*

The **Warner Collection,** which comprises several hundred paintings as well as dozens of artifacts and sculptures, is quite possibly the nation's largest private collection of American painting. It is displayed in two locations. The Asian-style, beautifully landscaped **Gulf State Paper Corporation Headquarters** houses a range of art, including numerous works by the Wyeths, Albert Bierstadt, Frederic Remington, Thomas Cole, and George Catlin. A short drive away you'll find an even more impressive collection in the exquisitely furnished **Mildred Warner House,** a log cabin built in 1822 (with a brick addition built in 1835). The comprehensive assortment of William Aiken Walker's revealing Southern folk paintings, which depict 19th-century African-American life, is enough to make a visit worthwhile. The walls are virtually covered with works of American Impressionists, including Mary Cassatt, Maurice Prendergast, Winslow Homer, John Singer Sargent, Childe Hassam, Georgia O'Keeffe, and James A. M. Whistler. *Gulf State Paper Corporation: 1400 River Rd. NE, ☎ 205/553–6200. ☛ Free. Tours offered weekdays at 5:30 and 6:30 PM, Sat. 10–7, Sun. 1–7. Mildred Warner House: 1925 8th St., ☎ 205/345–4062. ☛ Free. Tours offered on the hour Sat. 10–6, Sun. 1–6.*

Moundville

12 Fourteen miles south of Tuscaloosa on U.S. 69 is **Mound State Monument** in Moundville. The museum contains a number of artifacts found nearby that can be traced to the prehistoric forefathers of local Seminole, Creek, and Cherokee Native Americans. On the grounds are 20 earthen temple mounds, the largest of which supports a reconstructed Native American temple, a reconstructed Native American village, a nature trail leading to the Black Warrior River, picnic areas, and a campground. *Rte. 69S, ☎ 205/371–2572. ☛ $2 adults, $1 children 6–18 and senior citizens, children under 6 free. ⏲ Museum daily 9–5, ⏲ Park daily 8–8.*

What to See and Do with Children

Discovery 2000, Discovery Place. At this hands-on museum, a child can dress up in a police officer's hat and coat, climb on a fire truck, sit in an ambulance and sound the siren, or put together the bones of a skeleton. *1320 22nd Ave. S, ☎ 205/939–1176. ☛ (includes admis-*

sion to adjacent Red Mountain Museum): $2 adults, $1.50 children under 16. ⊙ Tues.–Fri. 9–3, Sat. 10–4, Sun. 1–4.

Ruffner Mountain Nature Center. Cutaway sections of the mountain ridge are labeled to explain the area's geologic history. There are also well-marked nature trails, a wildflower garden, and bird observation stations. *1214 81st St. S (about 1 mi east of downtown, take 77th St. Exit from I–59),* ☎ *205/333–8112.* ☞ *Free. ⊙ Tues.–Sat. 9–5, Sun. 1–5.*

U.S. Space and Rocket Center (*see* Exploring, *above*).

Off the Beaten Path

Southern Museum of Flight. Housed here is the Alabama Aviation Hall of Fame, the first Delta Airlines passenger plane, and World War II bombers built at a factory in Birmingham. See a portion of the Red Baron's propeller or watch an aircraft being restored to its original condition. *4343 73rd St. N (near airport),* ☎ *205/833–8226.* ☞ *$2 adults, $1 children 6–18, preschoolers free. ⊙ Tues.–Sat. 9:30–4:30, Sun. 1–4:30.*

Tannehill Historical State Park. Built around reconstructed ironworks and blast furnaces that produced munitions for the Confederacy, the park offers a museum, crafts demonstrations, a gristmill, a pioneer farm, a country store, and a train ride. The log-walled Furnace Master Inn specializes in home cooking. *Bucksville exit off I–59 (about 30 mi west of Birmingham),* ☎ *205/477–5711.* ☞ *$1 adults, 50¢ children 6–12, under 6 and over 65 free. ⊙ Daily 7 AM–sunset.*

Shopping

These days, shopping in the Birmingham area is done mostly in malls and centers in the suburban areas rather than downtown. Sales tax varies from 6% to 8% depending upon the town you're in.

Shopping Districts

A number of crafts and antiques shops and flea markets are clustered along the main street of **Mentone,** a Victorian resort village on AL 117 in the far northeastern part of the state.

Mountain Brook Village (Cahaba Rd.), a small, villagelike shopping area tucked away in the hollows of Birmingham's ritziest neighborhood, has a number of small specialty shops, including Pappagallo. Also here is Browdy's (☎ 205/879–8585), a New York–style deli-restaurant with imported beer.

Riverchase Galleria (intersection of I–459 and U.S. 31, ☎ 205/985–3039) is one of the largest shopping malls in the Southeast. Here you'll find more than 200 stores, including Macy's, Rich's, JC Penney, McRae's, Yieldings, and Parisian's department stores, plus such clothiers as Banana Republic and other purveyors of fashion high and low.

Discount Stores

Boaz Factory Outlets (Boaz, at U.S. 431 and AL 68 in northeast Alabama) are an outlet shopper's dream. The town has four large malls containing more than 150 discount stores, including London Fog, Anne Klein, Benetton, and Reebok.

Palisades Shopping Center (off Valley Avenue at Green Springs, ☎ 205/879–3040) is a complex of 15 to 20 discount shops, including Stein Mart (with name-brand clothing).

Antiques

The **Firm** (3000 Clairmont Ave., ☎ 205/322–3004) has a large selection of Depression glass, Oriental silver chests, and 19th–century memorabilia.

Participant Sports

Canoeing

North of Birmingham at Warrior, there are several outfitters on the **Black Warrior River** that offer whitewater canoeing. South of Birmingham, beginning and intermediate canoeing can be found on the **Cahaba River,** especially near Montevallo. The best guidebook is John Foshee's *Canoeing in Alabama.*

Fishing

The best fresh-water crappie or bass fishing in the Birmingham area is northeast of Birmingham at **Logan Martin Lake** (☎ 205/831–6860) or south at the smaller lakes in **Oak Mountain State Park** (☎ 205/620–2520) off I–65. Rentals are available at **Rabbit Branch Marina** (☎ 205/525–5562) or **Aeromarine Inc.** (☎ 205/595–2141).

Farther north, on the Tennessee River, the 66,000-acre **Lake Guntersville** reservoir is renowned for its largemouth and smallmouth bass; boat rentals are available at Guntersville Boat Mart (AL 69, ☎ 205/582–2038) and at Lake Guntersville State Park (☎ 800/548–4553). Bass, channel catfish, crappie, and freshwater drum can be found in **Wheeler Lake, Wilson Lake,** and **Pickwick Lake,** all Tennessee River reservoirs; for more information, call the Chamber of Commerce of the Shoals at 205/764–4661.

Golf

Golf in the northern part of the state isn't as much of a year-round activity as it is in southern Alabama, but it is possible to play here in the winter. Though some of the courses around the Tennessee River basin close during January or February, others stay open on a weather-permitting basis. Except for brief spells of cold weather, golfers around Birmingham can enjoy the sport all year.

Some of the most scenic and challenging courses in the state are part of the **Robert Trent Jones Golf Trail.** The "Trail" has a total of 18 courses spread out among seven locations around the state, providing 324 holes of some of the most challenging golf you'd ever hope to find. There is one toll-free number (☎ 800/949–4444) for reservations and information about golf at any of the locations. Rates for the Golf Trail courses are less than $40, including green fee and cart. In Huntsville, the trail includes **Hampton Cove,** where golfers challenge one of the two par 72 championship courses or play the par 3 short course. Farther south, in the Birmingham area, the Golf Trail continues with **Oxmoor Valley,** where, again, golfers can choose among three courses.

The state parks of the region offer outstanding public courses for golfers as well: In the northern region try **Joe Wheeler State Park** or **Lake Guntersville State Park. Oak Mountain State Park,** located in the Birmingham area, is both scenic and challenging. Call 800/252–7275 for further information on golf in the state parks. Greens fees with cart range from $30 to $40.

Hiking and Jogging

Oak Mountain State Park (☎ 205/620–2520), 15 miles south of Birmingham in Pelham, is laced with trails for hiking or jogging. Joggers also favor the quiet streets in and around Birmingham's Five Points South. **Buck's Pocket State Park** (☎ 205/659–2000), in northeast Alabama near Guntersville, is a hilly, wooded park with a mile-long trail into a 400-foot canyon.

Tennis

Birmingham's Park and Recreation Board (☎ 205/254–2391) maintains a number of public courts. **Lake Guntersville State Park** (☎ 800/548–4553) and **Joe Wheeler State Park** (☎ 205/247–1184) have lighted courts.

Spectator Sports

Baseball

The **Birmingham Barons,** a Chicago White Sox affiliate in the Southern League, play at Hoover Metropolitan Stadium (☎ 205/988–3200) in Hoover, south of Birmingham on AL 150.

Basketball

The **University of Alabama at Birmingham's Blazers** (☎ 205/934–7252) play most home games at the U.A.B. Arena (617 13th St. S, at 6th Ave. S, ☎ 205/975–8221).

Football

University of Alabama at Birmingham home games are often held at Legion Field (400 Graymont Ave. W, ☎ 205/254–2391).

Dining

As throughout Alabama, north of Mobile, Southern cooking dominates here. Popular dishes include fried chicken, barbecue, roast beef, and country fried steak, accompanied by fresh vegetables, biscuits, and cornbread. Dress is casual unless otherwise noted.

CATEGORY	COST*
$$$	$25–$35
$$	$15–$25
$	under $15

per person for a three-course meal, excluding drinks, service, and sales tax (7% in Birmingham, Guntersville, and Mentone; 8% in Decatur and Huntsville)

Birmingham

$$$ **Highlands: A Bar and Grill.** Owner-chef Frank Stitt, who worked at
★ Chez Panisse in Berkeley and with Richard Olney in France, has been praised by several national magazines. The room is a sophisticated peach and white, with paintings, an ornamental fireplace, brass candleholders, and fresh flowers—plus unhurried but efficient service. There's filet of sole with a light wine sauce; quail with raspberry sauce; and tomatoes stuffed with chunks of lobster, crab, shrimp, and corn—all superbly prepared. ✗ *2011 11th Ave. S, ☎ 205/939–1400. Dinner reservations advised. AE, DC, MC, V. Closed Sun., Mon.*

$$$ **Meadowlark Farms.** Owners Nick and Raphael Cairns have transformed this former farmhouse in suburban Alabaster into a charming European country inn. The intimate dining rooms gleam with fine china, silver, crystal, antiques, and fine art reproductions. Specialties include chateaubriand, lamb chops, duck with brandy fruit sauce, and stuffed red snapper. ✗ *20 min. south of downtown Birmingham. Take I–65 south to exit 242, then drive south on U.S. 31 to County Road 66/Industrial Road.* ☎ *205/663–3141. Reservations advised. AE, MC, V. No lunch Wed.–Sat.*

\$\$–\$\$\$ Bombay Café. The interior is attractive, with muted colors, an Italian marble fireplace, and white tablecloths, and the food—such as simple, perfectly grilled amberjack, and snapper *en papillote* (marinated in bèchamel sauce and baked in parchment with oysters and crabmeat)— is wonderful. ✗ *2839 Seventh Ave. S,* ☎ *205/322–1930. Reservations advised. AE, MC, V. Closed Sun.*

\$\$ Fish Market Restaurant. Fresh fish of all types is served here, from West Indies salad (with lump crabmeat) to seafood gumbo, grilled snapper to blackened redfish, fried scallops to raw oysters. Chef George Sarris is at his best with the Greek-style fish. The decor is restaurant nautical: fish nets, lobster traps, and carved fish. ✗ *611 21st St. S,* ☎ *205/322–3330. No reservations. D, MC, V. Closed Sun.*

\$\$ John's. Though there's not a thing fancy, John's has been consistently
★ rated best in local popularity polls. This nondescript family dining establishment seats 450 and serves some 1,200 meals daily. Owner George Hontzas serves the freshest seafood available and constantly gets raves on the trout almandine, whole red snapper, and jumbo shrimp fried in light batter. The coleslaw, with John's famous dressing, should be ordered with any meal. The corn sticks are an Alabama specialty. ✗ *112 21st St. N,* ☎ *205/322–6014. AE, DC, MC, V. Closed Sun.*

\$\$ Michael's Sirloin Room. This is one of the most popular steak houses in Birmingham. It's also a sports bar, with photos of all the local sports greats from Bear Bryant to Willie Mays on the Wall of Fame, and the television always tuned to the sport of the day. The specialty is a hearty cut of prime steer butt, usually at least 2 inches thick, charbroiled for a smoky taste, but other dishes are served, including veal, lamb, and pork cooked Greek style: heavy on the oregano and garlic. ✗ *431 20th St. S,* ☎ *205/322–0419. Reservations advised for groups of 6 or more. AE, D, DC, MC, V. Closed Sun.*

\$–\$\$ Browdy's of Mountain Brook. This Birmingham establishment has
★ shed its old grocery/bakery for a spiffy, contemporary look, executed in black-and-white walls with hot-pink–and-purple neon lights. The rotating daily specials, which always come with fresh vegetables, are very popular, as are the kosher sandwiches, baked beef short ribs, and beef brisket au jus with brown new potatoes and baby carrots. The restaurant also does a brisk carry-out business, including picnics and parties. ✗ *2713 Culver Rd.,* ☎ *205/879–8585. No reservations. AE, D, DC, MC, V.*

\$–\$\$ Cabana Café. This casual eatery went with nondescript, modern decor when it relocated to this new shopping mall location, but still offers an encyclopedic menu, including Mexican dishes. The Saturday champagne-brunch crowd crows over eggs Benedict and seafood salad. The shrimp gumbo and the Low Country Carolina chicken are very good. ✗ *217 Lakeshore Pkwy.,* ☎ *205/941–1390. Dinner reservations accepted. AE, MC, V. Closed Sun.*

\$ Cosmo's. This is an "in" place with U.A.B. students in the Five Points South neighborhood. The walls are paneled in pastel Formica, and the neon lighting makes for a colorful, lively mix. A glass wall fronting on Magnolia Street encourages people-watching. The specialty is gourmet pizza: pesto with prosciutto, sweet peppers, goat cheese, sun-dried tomatoes, and Italian sausage. ✗ *2012 Magnolia Ave.,* ☎ *205/930–9971. No reservations. AE, DC, MC, V.*

$ **Irondale Café.** This homey little restaurant was the inspiration for Fannie Flagg's Whistlestop Café in Fried Green Tomatoes. And yes, fried green tomatoes are always available, as well as a dozen other fresh vegetables, at least six entrées, and an array of desserts—all served cafeteria-style. Bill McMichael, who runs the restaurant with his family, has redecorated the place to include one room replicating the original café, which dates to Depression days; a '50s-and-'60s-style room; and a formal dining room. ✗ *1906 1st Ave. N, Irondale (east of Birmingham),* ☎ *205/956–5258. Reservations advised for groups. No credit cards. No dinner Sun. and Mon.; closed Sat.*

$ **Ollie's B-B-Q.** A Birmingham tradition, Ollie McClung's barbecue restaurant is a place where people go to meet while they eat. At this little hole-in-the-wall, the sauce is tangy, the pork tender. ✗ *515 University Blvd. off I–65,* ☎ *205/324–9485. No reservations. D, MC, V.* ☻ *Mon.–Sat. 9:30–8. Closed Sun.*

Decatur

$$–$$$ **Simp McGhee's.** Named after the riverboat captain who was an acquaintance of Kate Lackner, a famous turn-of-the-century madam, one of Alabama's best fish restaurants can be found in an early-1900s general store building in the historic district. The red brick and glass exterior is original, as is the large pub-style bar. The high ceiling is pressed tin, and the old red oak floor is stained dark. The downstairs dining room has a more casual, pub-like atmosphere, with a well-stocked bar and the owner's own carvings on the walls. Upstairs is a little more formal, with white linen tablecloths and candlelight—don't be surprised to see some diners decked out in their best dresses or tuxedos. The menu has a number of steak and chicken dishes, but most folks come here for fish. The fillet gumbo is a much-requested dish, but the house specialty is the pontchartrain: fresh fish of the day (usually snapper), topped with shrimp and crabmeat, in a butter and wine sauce, all served on a bed of wild rice. For dessert, try the Kentucky Derby pie, a cross between a giant chocolate chip cookie and a pecan pie, served hot and with vanilla ice cream. ✗ *725 Bank St.,* ☎ *205/353–6284. Reservations advised for groups of 5 or more. AE, D, DC, MC, V. Closed Sun.*

Guntersville

$$ **Chandelier Dining Room.** In the Lake Guntersville State Park Lodge, this restaurant is most notable for its location overlooking the gigantic man-made lake. The large cast-iron chandeliers, which give the place its name, are imposing; the floor is carpeted, and crisp white cloths cover the small wooden tables. The menu offers thick steaks, and chicken and seafood dishes. Try the seafood divan, a casserole of shrimp, crabmeat, mushrooms, and broccoli, with a secret sauce that makes all the difference, or the breast of chicken à la Eugénie, consisting of boneless chicken breast with ham, all in a light white wine sauce. Fried mushrooms and fried zucchini are tasty starters, and for dessert there are numerous pies and pastries, but the hot fudge cake is a notch above the rest. ✗ *Lake Guntersville State Park Lodge, 1155 Lodge Dr.,* ☎ *205/571–5448 or 800/548–4553. No reservations. AE, MC, V.*

Huntsville

$$ **Cafe Berlin.** This new restaurant is owned by the same couple that own Huntsville's Ol' Heidelberg Cafe. Paintings and photographs of European café scenes adorn the walls, and crisp black and white tablecloths and taped brass-band music ensure that the German theme is not forgotten. The menu is lighter than most teutonic-style restaurants, and while schnitzel and wurst are prepared a number of ways, you can also order fish, chicken, and steak dishes, and enormous salads. The Black Forest Gâteau is a favorite dessert. ✗ *505 Airport Rd.,* ☎ *205/880–9920. Reservations advised. AE, D, MC, V.*

$–$$ **Greenbrier Restaurant.** This rustic eatery, located in Madison (just west
★ of Huntsville), was built by hand in 1952 by the owner, Jack Webb, who then proceeded to build the tables as well. Although many modern conveniences have been added, the original hand-hewn decor makes eating here fun. If you close your eyes, you can almost see the country-and-western singers Mr. Webb once hired to stand on the roof and beckon to customers like mythical sirens. The food—catfish and barbecue ribs and chicken—makes this a local favorite. The chicken is served with a special white barbecue sauce. Add generous portions, tasty coleslaw, and hot hush puppies, and you'll know why people drive long distances to eat here. ✗ *27028 Old Highway 20, Madison (8 mi west of Huntsville),* ☎ *205/351–1800. No credit cards.*

Mentone

$ **Log Cabin Deli.** This early-1800s original pine log cabin was once used as an Native American fur trading post. Dine on the open front porch, the screened back porch, or in the main dining room, with a great rock fireplace that burns wood in winter. The hand-cut cedar tables, rough wooden floors, and upturned bushel baskets used as lighting fixtures complete the rustic effect. Everything here is truly home-cooked, and the deli has become famous throughout the south for its soups, hefty sandwiches (just try to finish the cabin roast beef special), baked chicken, country ham, southern-style vegetables, and exotic salad dressings. ✗ *Rte. 117,* ☎ *205/634–4560. No reservations. MC, V. Closed Mon.*

Tuscaloosa

$$ **Cypress Inn.** A series of signs on a small tree outside this multilevel cypress plank lodge records the dates and levels of the floods that have cursed this area since the 19th century. Perhaps that is the price this restaurant must pay for such an idyllic setting on the banks of the Black Warrior River. Inside, there's more cypress plank, along with huge windows looking out onto the river, and fresh flowers and hanging plants. There's also an outside deck with an old wooden covering where you can dine in good weather. The focus of the menu is definitely on fresh fish, and especially fried catfish. The Shrimp Cypress Inn is a casserole of sautéed shrimp and mushrooms in a white wine sauce, topped with a blend of cheeses and baked. Steak and chicken dishes are also available. Locals recommend the bread pudding or peanut butter pie for dessert. ✗ *501 Rice Mine Rd.,* ☎ *205/345–6963. Reservations accepted. AE, D, MC, V.*

$$ **Globe.** Ten minutes from downtown Tuscaloosa, across the Black Warrior River, you'll find the town of Northport and the big barnlike structure that once housed a dry goods store. The building was leased in 1992 by two actors who have turned it into what is perhaps the most adventurous dining establishment in the state. Named after Shakespeare's first theater, the restaurant continues this theme in the decor: A long

English tavern–style bar stands at the far end of one of the two spacious dining rooms and giant line drawings of famous scenes from Shakespeare's plays adorn the walls. But the international menu is the true star of this show, including such entrées as pan-sautéed orange roughy, tandoori chicken, stuffed pasta shells, vegetarian quesadillas, wild mushroom and sage pizzas, and broiled tilapia. The only thing that's typically Southern about this place is the service—very friendly but not exactly speedy. ✕ *430 Main Ave., Northport,* ☎ *205/391–0949. No Reservations. AE, MC, V.*

Lodging

Many hotels and motels offer weekend specials; inquire about special rates. In fall or winter, beware of football weekends in Birmingham: If the Alabama Crimson Tide or the Auburn Tigers are in town, you may find all hotels booked or at least very crowded.

CATEGORY	COST*
$$$$	OVER $95
$$$	$80–$95
$$	$50–$80
$	UNDER $50

All prices are for a standard double room, excluding tax (6% in Rogersville; 7% in Birmingham, Florence, Guntersville, and Mentone; and 8% in Cullman, Decatur, and Huntsville)

Birmingham

$$$$ **Pickwick Hotel.** Part of the Five Points South area, the eight-story Pick-
★ wick was built in 1931 as an office building and converted in 1986 to a bed-and-breakfast hotel. Rooms have been decorated in an art-deco style, with pink walls, green carpets, elegant period furnishings, and Liberty of London bedspreads. Suites have kitchenettes, wet bars, and dining tables. High tea is served every afternoon. ⌂ *1023 20th St. S, 35205,* ☎ *205/933–9555 or 800/255–7304,* FAX *205/933–6918. 35 rooms, 28 suites. Bar, breakfast room, meeting room. AE, DC, MC, V.*

$$$$ **Tutwiler.** A National Historic Landmark, the Tutwiler was built in 1913
★ as luxury apartments and converted into a hotel in 1987. The lobby is elegant, with marble floors, chandeliers, brass banisters, antiques, and lots of flowers. Rooms have antique reproductions, including armoires and high-back chairs, plus velour love seats. This one is pure class. ⌂ *Park Place at 21st St. N, 35203,* ☎ *205/322–2100 or 800/845–1787,* FAX *205/325–1183. 96 rooms, 53 suites. Restaurant, pub. AE, D, DC, MC, V.*

$$$$ **Wynfrey Hotel.** This deluxe hotel rises 15 stories above the Riverchase Galleria complex of 200 shops and restaurants (*see* Shopping, *above*). An Italian marble floor, Chippendale furniture, Oriental rug, enormous arrangement of fresh flowers, and brass escalator set a refined tone in the lobby. Rooms are furnished in English and French traditional styles, but don't measure up to the elegance of the lobby. The top two floors constitute the Chancellor's Club and have two bilevel suites each. ⌂ *U.S. 31, 1000 Riverchase Galleria, Hoover 35244,* ☎ *205/987–1600 or 800/476–7006,* FAX *205/988–4597. 310 rooms, 19 suites. Restaurant, café, 2 lounges, pool, health club. AE, DC, MC, V.*

$$$ **Radisson Hotel.** This 14-story hotel is near the University Medical Center and Five Points South. The pink-and-green lobby, with a piano lounge, has a marble floor and Queen Anne–style furnishings. Rooms are contemporary, in mauve and peach tones. ⌂ *808 20th St. S, 35205,* ☎ *205/933–9000 or 800/333–3333,* FAX *205/933–0920. 287 rooms,*

11 suites (3 with wet bars). Restaurant, lounge, pool, sauna, steam rooms. AE, DC, MC, V.

$$–$$$ **Courtyard Marriott.** Business travelers and families alike enjoy this attractive alternative to overpriced hotels. It offers beautifully landscaped grounds and attractive public areas. ☎ *500 Shades Creek Pkwy., 35209,* ☎ *205/879–0400 or 800/321–2211,* FAX *205/879–6324. 126 rooms, 14 suites. Restaurant, pool, hot tub, exercise room. AE, D, DC, MC, V.*

$$ **Holiday Inn–Redmont.** The city's oldest hotel, dating to 1925, has undergone a $9 million renovation and now sports a fresh look. The two-room suites, which include parlors and large baths, are very popular. The property is downtown, one block from the financial district and four blocks from I–59. Guests are treated to a welcome reception and have use of the YMCA nearby. ☎ *2101 5th Ave. N,* ☎ *205/324–2101,* FAX *205/324–0610. 110 rooms, 6 suites. Restaurant, lounge, airport shuttle. AE, D, DC, MC, V.*

$$ **Ramada Inn Airport.** Three minutes from the airport, this 12-story hotel is a typical Ramada, except for the eye-catching winding staircase in the chandeliered lobby. ☎ *5216 Airport Hwy., 35212,* ☎ *205/591–7900 or 800/272–6232,* FAX *205/592–6476. 186 rooms, 7 suites. Restaurant, lounge, pool, exercise room, meeting rooms. AE, D, DC, MC, V.*

Cullman

$ **Howard Johnson Lodge.** This complex of three low-rise, blue and gray buildings is one of the older motels in the Cullman area. At the Howard Johnson Lodge, rooms are small, neat, and modern, furnished with one king-size or two double beds. A few rooms also have microwaves and refrigerators. By the way, don't expect to get a drink here—this is a dry county. ☎ *Exit 308 off I–65, Box 267, 35056,* ☎ *205/739–4603,* FAX *205/734–8336. 96 rooms. Restaurant, pool. AE, D, DC, MC, V.*

Decatur

$$ **Holiday Inn Downtown.** You'll find nothing out of the ordinary about this five-story, sand-colored, concrete-stucco chain hotel. Accommodations are divided into three areas: the high-rise tower, with some rooms overlooking the Tennessee river; the "Holidome," whose rooms face the indoor pool; and motel-style rooms with their own entrances. All the rooms are simple, with burgundy and green color schemes, modern pine furnishings, and either king-size or double beds. A couple of suites also have a large parlor area. Every room comes with a coffeemaker. ☎ *11061 6th Ave., 35601,* ☎ *205/355–3150 or 800/553–3150,* FAX *205/350–5262. 225 rooms, 2 suites. Restaurant, bar, indoor and outdoor pools, hot tub, recreation room, airport shuttle. AE, D, DC, MC, V.*

Florence

$ **Best Western Executive Inn.** All of the commercial accommodations in Florence are basic, uninspired, and motel style, and this renovated two-story red brick building near the center of town, built in the 1960s as a Holiday Inn, is the best of them. Rooms have modern wood furnishings, a king-size or two double beds, coffeemakers, and simple blue and green wallpaper and carpets. All rooms have their own entrances. The Olympic-size pool is a pleasant extra. ☎ *504 S. Court St., 35630,* ☎ *205/766–2331 or 800/528–1234,* FAX *205/766–3567. 119 rooms, 1 suite. 2 restaurants, bar, pool, outdoor hot tub. AE, D, DC, MC, V.*

Guntersville

$$ **Lake Guntersville State Park Lodge.** Sixty miles southeast of Huntsville, at the meeting point of three distinct natural areas—5,559-acre Lake Guntersville State Park; Lake Guntersville, Alabama's largest lake, with 950 miles of shoreline; and the base of the Appalachian range—you'll find this rather prosaic, modern wood-and-stone building. Visitors are drawn to the lodge by its natural surroundings, not by the lodge itself: With the exception of the impressive high-ceilinged lobby with stuffed animals and birds everywhere, the lodge is a motel-type accommodation. The rooms in the main lodge are large, but the furnishings are nondescript and the color schemes standard. Rooms on the bluff side have balconies with great views of lake and forest. There are furnished cottages and A-frame chalets. The two-bedroom cottages are as modern and simple as the lodge rooms but have a sitting room and a kitchen, and they're right on the water. The chalets have living rooms and two bedrooms. ⌘ *115 Lodge Dr., 35976,* ☎ *205/571–5440 or 800/548–4553,* ℻ *205/571–5459. 94 rooms, 6 suites, 19 chalets, 16 cottages. Coffee shop, dining room, pool, 18-hole golf course, 2 tennis courts, boating. AE, MC, V.*

Huntsville

$$$ **Huntsville Hilton Inn.** Claiming the prize location in Huntsville, this hotel is within walking distance of the downtown square, the historic district, and museums, and many rooms overlook either Big Spring Park and Lake or the Von Braun Civic Center. While the four-story red brick building's exterior is nothing special, the lobby has an upscale, classical feel, complete with Oriental rugs, antique chairs and tables, and, on a dais, a grand piano, which provides entertainment most evenings. The spacious rooms are done in greens and burgundies and have oak and pine furnishings, cable TV, and coffeemakers. Suites and junior suites are also available. ⌘ *401 Williams Ave., 35801,* ☎ *205/533–1400 or 800/544–3197,* ℻ *205/533–1400, ext. 604. 268 rooms, 9 suites. Restaurant, bar, pool, hot tub, exercise room. AE, D, DC, MC, V.*

Mentone

$$ **Mentone Inn.** Lookout Mountain in northeastern Alabama forms the backdrop for this early 1900s country inn, a building perfectly suited to its environment. Flagstone paths lined with flowers and evergreens lead to the entrance. A stone foundation supports screened or glassed-in porches, which have rocking chairs and small tables. The living room has natural-colored pine paneling, comfortable beige furniture, a grandfather clock, and a stone fireplace; guests meet here to play dominoes or bridge. The bedrooms are furnished with 1920s pieces; one has a bookcase with glass doors and an elegant oval mirror on an unusual floor stand. All rooms have multicolored matching bedspreads and curtains, and most have art deco night tables. A full breakfast is included in the rate. ⌘ *Box 284, 35984* ☎ *205/634–4836. 12 rooms. Air-conditioning. No credit cards.*

Rogersville

$$ **Joe Wheeler State Park Lodge.** At the center of 3,400-acre Joe Wheeler State Park is this three-story fieldstone and redwood lodge. The lodge slopes down a hill, giving every room a view of Wheeler Lake. All rooms have balconies; suites have living rooms and tiny kitchenettes. Recreational opportunities abound: A marina is right at the back entrance to the lodge, and boats are available for trips on the lake; countless hiking trails lead to secluded spots and picnic areas throughout the park, and redwood walkways run from the guest rooms down to the pool area. Nearby are small, rustic log cabins, which are no-frills but comfortable. ▣ *U.S. 72, near Rogersville (between Decatur and Florence), Drawer K, Rogersville 35652,* ☎ *205/247–5461 or 800/544–5639,* FAX *205/247–5471. 69 rooms, 6 suites, 24 cabins. Bar, dining room, pool, 18-hole golf course, 4 tennis courts. AE, MC, V.*

The Arts

For an up-to-date listing of happenings in the arts, get the current issue of *Birmingham* magazine on the newsstand. For ticket information, contact the Greater Birmingham Convention & Visitors Bureau (*see* Visitor Information, *below*).

Concerts

Rock concerts are held at the **Civic Center, Sloss Furnaces's** covered amphitheater (☎ 205/324–1911), and the **Oak Mountain Amphitheater** in Pelham (☎ 205/985–9797). Organ shows on a "mighty Wurlitzer" accompany silent pictures at the **Alabama Theatre** (1817 3rd Ave. N, Birmingham, ☎ 205/252–2262).

Dance

The **State of Alabama Ballet** (☎ 205/252–2475) performs at the Civic Center from September through March.

Festival

For a month or more each spring, Birmingham celebrates the ballet, opera, painting, sculpture, literature, symphony, and other art forms of a single country at its **Festival of the Arts.** Performances and exhibits are staged at various locations throughout the city, though the Civic Center is usually the hub of activity. In June the city hosts another arts celebration, **City Stages,** in downtown Linn Park.

Opera

Birmingham Opera Theatre (Commerce Center, Suite 208, 2027 1st Ave. N, Birmingham 35203, ☎ 205/322–6737) presents two major and three minor productions each season (Sept.–May).

Theater

The **Birmingham Jefferson Civic Center (**☎ 205/251–4100)—a four-block complex with an exhibition hall, a theater, a concert hall, and the Coliseum—hosts touring Broadway companies, major rock concerts, and exhibitions. The **Terrific New Theatre** (☎ 205/328–0868) hosts touring drama groups. **Town and Gown Theatre** (☎ 205/934–5088), a semiprofessional community theater based on the U.A.B. campus (but not a college theater group), puts on five musical and dramatic works from October through May. **Birmingham Children's Theater** (☎ 205/324–0470), the nation's largest professional children's theatrical group, performs for children from October through May at the Civic Center.

Nightlife

Comedy

The Comedy Club (430 Green Springs Hwy., ☎ 205/444–0008) showcases nationally known and up-and-coming comedians nightly except holidays.

Country Music
Midnight Rodeo (5348 Oporto–Madrid Blvd. S, *n* 205/591–4885) offers the area's best country music and dancing.

Discos
Harry's Safari Club (at the Sheraton Perimeter, U.S. 280 at I–459, ☎ 205/972–8606) spins dance tunes nightly.

Jazz
True jazz aficionados frequent the **22nd Street Jazz Café and Brewery** (710 22nd St. S, ☎ 205/252–0407).

The Highlands Essentials

Arriving and Departing
BY BUS

Birmingham's **Greyhound Lines** (☎ 800/231–2222) terminal is on 19th Street North, between Fourth and Fifth avenues. Greyhound also serves Huntsville, Decatur, Florence, and Tuscumbia.

BY CAR

I–59 goes northeast from Birmingham to Chattanooga, southwest to Tuscaloosa and on into Mississippi. I–20 runs east to Anniston and Atlanta. I–65 goes north to Decatur and Nashville and south to Montgomery and Mobile. U.S. 72 and Alt. U.S. 72 run east–west across the northern part of the state and connect Florence, Tuscumbia, Decatur, and Huntsville.

BY PLANE

Birmingham International Airport (☎ 205/595–0533) is less than 3 miles from central downtown and is served by American, ComAir, Delta, Northwest Airlink, Southwest, TW Express, United, United Express, and USAir. Taxis are readily available; the fare to most hotels is about $10 for one passenger, $5 for each additional passenger. Many hotels provide limousine service from the airport by prior arrangement. If you're traveling by car, follow the clearly marked signs downtown.

Huntsville International Airport (☎ 205/772–9395), at Exit 7 off I–55, is served by American, Delta, Northwest, and United. **Muscle Shoals Airport** (☎ 205/381–2869) is served by Northwest Airlink.

BY TRAIN

The only **Amtrak** station (☎ 205/324–3033 or 800/872–7245) in the Highlands is on Morris Avenue, in downtown Birmingham. Northbound trains run on Monday, Wednesday, and Friday; southbound on Sunday, Tuesday, and Thursday.

Getting Around
A car is a necessity in the Highlands, including in Birmingham, whose sites and restaurants are spread throughout the city.

BY BUS

The **Metro Area Express** (MAX) (☎ 205/521–0101) serves the city. Buses require exact change (80¢ fare, 15¢ transfer), and run only during daytime hours (6–6).

BY TAXI

Birmingham's **Yellow Cab** (☎ 205/252–1131) charges $2.95 for the first mile, $1.20 for each additional mile.

Guided Tours

Not much exists in the way of guided tours, except for large groups. The **Greater Birmingham Convention & Visitors Bureau** (*see* Visitor Information, *below*) has free brochures for self-guided tours of the downtown and Five Points South areas.

Important Addresses and Numbers

EMERGENCIES

Dial 911 for **police** and **ambulance** in an emergency. The all-night emergency room closest to downtown Birmingham is at **University Hospital** (1900 5th Ave. S, ☎ 205/934–5105).

PHARMACY

Eckerd Drugs (Eastwood Shopping Plaza, ☎ 205/956–0400; ⊘ Daily 7 AM–midnight).

RADIO STATIONS

AM: WAGG 1320, modern rock; WYDE 850, talk. **FM:** WZZK 104.7, country; WAPI 94.5, pop; WZRR 99.5, classic rock; WXTX 98.1, country; WFFX 95.7, contemporary rock; WRSA 96.9, easy listening; WDRM 102.1, country; WAHR 99.1, adult contemporary.

VISITOR INFORMATION

Greater Birmingham Convention & Visitors Bureau (2200 9th Ave. N, 35203, ☎ 205/252–9825 or 800/458–8085). **Cullman Area Chamber of Commerce and Convention and Visitors Bureau** (211 2nd Ave., 35055, ☎ 205/734–0454). **Decatur Convention and Visitors Bureau** (corner of 6th Ave. and 4th St., 35602, ☎ 205/350–2028 or 800/524–6181). **Huntsville/Madison County Convention and Visitors Bureau** (700 Monroe St., Huntsville 35801, ☎ 205/533–5273). **Tuscaloosa Convention and Visitors Bureau** (1305 Greensboro Ave., 35401, ☎ 205/391–9200 or 800/538–8696).

PLANTATION COUNTRY, INCLUDING MONTGOMERY

Known as the Cradle of the Confederacy, Montgomery is a town steeped in antebellum history. While its population has grown to 200,500, the capital city is still reminiscent of a sleepy little town on the banks of the Alabama River. In the final year of the Civil War, Union troops, led by General John Wilson, passed through the city and burned artillery factories in Selma, but they did not destroy Montgomery. Many of the old houses have been restored.

The city bears witness to another of this country's great struggles as well. Here, in 1954, after black seamstress Rosa Parks was arrested for refusing to give up her seat on a city bus to a white man, a young black minister, Dr. Martin Luther King Jr., led the 1½-year bus boycott that spearheaded the civil rights movement. Completed in 1989, the dramatic Civil Rights Memorial in front of the Southern Poverty Law Center (400 Washington Ave., ☎ 334/264–0286) is the first phase of a long-range project. Created by Maya Lin, designer of the Vietnam Veterans' Memorial in Washington, D.C., the monument consists of an upper plaza and a pool from which water flows over a 40-foot-wide black granite wall. On it are inscribed words from Dr. King's "I have a dream . . . " speech and the names of many who gave their lives to the civil rights movement.

While Montgomery's history has been dramatic, its present makes it the capital of stage drama in the South. With the move of the Alabama Shakespeare Festival into world-class facilities (costing $21.5 million), some of the best actors in America have been lured to the area to perform at the 750-seat festival stage and the 225-seat Octagon theater. Also in the 250-acre Wynton M. Blount Cultural Park—named for the former postmaster general of the United States, who donated the land and the festival building to the city—is the $6.1 million Montgomery Museum of Fine Arts. The gardens are beautifully landscaped.

Montgomery is a good base for exploring the Old South plantations, historic sites, and big fishing lakes of central Alabama. The most interesting trips from Montgomery are to Selma, Demopolis, Tuskegee, Eufaula, and Troy.

Exploring

Montgomery
WALKING TOUR
Numbers in the margin correspond to points of interest on the Downtown Montgomery map.

★ ❶ Begin with the handsome **State Capitol,** which reopened in 1992 after an extensive restoration. It was built in 1851 and briefly (for a few months in 1861) served as the first capitol for the Confederate States of America. Just inside the huge double doors (with a bronze star marking the spot where Jefferson Davis stood to take the oath of office as president of the Confederacy) there is an amazing piece of interior design. The stairway curling up the sides of the circular hallway is free-standing, without visible support. The state's rich history has been caught by an artist's brush in great, colorful murals. In the large House chamber and smaller Senate chamber, the gigantic brick fireplaces are now fully operational following the renovation. *Bainbridge St. at Dexter Ave.,* ☎ *334/242–3184.*

❷ Walk west one block. On your left is **Dexter Avenue King Memorial Baptist Church,** where Dr. Martin Luther King Jr. began his career as a minister in 1955. The church's sanctuary and the basement Sunday-school rooms are open to visitors. A mural covering one basement wall depicts people and events associated with Dr. King and the Civil Rights Movement. *454 Dexter Ave.,* ☎ *334/263–3970.* ☛ *Free.* ☉ *For tours Mon.–Thurs. at 10 AM and 2 PM, Fri. at 2 PM, Sat. 10–2 by appointment only.*

❸ Returning to the capitol, turn right onto Bainbridge and pause where it meets Washington Avenue. Here the **Alabama Department of Archives and History** pays homage to the soldiers who lost their lives in World War I. It is lined with Alabama marble and contains outstanding exhibits of artifacts documenting the state's history from its Indian days. *624 Washington Ave.,* ☎ *334/242–4361.* ☉ *Weekdays 8–5, free guided tours Sat. 9–5.*

❹ At the corner of Washington Avenue and Union Street stands the **First White House of the Confederacy,** built in 1840. The house was occupied by Jefferson Davis and his family while the Confederacy was being organized at the State Capitol across the street. Today it contains many of their possessions, plus artifacts of the Civil War period. *644 Washington Ave.,* ☎ *334/242–1861. Free tours weekdays 8–4:30, weekends 9–4:30.*

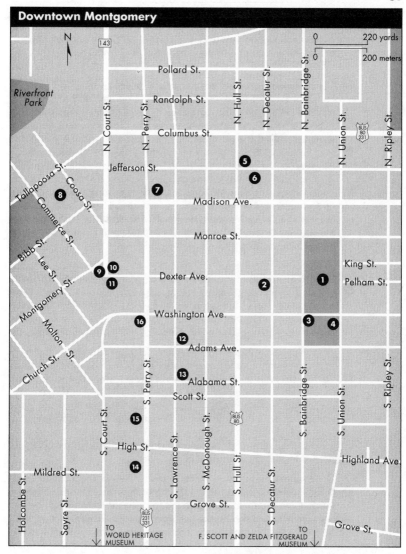

Downtown Montgomery

Alabama Department
of Archives and
History, **3**

Arts and Humanities
State Council
Building, **10**

Court Square
Fountain, **9**

Dexter Ave. King
Memorial Baptist
Church, **2**

First White House of
the Confederacy, **4**

Governor Shorter
Mansion, **13**

House of Mayors, **14**

Lower Commerce St.
Historic District, **8**

Lucas Tavern, **5**

Old Confederate Post
Office, **16**

Ordeman-Shaw
House, **6**

St. John's Episcopal
Church, **7**

St. Peter's Roman
Catholic Church, **12**

State Capitol, **1**

Teague House, **15**

Winter Building, **11**

The **Old North Hull Street Historic District** (also known as **Old Alabama Town**)—about six blocks northwest of the capitol, between Madison Avenue and Columbus Street—consists of 24 newly restored houses, barns, stores, and other structures from 1818 to the turn of the century.

⑤ The reception center for the district is in the old **Lucas Tavern** (310 N. Hull St., ☎ 334/240–4500), built in 1818 on the Old Federal Road traveled by early settlers to the area; in 1825, the French general Lafayette stayed at the tavern on his way to Montgomery. A free slide show here tells the story of the district. A self-guided cassette walking
⑥ tour covers 10 house museums. At the 11th—the **Ordeman-Shaw House** (230 N. Hull St., ☎ 334/240–4500), an Italianate town house with restored outbuildings and gardens—volunteers lead tours of the house, when it's available. Another section of restored buildings is just off Columbus Street on the district's north side. These include the **Cotton Gin and Cotton Museum, Haigler Plantation Office,** and the **Rose-Morris Craft Center.** *Cassette tour: $5 adults, $2 children 6–18, under 6 free.* ⊙ *Mon.–Sat. 9–3:30, Sun. 1–3:30.*

DRIVING TOUR

From North Hull Street, drive west on Madison Avenue for three
⑦ blocks. The imposing, high-spired church on the right is **St. John's Episcopal Church** (113 Madison Ave., ☎ 334/262–1937). Built in 1856, it has colorful stained-glass windows and a bronze plaque marking the pew where Jefferson Davis worshiped.

Continue west on Madison Avenue, veer left onto Bibb Street, then turn right onto Commerce Street. On your right, between Court Square and
⑧ the Riverfront, is the **Lower Commerce Street Historic District,** a group of renovated Victorian structures dating from the end of the last century and now used as office buildings. This area was the trade-and-transportation hub of the busy 19th-century town, which prospered from the business of the Alabama River; there cotton was loaded onto great riverboats and transported downstream and finally out to sea, headed for the textile mills of New England.

Drive south on Commerce Street to Dexter Avenue. At the junction is
⑨ **Court Square Fountain,** built in 1885. Hebe, cupbearer to the gods, looks north down Commerce Street to the river. To the left on Dexter is the
⑩ extraordinary **Arts and Humanities State Council Building** (1 Dexter Ave., ☎ 334/242–4076), patterned after a Venetian palazzo. Works by Alabama artists are always on display in the magnificent lobby with its banistered balcony. Free tours can be arranged.

⑪ Across the avenue is another newly renovated structure, the **Winter Building** (2 Dexter Ave.), built in the 1840s as the office of the Southern Telegraph Company. It was from here that the Confederate leaders sent a telegram ordering their soldiers to fire on Ft. Sumter, thereby starting the Civil War.

⑫ Drive east on Dexter Avenue, then south on Lawrence Street, to **St. Peter's Roman Catholic Church** (219 Adams Ave., ☎ 334/262–7304), built in 1852. Its unusual Spanish-style architecture may reflect the Cuban and Mexican origins of some of the building funds. To have a look inside, enter through the rectory.

Continue south on Lawrence Street past the Montgomery County
⑬ Courthouse. At the corner of Lawrence and Alabama streets is the **Governor Shorter Mansion** (305 S. Lawrence St.) with its Greek Revival

portico, home in the 19th-century to Governor John Gill Shorter. It has been renovated and now houses offices.

⑭ Turn right onto High Street and drive one block. To the left on South Perry Street is the brick **House of Mayors.** Once the home of Jack Thorington and Mordecai Moses, both mayors of Montgomery during the 19th century, and Joseph Norwood, who became mayor of nearby Ft. Deposit in the 1880s, this mansion now houses commercial offices.

⑮ One block north is the **Teague House** (468 S. Perry St.), a fine example of late Greek Revival architecture in the South and now owned by the Alabama Business Council. Continuing north on Perry Street,
⑯ you'll see the **Old Confederate Post Office** (39 S. Perry St., corner of Washington St.). One of the oldest buildings in town, it was once the law office of U.S. Congressman William Lowndes Yancey, who spoke eloquently in Congress in the mid-1800s about why the South should secede from the Union. The building served as the Confederate Post Office in 1861. Today it houses private offices.

Selma
Numbers in the margin correspond to points of interest on the Plantation Country map.

❶ Forty-nine miles west of Montgomery on U.S. 80, **Selma** is steeped in history. On March 21, 1965, following the aftermath of "Bloody Sunday" two weeks earlier, Dr. Martin Luther King Jr. led a group of civil-rights demonstrators on a 50-mile march from downtown Selma's Edmund Pettus Bridge to Montgomery. The journey resulted ultimately in the passing of the nation's Voting Rights Act.

Selma may always be remembered for its controversial role in the civil-rights movement, but history buffs of all periods will find plenty to see in this small city's rich array of museums and antebellum mansions. Each year in late March a **Historic Selma Pilgrimage** (☎ 800/272–2522) takes visitors through several renowned homes. In late April one of the largest annual **Civil War reenactments** (☎ 334/875–7241) in the nation draws thousands to the site of the Battle of Selma, on the Alabama River. Year-round you can stop by the Visitors Information Center for advice on what to see. *Off U.S. 80W, 2207 Broad St., ☎ 334/875–7485. ⊙ Daily 8–8.*

Demopolis
On U.S. 80, 40 miles west of Selma, this town takes great pride in its rich Southern heritage. A 5-mile self-guided-tour map provides detailed histories of the numerous antebellum homes in the area, and a cassette driving tour will take you past the 18th-century buildings in the his-
❷ toric downtown area. The 10,000-acre **Demopolis Lake** offers fishing, boating, swimming, picnicking, and campgrounds. *Take I–59S to U.S. 43W. Maps, cassettes, and tape players are available, free of charge, from the Demopolis Area Chamber of Commerce, 102 E. Washington St., Box 667, ☎ 334/289–0270, ⊙ Weekdays 8:30–5, or from the Information Center at the Best Western Hotel on Rte. 80, ☎ 334/289–5772, ⊙ Evenings and weekends.*

Two fine antebellum homes in Demopolis are open to the public. **Gaineswood,** built in 1860, has been called one of the finest Greek Revival mansions in the South. The house has been extensively restored, down to reproductions of the original French wallpapers. It contains the original furnishings, including carved four-posters and a flutina— a one-of-a-kind musical instrument invented by the original owner (who

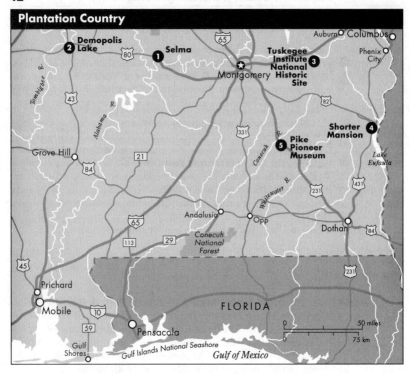

Plantation Country

also designed Gaineswood itself). Interior architectural elements include elaborate columns and pilasters; friezes and medallions of wood, plaster, cast iron, and leather; veined marble mantels; and ceiling-dome skylights. **Bluff Hall** was built in 1832 as a Federal-style house and remodeled in the Greek Revival style several years later. It stands on a chalky cliff above the Tombigbee River and features a columned front portico, a huge double parlor with Corinthian columns, and Empire and Victorian furnishings donated by friends and descendants of the original owner. Also on display is a collection of period clothing. Both are listed on the National Historic Register. *Gaineswood: 805 Whitfield St. E, ☎ 334/289–4846. ☛ $3 adults, $2 students, 50¢ children under 13. ⊙ Mon.–Sat. 9–5, Sun. 1–5. Bluff Hall: 405 N. Commissioners Ave., ☎ 334/289–1666. ☛ $3 adults, $1 children 5–12, children under 5 free. ⊙ Tues.–Sat. 10–5, Sun. 2–5.*

Tuskegee

A 35-mile drive east from Montgomery on U.S. 80 brings you to Tuskegee. The **Tuskegee Institute National Historic Site** (☎ 334/727–3200) includes the school founded by Booker T. Washington in 1881, one of America's first black universities; the Institute's Victorian buildings, many designed and constructed by students; a replica of the childhood home of Booker T. Washington; and his actual redbrick Victorian home, the Oaks. **The George Washington Carver Museum** on the campus includes Carver's original laboratory, his artwork, and a historical study of the **Tuskegee Institute.** A walking tour of the Historic Campus district originates at the Carver Museum. *U.S. 29S,*

Tuskegee Institute National Historic Site, ☎ *334/727–3200.* ☛ *Free.* ☉ *Daily 9–5.*

Northeast of Tuskegee, **Tuskegee National Forest** (☎ 334/727–2652), spread over 10,791 acres, offers fishing, quail hunting, and an 8-1/2-mile woodlands hiking trail.

Eufaula

On U.S. 431, 50 miles southeast of Tuskegee on a 45,000-acre Chattahoochee River reservoir, Eufaula is a town of antebellum homes and great fishing. Dozens of homes built between 1834 and 1911 are open during the Eufaula Spring Pilgrimage in early April. Open year round, ❹ the **Shorter Mansion,** a white-columned house museum built in 1884, is a fine example of Neoclassical Revival architecture and a showplace of the Seth Lore National Historic District. *Take U.S. 82S, 340 N. Eufaula Ave.,* ☎ *334/687–3793.* ☛ *$3 adults, 50¢ children under 12.* ☉ *Weekdays 9–4, Sat. 10–4, Sun. 1–4.*

Troy

❺ Troy is 40 miles south of Montgomery on U.S. 231. The **Pike Pioneer Museum** has captured the essence of 18th- and 19th-century Pike County in its 10,000 museum pieces, ranging from pioneer farm tools to turn-of-the-century household goods. These artifacts are displayed in 10 buildings that are themselves museum pieces, including a log house, a jail, a general store, and even an outhouse—all moved here from other parts of the state. *248 U.S. 231N, Troy,* ☎ *334/566–3597.* ☛ *$3 adults, $2 senior citizens, $1 students, children under 6 free.* ☉ *Mon.–Sat. 10–5, Sun. 1–5.*

What to See and Do with Children

Montgomery Museum of Fine Arts. Alabama's oldest fine arts museum reopened in 1988 in an impressive new facility within the same park that houses the Alabama Shakespeare Festival Theatre. It features ARTWORKS, a hands-on gallery for children and adults; a permanent gallery exhibiting the Blount, Inc. Corporate Collection of American Art; and a gift shop, auditorium, and print gallery, as well as new galleries for changing exhibitions. Patrons enjoy dining in the Terrace Cafe. *1 Museum Dr.,* ☎ *334/244–5700.* ☛ *Free.* ☉ *Tues.–Wed. and Fri.–Sat. 10–5, Thurs. 10–9, Sun. noon–5.*

Montgomery Zoo. Expanded from 6 to 40 acres, the zoo is home to 800 animals from five continents. Dining, a gift shop, and a train ride are offered as well. *329 Vandiver Blvd.,* ☎ *334/240–4900.* ☛ *$4.50 adults, $2 senior citizens, $1.50 children 4–12, under 4 free.* ☉ *May–Sept., daily 9–5; Oct.–Apr., daily 9–4.*

W. A. Gayle Planetarium. Images of the sun, moon, planets, stars, and other heavenly bodies are projected on a 50-foot dome. Shows are continuously updated. *1010 Forest Ave., Oak Park,* ☎ *334/241–4799.* ☛ *$2 adults, $1 children 6–17. Shows on some weekends at 2 PM (call first), closed last 2 weeks Dec.*

Off the Beaten Path

Hank Williams Memorial. Montgomery was the home of country-music singer and songwriter Hank Williams, and after his untimely death at age 29 on New Year's Day, 1953, he was brought here for one of the city's grandest funerals. It was held at City Hall, with the top country stars of the time delivering eulogies and singing sad songs. He was buried in the Oakwood Cemetery Annex (1305 Upper Wetumpka Rd., ☎ 334/264–4938), beneath a stone that depicts his likeness and sheet music from his most popular songs, such as "Your Cheatin' Heart."

Jasmine Hill Gardens and Outdoor Museum. Here, atop a wooded hill, are 17 acres of beautiful gardens with replicas of Greek sculptures and of the ruins of the Temple of Hera. Musical performances are sometimes given at the outdoor theater. *1500 Jasmine Hill Rd., Montgomery, ☎ 334/567–6463 or 334/263–1440.* ☛ *$3.50 adults, $2 children 6–12, under 6 free.* ☉ *Tues.–Sun. 9–5, closed Dec.–Feb.*

Scott and Zelda Fitzgerald Museum. Zelda Fitzgerald grew up in these parts, and some of her artwork still hangs at Montgomery's Museum of Fine Arts (*see* What to See and Do with Children, *above*). Her husband, F. Scott, is famous for such works as "The Great Gatsby," "Tender is the Night," and numerous short stories. Once the home of this colorful couple, it's now a museum containing many of the Fitzgeralds' belongings; you can also view a 25-minute video on their life in Montgomery. *919 Felder Ave. (via South Union St.), Montgomery, ☎ 334/264–4222.* ☛ *Free.* ☉ *Wed.–Fri. 10–2, weekends 1–5, and by appointment.*

Shopping

Shopping Centers and Malls

In addition to its anchor stores—Sears, Parisian's, McRae's, and Gayfer's—**Eastdale Mall** (on the Eastern Bypass and Atlanta Highway, 1000 Eastdale Mall, ☎ 334/277–7359) has a variety of specialty stores, record and book stores, restaurants, eight movie theaters, and Montgomery's only ice skating rink.

At **Zelda Place** (2960 Zelda Rd., ☎ 334/244–0440), you'll find a deco-style shopping area favored by the young professional crowd for its collection of small shops, including Nancy Blount (women's high fashion) and the New York Kitchen Shoppe. Joe's Delicatessen, a Montgomery tradition—serving whopping corned beef and pastrami sandwiches, is also here.

Antiques

Herron House (422 Herron St., ☎ 334/265–2063) has Montgomery's largest stock of porcelain, glass, and silver, plus 18th- and 19th-century furniture. **Bodiford's Antique Mall** (919 Hampton St., ☎ 334/265–4220) is a collection of 16 small stores gathered under one big roof.

Participant Sports

Bicycling

Cloverland Cycle Shop (3656 S. Perry St., ☎ 334/265–9427) rents bicycles for rides in Oak Park or in the country.

Fishing

A 45,000-acre reservoir on the Chattahoochee River, Lake Eufaula is noted for catfish, bream, crappie, and several species of bass. You can rent a boat at **Lakepoint State Park** (Rte. 2, off U.S. 431, ☎ 334/687–6676) or fish from the banks below the bluffs in downtown Eufaula. Lures and equipment are for sale at **Tom Mann's Fish World** (U.S. 431, 4 mi north of Eufaula, ☎ 334/687–3655).

Golf

Montgomery boasts **Lagoon Park** (☎ 334/271–7004), a very flat course with plenty of water hazards and trees, consistently rated by Golf Digest as one of the top 50 public courses in the United States. Other Montgomery area courses include **River Run** (☎ 334/271–2811) and **Oak Hills** (☎ 334/281–3344). Several sections of Alabama's **Robert Trent Jones Golf Trail** are also in this area: the **Grand National** course at Auburn/Opelika, **Highland Oaks** at Dothan, and **Cambrian Ridge** at Greenville (considered by many area golfers to be the most spectacular on the trail). The three sites combine to offer a variety of 7 courses. Some are long, some are short, but all are very challenging and scenic. For reservations and information about any of the state's "Trail" courses, call 800/949–4444. Greens fees with cart run $25–$40.

Miniature Golf

Mountasia Fantasy Golf (5671 Atlanta Hwy., ☎ 334/277–4653) takes golfers on a safari through and around a man-made mountain, large model elephants and other animals, and a cave.

Tennis

Montgomery's Lagoon Park (☎ 334/271–7001) has 17 lighted courts and is open 8 AM–10 PM. **Lakepoint State Park Resort** (*see* Fishing, *above*) has six lighted courts.

Spectator Sports

Dog Racing

Greyhound races are held at **Victoryland,** about 20 miles east of Montgomery, just off I–85N in Shorter (☎ 334/727–0540 or 800/688–2946). There's racing and pari-mutuel betting every night but Sunday, and several matinees during the week. No one under 19 is admitted.

Dining

Old Southern recipes, featuring lots of fresh vegetables and simple country dishes, are the focus of many restaurants in central Alabama, though a few eateries try to lean more toward fine dining and international (primarily Italian) cuisine. Dress is casual unless otherwise noted.

CATEGORY	COST*
$$$	over $25
$$	$15–$25
$	under $15

per person for a three-course meal, excluding drinks, service, and 8% sales tax

Montgomery

DOWNTOWN

$ **Chris' Hot Dog Stand.** A Montgomery tradition for over 50 years, this stand has booths and an old-fashioned lunch counter with stools. Mr. Chris's famous sauce combines chili peppers, onions, and a variety of herbs that give his hot dogs a one-of-a-kind flavor. For a special treat, try the hot dog with "kitchen chili," a heavy, hot chili of beans and onions that you have to eat with a knife and fork. ✕ *138 Dexter Ave.,* ☎ *334/265–6850. No reservations. No credit cards. Closed Sun.*

$ **Farmer's Market Cafeteria.** In a downtown industrial-style metal building, the cafeteria is about as plain as restaurants get, except for the photos on the walls reminding diners of past sports heroes. Fried chicken, catfish, country-smothered steak, and fresh vegetables are served. The hearty breakfast with smoked bacon and homemade biscuits is a local tradition. ✕ *315 N. McDonough St.,* ☎ *334/262–9163. No reservations. No credit cards. No dinner. Closed Sun.*

$ **Sassafras Tearoom.** You can buy the table you eat off of and enjoy a
★ superb meal in the Victorian atmosphere of this unusual century-old shop-cum-eatery in the Cottage Hill district. Operated by retired Colonel Jim Wallace and his wife, Mary, the restaurant, which serves lunch only, caters to professionals and antiques hunters alike. Sassafras tea, either hot or cold, accompanies the crunchy chicken salad, buttermilk pie, and other home-cooked delectables, which are served promptly and graciously. ✕ *532 Clay St.,* ☎ *334/265–7277. Lunch reservations advised for groups of 5 or more. MC, V. No dinner. Closed weekends.*

CLOVERDALE

$$$ **Vintage Year.** Chef Judy Martin's menu features snapper, tuna, shrimp,
★ salmon, and other fish prepared in a Northern Italian style, as well as the ever-popular pasta varieties. The decor is elegant, and the neighborhood bar is a popular meeting place. ✕ *405 Cloverdale Rd.,* ☎ *334/264–8463. Reservations advised. AE, MC, V. No lunch or breakfast. Closed Sun.–Mon.*

$$ **Jubilee Seafood Company.** In a very pleasant small café, Bud Skinner cooks some of the finest and freshest seafood dishes in town, including Dungeness crab, snapper prepared in a variety of ways (including Greek-style—sautéed in olive oil and spices and topped with roasted almonds), soft-shell crabs, crab claws, and other delicacies. For a real treat, try the barbecued shrimp, which are marinated in a secret red sauce, wrapped in bacon, and charbroiled. Bud also has a tasty West Indies salad with marinated crab. ✕ *1057 Woodley Rd., Cloverdale Plaza,* ☎ *334/262–6224. No reservations. AE, DC, MC, V. No lunch. Closed Sun.–Mon.*

$$ **Sahara Restaurant.** Joe and Mike Deep's Sahara, in Cloverdale, is one
★ of Montgomery's finest restaurants. Linen tablecloths and uniformed servers are part of the old South charm of the place. A choice of fresh snapper, grouper, and scampi are broiled to taste, and succulent steaks are grilled over coals. The seafood gumbo is wonderful: The okra is whole and not cooked to bits, and there's plenty of shrimp and oyster. ✕ *511 E. Edgemont Ave.,* ☎ *334/262–1215. Reservations accepted. AE, DC, MC, V. Closed Sun.*

$$ **Wesley's In Old Cloverdale.** Formerly Kat & Harri's Nice Place, Wesley's In Old Cloverdale has had a change in ownership, but is still one of Montgomery's most popular eateries and nightspots. Start with a plate piled high with their spicy nachos, and then enjoy one of the Italian, seafood, or Cajun entrées. On the lighter side, try a specialty pizza or calzone baked in their special wood-burning oven. The restaurant has recently added a pastry chef to the staff, making the menu offerings even better. There's a popular champagne brunch on Sunday. ✕ *1061 Woodley Rd.,* ☎ *334/834–2500. Reservations advised weekends. AE, MC, V.*

$ **Martin's Restaurant.** Martin's is plain but comfortable—in a shopping center, but here you'll find generous helpings of home-cooked fresh vegetables, Southern fried chicken, and delicious panfried catfish fresh from Alabama ponds. The cornbread sticks literally melt in your mouth. ✕ *1796 Carter Hill Rd.,* ☎ *334/265–1767. Reservations accepted. No credit cards. Closed Sat.*

Points Beyond

$$ **Green Lantern.** In a rustic country setting, with jukebox music, the Green Lantern is famous for its cheese biscuits, which many locals take home by the sackful. The waitresses bark out the menu, which is not printed. It consists of several types of steaks and excellent fried chicken. The best is the steak, with huge baked potatoes and all the cheese biscuits you can eat. ✗ *5725 Troy Hwy., 5 mi southeast on U.S. 231,* ☎ *334/288–9947. Reservations advised for groups. AE, MC, V. No lunch. Closed Sun.*

$ **Bates House of Turkey.** If you've a yen for turkey, don't miss this one-of-a-kind southern eatery. In a small but well-polished down-home dining room, with photographs of the biggest turkey farm in central Alabama, Bates House of Turkey serves nothing but turkey for lunch and dinner: turkey sandwiches, turkey chili, turkey sausage, even quick-frozen smoked turkey breasts. ✗ *1060 Eastern By-Pass, 1 block north of I–85,* ☎ *334/279–9775. No reservations. MC, V. No dinner Sun.*

Lodging

Several area lodgings offer special rates to theatergoers.

CATEGORY	COST*
$$$$	over $70
$$$	$50–$70
$$	$35–$50
$	under $35

All prices are for a standard double room, excluding 10% tax.

Montgomery

DOWNTOWN

$$$$ **Madison Hotel.** Elvis Presley slept here, but you're more likely to run into legislators and businessmen than rock stars. The six-story atrium lobby is furnished in Asian style and filled with lush greenery, and caged parrots and other birds that sing and talk throughout the day. The guest rooms carry on the Far East theme. The Civic Center is two blocks away. ⊞ *120 Madison Ave., 36104,* ☎ *334/264–2231 or 800/228–5586,* FAX *334/263–3179. 184 rooms, 5 suites. 2 restaurants, 2 lounges, pool, meeting rooms. AE, D, DC, MC, V.*

$$ **Red Bluff Cottage.** In the heart of downtown and overlooking the Al-
★ abama River, this raised cottage is bright and cheerful. Rooms are filled with antiques, some of them dating to the 18th century, collected by the Reverend Mark Waldo, who served an Episcopal parish in this city for many years, and his wife, Anne. Guests especially enjoy the music room/library containing a harpsichord, a piano, and lots of books. Full breakfast is served. ⊞ *551 Clay St., Box 1026, 36101,* ☎ *334/264–0056. 4 rooms with bath. No credit cards.*

$$ **Riverfront Inn.** A converted historic railway depot, the hotel retains many
★ original elements, resulting in an 1890s feel in the lobby and lounge. Every guest room has a brass bed; other furnishings vary from room to room. Second-floor rooms have cathedral ceilings and original brick and beams. The Civic Center is just a block away. ⊞ *200 Coosa St., 36104,* ☎ *334/834–4300,* FAX *334/265–5500. 124 rooms, 6 suites. Restaurant, coffee shop, lounge, pool, meeting rooms. AE, D, DC, MC, V.*

$$ **State House Inn.** The hotel has been attractively redecorated with a pleasing color scheme of mauve and gray throughout the terra-cotta-tiled lobby and the large guest rooms. Furnishings remain motel-basic—functional rather than attractive. The location is central; the State Capitol is a block away. ▦ *924 Madison Ave., 36104,* ☎ *334/265–0741 or 800/552–7099,* ⊠ *334/834–6126. 164 rooms, 2 suites. Restaurant, lounge, pool, meeting rooms. AE, D, DC, MC, V.*

OUTSKIRTS

$$$–$$$$ **Marriott Courtyard.** This handsome, contemporary low-rise motor inn
★ with a sunny gardenlike courtyard offers amenities popular with business travelers—spacious rooms, king-size beds, oversize work desks, excellent lighting, and hot water dispensers for in-room coffee. ▦ *5555 Carmichael Rd., near I–85 exit 6,* ☎ *334/272–5533 or 800/321–2211,* ⊠ *334/279–0853. 146 rooms, including 12 suites with refrigerators. Restaurant, lounge, pool, hot tub, exercise room, meeting rooms. AE, DC, MC, V.*

$$ **Best Western–Montgomery Lodge.** This is a two-story hotel 3 miles from the airport. The lobby bookcase is stocked for guests' use. Rooms have been redecorated in royal blue or cranberry; most have recliners, and three have king-size water beds. All have coffeemakers. ▦ *977 W. South Blvd., 36105,* ☎ *334/288–5740 or 800/528–1234,* ⊠ *334/288–5740. 100 rooms, 1 suite. Restaurant, lounge, pool, meeting rooms. AE, D, DC, MC, V.*

$$ **La Quinta Motor Inn.** The lobby has been remodeled in muted tones, with terra-cotta-tiled floor and silk flowers. Rooms are contemporary, in light earth tones. ▦ *1280 Eastern By-Pass, 36117-2231,* ☎ *334/271–1620 or 800/531–5900,* ⊠ *334/244–7919. 130 rooms, 2 meeting suites. Pool. AE, D, DC, MC, V.*

Selma

$ **Best Western Selma.** On U.S. 80, this two-story chain motel with an off-white stucco exterior houses typical motel rooms. Rooms are clean and a few have kitchenettes. Complimentary Continental breakfast is served in the lobby. ▦ *1915 Highland Ave., 36701,* ☎ *334/872–1900 or 800/528–1234,* ⊠ *334/872–6635. 51 rooms. Pool. AE, D, DC, MC, V.*

The Arts

For a listing of weekly events, get a current issue of *Montgomery!* magazine, which is given away in the lobbies of most hotels and motels.

Concerts

The **Montgomery Community Symphony Orchestra** (☎ 334/262–5182) performs at the Davis Theatre for the Performing Arts (251 Montgomery St., ☎ 334/241–9567). Other arts-related events are held at the 1,200-plus-seat auditorium as well.

Dance

The **Montgomery School of Ballet** and associated professional dance company (☎ 334/288–3110) performs at different locations in the city and throughout the region.

Theater

Alabama Shakespeare Festival. Shakespearean plays, modern drama, and musicals are performed on two stages at the multimillion dollar festival (☎ 334/271–5353) on the east side of Montgomery. (From downtown, drive east on I–85 to the Eastern By-Pass exit, then follow signs.) Stratford-upon-Avon drama authorities have called it the finest facility of its kind in the world. The season runs from November through August; tickets cost $16–$24.

A superb amateur theater group performs at the **Montgomery Little Theatre** (☎ 334/263–4856) in fall and winter. Traveling theater groups play at the large auditorium at Montgomery's **Civic Center** (300 Bibb St., ☎ 334/241–2105). At the campus theater of **Auburn University at Montgomery** (7300 University Dr., ☎ 334/244–3622), student actors perform drama and comedy.

Nightlife

Jazz

1048 East Fairview (1048 E. Fairview, Montgomery, ☎ 334/834–1048) offers live music nightly, with an emphasis on the blues Thursday, Friday, and Saturday evenings. Another option for jazz is **Dem Bonz** (600 E. South Blvd., Montgomery, ☎ 334/281–RIBS), featuring live music Friday and Saturday nights, as well as baby-back ribs and a variety of seafood.

Pop

T. P. Crockmier's Restaurant (5620 Calmar Dr., Montgomery, ☎ 334/277–1840) offers live music Wednesday through Sunday and prime rib steaks. **Wesley's In Old Cloverdale** (1061 Woodley Rd., ☎ 334/834–2500), in the heart of the old Cloverdale neighborhood, offers live entertainment on weekends and great food (*see* Dining, *above*). Guests enjoy the open-air deck.

Plantation Country Essentials

Arriving and Departing

BY BUS
Greyhound Lines (210 Court St., ☎ 334/834–1114 or 800/231–2222).

BY CAR
I–65 runs north to Birmingham and south to Mobile. I–85 begins in Montgomery and runs northeast to Atlanta. U.S. 80 runs west past the airport to Selma.

BY PLANE
Dannelly Field is 7 miles southwest of downtown Montgomery. It is served by American Eagle, Atlantic Southeast, Delta, Northwest Airlink, and USAir.

Taxis are readily available and relatively inexpensive at the airport. Many hotels provide transportation from the airport by prior arrangement. **By car,** take U.S. 80, which connects with U.S. 31, to the first major intersection. Turn right onto the South By-Pass, where some hotels are. To reach downtown, turn north onto I–65, follow signs to I–85, and take the first exit, Court Street.

BY TRAIN
The nearest **Amtrak** service to Montgomery and the Plantation Country area of Alabama is in Birmingham (☎ 800/872–7245).

Getting Around

BY BUS
Montgomery buses (☎ 334/262–7321) run from 5 AM to 4:30–6 PM, depending on the route. Exact change is required ($1 fare, 10¢ transfer).

BY CAR
U.S. 80 cuts east–west across the state, connecting Demopolis, Selma, Montgomery, and Tuskegee. U.S. 82 runs west through Montgomery and Eufaula.

BY TAXI
Taxis in Montgomery charge $1.50 for the first ¹⁄₁₀ mile, $1.10 for each additional mile. Try **Yellow Cab** (☎ 334/262–5225).

Guided Tours
Only guided group tours of Montgomery are available. The **Montgomery Visitors Center** (*see* Visitor Information, *below*) sells a cassette driving tour of the downtown area for $9 (tape and book) or $2 (book only); they also show a free 15-minute video about the city that will help you organize your own tour.

Important Addresses and Numbers
EMERGENCIES
Dial 911 for **police** or **ambulance** in an emergency, or, for medical emergencies, contact the **Montgomery Baptist Medical Center** (2105 E. South Blvd., ☎ 334/288–2100).

PHARMACY
Harco Drugs (Capitol Plaza Shopping Center, South By-Pass, Montgomery, ☎ 334/281–1312) is open weekdays 8 AM–midnight, weekends 8 AM–10 PM.

RADIO STATIONS
AM: WACV 1170, talk; WHHY 1440, light rock. **FM:** WLWI 92.3, country; WLNE 96.1, easy modern; WBAM 98.9, country; WSYA 103.2, rock.

VISITOR INFORMATION
Montgomery Area Chamber of Commerce & Visitor Division. Montgomery Visitors Center (401 Madison Ave., ☎ 334/262–0013). **Alabama Bureau of Tourism and Travel** (401 Adams Ave., ☎ 334/242–4169 or 800/252–2262 to request travel information).

MOBILE AND THE GULF COAST

Mobile, one of the oldest cities in Alabama, is perhaps the most graceful. Its main thoroughfare, Government Street, is bordered with live oaks, and many antebellum buildings survive as a bridge to its treasured past. The city has profuse plantings of azaleas—a feature that is highlighted each spring with the Azalea Trail Festival. Nearby is Bellingrath Gardens, one of the most spectacular public gardens in the country, especially in spring, when more than 250,000 plants are indeed resplendent.

Mardi Gras began in Mobile, long before New Orleans ever celebrated Fat Tuesday, and today the city celebrates the pre-Lenten season, usually in February, with parades and merrymaking day and night.

The area of the Gulf Coast around Gulf Shores, to the south of Mobile, encompasses about 50 miles of pure white-sand beach, including a former peninsula called Pleasure Island and Dauphin Island to the west. Though hotels and condominiums take up a good deal of the beachfront, some of it remains public. Here you'll find small-town Southern beach life, with excellent deep-sea fishing, as well as freshwater fishing in the bays and bayous, plus water sports of all types.

Those with more time might explore the eastern shore of Mobile Bay—Spanish Fort, Daphne, and Fairhope—where, sometime between June and September, locals and tourists eagerly await the mythical phenomenon, "Jubilee." Supposedly, fish, crabs, and shrimp venture into shallow water at this time, become dazed and disoriented, and fall prey to fisherfolk in great quantities. The Eastern Shore revels in the laid-back atmosphere of yesteryear: live oaks laced with Spanish moss; sprawling clapboard houses with wide porches overlooking the lazy, dark water of the bay; and interesting watering holes where local artists and writers meet informally. At Point Clear, south of Fairhope, is the Victorian-style Marriott's Grand Hotel, host since the mid-19th century to the vacationing wealthy.

Exploring

Mobile

Numbers in the margin correspond to points of interest on the Mobile and the Gulf Coast map.

❶ The busy port city of **Mobile,** on the western bank of the Mobile River and at the top of Mobile Bay, overlaps past and present. Gracious old mansions with iron-grillwork balconies and lovely gardens abound—belying the madness of the city's annual Mardi Gras (for 10 days preceding Shrove Tuesday, in February). Many businesses in town are conducted from buildings that predate the Civil War.

Ft. Condé was the name the French gave the site in 1711; around it blossomed the first white settlement in what is now Alabama. For eight years it was the capital of the French colonial empire, and it remained under French control until 1763, long after the capital had moved to New Orleans. This French connection survives in the area's strong Creole-flavor cuisine that rivals New Orleans in fieriness.

Ft. Condé, too, survives, thanks to a $2.2-million restoration, which preserved it when its remains were discovered—150 years after the fort was destroyed—during construction of the I–10 interchange (an I–10 tunnel now runs under the fort). A reconstructed portion houses the visitor center for the city, as well as a museum and several re-created rooms. Costumed guides interpret and enlighten. *150 S. Royal St.,* ☎ *334/434–7304.* ☛ *Free.* ⊙ *Daily 8–5.*

Mobile today is noted for its tree-lined boulevards fanning out from **Bienville Square.** At the center of the city, the lovely park is shaded by moss-draped live oaks, with an ornate cast-iron fountain in the center. Part of a downtown revival, bands play here during weekday lunch hours for downtown office workers and visitors who eat their lunches in the square. Also during the week, fresh fruit, vegetables, and flowers are sold at an open market alongside the square.

The city's main thoroughfare is Government Street, in the Oakleigh Garden Historic District, a block north of Ft. Condé. From here, signs lead to **Oakleigh,** an imposing Greek Revival mansion with a stairway circling under ancient live oaks to a small portico. The high-ceilinged half-timbered house was built between 1833 and 1838 and is typical of the most expensive dwellings of its day. Fine period furniture, portraits, silver, jewelry, kitchen implements, toys, and more are displayed throughout. Tickets can be purchased next door at the **Cox-Deasy House,** another antebellum home that is not quite as old as Oakleigh

Mobile and the Gulf Coast

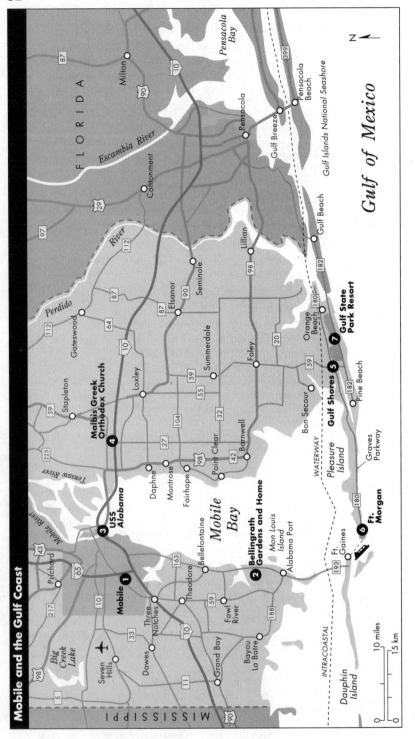

(1850) and by no means as grand. A raised cottage, it was not meant to be a showplace for the planter society, but rather a warm, comfortable home. *350 Oakleigh Pl., ☎ 334/432–1281. ☞ $4. ⊙ Mon.–Sat. 10–4, Sun. 2–4. Guided tours conducted every half hour.*

Several of Mobile's churches figure prominently in the area's rich African-American history: The **State Street A.M.E. Zion Church** (502 State St., ☎ 334/432–3965) is one of the oldest and most striking African-American Methodist churches in town and the **St. Louis Street Missionary Baptist Church** (108 North Dearborn St., ☎ 334/438–3823) hosted a conference that established Selma University. You can also visit the **Slave Market Site** (St. Louis and Royal Sts.), where a memorial now stands commemorating Cudjoe Lewis, the last survivor of the *Clotilde,* America's last slave ship, which arrived in 1859.

★ ❷ Fewer than 20 miles south of Mobile off I–10 (turn south onto Bellingrath Rd. at the town of Theodore) is **Bellingrath Gardens and Home,** site of one of the world's most magnificent azalea gardens. Here, set amid a 905-acre semitropical landscape, are some 65 spectacular acres of gardens. Showtime for its azaleas is spring, when some 250,000 plantings of 200 different species are ablaze with color. But Bellingrath is a year-round wonder. In summer, 2,500 rosebushes are in bloom; in autumn, 60,000 chrysanthemum plants; in winter, fields of poinsettias. And countless other species and varieties of flowering plants spring up along a river or stream or around a lake populated by ducks and swans.

Guides are on hand throughout the gardens to assist or explain, but a free map lets you plan your own strolls along flagstone paths and charming bridges. One special area is the Oriental-American Garden, a lovely, tranquil setting with teahouses and bridges. The gardens are a sanctuary to over 200 species of birds; especially good times to visit for those ornithologically inclined are April and October, when large numbers of migratory birds drop by.

Coca-Cola bottling pioneer Walter D. Bellingrath began the nucleus of the gardens in 1917, when he and his wife bought a large tract as a fishing camp. Their travels, however, prompted them to create, instead, a garden rivaling some they had seen in Europe, and before long they opened it to the public. Today their brick home on the property is also open to visitors and offers one of the finest collections of antiques in the Southeast. Along with furniture, Meissen porcelain figurines, Dresden china, and other objets d'art amassed by Mrs. Bellingrath is the world's largest collection of Boehm porcelain birds. *Bellingrath Rd., Theodore, ☎ 334/973–2217. ☞ To gardens: $6.83 adults, $3.41 children 6–11, under 6 free. ☞ To gardens and house: $14.70 adults, $11.55 children 6–11, $8.93 under 6, "babes in arms" free. ⊙ Gardens daily 8 AM–sunset, house daily 8:30–4:30.*

Mobile is at its loveliest during the **Azalea Trail Festival** in March or April, on the Saturday following the 10K Azalea Trail Run. The trail twines for 27 well-marked miles in and around the city, showing off azaleas at their best. Throughout the preceding week, scores of special events celebrate the yearly blossoming, from concerts to art exhibits, and in summer there's the crowning of America's Young Woman of the Year.

March is also the time of the **Historic Mobile Homes Tour,** when 19th-century Federal-style town houses, Creole cottages, and antebellum plantation homes—22 in all, public and private—are opened to visitors for daytime and candlelight tours. *For information, write to Historic Mobile Homes Tours, Box 66247, Mobile 36660, or call 334/434–7659.*

To the Shore

From Mobile, there are two ways to reach Pleasure Island, a 30-mile region along the Gulf of Mexico. One is to take a scenic drive south along Routes 163 and 193, perhaps stopping off at Bellingrath Gardens, and cross over the bridge to Dauphin Island, site of historic Ft. Gaines, captured by Union forces during the Civil War Battle of Mobile Bay. Then you catch the **Mobile Bay Ferry** (☎ 904/434–7345 or 334/540–7787; outside AL, 800/634–4027) for the 30-minute trip over to Ft. Morgan, at the tip of Pleasure Island. This coastal route is shorter in mileage, though probably not in time. The other approach—the one our tour follows—is via U.S. 90E through the Bankhead Tunnel, then south on AL 59.

❸ On the way, stop to pay a call aboard the **USS *Alabama,*** anchored in Mobile Bay just east of Mobile off I–10. Public subscription saved the mighty gray battleship from being scrapped ignominiously after her heroic World War II service, which ranged from Scapa Flow to the South Pacific. A tour of the ship gives a fascinating look into the life of a 2,500-member crew. Anchored next to the battleship is the submarine USS *Drum,* another active battle weapon during World War II, also open to visitors. Other exhibits in the 100-acre Battleship Park include a B-52 bomber called *Calamity Jane* and a P–51 Mustang fighter plane. *Battleship Pkwy.,* ☎ *334/433–2703.* ☛ *$6 adults, $3 children 6–11, under 6 free. Parking: $2.* ☉ *8:30–7 (park closes at 5 PM in winter).*

Twelve miles east of Mobile, on U.S. 90, the Malbis exit off I–10, is **❹** the **Malbis Greek Orthodox Church,** a replica of a beautiful Byzantine church in Athens, Greece. It was built in 1965, at a cost of more than $1 million, as a memorial to the faith of a Greek immigrant and former monk, Jason Malbis, who founded the community but died before his dream for a cathedral could be realized. The marble for the interior was imported from the same quarries that provided stone for the Parthenon, and a master painter was brought over from Greece to paint murals on the walls and the 75-foot dome of the rotunda. The stained-glass windows are stunning. *County Rte. 27,* ☎ *334/626–3050.* ☛ *Free. Tours daily 9–noon, 2–5.*

When you're ready for some sun and surf, take AL 59 south to the end. At AL 182, head west. A block later, turn right for a circular drive next **❺** to the **Gulf Shores** public beach area, crowded with Alabama high school and college students on spring break and everyone in summer. There's ample free parking—though the traffic is bumper-to-bumper at peak times—and the beach is as white as snow.

At the western tip of Pleasure Island, 20 miles from Gulf Shores at the **❻** end of AL 180, is **Ft. Morgan,** built in the early 1800s to guard the entrance to Mobile Bay. The fort saw fiery action during the Battle of Mobile Bay in 1864: Confederate torpedoes sank the ironclad Tecumseh, on which Admiral David Farragut gave his famous command "Damn the torpedoes! Full speed ahead!" The original outer walls still stand; inside, a museum chronicles the fort's history and displays artifacts from Indian days through World War II, with an emphasis on the Civil War. *Mobile Point,* ☎ *334/540–7125.* ☛ *$2 adults, $1 over 61 and children 6–18, under 6 free.* ☉ *Daily 9–5.*

★ **❼** Five miles east of Gulf Shores on AL 182 is **Gulf State Park Resort,** which covers more than 6,000 acres of Pleasure Island. Along with 2½ miles of pure white beaches and glimmering dunes, the park also has two freshwater lakes with canoeing and fishing, plus biking, hiking, and jogging trails through pine forests. There is a large beach pavilion, and nearby is a concrete fishing pier that juts 825 feet into the Gulf. There is also a resort inn and convention center, 468 campsites, and 21 cottages, plus tennis courts and an 18-hole golf course. *For information, write Gulf State Park, HC 79, Box 9, Gulf Shores 36542, ☎ 800/252–7275.*

What to See and Do with Children

Exploreum Museum of Discovery offers hands-on exhibits that are educational and fun. *2.5 mi east of Spring Hill Ave. Exit off I–65, ☎ 334/476–6873. ☛ $3 adults, $2 children 2–17, under 2 free. ☉ Tues.–Fri. 9–5, weekends 1–5. Closed Mon. and major holidays.*

Ft. Condé (*see* Mobile *in* Exploring, *above*).

Ft. Morgan (*see* To the Shore *in* Exploring, *above*).

Gulf State Park (*see* To the Shore *in* Exploring, *above*).

USS *Alabama* (*see* To the Shore *in* Exploring, *above*).

Waterville USA. This water park set on 17 acres has a 750,000-gallon wave pool (creates 3-foot waves), seven exciting water slides, and a lazy river ride around the park. For younger children there are gentler rides in a supervised play area. There is also a 36-hole miniature golf course and a video-game arcade. *AL 59, Gulf Shores, ☎ 334/948–2106. ☛ $9.95 adults, children under 3 free. ☉ Memorial Day–Labor Day.*

Wildland Expeditions, led by Captain Gene Burrell on the Gator Bait, explores the Mobile–Tensaw Delta, with close-up views of plants and animals. *7536 Tung Ave. N, Theodore 36582, ☎ 334/460–8206. ☛ $20 adults, $10 children under 13.*

Off the Beaten Path

Naval Aviation Museum. At the Naval Air Station in Pensacola, many planes used in both world wars and later—including a Gemini space capsule, F-18s, Corsairs, and Spitfires—are displayed. And they're everywhere—outdoors, in hangars, or inside, on the floor or suspended from the ceiling. From Gulf Shores, follow the Beach Road east to Blue Angel Parkway, then to Sherman Field, where the precision-flying team the Blue Angels is based. (They practice here during the week when they are not doing shows elsewhere.) When the USS *Lexington* aircraft carrier is in port, you can go aboard between 9 and 3 on weekends. *☎ 904/452–3604. ☛ Free. ☉ Daily 9–5.*

Shopping

Mobile

Most shopping in Mobile is done in malls and centers in the suburban areas. Stores are generally open Monday–Saturday 10–9, Sunday 1–6. Sales tax is 7%.

SHOPPING DISTRICTS

At the **Bel Air Mall** (one block east of I–65 Beltline off Airport Blvd., ☎ 334/478–1893), you'll find some 175 stores under one roof, including JC Penney and Sears, and a food court. **Springdale Mall-Plaza** (Airport Blvd. and I–65, ☎ 334/479–9871), anchored by Gayfer's, McRae's, and Montgomery Ward, has more than 100 stores.

Antiques buffs love Mobile because it offers over 25 individual shops and three malls that specialize in antiques. **Red Barn Antique Mall** (418 Dauphin Island Pkwy., ☎ 334/473–9227) has at least 15 shops offering a variety of antiques from glassware and books to furniture. **Al Atchison Antiques** (601 Government St., ☎ 334/438–9421 or 334/432–8423), one of the largest antiques dealers in the South, is packed with antique brass beds and other American and European antique furniture.

SOUVENIRS

Tanner Mercantile Company (2101 Airport Blvd., ☎ 334/476–5282), operated by Joel and Catherine Turner, specializes in Mobile souvenirs and gourmet coffees, including their trademark blend, Café Pecan Mobile. **Museum Gift Shoppe** (355 Government St., ☎ 334/694–0069) is a good place to pick up souvenirs, books, and local art items.

Gulf Shores

BEACH GEAR

Beach Bazaar (Gulf Shores Pkwy., ☎ 334/948–7233) has a large selection of beach wear items, souvenirs, camera supplies, and sunscreen.

GIFTS

Riviera Centre (AL 59 S, Foley, ☎ 334/943–8888 or 800/523–6873), a handsome complex of outlet stores 45 miles from Mobile, offers savings of up to 75% off regular retail prices. Stores include Danskin, Calvin Klein, Liz Claiborne, American Tourister, Polo/Ralph Lauren, Manhattan, Bass Shoes, Pfaltzgraff, and other top names. ☺ *Mon.–Sat. 9–9, Sun. 10–6.*

Participant Sports

Biking

Gulf State Park Resort (☎ 800/252–7275) in Gulf Shores has biking trails through pine forests and rents bicycles. **Island Recreation Services** (☎ 334/948–7334) in Gulf Shores rents bikes, mopeds, and watersports equipment (*see* Watersports, *below*).

Canoeing

Sunshine Canoe Rentals (☎ 334/344–8664) runs canoe trips at Escatawpa River, 15 miles west of Mobile. The river has no rapids but makes for pleasant, leisurely travel past lots of white sandbars.

Fishing

Freshwater and saltwater fishing in the Gulf area is excellent. **Gulf State Park Resort** has fishing from an 825-foot pier and rents flat-bottom boats for lake fishing. Deep-sea fishing from charter boats is very popular; in Gulf Shores, you can sign on board the *Moreno Queen* (☎ 334/981–8499) for a full- or half-day fishing expedition, and Orange Beach has 40 boats to choose from. For a brochure on Orange Beach's offerings, call 334/981–8000. Catches from these deep-sea expeditions include king mackerel, amberjack, tuna, white marlin, blue marlin, grouper, bonito, sailfish, and red snapper. Nonresidents 16 or over may not fish anywhere in Alabama without a valid fishing license; for information, call 334/242–3260.

Golf

In recent years, coastal Alabama has developed into one of the newest and nicest golfing resort destinations in the Southeast. New courses are springing up with surprising regularity, and the names of the course architects read like a Who's Who in the golfing world—Robert Trent Jones Sr., Arnold Palmer, and Jerry Pate, to name just a few. With winter temperatures averaging in the 60° range, and pleasant off-shore breezes, the area has become a true year-round fun spot.

The Gulf Shores area is leading the way for this golf resort bonanza. The new **Kiva Dunes** course at Gulf Shores Plantation Resort (13 mi west of Gulf Shores on Rte. 180, ☎ 800/554–0344), designed by Jerry Pate, is spectacular, and combines oceanfront dunes golf with Scottish-style links golf. The Craft Farms complex on Rte. 59 just north of Gulf Shores has 27 holes on the Arnold Palmer–designed course at **Cotton Creek** (☎ 800/327–2657), and another 18 on the new **Woodlands** course (☎ 334/968–4133), designed by Larry Nelson. Another new course, the **Dunes at Glenlakes** (☎ 334/943–8000), designed by Bruce Devlin, has 18 very challenging holes and plays over 7,000 yards. The course at **Gulf State Park** (800/252–7275) isn't quite as new and challenging, but it is one of the most scenic and best maintained courses along the coast. Prices for all the courses range from about $28–$40 for greens fees and a cart.

In the Mobile area, you have **Magnolia Grove** (☎ 800/949–4444), the southernmost offering of Alabama's Robert Trent Jones Golf Trail. The Magnolia Grove facility has 54 holes of championship golf: 2 par 72 courses and an 18-hole par three course that is anything but easy. Other very interesting Mobile area courses include **Timber Creek** (☎ 334/621–9900) and **Rock Creek** (☎ 334/928–4223), both located in the town of Daphne, on the eastern shore; and the **Spring Hill College Golf Course** (☎ 334/343–2356) and **Azalea City Golf Club** (☎ 334/342–4221), both in Mobile.

Horseback Riding

Horseback Beach Rides (☎ 334/943–6674) offers guided group rides along country trails or along the beach at Gulf Shores.

Jogging

Gulf State Park Resort (*see* Biking, *above*) has trails through a forest.

Sailing

Sailboats that can be rented with captain include the *Cyrus King* (at **Island Sailing Center,** ☎ 334/981–9706) and the *Daedalus* (☎ 334/986–7018) in Gulf Shores. **Island Recreation Services** (☎ 334/948–7334), in Gulf Shores, and **Land 'N' Sea** (☎ 334/943–3600), in Foley, rent sailboats without captain.

Tennis

Gulf State Park Resort (*see* Biking, *above*) has four lighted courts.

Water Sports

Fun Marina (☎ 334/981–8587) in Orange Beach rents Jet Skis, pontoon boats, and 16-foot bay-fishing boats. In Gulf Shores, **Island Recreation Services** (☎ 334/948–7334) rents boogie boards, body boards, surf boats, and sailboats.

Spectator Sports

Dog Racing

At the **Mobile Greyhound Park** (off I–10W, about 10 mi from Mobile, ☎ 334/653–5000) and at the **Pensacola Greyhound Track** (U.S. 98, about 40 mi east of Gulf Shores in Florida, ☎ 904/455–8595 or 800/345–3997), there's pari-mutuel betting and a restaurant overlooking the finish line.

Dining

In Mobile and throughout the Gulf area, the specialty is fresh seafood, often prepared in Creole style, with peppery spices, crabmeat dressing, and sometimes a tomato-based sauce. Mobile, in fact, prides itself on being the only city in Alabama with a cuisine of its own, whose precedence (in time, at least) over New Orleans's it has been claiming for years. The basis of the claim is history: The founders of Mobile, French explorers Bienville and Iberville, came here first, then moved west to New Orleans. Dress is casual unless otherwise noted.

CATEGORY	COST*
$$$	$25–35
$$	$15–$25
$	under $15

*per person for a three-course meal, excluding drinks, service, and tax (10% in Mobile, 8% along the rest of the coast)

Mobile

$$$ **La Louisiana.** This antiques-filled old house on the outskirts is a delightful dinner setting. Fresh seafood is prepared with a touch of French Creole. Shrimp dishes are heavy with cream sauces unless you order them lightly fried. The seafood gumbo is made the Mobile way: heavy on shrimp, oysters, and okra. ✕ 2400 Airport Blvd., ☎ 334/476–8130. Reservations preferred. Jacket and tie. AE, DC, MC, V.

$$$ **Pillars.** Sitting amid fine antiques from the 18th and 19th centuries in
★ a huge old mansion with wide porches overlooking the live oaks in the yard, it is easy to imagine oneself in another time, listening to the latest news from the battlefront at Vicksburg or Shiloh. The beautifully cooked snapper with a white-wine-and-cream sauce and the snapper with crabmeat and a pecan Creole sauce are delicious. The lamb chops are cut thick and cooked just the way you like them over a charcoal grill. ✕ 1757 Government St., ☎ 334/478–6341. Reservations advised. Jacket and tie. AE, DC, MC, V. No lunch. Closed Sun.

$$ **Malaga Restaurant.** This is a small, intimate restaurant in the former carriage house of the Malaga Inn (see Lodging, below). At the end of one of its two rooms, a set of French doors lets in lots of light and a view out to the pool, landscaped with banana trees and other tropical plants. The walls are a mixture of old brick and a cream-and-green floral-print wallpaper. The menu is a mix of Creole-style seafood and Continental dishes. One of the most popular choices is snapper Brennan—fresh Gulf snapper served with a sauce of crabmeat, mushrooms, wine, and other delights. Continental choices include chateaubriand and steak Diane. ✕ 359 Church St., ☎ 334/433–5858. Reservations advised for dinner. AE, DC, MC, V.

$$ **Roussos Restaurant.** A local favorite, with a nautical look created by
★ lots of fishnets and scenes of ships at sea, Roussos is known for its crab claws, fried in a light batter and served with a catsup-horseradish sauce. Diners have a choice of having their seafood fried, broiled, or

served Greek-style (the blend of spices and oils helps bring out the fresh flavor). In addition to a very large selection outstanding seafood entrées, the appetizers are big favorites as well—especially the Roussos baked oysters and Mr. George's seafood gumbo. ✗ *166 S. Royal St.,* ☎ *334/433–3322. Reservations accepted. AE, DC, MC, V.*

$$ **Weichman's All Seasons.** Old Mobile elegance is reflected in the decor, and the outstanding menu features such mainstays as fresh Gulf seafood, prime cuts of beef, and gourmet veal delicacies. The wine selection is one of the largest in Alabama. ✗ *168 S. Beltline Hwy. (on the West Service Rd. off I–65),* ☎ *334/344–3961. Reservations advised. AE, DC, MC, V.*

Gulf Coast

$$–$$$ **Original Oyster House.** A rustic but very clean, plant-filled restaurant overlooking the bayou, this has become a Gulf Shores tradition. Oysters on the half-shell, fresh out of nearby Perdido Bay, are the specialty of the house. The Cajun-style gumbo—a concoction of crab claws, shrimp, amberjack, grouper, redfish, okra and other vegetables, and Cajun spices—has won 20 major awards. ✗ *Bayou Village Shopping Ctr., AL 59, Gulf Shores,* ☎ *334/948–2445. No reservations. AE, DC, MC, V.*

$$–$$$ **Voyagers.** Roses in crystal vases and art-deco touches set the tone for
★ this airy, elegant dining room. Two-level seating allows beach or poolside views from every table. The specialties include trout with roasted pecans in Creole meunière sauce and soft-shell crab topped with Creole sauce Choron. Follow up with fried-apple beignet topped with French vanilla sauce or crepe soufflé praline. Service is deft, sophisticated, and there's an extensive wine selection. ✗ *Perdido Beach Hilton, Rte. 182, Orange Beach,* ☎ *334/981–9811. Reservations advised. Jacket and tie. AE, DC, MC, V.*

$ **Dempsey's Restaurant.** The setting is tropical, enhanced by a 20-foot waterfall, at this lakeside dining room. Cajun seafood specialties are arranged temptingly at the all-you-can-eat dinner buffet that includes such seafood dishes as stuffed jumbo shrimp. Live entertainment is offered nightly during the summer months and on weekends the rest of the year. ✗ *AL 182, Orange Beach,* ☎ *334/981–6800. No reservations. AE, D, MC, V.*

$ **Hazel's Family Restaurant.** This plain but tasteful family-style restaurant serves a good, hearty breakfast, soup-and-salad lunches, and adequate buffet dinners featuring such seafood dishes as flounder Florentine or crab-stuffed broiled snapper. ✗ *Gulf View Square Shopping Ctr., Orange Beach,* ☎ *334/981–4628. No reservations. AE, D, DC, MC, V.*

$ **Zeke's Landing Restaurant and Oyster Bar.** Overlooking a marina, the
★ large dining rooms are highlighted by bleached woods, black lacquer, and brass. Service is deft, unhurried, and friendly. There's an excellent, modestly priced selection of fried or grilled seafood, steaks, garden salads, and sandwiches, such as the seafood melt—crab and shrimp with Cheddar-cheese sauce over an open-faced English muffin. ✗ *Beach Rte. 180, Orange Beach, 8 mi east of Gulf Shores,* ☎ *334/981–4001. No reservations. AE, DC, MC, V.*

Lodging

CATEGORY	COST*
$$$$	over $95
$$$	$70–$95
$$	$50–$70
$	under $50

All prices are for a standard double room, excluding tax (10% in Mobile, 8% on the coast)

Mobile

$$$$ **Adam's Mark Mobile.** Formerly a Stouffer's property, this 28-story waterfront hotel is connected to the new Mobile Convention and Exhibition Center by an enclosed skywalk. The large guest rooms are freshly renovated and have floor-to-ceiling windows offering views of downtown Mobile or Mobile Bay, and a separate dressing area with a full-length mirror. The newly renovated lobby and restaurants have oak paneling and are done in shades of rose and soft jade. The Riverview Cafe and Grill specializes in Gulf Coast seafood; there's lighter fare and live entertainment six nights a week in the Tiffany Rose Restaurant. ⌕ *64 S. Water St., 36602,* ☎ *334/438–4000 or 800/444–2326,* FAX *334/415–3060. 375 rooms, 12 suites. 2 restaurants, bar, pool, hot tub, sauna, exercise room, gift shop, meeting rooms. AE, D, DC, MC, V.*

$$$ **Radisson Admiral Semmes Hotel.** This old hotel is a favorite with local
★ politicians. It is also popular with partygoers, particularly during Mardi Gras, because of its excellent location directly on the parade route. Rooms are furnished in Queen Anne and Chippendale styles. This is a favorite because there's really no competition in this price category in Mobile. ⌕ *251 Government St., Box 1209, 36633,* ☎ *334/432–8000 (fax ext. 7111) or 800/333–3333. 147 rooms, 22 suites. Restaurant, lounge. AE, D, DC, MC, V.*

$–$$ **Malaga Inn.** A delightful, romantic getaway place, the Malaga comprises
★ two town houses built by a wealthy landowner in 1862. The lobby is furnished with 19th-century antiques and opens onto a tropically landscaped central courtyard with a fountain. The rooms are large, airy, and furnished with massive antiques. Ask for the front suite, with 14-foot ceilings and crimson velveteen wallpaper. The inn's restaurant (*see Dining, above*) serves a mixture of Creole and Continental fare. ⌕ *359 Church St., 36602,* ☎ *and* FAX *334/438–4701 or* ☎ *800/235–1586. 40 rooms. Restaurant, lounge, pool. AE, DC, MC, V.*

Gulf Coast

$$$$ **Marriott's Grand Hotel.** Nestled amid 550 acres of beautifully land-
★ scaped grounds, the "Grand" has been a cherished tradition since 1847. Extensively refurbished by Marriott, it is one of the South's premier resorts. Its two-story cypress-paneled and beamed lobby evokes an aura of traditional elegance. Spacious rooms and cottages are also traditionally furnished. ⌕ *On Mobile Bay, U.S. Scenic 98, Point Clear 36564,* ☎ *334/928–9201 or 800/544–9933,* FAX *334/928–6271. 277 units, 23 suites. Coffee shop, 3 dining rooms, lounge, pool, hot tub, sauna, 2 18-hole golf courses, tennis, horseback riding, beach, boating, fishing, bicycles, children's programs, playground. AE, DC, MC, V.*

$$$$ **Perdido Beach Resort.** The eight- and nine-story towers are Mediter-
★ ranean stucco and red tile. The lobby is tiled in terra-cotta and decorated with mosaics by Venetian artists and a brass sculpture of gulls in flight. Rooms are furnished in luxurious Mediterranean style, and

all have a beach view and balcony. The location and scenic views here are outstanding. ⌕ *AL 182E, Box 400, Orange Beach 36561,* ☎ *334/981–9811 or 800/634–8001,* 𝔽𝔸𝕏 *334/981–5670. 333 rooms, 12 suites. Restaurant, café, piano bar, indoor-outdoor pool, 2 hot tubs, 2 saunas, 4 tennis courts, exercise room, nightclub, pool bar, video games. AE, DC, MC, V.*

$$$–$$$$ **Quality Inn Beachside.** This spacious motel is made up of one three-story and one six-story building. All the guest rooms are modern, decorated in pastels, with private balconies; most face the Gulf; half have kitchens. In the art deco–style atrium lobby, with glass-brick walls, is a 70-foot swimming pool and a waterfall. Glass-walled elevators rise six stories. ⌕ *921 W. Gulf Beach Blvd. (Rte. 182), Box 1013, Gulf Shores 36542,* ☎ *334/948–6874 or 800/228–5151. 158 rooms. Restaurant, deli, piano room, outdoor and indoor pools, hot tub, exercise room, pool bar. AE, D, DC, MC.*

$$–$$$ **Gulf Shores Plantation.** This 320-acre family resort, 8 miles east of Ft. Morgan on the Gulf, has condominiums with fully equipped kitchens in high rises overlooking the beach. Abundant recreational activities are available. ⌕ *Rte. 180W, Box 1299, 36547,* ☎ *334/540–2291 or 800/554–0344,* 𝔽𝔸𝕏 *334/540–6050. 400 units. Café, pizzeria, lounge, indoor and outdoor pools, 18-hole golf course, 9 tennis courts, watersports, gift shop. AE, MC, V.*

$$–$$$ **Lighthouse.** This complex of five two- to four-story buildings, surrounded by brightly colored exotic flowers, is set on a 580-foot private beach. The waterfront rooms have private balconies, and some units have kitchens. All have contemporary furnishings. ⌕ *455 E. Beach Blvd., Box 233, Gulf Shores 36547,* ☎ *334/948–6188. 124 rooms. 2 pools (1 heated, with hot tub). AE, D, DC, MC, V.*

$$–$$$ **Original Romar House.** This unassuming beach cottage is filled with surprises—from the Caribbean-style upstairs sitting area to the Purple Parrot Bar to the luxurious art deco–style guest rooms. A full breakfast is included in the rate. ⌕ *23500 Perdido Beach Blvd. (Rte. 182), 36561,* ☎ *334/981–6156 or 800/487–6627. 6 rooms (3 with private bath). Bar, breakfast room, hot tub. MC, V.*

The Arts

Theater

The **Joe Jefferson Players** (☎ 334/471–1534), a well-established group of amateur actors and actresses, perform plays and musicals at various locations around Mobile throughout the year. They often perform at the Saenger Theater (☎ 334/433–2787) or the Mobile Municipal Auditorium (☎ 334/434–7381), as do the Playhouse in the Park's **Pixie Players** (☎ 334/344–1537), a children's theatrical group.

Nightlife

Honky-Tonk

On the Alabama–Florida line is the **Flora-Bama Lounge** (Beach Rd., ☎ 334/981–8555), with country-and-western music performed nightly by a local band and vocalist. It's the place where Mobile native Jimmy Buffett got his start.

Swing

At **Shirley & Wayne's** (AL 182, Romar Beach, ☎ 334/981–4818), Wayne Perdew and his band play swing and country Monday–Saturday nights while you dine and/or dance.

Mobile and the Gulf Coast Essentials

Arriving and Departing, Getting Around

BY BUS

Greyhound (☎ 800/231–2222) has stations in Mobile (2545 Government Blvd., ☎ 334/478–6089) and Pensacola (505 W. Burgess Rd., ☎ 904/476–4800).

BY CAR

I–10 travels east from Mobile into Florida through Pensacola, west into Mississippi. I–65 slices Alabama in half vertically, passing through Birmingham and Montgomery and ending at Mobile. Gulf Shores is connected with Mobile via I–10 and Route 59; Routes 180 and 182 are the main beach routes.

BY PLANE

The **Mobile Municipal Airport at Bates Field** (☎ 334/633–0313), about 5 miles west of the city, is served by American, Delta, Northwest Express, and USAir. Air New Orleans, Continental, Delta, and USAir have flights into the **Pensacola Regional Airport** (☎ 904/433–7800), some 40 miles east of Gulf Shores in Florida.

BY TRAIN

Amtrak's (☎ 800/872–7245) *Sunset Limited* links Mobile with both the East and West coasts.

Guided Tours

Gray Line Tours (☎ 334/432–2229 or 800/338–5597), in Mobile, offers one- to 3½-hour trolley or motorcoach tours, departing from Ft. Condé daily, to Mobile's historic points of interest, as well as to Bellingrath Gardens and the USS *Alabama*.

Memorable Mobile Tours, Inc. (☎ 800/441–1146) conducts customized guided tours of Mobile's historic homes and museums, accommodating groups of three or more.

Important Addresses and Numbers

EMERGENCIES

Dial 911 for **police** or **ambulance** in an emergency. All-night medical care is available in Mobile at the emergency room of **University of South Alabama Hospital** (2451 Fillingjim St., ☎ 334/471–7000).

RADIO STATIONS

AM: WBLX 660, gospel; WGOK 900, rhythm & blues; WNTM 710, talk. **FM:** WZBA 104.9, country; WMEZ 94.1, easy listening; WGCX 92.1, classic rock; WAVH 106.5, oldies; WABB 97.5, country rock; WWRO 100.7, rock and roll.

VISITOR INFORMATION

Mobile Chamber of Commerce is housed in **Ft. Condé**, the official visitor center for Mobile (150 S. Royal St., ☎ 334/434–7304 or 800/252–3862). **Alabama Gulf Coast Area Convention and Visitors Bureau** (Rte. 59, 3150 Gulf Shores Pkwy., Drawer 457, Gulf Shores 36542, ☎ 334/968–7511 or 800/745–7263). **Orange Beach Chamber of Commerce** (Rte. 182, Drawer 399, Orange Beach 36561, ☎ 334/981–8000).

3 Georgia

Georgia is notable for its contrasting landscapes and varied cities and towns, each reflecting its own special Southern charm. The northern part of the state has the Appalachian Mountains and their waterfalls; Atlanta, a fast-growing banking center and host for the 1996 Summer Olympics; and Macon, an antebellum town with thousands of cherry trees. Five hours southeast of Atlanta is Savannah, which has the nation's largest historic district, filled with restored Colonial buildings. Along the state's 100-mile coast are the lush, subtropical Golden Isles.

Updated by
Mark Beffart

GEORGIA IS LIKE A CLEVERLY MADE PATCHWORK quilt. First, consider its wildly varied landscapes: from the Appalachian mountains in the north to the pristine white beaches of the Atlantic; to the pine barrens dotted with azaleas and the black-water, gator-infested swamps that make up the state's southern portion. Next, observe its towns, each with its own brand of southern charm: from Dahlonega, site of the nation's first gold rush in 1828; to Helen, a re-created Bavarian-style alpine village in the Blue Ridge Mountains; to graceful Savannah, so beautiful that General Sherman spared the city during the Union Army's destructive march to the sea; to Macon, full of flowering Japanese cherry trees and the ghosts of the antebellum South.

Atlanta, a world apart from all of these, catapulted into the international spotlight when it was named the host city for the 1996 Olympic Games. The undisputed boomtown of the southeast, Atlanta is a vibrant city with a gleaming skyline, largely designed by local architect John Portman. Yet despite the progress, Atlanta has retained its reputation as a city of trees; a bird's eye view of the city from one of those skyscrapers will tell you why.

A five-hour car ride away lies another world. Georgia's 100-mile coast runs from the mouth of the Savannah River south to the mouth of the St. Mary's River. Colonial Savannah lures visitors to its 21 cobblestone squares, giant parterre gardens, waterfront gift shops, jazz bars, and parks draped in Spanish moss.

The seaside resort communities blend southern elegance with a casual sensibility. St. Simons Island, about 70 miles south, attracts a laid-back crowd of anglers, beach-goers, golfers, and tennis players. On nearby Jekyll Island, the lavish lifestyle of America's early 19th-century rich and famous is still evident in their stately Victorian "cottages." Cumberland Island's protected forests and miles of sandy coastline and the dark waters of Okefenokee Swamp are favorite haunts of nature lovers.

Other historical riches include thousand-year-old Native American homesites and burial mounds, antebellum mansions, war heroes' memorials, and intriguing monuments built by eccentric folk artists and obsessive gardeners. Georgia's large number of state parks offer superb facilities for white-water rafting, canoeing, fishing, golf, and tennis, plus nature trails through mountain forests delicately laced with wild rhododendron, dogwoods, and azaleas.

ATLANTA

"Her patron saint is Scarlett O'Hara," the writer James Street once said of Atlanta, "and the town is just like her—shrewd, proud and full of gumption—her Confederate slip showing under a Yankee mink coat."

Although no born-and-bred Atlantan would ever claim to have been influenced by a Yankee, transplanted northerners and those from elsewhere, who account for 50% of the population, have undeniably affected the mood and character of the city. The traditional South, which in a romantic version consists of lacy moss dangling from tree limbs, thick sugary Southern drawls, a leisurely pace, and luxurious antebellum mansions, is rarely found here. Still viewed by diehard Southerners as the heart of the Old Confederacy, Atlanta has emerged from a backward and negative past to become the best example of the New South, a fast-paced, modern city proud of its heritage (the daily newspaper still calls its regional news section "Dixie Living," while a top tourist attraction depicts the Battle of Atlanta during the Civil War) yet one forcefully moving into the future.

From its founding in 1837, Atlanta—then called Terminus—was a vital railroad freight center. Today it's called the "Crossroads of the South," as three interstates converge near downtown and Hartsfield Atlanta International Airport is the nation's third busiest airport in daily passenger flights. Atlanta has emerged as a banking center, and the city is the world headquarters for such Fortune 500 companies as CNN, Coca-Cola, Delta Air Lines, Georgia-Pacific, Holiday Inn Worldwide, Home Depot, Scientific-Atlanta, and United Parcel Service.

Part of the city's vibrancy comes from its international community. Direct flights to Europe, South America, and Asia have made Atlanta easily accessible to the 1,200 international businesses that operate here, and the 48 countries that have representation in the city through consulates, trade offices, and foreign chambers of commerce.

For more than three decades, Atlanta has been linked to the civil rights movement. Among the many accomplishments of Atlanta's African-American community is the Nobel Peace Prize that Martin Luther King Jr. won in 1964. Dr. King's widow, Coretta Scott King, continues to operate the King Center, which she founded after her husband's assassination in 1968, and their four children maintain high profiles in the community. In 1972, Andrew Young was elected the first black congressman from the South since Reconstruction. After serving as Ambassador to the United Nations during President Jimmy Carter's administration, Young was elected mayor of Atlanta. Today, he serves on the city's Olympic committee.

The 1996 Summer Olympics have had a great impact on Atlanta as several new facilities have been created and existing buildings from offices to shopping centers have been renovated and spruced up. Atlanta was picked to join the 20 international cities that have hosted the summer games since 1896 in Athens, Greece. Athletes from 200 countries will descend on Atlanta in July, accompanied by an estimated 2 million other visitors.

Exploring

In the past two decades, Atlanta has experienced unprecedented growth. A good measure of that is its ever-changing downtown skyline, along with skyscrapers constructed in the Midtown, Buckhead, and outer Perimeter business districts. Since the late 1970's, dozens of architecturally dazzling skyscrapers have reshaped the city's profile. Architect John Portman, who graduated from Atlanta's Georgia Tech in 1950, has designed numerous projects, including Peachtree Center, notable as a city within the city. Residents, however, are less likely to measure the city's growth by skyscrapers than by increasing traffic jams, crowds, higher prices, and the ever-burgeoning subdivisions that continue to push the city's limits further and further into surrounding rural areas. Although the Chamber of Commerce advertises Atlanta as a 20-county metropolitan area, the core of Atlanta revolves around five counties. The City of Atlanta is primarily in Fulton and DeKalb counties, with the southern part and the airport in Clayton County. Outside of I–285, Cobb and Gwinnett counties on the northwest and northeast corners of the city are experiencing much of Atlanta's population increase.

Georgia

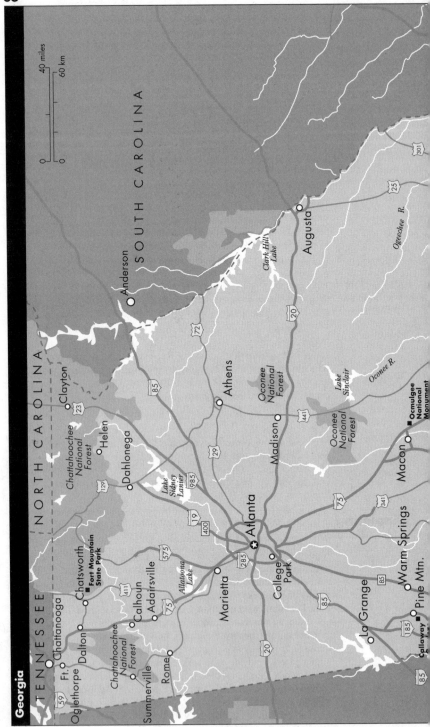

40 miles

60 km

TENNESSEE

NORTH CAROLINA

SOUTH CAROLINA

Chattanooga
Ft.
Oglethorpe
59
Dalton
Chattahoochee
National
Forest
Summerville
Chatsworth
Fort Mountain
State Park
411
Calhoun
Adairsville
75
Rome
Chattahoochee
National
Forest
129
Helen
Clayton
23
Dahlonega
Chattahoochee
National
Forest
575
Allatoona
Lake
Lake
Sidney
Lanier
985
Marietta
285
9
400
Atlanta
College
Park
20
85
La Grange
85
85
Warm Springs
Pine Mtn.
Callaway
85
341
Macon
75
Ocmulgee
National
Monument
Madison
441
Oconee
National
Forest
Lake
Sinclair
Oconee R.
Oconee
National
Forest
Athens
29
85
72
Anderson
Clark Hill
Lake
20
Augusta
25
Ogeechee R.
301

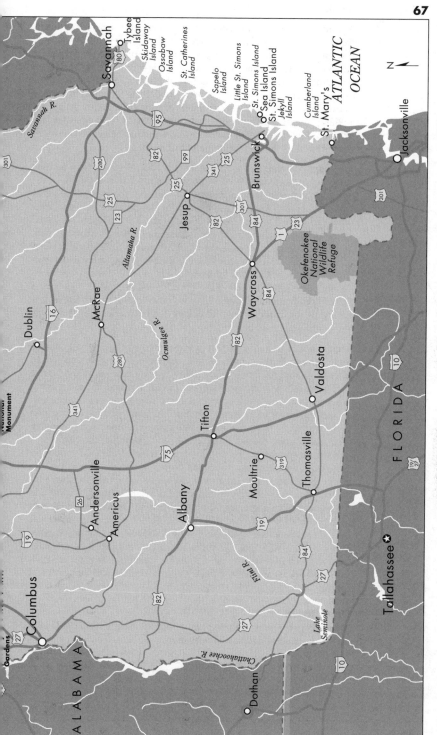

Although downtown offers interesting architecture and some excellent restaurants, it is practically empty during nighttime and weekends (except for Underground Atlanta); for locals, a night on the town usually means a visit to the Buckhead, Virginia-Highland, or Little Five Points neighborhoods. Residents love the area's recreational opportunities—from "shooting the "Hooch" (local talk for riding the rapids of the Chattahoochee River) to waterskiing at Lake Lanier. Atlanta is a young city. At last count, the median age was 28. This youthful face helps account for much of the energy here and has helped Atlanta gain a reputation for nightlife, especially live music.

The main complaint of most residents is traffic—and it may become yours when you visit. With attractions scattered and public transportation limited in some areas, it can be difficult to get to all the sights without your own wheels. Rush-hour traffic runs from about 7 AM (sometimes earlier) to 9 AM and from 4:30 PM to about 7 PM. If you can, avoid interstates and such main streets as Piedmont Road, Peachtree Road, and Ponce de Leon Avenue during these hours. In particular, steer clear of I–285, which encircles the city and is always jam-packed with traffic. Known by locals as "the perimeter," it is filled with trucks who cannot come into Atlanta on the other interstates unless they have a delivery, and commuters who have no other choice but to use it. It is notorious for traffic snarls and delays due to accidents, bad drivers, and continuous road construction.

Atlanta's lack of a grid system in most parts of the city will confuse some drivers. With many hills and meandering streets, locals like to tell visitors that the city's streets follow ancient cow paths and Native American trails, which have since been paved, renamed, and given lights. Whether this is the truth or legend doesn't help you much when you are looking for an address on a winding road and trying to pay attention to the traffic. At the same time, you'll discover some streets changing their name along the same stretch of road, including the city's most famous thoroughfare, Peachtree Street, which follows a mountain ridge from downtown to suburban Norcross outside of north I-285; it becomes Peachtree Road after it crosses I-85 and then Peachtree Industrial Boulevard beyond the Buckhead neighborhood. And to add to the confusion, there are 60 other streets in the metropolitan area with the word Peachtree in their names. Before setting out anywhere, get the complete street address of your destination, including whether it has a NE, NW, SE, or SW suffix at the end of address (which indicates the part of town you need to be in); Peachtree Street is the division line for east and west, and Five Points (downtown) for north and south.

Downtown

Numbers in the margin correspond to points of interest on the Downtown Atlanta and Atlanta Vicinity maps.

The Martin Luther King Jr. National Historic District occupies several blocks on Auburn Avenue, a few blocks east of Peachtree Street. In the black business community of Sweet Auburn, the neighborhood was the birthplace of Martin Luther King Jr., the undisputed leader of the civil rights movement, in 1929. After his assassination in 1968, King's widow, Coretta Scott King, established the **King Center.** It contains a museum with King's Nobel Peace Prize, bible, and typewriter, as well as photos chronicling the Civil Rights Movement, plus a library, souvenir gift shop, and meeting rooms for educational programs. If enough funding is available, a **Civil Rights Museum** will open at the center in

1996. In the courtyard, on a circular brick pad in the middle of a rect-angular "meditation" pool, is King's white marble tomb, where an eter-nal flame burns and the inscription reads, "Free at last!" Tours of Sweet Auburn, given by National Park Service guides, commence from here. *449 Auburn Ave.,* ☎ *404/524–1956.* ☛ *Free.* ⊘ *Daily 9–5:30.*

② Next door is **Ebenezer Baptist Church** (407 Auburn Ave., ☎ 404/688–7263), a Gothic-Revival style building completed in 1922, which be-came known as the spiritual center for the movement after Dr. King won the Nobel Peace Prize in 1964. Members of the King family have preached at the church for three generations; Dr. King's funeral was here.

③ **Dr. King's birthplace** (501 Auburn Ave., ☎ 404/331–1590), a Queen Anne–style bungalow, is managed by the National Park Service and is open to the public daily.

④ **Auburn Avenue** is still the heart of the black community's entrepreneurial district. The landmark **Atlanta Life Insurance Company,** founded by Alonzo Herndon, was located in modest quarters at 148 Auburn Av-enue until the modern complex at No. 100 was opened in 1980.

⑤ At 145 Auburn Avenue is the **Atlanta Daily World** building, home of one of the nation's oldest black newspapers. The church with the "Jesus Saves" sign on its steeple is the Big Bethel African Methodist
⑥ Episcopal Church. Nearby is the **Royal Peacock** (186 Auburn Ave., ☎ 404/880–0745, ⊘ daily 4 PM–2 AM), the club where the king and queen of soul—James Brown and Aretha Franklin—frequently held court in the '60s. Now it's the home of reggae, hip-hop, and international music.

⑦ For a history of Sweet Auburn, view the permanent exhibit at the **African American Panoramic Experience(APEX);** there are also changing exhibits on African-American culture. *135 Auburn Ave.,* ☎ *404/521–2739.* ☛ *$2 adults, $1 children.* ⊘ *Tues.–Sat. 10–5.*

⑧ On Edgewood Avenue is the **Sweet Auburn Curb Market** (209 Edge-wood Ave., ☎ 404/659–1665, ⊘ Mon.–Sat. 8 AM–5:45 PM), a thriv-ing food market where you can buy every part of the pig but the oink—as well as vegetables, fish, and meat. At 125 Edgewood Avenue is the site of the first bottling plant for the Coca-Cola Company—today
⑨ occupied by the **Baptist Student Center** for the adjoining campus of **Geor-gia State University.** Take a shortcut through the urban GSU campus
⑩ toward the glittering gold dome of the **Georgia State Capitol,** a Re-naissance-style building dedicated on July 4, 1889. The capitol's dome was gilded in 1958 with gold leaf mined from Dahlonega, a small town in north Georgia. In addition to housing politicos, it also contains a Georgia history museum, which is open to the public. State historical markers on the grounds commemorate the 1864 Battle of Atlanta, which destroyed 90% of the city. *206 Washington St.,* ☎ *404/656–2844. Free guided tours every ½ hr, weekdays 9:30–11:30, 1–2.*

⑪ Across the street from the capitol's southwest corner is Atlanta's **City Hall** (68 Mitchell St.). When this 14-story, neo-Gothic structure with lavish marble interior was built in 1926, critics dubbed it "The Painted Lady of Mitchell Street."

⑫ The **Five Points MARTA** station (corner of Peachtree and Alabama streets, downtown) services Underground Atlanta and nearby Woodruff Park, Georgia State University, city and county government offices, and numerous businesses. Stand on the corner of Peachtree and Alabama streets, outside the station, and notice the old-fashioned gas street

Downtown Atlanta

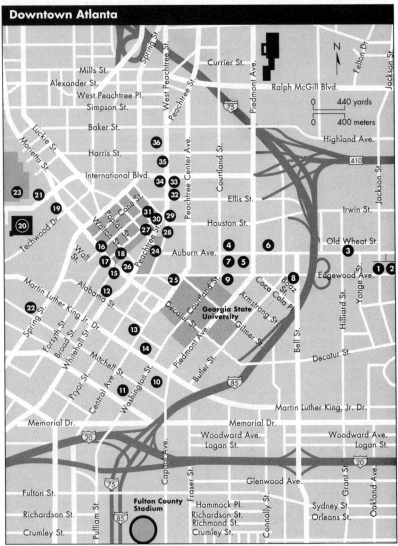

African American
Panoramic
Experience, **7**
Atlanta Daily
World, **5**
Atlanta-Fulton
County Public
Library, **31**
Atlanta History
Center, **46**
Atlanta Life Insurance
Company, **4**
Bank of the South
Building, **16**

Baptist Student
Center, **9**
The Candler
Building, **28**
Capital City Club, **36**
City Hall, **11**
CNN Center, **19**
Dr. King's
Birthplace, **3**
Ebenezer Baptist
Church, **2**

Fay Gold Gallery, **45**
Fernbank Museum of
Natural History, **52**
Fernbank Science
Center, **53**
Five Points MARTA, **12**
The Flatiron
Building, **27**

Fox Theatre, **38**
Georgia Dome, **23**
Georgia Governor's
Mansion, **47**

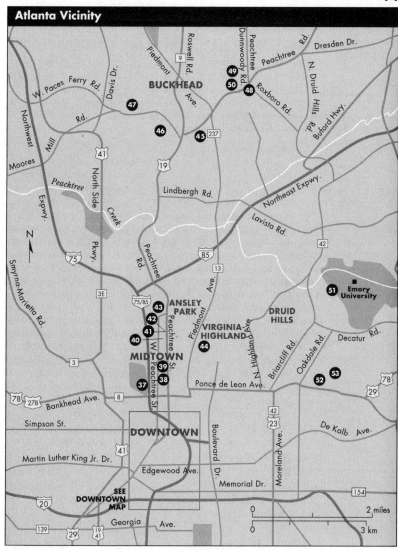

Atlanta Vicinity

Georgia-Pacific
Building, **29**

Georgia State
Capitol **10**

Healy Building, **18**

High Museum
of Art, **42**

The Hurt Building, **25**

King Center, **1**

Lenox Square, **48**

Margaret Mitchell
Park, **30**

Michael C. Carlos
Museum, **51**

Nation's Bank
Building, **15**

Nation's Bank Plaza
Tower, **37**

Omni, **20**

One Atlantic Center/
IBM Tower, **40**

One Ninety
OnePeachtree
Tower, **33**

Peachtree Center, **35**

Phipps Plaza, **49**

Piedmont Park, **44**

Rhodes Memorial
Hall, **43**

Richard B. Russell
Federal Building, **22**

Ritz-Carlton
Buckhead, **50**

Ritz-Carlton Hotel, **32**

Road to Tara
Museum, **39**

Royal Peacock, **6**

Sweet Auburn Curb
Market, **8**

Statue of Henry
Grady, **17**

Underground
Atlanta, **13**

Westin-Peachtree
Plaza Hotel, **34**

The William Oliver
Building, **26**

Woodruff Arts
Center, **41**

Woodruff Park, **24**

World Congress
Center, **21**

The World of
Coca-Cola, **14**

light, with its historic marker proclaiming it as the **Eternal Flame of the Confederacy.**

Across from the Five Points MARTA Station and at Plaza. Depot are entrances to **Underground Atlanta** (☎ 404/523–2311). This six-block entertainment and shopping district was created from the web of underground brick streets, ornamental building facades, and tunnels that fell into disuse in 1929, when the city built viaducts over the train tracks. Merchants moved their storefronts to the new viaduct level, leaving the original street level for storage.

Developed as a tourist attraction in the late 1960's, then closed in the late 1970's due to a lack of popularity and crime problems, Underground was resurrected in 1989 by the Rouse Company, the creators of Baltimore's highly successful Harborplace. Given their track record, it was expected to draw scores of residents and visitors back to the downtown area. Unfortunately, most residents, especially suburbanites, avoid downtown due to its reputation for crime (not totally unfounded, so exercise caution, especially at night). Therefore, the result has been disappointing, with conventioneers and tourists a stronger presence than locals, who opt for Midtown, Buckhead, and Virginia-Highland night spots instead. Still, Underground's atmosphere is lively enough—if a bit contrived—on weekend nights. The complex accommodates 50 specialty shops, as well as 22 fast-food vendors and 15 restaurants and nightclubs on three levels. Merchants—45–50—selling their wares from push-carts add to the carnival atmosphere. The entertainment strip, Kenny's Alley—once occupied by saloons and livery stables—styles itself as Atlanta's version of New Orleans's Bourbon Street, with bars and night spots offering comedy acts, a variety of music (rock, country, pop, folk, jazz), and dancing. **Dante's Down the Hatch** stars live alligators, fondue, and jazz and is a favorite of locals and tourists alike. Underground's main entrance is highlighted by the Peachtree Fountains Plaza, with its distinctive 138-foot light tower, a stage where various special events take place, and a series of cascading waterfalls and splashing fountains. Two parking garages are on Martin Luther King Jr. (locally, MLK) Drive.

Look closely for the historic markers that dot Underground Atlanta. Opposite the Plaza Depot entrance is downtown's oldest building, the Georgia Railroad Freight Depot. Built in 1869 with three stories (to replace the one torched by Sherman's troops in 1864), it was once the city's tallest building, but a fire reduced it to a single story in 1935. It is now used by several downtown companies as a meeting hall and for special events.

Across the plaza from the Depot and the entrance to Kenny's Alley is the **World of Coca-Cola** (55 Martin Luther King Jr. Dr., ☎ 404/676–5151), where you can sip samples of more than 100 Coke products from around the world and marvel over memorabilia from more than a century's worth of corporate archives in this four-story, $10 million facility.

From Five Points (Peachtree and Marietta Sts.) head down Marietta Street into Atlanta's banking district, stopping at the **NationsBank Building** (35 Broad St.) to see the lavish lobby designed by noted architect Philip Shutze and the 21-story **Bank of the South Building** (55 Marietta St.), Atlanta's tallest building from 1955–64.

At the corner of Marietta and Forsyth streets is a bronze **statue of Henry Grady,** the post–Civil War editor of the *Atlanta Constitution* and early champion of the so-called "New South." To the right at 57 Forsyth

⑱ Street is the **Healy Building,** an early skyscraper (1913) with Tudor decoration. At 72 Marietta Street are the offices of the *Atlanta Journal-Constitution.* Its lobby features a display of front page news documenting historic events and photographs of famous individuals who have worked for the paper. Next door is the **Federal Reserve Bank.** Tours of its monetary museum can be arranged. *104 Marietta St.,* ☎ *404/521–8747.* ☛ *Free.* ☺ *Weekdays 9–4.*

⑲ Two blocks away, at the corner of Marietta Street and Techwood Drive, is **CNN Center,** the home of Ted Turner's Cable News Network. The 45-minute CNN studio tour begins with a ride up the world's longest escalator to an eighth-floor exhibit on Turner's global broadcasting empire. This center will serve as the command post to thousands of international journalists during the Olympics. *1 CNN Center,* ☎ *404/827–2300. Tour reservations strongly recommended.* ☛ *$6 adults, $4 senior citizens, $3.50 children under 13. Not recommended for children under.6.* ☺ *Daily 9–5:30. Closed major holidays.*

⑳ Behind the CNN Center is the **Omni** (100 Techwood Dr.), home to the Atlanta Hawks NBA basketball team and Atlanta Knights minor league hockey team, as well as the site of special events, from rock concerts to the 1988 Democratic National Convention. The Hawks plan to build a new arena in the north suburbs by 1996, leaving the Omni's future ㉑ in doubt. The **World Congress Center** (285 International Blvd.), used primarily for large conventions and trade shows, is across the street. ㉒ A couple of blocks south is the **Richard B. Russell Federal Building** (Spring St. between Mitchell St. and Martin Luther King Jr. Dr.), the largest building in Atlanta owned by the U.S. government; its lobby features magnificent tile mosaics and art.

㉓ The 70,500-seat **Georgia Dome** (1 Georgia Dome Dr.), with a white, plum, and turquoise facade, is the site of Atlanta Falcons football games, major rock concerts, conventions, and trade shows. A design team of local architects crowned the 1-million-square-foot facility with the world's largest cable-supported oval, giving the roof a circus-tent top.

㉔ Returning to Five Points by foot or MARTA Rail, visit **Woodruff Park** (Peachtree St. and Park Pl.), named after the city's great philanthropist, Robert W. Woodruff, the late Coca-Cola magnate; it presents a cross section of Atlanta life. During lunchtime on weekdays, the park is filled with executives, street preachers, politicians, Georgia State University students, and homeless people.

Not much of old Atlanta still exists downtown, although a few turn-of-the-century buildings remain. These elaborately decorated structures stand in sharp contrast to the postmodern skyscrapers of recent years. ㉕ The **Hurt Building** (45 Edgewood Ave.) features intricate grillwork and ㉖ an elaborate marble staircase. The **William–Oliver Building** (32 Peachtree St.) is an Art Deco gem. Walk through its lobby and admire the ceil- ㉗ ing mural, brass grills, and elevator doors. The **Flatiron Building** (84 Peachtree St.) dates from 1897 and is the city's oldest high rise. The ㉘ magnificent mosaic lobby of the **Candler Building** (127 Peachtree St.) shouldn't be missed.

㉙ The towering, 52-story **Georgia-Pacific Building** (133 Peachtree St. at John Wesley Dobbs Ave.) occupies hallowed ground, the site of the old Loew's Grand Theatre, where *Gone with the Wind* premiered in 1939. One of the architectural oddities of this red-marble high rise is that from certain angles the building appears to be two-dimensional, or flat against the sky. The **High Museum of Art Folk Art and Photography**

Galleries is inside the building. *30 John Wesley Dobbs Ave.,* ☎ *404/577–6940.* ☛ *Free.* ☉ *Mon.–Sat. 10–5.*

㉚ Across from the Georgia-Pacific building is the miniscule **Margaret Mitchell Park,** with its cascading waterfall and columned sculpture. Within sight of the park named for Atlanta's most famous author is **㉛** the **Atlanta–Fulton County Public Library** (126 Carnegie Way), which houses a large collection of *Gone with the Wind* memorabilia and newspapers from most major cities in the United States and elsewhere on its fourth floor.

㉜ On the next corner is the downtown **Ritz-Carlton Hotel** (181 Peachtree St.), elegant with the company's trademark 18th- and 19th-century En-**㉝** glish antiques. The Ritz-Carlton's neighbor is **One Ninety One Peachtree Tower,** designed by Philip Johnson.

Across the street is **Macy's** department store (180 Peachtree St.), and **㉞** next to it is the 73-story **Westin Peachtree Plaza Hotel** (210 Peachtree St.). Designed by Atlanta architect John Portman, the glassy, cylindrical tower with its trademark exterior elevator features a postmodern interior and the Sundial, a revolving bar/restaurant offering the best panoramic view of the city. Until a few years ago, it was the tallest building in the city.

㉟ In the next block, on both sides of the street, is **Peachtree Center,** also designed by John Portman. This complex, with its connecting skywalks, includes the massive **Atlanta Market Center,** housing the **Merchandise Mart, Apparel Mart, Gift Mart and Inforum** (technological companies); and the twin office towers of Peachtree Center, with an underground shopping and restaurant area. The adjacent **Hyatt Regency Hotel,** a block north on Peachtree Street and connected to the center by a skywalk, is another Portman creation, a model when it was built in 1967 for other American hotels with its bunkerlike exterior, low entrance, soaring atrium, and blue-domed Polaris Lounge.

Behind Peachtree Center in the Marriott Marquis Two Tower is the **Atlanta International Museum of Art and Design,** which exhibits art and crafts from around the globe. *285 Peachtree Center Ave.,* ☎ *404/688–2467.* ☛ *Free.* ☉ *Tues.–Sat. 11–5.*

Dwarfed by the skyscrapers around it, the modestly sized Italian Re-**㊱** naissance-style **Capital City Club** (7 Harris St.), built in 1911, continues to attract the city's power brokers.

Midtown

Just north of downtown lies this thriving area, a former hippie hangout in the late '60s and '70s, now populated by a large segment of the city's gay population who reside in the area. Formerly in decline, a massive gentrification program during the past decade has transformed Midtown into one of the city's most interesting neighborhoods. Its gleaming new office towers give it a skyline to rival downtown, and the renovated mansions and bungalows in its residential section have made it a city showcase. As the city's primary art and theater district, complimented by several interesting bars and restaurants, it is a favorite of Atlantans for nighttime entertainment. Our tour takes you north along Peachtree Street and then east to Piedmont Park.

㊲ Built in 1992, the **NationsBankPlaza Tower** (600 Peachtree St. at North Ave.), its graceful birdcage roof easily visible from the interstate, is the South's tallest building at 1,023 feet. Its elegant and marbled central lobby is worth seeing.

38 The not-to-be-missed **Fox Theatre** is one of only a handful of classic movie palaces in the nation saved from the wrecker's ball. It was built in 1929 in a fabulous Moorish-Egyptian style to be the headquarters for the Shriner's Club. The interior's crowning glory is its "sky" ceiling—complete with clouds and stars above Alhambralike minarets. The Fox is still a prime venue for Broadway shows, rock concerts, dance performances, and film festivals. *660 Peachtree St., ☎ 404/881–2100 or 404/876–2040. ☛ Tour $5 adults, $4 senior citizens, $3 students. Tours given Mon. and Thurs. at 10 AM, Sat. at 10 AM and 11:30 AM.*

TIME OUT A few blocks from the Fox, in an old drugstore with the original tile floors and pressed-tin ceilings, is a branch of **Mick's** (557 Peachtree St. at Linden St., ☎ 404/875–6425), a popular Atlanta chain featuring great burgers and traditional American food.

39 Across the street from the Fox is the **Road to Tara Museum.** This museum, named for the original title of *Gone with the Wind,* houses an impressive collection of *Gone with the Wind* memorabilia from around the world. Especially peachy are the David O. Selznick Screening Room, where clips on the making of the film classic are shown, and the new costume gallery. *Georgian Terrace Apartments, 659 Peachtree St., ☎ 404/897–1939. ☉ Mon.–Sat. 10–6, Sun. 1–6.*

At Peachtree and 10th streets once stood a piece of Atlanta history, the dilapidated apartment house where Margaret Mitchell penned *Gone with the Wind.* Fought over for years by historical preservationists who wanted to make it a national landmark and developers who highly desired the land on which it stood, the building was destroyed by arson in September 1994. Daimler-Benz, AG of Stuttgart, Germany, makers of Mercedes-Benz automobiles, have pledged to rebuild it in time for the 1996 Summer Olympics.

40 Down 14th Street is **One Atlantic Center** (1201 W. Peachtree St.), also known as the **IBM Tower.** Visible from many parts of the city, this pyramid-topped office tower with a Gothic motif, built in 1987, was designed by Philip Johnson.

41 The **Woodruff Arts Center** (1280 Peachtree St.) is home to the world-renowned **Atlanta Symphony Orchestra** and the **Alliance Theatre.** The Alliance has a primary stage, where mainstream works are produced for general audiences, and a downstairs studio that offers innovative productions.

42 Next door is the bold white porcelain–paneled **High Museum of Art,** a building that many call far superior to the collection within. This high-tech showplace built in 1983 is the award-winning design of premier architect Richard Meier. In 1991, the American Institute of Architects listed the sleek museum among the 10 best works of American architecture of the 1980s. Best bets among the museum's permanent collection are its American decorative arts collection and its African folk art collection. Several temporary exhibits featuring major artists and art movements are held here each year. *1280 Peachtree St., ☎ 404/733–4444 for recorded information. ☛ $6 adults, $4 students and senior citizens, $2 children 6–17; free Thurs. after 1. Special exhibits often have an additional charge. ☉ Tues.–Thurs. 10–5, Fri. 10–9, Sat. 10–5, Sun. noon–5.*

43 North on Peachtree Street, **Rhodes Memorial Hall,** headquarters of the **Georgia Trust for Historic Preservation,** is one of the finest works of Willis F. Denny II. Built of Stone Mountain granite in 1904 for Amos Giles Rhodes, the wealthy founder of a local furniture chain, the hall now shelters a permanent exhibit on Atlanta architecture of bygone eras. *1516 Peachtree St., ☎ 404/881–9980. ☛ $2. ⊘ Weekdays 11–4.*

㊹ A few blocks off Peachtree Street is beautiful **Piedmont Park,** the city's outdoor recreation center and the site of most *plein air* festivals and events in Atlanta's calendar (a source of rancor for those who say the numerous mega-events scheduled there each year result in damage to the park and excessive traffic congestion in and around the area during the events). Tennis courts; a swimming pool; and paths for walking, jogging, and rollerblading are part of the attraction, but many retreat to the park's great lawn for picnics with a smashing view of the Midtown skyline. Each April the park hosts the popular Dogwood Festival, and in September is the nine-day Arts Festival of Atlanta. The **Atlanta Botanical Garden** (1345 Piedmont Ave. at the Prado, ☎ 404/876–5859), occupying 60 acres inside the park, has 15 acres of formal gardens; a 15-acre hardwood forest with walking trails; a serene Japanese garden; and the Fuqua Conservatory, featuring unusual and threatened flora from tropical and desert climates. A whimsical dragon topiary guards the entrance. ☛ *$6.50 adults, $4.75 children 6–12 and senior citizens; free Thurs. 1–6. ⊘ Tues.–Sun. 9–6.*

Buckhead

Take to the road for the remainder of the tours; Atlanta's sprawl doesn't lend itself to walking. Drive north on Peachtree Road to **Buckhead,** the heart of affluent and trendy Atlanta. Many of Atlanta's see-and-be-seen restaurants, music clubs, chic shops, and hip art galleries are concentrated in this neighborhood. Finding a parking spot on the weekends can be a real headache, and waits of two hours or more are common in the hottest restaurants.

㊺ Start a tour at the **Fay Gold Gallery** (247 Buckhead Ave., ☎ 404/233–3843; ⊘ Tues.–Fri. 9:30–5:30, Sat. 10–6), noted for its shows of nationally renowned contemporary artists. Fine photography is sold at the **Jackson Fine Art Gallery** (3115 E. Shadowlawn, ☎ 404/233–3739).

TIME OUT **Café Tu Tu Tango** (220 Pharr Rd., ☎ 404/841–6222), a small space with local art—and artists—in every nook and cranny, serves tasty tapas throughout the day. At night, the crush of Buckhead's beautiful people often means two-hour waits for tables.

㊻ A short distance west of the Buckhead commercial district is the **Atlanta History Center**. The 28-foot-high atrium in its museum highlights materials native to Georgia, with a floor of heart pine and polished Stone Mountain granite. Displays are provocative, juxtaposing *Gone with the Wind* romanticism with the grim reality of Ku Klux Klan racism. Also on the 32-acre site, but not new to it, are the elegant **Swan House,** a Palladian mansion designed by architect Philip Trammell Shutze in 1926; the **Tullie Smith Plantation,** a two-story plantation house (1845) brought here from another Georgia site; **McElreath Hall,** an exhibition space for artifacts from Atlanta's history, with lectures given in its auditorium; and the **Coach House Restaurant.** *130 W. Paces Ferry Rd., ☎ 404/814–4000. ☛ $7 adults, $5 senior citizens and students, $3 children 5–17, under 5 free. ⊘ Mon.–Sat. 10–5:30, Sun. noon–5.*

㊼ The **Georgia Governor's Mansion** is a few blocks farther on West Paces Ferry Road. Built in the late 1970s in Greek Revival style, the house features Federal-period antiques in its public rooms. *391 W. Paces*

Ferry Rd., ☎ 404/261–1858. ☛ *Free. Guided tours Tues.–Thurs. 10–11:30 AM.*

Beyond here, look for the green-and-white "Scenic Drive" signs along Tuxedo, Valley, and Habersham roads to get a look at the lawns, gardens, and mansions of Atlanta's well-to-do. Greek Revival, Spanish, Italianate, English Tudor, and French château mansions vie for viewers' attention.

At the intersection of Peachtree Street and Lenox Road are Atlanta's two premier shopping malls: **Lenox Square,** which boasts 268 stores with its new second level, and the newly refurbished and enlarged **Phipps Plaza,** which now has 200 stores. At the latter, catering to well-to-do shoppers, such amenities as valet parking and concierge service are taken in stride. Break up boutique visits with a stop at **Il Centro,** the center's chic coffee bar, or one of several restaurants here.

Across the street lies the **Ritz-Carlton Buckhead,** next door to the luxury hotel chain's headquarters. Considered one of the finest hotels in the country, it contains one of the South's most valuable private art collections, primarily 18th- and 19th-century American and European painting, sculpture, and porcelain. It's also home to Atlanta's only five-star restaurant, the **Dining Room** (*see* Dining, *below*).

Virginia-Highland and the Emory Area
Restaurants, bars, and art galleries are the backbone of the eclectic Virginia-Highland/Morningside neighborhood, northeast of Midtown. Emory University, site of the Centers for Disease Control and one of the city's cultural and academic hubs, lies east of here. A number of museums and other attractions are scattered throughout the area.

The postmodern **Michael C. Carlos Museum**'s interior was designed by architect Michael Graves. Exhibits range from an Egyptian mummy to contemporary art. *Emory University, 571 Kilgo St., ☎ 404/727–4282. Suggested donation: $3.* ☉ *Mon.–Sat. 10–4:30, Fri. 10–9, Sun. noon–5; closed major holidays.*

Drive east on North Decatur Avenue, turn right on Clifton Road, and continue for 1 mile to the **Fernbank Museum of Natural History,** which maintains the largest natural history collection south of the Smithsonian. A permanent exhibit, "A Walk Through Time in Georgia," takes the visitor through 15 galleries to explore the beauty of the state. The museum's IMAX theater shows films on a six-story screen. *767 Clifton Rd., ☎ 404/370–0960, 404/370–0019 (IMAX only), or 404/370–0850 (directions hot line).* ☛ *$5.50 adults, $4.50 students and senior citizens, under 2 free; prices vary for IMAX.* ☉ *Tues.–Thurs., Sat. 10–5, Fri. 10–9, Sun. noon–5; closed Dec. 25.*

From the museum, turn left on Ponce de Leon Avenue and left again on Altwood Road. A right onto Heaton Park Drive takes you to the large planetarium at the **Fernbank Science Center,** the only one in the nation owned by a public school system. This small museum focuses on geology, space exploration, and ecology; older children will likely find its displays outdated. *156 Heaton Park Dr., ☎ 404/378–4311.* ☛ *Museum free (planetarium shows: $2 adults, $1 students).* ☉ *Mon. 8:30–5 (except for Planetarium), Tues.–Fri. 8:30–10, Sat. 10–5, Sun. 1–5.*

Although you can walk much of the Virginia-Highland area, with most points of interest being along or off North Highland Avenue, you'll often find clusters of shops, restaurants, and galleries separated by longish stretches of residential area. If you plan to do the entire area, a car is your best bet; parking is usually available along the street or in lots behind or next to stores. Virginia-Highland's funky galleries specialize in works by local and regional contemporary artists. The **Modern Primitive Gallery** (1402 N. Highland Ave., ☎ 404/892–0556) features the folk art of Howard Finster, an internationally recognized artist who has done album covers for the rock bands REM and the Talking Heads. For a touch of nostalgia, check out **20th Century Antiques** (1044 N. Highland Ave., ☎ 404/892–2065).

Nearby, about 2 miles south of Virginia Avenue via North Highland Avenue, is the **Carter Presidential Center,** located on the site where General Sherman orchestrated the Battle of Atlanta. The museum and archives focus on Jimmy Carter's political career, while the center sponsors foreign affairs conferences and projects on such issues as world food supply. Outside, its Japanese garden is a serene spot to unwind. *1 Copenhill Ave., ☎ 404/420–5100. ☛ $4 adults, $3 senior citizens, children under 16 free. ⊙ Mon.–Sat. 9–4:45, Sun. noon–4:45 except major holidays. Cafeteria open Mon.–Sat. 11–4, Sun. noon–4:30.*

When you tire of gallery-hopping, some of the city's best restaurants and bars are here (*see* Dining, *below*).

What to See and Do with Children

The "Weekend" tabloid section of Saturday's *Atlanta Journal-Constitution* has a listing called "Kids," which highlights special happenings around the city for youngsters.

American Adventures/White Water Atlanta. The former, with a $1 million tree house, 15 indoor and outdoor rides, miniature golf, a race-car track, and Imagination Station, will keep your children busy for hours. The latter features more than 40 water attractions, including the largest kid's water playground in the country. After you've worked up an appetite, visit one of the attraction's five restaurants. *250 North Cobb Parkway, Marietta, ☎ 404/424–9283. ☛ From $9.99 per child, depending on what park you visit, age, and few other factors; $2 for parking. ⊙ Memorial Day–Labor Day, Mon.–Thurs. 11–7, weekends 10–9; Labor Day–Memorial Day, hours vary—call ahead.*

Center for Puppetry Arts. This center, designed to teach visitors about the craft, displays puppets from all over the world. Children who attend a workshop on puppet making take home their creations. Performances by professional puppeteers leave youngsters spellbound. *1404 Spring St. at 18th St., ☎ 404/873–3391. ☛ $3 adults, $2 children 13 and under. Not recommended for children below age 4. ⊙ Mon.–Sat. 9–5.*

Chattahoochee Nature Center. Birds and animals in their natural habitats may be seen from nature trails and a boardwalk winding through 100 acres of woodlands and wetlands. *9135 Willeo Rd., Roswell, ☎ 404/992–2055. ☛ $2 adults, $1 children and senior citizens. ⊙ Daily 9–5.*

SciTrek. The Science and Technology Museum of Atlanta covers 96,000 square feet of space and has about 100 hands-on exhibits in four halls: Simple Machines; Light, Color, and Perception; Electricity and Magnetism; and Kidspace, for children ages two to seven. *395 Piedmont Ave., ☎ 404/522–5500. ☛ $7 adults, $5 children 3–17 and senior citizens, under 3 free. ⊙ Mon.–Sat. 10–5, Sun. noon–5.*

Six Flags Over Georgia. This is Atlanta's major theme park, with more than 100 rides, many of them heart-stopping roller coasters and water rides (the latter best saved for last to prevent being damp all day). An especially popular spectacle is the Batman Stunt Show. The park also features well-staged musical revues, diving demonstrations, concerts by top-name artists, and other performances. *I–20W at 7561 Six Flags Rd., Austell,* ☎ *404/739–3400.* ☛ *(all-inclusive 1-day pass) $28 adults, $14 ages 55 and older, $19 children 3–9, under 3 free; $5 parking fee.* ☉ *10 AM–11 PM daily in summer, with weekend-only operations Mar.–May and Sept.–Oct. Closed Nov.–Feb.; closing times vary. Take MARTA's West Line to Hightower Station and then Six Flags bus (No. 201).*

Stone Mountain Park. This park features the largest exposed granite outcropping on earth. The Confederate Memorial on the north face of the 825-foot-high domed mountain is the world's largest sculpture. The 3,200-acre state park has a skylift to the mountaintop, a steam locomotive ride around the mountain's 5-mile-diameter base, an antebellum plantation, two golf courses, a swimming beach, a campground, two hotels, a resort and conference center, an upscale restaurant, a paddle wheel steamboat, and a Civil War museum. Summer nights are capped with a laser light show, and annual events like the Yellow Daisy Festival and the Scottish Highland Games are well attended. *U.S. 78, Stone Mountain Pkwy.,* ☎ *404/498–5600.* ☛ *$5 per car, $20 annual pass; additional fees for attractions and special events.* ☉ *Daily 6 AM–midnight.*

Zoo Atlanta. Recently named by *Good Housekeeping* magazine as one of the top 10 zoos in the United States, Zoo Atlanta has more than 1,000 animals inhabiting its property. An ongoing $35-million renovation program has already produced the Birds of Prey Amphitheater, the Ford African Rain Forest, Flamingo Lagoon, Masai Mara (re-created plains of Kenya), Sumatran Tiger Exhibit, and the new Sea Lion Cove. Longtime resident gorilla, Willie B., and his child, Kudzu, who was conceived a few years ago after a decade of trying, are always hits with zoo visitors. *Grant Park, 800 Cherokee Ave.,* ☎ *404/624–5600.* ☛ *$6 adults and children 12 and older, $4 children 3–11, under 3 free.* ☉ *Daily 10–4:30 (10–5:30 on weekends during daylight savings time); closed major holidays.*

Off the Beaten Path

Just 30 minutes north of Atlanta, **Chateau Elan** (7000 Old Winder Hwy., I–85 to GA 211, exit 48, Braselton, ☎ 404/932–0900 or 800/233–9463, ⟨FAX⟩ 404/271–6005), a 16th-century–style French chateau and Georgia's premiere winery, sits on 2,400 rolling acres. Winery tours and tastings are free; European luxury blends with southern hospitality at the 144-room inn and newly opened spa. Rounding out the offerings are two golf courses, fishing, tennis, an equestrian center, an art gallery, a restaurant, a wine market, and a gift shop.

Shopping

Atlanta is second only to Chicago in space devoted to shopping areas, and its department stores, specialty shops, large enclosed malls, and antiques markets draw shoppers from across the Southeast. Most stores are open Monday–Saturday 10–9:30, Sunday noon–6. Many downtown stores close Sunday. Sales tax is 6% in the city of Atlanta and Fulton County, and 4%–5% in the suburbs.

Unlike many urban centers, downtown stores—although not abundant—do a steady business. Stores here are anchored on the north by Peachtree Center's **Mall**, with 30 retailers, including **Brooks Brothers** (235 Peachtree St., ☎ 404/577–4040) in its Gaslight Tower, and by **Underground's** 46 retailers on the south end. In between are **Macy's** (180 Peachtree St., ☎ 404/221–7221) and the **Limited** (209 Peachtree St., ☎ 404/523–1728).

At the intersection of Peachtree and Lenox roads, 8 miles north of downtown, are two of Atlanta's oldest and most popular shopping malls (*see* Buckhead, *above*). **Lenox Square Mall**, the largest shopping space (per square foot) in Atlanta, has branches of **Neiman Marcus, Macy's, Rich's;** 265 other specialty stores ; and restaurants and fast food chains in its large food court. Diagonally across the street from Lenox is the upscale **Phipps Plaza,** catering more to the tastes of the affluent with branches of **Saks Fifth Avenue, Lord & Taylor, Parisian, Gucci, Tiffany & Co., Abercrombie & Fitch,** and other small specialty shops. Phipps will more than double its size from 90 to 200 stores by July 1996, with a new wing that includes a branch of **Bloomingdale's.**

Cumberland Mall (Cobb Parkway at I–285) and the more upscale **Galleria Specialty Mall** (One Galleria Parkway) offer prime shopping for residents of Atlanta's northwestern suburbs. The refurbished **Northlake Mall,** east of the I–85/I–285 intersection, is anchored by **Macy's** and a new **Parisian** department store. The newest entry on the mall scene, the vast **North Point Mall** (1000 North Point Circle, Alpharetta), has five department stores. About 15 minutes north of Lenox Square Mall, in the affluent suburb of Dunwoody, is **Perimeter Mall** (4400 Ashford–Dunwoody Rd.), known for upscale family shopping, with shops such as the **High Museum of Art Gift Shop, Gap Kids,** and the **Nature Company.** Also child-friendly are **Town Center** (400 Barrett Parkway, Kennesaw) and **Gwinnett Place Mall** (2100 Pleasant Hill Rd., Duluth), both with on-site child-care facilities.

Outlets

Atlanta and surrounding towns are a bargain-hunter's delight. For new clothes and shoes, **Macy's Close-Out** at **Avondale Mall** (3588 Memorial Dr., Decatur, tel 404/286–0829) and **Rich's Finale** at **Greenbriar Mall** (2841 Greenbriar Parkway, ☎ 404/346–2615) are two of the best discounters here. **Ballard's Backroom Catalog Clearance Center** (1670 Defoor Ave., ☎ 404/352–2776) carries the uniquely designed rugs, lamps, tables, and pillows usually available only through Ballard Design's stylish catalogs.

The **Dalton Factory Stores** (80 mi north of Atlanta; exit 136 off I–75) offer **Jones of New York, West Point Pepperell,** and more. **Outlets Ltd. Mall** (3750 Venture Dr., Duluth) yields good buys in men's, women's, and children's clothing, as well as numerous specialty items. **Outlet Square of Atlanta** (4166 Buford Hwy.) is anchored by the **Burlington Coat Factory, Rack Room Shoes,** and **Marshall's.**

Specialty Shops

ANTIQUES

Buckhead is home to several antiques shops, with most of them along or near Peachtree Road. Expect rare goods and high prices in many stores. More than 25 shops line the cobblestone courtyard of Buckhead's **2300 Peachtree Road** complex. Along **Miami Circle**, off Piedmont Road, is another enclave for antiques and decorative arts lovers.

The **Stalls** (116 Bennett St., ☎ 404/352–4430) is an upscale flea market.

"Junking" addicts find nirvana in **Little Five Points,** at the intersection of Moreland and Euclid avenues. The neighborhood, Atlanta's version of Greenwich Village, is characterized by vintage clothing stores, art galleries, used record and book shops, and some stores that defy description.

Other fertile ground for serious antiques shoppers includes suburban Chamblee's "Antiques Row," a few blocks off Peachtree Industrial Boulevard with some shops near the Chamblee MARTA rail station, and historic Roswell, about a 30-minute drive north of downtown.

BOOKS
Atlanta's largest selection of books and newspapers is at **Oxford Books at Buckhead** (360 Pharr Rd., ☎ 404/262–3333), a local institution where frequent book signings are prominently noted on the store's marquee. Oxford's narrow balcony is a coffee shop, and the store also contains a full-service art gallery that emphasizes local artists' works. New to the neighborhood, the nearby **Barnes & Noble** (2900 Peachtree Rd., ☎ 404/261–7747), adjoined by a **Starbucks** (the famed coffee shop chain that began in Seattle), promises competition.

FOOD
DeKalb Farmers Market (3000 E. Ponce de Leon Ave., Decatur, ☎ 404/377–6400) has 140,000 square feet of exotic fruits, cheeses, seafood, sausages, breads, and delicacies from around the world. Gourmands stock up at **Harry's Farmers Markets** (1180 Upper Hembree Rd., Alpharetta, ☎ 404/664–6300; 2025 Satellite Blvd., Duluth, ☎ 404/416–6900) north of the city, with their dazzling array of prepared foods as well as produce, meats, seafood, and wines.

Participant Sports

In a city where outdoor recreation is possible almost year-round, sports play a major role. At almost any time of the year, in parks, private clubs, and neighborhoods throughout the city, you'll find Atlantans pursuing everything from tennis to soccer to rollerblading. *Atlanta Sports & Fitness Magazine* (☎ 404/842–0359), available for free at many grocery stores and health clubs, is a good link to Atlanta's athletic community.

Bicycling and Rollerblading
Piedmont Park (Piedmont Ave. between 10th and 14th Sts.) is closed to traffic and popular for rollerblading. **Skate Escape** (across from the park at 1086 Piedmont Ave., ☎ 404/892–1292) has rental bikes, Rollerblades, and skates. The **Southern Bicycle League** (☎ 404/594–8350) and **Cycle South** (☎ 404/991–6642) offer regularly scheduled tours.

Golf
Golf is enormously popular here, as the many courses will attest. The only public course within sight of downtown Atlanta is the **Bobby Jones Golf Course** (384 Woodward Way, ☎ 404/355–1009), named after the famed golfer and Atlanta native and located on a portion of the site of the Battle of Peachtree Creek. Despite having some of the city's worst fairways and greens, the immensely popular 18-hole, par 71 course is always crowded. Another club on a Civil War site is the **Alfred Tup Holmes Club** (2300 Wilson Dr., ☎ 404/753–6158), built upon a former Con-

federate breastworks; golf-wise, it's known for numerous doglegs and blind shots. Also within I–285 are the **Browns Mill Golf Course** (480 Cleveland Ave., ☎ 404/366–3573), considered the best operated by the City of Atlanta, and **North Fulton Golf Course** (216 W. Wieuca Rd., ☎ 404/255–0723), offering one of the best layouts, but also some of the smallest greens. The **Sugar Creek Golf Course** (2706 Bouldercrest Rd., ☎ 404/241–7671), straddling I–285 (11 holes on one side, seven on the other) in southeast Atlanta, is a challenging course with several long drives and good Bermuda greens. Outside I–285 in the suburbs, the best public course is the **Southerness Golf Club** (4871 Flat Bridge Rd., Stockbridge, ☎ 404/808–6000), with a great variety of challenging holes—from long par fours to shots over water requiring pinpoint accuracy. Among Stone Mountain Park's (U.S. 78, ☎ 404/498–5715) two 18-hole courses, **Stonemont** is the best, with several challenging and scenic holes; it was voted one of the top 75 public courses by *Golf Digest*. The former private **Lakeside Country Club** (3600 Old Fairburn Rd., ☎ 404/344–3620), just outside I–285 in southwest Atlanta, offers many challenges, with a dogleg on nearly every hole. **Eagle Watch Golf Club** (3055 Eagle Watch Dr., Woodstock, ☎ 404/591–1000), designed by Arnold Palmer, is a huge course that will please long distance drivers.

Health Clubs

SportsLife (3340 Peachtree Rd., ☎ 404/ 262–2120; six other locations) and the **YMCA** (☎ 404/588–9622; 15 locations) are both open to the public. Hotels with health clubs include the **Ritz-Carlton Buckhead, Westin Peachtree Plaza, Hotel Nikko,** the **Swissotel,** and the **Atlanta Marriott Marquis** (*see* Lodging, *below*).

Jogging

This is one of the city's most popular sports. The **Peachtree Road Race 10K,** held annually on July 4, has become so popular that there are no longer enough slots for those wanting to sign up (up to 25,000 runners allowed). Atlanta's hills provide joggers with plenty of challenges. On the plus side, most streets are heavily shaded, offering some respite from the miserable summer humidity. Traffic-free **Piedmont Park** is ideal for running, as is the **Chattahoochee National Recreation Area.** Contact the **Atlanta Track Club** (3097 Shadowlawn Ave., ☎ 404/231–9064) or **Chattahoochee Road Runners** (Box 724745, 31139, ☎ 404/916–2820) for other suggestions.

Rafting and Rowing

The **Chattahoochee River** is a favorite among rafters and rowers alike. The **Atlanta Rowing Club** (☎ 404/993–1879) provides information.

Swimming

White Water Park (*see* What to See and Do with Children, *above*) has a huge wave pool, several water slides, picnic areas, lockers, and showers. **Lake Lanier,** 45 minutes northeast of Atlanta (I–85 to I–985), is frequented by swimmers and boaters during the summer months.

Tennis

Bitsy Grant Tennis Center (2125 Northside Dr., ☎ 404/351–2774; ◷ Weekdays 8:30–7, weekends 8:30–6), with 13 clay courts and 10 hard courts, is the area's best public facility. **Piedmont Park** (☎ 404/872–1507) has 12 hard courts with night lights available, but no locker facilities (◷ Weekdays noon–9, weekends 9–5).

Waterskiing
Lake Lanier and **Callaway Gardens** both offer superior waterskiing, although the former can be extremely crowded on weekends. Contact the **Atlanta Water Ski Club** (☎ 404/425–7166).

Spectator Sports

As much as they play sports, Atlantans love to watch them. Sports fever grew in 1991 and 1992, when the Atlanta Braves won back-to-back National League titles. The Braves currently play home games at **Atlanta–Fulton County Stadium** (521 Capitol Ave., ☎ 404/ 249–6400). In 1997, they will cross the street to occupy Olympic Stadium, which will be converted into baseball stadium dimensions after the 1996 Summer Olympics. The National Basketball Association's Atlanta Hawks play home games at the **Omni Coliseum** (100 Techwood Dr., ☎ 404/827–DUNK). The National Football League's Atlanta Falcons play home games at the **Georgia Dome** (1 Georgia Dome Dr., ☎ 404/223–8000). The International Hockey League's 1994 champions, the Atlanta Knights, play at the **Omni** (☎ 404/525–8900).

Dining

Updated by
Jane Schneider

From a million-dollar Patrick Kuleto–designed diner to a humble meat-and-three establishment, one can find almost anything in the capital of the New South: prestigious kitchens run by world-class chefs; a multitude of ethnic restaurants; and such regional favorites as fried chicken, Brunswick stew, fried catfish, and hush puppies.

As is probably inevitable in a city where enthusiasm and growth has outstripped experience, however, some of the so-called hottest or trendiest Atlanta restaurants can be something of a letdown. Service, too, has a long way to go at many popular establishments. Wine enthusiasts will marvel at some of the wine lists assembled in the city's finer restaurants, and find others exasperating. Visitors would do well to approach each meal here with cautious optimism.

The local taste for things sweet and fried holds true for restaurants serving traditional Southern food. To taste Southern iced tea, order it sweet. (When ordering tea in the South, it is assumed you want iced tea. To get hot tea, specify hot.) Don't pass up desserts in the South; they're legendary. And fried chicken, seafood, collard greens, and okra are the staples of Southern cooking for all Southerners. Catch the flavor of the South at breakfast and lunch in modest establishments that serve only these two meals. Reserve evenings for culinary exploration, including some of the new Southern-style restaurants that present regional dishes and traditional ingredients in fresh and inventive ways

CATEGORY	COST*
$$$$	over $45
$$$	$35–$45
$$	$25–$35
$	under $25

per person for a three-course meal, excluding drinks, service, and 6% tax.

What to Wear
Dress in Atlanta is casual unless noted otherwise.

Downtown

$$$$ **City Grill.** This posh but breezy restaurant has made the most of its grand
★ location in the elegantly renovated historic Hurt building. The bustle
of success greets you at the door, while bucolic murals and stunning
high ceilings create a feeling of glamour. Chef Roger Kaplan's regional
American menu chiefly explores the specialties of the South and Southwest. The excellent wine list covers the world, offering many unusual
selections. City Grill is a top Atlanta "power lunch" spot. ✗ *50 Hurt
Plaza,* ☎ *404/524–2489. Reservations recommended far in advance
for weekend dining. AE, D, DC, MC, V. No lunch Sat. Closed Sun.*

$$$$ **The Restaurant, Ritz-Carlton, Atlanta.** The elegant, clublike interior of
the Restaurant is an ideal business dining spot. Lunch is a buffet arrangement, serving dishes that change daily. Save this one for dinner.
Chef Daniel Schaffhauser, a native of Alsace, presents an international
menu with regional American touches. Braised Georgia quail partners
with roasted garlic polenta. Venison chops are paired with Napa cabbage and a confit of apples and pecans. The well-selected wine list is
ably administered by a knowledgeable sommelier. ✗ *181 Peachtree St.,*
☎ *404/659–0400, ext. 6450. Reservations advised. Jacket and tie. AE,
D, DC, MC, V. No lunch Sat. Closed Sun.*

$$$ **Savannah Fish Company.** Have a drink in the revolving lounge at the
top of the hotel, but come to the ground floor for a smashingly good
and simple meal of fresh grilled or sautéed fish. Begin with the restau-
rant's famous smoked bluefish spread, a complimentary opener.Enjoy
the house's saffron- and fennel-flavored fish stew. And don't forget to
save room for the simple Savannah hot puffs, fried dough sprinkled
with sugar and cinnamon and served with three sauces. ✗ *Westin
Peachtree Plaza, 210 Peachtree St. at International Blvd.,* ☎ *404/589–
7456. No reservations at dinner. AE, D, DC, MC, V*

$$ **Dailey's.** The downstairs dining room of this enormous converted
warehouse is casual fun. Upstairs there's spectacular decor (merry-go-
round horses and huge shop lamps) and more serious dining: swordfish au poivre, Georgia peach rack of lamb, duck in apple brandy, and
fried yeast rolls. Revved-up versions of pastry classics are paraded before the adoring eyes of the crowd. ✗ *17 International Blvd.,* ☎
*404/681–3303. No reservations; expect a wait. AE, D, DC, MC, V.
Entertainment nightly in downstairs lounge. No lunch Sun.*

$ **Deacon Burton's Soul Food Restaurant.** The deacon who presided over
this temple of Southern cooking is gone, but his affable son stands in,
presiding over some of the best fried chicken in town. Opposite the
Inman Park/Reynoldstown MARTA station, this humble eatery serves
up perfectly prepared down-home collards, hoe cakes, mashed potatoes and gravy, and peach cobbler. No alcohol is served. ✗ *1029 Edgewood Ave.,* ☎ *404/658–9452. No reservations. No credit cards. No
dinner. Closed weekends and Aug.*

$ **Delectables.** One of downtown's best-kept secrets; don't let the loca-
tion (inside the central branch of the Atlanta–Fulton Public Library)
or the format (cafeteria) deter you. This is a sophisticated little operation serving ravishing salads, wholesome soups, yummy cookies, and
freshly baked cakes. Enjoy your meal to the strains of classical music
and sunshine on the patio. ✗ *Atlanta–Fulton Public Library, corner
of Margaret Mitchell Sq. and Carnegie Way (enter through Carnegie
Way),* ☎ *404/681–2909. AE, MC, V. No dinner. Closed weekends.*

$ **Harold's Barbecue.** Legislators, political groupies, and small fry from
the capitol sit side by side, wolfing down delicious sliced pork sandwiches, huge platters of freshly sliced meat, and overflowing bowls of
Brunswick stew. Don't miss the crackling bread. The knotty pine,

Dining

Ciboulette, **3**

City Grill, **17**

Dailey's, **12**

Deacon Burton's Soul Food Restaurant, **16**

Delectables, **15**

French Quarter Food Shop, **4**

Harold's Barbecue, **18**

Indigo Coastal Grill, **6**

Partners Morningside Cafe, **7**

The Restaurant, The Ritz-Carlton Atlanta, **14**

Savannah Fish Company, **11**

The Varsity, **5**

Lodging

Ansley Inn, **2**

Atlanta Marriott Marquis, **8**

Barclay Hotel, **10**

Colony Square Hotel, **1**

Atlanta Hyatt Regency, **9**

Omni Hotel at CNN Center, **13**

The Ritz-Carlton Atlanta, **14**

Westin Peachtree Plaza, **11**

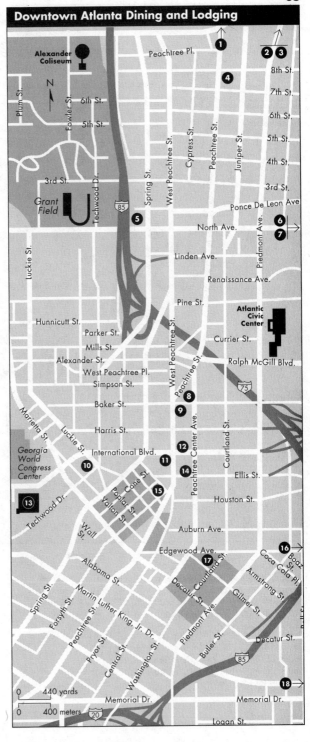

Downtown Atlanta Dining and Lodging

Atlanta Vicinity Dining and Lodging

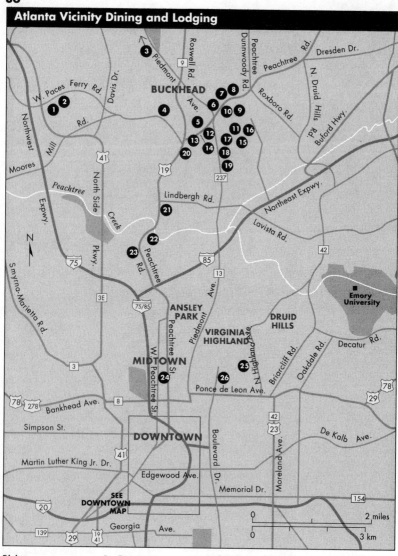

Dining

Abruzzi Ristorante, **21**
Annie's Thai Castle, **5**
Atlanta Fish Market, **11**
Azalea, **12**
Bacchanalia, **18**
Basil's Mediterranean Cafe, **17**
Bone's, **14**
Buckhead Diner, **19**
Dining Room, in the Ritz-Carlton Buckhead, **8**
Horseradish Grill, **3**
Kudzu Cafe, **13**

La Grotta, **20**
Luna Sí, **22**
OK Café, **1**
103 West, **4**
Pano's and Paul's, **2**
Pricci, **15**
Rocky's Brick Oven Pizzeria, **23**
South City Kitchen, **24**
Surin of Thailand, **25**
Tortillas, **26**

Lodging

Embassy Suites, **10**
Hotel Nikko, **6**
JW Marriott, **16**
The Ritz-Carlton, Buckhead, **8**
Swissôtel, **9**
Windham Garden Hotel, **7**

tacky art, and management haven't changed in a half century. It's a short distance from downtown, but worth the ride. ✕ *171 McDonough Blvd.,* ☏ *404/627–9268. No reservations. No credit cards. Closed Sun.*

$ **The Varsity.** Part of Atlanta's collective past, this sprawling diner near the Georgia Tech campus pioneered the drive-in eatery concept. It attracts people from all walks of life who come for the famous chili dogs, hamburgers, and gigantic orders of fresh and delicious—but greasy—onion rings. Line up behind the locals and pay close attention to the lingo: "One naked dog, walkin' and a bag o' rags," will get you a plain hot dog and some potato chips. Connoisseurs drink orange frosties. Folks in a hurry get curb service. ✕ *61 North Ave.,* ☏ *404/881–1706. No reservations. No credit cards.*

Midtown

$$$ **Ciboulette.** French-bistro food and atmosphere from Tom Coohill have Atlantans lining up for hot smoked salmon with wild mushrooms and ginger, Lyonnaise sausage in crust with warm lentil salad, and lamb with garlic mashed potatoes. Game dishes are frequent specials in season. The wine list is well chosen and embraces many good selections by the glass. The dining room is a bit tight, making intimate conversation difficult, but the counter seats, with their kitchen view, provide a true bistro ambience. ✕ *1529 Piedmont Ave. NE,* ☏ *404/874–7600. Reservations accepted weekdays. AE, DC, MC, V. No lunch. Closed Sun.*

$$–$$$ **Indigo Coastal Grill.** Trendy coastal cuisine packs them in at this lively Virginia–Highland eatery. Cuisine is more fun than fabulous, with some dishes suffering from overwrought flavors and mediocre preparation. Popular here are conch fritters, heavy-cream biscuits, lobster corn chowder, and fish and fresh herbs in a twist of parchment. Don't miss the refreshing Key lime pie or the sautéed bananas with rum and lime. Sunday brunch is served. ✕ *1397 N. Highland Ave.,* ☏ *404/876–0676. No reservations; expect a wait. AE, MC, V. No sit-down lunch, but take-out service available.*

$$–$$$ **Partners Morningside Cafe.** This upbeat, noisy, and colorful spot is next door to Indigo Coastal Grill (*see above*), its companion operation. Cuisine blends several influences, particularly Mediterranean and Pacific Rim. Ravioli stuffing and sauce changes daily; there's also grilled portobello mushrooms, pasta specials that change daily, Vietnamese chicken cakes, and nostalgic, old-fashioned desserts. An appealing small wine list is full of good values. ✕ *1399 N. Highland Ave.,* ☏ *404/876–8104. No reservations; expect a wait. AE, MC, V. No lunch.*

$$–$$$ **South City Kitchen.** The food traditions of South Carolina's coastal low country inspire the cooking at this bright, very popular in-town restaurant. The clean, spare, art-filled interior of this former modest residence attracts a frisky crowd of hip in-towners. This is the place for catfish, prepared in a variety of intriguing ways, such as in a unique Reuben sandwich or on a bed of grits. The very good, well-priced wine list focuses on American wines. ✕ *1144 Crescent Ave.,* ☏ *404/873–7358. Reservations accepted for dinner. AE, MC, V.*

$ **French Quarter Food Shop.** Sandwiched between two bars, this ultracasual eatery has a pleasant sidewalk café. Sit down to some crawfish étouffée, shrimp jambalaya, gumbo, a huge muffaletta that could easily serve two, or a shrimp or oyster po'boy; takeout is also available. ✕ *923 Peachtree Rd.,* ☏ *404/875–2489. No reservations. AE, D, DC, MC, V. Closed Sun.*

$ **Surin of Thailand.** This dining spot opened in 1991 in a renovated drugstore in Virginia-Highland. Big windows let in plenty of light, and the owners' own photographs of Thailand hang on the yellow walls. Try the French basil rolls stuffed with shrimp, cucumber, and pork—one of Chef Surin Techarukpong's best dishes—and save room for the delicately flavored, homemade coconut or mango ice cream for dessert. ✕ *810 N.Highland Ave.,* ☎ *404/892–7789. No reservations. AE, D, MC, V.*

$ Tortillas. This funky California–Spanish joint rates raves from the business and student crowd it attracts at lunch. Weekends and evenings find it packed with 20-somethings. The burritos stuffed with pork or shrimp, the cheese-stuffed quesadillas, and freshly prepared extras like green salsa, guacamole, and potatoes taste authentic and satisfying. ✕ *774 Ponce de Leon Ave.,* ☎ *404/892–0193. No reservations. No credit cards.*

Buckhead

$$$$ Bone's. In this brash, New York–style steakhouse, sports celebs and fast-track businesspeople rub egos and compare lifestyles over excellent prime beef, chops, Maine lobster, and potatoes baked in a crust of salt. Silky, aromatic lobster bisque warms the heart. The award winning wine list strikes a balance between French and American wines, and includes a fair number of Italian vintages. Good wines are available by the glass. Most patrons wear jackets, but if your idea of fun is spending big bucks in a sport shirt, they won't turn you down. Private dining rooms are available. ✕ *3130 Piedmont Rd.,* ☎ *404/237–2663. Reservations advised. AE, DC, MC, V. No lunch weekends.*

$$$$ The Dining Room, Ritz-Carlton, Buckhead. This is the best restaurant in town and among the country's 10 greatest. Under Chef Guenter Seeger, haute cuisine is not flashy or ostentatious. Strictly limiting himself to the freshest regional products, Seeger doesn't like calling attention to the culinary process. The menu, handwritten every day, is likely to involve local sun-dried sweet potatoes (in ravioli), Vidalia onions (with lobster and lobster coral sauce), or persimmons (in a mousse with muscadine sorbet and Georgia golden raspberries). Don't ask for your food to be well-done. Surrender to this imperious genius and the exquisite, discreet service. The wine list and service are extraordinary, worthy of the awards both have won. ✕ *3434 Peachtree Rd.,* ☎ *404/237–2700. Reservations required, several days ahead for weekend dining. Jacket and tie. AE, D, DC, MC, V. No lunch. Closed Sun.*

$$$$ Horseradish Grill. One of *Bon Appétit* magazine's 1994 "10 best new restaurants" selections is a must stop for anyone looking for good Southern-style food. Horseradish Grill reflects the expertise of Alabama native Scott Peacock and his mentor, Edna Lewis, of Virginia. Perfect fried chicken and cream gravy is just one example. The juicy hot browns, an open-faced sandwich originating in Kentucky, feature succulent turkey smoked on the premises over all-natural hickory wood that has not been treated with chemicals. The menu changes often, but Southern ingredients hold sway. The wine list is extensive and growing, as many more selections by the glass are being added. ✕ *4320 Powers Ferry Rd.,* ☎ *404/255–7277. No reservations. AE, MC, V. No lunch Sat.*

$$$$ La Grotta. Despite its odd location in the basement of a posh Buckhead condominium, this is one of the best-managed dining rooms in town. Magnetic, dynamic Sergio Favalli is a superb host, and waiters are on their toes. The kitchen experiments cautiously with new concepts and trendy ingredients, but old Northern Italian favorites remain at the core of the menu. Don't miss the warm grilled portobello mushrooms, the baby quails over polenta, or the tiramisù. Veal and fresh pasta are outstanding. There's an excellent wine list. ✕ *2637 Peachtree Rd.,* ☎ *404/231–1368. Reservations required well in advance for* *weekend dining. Jacket and tie. AE, D, DC, MC, V. No lunch. Closed Sun.*

$$$ Abruzzi Ristorante. "Understated elegance" is the buzz phrase for this modern yet traditional restaurant frequented by the city's old guard. If you're not taken with one of the myriad menu offerings, have managing partner Nico Petrucci suggest a specialty. Excellent dishes include salmon carpaccio, green-and-white *gnocchi* in pesto, sautéed sweetbreads, veal chop, baked fish with rosemary, and ricotta cheesecake. ✗ *2355 Peachtree Rd.,* ☎ *404/261–8186. Reservations advised. AE, DC, MC, V. No lunch Sat., closed Sun.*

$$$ Bacchanalia. *Bon Appétit* magazine included Bacchanalia in its annual list of 10 best new restaurants in 1993. Chefs and companions, Anne Quatrano and Clifford Harrison dazzle diners with dishes that the pair labels "new American," but that take inspiration chiefly from country Mediterranean sources, with occasional touches of Asian ingredients. The four-course fixed-price menu ($35 without wine; $55 with three preselected wines) offers plenty of options. The dishes changes weekly, while exhibiting seasonal emphasis, and may include, for starters, a perfect risotto topped with a generous sprinkle of aromatic fresh white truffle or a roasted butternut squash and apple soup made surprising with a slice of pan-seared foie gras. Main courses range from fish through fowl and red meats, but vegetarians will enjoy offerings tailored to their requirements. Turbot encrusted in potato, sautéed and served with braised leeks is perfect with any one of the wine list's many Pinot Noirs. The wine list, while maddeningly short on offerings by the glass, contains a host of unusual selections, including a separate list of Viogniers. À la carte ordering is available upon request. ✗ *3125 Piedmont Rd.,* ☎ *404/365–0410. Reservations strongly advised. AE, DC, MC, V. No smoking. No lunch. Closed Sun. and Mon.*

$$$ Pano's and Paul's. This is an Atlanta classic that's known for stylish pampering. Pano Karatassos and Paul Albrecht hit gold with their single-minded devotion to their customers' needs, from whims to dietary restrictions. Many new ideas percolate through the kitchen; state-of-the-art dishes are introduced as specials and eventually included in the menu. Look for lemon-roasted, farm-raised chicken with a crisp, celery-potato cake, sautéed gulf red snapper fillet, and jumbo cold lobster tail fried in a light batter and served with Chinese honey mustard. ✗ *1232 W. Paces Ferry Rd.,* ☎ *404/261–3662. Reservations required (days, sometimes weeks ahead for a prime slot). Jacket required. AE, D, DC, MC, V. No lunch. Closed Sun.*

$$–$$$ Atlanta Fish Market. An overwhelming selection of fresh seafood is served in this cavernous space, reminiscent of an old train station. Swordfish with roasted cashew and cracked-pepper crust, served with white-corn cheese grits, exemplifies the creatively prepared cuisine on the ever-changing menu. The wine list has many good choices by the glass. The noise level is high, but the more intimate Geechee Porch presents a quieter ambiance adjacent to the main dining room. ✗ *265 Pharr Rd.,* ☎ *404/262–3165. Reservations limited. AE, D, DC, MC, V. No lunch Sun.*

$$–$$$ Buckhead Diner. This million-dollar fantasy by the owners of Pano's and Paul's is still one of the hottest restaurants in town, a shimmering faux-diner wrapped in luscious hues of neon. Inlaid wood, Italian leather, hand-cut marble and mellow lights establish a languorous ambience reminiscent of the Orient Express. The cuisine is anything but diner: salt-and-pepper squid, fresh goat cheese and tomato fondue, veal-and-wild-mushroom meat loaf, and white chocolate banana cream pie are a sampling. Interesting wines are available by the glass. ✗ *3073*

Piedmont Rd., ☎ *404/262–3336. No reservations; expect a long wait. AE, D, DC, MC, V.*

$$–$$$ **Kudzu Cafe.** Come here for witty, updated southern food that includes fresh vegetables, such as fried green tomatoes. Savannah crab cakes with creole sauce are also worth the trip, and don't forget the pecan pie for dessert. Have someone here tell you the history of kudzu. ✗ *3215 Peachtree Rd.,* ☎ *404/262–0661. No reservations. AE, MC, V. No lunch weekends.*

$$–$$$ **Pricci.** The stamp of acclaimed designer Patrick Kuleto is apparent in the chic mirrored and windowed decor of this high-style hot spot. Deceptively simple southern Italian fare is accompanied by Pricci's own freshly baked breads. The homemade spinach-filled tortellini is delicious. ✗ *500 Pharr Rd.,* ☎ *404/237–2941. Reservations advised. AE, D, DC, MC, V. No lunch weekends.*

$$ **Basil's Mediterranean Café.** Tucked down a side street, in a renovated bungalow, this restaurant is handsomely decorated with original art. In good weather you can dine on the front deck. Dishes—mostly seafood—are well-seasoned, and each plate is an artistic masterpiece. The Greek-style shrimp with artichoke hearts, sun-dried tomatoes, olives, and feta cheese is superb. Dishes reflect the influence of Mediterranean cooking, from southern France to the Middle East and Morocco. Pasta may come topped with tomato and seafood, a spicy tomato sauce, or steamed vegetables. ✗ *2985 Grandview,* ☎ *404/233–9755. Reservations accepted. AE, D, DC, MC, V. Closed Sun.*

$ **Annie's Thai Castle.** A family-run delight transplanted from a suburban location into the heart of Buckhead, this small restaurant is lovingly decorated with objets d'art from Annie's native Thailand. Soups are perfectly flavored with spices and lemon grass, and the seafood salad, aromatic with garlic and lime, dazzles. *Nam sod*, chicken satay, and spicy catfish are excellent choices. Traditional curries and noodle dishes seem to have an extra dash of finesse. ✗ *3195 Roswell Rd.,* ☎ *404/264–9546. Reservations advised on weekends. AE, MC, V.*

$ **Azalea.** East meets West on the menu at this see-and-be-seen restaurant, with its black-on-white contemporary decor. Try the potato-crusted salmon with a wild mushroom cream sauce. Whole sizzling catfish with black bean chile sauce has been a hit from the beginning. Excellent wines by the glass are a specialty. ✗ *3167 Peachtree Rd.,* ☎ *404/237–9939. Reservations accepted Sun.–Thurs. AE, D, DC, MC, V. No lunch.*

$ **Luna Sí.** The emphasis is on fun at this New York loft–style restaurant where Latin music blares, and customers are encouraged to write on the walls. The menu, which changes weekly, is dominated by seafood—seared Atlantic salmon with a ginger crust is a favorite. The chef eschews cream and butter in the preparations. The entire restaurant is nonsmoking. ✗ *1931 Peachtree Rd.,* ☎ *404/355–5993. Reservations accepted for large parties. AE, D, MC, V. No lunch. Closed Mon.*

$ **OK Café.** Go "back to the future" in this witty take-off on small-town eateries. The cheeky waitresses, whimsical art, and roomy, comfortable booths make this a favorite hangout for Atlanta's artsy crowd—and lots of ordinary folk besides. The fried chicken ginger salad is popular. Vegetable plates are supremely satisfying. Mammoth breakfasts, old-fashioned blue-plate specials, and chocolate shakes satisfy that high-cholesterol craving in all of us. ✗ *1284 W. Paces Ferry Rd.,* ☎ *404/233–2888. No reservations. AE, MC, V.*

$ **Rocky's Brick Oven Pizzeria.** It's a find in a city where good pizza is hard to come by. The bustling kitchen turns out thick, square Sicilian pizzas and thin-crusted Neapolitan pies with the city's most appealing combination of toppings. Clientele includes well-heeled parents with tots in tow, art school students, and rocker Mick Jagger, who frequented it while filming a movie. ✕ *1770 Peachtree St.,* ☏ *404/876–1111. No reservations. AE, D, DC, MC, V.*

Lodging

One of America's three most popular convention destinations, Atlanta offers a broad range of lodgings. More than 12,000 rooms are in the compact downtown area, close to the Georgia World Congress Center, Atlanta Civic Center, Atlanta Merchandise Mart, and Omni Coliseum. Other clusters are in Buckhead, in the north I–285 perimeter, and around Hartsfield Atlanta International Airport.

CATEGORY	COST*
$$$$	over $160
$$$	$115–$160
$$	$80–$115
$	under $80

All prices are for a standard double room, excluding 11% tax.

Downtown and Midtown

$$$$ **Atlanta Marriott Marquis.** Immense and coolly contemporary, the Marquis seems to go on forever as you stand under the lobby's huge fabric sculpture that appears to float from the sky-lit roof 48 stories above. Each guest room—of average size and with standard-issue hotel decor—opens onto this atrium. ☎ *265 Peachtree Center Ave., 30303,* ☏ *404/521–0000 or 800/328–9290,* 🖷 *404/586–6299. 1,671 rooms, 71 suites. 5 restaurants, 4 bars and lounges, indoor-outdoor pool, health club. AE, D, DC, MC, V.*

$$$$ **Omni Hotel at CNN Center.** The hotel is adjacent to the CNN Center, home of Ted Turner's Cable News Network. The lobby combines Old World and modern accents, with marble floors, Oriental rugs, exotic floral and plant arrangements, and contemporary furnishings. Rooms are large and decorated in shades of mauve. Guests have access to the Downtown Athletic Club. ☎ *100 CNN Center (MARTA's Omni rail station is adjacent to CNN Center), 30305,* ☏ *404/659–0000 or 800/843–6664,* 🖷 *404/525–5050. 465 rooms. 2 restaurants, lounge. AE, D, DC, MC, V.*

$$$$ **Ritz-Carlton, Atlanta.** The mood here is set by traditional afternoon tea served in the intimate, sunken lobby beneath an 18th-century chandelier. Notice the 17th-century Flemish tapestry when you enter from Peachtree Street. Spacious guest rooms are luxuriously decorated with marble writing tables, plump sofas, four-poster beds, and white marble bathrooms. The Cafe's Sunday brunch spread is spectacular. In the evenings, live jazz music is performed at the Bar upstairs. Service is very European, cold but efficient. ☎ *181 Peachtree St. (entrance to MARTA's Peachtree Center rail station is across the street), 30303,* ☏ *404/659–0400 or 800/241–3333,* 🖷 *404/577–8366. 447 rooms. 2 restaurants, bar, exercise room. AE, D, DC, MC, V.*

$$$$ **Westin Peachtree Plaza.** Every photograph of Atlanta's skyline taken in the last 10 years features this cylindrical glass tower, the second tallest hotel in North America. Designed by John Portman, its blockhouse-like entrance at Peachtree Street leads to a five story atrium surrounding the narrow glass elevator attached to the outside of the building. For the best views of Atlanta, have a drink or meal in the revolving, multi-level Sun Dial Restaurant & Lounge atop the hotel. ☎ *210 Peachtree St. at International Blvd., 30303,* ☏ *404/659–1400 or 800/228–*

3000, FAX *404/589–7591. 1,074 rooms. 3 restaurants, 3 bars, indoor-outdoor pool, sauna, health club. AE, D, DC, MC, V.*

$$$ **Ansley Inn.** Above a sloping lawn a block from Piedmont Park and in the heart of Ansley Park, one of Atlanta's most beautiful neighborhoods, stands this handsome three-story brick Tudor mansion. Its oversize guest rooms with private baths and common areas are furnished with Chinese porcelains, antiques, and original art. A Continental breakfast is included in the price. Guests have access to an athletic club ($10 per visit). ☎ *253 15th St., 30309,* ☎ *404/872–9000 or 800/446–5416,* FAX *404/892–2318. 15 rooms. AE, D, DC, MC, V.*

$$$ **Colony Square Hotel.** Theatricality and opulence are epitomized by the dimly lit lobby with overhanging balconies, piano music, and fresh flowers. Rooms are modern and done in muted tones—those on higher floors have nice city views. The hotel is three blocks from MARTA's Art Center station and two blocks from the Woodruff Arts Center and the High Museum of Art; it anchors the Colony Square office/residential/retail complex. Several restaurants are within or near the center. Guests have access (for a fee) to the Colony Club health club, racquetball courts, and pool. ☎ *Peachtree and 14th Sts., 30361,* ☎ *404/892–6000 or 800/422–7895,* FAX *404/872–9192. 428 rooms, 33 suites. Restaurant, lobby lounge. AE, D, DC, MC, V.*

$$$ **Hyatt Regency Atlanta.** The Hyatt's 23-story lobby (built in 1965) launched the chain's "atrium look." Easily identified at night by its brightly lit blue bubble dome over the rooftop Polaris restaurant, it remains one of Atlanta's more unique hotels. ☎ *265 Peachtree St. (connected by skywalk to Peachtree Center), 30303,* ☎ *404/577–1234 or 800/233–1234,* FAX *404/588–4808. 1,278 rooms, 58 suites. 4 restaurants, pool, sauna, health club. AE, D, DC, MC, V.*

$ **Barclay Hotel.** This quiet, older downtown hotel, two blocks off of Peachtree Street, was renovated in 1994. The teal-carpeted lobby dominated by two modern chandeliers features works by black artists. Done in mauve with floral accents, each room has a view of downtown; some rooms have balconies. The Celebrity Cafe is known for its waffles and fried chicken. ☎ *89 Luckie St., 30303,* ☎ *404/524–7991,* FAX *404/525–0672. 73 rooms. 2 restaurants, pool. AE, DC, MC, V.*

Buckhead

$$$$ **Hotel Nikko.** A dual-height lobby facing a courtyard with Japanese garden and cascading 35-foot waterfall is the opening statement of this modern, towering hotel. The understated decor features mainly hues of black, gray, and purple. Rooms are spacious and comfortable, with a style that's more American than Japanese. Japanese and Mediterranean cuisine are featured in the hotel's two restaurants. ☎ *3300 Peachtree Rd., 30305,* ☎ *404/365–8100 or 800/645–5687,* FAX *404/233–5686. 439 rooms, 32 suites. 2 restaurants, bar, lounge, pool, health club, 14 meeting rooms. AE, D, DC, MC, V.*

$$$$ **Ritz-Carlton, Buckhead.** Decorated with the Ritz's signature 18th- and 19th-century antiques, this elegant gem bids a discreet welcome to locals and visitors alike. Shoppers from nearby Lenox Mall and Phipps Plaza often revive here over afternoon tea or cocktails in the richly paneled Lobby Lounge; the Café and the Bar offer other spots to relax within luxurious surroundings. The Dining Room (*see* Dining, *above*) is the city's finest restaurant. The spacious rooms are furnished with traditional reproductions and have luxurious white-marble baths. From the hotel's club floors you get a view of Buckhead and an understanding of why Atlanta is known as a city of trees. ☎ *3434 Peachtree Rd., 30326,*

☎ 404/237–2700 or 800/241–3333, ⟨FAX⟩ 404/239–0078. 524 rooms, 29 suites. Restaurant, 2 bars, lounge, indoor pool, hot tub, health center. AE, D, DC, MC, V.

$$$$ Swissôtel. Sleek and efficient, this stunner boasts a chic contemporary glass-and-white-enamel exterior and sophisticated Biedermeier-style interiors. Comfortable sofas and chairs beckon in common areas. Handy to Lenox Square Mall, a prime location for shopping and dining, the hotel is a favorite with business travelers. ⟨T⟩ 3391 Peachtree Rd., 30326, ☎ 404/365–0065 or 800/253–1397, ⟨FAX⟩ 404/365–8787. 362 rooms, 15 suites. Restaurant, lounge, indoor pool, health club, meeting rooms. AE, D, DC, MC, V.

$$$ JW Marriott. This elegant 25-story hotel, connected to Lenox Square Mall, is traditionally decorated with reproduction furniture, hunter green and floral hues, and accents of brass and crystal. Irregularly shaped rooms have spacious baths with separate shower stall and tub. ⟨T⟩ 3300 Lenox Rd., 30326, ☎ 404/262–3344 or 800/328–9290, ⟨FAX⟩ 404/262–8689. 371 rooms, 30 suites. Restaurant, 2 lounges, indoor pool, health club, meeting rooms. AE, D, DC, MC, V.

$$$ Embassy Suites. This contemporary high-rise in Buckhead is just blocks from thePhipps Plaza and Lenox Square malls. A variety of suites ranging from deluxe presidential (with wet bars) to more basic sleeping- and sitting-room combinations are available, as are a limited number of double-bed rooms. ⟨T⟩ 3285 Peachtree Rd., 30305, ☎ 404/261–7733 or 800/362–2779, ⟨FAX⟩ 404/261–6857. 313 suites, 15 rooms. Restaurant, lounge, indoor-outdoor pool, exercise room. AE, D, DC, MC, V.

$$ Wyndham Garden Hotel. In the shadow of Hotel Nikko, this hotel's neat rooms are spacious and decorated with botanical prints, and rates are reasonable given the excellent location. Service is adequate, but doesn't compare with the luxury establishments in the area. Guests have access to a health club. ⟨T⟩ 3340 Peachtree Rd., 30326, ☎ 404/231–1234 or 800/822–4200, ⟨FAX⟩ 404/231–5236. 221 rooms. Restaurant, pool. AE, D, DC, MC, V.

The Arts

For the most complete schedule of cultural events, check the *Atlanta Journal-Constitution*'s Friday "Weekend Preview" or Saturday "Leisure" sections. Also, check *Creative Loafing*, a lively community weekly distributed free at Atlanta restaurants, bars, and stores. You can also call the 24-hour **Arts Hotline** (☎ 404/853–3ART) or connect with **Access Atlanta,** via computer modem (☎ 800/224–5285, ext. 79 for hookup).

TicketMaster (☎ 404/249–6400 or 800/326–4000) and **Tic-X-Press, Inc.** (☎ 404/231–5888) handle tickets for the Fox Theatre, Atlanta Civic Center, and other locations. However, most companies sell tickets through their own box offices.

Concerts

The world-class **Atlanta Symphony Orchestra (ASO)** (☎ 404/733–5000), under the musical direction of Yoel Levi, recently celebrated its 50th anniversary. It performs its fall–spring subscription series in the 1,800-seat Symphony Hall at Woodruff Arts Center (1280 Peachtree St., tel 404/733–5000). During the summer, the orchestra occasionally accompanies big-name artists in Chastain Park's outdoor amphitheater (4469 Stella Dr.). Despite its international reputation, the ASO fails to sell out most local performances and suffers from financial problems and an acoustically flawed performance space. The acoustically magnificent little **Spivey Hall** (☎ 404/898–1189), located at Clayton State College 15 miles south of Atlanta in Morrow, is widely considered to be one of the finest concert venues in the country. Internationally renowned musicians perform everything from choral works to chamber music to jazz.

Modeled after the Vienna Boys' Choir, the **Atlanta Boys' Choir** (☎ 404/378–0064) performs frequently at Atlanta locations and makes national and international tours. The long-established **Atlanta Chamber Players** (☎ 404/651–1228) perform classical works at various Atlanta locations.

Dance
Atlanta Ballet Company (☎ 404/873–5811), founded in 1929, has received international recognition for its high-quality productions of classical and contemporary works. Performances are at the Fox Theatre and Atlanta Civic Center. Although, it is the nation's oldest continually operating professional ballet company, it is constantly plagued by financial problems, which limits its productions. New artistic director John McFall, only the third in its history after an exceptional 32-year stint by Robert Barnett, brings new ideas and vision to the group.

Opera
Atlanta Opera Association (☎ 404/355–3311), made up of local singers and musicians, is augmented by internationally known artists.

Theater
Consistently one of the region's best, the **Alliance Theatre** performs everything from Shakespeare to the latest Broadway and off-Broadway shows in the Woodruff Arts Center (*see* Exploring, *above*). The **Horizon Theatre Co.** (1083 Austin Ave., ☎ 404/584–7450) in Little Five Points produces new works by contemporary playwrights. **Theatrical Outfit** (1012 Peachtree at 10th St., ☎ 404/872–0665) produces original and nationally known contemporary works.

Actor's Express (887 W. Marietta St., ☎ 404/607–7469) presents an eclectic selection of cutting-edge productions that take place in the 150-seat theater of the King Plow Arts Center, a stylish artist's complex hailed by local critics as a showplace of industrial chic.

Touring Broadway musicals, pop music, and dance concerts are presented in the **Atlanta Civic Center** (395 Piedmont Ave., ☎ 404/523–6275), **Center Stage** (1374 W. Peachtree St., ☎ 404/874–1511), and at the **Fox Theatre** (660 Peachtree St., ☎ 404/881–2100; *see* Exploring, *above*).

Nightlife

The pursuit of entertainment—from Midtown to Buckhead—is known as the "Peachtree Shuffle." Atlanta's vibrant nightlife can mean anything from coffee bars to sports bars, from country line dancing to high-energy dance clubs. Atlanta has long been known for having more bars than churches, and in the South, that's an oddity.

Most bars and clubs are open seven nights, until 2–4 AM. Those with live entertainment usually have a cover charge. Consult *Creative Loafing* and the *Atlanta Journal-Constitution*.

Bars
Limerick Junction (822 N. Highland Ave., ☎ 404/874–7147) is a lively Irish pub.

The antithesis of hip-and-trendy, 33-year-old **Manuel's Tavern** (602 N. Highland Ave., ☎ 404/525–3447)—ancient by Atlanta standards—is a neighborhood saloon in the truest sense. Families, politicians, writers, students, professionals, and blue-collar workers enjoy drinks, bar food (chili dogs, french fries, strip steaks), and conversation.

Prince of Wales (1144 Piedmont Ave, ☎ 404/876–0227) is a cozy, authentic English pub with live music, from alternative rock to jazz.

For great burgers, try the **Vortex** (1041 W. Peachtree St., ☎ 404/875–1667). The atmosphere is friendly and the beer list is long.

Country
Hot spots for boot-scoot and boogie include the **Buckboard Country Music Showcase** (2080 Cobb Parkway in Windy Hill Plaza, ☎ 404/955–7340) and the **Crystal Chandelier** (1750 North Roberts Rd., Kennesaw, ☎ 404/426–5006), both north of the city.

Jazz and Blues
New Orleans–style blues sends jam-packed crowds into a frenzy at **Blind Willie's** (828 N. Highland Ave., ☎ 404/873–2583), a storefront club in Virginia-Highland.

Cafe 290 (290 Hilderbrand Dr., ☎ 404/256–3942) showcases talented local jazz bands in a casual neighborhood restaurant/bar setting.

Dante's Down the Hatch's venues (3380 Peachtree Rd., ☎ 404/266–1600; Underground Atlanta, Lower Pryor St., ☎ 404/577–1800) are two of the city's most popular nightspots. In Buckhead, the Paul Mitchell Trio conjures silky-smooth jazz sounds in the "hold" of a make-believe sailing ship. Downtown, jazz entertainers perform nightly. Swiss fondue and a large wine selection are part of the Dante's experience.

Just Jazz (595 Piedmont Ave., ☎ 404/897–1555; closed Mon.–Tues.) and the upscale **Echelon** (585 Franklin Rd., Marietta, ☎ 404/419–3393) feature jazz musicians from around the country.

Rock
The **Cotton Club** (1021 Peachtree St., ☎ 404/874–9524) is a loud, usually packed, Midtown club that features local and national performers in a variety of musical styles.

The **Masquerade** (695 North Ave., ☎ 404/577–8178), a tri-level grunge hangout, features just about everything in popular music, from disco to techno to industrial rock. Crowds are an odd mix that reflects the club's three separate spaces, dubbed Heaven, Hell, and Purgatory.

The **Point** (420 Moreland Ave., ☎ 404/ 659–3522) in Little Five Points showcases up-and-coming rock and progressive music groups in a small club setting.

Rupert's (3330 Piedmont Rd., ☎ 404/266–9834) attracts the Buckhead after-work crowd with its 10-piece orchestra playing big band and contemporary dance music. The club's multi-tiered balcony overlooks the large dance floor.

More than one generation dances to the beat at **Axys** (1150-B Peachtree St., ☎ 404/607–0922), an upscale, high-tech dance club in Midtown.

Atlanta Essentials

Arriving and Departing

BY BUS

Greyhound Bus Lines (81 International Blvd., ☎ 404/522–6300 or 800/231–2222) provides transport to downtown Atlanta.

BY CAR

Some refer to Atlanta as the Los Angeles of the South, because travel by car is virtually the only way to get to most parts of the city. Although the congestion isn't comparable to L.A.'s yet, Atlantans have grown accustomed to frequent delays at rush hour. Beware, the South as a whole may be laid back, but Atlanta drivers are not; they tend to drive faster than drivers in other southern cities. Visiting drivers should be vigilant.

The city is encircled by I–285. Three interstates—I–85, running northeast–southwest from Virginia to Alabama; I–75, north–south from Michigan to Florida; and I–20, east–west from South Carolina to Texas—also crisscross Atlanta.

BY PLANE

Hartsfield Atlanta International Airport, off I–85 and I–285, 13 miles south of downtown, is served by the following airlines: **Aero Costa Rica, AreoMexico, Air Jamaica, Air South, ALM Antillean, AMC, ASA, America West, American, British Airways, Cayman Airways, Continental, Delta, GP Express, Japan Airlines, Kiwi International, KLM, Korean Air, Leisure Air, Lufthansa, Markair, Midwest Express, National, Northwest, Sabena, Swissair, TWA, United, USAir, ValuJet,** and **VARIG Brazilian.**

Atlanta Airport shuttle vans (☎ 404/766–5312) operate every half hour between 7 AM and 11 PM. The downtown trip ($8 one-way, $14 round-trip) takes about 20 minutes and stops at major hotels. Vans also go to Emory University and Lenox Square ($12 one-way, $20 round-trip).

If your luggage is light, you can take **MARTA**'s (Metropolitan Atlanta Rapid Transit Authority, ☎ 404/848–4711) high-speed trains between the airport and downtown and other locations. Trains operate 4:34 AM– 1:17 AM (weekdays) and 5:30 AM–1:30 AM (weekends). The trip downtown takes about 15 minutes to the Five Points station, and the fare is $1.25.

Taxi fare between the airport and downtown hotels is fixed at $15 for one person; $8 each for two people; $6 each for three people. Taxi drivers, many of whom are recent immigrants and speak poor English, sometimes appear as befuddled as the visitor by Atlanta's notoriously winding and hilly streets, which often complicates the finding of an address if it is off a popular thoroughfare like Peachtree Street. The problem gets worse when big events are in town, because out-of-town operators come into Atlanta to pick up business. These drivers are even less familiar with the roads, so come armed with directions if your destination is something other than a major hotel or popular sight. Supposedly, the city is tightening up its rules on who can get a taxi permit, so the situation may get better in the future..

BY TRAIN

Amtrak's *Crescent* (☎ 404/881–3060 or 800/872–7245) operates daily to New Orleans, Greenville; Charlotte; Washington, DC; Baltimore; Philadelphia; and New York from Atlanta's Brookwood Station (1688 Peachtree St.). Its *Gulf Breeze* travels from Atlanta to Birmingham and Mobile, Alabama.

Getting Around

BY BUS

The **Metropolitan Atlanta Rapid Transit Authority (MARTA)** (☎ 404/848–4711), with a fleet of 700 buses, operates 150 routes covering 1,500 miles. The fare is $1.25, and exact change is required. Weekly and monthly *TransCards,* giving you a slight ride discount, are available, too. Outside the perimeter set by I–285, except for a few important areas of Clayton, DeKalb, and Fulton counties, service is very limited.

BY SUBWAY

MARTA's clean and safe rapid-rail subway trains have somewhat limited routes, but do link downtown with many major landmarks. The rail system's two main lines cross at the **Five Points Station** downtown, where TransCards and information on public transportation are available at the **Ride Store** (weekdays 7–7 and Sat. 8:30–5). Trains run 4:34 AM– 1:17 AM, and large parking (free) lots are at most stations beyond downtown. Tokens, costing $1.25 each, required to enter the station, can be bought from machines outside the station entrance or at the Ride Store. Free transfers, needed for some bus routes, are available by pressing a button on the subway turnstile or requesting one from the bus driver.

BY TAXI

Taxi fares start at $1.50 for the first ⅛ mile and 20¢ for each additional ⅛ mile; 50¢ per extra passenger and $12 per hour waiting time. Each additional person is charged another $1. Within the Downtown Convention Zone a flat rate of $4 for one person or $2 each for more than one will be charged for any destination. **Executive Limousine** (☎ 404/223–2000), **Checker Cab** (☎ 404/351–1111), and **Buckhead Safety Cab** (☎ 404/233–1152) offer 24-hour service.

Guided Tours

ORIENTATION

Gray Line of Atlanta (☎ 404/767–0594; 3½-hour tour $16.50 per person, full-day tour $27.50 per person) gives tours of Downtown, Midtown, and Buckhead, plus a day-long tour that includes Stone Mountain and the King Center. **Historic Air Tours** (1954 Airport Rd., Suite 215, Chamblee 30341, ☎ 404/457–5217; 3 tours lasting 20–55 min; $35-$85 per person) takes visitors high above the city in a private airplane.

WALKING TOURS

The **Atlanta Preservation Center** (156 7th St., Suite 3, ☎ 404/876–2041 or 404/876–2040) offers 10 walking tours of historic areas and neighborhoods ($5 adults, $4 senior citizens, $3 students; children under 19 free; tours conducted primarily on weekends). Especially noteworthy are tours of Sweet Auburn, the neighborhood associated with Martin Luther King Jr. and other leaders in Atlanta's African-American community; Druid Hills, the verdant, genteel neighborhood where *Driving Miss Daisy* was filmed; and the Fox Theatre, the elaborate, Moorish 1920s picture palace.

1996 Summer Olympics

The Atlanta Committee for the Olympic Games has spent over $1.6 billion to ready Atlanta for the event. Built on the former south parking lot of Atlanta–Fulton County Stadium (521 Capitol Ave., ☎ 404/

249–6400)—home of the Atlanta Braves baseball team—Olympic Stadium seats 85,000 people and will be converted into a baseball arena for use by the Braves beginning with the 1997 season. The Velodrome, an indoor bicycle race track, has been constructed at Stone Mountain Park, and the Olympic Village, where athletes and their families will stay, is on the Georgia Institute of Technology campus in the heart of the city. By the opening day ceremony, nearly 11 million tickets are expected to have been sold. For ticket information, contact the ACOG (*see* Visitor Information, *above*).

Important Addresses and Numbers

EMERGENCIES

Dial 911 for assistance. Both **Grady Memorial Hospital** (80 Butler St., ☎ 404/616–4307) and **Georgia Baptist Medical Center** (300 Blvd., ☎ 404/653–4000) have 24-hour emergency rooms. **Big B Drug** (1061 Ponce de Leon Ave., ☎ 404/876–0381) is open 24 hours, seven days a week.

RADIO STATIONS

AM: WPLO 610, country; WGST 640, news/talk; WCNN 680, sports/talk; WSB 750, news/talk; WQXI 790, music/talk; WAEC 860, Christian talk/music. **FM:** WABE 90.1, National Public Radio/classical; WCLK 91.9, jazz/soul; WZGC 92.9, classic rock; WPCH 94.9, light rock; WKLS 96.1, album rock; WFOX 97.1, oldies; WKHX 101.5, country; WVEE 103.3, top 40/soul.

VISITOR INFORMATION

To plan your trip, write to the **Georgia Department of Industry, Trade, and Tourism** (Box 1776, 30301, ☎ 800/847–4842, FAX 404/656–3567) or, for Atlanta only, contact the **Atlanta Convention & Visitors Bureau** (ACVB; 233 Peachtree St., Suite 2000, 30303, ☎ 404/222–6688 or 800/285–2682). For information on the 1996 Olympic Games (July 19–Aug. 4), contact the **Atlanta Committee for the Olympic Games** (ACOG; Box 1996, Atlanta 30301-1996, ☎ 404/224–1996). Once in Atlanta, the ACVB has five visitor information centers stocked with maps and brochures: **Hartsfield Atlanta International Airport** (north terminal at west crossover), **Peachtree Center Mall** (233 Peachtree St.), **Underground Atlanta** (65 Upper Alabama St.), **Georgia World Congress Center** (285 International Blvd.), and **Lenox Square Mall** (3393 Peachtree Rd.). ACOG also runs **The Olympic Experience,** a public information/gallery/gift shop at Underground Atlanta, plus a booth at Lenox Square and other major malls.

SAVANNAH

By Honey
Naylor

The very sound of the word Savannah conjures up misty images of mint juleps, live oaks dripping with Spanish moss, handsome mansions, and a somewhat decadent city moving at a lazy Southern pace. Why, you can hardly say "Savannah" without drawling.

Well, brace yourself. The mint juleps are there all right, along with the moss and the mansions and the easygoing pace, but this Southern belle rings with surprises.

Take, for example, St. Patrick's Day: Why on earth does Savannah, of all places, have a St. Patrick's Day celebration second only to New York's? The greening of Savannah began more than 164 years ago and nobody seems to know why, although everybody in town talks a blue (green) streak about St. Patrick's Day. Everything turns green on March 17, including the faces of startled visitors when green scrambled eggs and green grits are put before them. One year, some well-oiled revelers even tried to dye the Savannah River green.

Savannah's beginning was February 12, 1733, when English General James Edward Oglethorpe and 120 colonists arrived at Yamacraw Bluff on the Savannah River to found the 13th and last colony in the New World. As the port city grew, Englishmen, Scottish Highlanders, French Huguenots, Germans, Austrian Salzburgers, Sephardic Jews from Spain and Portugal, Moravians, Italians, Swiss, Welsh, and the Irish all arrived to create what could be called a rich gumbo.

In 1793, Eli Whitney of Connecticut, who was tutoring on a plantation near Savannah, invented a mechanized means of "ginning" seeds from cotton bolls. Cotton soon became king, and Savannah, already a busy seaport, flourished under its reign. Waterfront warehouses were filled with "white gold," and brokers trading in the Savannah Cotton Exchange set world prices. The white gold brought in solid gold, and fine mansions were built in the prospering city.

In 1864, Savannahians surrendered their city to Union General Sherman rather than see it torched. Following Reconstruction and the collapse of the cotton market, the city itself virtually collapsed, and languished for more than 50 years. Elegant mansions were either razed or allowed to decay, and cobwebs replaced cotton in the dilapidated riverfront warehouses.

But in 1955, Savannah's spirits rose again. News that the exquisite Isaiah Davenport home (324 E. State St.) was to be destroyed prompted seven outraged ladies to raise enough money to buy the house. They saved it the day before the wrecking ball was to swing.

Thus was born the Historic Savannah Foundation, the organization responsible for the restoration of downtown Savannah, where more than 1,000 restored buildings form the 2.5-square-mile Historic District, the nation's largest. Many of these buildings are open to the public during the annual tour of homes, and today Savannah is recognized as one of the top 10 cities in the U.S. for walking tours.

John Berendt's wildly popular *Midnight in the Garden of Good and Evil*, published in 1994, has dispatched many new visitors to Savannah. A nonfiction account of a notorious murder that took place in the city during the 1980s, the book brings to life such Savannah sites as Monterey Square, Mercer House, and Bonaventure Cemetery.

Exploring

Numbers in the margin correspond to points of interest on the Savannah Historic District map.

Georgia's founder, General James Oglethorpe, designed the original town of Savannah and laid it out in a perfect grid. The Historic District is neatly hemmed in by the Savannah River, Gaston Street, East Street, and Martin Luther King Jr. Boulevard. Streets are arrow-straight, public squares of varying sizes are tucked into the grid at precise intervals, and each block is sliced in half by a lane. Bull Street, anchored on the north by City Hall and the south by Forsyth Park, charges down the center of the grid and lunges around the five public squares that stand in its way. (Maneuvering a car around Savannah's squares is a minor art form.)

The Historic District

❶ Make your first stop the **Savannah Visitor's Center** (*see* Important Addresses and Numbers, *below*), to pick up the maps and brochures you'll need for exploring, and to look at the structure that houses the Center. The big redbrick building with its high ceilings and sweeping arches was the old Central of Georgia railway station, completed in 1860.

The Visitor's Center lies just north of the **site of the Siege of Savannah.** In 1779, the Colonial forces, led by Polish Count Casimir Pulaski, laid siege to Savannah in an attempt to retake the city from the Redcoats. They were beaten back, and Pulaski was killed while leading a cavalry charge against the British. On the battle site, adjacent to the

❷ Visitor's Center, the **Savannah History Museum,** in a restored shed of the railway station, offers an excellent introduction to the city. Two theaters present special-effects depictions of Oglethorpe's landing and of the siege. Exhibits range from old locomotives to a tribute to Savannah-born songwriter Johnny Mercer. There are two restored dining cars that aren't going anywhere, but you can climb aboard for a bite to eat. *303 Martin Luther King Jr. Blvd.,* ☎ *912/238–1779.* ☛ *$3 adults, $2.50 senior citizens, $1.75 children 6–12, under 6 free.* ☉ *Weekdays 8:30–5, weekends 9–5.*

❸ Turn left on Broad Street and walk two blocks to the **Scarbrough House** (41 Martin Luther King Jr. Dr.). The exuberant Regency mansion was built during the 1819 cotton boom for Savannah merchant prince William Scarbrough and designed by English architect William Jay. A Doric portico is capped by one of Jay's characteristic half-moon windows. Four massive Greek Doric columns form a peristyle in the atrium entrance hall. Three stories overhead is an arched, sky-blue ceiling with sunshine filtering through a skylight. Visitors can admire its Regency architecture from outside; Scarbrough House is not open to the public.

Continue east across Franklin Square and stroll through City Market, which includes an art center with working studios of 35 area artists, along with sidewalk cafés, jazz joints, and shops. Now head east on

❹ St. Julian Street to **Johnson Square.** Laid out in 1733 and named for South Carolina Governor Robert Johnson, this was the earliest of Oglethorpe's original 24 squares. The square was once a popular gathering place, where Savannahians came to welcome President Monroe in 1819, to greet the Marquis de Lafayette in 1825, and to cheer for Georgia's secession in 1861.

As you stand at the foot of Bull Street, the building to the north with the glittering dome (regilded in 1987) is **City Hall,** dating from 1905. Its lower stories face the spot from which the SS *Savannah* set sail in 1819, the first steamship to cross an ocean. Just west of City Hall, on Yamacraw Bluff, is a marble bench, appropriately called **Oglethorpe's Bench,** marking the site of the general's field tent.

❺ Cobblestone ramps lead from Bay Street down to **Factors Walk** and,
❻ below it, to **River Street.** Cars can enter Factors Walk via the ramps, and so can pedestrians. (These are serious cobblestones, and you will suffer if you wear anything but the most comfortable shoes you own.) There is also a network of iron walkways connecting Bay Street with the multistoried buildings that rise up from the river level, and iron stairways descend from Bay Street down to Factors Walk.

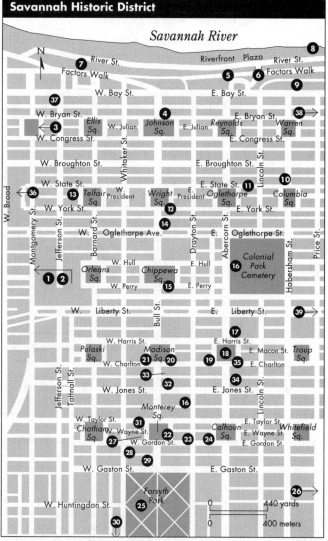

Savannah Historic District

Children enjoy the **River Street Train Museum,** which offers guided tours of antique train displays and railroad memorabilia. *315 W. River St.,* ☎ *912/233–6175.* ☛ *$1.50 adults, 50¢ children 5–12, under 5 free.* ☉ *Mon.–Sat. 11–5:30, Sun. 1–6.*

Foreign vessels still call at the Port of Savannah, the largest port between Baltimore and New Orleans. Paper and other products have replaced the cotton exports, and in 1977 a multimillion-dollar riverfront revitalization transformed the decayed warehouses into a nine-block marketplace housing unique boutiques alongside musty taverns.

Benches line **Riverfront Plaza,** where you can watch a parade of freighters and pug-nosed tugs; youngsters can play in the tugboat-shaped sandboxes here. Each weekday, Dixieland music can be heard from the cabin of the ***River Street Rambler,*** a brightly painted freight train that rumbles down River Street to the port. River Street is the main venue for many of the city's celebrations, including the First Saturday festivals when flea marketeers, artists, and craftspeople display their wares and musicians entertain the crowds.

Even landlubbers can appreciate the fine craftsmanship of the ship models in the **Ships of the Sea Museum.** The four floors of the museum contain models of steamships, nuclear subs, China clippers with their sails unfurled, Columbus's ships, a showcase filled with ships-in-bottles, and a collection of fine Royal Doulton porcelain seafarers. *503 East River St. and 504 East Bay St.,* ☎ *912/232–1511.* ☛ *$3 adults, $1.50 children 7–12, under 7 free.* ☼ *Daily 10–5.*

If you entered the museum at the River Street entrance and worked your way up all four floors, you'll be topside again on Bay Street. The tree-shaded park along Bay Street is **Emmet Park,** named for Robert Emmet, a late 18th-century Irish patriot and orator. Walk west along Bay Street and turn left onto Abercorn Street. In **Reynolds Square** you'll see the statue of John Wesley, who preached in Savannah and wrote the first English hymnal here in 1736. The monument to the founder of the Methodist Church is shaded by greenery and surrounded by park benches. On the square is the **Olde Pink House** (23 Abercorn St.). Built in 1771, it is one of the oldest buildings in town. The porticoed pink stucco Georgian mansion has been a private home, a bank, and headquarters for a Yankee general during the war. It is now a restaurant (*see* Dining, *below*).

From Reynolds Square walk south on Abercorn Street, turn left onto Broughton Street, and two blocks down turn right onto Habersham Street. Ahead stands the **Isaiah Davenport House.** Semicircular stairs with wrought-iron trim lead to the recessed doorway of the redbrick Federal mansion that master builder Isaiah Davenport built for himself in 1815, using architectural texts available in his day. Three dormer windows poke through the sloping roof of the stately house, and inside there are polished hardwood floors, fine woodwork and plasterwork, and a soaring elliptical staircase. The furnishings are Hepplewhite, Chippendale, and Sheraton, and in the attic there is a collection of antique dolls and a dollhouse with tiny 19th-century furnishings. *324 E. State St.,* ☎ *912/236–8097.* ☛ *$4 adults, $3 children 6–18.* ☼ *Daily 10–4.*

Walk west on State Street two blocks to the **Owens Thomas House & Museum.** This was William Jay's first Regency mansion in Savannah, built in 1816, and it is the city's finest example of that architectural style. The thoroughly English house was built largely with local materials, including tabby—a mixture of oyster shells, sand, and water that resembles concrete. The entry portico is of Doric design with curving stairs leading to a recessed door topped by a fanlight. Of particular note are the curving walls of the house, Greek-inspired ornamental molding, Jay's half-moon arches, stained-glass panels, and Duncan Phyfe furniture. You'll find canopied beds, a pianoforte, and displays of ornate silver. From a wrought-iron balcony, in 1825, the Marquis de Lafayette bade a two-hour au revoir to the crowd below. *124 Abercorn St.,* ☎ *912/233–9743.* ☛ *$5 adults, $3 students, $2 children 6–12, under 6 free.* ☼ *Sun. 2–4:30, Tues.–Sat. 10–4:30.*

Stroll through **Oglethorpe Square,** across State Street, and continue two blocks west to **Wright Square.** The square was named for James Wright, Georgia's last Colonial governor. The centerpiece of the square is an elaborate monument erected in honor of William Washington Gordon, founder of the Central of Georgia Railroad. A slab of granite from Stone

Mountain marks the grave of Tomo-Chi-Chi, the Yamacraw chief who befriended General Oglethorpe and the colonists.

⑬ Continue west on State Street, strolling through **Telfair Square** to reach the **Telfair Mansion and Art Museum.** The South's oldest public art museum is housed in yet another of Jay's Regency creations, this one designed in 1819. Within its marbled halls are American, French, and Dutch Impressionist paintings; German Tonalist paintings; a large collection of works by Kahlil Gibran; plaster casts of the Elgin Marbles, the Venus de Milo, and the Laocoön, among other classical sculptures; and a room that contains some of the Telfair family furnishings, including a Duncan Phyfe sideboard and Savannah-made silver. *121 Barnard St., ☎ 912/232–1177. ☛ $3 adults, $1 students and senior citizens, 50¢ children 6–12; free on Sun. ☼ Tues.–Sat. 10–5, Sun. 2–5.*

⑭ At the next corner, turn left onto Oglethorpe Avenue and cross onto Bull Street to reach the **Juliette Gordon Low Birthplace.** This majestic Regency mansion is attributed to William Jay and in 1965 was designated Savannah's first National Historic Landmark. "Daisy" Low, founder of the Girl Scouts, was born here, and the house is now owned and operated by the Girl Scouts of America. Mrs. Low's paintings and other artworks are on display in the house, restored to the style of 1886, the year of Mrs. Low's marriage. *142 Bull St., ☎ 912/233–4501. ☛ $5 adults, $4.50 senior citizens, $4 children under 18; discounts for Girl Scouts. ☼ Mon.–Tues. and Thurs.–Sat. 10–4, Sun. 12:30–4:30.*

⑮ **Chippewa Square** is a straight shot south on Bull Street. There you can see Daniel Chester French's imposing bronze statue of the general himself, James Edward Oglethorpe. Also note the Savannah Theatre, the longest continuously operated theater site in North America.

⑯ From Chippewa Square, go east on McDonough Street to reach the **Colonial Park Cemetery.** Savannahians were buried here from 1750 to 1853. Shaded pathways lace through the park, and you may want to stroll through and read some of the old inscriptions. There are several historical plaques in the cemetery, one of which marks the grave of Button Gwinnett, a signer of the Declaration of Independence.

⑰ The **Cathedral of St. John the Baptist** soars like a hymn over the corner of Abercorn and Harris streets, two blocks south of the cemetery. The French Gothic cathedral, with the pointed arches and free-flowing traceries characteristic of the style, is the seat of the Diocese of Savannah. It is the oldest Roman Catholic church in Georgia, having been founded in the early 1700s. Fire destroyed the early structures, and the present cathedral dates from 1876. Most of the cathedral's impressive stained-glass windows were made by Austrian glassmakers and imported around the turn of the century. The high altar is of Italian marble, and the Stations of the Cross were imported from Munich.

⑱ Across from the cathedral is **Lafayette Square,** named for the Marquis de Lafayette. The graceful three-tier fountain in the square was donated by the Georgia chapter of the Colonial Dames of America.

⑲ Across the square is the **Andrew Low House.** The house was built for Andrew Low in 1848, and later belonged to his son William, who married Juliette Gordon. After her husband's death, "Daisy" Low founded the Girl Scouts in this house on March 12, 1912. Robert E. Lee and William Thackeray were both entertained in this mansion. In addition to its historical significance, the house boasts some of the finest ornamental ironwork in Savannah. Members and friends of the Colonial

Dames have donated fine 19th-century antiques and stunning silver to the house. *329 Abercorn St., ☎ 912/233–6854. ☞ $5 adults, $2 students, $1 children and Girl Scouts. ☉ Mon.–Wed. and Fri.–Sat. 10:30–4:30, Sun. noon–4:30.*

⑳ Two blocks to the west is **Madison Square,** laid out in 1839 and named for James Madison. The statue depicts Sergeant William Jasper hoisting a flag and is a tribute to his bravery during the Siege of Savannah. Though mortally wounded, he rescued the colors of his regiment in the assault on the British lines.

㉑ On the west side of the square is the **Green-Meldrim House,** designed by New York architect John Norris and built in about 1850 for cotton merchant Charles Green. The house was bought in 1892 by Judge Peter Meldrim, whose heirs sold it to St. John's Episcopal Church, for which it is now the working parish house. It was here that General Sherman lived after taking the city in 1864—in the splendid Gothic Revival mansion, complete with crenellated roof and oriel windows. The gallery that sweeps around three sides of the house is awash with filigreed ironwork. The mantels are Carrara marble, the woodwork is carved black walnut, and the doorknobs and hinges are silver-plated. There is a magnificent skylight above a gracefully curved staircase. The house is furnished with 16th- and 17th-century antiques. *14 West Macon St. on Madison Sq., ☎ 912/233–3845. ☞ $3. ☉ Oct.–Feb., Tues. and Thurs.–Sat. 10–4; Mar.–Sept., Mon. and Wed. 1–4. Closed the first Wed. of each month.*

TIME OUT Students from the Savannah College of Art and Design buy art supplies and books at **Design Works Bookstore.** There is also a soda fountain and tables in this old Victorian drugstore, where you can get short orders, burgers, and deli sandwiches. *Corner of Bull and Charlton Sts., ☎ 912/238-2481. ☉ Weekdays 9–5, Sat. 10–2.*

The fifth and last of Bull Street's squares is **Monterey Square,** which commemorates the victory of General Zachary Taylor's forces in Monterrey, Mexico, in 1846. The square's monument honors General Casimir Pulaski, the Polish nobleman who lost his life in the Siege of Savannah during the Revolutionary War.

㉒ On the east side of the square stands **Temple Mickve Israel,** home to the third oldest Jewish congregation in America, who settled in town five months after the founding of Savannah in 1733. The original congregation, a group of Spanish and German Jews, brought with them the prized "Sephar Torah" now in the present temple, which was consecrated in 1878. The splendid Gothic Revival synagogue contains a collection of documents and letters (some from George Washington and Thomas Jefferson) pertaining to early Jewish life in Savannah and Georgia. *20 E. Gordon St., ☎ 912/233–1547. ☞ Free. ☉ Weekdays 10–noon and 2–4.*

㉓ A block east of the temple is a Gothic Revival church memorializing the founders of Methodism. The **Wesley Monumental Church,** patterned after Queen's Kirk in Amsterdam, celebrated a century of service in 1968. The church is noted for its magnificent stained-glass windows. In the Wesley Window there are busts of John and Charles Wesley.

㉔ At the **Massie Heritage Interpretation Center,** in addition to a scale model of the city, maps and plans, and architectural displays, is a "Heritage Classroom" that offers schoolchildren hands-on instruction about early Colonial life. *207 E. Gordon St., ☎ 912/651–7022. ☞ Free, but a donation of $1.50 is appreciated. ☉ Weekdays 9–4:30.*

㉕ The southern anchor of Bull Street is **Forsyth Park,** with 20 luxuriant acres. The glorious white fountain, dating from 1858, was restored in 1988. In addition to its Confederate and Spanish-American War memorials, the park contains the Fragrant Garden for the Blind, a project of Savannah garden clubs. There are tennis courts and a tree-shaded jogging path. The park is often the scene of outdoor plays and concerts.

㉖ The **King-Tisdell Cottage,** perched behind a picket fence, is a museum dedicated to the preservation of African-American history and culture. The Negro Heritage Trail Tour (*see* Special-interest Tours in Guided Tours, *below*) visits here, in this little Victorian house. Broad steps lead to a porch that's loaded with gewgaws, and dormer windows pop up through a steep roof. The interior is furnished to resemble an African-American coastal home of the 1890s. *514 E. Huntingdon St.,* ☎ *912/234–8000.* ☛ *$2.50.* ◷ *Tues.–Fri. 1–4:30.*

Other houses of interest in the Victorian district are at **118 E. Waldburg Street** and **111 W. Gwinnett Street.** A stroll along **Bolton Street** will be especially rewarding for fans of fanciful architecture. Of particular note is the entire 200 block, 114 W. Bolton Street, 109 W. Bolton Street, and 321 E. Bolton Street.

Tour 2: Midnight in the Garden of Good and Evil

A true town gossip can give you the best introduction to a city and, as author John Berendt discovered, Savannah's not short on them. In his 1994 bestseller, *Midnight in the Garden of Good and Evil,* Berendt shares the juiciest of tales imparted to him during the eight years he spent here wining and dining with Savannah's high-society and dancing with her Grand Empress drag queen, the Lady Chablis, among others. By the time he left, there had been one scandalous homicide and several follow-up trials, each played out among lavishly drunken party after party.

Before you enter the city limits, first try to grab a copy of the book, pour yourself a cool martini, and enter an eccentric world of killers and backstabbers, voodoo witches and garden-club women, all surrounded by graveyards and inhabiting mansions. After you've read the book, slip on a pair of comfortable shoes and head over to the historic district to follow the characters steps to their homes and haunts. By the end of this walking tour, you'll be hard-pressed to find the line between Berendt's creative nonfiction and Savannah's reality. *Note: Unless otherwise indicated, the sights on this tour are not open to the public.*

㉗ Begin this tour at **Mercer House** at 429 Bull Street. Songwriter and crooner Johnny Mercer's great-grandfather began building the residence in 1860 but dropped the project on the eve of the Civil War. A redbrick Italianate mansion on the southwest corner of Monterey Square, the house became the Taj Mahal of the book's main character Jim Williams; here he ran a world-class antique dealership, held *the* Christmas party of the season, and shot and killed his sometime house partner Danny Hansford. Williams himself died in 1990 in the den near the very spot where Hansford fell. Today, his sister lives there quietly among the remnants of his Fabergé collection, and Joshua Reynolds paintings, in rooms lit by Waterford crystal chandeliers.

㉘ Next, walk south on Bull Street to West Gordon Street and take a right until you come to **Serena Dawes's house** (17 W. Gordon St.). Serena, who in real life went by the name of Helen Driscoll, was a high-profile beauty in the 1930s and '40s who married into the fortunes of a Pennsylvania steel family. After her husband accidentally and fatally shot himself in the head, she retired here, back in her hometown. Dawes, Berendt writes, "spent most of her day in bed, holding court, drinking martinis and pink ladies, playing with her white toy poodle, Lulu." One neighbor remarked to the author that Serena's callers were all gentlemen, and chief among them was Luther Driggers, rumored to possess a poison strong enough to wipe out the entire city.

㉙ Head back to Bull Street and take a right, walking south toward Forsyth Park, until you reach the **Armstrong House** (447 Bull St.), where Jim Williams once lived and worked before purchasing the Mercer House. This unique mansion was on Berendt's jogging path, and he occasionally strolled by during his late afternoon walks. On its surrounding sidewalk, he met Mr. Simon Glover, the 86-year-old singer and porter for the law firm of Bouhan, Williams, and Levy, who occupy the building. Glover's daily jaunts lead him up and down Bull street to earn a weekly $10 for walking one of the firm's former partner's deceased dogs. Baffled? So was the author. Behind the house's cast-iron gates, are the offices of Jim Williams's attorney, who doubles as keeper of Uga, the Georgia Bulldog mascot.

㉚ Continue south on Bull Street until you come to the northwest corner of Forsyth Park. Take a right there, down West Gaston till it crosses Whitaker, and proceed south till you get to the **Forsyth Parkside Apartments** (Whitaker and Gwinnett streets). This complex became Berendt's second home in Savannah, and from his fourth-floor rooms he pieced together the majority of the book. Parking his newly acquired 1973 Pontiac Grand Prix outside these apartments, Berendt first met the Lady Chablis coming out of her nearby doctor's office, freshly feminine from a new round of hormone shots.

Walk through Forsyth Park, heading north back to Monterey Square, to complete the first circle of the walking tour. At the southeast corner of the Square, you'll find **Temple Mickve Israel** (20 E. Gordon St., *see* Tour 1, *above*) near the intersection of Bull and East Gordon streets. The Mercer House (*see above*) is in easy view of the temple, as was the Nazi swastika flag Jim Williams once flew from his windows, supposedly to disrupt the filming of a TV movie. His antics temporarily stopped the shooting, but did deeper damage, offending the temple's congregation and the rest of the neighborhood.

㉛ Cross the square heading west, back toward the Mercer House, and walk north to **Lee Adler's Home** (425 Bull St.). One of Williams's biggest adversaries, Adler lives in half of the double town house facing West Wayne Street, where he runs his business of restoring historic Savannah properties. Adler's howling dogs drove Williams to his pipe organ, where he churned out a deafening version of César Franck's *Pièce Heroique*. Later, Adler stuck reelection signs in his front lawn, showing his support for the District Attorney who prosecuted Williams three time before he was finally found not guilty.

TIME OUT By now, you should have worked up a pretty good appetite, so head over to **Mrs. Wilkes Dining Room** (107 W. Jones St., *see* Dining, *below*) and sample some of the fare that Jim Williams had delivered to him while in jail at Chatham County Courthouse. Go west away from Monterey Square, till you get to Whitaker Street. Then go north until you find West Jones Street.

㉜ Head east on Jones Street to view the **first of Joe Odom's homes** (16 E. Jones St.). Odom, a combination tax lawyer, real-estate broker, and piano player, played host to a 24-hour steady stream of visitors in this stucco town house. The author met Odom through his fourth fiancée-in-waiting, Mandy, a former Miss Big Beautiful Woman, who stopped by to borrow ice for yet another party, when their power had been cut off yet another time.

33 Within earshot of 16 East Street, you'll find **Berendt's first Savannah residence,** one street north on Charlton Lane, on the backside of 22 East Jones Street. Here, from the second story of the redbrick carriage house, Berendt first heard Joe's all-night parties, as the music and laughter filtered into his tiny magnolia-and-banana-tree-stocked garden below.

Next, take the East Jones Street sidewalk east toward Abercorn Street. **34** At the southeast corner of Abercorn and East Jones, look for **Clary's Café** at 402 Abercorn Street. John Berendt came here following his morning jogs to load up on a typical greasy spoon–style breakfast, and to catch the latest gossip. With locals gathered at tables and along the soda fountain counter, Clary's makes for some fine people-watching. Berendt first observed Serena Dawes's tormented boyfriend Luther Driggers at Clary's, while the man sat in front of his usual eggs and bacon and milk of magnesia breakfast, with thread-leashed flies attached to his clothes.

From Clary's, go right on Abercorn Street toward Lafayette Square. At the southeastern corner of the square, you will see the towering hulk **35** of the sturdily elegant **Hamilton-Turner House** (330 Abercorn St.). After one too many of Odom's deals went sour, Mandy left him and took over his third residence, a Second Empire–style mansion from 1873. Mandy (or Nancy Hillis, as her driver's license reads) filled it with 17th- and 18th-century antiques and has since transformed it into a successful museum through which she sometimes leads tour groups. ☎ 912/233–4800. ☛ $5. ⊗ For tours mid-Apr.–Sept., daily 10–5; Oct.–mid.-Apr., daily 11–4.

Leave the Hamilton-Turner House and head west on East Charlton Street till you find Bull Street once again. Go right on Bull Street, through Chippewa Square, then turn left onto Oglethorpe Avenue till you come **36** to the **Chatham County Courthouse** at 133 Montgomery Street. Here, Williams was triple-tried for murder over the course of about eight years. An underground tunnel leads from the courthouse to the jail where he was held in a specially modified cell that allowed him to conduct his antiques business.

Three more essential stops from the book are best taken in as they were **37** in the book—at nightfall or later. Don't miss a trip to the gay bar **Club One** (1 Jefferson St.), where the Lady Chablis still bumps and grinds her wild way down the catwalk, lip-syncing disco tunes in a shimmer of sequin and satin gowns. Call 912/232–0200 to find out when Chablis sings. ☛ $5 adults, $10 ages 18–20. Shows at 10:30 PM and 1 AM.

For tunes that are a little more low-key but no less flamboyant, head **38** over to **Hard Hearted Hannah's East** (upstairs in the Pirates' House, 20 E. Broad St.) to find Emma Kelly pouring out her best show tunes and blues bits. Emma moved here after her self-named club went bankrupt under Joe Odom's direction. Nicknamed "The Lady of 6,000 Songs" by Johnny Mercer, who convinced her to start singing, Miss Kelly has got quite a repertoire. Yes, she does take requests, so come prepared to be serenaded by this lovely woman who has entertained countless church groups and Lions clubs, not to mention three presidents and at least 20 governors. ☎ *912/233–2225. Cover: $3 Fri. and Sat. Ms. Kelly performs Tues. and Wed. 6–11 PM, Thurs.–Sat. 6–9 PM.*

③⑨ Last of all, end your pilgrimage at the **Bonaventure Cemetery** by following Wheaton Street west out of downtown to Bonaventure Road. (Note: get there before sundown, when it closes). Once the grounds of a magnificent live oak-choked plantation, whose mansion burned to the ground in the midst of a dinner party, Bonaventure is the final resting place for both Jim Williams and Danny Hansford. While you may be able to find their markers, don't look too hard for the haunting female tombstone figure from the book's cover. Apparently, Berendt fans beat too tough a path to her feet, and she was removed to protect surrounding graves. Savannah, no matter how wild the city was portrayed, seems to know how to pay last respects.

Day-Tripping to Tybee Island

Tybee Island, which lies 18 miles east of Savannah on the Atlantic Ocean, offers all manner of water and beach activities. Take Victory Drive (U.S. 80), which sometimes takes the alias of Tybee Road. There are two historic forts to visit on the way.

Fort Pulaski National Monument is 14 miles east of downtown Savannah. You'll see the entrance on your left just before U.S. 80E reaches Tybee Island. A must for Civil War buffs, the fort was built on Cockspur Island between 1829 and 1847 and named for Casimir Pulaski, a Polish count who was a Revolutionary War hero. Robert E. Lee's first assignment after graduating from West Point was as an engineer here. During the Civil War the fort fell on April 12, 1862, after a mere 30 hours of bombardment by newfangled rifled cannons. It was the first time such cannons had been used in warfare—and the last time a masonry fort was thought to be impregnable. The restored fortification, operated by the National Park Service, is complete with moats, drawbridges, massive ramparts, and towering walls. The visitor center includes museum exhibits and an audiovisual program. The park has self-guided trails and ample picnic areas. *U.S. 80, ☎ 912/786–5787.* ☛ *$2 adults, children 16 and under free.* ☉ *Daily 8:30–5, hours extended during summer.*

Three miles farther along U.S. 80 is **Tybee Island.** "Tybee" is an Indian word meaning salt. The Yamacraw Indians came to the island to hunt and fish, and legend has it that pirates buried their treasure here. The island is about 5 miles long and 2 miles wide, with a plethora of seafood restaurants, chain motels, condos, and shops, most of which sprung up during the 1950s and haven't changed much since. The entire expanse of white sand is divided into a number of public beaches, where visitors go shelling and crabbing, play on waterslides, charter fishing boats, swim, and build sand castles. Contact Tybee Island Beach Visitor Information (Box 1628, Savannah 31402, ☎ 800/868–2322).

The **Tybee Museum and Lighthouse** are at the island's tip. In the museum you'll see Indian artifacts, pirate pistols, powder flasks, old prints tracing the history of Savannah, even some sheet music of Johnny Mercer songs. The Civil War Room has old maps and newspaper articles pertaining to Sherman's occupation of the city. On the second floor there are model antique cars and ship models, and a collection of antique dolls. The lighthouse across the road is Georgia's oldest and tallest, dating from 1773, with an observation deck 145 feet above the sea. Bright red steps—178 of them—lead to the deck and the awesome Tybee

Light. The view of the ocean will take away whatever breath you have left after the climb. *30 Meddin Dr., ☎ 912/786–4077.* ☛ *To both lighthouse and museum: $2.50 adults, $1.50 senior citizens, 75¢ children 6–12.* ☉ *Both daily 10–6 in summer; Mon., Wed.–Fri. noon–4, weekends 10–4 in winter.*

TIME OUT Spanky's Pizza Galley & Saloon has fried shrimp, burgers, chicken fingers, and salads. *317 E. River St., ☎ 912/236–3009. AE, MC, V.* ☉ *Daily 11 AM–midnight.*

Heading west back to Savannah, take the Islands Expressway, which becomes the President Street Extension. About 3½ miles outside the city you'll see a sign for **Fort Jackson,** located on Salter's Island. The Colonial fort was purchased in 1808 by the federal government and is the oldest standing fort in Georgia. It was garrisoned in 1812 and was the Confederate headquarters of the river batteries. The brick fort is surrounded by a tidal moat, and there are 13 exhibit areas. Battle reenactments, blacksmithing demonstrations, and programs of 19th-century music are among the fort's schedule of activities. The Trooping of the Colors and military tattoo take place at regular intervals during summer. *1 Ft. Jackson Rd., ☎ 912/232–3945.* ☛ *$2.50 adults; $2 students, senior citizens, and military personnel; children 6 and under free.* ☉ *Daily 9–5.*

What to See and Do with Children

Forts Pulaski and **Jackson** (*see* Day-tripping to Tybee Island, *above*).

Juliette Gordon Low Girl Scout National Center (*see* Exploring, *above*).

Oatland Island Education Center. This 175-acre maritime forest, 5 minutes from downtown, is a natural habitat for coastal wildlife, including timber wolves and panthers. The center also houses the coastal offices of the Georgia Conservancy. *711 Sandtown Rd., tel 912/897–3773. Donation (about $1) requested.* ☉ *Weekdays 8:30–5; special events and programs take place Oct.–May, on the 2nd Sat. of each month 11–5.*

Exhibits at the **Savannah Science Museum** include a Plexiglas "crawl through" that allows kids to view reptiles and amphibians; a discovery room; a 32-foot, two-deck boat; an 800-gallon aquarium; Indian artifacts; and planetarium shows. *4405 Paulsen St., ☎ 912/355–6705.* ☛ *$3 adults; $2 senior citizens, students, and children 12 and under.* ☉ *Tues.–Sat. 10–5, Sun. 2–5; free planetarium shows every second Sun. at 3.*

Skidaway Island Marine Science Complex. On the grounds of the former Modena Plantation, the complex features a 12-panel, 12,000-gallon aquarium with marine and plant life of the Continental Shelf. Other exhibits highlight coastal archaeology and fossils of the Georgia coast. Nature trails overlook marsh and water. *30 Ocean Science Circle, Skidaway Island, ☎ 912/598–2325.* ☛ *$1, children under 7 free.* ☉ *Weekdays 9–4, Sat. noon–5.*

Tybee Island Museum and Lighthouse (*see* Day-Tripping to Tybee Island, *above*).

Off the Beaten Path

If your tastebuds crave down-home barbecue, head for **Walls',** place your order at the counter, then wait at an orange plastic booth. Entertainment is provided by a small color TV set. Drinks are serve-yourself from the refrigerator case, and your food comes in Styrofoam cartons. A sign taped above the counter reads, "When I work, I works hard. When I sit, I sits loose—when I think, I falls asleep." Plain? Not really. Barbecued spare ribs, barbecued sandwiches, and deviled crabs—the only items on the menu—are plenty rich. A large carton of ribs costs $8.50. *515 E. York La., between Oglethorpe Ave. and York St., ☎ 912/232-9754. No credit cards. ⊙ Wed. 11-5, Thurs. 11-10, Fri. and Sat. 11-10:30.*

Shopping

Find your own Low Country treasures among a bevy of handcrafted wares—handmade quilts and baskets; wreaths made from Chinese tallow trees and Spanish moss; preserves, jams, and jellies. The favorite Savannah snack, and a popular gift item, is the benne wafer. It's about the size of a quarter and comes in a variety of flavors.

Shopping Districts

Riverfront Plaza/River Street is nine blocks of shops housed in the renovated waterfront warehouses, where you can find everything from popcorn to pottery. **City Market,** located on West St. Julian Street between Ellis and Franklin squares, has sidewalk cafés, jazz haunts, shops, and art galleries. If you're in need of anything from aspirin to anklets, head for **Broughton Street** and wander through its many variety and specialty stores.

Oglethorpe Mall (7804 Abercorn Extension, ☎ 912/354-7038) is an enclosed center with four department stores (Sears, JC Penney, Belks, and Rich's) and more than 140 specialty shops and fast-food and full-service restaurants. The **Savannah Mall** (14045 Abercorn St. and Rio Rd., ☎ 912/927-7467) just off I-95 also has four major anchor stores (JB White's, Belks, Parisians, and Montgomery Ward), along with more than 100 specialty shops and fast-food and full-service restaurants. Kids delight in its old-fashioned carousel. **Savannah Festival Factory Stores** (11 Gateway Blvd. S, ☎ 912/925-3089) has manufacturers' merchandise at 25%-75% off.

Specialty Shops

ANTIQUES

Arthur Smith (1 W. Jones St., ☎ 912/236-9701) houses four floors of 18th- and 19th-century European furniture, porcelain, rugs, and paintings. At **Claire West Antiques and Fine Linen** (411-413 Whitaker St., ☎ 912/236-8163) you will find two buildings filled with an extensive collection of fine European linens, antiques, prints and engravings, old and new decorative tabletop objects, and a children's boutique with handmade bonnets and pinafores.

ARTWORK

Exhibit A Gallery (340 Bull St., ☎ 912/238-2480), the gallery of the Savannah College of Art and Design, has hand-painted cards, handmade jewelry, and paintings by regional artists. **Gallery 209** (209 E. River St., ☎ 912/236-4583) is a co-op gallery with paintings, watercolors, pottery, jewelry, batik, stained glass, and sculpture by local artists. Original artwork, prints, and books by internationally acclaimed artist Ray Ellis are sold in the **Compass Prints, Inc. Ray Ellis Gallery** (205 W. Congress St., ☎ 912/234-3537).

BENNE WAFERS

You can buy boxed bennes in most gift shops, but the **Byrd Cookie Company, Inc.** (2233 Norwood Ave., ☎ 912/355-1716) is where they originated in 1924. The popular cookies are sold in 50 gift shops around town or on site at the **Cooky Shanty.**

BOOKS
The 12 rooms of **E. Shaver's, Bookseller** (326 Bull St., ☎ 912/234–7257) are stocked with books on architecture and regional history, among other great finds. The **Book Lady** (17 W. York St., ☎ 912/233–3628) specializes in used, rare, and out-of-print books; it also provides a search service.

COUNTRY CRAFTS
At **Charlotte's Corner** (1 W. Liberty St., ☎ 912/233–8061) browse through regional cookbooks, children's clothes and handmade toys, and potpourris. **Georgia Gifts** (217 W. St. Julian St., ☎ 912/236–1220) has handmade baskets, jams, jellies, preserves, and wreaths.

Participant Sports

Bicycling
Pedaling is a breeze on these flatlands. Rental bikes are available at **Cyclological** (322 W. Broughton St., ☎ 912/233–9401) beginning in March.

Boating
Saltwater Charters (111 Wickersham Dr., ☎ 912/598–1814) operates everything from two-hour sightseeing tours to 13-hour deep-sea fishing expeditions. Pedal boats can be rented for tooling around **Lake Mayer** (Lake Mayer Park, Sallie Mood Dr. and Montgomery Crossroads Dr., ☎ 912/652–6780). There are public boat ramps at **Bell's Landing** on the Forest River (Apache Rd. off Abercorn St.); **Islands Expressway** on the Wilmington River (Islands Expressway adjacent to Frank W. Spencer Park); and **Savannah Marina** on the Wilmington River in the town of Thunderbolt.

Golf
Try the 27-hole course at **Bacon Park** (Shorty Cooper Dr., ☎ 912/354–2625) and the 9-hole course at **Mary Calder** (W. Lathrop Ave., ☎ 912/238–7100).

Health Clubs
Jewish Educational Alliance (5111 Abercorn St., ☎ 912/355–8111) has racquetball courts, a gymnasium, weight room, sauna, whirlpool, outdoor Olympic-size pool, and aerobic dance classes.

Savannah Downtown Athletic Club (7 E. Congress St., ☎ 912/236–4874) has Lifecycles, StairMasters, Nautilus and free-weight equipment, sauna, swimming pool, aerobics, and tae kwon do classes.

YMCA Family Center (6400 Habersham St., ☎ 912/354–6223) offers a gymnasium, aerobics, racquetball, pool, and tennis.

Jogging
Flat-as-a-benne wafer **Forsyth Park** and the beach at **Tybee Island** are favorites with runners. Suburbanites favor the jogging trails in **Lake Mayer Park** (Montgomery Crossroads Rd. at Sallie Mood Dr.) and **Daffin Park** (1500 E. Victory Dr.).

Tennis
There are 14 lighted courts in **Bacon Park** (Skidaway Rd., ☎ 912/351–3850), four lighted courts in **Forsyth Park** (Drayton and Gaston Sts.,

☎ 912/351–3852), and eight lighted courts in **Lake Mayer Park** (Montgomery Crossroads Rd. and Sallie Mood Dr., ☎ 912/652–6780). Five other local parks have courts as well.

Dining

On a river, 18 miles inland from the Atlantic Ocean, Savannah naturally has excellent seafood restaurants. Locals also have a passion for spicy barbecue. The Historic District yields culinary treasures among its architectural diamonds—especially along River Street. Savannahians also like to drive out to eat in Thunderbolt and on Skidaway, Tybee, and Wilmington islands.

CATEGORY	COST*
$$$$	over $30
$$$	$25–$30
$$	$15–$25
$	under $15

per person for a three-course meal, excluding drinks, service, and tax

What to Wear
Dress in Savannah is casual except where noted otherwise.

American

$$$$ **45 South.** This popular southside eatery moved in 1988 to the sprawling Pirates' House complex. It's a small, stylish restaurant with contemporary decor in lush mauve and green (typical of Savannah) colors. The ever-changing menu includes contemporary American dinner entrées such as sliced breast of duck with au gratin potatoes and grilled tuna with black angel-hair pasta and a pomeray mustard butter sauce. ✕ *20 E. Broad St.,* ☎ *912/233–1881. Reservations advised. AE, MC, V. No lunch. Closed Sun.*

$$$ **Olde Pink House.** The brick Georgian mansion was built for James Habersham, one of the wealthiest Americans of his time, in 1771. The elegant tavern, one of Savannah's oldest buildings, has original Georgia pine floors, Venetian chandeliers, and 18th-century English antiques. The new owners have taken great pains to research Colonial cooking style and have introduced it where appropriate. Signature dishes are a colonial version of crisp roast duck with a savory wild-berry compote, and black grouper stuffed with blue crab and finished with Vidalia onion sauce. The restaurant is graced with one of the largest wine cellars in the state of Georgia—fitting, as the Habersham family dominated the Madeira trade for years. Piano jazz (Tues.–Sun. 7:30–midnight) is played downstairs at Planters Tavern, where Martha Washington chairs and a Queen Anne settee are pulled up to the original cooking hearths on cool days. ✕ *23 Abercorn St.,* ☎ *912/232–4286. Reservations advised. AE, MC, V.*

$$ **Bistro Savannah.** This Beaux Arts–style gallery setting featuring new works by rising local artists is the place to see and be seen. Tucked in a historic building and featuring Savannah-gray brick walls, marble tables, and wicker chairs, this bistro has emerged as a favorite meeting and feeding spot among locals who love the Southern coastal cuisine. Items on the changing menu might include sweet onion-crusted North American red snapper with Madeira sauce and a 20-ounce "cowboy steak" with homemade smoked tomato-mustard barbecue sauce. Late-night cappuccino is popular here. ✕ *309 W. Congress St.,* ☎ *912/233–6266. Reservations accepted. AE, MC, V. No lunch.*

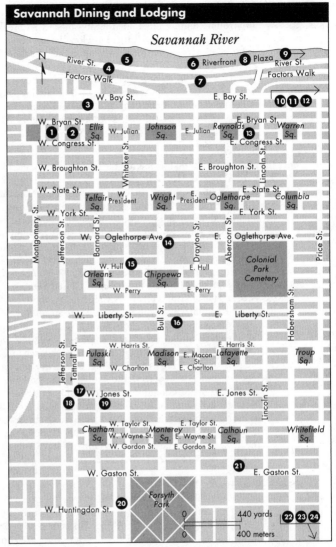

Savannah Dining and Lodging

$$ **Garibaldi's Cafe.** The 19th-century Savannah Germantown Firehouse houses this fanciful eatery with antique tin ceilings, hand-painted murals depicting the African tropics, and original oil paintings. Here the emphasis is on fresh fish—caught daily by the restaurant's small fleet. Try the crisp local flounder with apricot-shallot glaze or the local lump blue crab fettucine with pepper cream. ✕ *315 W. Congress St., ☎ 912/232–7118. Reservations accepted. AE, MC, V. No lunch.*

$ **Crystal Beer Parlor.** This comfortable family tavern is famed for hamburgers, thick-cut french fries, huge onion rings, and frosted mugs of draft beer. The menu also offers fried oyster sandwiches, gumbo, and shrimp salad. ✕ *301 W. Jones St. at Jefferson St., ☎ 912/232–1153. No reservations. MC, V. Closed Sun.*

$ **Johnny Harris.** What started as a small roadside stand in 1924 has grown into one of the city's mainstays, with a menu that includes steaks, fried chicken, seafood, and a variety of barbecued meats spiced with the restaurant's famous sauce. ✕ *1651 E. Victory Dr., ☎ 912/354–7810. Reservations recommended for weekends. AE, DC, MC, V. Closed Sun.*

$ **Mrs. Wilkes Dining Room.** There's no sign out front, but you won't have
★ any trouble finding this famed establishment. At breakfast time and
noon (no dinner is served) there are long lines of folks waiting to get
in for a culinary orgy. Charles Kuralt and David Brinkley are among
the celebrities who have feasted on the fine Southern food, served
family-style at big tables. For breakfast there are eggs, sausage, piping
hot biscuits, and grits. At lunch, bowl after bowl is passed around the
table. Fried or roast chicken, collard greens, okra, mashed potatoes,
cornbread, biscuits—the dishes just keep coming. ✕ *107 W. Jones St.,*
☎ *912/232–5997. No reservations. No credit cards. No dinner.*

Seafood

$$$ **Elizabeth on 37th.** Elizabeth is the chef, and her namesake was recently
★ toasted by *Food & Wine* magazine as one of the top 25 restaurants in
America. Elizabeth and Michael Terry's restaurant is located in the city's
Victorian District, in an elegant turn-of-the-century mansion with
hardwood floors and spacious rooms. Among the chef's seasonal spe-
cialties are shad stuffed with sautéed shad roe and stuffed Vidalia
onions. While the emphasis is on sea creatures served in delicate sauces,
there are other excellent offerings, including beef tenderloin, quail, lamb,
and chicken dishes. ✕ *105 E. 37th St.,* ☎ *912/236–5547. Reserva-
tions advised. AE, MC, V. No lunch. Closed Sun.*

$$$ **Pirates' House.** You'll probably start hearing about the Pirates' House
about 10 minutes after you hit town. There are all sorts of legends about
it involving shanghaied sailors and ghosts. It's a sprawling complex
with nautical and piratical trappings, and 15 rooms with names like
the Jolly Roger and the Buccaneer's Room; children love the place. The
menu is almost as big as the building, with heavy emphasis on sea critters. For starters, try oysters, crab-stuffed mushrooms, or soft-shell crabs.
The large portions of gumbo and seafood bisque come in iron kettles.
Flounder Belle Franklin is crabmeat, shrimp, and fillet of flounder baked
in butter with herbs and wines and a glaze of cheeses and toasted almonds. The Key lime pie is the best choice among the 40 listings on
the dessert menu. Hard Hearted Hannah's Jazz Club is upstairs. ✕ *20
E. Broad St.,* ☎ *912/233–5757. Reservations accepted. AE, DC, MC,
V.*

$$–$$$ **River House.** This stylish restaurant sits over the spot where the SS *Sa-
vannah* set sail for her maiden voyage across the ocean in 1819. A number of mesquite-grilled entrées, including swordfish topped with
raspberry-butter sauce and grouper Florentine, served with creamed
spinach and a fresh dill and lemon-butter sauce, are good. Entrées are
served with freshly baked loaves of sourdough bread, and fish dishes
come with homemade angel-hair pasta. ✕ *125 W. River St.,* ☎ *912/234–
1900. Reservations accepted. AE, DC, MC, V.*

$–$$ **Sea Shell House.** It may not look like much from the outside, but the
★ steamed and fried seafood inside is regarded by many to be the city's
best. Specialties are crab, shrimp, and oysters, as well as a Low Country Boil that includes shrimp, sausage, corn, and whatever else comes
to mind that day. It also features a seafood platter second to none. The
restaurant's pastry chef prepares a beautiful bananas Foster flambé.
French-style coffee is brewed tableside. ✕ *3111 Skidaway Rd.,* ☎
912/352–8116. No reservations. MC, V.

$–$$ **Shrimp Factory.** Like all of Savannah's riverfront restaurants, this was
once an old warehouse. Now it's a light and airy place with exposed
brick, wood paneling, beamed ceilings, and huge windows that let you
gaze at the passing parade of ships. A house specialty is pine bark stew—
five native seafoods simmered with potatoes, onions, and herbs, and
served with blueberry muffins. Blackened dolphinfish fillet is smoth-

ered with herbs and julienned sweet red peppers in butter sauce. Baked deviled crabs are served with chicken-baked rice, and fish entrées come with angel-hair pasta. ✗ *313 E. River St.,* ☎ *912/236–4229. Reservations accepted. AE, DC, MC, V.*

Lodging

While Savannah has its share of chain hotels and motels, the city's most distinctive lodgings are the more than two dozen historic inns, guest houses, and bed-and-breakfasts gracing the Historic District.

If "historic inn" brings to mind images of roughing it in shabbily genteel mansions with slightly antiquated plumbing, you're in for a surprise. Most of the inns are in mansions with the requisite high ceilings, spacious rooms, and ornate carved millwork. Most have canopied, four-poster, or Victorian brass beds that dominate most quarters. And amid antique surroundings, modern luxury: enormous baths, many with whirlpools, hot tubs, or Jacuzzis; film libraries for in-room VCRs; and turn-down service with a chocolate, praline, or even a discreet brandy on your nightstand. Continental breakfast and afternoon refreshments are often included in the rate.

CATEGORY	COST*
$$$$	over $100
$$$	$75–$100
$$	$50–$75
$	under $50

All prices are for a standard double room, excluding TK tax.

Inns and Guest Houses

$$$$ **Ballastone Inn & Townhouse.** This sumptuous inn within a mansion,
★ dating from 1838, once served as a bordello. Notable for the wildly dramatic designs of its Scalamandre wallpaper and fabrics, each of its 17 rooms has a different theme. In Scarborough Fair, a deep China blue and yellow room, the fabric pattern was adapted from a Victorian china serving platter in the Davenport House. This exquisite third-floor room has two queen-size Victorian brass beds, a Queen Anne lowboy and writing desk, and a Victorian slipper chair. On the garden level, rooms are small and cozy, with exposed brick walls, beamed ceilings, and, in some cases, windows at eye level with the lush courtyard. One such room is the Sorghum Cane, trimmed in the bronze color of sug-arcane molasses; it has two queen-size brass beds, wicker furniture, and wall fabric patterned after the etched glass window of a restored local house. Rooms have fireplaces and whirlpool baths. The townhouse, four blocks away, houses another five units (one room and four suites). Built in 1830, it's the oldest building south of Liberty Street. ▥ *14 E. Oglethorpe Ave., 31401,* ☎ *912/236–1484 or 800/822–4553. 17 rooms with bath. In-room VCRs, concierge. AE, MC, V.*

$$$$ **Gastonian.** Hugh and Roberta Lineburger's inn will probably, to put
★ it modestly, knock your socks off. The mansion was built in 1868, and each of its 13 sumptuous suites is distinguished with vivid Scalamandre colors. The Caracalla Suite is named for the marble bath with an eight-foot whirlpool tub. The huge bedroom has a king-size canopy bed, two working fireplaces, and a lounge with a mirrored wet bar. The Layfayette Room, resembling a 19th-century French boudoir, is done in blues and whites, with Oriental rugs and flocked wallpaper. All rooms have working fireplaces and antiques from the Georgian and Regency periods. At bedtime, a turn-down service leaves schnapps by your bedside and Savannah pralines on your pillow. In the morning, a full breakfast is served in the formal dining room—or you can opt

for a Continental breakfast in your room. Each guest receives a fruit basket and split of wine upon arrival. ☎ *220 E. Gaston St., 31401,* ☎ *912/232–2869, fax 912/232–0710. 13 rooms, 6 with oversize hot tubs. Outdoor hot tub, concierge. AE, MC, V.*

$$$–$$$$ **Olde Harbour Inn.** The building dates from 1892, when it was built on the riverfront as an overall factory, but the old inn is actually a thoroughly modern facility that housed condos until 1987. Each suite has a fully equipped kitchen, including dishwasher and detergent. All suites overlook the river and have wall-to-wall carpeting, exposed brick walls painted white, and a four-poster bed. There are studio suites; regular suites with living room, bedroom, kitchen, and bath; and loft suites. (The latter are lofty indeed, with 25-foot ceilings, balconies overlooking the water, huge skylights, and ample room to sleep six.) Each evening a dish of ice cream is brought to your room and placed in the freezer. Cereal, fruit, hot muffins and biscuits, juice, tea, and coffee are served in a cozy breakfast room each morning. ☎ *508 E. Factors Walk, 31401,* ☎ *912/234–4100 or 800/553–6533;* FAX *912/233–5979. 24 housekeeping suites with bath. Laundry service, concierge, parking. AE, DC, MC, V.*

$$$ **Forsyth Park Inn.** Rooms in this Victorian mansion across the street
★ from Forsyth Park are outfitted with 19th-century furnishings, including king- and queen-size four-poster beds, and have working fireplaces and large marble baths (some with whirlpools). The carriage house, just off the courtyard, has a suite with bath, a complete kitchen, and a new intimate deck. In the foyer is a grand piano, and afternoon wine is served here. ☎ *102 W. Hall St., 31401,* ☎ *912/233–6800. 9 rooms with bath, 1 private guest cottage. AE, D, MC, V.*

Bed-and-Breakfasts

$$$ **Jesse Mount House.** The Georgian home of Sue Dron has two two-bed-
★ room suites, a garden suite with a kitchen and whirlpool, and a one-bedroom suite. All units have their own fireplace with gas logs. Full breakfast is served in your room or in the formal dining room. ☎ *209 W. Jones St., 31401,* ☎ *912/236–1774. 4 suites with bath. VCRs. AE, D, MC, V.*

Hotels and Motels

$$$–$$$$ **DeSoto Hilton.** Three massive chandeliers glisten over the jardinieres and discreetly placed conversation areas of the spacious, newly redecorated lobby. The chandeliers are from the historic DeSoto Hotel that stood on this site long ago. Guest rooms are on the cushy side, in Savannah peach and green, with wall-to-wall carpeting, traditional furniture, and king-size, queen-size, or two double beds. (The best view is from the corner king-size rooms, which have the added attraction of coffeemakers.) Suites come with refrigerators upon request, and custom-made furnishings fill the bedroom, sitting room, and dining area. Golf, tennis, and athletic club privileges in the area are available to guests. ☎ *15 E. Liberty St., 31401,* ☎ *912/232–9000 or 800/426–8483, fax 912/232–6018. 250 rooms, 6 suites with bath. 2 restaurants, lounge, outdoor heated pool, concierge. AE,D, DC, MC.*

$$$–$$$$ **Hyatt.** When this riverfront hotel was built in 1981, preservationists opposed a seven-story modern structure in the historic district. Although it doesn't blend well with its surroundings, the hotel has some points to recommend it. The main architectural features are the towering atrium and a pleasant central lounge, as well as glass elevators. Rooms have mauve furnishings and balconies overlooking the atrium and the Savannah River. MD's Lounge is the ideal spot to have a drink and watch the river traffic drift by. ☎ *2 W. Bay St.,* ☎ *912/238–1234 or 800/233–*

1234, ℻ 912/944–3678. *346 rooms with bath.* Restaurant, lounge, indoor pool. AE, DC, MC, V.

$$$–$$$$ **Marriott.** Located in the Historic District, the eight-story property with rounded balconies facing the river occupies a choice spot on the city's riverfront, adjacent to River Street and Factor's Walk. *100 Gen. McIntosh Blvd., 31401,* ☎ *912/233–7722 or 800/228–9290,* ℻ *912/233–3765. 386 rooms, 46 suites with bath. 2 restaurants, lobby lounge, indoor-outdoor pools, hot tub, health club.* AE, D, DC, MC, V.

$$$–$$$$ **Mulberry Inn.** So many objets d'art fill the public rooms that the man-
★ agement has obligingly provided a walking tour brochure. Treasures include 18th-century oil paintings, an English grandfather clock dating from 1803, Chinese vases from the Ch'ing Dynasty, and an ornate Empire game table. The restaurant is a sophisticated affair, with crystal chandeliers and mauve velvet Regency furniture. The spacious courtyard is covered with a mosquito net, which keeps it about 10 degrees cooler in the summer. The guest rooms are in a traditional motif; suites have king-size beds and wet bars. Accommodations are available for nonsmokers and those with disabilities. ⌖ *601 E. Bay St., 31401,* ☎ *912/238–1200 or 800/465–4329,* ℻ *912/236–2184. 122 rooms, 22 suites with bath. Restaurant, bar, pool, outdoor hot tub.* AE, DC, MC, V.

$$$–$$$$ **River Street Inn.** This elegant hotel offers panoramic views of the Savannah River. Rooms are furnished with antiques and reproductions from the era of King Cotton. Amenities include turn-down service. The interior is so lavish, it's difficult to believe it was only recently a vacant warehouse dating back to 1817. One floor includes charming shops and a New Orleans–style restaurant. ⌖ *115 E. River St.,* ☎ *912/234–6400 or 800/253–4229. 44 rooms with bath.* 3 restaurants, 3 bars. AE, MC, V.

$$ **Days Inn/Days Suites.** This downtown hotel is located in the Historic District near the City Market, only a block off River Street. Its compact rooms have modular furnishings and most amenities, including HBO/ESPN on the tube. Interior corridors and an adjacent parking garage minimize its motel qualities. ⌖ *201 W. Bay St.,* ☎ *912/236–4440 or 800/325–2525. 253 rooms with bath. Restaurant, pool, health club.* AE, DC, MC, V.

Nightlife

Savannah's nightlife is a reflection of the city's laid-back, easy-going personality. Some clubs feature live reggae, hard rock, and other contemporary music, but most stay with traditional blues, jazz, and piano bar vocalists. After-dark merrymakers usually head for watering holes on Riverfront Plaza or the south side.

Jazz Clubs

Crossroads (219 W. Saint Julian St., ☎ 912/234–5438) is Savannah's sole blues nightclub, featuring live performances by local and national talent Monday through Saturday.

Hard Hearted Hannah's East (20 E. Broad St., ☎ 912/233–2225) features Emma Kelly, the undisputed "Lady of 6,000 Songs," performing Tuesday through Saturday.

Bars and Nightclubs

Axis (121 W. Congress St., ☎ 912/236–6266) is the city's liveliest music hall, featuring a variety of name performers in rock, blues, jazz, reggae, folk, country, and comedy. The age of the crowd on the tiny dance floor depends on who's on the bandstand.

Bottom Line (206 W. Julian St., ☎ 912/232–0812) is the place to swing and sway to big band music.

Kevin Barry's Irish Pub (117 W. River St., ☎ 912/233–9626), a cozy pub with a friendly bar and traditional Irish music, is *the* place to be on St. Patrick's Day. The rest of the year there's a mixed bag of tourists and locals, young and old.

Savannah Essentials

Arriving and Departing

BY BUS

The **Greyhound/Trailways** station (☎ 912/232–2135) is downtown at 610 W. Oglethorpe Avenue.

BY CAR

I–95 slices north–south along the Eastern Seaboard, intersecting 10 miles west of town with east–west I–16, which dead-ends in downtown Savannah. U.S. 17, the Coastal Highway, also runs north–south through town. U.S. 80, which connects the Atlantic to the Pacific, is another east–west route through Savannah.

BY PLANE

Savannah International Airport (☎ 912/964–0514), 8 miles west of downtown, is served by **Delta, Continental, USAir, and ValuJet.** Despite the name, international flights are nonexistent.

Vans operated by **McCall's Limousine Service** (☎ 912/966–5364 or 800/673–9365) leave the airport daily 6 AM–10 PM, after the arrival of each flight, bound for downtown locations. The trip takes 15 minutes, and the one-way fare is $12.

Taxi fare from the airport to downtown is $15 for one person, $3 for each additional person.

By car, drive south on Dean Forest Drive to I–16, then east on I–16 into downtown Savannah.

BY TRAIN

Amtrak (☎ 800/872–7245) has regular service along the Eastern Seaboard, with daily stops in Savannah. The Amtrak station (2611 Seaboard Coastline Dr., ☎ 912/234–2611) is 4 miles southwest of downtown. Cab fare into the city is $5–$10.

Getting Around

Despite its size, the downtown Historic District should be explored on foot. Its grid shape makes getting around a breeze, and you'll find any number of places to stop and rest.

BY BUS

Buses require $1 in exact change, and 5¢ extra for a transfer. **Chatham Area Transit (CAT)** (☎ 912/233–5767) operates buses in Savannah and Chatham County Monday–Saturday from 6 AM to midnight, Sunday 7 AM to 7 PM.

BY TAXI

Taxis start at 60¢ and cost $1.20 for each mile. **Adam Cab Co.** (☎ 912/927–7466) is a reliable, 24-hour taxi service.

Guided Tours

LOWCOUNTRY

The **Associated Guides of the Low Country** (☎ 912/234–4088 or 800/627–5030; closed Mon.), and **Gray Line** (☎ 912/234–8687) make four-hour excursions to the fishing village of Thunderbolt; the Isle of Hope, with stately mansions lining Bluff Drive; the much-photographed Bonaventure Cemetery on the banks of the Wilmington River; and Wormsloe Plantation Site, with its mile-long avenue of arching oaks.

ORIENTATION

Gray Line Tours (☎ 912/234–8687) is the official tour organization for the Historic Savannah Foundation. Knowledgeable and enthusiastic guides whisk you about in 20-passenger, climate-controlled vans. Tours of the Historic District and of the Victorian District take about two hours each. **Old Town Trolley Tours** (☎ 912/233–0083) offers tours providing an old-time view of the Historic District. Trolleys come by nine designated stops every half hour from 9–4:30 (cost: $14).

SPECIAL-INTEREST

In May, the **Garden Club of Savannah** (☎ 912/238–0248) takes you into private gardens tucked behind old-brick walls and wrought-iron gates. For groups of five or more, the **Negro Heritage Trail Tour** (☎ 912/234–8000) provides a knowledgeable guide who traces the city's more than 250 years of Black history. Tours commence at the Savannah Visitor's Center.

Carriage Tours of Savannah (10 Warner St., ☎ 912/236–6756 or 800/442–5933) show you the Historic District by day or by night at a 19th-century clip-clop pace, with coachmen spinning tales and telling ghost stories along the way. A romantic evening champagne tour in a private carriage will set you back $60, plus $16 per bottle of bubbly. Regular tours are a more modest $13 adults, $5 children 11 and under.

WALKING TOURS

A Ghost Talk Ghost Walk Tour (☎ 912/233–3896) will send chills up your spine during a two-hour jaunt through the Old Colonial City. Call for reservations; cost: $10 adults, $5 children.

The **Square Routes** (☎ 912/232–6866 or 800/868–6867) offers customized strolls through the Historic District and along Tybee Beach. In-town tours focus on the city's architecture and gardens, and specialized tours include the *Midnight in the Garden of Good and Evil* walk based on the current bestseller. Tours usually last two hours and cost from $15 to $25.

Important Addresses and Numbers

EMERGENCIES

Dial 911 for **police** and **ambulance** in an emergency.

HOSPITALS

Area hospitals with 24-hour emergency rooms are **Candler Hospital** (5353 Reynolds St., ☎ 912/354–9211) and **Memorial Medical Center** (4700 Waters Ave., ☎ 912/350–8000).

24-HOUR PHARMACY

Revco Drug Center (Medical Arts Shopping Center, 4725 Waters Ave., ☎ 912/355–7111).

VISITOR INFORMATION

For trip planning information, write to the **Savannah Area Convention & Visitor's Bureau** (222 W. Oglethorpe Ave., Savannah 31401, ☎ 912/944–0456 or 800/444–2427). The **Savannah Visitor's Center** (301 Martin Luther King Jr. Blvd., ☎ 912/944–0455) has free maps and brochures, lots of friendly advice, and an audiovisual overview of the city. The center is also the starting point for a number of guided tours. ⊙ *Weekdays 8:30–5, weekends and holidays 9–5.*

THE GOLDEN ISLES AND OKEFENOKEE SWAMP

The Golden Isles are a string of lush, subtropical barrier islands meandering lazily down Georgia's Atlantic coast from Savannah to the Florida border. They have a long history of human habitation; Indian relics have been found on these islands that date to about 2500 BC. According to legend, the Indian nations agreed that no wars would be fought there and that tribal members would visit only in a spirit of friendship. In a latter-day spirit of friendship today, all of Georgia's beaches are in the public domain. Each Golden Isle has a distinctive personality, shaped by its history and ecology. Three of them—Jekyll Island, Sea Island, and St. Simons Island—are connected to the mainland by bridges in the vicinity of Brunswick; these are the only ones accessible by automobile. The Cumberland Island National Seashore is accessible by ferry from St. Mary's. Little St. Simons Island, a privately owned retreat with a guest lodge, is reached by a private launch from St. Simons. About 50 miles inland is the Okefenokee Swamp National Wildlife Refuge, which has a character all its own.

Cumberland Island National Seashore

Numbers in the margin correspond to points of interest on the Golden Isles map.

The largest, most southerly, and most accessible of Georgia's primitive coastal islands is **Cumberland,** a 16-by-3-mile sanctuary of marshes, dunes, beaches, forests, lakes and ponds, estuaries, and inlets. Waterways are home to gators, sea turtles, otters, snowy egrets, great blue herons, ibis, wood storks, and more than 300 other species of birds. In the forests are armadillos, wild horses, deer, raccoons, and an assortment of reptiles.

After the ancient Guale Indians came 16th-century Spanish missionaries, 18th-century English soldiers, and 19th-century planters. During the 1880s, Thomas Carnegie of Pittsburgh built several lavish homes here, but the island remained largely as nature created it. In the early 1970s, the federal government established the Cumberland Island National Seashore and opened this natural treasure to the public.

There is no transportation on the island itself, and the only public access to the island is on the *Cumberland Queen,* a reservations-only, 146-passenger ferry based near the National Park Service Information Center at St. Mary's. Ferry bookings are heavy in summer, but cancellations and no-shows often make last-minute space available. *Cumberland Island National Seashore, Box 806, 31558, ☎ 912/882–4335. Roundtrip fare: $10.07 adults, $7.95 senior citizens, $5.99 children 12 and under. Mid-May–Sept., ferry departure from St. Mary's daily 9 AM and 11:45 AM, from Cumberland 10:15 AM and 4:45 PM. No ferry service Tues.–Wed. Oct.–May 14.*

Exploring

From the Park Service docks at the island's southern end, you can follow wooded nature trails, swim and sun on 18 miles of undeveloped beaches, go fishing and bird-watching, and view the ruins of Carnegie's great estate, **Dungeness.** You can also join history and nature walks led by Park Service rangers. Bear in mind that summers are hot and humid, and that you must bring your own food, soft drinks, sun-

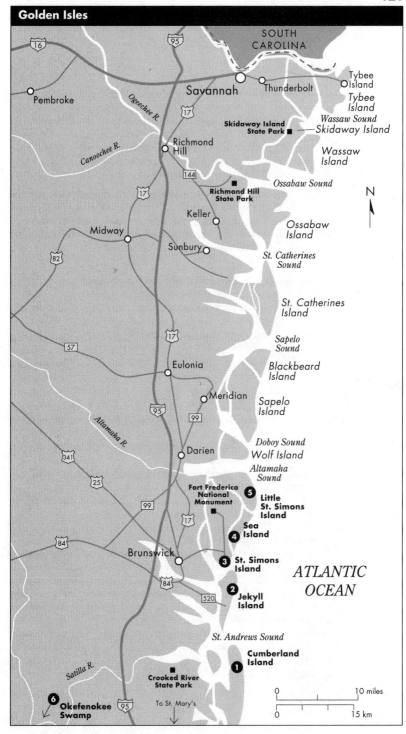

Golden Isles

SOUTH CAROLINA

Pembroke

Savannah
Thunderbolt
Tybee Island
Tybee Island

Ogeechee R.

Skidaway Island State Park
Skidaway Island

Canoochee R.

Richmond Hill

Wassaw Sound
Wassaw Island

144

Richmond Hill State Park

17

Ossabaw Sound

Keller

Ossabaw Island

Midway

82

Sunbury

St. Catherines Sound

17

St. Catherines Island

57

Sapelo Sound

Eulonia

Blackbeard Island

Meridian

Sapelo Island

95

99

341

Darien

Doboy Sound
Wolf Island
Altamaha Sound

Altamaha R.

25

Fort Frederica National Monument

5 Little St. Simons Island

99

17

4 Sea Island

84

Brunswick

3 St. Simons Island

ATLANTIC OCEAN

84

520

2 Jekyll Island

St. Andrews Sound

1 Cumberland Island

Satilla R.

6 Okefenokee Swamp

95

Crooked River State Park

To St. Mary's

N

0 — 10 miles
0 — 15 km

screen, and a reliable insect repellent. All trash must be transported back to the mainland by campers and picnickers. Nothing can be purchased on the island.

Lodging

ISLAND

$$$$ **Greyfield Inn.** The island's only accommodations are in a turn-of-the-century Carnegie family home. Greyfield's public areas are filled with family mementoes, furnishings, and portraits (you may feel as though you've stepped into one of Agatha Christie's mysterious Cornwall manors). Prices include all meals, transportation, tours led by a naturalist, and bike rentals. ⊞ *Box 900 Fernandina Beach, FL 32035,* ☏ *904/261–6408. 11 rooms, 1 suite. MC, V.*

Novice campers usually prefer **Sea Camp,** a five-minute walk from the *Cumberland Queen* dock, with rest rooms and showers adjacent to campsites. The beach is just beyond the dunes. Experienced campers will want to hike 3–10 miles to several areas where cold-water spigots are the only amenities.

MAINLAND

$ **Charter House Inn.** Two miles from the Cumberland ferry dock is a 120-room motel, whose accommodations are spartan but air-conditioned. Rooms have kitchenettes with microwaves for those who like to haul their own grub, and the on-site restaurant serves reasonably priced breakfasts, lunches, and dinners. ⊞ *2710 Osborne St., St. Mary's 31558,* ☏ *800/768–6250. 120 rooms. Restaurant, lounge. AE, D, DC, MC, V.*

Jekyll Island

➋ For 56 winters, between 1886 and 1942, America's rich and famous faithfully came south to **Jekyll Island.** Through the Gilded Age, the Great War, the Roaring '20s, and the Great Depression, Vanderbilts and Rockefellers, Morgans and Astors, Macys, Pulitzers, and Goodyears shuttered their Fifth Avenue castles and retreated to the serenity of their wild Georgia island. There they built elegant "cottages," played golf and tennis, and socialized. Early in World War II, the millionaires departed for the last time. In 1947, the state of Georgia purchased the entire island for the bargain price of $675,000.

Tourist Information

The **Jekyll Island Welcome Center,** at the end of the causeway, offers ninety-minute open-air trolley tours of the Jekyll Island Club Historic Landmark District. Tours originate at the Museum Orientation Center on Stable Road and include several restored homes and buildings in the 240-acre historic district. Faith Chapel, illuminated by Tiffany stained-glass windows, is open for meditation Sunday–Friday 2–4. Audiovisual orientations are presented before each tour departs. *Go north on 95 to Exit 6, south on 95 to Exit 8, Box 13186, Jekyll Island Causeway, Jekyll Island 31527,* ☏ *912/635–3636 or 800/841–6586.* ☛ *$8 adults, $6 students 6–18.* ☉ *Daily 9–5, tours daily 10–3.*

Exploring

Jekyll Island is still a 7½-mile playground, but no longer restricted to the rich and famous. The golf, tennis, fishing, biking, jogging, water park, and picnic grounds are open to all. One side of the island is flanked by nearly 10 miles of hard-packed Atlantic beaches; the other, by the Intracoastal Waterway and picturesque salt marshes. Deer and wild turkeys inhabit interior forests of pine, magnolia, and moss-veiled live oaks. Egrets, pelicans, herons, and sandpipers skim the gentle surf.

Jekyll's clean, mostly uncommercialized public beaches are free and open year-round. Bathhouses with rest rooms, changing areas, and showers are open at regular intervals along the beach. Beachwear, suntan lotion, rafts, snacks, and drinks are available at the **Jekyll Shopping Center,** facing the beach at Beachview Drive.

Participant Sports

GOLF

Jekyll's 63 holes of golf include three 18-hole courses with a main clubhouse on Capt. Wylly Road (☎ 912/635–2368) and a 9-hole course on Beachview Drive (☎ 912/635–2170).

TENNIS

Eight courts include J. P. Morgan's indoor court (☎ 912/635–2600, ext. 1060) and the Kelly Gunterman tennis school (☎ 800/426–3930).

WATER PARK

Summer Waves, the 11-acre water park, has an 18,000-square-foot wave pool, eight water slides, a children's activity pool with two slides, and a 1,000-foot river for tubing and rafting. *210 S. Riverview Dr.,* ☎ *912/635–2074.* ☛ *$11.95 adults, $9.95 children under 48".* ⊗ *May 28–Sept. 5, Sun.–Fri. 10–6, Sat. 10–8.*

Dining

$$$ **Grand Dining Room.** In the Jekyll Island Club Hotel the dining room sparkles with silver and crystal. Low Country cuisine by the hotel's young chef includes delicately flavored fresh seafood, beef, veal, and chicken. ✕ *371 Riverview Dr.,* ☎ *912/635–2600, ext. 1002. Reservations advised. Jacket required at dinner. AE, DC, MC, V.*

Lodging

$$$–$$$$ **Jekyll Island Club Hotel.** Built in 1887, the four-story clubhouse with wraparound verandas and Queen Anne–style towers and turrets once served as the winter hunting retreat for wealthy financiers. In 1985, a group of Georgia businessmen spent $17 million restoring it to a splendor that would astonish even the Astors and Vanderbilts. The guest rooms and suites are custom-decorated with mahogany beds, armoires, and plush sofas and chairs. Some have flowery views of the Intracoastal Waterway, Jekyll River, and the hotel's croquet lawn. Several suites have Jacuzzis. The adjacent Sans Souci Apartments, built in 1896 by William Rockefeller, have been converted into spacious guest rooms. The hotel is operated as a Radisson resort; it has 22 miles of bicycle trails and a free shuttle to area beaches. ☷ *371 Riverview Dr., Jekyll Island 31527,* ☎ *912/635–2600 or 800/333–3333,* ☷ *912/635–2818. 134 units. Restaurant, pool, 8 tennis courts, croquet. AE, DC, MC, V.*

$$–$$$$ **Best Western Jekyll Inn.** Located on a landscaped 15-acre site, these oceanfront units, the largest facility on the island, recently underwent a $2.5 million renovation. Rooms were redecorated with new lighting and carpeting. Units include some villas with kitchenettes. ☷ *975 N. Beachview Dr., Jekyll Island 31527,* ☎ *912/635–2531 or 800/736–1046. 264 units. Restaurant, pool, bicycles, playground. AE, D,DC, MC, V.*

$–$$$ **Holiday Inn Beach Resort.** Nestled amid natural dunes and oaks in a secluded oceanfront setting, this hotel has a private beach, but its rooms with balconies still don't have an ocean view. ☷ *200 S. Beachview Dr., Jekyll Island 31527,* ☎ *912/635–3311 or 800/753–5955. 205* rooms. *Restaurant, lounge, pool, golf course, tennis courts, bicycles, playground. AE, D, DC, MC, V.*

RENTALS
Jekyll's more than 200 rental cottages and condos are handled by **Jekyll Realty** (912/635–3301) and **Parker-Kaufman Realty** (912/635–2512).

St. Simons Island

As large as Manhattan, with more than 14,000 year-round residents, ❸ **St. Simons** is the Golden Isles' most complete resort destination. Fortunately, the accelerated development in recent years has failed to spoil the natural beauty of the island's regal live oaks, beaches, and salt marshes. Visits are highlighted by swimming and sunning on hard-packed beaches, golf, biking, hiking, fishing, horseback riding, touring historic sites, and feasting on fresh local seafood at more than 50 restaurants.

Tourist Information
St. Simons Island Chamber of Commerce (530 Beachview Dr., St. Simons Island 31522, ☎ 912/638–9014 or 800/525–8678, FAX 912/638–2172; closed Sun.) provides helpful information.

Exploring
Many sights and activities are in the **village** area along Mallery Street at the more developed south end of the island, where there are shops, several restaurants, pubs, and a popular public pier. A quaint "trolley" takes visitors on a 1½-hour guided tour of the island, leaving from near the pier, several times a day in high season, less frequently in winter ($10 adults, $6 children).

Also at the island's south end is **Neptune Park,** which includes picnic tables, a children's play park, miniature golf, and beach access. A freshwater swimming pool, with showers and rest rooms, is open each summer in the **Neptune Park Casino** (☎ 912/638–2393), which also has a recreation room and snack bars. Also in the park is **St. Simons Lighthouse,** a beacon since 1872. The **Museum of Coastal History** in the lightkeeper's cottage has a permanent exhibit of coastal history. ☎ *912/638–4666. ☞ (including the lighthouse): $3 adults, $1 children 6–12. ☉ Tues.–Sat. 10–5, Sun. 1:30–5.*

At the burgeoning north end of the island there's a marina, a golf club, and a housing development, as well as **Fort Frederica National Monument.** Tabby ruins remain of a fort built by English troops in the mid-1730s as a bulwark against a Spanish invasion from Florida. Around the fort are the foundations of homes and shops. Start at the **National Park Service Visitors Center,** which has a film and displays. ☎ *912/638–3639. ☞ $4 per car. ☉ Daily 9–5.*

On your way to Fort Frederica, pause at **Christ Episcopal Church** (donations welcome) on Frederica Road. Consecrated in 1886 following an earlier structure's desecration by Union troops, the white frame Gothic structure is surrounded by live oaks, dogwoods, and azaleas. The interior is highlighted by beautiful stained-glass windows.

Dining
$$ **Alfonza's Olde Plantation Supper Club.** Down-home versions of seafood, superb steaks, and plantation fried chicken are served in a gracious and relaxed environment. ✕ *Harrington La.,* ☎ *912/638–9883. Reservations advised. D, DC, MC, V. No lunch. Closed Sun.*

$$ **Blanche's Courtyard.** In the village, this lively restaurant/nightclub is gussied up in "Bayou Victorian" dress, with lots of antiques and nostalgic memorabilia. True to its bayou decor, the menu features Cajun-style seafood as well as basic steak and chicken. A ragtime band plays for dancers on Saturday. ✗ *440 Kings Way,* ☎ *912/638–3030. Reservations accepted. AE, DC, MC, V.*

$ **CJ's.** This tiny village-area restaurant serves the island's best Italian food. Deep-dish and thin-crust pizzas, pastas, and all of the menu's sandwiches draw a faithful local clientele. The limited seating capacity creates lengthy waits, but the cuisine is worth your patience, and take-out is available. ✗ *405 Mallory St.,* ☎ *912/634–1022. No reservations. No credit cards; local checks accepted. Lunch served late Mar.–late Sept.*

$ **Crab Trap.** One of the island's most popular spots, the Crab Trap offers a variety of fried, blackened, and broiled fresh seafood; oysters on the half shell; blue crab soup; heaps of batter fries; and hush puppies. The atmosphere is rustic-casual—there's a hole in the middle of every table to deposit corn cobs and shrimp shells. ✗ *1209 Ocean Blvd.,* ☎ *912/638–3552. No reservations. MC, V.*

Lodging

$$–$$$ **King and Prince Beach and Golf Resort.** This hotel faces the beach. Guest rooms are spacious, and villas offer two or three bedrooms. ⊞ *Box 20798, 201 Arnold Rd., St. Simons Island 31522,* ☎ *912/638–3631 or 800/342–0212. 137 rooms, 47 villas. Restaurant, lounge, indoor pool, 4 pools, bicycles. AE, D, DC, MC, V.*

$$$ **Sea Palms Golf and Tennis Resort.** A contemporary resort complex with fully furnished villas nestles on an 800-acre site. ⊞ *5445 Frederica Rd., St. Simons Island 31522,* ☎ *912/638–3351. 163 rooms. 2 pools, 27-hole golf course, tennis, bicycles, children's programs. AE, DC, MC, V.*

$$ **Days Inn of America.** This facility opened in 1989 on an inland stretch of the island's main thoroughfare. Each room has a built-in microwave and refrigerator. Continental breakfast is included in the rate. ⊞ *1701 Frederica Rd., St. Simons Island 31522,* ☎ *912/634–0660,* FAX *912/638–7115. 101 rooms. Pool. AE, MC, V.*

$$ **Island Inn.** On wooded land just off one of the island's main streets, this newer antebellum-style motel offers convenience and privacy with its efficiency accommodations. Continental breakfast is included, and complimentary wine and cheese are served weekdays from 5:30 to 6:30. *301 Main St.,* ☎ *912/638–7805. 74 rooms. Pool, hot tub, meeting rooms. AE, MC, V.*

$$ **Queen's Court.** This family-oriented complex in the village has clean, modest rooms with shower-baths, some with kitchenettes. The grounds, with their ancient live oaks, are beautiful. *437 Kings Way, St. Simons Island 31522,* ☎ *912/638–8459. 23 rooms. Pool. MC, V.*

RENTALS
For St. Simons condo and cottage rentals, contact **Trupp–Hodnett Enterprises** (☎ 800/627–6850) or **Golden Isles Realty** (☎ 912/638–8623).

Sea Island

❹ **Sea Island** has been the domain of the **Cloister Hotel** since 1928. Separated from St. Simons Island by a narrow waterway and a good many steps up the social ladder, this famed resort lives up to its celebrity status. Guests lodge in spacious, comfortably appointed rooms and suites in the Spanish Mediterranean hotel. The owners of the 500 or so private cottages and villas treat the hotel like a country club, and their tenants may use the hotel's facilities. Contact **Sea Island Cottage Rentals** (☎ 912/638–5112) to arrange to rent one.

For recreation, there's 54 holes of golf, tennis, swimming in pools or at the beach, skeet shooting, horseback riding, sailing, biking, lawn games, and surf and deep-sea fishing. After dinner, guests dance to live music in the lounge. All meals are included in the rate.

Like a person of some years, the Cloister has its eccentricities. Guest rooms were only recently equipped with TVs. Credit cards are not honored, but personal checks are accepted. Gentlemen must cover their arms in the dining rooms, even at breakfast. A complete and superb spa facility opened in 1989 in a beautiful building of its own by the pool and beach and features a fully equipped workout room, daily aerobics classes, personal trainers, facials and massages, and other beauty treatments.

There is no entrance gate, and nonguests are free to admire the beautifully planted grounds and to drive past the mansions lining Sea Island Drive. Space permitting, they may also play at the Sea Island Golf Course (on St. Simons) and dine in the main dining room. *The Cloister, Sea Island 31561, ☎ 912/638–3611 or, for reservations, 800/732–4752. 262 rooms. 4 restaurants, 2 pools, spa, golf, tennis, health club, airport shuttle. No credit cards; personal checks are accepted.* **$$$$** *($288–$552 for 2 in high season).*

Little St. Simons Island

❺ Six miles long, 2 to 3 miles wide, skirted by Atlantic beaches and salt marshes teeming with birds and wildlife, **Little St. Simons** is custom-made for Robinson Crusoe–style getaways. The island has been owned by one family since the early 1900s, and the only development is a rustic but comfortable guest compound.

The island's forests and marshes are inhabited by deer, armadillos, horses, raccoons, gators, otters, and over 200 species of birds. Guests are free to walk the 6 miles of undisturbed beaches, swim in the mild surf, fish from the dock, and seine for shrimp and crabs in the marshes. There are also horses to ride, nature walks with experts, and other island explorations via boat or the back of a pickup truck. From June through September, up to 10 nonguests per day may visit the island by reservation; the $60 cost includes the ferry to the island, an island tour by truck, lunch at the lodge, and a beach walk.

Dining and Lodging

$$$$ **River Lodge** and **Cedar House.** Up to 24 guests can be accommodated in the lodge and house. Each has four bedrooms with twin or king-size beds, private baths, sitting rooms, and screened porches. Two other lodges have two bedrooms each; one with private and the other with shared baths. None of the rooms are air-conditioned, but ceiling fans make sleeping comfortable. The rates include all meals and dinner wines (cocktails available at additional cost). Meals, often featuring fresh fish, pecan pie, and home-baked breads, are served family-style in the lodge dining room. The properties also provide transportation from St. Simons Island, transportation on the island, and interpretive guides. ⌧ 21078 Little St. Simons Island 31522, ☎ 912/638–7472, FAX 912/634–1811. *Pool, beach, fishing. Minimum 2-night reservations. MC, V.*

Okefenokee Swamp National Wildlife Refuge

⑥ Covering more than 700 square miles of southeast Georgia and spilling over into northeast Florida, the mysterious rivers and lakes of the **Okefenokee Swamp** bristle with seen and unseen life. Scientists agree that Okefenokee is not duplicated anywhere else on earth. The swamp is actually a vast peat bog, remarkable in geologic origin and history. Once part of the ocean floor, it now rises more than 100 feet above sea level.

As you travel by canoe or speedboat among the water-lily islands and the great stands of live oaks and cypress, be on the lookout for otters, egrets, muskrats, herons, cranes, and gators cruising the dark channels like iron-clad subs. The Okefenokee Swamp Park, 8 miles south of Waycross, is a major visitor gateway to the refuge. The Swamp Park is a nonprofit development operating under a long-term lease. There are two other gateways to the swamp: an eastern entrance in the Suwanee Canal Recreation Area, near Folkston; and a western entrance at Stephen C. Foster State Park, outside the town of Fargo.

Seminole Indians, in their migrations south toward Florida's Everglades, once took refuge in the Great Okefenokee. Noting the many floating islands, they provided its name—"Land of the Trembling Earth."

Exploring

Okefenokee Swamp Park. South of Waycross, via U.S. 1, the park offers orientation programs, exhibits, observation areas, wilderness walkways, an outdoor museum of pioneer life, and boat tours into the swamp that reveal its ecological uniqueness. A boardwalk and 90-foot tower are excellent places to glimpse cruising gators and a variety of birds. Gate admission includes a guided boat tour and all exhibits and shows. You may also arrange for lengthier explorations with a guide and a boat. *Waycross 31501,* ☎ *912/283–0583.* ☛ *$10 adults, $7 children 4–11.* ☼ *Summer, daily 9–6:30; spring, fall, and winter, 9–5:30.*

Suwanee Canal Recreation Area. This area, 8 miles south of Folkston via GA 121/23, is administered by the U.S. Fish and Wildlife Service. Stop first at the Visitor Information Center, which has an orientation film and exhibits on the Okefenokee's flora and fauna. A boardwalk takes you over the water to a 40-foot observation tower. At the concession building you may purchase snacks and sign up for guided boat tours into an 11-mile waterway, which resulted from efforts to drain the swamp a century ago. Hikers, bicyclists, and private motor vehicles are welcome on the Swamp Island Drive; several interpretive walking trails may be taken along the way. Picnicking is allowed. *Rte. 2, Folkston 31537,* ☎ *912/496–7156.* ☛ *To the park is free (there's a $4 charge per car). 1-hr tours: $7.50 adults, $3.75 children 5–11, $2.50 children 1–4; 2-hr tours: $15 adults, $7.50 children 5–11, $5 children 1–4. Refuge open Mar.–Sept. 10, daily 7 AM–7:30 PM; Sept. 11–Feb., daily 8–6; tours offered 10–2.*

Stephen C. Foster State Park. Eighteen miles from Fargo, via GA 11, is an 80-acre island park entirely within the Okefenokee Swamp National Wildlife Refuge. The park encompasses a large cypress and black gum forest, a majestic backdrop for one of the thickest growths of vegetation in the southeastern United States. The lush terrain and the mirrorlike black waters of the swamp provide at least a part-time home for more than 225 species of birds, 41 species of mammals, 54 species of reptiles, 32 species of amphibians, and 37 species of fish.

Park naturalists leading boat tours will spill out a wealth of swamp lore as riders observe gators, many bird species, and native trees and plants. You may also take a self-guided excursion in rental canoes and fishing boats. Camping is also available here (*see* Lodging, *below*). *Fargo 31631,* ☎ *912/637–5274.* ☛ *$4 to National Wildlife Refuge.* ☉ *Mar.–Aug., daily 6:30 AM–8:30 PM; Sept.–Feb., 7 AM–7 PM.*

Lodging
CAMPING

$–$$ **Stephen C. Foster State Park.** The park has furnished two-bedroom cottages and campsites with water, electricity, rest rooms, and showers. Because of roaming wildlife and poachers, the park's gates close between sunset and sunrise. If you're staying overnight, stop for groceries in Fargo beforehand. ▥ *Park Supt., Fargo 31631,* ☎ *912/637–5274.*

$ **Laura S. Walker State Park.** Nine miles from Okefenokee Swamp Park are campsites ($11) with electrical and water hookups. Be sure to pick up food and supplies on the way to the park. ▥ *Park Supt., Waycross 31503,* ☎ *912/287–4900. Picnic areas, pool, fishing, playground.*

The Golden Isles and Okefenokee Swamp Essentials

Getting There and Getting Around
BY CAR
From Brunswick by car, take the Jekyll Island Causeway ($2 per car) to Jekyll Island, and the Torras Causeway to St. Simons and Sea Island. You can get by without a car on Jekyll Island and Sea Island, but you'll need one on St. Simons. You cannot bring a car to Cumberland Island or Little St. Simons.

BY FERRY
Cumberland Island and Little St. Simons are accessible only by ferry (*see above*).

BY PLANE
The Golden Isles are served by **Glynco Jetport,** 6 miles north of Brunswick, which is served in turn by Delta affiliate **Atlantic Southeast Airlines** (☎ 800/282–3424), with flights from Atlanta.

ELSEWHERE IN THE STATE

Alpine Helen. The idea is an Alpine village in the Georgia mountains; the look is Bavaria; the attractions are mostly of the fun-and-fudge variety. The town's annual Oktoberfest draws crowds. *Rte. 385N from Atlanta to U.S. 129N to Cleveland, then Rte. 75N to Helen.*

Andersonville National Historic Site. Andersonville, which opened in 1864, was the Civil War's most notorious prisoner-of-war site: 13,000 prisoners died here, and at war's end the commandant was tried, convicted, and hanged. Earthworks, palisades, and some structures remain. Today it is the site of a memorial to prisoners of war. *I–75S from Macon to Rte. 26, then east to Oglethorpe, then Rte. 49 to Andersonville,* ☎ *912/924–0343.* ☛ *Free.* ☉ *Daily 8–5.*

Athens. The home of the University of Georgia, this college town has an appeal that's a cross between Mayberry R.F.D. and M-TV—the latter owing to its reputation as a breeding ground for new and alternative music. Athens has several splendid Greek Revival buildings, including, on campus, the **University Chapel** (built in 1832) and the **University President's House,** built in the late 1850s (570 Prince Ave.,

☎ 706/354–4096; open by appointment). The **Taylor-Grady House** (634 Prince Ave., ☎ 706/549–8688; ☞ $2.50; open Tues.–Fri. 10–3:30), down the street, was constructed in 1844. The **Franklin Hotel** (480 E. Broad St.), also built in 1844, was recently restored and reopened as an office building. Contact the **Athens Convention and Visitors Bureau** (☎ 706/546–1805).

Barnsley Gardens, near Adairsville. The Civil War halted construction of Godfrey Barnsley's 26-room Italianate house, and in 1988 the estate and its gardens lay in ruins. A German prince, Hubertus Fugger-Babenhausen, and his wife, Princess Alexandra, bought it and started work on restoration. Today there are 30 acres of shrubbery, trees, ponds, fountains, and flowers, designed in the style of Mr. Barnsley's time. At press time, a restaurant was planned. *Barnsley Gardens Rd. off Hall Station Rd.,* ☎ *404/773–7480.* ☞ *$6.50 adults, $5.75 senior citizens, children under 12 free.* ☉ *Tues.–Sat. 10–6, Sun. noon–6.*

Callaway Gardens, in Pine Mountain. This 14,000-acre family-style golf and tennis resort is best known for its impressive gardens and its not-to-be-missed butterfly conservatory. The gardens were developed in the 1930s by a couple determined to breathe new life into the area's dormant cotton fields. On the grounds are four nationally recognized golf courses, 17 tennis courts, bicycling trails, and a lakefront beach. The **Day Butterfly Center** contains more than 1,000 varieties flying free. Mountain Creek Lake is well stocked with large-mouth bass and bream. If you visit here in the height of the spring season or during the garden's annual holiday light spectacular in December, you may find yourself in a traffic jam in the middle of rural Georgia. *U.S. 27S,* ☎ *706/663–2281 or 800/282–8181.* ☞ *$7.50 adults, $1.50 children 6–11, children under 6 free.* ☉ *Daily 7–6.*

Chickamauga and Chattanooga National Military Park. Established in 1890 and the nation's first military park, this was the site of one of the Civil War's bloodiest battles; casualties totaled more than 30,000. Though the Confederates routed the Federals early, General Ulysses Grant eventually broke the siege of Chattanooga and secured the city as a base for Sherman's march through Atlanta and on to the sea. Monuments, battlements, and weapons adorn the road that traverses the 8,000-acre park, with markers explaining the action. *U.S. 27 off I–75, south of Chattanooga,* ☎ *706/866–9241.* ☞ *Free.* ☉ *Daily 8–4:45.*

Clayton. This unassuming mountain town is near spectacular Tallulah Gorge, the deepest canyon in the U.S. besides the Grand Canyon, and a popular turn-of-the-century destination for Atlantans. The state of Georgia recently acquired the site for a state park, and vast improvements are planned. In Clayton, the **Main Street Gallery** (☎ 706/782–2440), one of the state's best sources for folk art, features works by regional artists such as O.L. Samuels, Sarah Rakes, and Jay Schuette, and North Carolina's reclusive James Harold Jennings. About 10 miles north of Clayton on U.S. 441 is the **Dillard House,** justifiably famous for its spread of country food served family-style. ☎ *706/746–5348 or 800/541–0671. No early breakfast Sun.*

Dahlonega. Gold was mined here before the Civil War, and a U.S. mint operated in this modest boom town from 1838 to 1861. In the present-day courthouse on the town square is the Gold Museum, with coins, tools, and a 5½-ounce nugget. The square is ringed with a mixture of tourist-oriented boutiques and old small-town businesses. *About 55 mi northeast of Atlanta,* ☎ *706/864–2257.* ☞ *$2 adults, $1 children under 18.* ☉ *Daily.*

Fort Mountain State Park. Amid the deep woods and spectacular views in this out-of-the-way park in the Chattahoochee National Forest, nature is the main attraction, with a wide variety of trees and other flora. *Rte. 52 east of Chatsworth, ☎ 706/695–2621. ☛ $2 per vehicle, free on Wed. ⏲ Sat.–Thurs. 8–5, Fri. 8–10.*

Macon. This antebellum town features more than 100,000 flowering cherry trees. The Hay House (1860), considered one of the South's finest Italianate villas, contains 19 marble mantlepieces and other fine architectural detailing. *934 Georgia Ave., ☎ 912/742–8155. ☛ $6.30 adults, $5.25 senior citizens, $2.10 children 12–18, $1.05 children 6–12. ⏲ Mon.–Sat. 10–5, Sun. 1–5; last tour 4:30.*

The **Harriet Tubman African American Museum** is a tribute to the former slave who led more than 300 people to freedom as one of the "conductors" on the Underground Railroad. A mural that spans two walls and several centuries depicts black history and culture. The museum also has an African artifacts gallery and regularly changing exhibits. *340 Walnut St., ☎ 912/743–8544. ☛ $2 adults, $1 children 6–18. ⏲ Mon.–Sat. 10–5, Sun. 2–5.*

Madison. This town remains virtually unchanged architecturally from the 1830s. The **Madison-Morgan Cultural Center** is housed in a turn-of-the-century schoolhouse built in Romanesque Revival style. Besides a restored classroom of the period, the center contains artifacts and information and printed guides for other historic sites in town. *434 S. Main St., ☎ 706/342–4743. ☛ $2.50 adults, $1.50 students. ⏲ Tues.–Sat. 10–4:30, Sun. 2–5.*

New Echota State Historic Site. From 1825 to 1838, New Echota was the capital of the Cherokee nation, whose constitution was patterned after that of the United States. There was a courthouse, a Supreme Court building, and the *Cherokee Phoenix,* a newspaper that utilized the Cherokee alphabet developed by Sequoyah. Some buildings have been reconstructed. *Rte. 225, 1 mi east of I–75N, near Calhoun, ☎ 706/629–8151. ☛ $2 adults, $1 children 6–18, under 5 free. ⏲ Tues.–Sat. 9–5, Sun. 2–5:30.*

Ocmulgee National Monument. This archaeological site, occupied for more than 10,000 years, was at its peak under the Mississippian peoples who lived here between 900 and 1100. There's a reconstructed earth lodge and displays of pottery, effigies, and jewelry of copper and shells discovered in the burial mound. *Rte. 80 just east of Macon, ☎ 912/752–8257. ☛ Free. ⏲ Daily 9–5.*

Spring Place. Chief James Vann, a leader of the Cherokee Nation around 1800, hired Moravian artisans to build this two-story brick house in 1805. The interior is intricately carved and beautifully restored. *Rte. 52A just west of Chatsworth, ☎ 706/695–2598. ☛ $2 adults, $1.50 children 6–18, under 6 free. ⏲ Tues.–Sat. 9–5, Sun. 2–5:30.*

Summerville. Paradise Garden is the vision-come-to-life of the Rev. Howard Finster, preacher and folk artist. His artwork has been used for album covers by Talking Heads and R.E.M., and his eccentric visions are also in the collection of Atlanta's High Museum of Art. The garden, which occupies several city blocks, is dominated by the chapel built by Finster and members of his family. A tower built of old bicycle parts serves as a sentry for the spectacle. Artwork is for sale in the shop. *Off U.S. 27, near Pennville, ☎ 706/857–2926. ☛ Free, donations accepted. ⏲ Daily 10–6.*

Warm Springs. President Franklin Delano Roosevelt first visited here in 1924 and in 1932 built the "Little White House," a simple, three-bedroom house where he stayed when taking the therapeutic hot waters of the area. Now restored, it contains two hand-operated automobiles among his personal effects. *Rte. 85 W,* ☎ *706/655–5870.* ☛ *$4 adults, $2 children 6–18, under 6 free.* ☉ *Daily 9–5.*

4 Louisiana

Louisiana is a state divided, both physically and philosophically. North Louisiana, with its rolling hills and piney woods, is strongly southern in flavor and appeal, while flatter, marshy Southern Louisiana is considered Cajun Country, with sharp differences in food, music, and even language. Riverboats ply the mighty Mississippi and antebellum homes line the wayside in both regions, but it's New Orleans, home of the famous Mardis Gras festivities, that garners the lions' share of attention, drawing most visitors to Southern Louisiana.

By Honey
Naylor

THE VARIOUS REGIONS WITHIN MOST STATES are vaguely referred to by locals as "upstate," "to the south," and so on. Such is not the case in Louisiana. In "Sportsman's Paradise" (or the "Bayou State" or the "Pelican State," as it is also called), the land is clearly divided. Louisianians almost to a person say "North Louisiana" and "South Louisiana," and even in conversation you can detect a capitalized distinction. The truth is, North Louisiana and South Louisiana have about as much in common as North Dakota and South Carolina. North Louisiana is southern, and South Louisiana is not. (A South Louisiana exception is the area north of Baton Rouge, in the Feliciana Parishes, where both terrain and customs are akin to those in North Louisiana.) Peace reigns 'twixt the twain, of course. But it is no accident that construction of I–49, the north–south interstate, dragged on for years. Now, at least the North and the South are physically—though not philosophically—connected.

Louisiana's Mason-Dixon line is Alexandria, in the state's mid-section, known to all as Alex and pronounced "Elleck" by most. North of Alexandria are rolling hills and piney woods, acres of hiking and happy hunting grounds, and lakes where you can fish and camp.

The terrain flattens out and becomes marshy south of Alexandria. In Cajun Country (also known as Acadiana and French Louisiana), Cajun fiddles tune up for fais-do-do (dances); tables are laden with crawfish, jambalaya, and gumbo; and pirogues (small, flat-bottom boats) are poled through bayous. Gracious antebellum homes decorate the Great River Road between Baton Rouge and New Orleans, frilly riverboats play upon the Mississippi, and tour boats sneak beneath lacy gray Spanish moss into mysterious cypress swamps and sloughs.

Not a month goes by without a festival of some sort. South Louisiana is particularly festive. It's home, after all, to the state's most famous city—New Orleans—and the splashiest celebration in all of North America—Mardi Gras.

NEW ORLEANS

When Rhett Butler took Scarlett O'Hara to New Orleans on their honeymoon, the city was scarred by war, carpetbaggers were looting the town, and decent folk feared for their lives. But gone with the wind the city wasn't. Captain Butler and his bride were entertained at a continuous round of lavish parties, suppers, and plays.

Since the 1980s, New Orleans, like most other cities, has had its problems with crime and a depressed economy. But its reputation as a good-time town has remained intact. Despite its problems, New Orleans is forever finding something to celebrate. As well as world-famous Mardi Gras, new festivals crop up at the drop of a Panama hat. New Orleans party animals even celebrate each new addition to the Audubon Zoo.

The city's most famous party place is the French Quarter. Also called the Vieux Carré (Old Square), the Quarter is the original colony, founded in 1718 by French Creoles. As you explore its famous restaurants, antiques shops, and jazz haunts, try to imagine a handful of determined early 18th-century settlers living in crude palmetto huts, battling swamps, floods, hurricanes, and yellow fever. Two cataclysmic

Louisiana

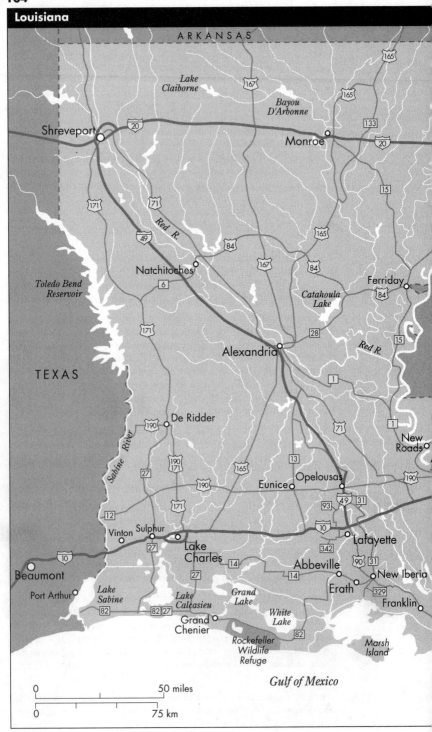

ARKANSAS

Lake Claiborne

Bayou D'Arbonne

[165]

[165]

[133]

Shreveport

[20]

Monroe

[20]

[15]

[171]

[71]

Red R.

[84]

[165]

[49]

[167]

[84]

Ferriday

Natchitoches

[6]

Catahoula Lake

[84]

Toledo Bend Reservoir

[171]

[28]

Red R.

[15]

TEXAS

Alexandria

[1]

[171]

De Ridder

[71]

[1]

New Roads

[190]

Sabine River

[190]
[171]

[165]

[13]

Opelousas

[190]

[27]

[190]

Eunice

[93] [49] [31]

[12]

[10]

Vinton Sulphur

[171]

[342]

Lafayette

[10]

Lake Charles

[27]

[14]

Abbeville

[90] [31]

New Iberia

Beaumont

[14]

Erath

[329]

Port Arthur

Lake Sabine

[27]

Grand Lake

Franklin

[82]

Lake Calcasieu

White Lake

Marsh Island

[82] [27]

Grand Chenier

Rockefeller Wildlife Refuge

[82]

Gulf of Mexico

0 —————— 50 miles

0 —————— 75 km

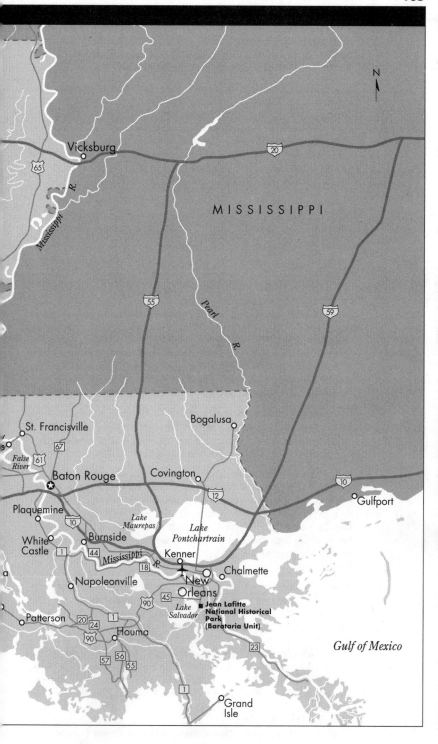

N

Vicksburg

`65`

`20`

M I S S I S S I P P I

Mississippi R.

Pearl R.

`55`

`59`

Bogalusa

St. Francisville

False River

`67`

`61`

Covington

Baton Rouge

`12`

`10`

Gulfport

Plaquemine

`10`

Lake Maurepas

Lake Pontchartrain

White Castle

`1`

Burnside

`44`

Mississippi R.

Kenner

`18`

Chalmette

Napoleonville

Lake Salvador

New Orleans

■ Jean Lafitte National Historical Park (Baratria Unit)

Patterson

`20` `24`

`1`

`90`

`45`

Houma

`90`

`57` `56`

`55`

`23`

Gulf of Mexico

`1`

Grand Isle

fires in the late 18th century virtually leveled the town. The Old Ursuline Convent on Chartres Street is the only remaining original French
Colonial structure. Survival was a struggle for the Creoles, and the so-
briquet "The City That Care Forgot" stems from a determination not
only to live life but to celebrate it, come what may.

Necessity may be the mother of invention, but it was the Father of Waters that forced Crescent City denizens to devise a new vocabulary for
dealing with directions. The Mississippi River moves in mysterious waves,
looping around the city and wreaking havoc with ordinary directions.
New Orleanians, ever resourceful, refer instead to lakeside (toward Lake
Pontchartrain), riverside (toward the Mississippi), upriver (also called
uptown), and downriver (downtown).

Exploring

*Numbers in the margin correspond to points of interest on the Down-
town New Orleans map.*

Bordered by Canal Street, Esplanade Avenue, North Rampart Street,
and the Mississippi River, the French Quarter—also known as Vieux
Carré—is a carefully preserved historic district. But the Quarter is
also home to some 3,600 residents, some of the most famous of the
French Creole restaurants, and many a jazz club. An eclectic crowd,
which includes some of the world's best jazz musicians, ambles in and
out of small two- and three-story frame, old-brick, and pastel-painted
stucco buildings. Baskets of splashy subtropical plants dangle from the
eaves of buildings with filigreed galleries, dollops of gingerbread, and
dormer windows. Built flush with the banquettes (sidewalks), the
houses, most of which date from the early to mid-19th century, front
secluded courtyards awash with greenery and brilliant blossoms.

In the early 19th century, the American Sector was just upriver of the
French Quarter. For that reason, street names change as you cross Canal
Street from the French Quarter: Bourbon Street to Carondelet Street,
Royal Street to St. Charles Avenue, and so on.

Nerve center of the nation's second-largest port and main parade route
during Mardi Gras, the CBD (Central Business District) cuts a wide
swath between Uptown and Downtown, with Canal Street the official
dividing line. Bordered by Canal Street, the river, Howard Avenue, and
Loyola Avenue, the CBD has the city's newest high-tech convention
hotels, along with ritzy new shopping malls, age-old department stores,
foreign agencies, fast-food chains, monuments, and the monumental
Superdome.

Nestled in between St. Charles Avenue, Louisiana Avenue, Jackson Avenue, and Magazine Street, the Garden District is aptly named. The
Americans who built their estates upriver surrounded their homes
with lavish lawns, forgoing the Creoles' preference for secluded courtyards. Many of the elegant Garden District homes were built during
New Orleans's Golden Age, from 1830 until the Civil War. Magazine
Street is heaven on earth for shoppers. Joggers, golfers, tennis buffs,
and horseback riders head for Audubon Park, and animal lovers can
get close to many different species at the Audubon Zoo.

The French Quarter

Make your first stop the **New Orleans Welcome Center** (529 St. Ann
St.), for free maps, brochures, and friendly advice.

❶ The **Welcome Center** is in the heart of **Jacks**

★ ❷ equestrian statue of General Andrew Jackson
named. Jackson Square was known as Place u
it was renamed in the mid-19th century for the man
British in the Battle of New Orleans. Place d'Armes was
all Colonial life, home to parading militia, religious ceremonie
gatherings, food vendors, entertainers, and pirates. The square
mains a social hub today. Pirate attire is not uncommon in the colorful crowd that flocks to the square. The only thing missing is the
militia.

❸ **St. Louis Cathedral** (Jackson Sq., on the 700 block of Chartres St., ☎
504/525–9585), soaring above the earthly activity taking place right
in its front yard, is a quiet reminder of the spiritual life of New Orleans citizens. The present church dates from 1794, and it was restored
in 1849. Tours are conducted daily (on the half hour from 9–5) except during services.

Alongside the church are **Pirate's Alley** and **Père Antoine's Alley.** Those
cracked-flagstone passageways are redolent of infamous plots and pirate intrigue—but, alas, the streets were laid long after Jean Lafitte and
his Baratarian band had vanished. William Faulkner wrote his first novel,
A Soldier's Pay, while living at **624 Pirate's Alley.**

The church is flanked by two buildings of the **Louisiana State Museum.**
❹ ❺ As you face the church, the **Cabildo** is on the left, the **Presbytère** on
the right. Transfer papers for the Louisiana Purchase of 1803 were signed
on the second floor of the Cabildo. Exhibits here trace the multicul-
tural historic contributions to the region. Among the artifacts is a
death mask of Napoleon, who was a hero for many a New Orleanian.

The Presbytère was built to house priests of the church, but was never
used for this purpose. Like the Cabildo, it is also a museum, with changing exhibits. The odd-shaped structure in the arcade of the Presbytère
is a Confederate submarine. Hours and admission charges for the Cabildo and Presbytère are the same. *Jackson Sq., ☎ 504/568–6968.* ☛
*To each building: $4 adults, $2 students and senior citizens, children
under 12 free. ☺ Tues.–Sun. 10–5.*

You can see what life was like for upscale 19th-century Creole apart-
❻ ment dwellers on a guided tour in the **1850s House,** another compo-
nent of the Louisiana State Museum. In the lower Pontalba Buildings
(lower because it's on the downriver side of the square), the building
contains period furnishings, antique dolls, and evidence of cushy Creole living. *523 St. Ann St., Jackson Sq., ☎ 504/568–6968.* ☛ *$4
adults, $2 students and senior citizens, children under 12 free. ☺
Tues.–Sun. 10–5.*

The **Pontalba Buildings** that line either side of Jackson Square on St.
Ann and St. Peter streets are among the oldest apartment houses in the
country. Built between 1849 and 1851, they were constructed under
the supervision of the baroness Micaela Pontalba, who occasionally
lent the laborers a helping hand.

The promenade of **Washington Artillery Park,** opposite Jackson Square
on Decatur Street, affords a splendid perspective of the square on one
side and Old Man River rolling along on the other. On the **Moon Walk**
promenade, across the tracks from the park, you can sit on a bench or
stroll down the steps to the water's edge.

❼ Washington Artillery Park is anchored on the upriver side by the **Jackson Brewery and Millhouse,** and downriver by the **French Market.** Jax

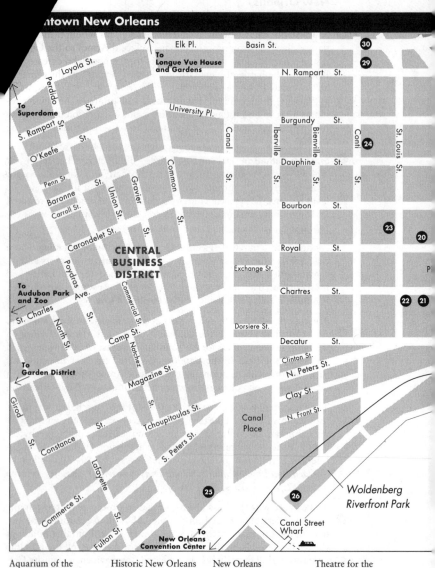

Aquarium of the
Americas, **26**

Beauregard-Keyes
House, **11**

Cabildo, **4**

Café du Monde, **8**

Cornstalk Fence, **14**

1850s House, **6**

First Skyscraper, **18**

Gallier House, **12**

Harrah's Casino New
Orleans, **25**

Hermann-Grima
House, **23**

Historic New Orleans
Collection, **20**

Jackson Brewery and
Millhouse, **7**

Jackson Square, **2**

LaBranche House, **17**

Lafitte's Blacksmith
Shop, **13**

Louis Armstrong
Park, **27**

Madame John's
Legacy, **16**

Musée Conti Wax
Museum, **24**

Napoleon House, **22**

New Orleans
Pharmacy Museum, **21**

Old Ursuline
Convent, **10**

Old U.S. Mint, **9**

Our Lady of
Guadalupe Catholic
Church, **29**

Presbytère, **5**

Preservation Hall, **19**

St. Louis Cathedral, **3**

St. Louis Cemetery
No. 1, **30**

Theatre for the
Performing Arts, **28**

Voodoo Museum, **15**

Welcome Center, **1**

139

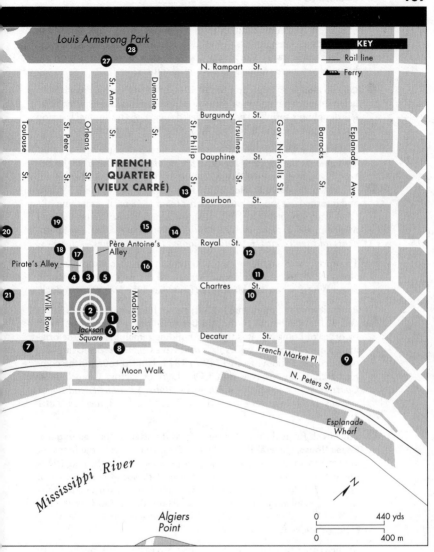

Beer used to be brewed in the brewery, and the market is on the site of a late-17th-century Indian trading post. Both are now filled with boutiques and restaurants. Toward Canal Street on Decatur Street is the Jackson Brewery Corporation's **Marketplace,** on Decatur Street, home of yet more restaurants and retail outlets.

8 **Café du Monde** (800 Decatur St., ☎ 504/525–4544), in the French Market, a 24-hour haven for café au lait and beignets (square, puffy, holeless doughnuts sprinkled with powdered sugar), is a traditional last stop after a night out on the town, and a New Orleans institution.

Make a right and continue along Decatur Street to Esplanade Avenue. *This area on the fringe of the Quarter should be avoided at night,* but you'll be safe during the day when you visit the Jazz and Mardi Gras **9** Exhibits in the **Old U.S. Mint.** This was the first branch of the U.S. Mint, and it turned out money hand over fist from 1838 until something (the Civil War) stopped it in 1861. It's now a part of the Louisiana State Museum. *400 Esplanade Ave., ☎ 504/568–6968. ☛ $4 adults, $2 students and senior citizens, children under 12 free. ☉ Tues.–Fri. 10–5.*

The upriver trip is a breeze on the Riverfront Streetcar. It rumbles right along the river from Esplanade Avenue all the way up to the Robin Street Wharf, where the *Mississippi Queen* and the *Delta Queen* dock.

After viewing the mint, make a left; turn left again at Chartres Street **10** and walk three blocks to the **Old Ursuline Convent.** Erected in 1749 by order of Louis XV, it is the only building remaining from the original colony. The Sisters of Ursula, who arrived in New Orleans in 1727, occupied the building from 1749 to 1824. Guided tours of the complex include the lovely restored Our Lady of Victory Chapel. *1100 Chartres St., ☎ 504/529–3040. ☛ $4 adults, $2 students and senior citizens, children under 8 free. Tours: Tues.–Fri. 10–3, weekends at 1 and 2.*

11 The Greek Revival raised cottage across the street is the **Beauregard-Keyes House.** General P. G. T. Beauregard, who ordered the first shot at Fort Sumter, lived in the house after the Civil War. In the mid-1940s the house was bought by novelist Frances Parkinson Keyes (author of *Dinner at Antoine's*), whose office was in the slave quarters. Docents will tell you all about the dwelling and its dwellers. *1113 Chartres St., ☎ 504/523–7257. ☛ $4 adults, $3 senior citizens and students, $1.50 children under 12. ☉ Mon.–Sat. 10–3.*

At the corner turn right onto Ursulines Street and walk one block to **12** Royal Street, where you'll find the **Gallier House.** Built about 1857 by famed architect James Gallier Jr., this is one of the best-researched house museums in the city. The Galliers were Irish, but this is a fine example of how well-heeled Creoles lived. *1118 Royal St., ☎ 504/523–6722. ☛ $5 adults, $4 senior citizens, AAA members, and students, $2.50 children 6–12. Tours Mon.–Sat.10–4:30, occasionally Sun. noon–4.*

Back on Ursulines Street, turn right and walk one block away from the river, turn left onto Bourbon Street, and go one more block. The **13** tattered cottage on your right is **Lafitte's Blacksmith Shop** (941 Bourbon St., ☎ 504/523–0066). The house dates to 1772, and it is typical of houses built by the earliest settlers. According to a cherished legend, the cottage was once a front for freebooter Jean Lafitte's smuggling and slave trade. Today it's a neighborhood bar, and for a long time it has been a favorite haunt of artists and writers, the well known and the never known.

⑭ Return to Royal Street via St. Philip Street and turn right for the **Cornstalk Fence** (915 Royal St.). Morning glories and ears of corn are intricately intertwined in the cast-iron fence.

⑮ At the corner of Royal Street turn right onto Dumaine Street. The **Voodoo Museum** is an "only in New Orleans" phenomenon and either spooky or campy (or both), depending upon what spirits move you. Remembrances of voodoo queen Marie Laveau are prominently displayed, along with altars, artifacts, and everything you need for a voodoo to-do. *724 Dumaine St., ☎ 504/523–7685. ☛ $5.25 adults, $4.20 senior citizens, $3.15 students, $2.50 children. ☉ Daily 10–7.*

⑯ As you leave the museum, turn right and walk one block toward the river on Dumaine Street. **Madame John's Legacy** (632 Dumaine St.) is so named for a character in the short story "Tite Poulette," by 19th-century New Orleans writer George Washington Cable. The West Indies–style house was built in 1788 on the site of the birthplace of Renato Beluche, a Lafitte lieutenant who helped Andrew Jackson in the Battle of New Orleans. Owned by the Louisiana State Museum (☎ 504/568–6968), the house is not open to the public.

⑰ Return to Royal Street, turn left and walk two blocks past the quiet, green **Cathedral Garden,** which is at the rear of St. Louis Cathedral. One block more will bring you to St. Peter Street and the most-photographed building in the city: The **LaBranche House** (700 Royal St.), dating from about 1840, wraps around the corner of Royal Street and runs halfway down St. Peter Street. Its filigreed double galleries are cast iron with an oak-leaf-and-acorn motif. Shops and restaurants on the ground floor are open to the public.

⑱ Directly across the street is the **First Skyscraper** (640 St. Peter St.). Built between 1795 and 1811, it was a three-story high rise; rumor has it that the fourth floor was added later so that it might retain its towering title. Shops on the ground floor are open to the public. Up St. Peter **⑲** Street, behind weathered walls is **Preservation Hall** (726 St. Peter St., ☎ 504/522–2238), home of the world's best traditional and Dixieland jazz (*see* Nightlife, *below*).

⑳ Continue on Royal Street one block to the **Historic New Orleans Collection.** The **Merieult House** was one of the few buildings to survive the fire of 1794 and now contains an extensive collection of documents and research materials pertaining to the city. Exhibits in the **Williams Gallery** on the ground floor can be seen for free, and for a fee you can take a guided tour and hear the legends of the historic house. *533 Royal St., ☎ 504/523–4662. Tour: $2. ☉ Tues.–Sat. 10–4:45.*

㉑ Turn left and then right onto Toulouse Street, walk toward the river, and turn right onto Chartres Street. The **New Orleans Pharmacy Museum** is a musty old place where Louis Dufilho had his pharmacy in 1823. It's full of ancient and mysterious medicinal items, and there is an Italian marble fountain used by 19th-century soda jerks. *514 Chartres St., ☎ 504/565–8027. ☛ $3. ☉ Tues.–Sun. 10–5.*

㉒ At the corner of Chartres and St. Louis streets is the **Napoleon House** (500 Chartres St., ☎ 504/524–9752), a long-time favorite haunt of artists and writers. The bar fairly oozes atmosphere from every splinter, with peeling sepia walls, Napoleonic memorabilia, and taped classical music to back up your libation. It is entirely possible—and this is a proven fact—to laze away an entire afternoon sitting by an open door watching rain splatter down on the pavement.

If you can wrench yourself away, turn right at the corner and walk along St. Louis Street past Antoine's Restaurant and go one more block to the **Hermann-Grima House.** Guides will steer you through the American-style town house–museum, built in 1831, and on winter Thursdays you can get a taste of Creole during cooking demonstrations. *820 St. Louis St.,* ☎ *504/525–5661.* ☛ *$4 adults, $3 senior citizens and students, $2 children 8–18, under 8 free.* ☉ *Mon.–Sat. 10–4; last tour at 3:30.*

Continue along St. Louis Street, turning left onto Dauphine Street, then right onto Conti Street where you'll come upon the **Musée Conti Wax Museum.** The museum waxes lifelike on Louisiana legends, among them Andrew Jackson, Jean Lafitte, Marie Laveau, and governor Edwin Edwards. *917 Conti St.,* ☎ *504/525–2605.* ☛ *$5.75 adults, $5.25 senior citizens, $3.50 children 4–18.* ☉ *Daily 10–5.*

Foot of Canal

At press time, work had finally begun on Louisiana's most highly publicized land-based casino. (It is not the first, or the only, land-based casino in the state; there are thriving casinos on three Indian reservations.) The Rivergate Exhibition Center is being demolished to make way for **Harrah's Casino New Orleans.** With 250,000 square feet, the $790 million facility will be the world's largest casino. Completion is scheduled for April 1996. Until then, Harrah's will operate a temporary casino in the Municipal Auditorium in Armstrong Park (scheduled to open in July 1995).

Near the casino site, at the end of Canal Street, is the **Aquarium of the Americas,** whose spectacular design lets viewers feel part of the watery world by offering close-up encounters with the 7,000 aquatic creatures in 60 separate displays in four major environments. The beautifully landscaped 16-acre **Woldenberg Riverfront Park** around the aquarium is a tranquil spot with an excellent view of the river. *Foot of Canal St.,* ☎ *504/861–2538.* ☛ *$9.75 adults, $7.75 senior citizens, $5 children 2–12.* ☉ *Sun.–Thurs. 9:30–6, Fri.–Sat. 9:30–7.*

TIME OUT   Nearby **Arnaud's Grill** has mosaic-tile floors, ceiling fans, and a player piano as the backdrop for its mixed drinks. *813 Bienville St.,* ☎ *504/523–5433. AE, DC, MC, V.*

North Rampart Street

At press time, unattractive, rundown North Rampart Street was on the brink of a much-needed face-lift. The "Renaissance on Rampart" was spurred by plans for Harrah's temporary casino in **Louis Armstrong Park.** The park's **Municipal Auditorium,** formerly used for Carnival balls, is being renovated to house the temporary casino until completion of the permanent Harrah's New Orleans Casino at the foot of Canal Street (*see above*). (It is widely believed locally that the "temporary" casino will continue to function even after the Canal Street facility opens). The city has long had plans for a "Jazz Alley" and an African-American Music Hall of Fame and Museum in the park, but so far nothing much has happened toward that goal. There are also plans for sidewalk cafés and other attractions in the vicinity of the casino. North Rampart Street and Louis Armstrong Park have long been *unsafe day or night,* but it is hoped that beefed-up security and large crowds of people will change that situation.

At St. Ann Street, a large glittering arch hovers over the entrance to the park, which is named for native son Louis "Satchmo" Armstrong.

Municipal Auditorium is on the site of Congo Square, scene of 18th- and 19th-century slave gatherings. Congo Square is believed to have been the birthplace of jazz, with the voodoo Afro-Caribbean rhythms of the slaves' songs and chants influencing the new music. Not far from the auditorium is the **Theatre for the Performing Arts,** in which the opera and ballet perform.

㉙ **Our Lady of Guadalupe Catholic Church** (411 N. Rampart St., ☎ 504/525–1551) was dedicated in 1827, when it was known as the Mortuary Chapel. It was originally used only for funerals, usually for victims of yellow fever and cholera. This church is home to one of the city's legends, St. Expedite. The story is that a statue was delivered to the church in a crate marked simply "Expedite." It was expeditiously mounted, and it can be seen to the right as you enter the church.

㉚ Just behind the church on Basin Street is **St. Louis Cemetery No. 1,** between St. Louis and Conti streets. This is New Orleans's oldest City of the Dead, so called because the stark white aboveground tombs resemble tiny houses. The cemetery dates from 1789, and well-worn paths lead through a maze of tombs and mausoleums, many with the same ornate grilles and ironwork as the houses where live folks live. Many a well-known early New Orleanian is buried here, and voodoo doings mark the tomb believed to be that of voodoo queen Marie Laveau. (Some say she is really buried in St. Louis Cemetery No.2.) *Warning: The cemetery is adjacent to a crime-ridden housing project, and you should not visit it alone. Go on a group tour (see Guided Tours, below).*

Audubon Park and Zoo

★ Rolled out across St. Charles Avenue from Tulane and Loyola universities is **Audubon Park and Zoo.** You can board the **St. Charles Streetcar** at Poydras Street and St. Charles Avenue to tool off Uptown. The Friends of the Zoo operate a free shuttle that boards in front of Tulane every 15 to 20 minutes for a ride to the zoo, which lies on the 58 acres of the park nearest the river. It is entirely possible to while away an entire day exploring Audubon Zoo. A wooden walkway strings through the zoo, and a miniature train rings around a part of it. More than 1,800 animals roam about in natural habitats, such as the **Australian exhibit,** where kangaroos hop-nob with wallabies, and the **Louisiana Swamp exhibit,** where alligators bask on the bayou. A special treat is the feeding of the sea lions, which is marked by a great deal of flapping about and barking. The **Wisner Children's Village** has a petting zoo and elephant and camel rides. ☎ *504/861–2537.* ☛ *$7.75 adults, $3.75 senior citizens and children 2–12.* ☉ *Weekdays 9:30–5; weekends (winter) 9:30–5, during daylight saving time 9:30–6.*

The 400-acre Audubon Park, with live oaks and lush tropical plants, was once part of the plantation of Etienne de Bore and his son-in-law Pierre Foucher. In 1795, de Bore figured out how to granulate sugar for commercial purposes, thereby revolutionizing the sugar industry.

In addition to the 18-hole golf course, there is a 2-mile jogging track with 18 exercise stations along the way, a stable that offers guided trail rides, and 10 tennis courts. The park is also eminently suitable for lolling about under a tree and doing nothing. Note, however, that you should *stay out of the park after dark.*

Around Town

City Park Avenue, Bayou St. John, Robert E. Lee Boulevard, and Orleans Avenue embrace the 1,500 luxuriant acres of **City Park,** which can be reached via Esplanade Avenue or the City Park bus. You can spend a great deal of time simply admiring the lagoons and majestic live oaks, whose gnarled branches bow and scrape to Mother Earth, but there is plenty to keep you busy if you are not an idler. There are four 18-hole golf courses, a double-deck driving range, 39 lighted courts in the Wisner Tennis Center, Botanical Gardens, baseball diamonds, and stables. At the casino on Dreyfous Avenue you can rent bikes, boats, and canoes—or just have a bite to eat—and at the amusement park, you can ride the turn-of-the-century carousel and miniature train. **Storyland** (☎ 504/483–9382) has puppet shows, talking storybooks, storybook exhibits, and storytelling—hence its name. Unfortunately, it is no fairy tale that City Park is *not safe at night.*

The **New Orleans Museum of Art** (NOMA), in the park, is housed in a white neoclassical building. A $23 million expansion in 1994 enabled NOMA to display virtually all of its collections of Italian paintings from the 13th to 18th centuries, 20th-century European and American paintings and sculptures, Chinese jades, and the Imperial Treasures by Peter Carl Fabergé. *City Park on Lelong Ave., ☎ 504/488–2631. ☛ $6 adults, $3 senior citizens and children 3–17; free to LA residents Thurs. 10–noon. ☉ Tues.–Sun. 10–5.*

To reach the **Pitot House** from NOMA, walk along Lelong Avenue, cross over the Bayou St. John Bridge, and make a right turn on Moss Street. Continue following Moss Street as it winds alongside the bayou, and look for the house on your left. The West Indies–style house was built in the late 18th century and bought in 1810 by New Orleans mayor James Pitot. It is furnished with Louisiana and other American 19th-century antiques. *1440 Moss St., ☎ 504/482–0312. ☛ $3 adults, $2 senior citizens, $1 children under 12. ☉ Wed.–Sat. 10–3, last tour 2:15. Sometimes closed Sat.*

★ **Longue Vue House & Gardens,** on the border between Orleans and Jefferson parishes, is about an $8 cab ride from the Quarter. It is also on the Gray Line Loop Tour (*see* Guided Tours, *below*). To describe this mansion, the word "opulent" immediately comes to mind. The house, furnished with elegant antiques, is on 8 acres of landscaped gardens. Yes, opulent is the word. *7 Bamboo Rd., ☎ 504/488–5488. ☛ $7 adults, $3 students and children, free children under 5. ☉ Mon.–Sat. 10–4:30, Sun. 1–5. Last tour begins 45 min before closing.*

What to See and Do with Children

Aquarium of the Americas (*see* Foot of Canal *in* Exploring, *above*).

Audubon Zoo (*see* Audubon Park and Zoo *in* Exploring, *above*).

City Park (*see* Around Town *in* Exploring, *above*).

Jackson Square (*see* The French Quarter *in* Exploring, *above*).

Le Petit Théâtre du Vieux Carré (616 St. Peter St., ☎ 504/522–2081). The Children's Corner often puts on plays for the little ones.

Louisiana Children's Museum has a host of educational hands-on exhibits, including a market, a TV station, and a small port. *428 Julia St. (in the Warehouse District), ☎ 504/523–1357. ☛ $4. ☉ Tues.–Sat. 9:30–5:30, Sun. noon–5:30.*

Louisiana Nature and Science Center offers an in-town taste of the surrounding swamps, an interpretive center, nature trails, and a planetarium. *11000 Lake Forest Blvd. (E. New Orleans), ☎ 504/246–5672. ☛ $4 adults, $2 children, $3 senior citizens. ☉ Tues.–Fri. 9–5, weekends noon–5.*

Musée Conti Wax Museum (*see* the French Quarter section *in* Exploring, *above*).

Riverboat Rides. Steamboat and ferry rides on the Mississippi hold a particular fascination for children. Aside from the view of the city and the water lapping at the sides of the boats, kids love to watch the big stern wheel turning. The **New Orleans Steamboat Company** (☎ 504/586–8777 or 800/233–2628) runs the mighty *Steamboat Natchez,* which cruises the harbor; the little *John James Audubon,* which cruises between the Aquarium and the Audubon Zoo; and the *Cotton Blossom,* which churns into the bayous on naturalist-narrated excursions.

Roman Candy Man. Look for the old-fashioned horse-drawn cart of the candy man just outside the zoo.

St. Charles Streetcar (*see* Getting Around, *below*).

Off the Beaten Path

Just 45 minutes by car from the French Quarter, you can sample Louisiana's exotic natural splendors in the 8,000-acre **Barataria Unit** of the **Jean Lafitte National Historical Park.** Paved walkways lace alongside bayous, over which hang frayed canopies of Spanish moss, and in which alligators, snakes, and other critters slither. Park rangers conduct free walking tours daily, but you can also wander along the trails on your own. At the **Bayou Barn** (intersection of Rtes. 31, 34, and 45, ☎ 504/689–2663 or 800/862–2968, FAX 504/689–4554), the intrepid can rent a canoe and paddle off alone ($7.50 per person for 2 hrs); the less adventuresome can hook up with one of Bayou Barn's guided tours ($20 for two hrs); and all can enjoy the fresh gumbo and jambalaya dished up daily by the friendly folks at the shop. *Just below Marrero on Lake Salvador (via U.S. 90, south of New Orleans, and Rte. 45), ☎ 504/589–2330.*

Shopping

Louisiana is the first state to grant a sales tax–rebate to non-U.S. shoppers. Look for shops, restaurants, and hotels that display the tax-free logo, then ask for a voucher for the tax, which varies from parish to parish, that's tacked onto most purchases. Present vouchers with your passport and airline ticket at the tax rebate office in New Orleans International Airport, and receive up to $500 cash back. Rebates exceeding $500 will be mailed to your home address.

Pralines, chicory coffee, Mardi Gras masks, vintage clothing, and jazz records are usually hot tickets for tourists (as well as for locals). The packaging of New Orleans food to go is a growing trend.

Shopping Districts

New Orleans shops string along the Mississippi all the way from the French Quarter to Riverbend (at the Uptown bend in the river) and beyond. The **French Quarter** is the place to search for antiques shops, art galleries, designer boutiques, bookstores, and all sorts of shops in all sorts of edifices. Among **Canal Place's** (333 Canal St.) lofty tenants you'll find Saks Fifth Avenue, Laura Ashley, Gucci, Brooks Brothers, and the wares of New Orleans jewelry designer Mignon Faget. **Riverwalk** (1 Poydras St.) is a long, tunnel-like marketplace brightened by more than 200 splashy shops, restaurants, food courts, and huge windows overlooking the Mississippi. The tony **New Orleans Centre,** between the Hyatt Regency Hotel and the Superdome on Poydras St., has more than 100 occupants, including Macy's and Lord & Taylor. Along

6 miles of **Magazine Street** are Victorian houses and small cottages filled with antiques and collectibles. Stop at the **New Orleans Welcome Center** for a copy of the shopper's guides published by the Magazine Street Merchants Association and the Royal Street Guild. Turn-of-the-century Creole cottages cradle everything from toy shops to designer boutiques and delis in the **Riverbend** (Maple St. and Carrollton Ave.). Macy's and Mervyn's are among the 155 shops in Metairie's glittering three-level **Esplanade Mall** (1401 W. Esplanade Ave.). The **Warehouse District** (bounded roughly by Girod St., Howard Ave., Camp St., and the river), particularly Julia Street, has become a major center for the visual arts, not unlike New York City's SoHo.

Department Stores

Maison Blanche department store (901 Canal St., ☎ 504/566–1000) is in the CBD, with branches in the suburban shopping centers. It carries designer labels as well as full lines of appliances and home furnishings.

Woolworth's (737 Canal St., ☎ 504/522–6426) has budget shopping to a New Orleans beat.

Specialty Stores

As You Like It (3025 Magazine St., ☎ 504/897–6915 or 800/828–2311) carries obsolete patterns in silver and silverplate.

ANTIQUES

Shoulder to shoulder along **Royal Street** are some of the finest—and oldest—antiques stores in New Orleans. **French Antique Shop** (225 Royal St., ☎ 504/524–9861) has a large selection of European chandeliers and furniture, as well as some Creole and local designs. **Lucullus** (610 Chartres St., ☎ 504/528–9620) carries fine Continental and English 17th- to 19th-century furniture, art, and cookware. **Manheim Galleries** (403–409 Royal St., ☎ 504/568–1901) has the city's largest collection of antique English, Continental, and Asian furnishings; porcelains; paintings; silver; and jade. This is the agent for Boehm Birds. **Miscenich Antiques** (834 Chartres St., ☎ 504/523–4718) has a complete selection of Baroque and Renaissance art. **Moss Antiques** (411 Royal St., ☎ 504/522–3981) has a large selection of antique and estate jewels, as well as fine French and English furnishings, paintings, and bric-a-brac. **Patout Antiques** (920 Royal St., ☎ 504/522—582) is the best place in town for antiques from Louisiana plantation houses. **M. S. Rau** (630 Royal St., ☎ 504/523–5660 or 800/544–9440) stocks American, French, English, Oriental furniture, china, glass, silver, ornamental iron, and American cut glass. **Rothschild's Antiques** (241 Royal St., ☎ 504/523–5816; 321 Royal St., ☎ 504/523–2281) has a large collection of furniture, silver, jewelry, mantels, and clocks from 18th to 20th century. **Royal Antiques** (307–309 Royal St., ☎ 504/524–7033) specializes in French and English 18th-century furnishings. **Waldhorn Company** (343 Royal St., ☎ 504/581–6379), the city's oldest antiques store, was established in 1881; specialties are English furniture, Victorian and Early American jewelry, and antique English porcelain and silver.

ART

The French Quarter is known for its many art galleries, most of which are on Royal Street. **Bergen Galleries** (730 Royal St., ☎ 504/523–7882) offers posters and collectibles by local artists. The **Black Art Collection** (309 Chartres St., ☎ 504/529–3080) displays and sells works by local and national African-American artists. **Dyansen Gallery** (433 Royal St., ☎ 504/523–2902) features the work of modern and contemporary artists. **Kurt E. Schon, Ltd.** (523 Royal St., ☎ 504/523–5902) has classic paintings from the 17th through the 20th centuries. **Merrill B. Domas American Indian Art** (824 Chartres St., ☎ 504/586–0479) offers antique and contemporary art and crafts by Native American artists. **Southern Expressions** (521 St. Ann St. at Jackson Sq., ☎ 504/525–4530) shows the work of regional artists.

FLEA MARKET
Jazz is within earshot and "junque" at your fingertips, at the **French Market Flea Market** (French Square, ☎ 504/522–2621) daily from 7 to 7.

FOOD TO GO
Bayou To Go (New Orleans International Airport, Concourse C, ☎ 504/468–8040) has a full line of Louisiana food products, including fresh, frozen, and cooked seafood packed to check or carry on the plane.

JAZZ RECORDS
You'll find the hard-to-find vintage stuff at **Record Ron's** (1129 Decatur St. and 407 Decatur St., ☎ 504/524–9444).

MASKS
For exotic handmade masks to decorate your face or your wall, try **Rumors** (513 Royal St., ☎ 504/525–0292).

PRALINES
For the best pralines in town, try **Old Town Praline Shop** (627 Royal St., ☎ 504/525–1413).

Participant Sports

Biking
In the French Quarter, Bourbon and Royal streets are often closed to all but pedalers and pedestrians. Rentals are available at **Bicycle Michael's** (622 Frenchmen St., ☎ 504/945–9505), at rates of $3.50 per hour and $12.50 per day. **French Quarter Bicycles** (522 Dumaine St., ☎ 504/529–3136) rents mountain bikes, baby strollers, and baby carriages.

Horseback Riding
Cascade Stables (6500 Magazine St., ☎ 504/891–2246) has guided 45-minute trail rides, costing $20 per person, in Audubon Park.

Tennis
There are 39 courts in the **City Park Wisner Tennis Center** (1 Dreyfous Ave. in City Park, ☎ 504/483–9383). **Audubon Park** (☎ 504/895–1042) has 10 courts near Tchoupitoulas Street.

Spectator Sports

Baseball
The AAA **New Orleans Zephyrs**, a farm team of the Milwaukee Brewers, play ball at the University of New Orleans's Privateer Park (☎ 504/282–6777). The **University of New Orleans Privateers** take on foes at the Lakefront (☎ 504/286–7240). The **Tulane Green Wave** plays home games at the school's St. Charles Avenue campus (☎ 504/861–3661).

Basketball

The **Sugar Bowl Basketball Classic** (tel 504/525–8573) is played in the Superdome the week preceding the annual football classic.

Football

The **New Orleans Saints** (☎ 504/522–2600) play NFL games in the Superdome. Home games of **Tulane University** (☎ 504/861–3661) are also played in the Dome. The annual **Sugar Bowl Football Classic** (☎ 504/525–8573) is played in the Dome on New Year's Day, and in late November the **Bayou Classic** (☎ 504/587–3663) pits Southern University against Grambling University. In 1997, the Superdome will host the Super Bowl.

Dining

By Gene Bourg

New Orleans usually means excellent dining. The Big Easy is recognized almost as much for hot and spicy culinary delights as it is for hot and steamy jazz. Louisiana styles of cooking are becoming increasingly popular worldwide—but what is a fad elsewhere is a tradition here.

Apart from Galatoire's, where people stand in line to be served on a first-come basis, you are strongly advised to make reservations and to book well in advance for weekends, particularly during holiday periods or conventions.

Lunch hours are 11:30 AM to 2:30 PM. Dinner is almost always served from 6 to 10 PM, although some restaurants offer "early bird" dinner specials for those who don't mind eating about 5:30 PM.

As a general rule, expect to tip from 15% to 20%. Most establishments do not automatically add a service charge.

What to Wear

Pricey restaurants adhere to a moderate dress code—jackets for men, and in some places, a tie. New Orleans is a conservative city; dining out is an honored ritual, and people are expected to dress the part. A man in faded jeans and sports coat may be turned away, and even if he isn't he may not feel entirely welcome. Credit cards are accepted in most, but not all, dining establishments; it's wise to check in advance.

The following terms will appear frequently throughout this section:

Andouille (an-*dooey*)—Cajun sausage made with pork blade meat, onion, smoked flavorings, and garlic.
Bananas Foster—a dessert of bananas sautéed with butter, brown sugar, and cinnamon, flambéed in white rum and banana liqueur, and served on ice cream.
Barbecue shrimp—large shrimp baked in the shell, covered with butter, rosemary, herbs, and spices. They are not barbecued at all.
Boudin (boo-*dan*)—hot, spicy pork with onions, rice, and herbs stuffed in sausage casing.
Courtbouillon (coo-bee-*yon*)—a thick, hearty soup made with a roux, vegetables, and fish, and served over rice.
Crawfish—also known as "mud-bugs," because they live in the mud of freshwater streams. They resemble miniature lobsters and are served in a great variety of ways.
Etouffée (ay-too-*fay*)—crawfish étouffée is made with a butter and flour roux of celery and onion, then cooked for a short period of time and served over rice. Shrimp étouffée is heartier, made with an oil and flour

roux or tomato paste, celery, onion, bell pepper, tomatoes, and chicken stock, cooked for approximately an hour and served over rice.

Filé (fee-*lay*)—ground sassafras, used to season gumbo and many other Creole specialties.

Grillades (gree-*yads*)—bite-size pieces of veal rounds or beef chuck, braised in red wine, beef stock, garlic, herbs, and seasoning, served for brunch with grits and with rice for dinner.

Gumbo—a hearty soup prepared in a variety of combinations (okra gumbo, shrimp gumbo, chicken gumbo, to name a few).

Jambalaya (jum-bo-*lie*-yah)—a spicy rice dish cooked with stock and chopped seasoning, and made with any number of ingredients including sausage, shrimp, ham, and chicken.

Muffuletta—a large, round loaf of bread filled with cheese, ham, and salami smothered in a heavy, garlicky olive salad.

Praline (*praw*-leen)—candy patty most commonly made from sugar, water or butter, and pecans. There are many different flavors and kinds.

Rémoulade—a cold dressing that accompanies shrimp (sometimes crabmeat) over shredded lettuce, made of mayonnaise and Creole mustard, oil and vinegar, horseradish, paprika, celery, and green onion.

New Orleans is renowned for *Creole* cuisine. A Creole, by definition, is a person of French or Spanish ancestry born in the New World. However, Creole is also a word of elastic implications, and in culinary terms, Creole refers to a distinctive cuisine indigenous to New Orleans that has its roots in European dishes, enhanced by the liberal usage of local seasonings such as filé. The French influence is also strong, but the essence of Creole is in sauces, herbs, and the prominent use of seafood.

In recent years the term *Nouvelle Creole* has been popularized by local restaurateurs. Instead of gumbo or jambalaya, a nouvelle menu might include hickory-grilled items, seafood served with pasta, or smoked meats and fish. There has also been a strong Italian influence in Creole cuisine in the last decade, creating yet another marriage of styles.

The initial restaurant listings here are divided into four Creole categories: *Classic Creole,* restaurants devoted to traditional Louisiana cuisine with minimal French overtones; *French Creole,* indicating a more expansive Continental accent; *Soul Creole,* black cuisine of Creole origin; and *Creole-inspired,* meaning the newer breed of cooking styles that incorporate Nouvelle Creole dishes, new American cooking, and classic Creole. Please note that the above categories often overlap; it is not unusual to find a blend of varying Creole cuisines on any given menu.

Cajun cuisine was brought from Nova Scotia to the bayou country by the Acadians more than 250 years ago. Cajun cooks generally use less expensive ingredients than their Creole counterparts, and they are heavy-handed on the herbs and spices.

Cajun cuisine is rarely served in its purest form in New Orleans; rather it is often blended with Creole to create what's known as "New Orleans–style" cooking. There is a difference, though, between the two: Creole is distinguished by its rich and heavy sauces; Cajun, by its tendency to be spicy and hot.

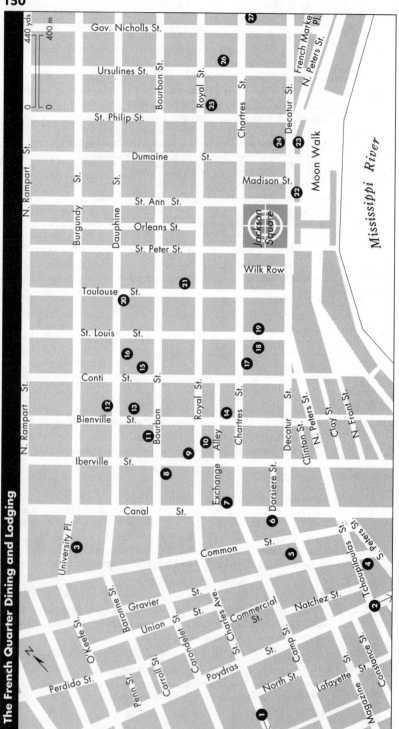

The French Quarter Dining and Lodging

Gov. Nicholls St.

Ursulines St.

St. Philip St.

Bourbon St.

Royal St.

Chartres St.

Decatur St.

N. Peters St.

French Market Pl.

Dumaine St.

Madison St.

Moon Walk

Mississippi River

N. Rampart St.

Burgundy St.

Dauphine St.

St. Ann St.

Orleans St.

St. Peter St.

Jackson Square

Wilk Row

Toulouse St.

St. Louis St.

Conti St.

Bourbon St.

Royal St.

Chartres St.

Decatur St.

Clinton St.

N. Peters St.

Clay St.

N. Front St.

Bienville St.

Iberville St.

Exchange Alley

Dorsiere St.

Canal St.

University Pl.

Common St.

S. Peters St.

Tchoupitoulas St.

Baronne St.

Gravier St.

Union St.

St. Charles Ave.

Commercial St.

Natchez St.

O'Keefe St.

Carondelet St.

Camp St.

Magazine St.

Constance St.

Penn St.

Carroll St.

Poydras St.

North St.

Lafayette St.

Perdido St.

440 yds
400 m

N

151

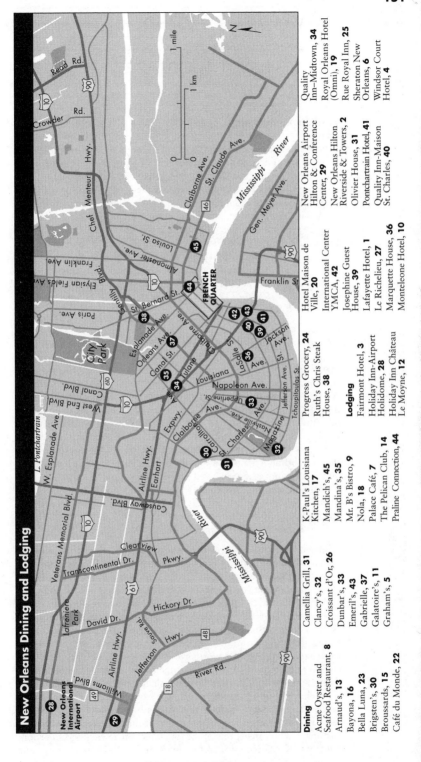

New Orleans Dining and Lodging

Dining
Acme Oyster and
Seafood Restaurant, **8**
Arnaud's, **13**
Bayona, **16**
Bella Luna, **23**
Brigsten's, **30**
Broussards, **15**
Café du Monde, **22**

Camellia Grill, **31**
Clancy's, **32**
Croissant d'Or, **26**
Dunbar's, **33**
Emeril's, **43**
Gabrielle, **37**
Galatoire's, **11**
Graham's, **5**

K-Paul's Louisiana
Kitchen, **17**
Mandich's, **45**
Mandina's, **35**
Mr. B's Bistro, **9**
Nola, **18**
Palace Café, **7**
The Pelican Club, **14**
Praline Connection, **44**

Progress Grocery, **24**
Ruth's Chris Steak
House, **38**

Lodging
Fairmont Hotel, **3**
Holiday Inn-Airport
Holidome, **28**
Holiday Inn Château
Le Moyne, **12**

Hotel Maison de
Ville, **20**
International Center
YMCA, **42**
Josephine Guest
House, **39**
Lafayette Hotel, **1**
Le Richelieu, **27**
Marquette House, **36**
Monteleone Hotel, **10**

New Orleans Airport
Hilton & Conference
Center, **29**
New Orleans Hilton
Riverside & Towers, **2**
Olivier House, **31**
Pontchartrain Hotel, **41**
Quality Inn-Maison
St. Charles, **40**

Quality
Inn-Midtown, **34**
Royal Orleans Hotel
(Omni), **19**
Rue Royal Inn, **25**
Sheraton New
Orleans, **6**
Windsor Court
Hotel, **4**

CATEGORY	COST*
$$$$	over $35
$$$	$25–$35
$$	$15–$25
$	under $15

*per person for a three-course meal, excluding drinks, service, and 9% sales tax

Louisiana Cuisine

CAJUN-INSPIRED

$$$ K-Paul's Louisiana Kitchen. Chef Paul Prudhomme started the blackening craze and added "Cajun" to America's culinary vocabulary in this rustic French Quarter café. Almost a decade later, thousands still consider a visit to New Orleans partly wasted without a long wait outside for his inventive gumbos, fried crawfish tails, blackened tuna, roast duck with rice dressing, and sweet potato–pecan pie. Although servings are generous, the prices are steep at dinner but moderate at lunch. Some diners may be put off by the community seating downstairs, and the custom of putting a gold paper star on your cheek if you clean your plate. The jalapeño-laced martinis are served in canning jars, and the guru himself makes an occasional appearance. ✗ *416 Chartres St., French Quarter,* ☎ *504/524–7394. Reservations accepted for dinner upstairs. AE. Closed Sun. and Mon.*

CLASSIC CREOLE

$$$$ Arnaud's. This is one of the grandes dames of classic Creole restaurants, and it still sparkles, thanks to a major face-lift made a decade ago. The main dining room's outside wall of ornate etched glass reflects light from the charming old chandeliers, while the late founder, Arnaud Cazenave, gazes from an oil portrait near the extra-high ceiling. When the main room fills up, the overflow spills over into a labyrinth of plush banquet rooms and bars. The big, ambitious menu includes classic dishes that have been around for decades, as well as some new creations in a more contemporary style. Always reliable are the cold shrimp Arnaud in a superb rémoulade, the creamy oyster stew, and rich shrimp bisque, as well as the fish in crawfish sauce, the beef Wellington, and the fine crème brûlée. Expect hurried service on especially crowded nights, but rely on the reservations desk to perform efficiently. ✗ *813 Bienville St., French Quarter,* ☎ *504/523–5433. Reservations required. Jacket required. AE, D, DC, MC, V.*

$$$ Brigtsen's. Chef Frank Brigtsen's fusion of Creole refinement and Aca-
★ dian earthiness reflects his years as a protégé of Paul Prudhomme. The owner-chef's ever-changing menus add up to some of the best South Louisiana cooking you'll find anywhere. Everything is fresh and filled with the deep and complex tastes that characterize Creole-Cajun food. The cream of oysters Rockefeller soup is a revelation. Rabbit and chicken dishes, usually presented in rich sauces and gravies, are full of robust flavor. The roux-based gumbos are thick and intense, and the fresh banana ice cream is worth every calorie. Fans of blackened food couldn't do better than with this prime rib, in a spicy charred coating that is perfect with the meat flavors. Fish dishes are likewise elaborate, often showing up as crawfish, shrimp, or oysters in buttery, seasoned sauces. The simple surroundings remain as they were when this was a long, narrow-frame cottage at the turn of the century. Lucky are the customers who can get one of the two tables on an enclosed sun room out front. ✗ *723 Dante St., Uptown,* ☎ *504/861–7610. Reservations required (call a week or more in advance). AE, MC, V. Closed Sun. and Mon.*

$$$ Clancy's. The easy, sophisticated charm and consistently classy menu have made this minimally decorated bistro a favorite with professional and business types from nearby uptown neighborhoods. Most of the dishes are imaginative treatments of New Orleans favorites. Some specialties, like the fresh sautéed fish in cream sauce flavored with crawfish stock and herbs, are exceptional. Other signs of an inventive chef are the sweetbreads in cream, mustard, and basil; the expertly fried oysters matched with warm Brie; the grilled chicken breast in lime butter; and a marvelous peppermint ice-cream pie. Simpler dishes like fettucine Alfredo and filet mignon in Madeira sauce benefit from careful and knowledgeable preparation. The decor is neutral, with grey walls and a few ceiling fans above bentwood chairs and white linen cloths. The small bar separating the two rooms is usually filled with regulars who know each other. ✗ *6100 Annunciation St., Uptown,* ☎ *504/895–1111. Reservations advised. AE, MC, V. No lunch Mon. and Tues. Closed Sun.*

$$$ Gabrielle. This bright and energetic newcomer, about five minutes by
★ taxi from the French Quarter, was an immediate hit with locals, thanks to chef Greg Sonnier's marvelous interpretations of earthy and spicy South Louisiana dishes. Spaces are tight in the single dining room, its pale walls hung with pleasant pastel still lifes. Regulars come for the spicy rabbit and veal sausages, buttery oysters gratinéed with artichoke and Parmesan, a slew of excellent gumbos and étouffées, and Mary Sonnier's fresh-fruit cobblers and shortcakes. Servings are generous and sauces are rich, so you may want to skip lunch before dining here. ✗ *3201 Esplanade Ave., Mid-City,* ☎ *504/948–6233. Reservations advised. AE, DC, MC, V. No lunch Tues.–Thurs. and Sat. Closed Sun. and Mon.*

$$ Mandich's. This many-faceted favorite of locals resists categorizing. It occupies a neat but unremarkable building in a blue-collar neighborhood. The decor—a mix of bright yellow paint, captain's chairs, and wood veneer—won't win prizes. The food ranges from straight-forward, home-style dishes to ambitious trout and shellfish dishes. Fried oysters are swathed in a finely balanced butter sauce with garlic and parsley. Shrimp and andouille sausages trade flavors on the grill. The breaded trout Mandich has become a classic of the genre, and more garlic boosts slices of buttery roasted potatoes. Prices are rather steep for a restaurant that invests little in decoration, accepts no reservations, and opens for dinner only two nights a week. ✗ *3200 St. Claude Ave., Ninth Ward,* ☎ *504/947–9533. MC, V. No dinner Tues.–Thurs., no lunch Sat. Closed Sun. and Mon.*

CREOLE-INSPIRED

$$$ Emeril's. For many seasoned restaurant goers in New Orleans, Emeril's
★ is the pacesetter for Creole cuisine in the 1990s. Proprietor-chef Emeril Lagasse, former executive chef at Commander's Palace, opened this large, noisy, and decidedly contemporary restaurant in early 1990 with an ambitious menu that gives equal emphasis to Creole and modern American cooking. On the plate, this translates as a fresh corn crêpe topped with Louisiana caviar, grilled andouille sausage in the chef's own Worcestershire sauce, a sauté of crawfish over jambalaya cakes, fresh fruit cobblers, and a cornucopia of other creative dishes. Singles and couples can grab a stool at a food bar and get close-up views of the chef at work while they eat. The looks of the place are appropriately avant-garde—brick and glass walls, gleaming wood floors, burnished-aluminum lamps, and a huge abstract-expressionist oil painting. ✗ *800 Tchoupitoulas St., Warehouse District,* ☎ *504/528–9393.*

Reservations strongly advised, at least several days in advance. AE, DC, MC, V. No lunch Sat. Closed Sun.

$$$ Mr. B's Bistro. The energy never seems to subside in this attractive, smart French Quarter restaurant, with waiters darting between the wood and glass screens that reduce the vastness of the dining room. On the green vinyl banquettes, diners choose from a dependable contemporary-Creole menu centering on meats and seafood from a grill fueled with hickory and other aromatic woods. The barbecue shrimp is one of the best versions in town. Pasta dishes, especially the pasta jambalaya with andouille sausage and shrimp, are fresh and imaginative. The traditional-style bread pudding with Irish whiskey sauce is excellent, too. Lunchtime finds most of the tables taken up by locals, who like the correctly composed club sandwich, pasta carbonara, and other main attractions from the fixed-price menu. ✕ *201 Royal St., French Quarter,* ☎ *504/523–2078. Reservations advised. AE, D, DC, MC, V.*

$$$ Nola. Fans of chef Emeril Lagasse's who can't get a table at Emeril's in the Warehouse District now have this sassy and vibrant French Quarter restaurant as an alternative. Lagasse has not lowered his sights with Nola's menu, as lusty and rich as any in town. He stews boudin sausage with beer, onions, cane syrup, and Creole mustard before landing it all onto a sweet-potato crouton. Trout is swathed in a horseradish-citrus crust before it's plank-roasted in a wood oven. Pasta comes laden with sautéed eggplant and a sauce of smoked tomatoes and Parmesan. The combinations seem endless. At dessert time, go for the coconut cream or apple-buttermilk pie with cinnamon ice cream ✕ *534 St. Louis St., French Quarter,* ☎ *504/522–6652. AE, D, DC, MC, V. No lunch Sun.*

$$$ Palace Café. Members of the Commander's Palace branch of the Brennan family operate this big and colorful new restaurant on Canal Street just a few blocks from the Mississippi riverfront. Crafted from a multistory building that was the city's oldest music store, the Palace is a convivial spot to try some of the more imaginative contemporary Creole dishes. The crab chops, rabbit ravioli in piquante sauce, grilled shrimp with fettucine, and seafood Napoleon represent the best in both traditional and modern New Orleans cookery. Desserts, especially the white-chocolate bread pudding and Mississippi mud pie, are luscious. An easy elegance pervades the restaurant's two levels. Out front, the sidewalk tables are an excellent vantage point for people-watching along bustling Canal Street. ✕ *605 Canal St., Central Business District,* ☎ *504/523–1661. Weekend reservations advised. AE, DC, MC, V.*

FRENCH CREOLE

$$$$ Broussards. No French Quarter restaurant surpasses Broussard's for old-fashioned spectacle. A complete overhaul in the 1970s turned a dowdy Creole bistro into a soft-edged, glittery mix of elaborate wall coverings, chandeliers, porcelain, and polished woods, with a manicured courtyard to boot. If the menu blazes no trails, it contains respectable renditions of the fancier Creole standbys further upgraded with Continental touches. The savory cheesecake of crab and shrimp with dill and roasted sweet peppers is a star among the appetizers, along with lumps of backfin crab in a spicy sauce. Other luxurious sauces crown fillets of fresh pompano, braised quail, and a rack of lamb. Desserts are especially fancy, such as the layers of ice creams and sorbets wrapped in meringue. ✕ *819 Conti St., French Quarter,* ☎ *504/581–3866. Reservations advised. AE, D, DC, MC, V. No lunch Sat.–Thurs.*

$$ **Galatoire's.** A 90-year-old restaurant that seems as fresh as it was at 20, Galatoire's epitomizes the old-style French-Creole bistro. Few customers tire of the lengthy menu, filled with sauces that can be humdrum in lesser restaurants but somehow escape staleness in this one. The answer may lie in the staff's high standards for ingredients and recipes, which have been fine-tuned over decades. Fried oysters and bacon en brochette court excess but are worth every calorie. The brick-red rémoulade sauce is the touchstone to measure all others against. Lumps of crabmeat, served either cold in a seasoned mayonnaise or warm atop buttery broiled pompano, never tasted better. Others on the long list of time-tested winners include a Creole-based bouillabaisse, meaty veal or spring lamb chops in béarnaise sauce, seafood-stuffed eggplant, and earthy lyonnaise potatoes. The setting is close to perfect—a single, narrow dining room lit with glistening brass chandeliers, swathed in white-framed mirror panels, and bordered with polished brass coat hooks. The bentwood chairs at the white-clothed tables add to the timeless atmosphere. The quality of service varies from waiter to waiter; the best strategy is to ask for recommendations and then be assertive. Long waits in the line outside sometimes can be avoided by eating early. ✕ 209 Bourbon St., French Quarter, ☎ 504/525–2021. No reservations. Jacket required at dinner. MC, V. Closed Mon.

SOUL CREOLE

$ **Dunbar's.** Red tufted booths and homey, brightly colored paintings perk up the atmosphere at this diamond-in-the-rough, where home-style Creole cooking is king. Owner-chef Tina Dunbar's fried chicken takes a back seat to none other, and her stuffed sweet peppers, red beans, fried-seafood po-boys, and mustard greens are state-of-the-art as well. Prices are the next best thing to free, and students who produce ID cards get free iced tea. You're not likely to spend more than $5 or $6 for a very filling dinner here, and substantial breakfasts can be had for about $2, all-inclusive. ✕ 4927 Freret St., Uptown, ☎ 504/899–0734. Reservations for large groups only. MC, V.

$ **Praline Connection.** Down-home cooking in the Southern-Creole style
★ is the forte of this laid-back and likeable restaurant a couple of blocks from the French Quarter, with a branch in the Warehouse District as well. The food is the no-nonsense kind that has fueled generations of Southern families, urban and rural, rich and poor. The fried or stewed chicken, smothered pork chops, barbecued ribs, and collard greens are definitively done. And the soulful filé gumbo, crowder beans, bread pudding, and sweet-potato pie are among the best in town. Add to all this some of the lowest prices anywhere, a congenial service staff, and a neat-as-a-pin dining room and the sum is a fine place to spend an hour or two. The adjacent sweet shop holds such home-style delights as sweet-potato cookies, several types of Creole pralines, and all sorts of pies and confections. ✕ 542 Frenchmen St., Faubourg Marigny, ☎ 504/943–3934.; 901 S. Peters St., Warehouse District, ☎ 504/523–3973. MC, V. No lunch Sat. Closed Sun.

Avant-Garde

$$$ **Bayona.** "New World" is the label chef Susan Spicer applies to her cook-
★ ing style—such dishes as turnovers filled with spicy crawfish tails; a bisque of corn, leeks, and chicken; or fresh salmon fillet in white-wine sauce with sauerkraut. Her grilled duck breast with pepper-jelly glaze and shrimp with coriander sauce are among the creations that originally made Spicer's reputation at her previous post, the Bistro at Maison de Ville. These and myriad other imaginative dishes are served in an early 19th-century Creole cottage on a quiet French Quarter street.

The chef herself supervised the renovation of the handsome building, now fairly glowing with oversized flower arrangements, elegant photographs, and, in one small dining room, trompe l'oeil murals suggesting Mediterranean landscapes. In good weather drinks and meals are served in a rear patio overflowing with tropical greenery. ✗ *430 Dauphine St., French Quarter,* ☎ *504/525–4455. Reservations strongly advised. AE, DC, MC, V. Closed Sun.*

$$$ **Bella Luna.** If luxurious surroundings, imaginative food, and a knock-out view of the Mississippi River are high on your list of priorities, this elegantly turned out restaurant in the French market complex should fill the bill. Handsome French-style windows line one wall in the plush main dining room, offering overhead views of the riverbank and the ships and excursion boats gliding by. The second dining space is enclosed on three sides by even more glass, exposing the river on one side, the city skyline straight on, and French Quarter rooftops on the other side. The kitchen takes an eclectic approach, although the strongest accent is Italian. Good bets are the pastas, especially penne with roasted eggplant, Gorgonzola, peppers, and fried herbs in Fontina Sauce. The robust osso buco is a straightforward delight, as is the coconut meringue pie. Fancier fare includes a delicious grouping of quesadillas filled with smoked shrimp and spicy goat cheese. ✗ *French Market complex near the corner of Decatur and Dumaine Sts., French Quarter,* ☎ *504/529–1583. Reservations advised. AE, DC, MC, V. No lunch.*

$$$ **Graham's.** Not so much as a swatch of fabric hangs on the 10 tall arched windows in the dining room at Graham's, and little else intrudes on the flat whiteness of the walls. Although the kitchen puts a premium on simply prepared dishes, the food supplies most of the color at this establishment, with its bare tabletops of dark-green granite. From the Windsor Court Hotel, his previous post, English-born proprietor-chef Kevin Graham has brought over a few of his most celebrated dishes, most notably the duck "lacquered" with chicory coffee and oranges. A luxurious cream sauce covers his roasted monkfish and horseradish-glazed oysters. Seared yellowfin tuna is glossed with a marmalade of star anise and lemon, and one of the soups is a match-up of aromatic vegetable bisques, mushroom, and tomato in a single bowl. Desserts can be uncomplicated, as in a crumbly almond tart with amaretto, or very innovative, as in the warm, sweetened polenta flavored with vanilla and topped with mascarpone. The modest wine list takes a back seat to the food. And all the hard surfaces make for a high noise level. ✗ *200 Magazine St., in the Pelham Hotel, Central Business District,* ☎ *504/524–9678. Reservations advised. AE, DC, MC, V. No lunch Sat.*

$$$ **Pelican Club.** Sassy New York flourishes are found throughout the menu
★ of this smartly decorated but eminently comfortable place in the heart of the French Quarter. Still, evidence of chef Richard Hughes' South Louisiana origins also keeps popping up. Hughes spent seven years in Manhattan as the top chef of the acclaimed Memphis. In three handsome dining rooms inside a balconied old town house, he turns out a stew of shellfish that's a clever improvisation on both San Francisco's cioppino and Louisiana's bouillabaisse. A touch of saffron in his jambalaya of chicken, sausage, and shellfish makes it a cousin of Spain's paella. Closer to home are red snapper stuffed with crabmeat; a bisque of bourbon, crab, and corn; and a crème brûlée in the grandest French-Creole tradition. Each of the dining rooms, hung with consignment art from local galleries, has its own ambience. ✗ *615 Bienville St., French*

Quarter, ☎ *504/523–1504. Reservations advised. AE, D, DC, MC, V. No lunch.*

Back to Basics

DESSERT

$ Croissant d'Or. Locals compete with tourists for a table in this color-
★ ful and pristine pastry shop that serves excellent and authentic French croissants, pies, tarts, and custards, as well as an imaginative selection of soups, salads, and sandwiches. Wash them down with real French breakfast coffee, cappuccino, or espresso. In good weather, the cheerful courtyard, with its quietly gurgling fountain, is the place to sit. A filling lunch can be had for less than $10. ✕ *617 Ursulines St., French Quarter,* ☎ *504/524–4663. No credit cards.* ☉ *Daily 7 AM–5 PM.*

GRILLS AND COFFEE SHOPS

$ Café du Monde. For most visitors, no trip to New Orleans would be
★ complete without a cup of chicory-laced café au lait and a few sugar-dusted beignets in this venerable Creole institution. The dozens of tables, inside or out in the open air, are jammed at almost any hour with locals and tourists feasting on the views of Jackson Square and the hubbub on Decatur Street. The magical time to go is just before dawn, when the bustle subsides and you can almost hear the birds in the crepe myrtles across the way. ✕ *In the French Market, Decatur and St. Ann Sts., French Quarter,* ☎ *504/525–4544. No credit cards.* ☉ *Daily 24 hrs.*

$ Camellia Grill. Every diner should be as classy as Camellia Grill, a one-
★ of-a-kind eatery that deserves its following. Locals vie until the early morning hours for one of the 29 stools at the gleaming counter, each place supplied with a large, fresh linen napkin. The hamburger—four ounces of excellent beef on a fresh bun with any number of embellishments—is unexcelled in the city. Other blue-ribbon dishes are the chili, the fruit and meringue pies, the garnished omelets, and the "cannibal special"—uncooked hamburger and egg with chopped onion on rye. To wash it down, try an orange or coffee freeze with ice cream. Everything's made on the premises and served by bow-tied, white-waist coated waiters with the fastest feet in the business. ✕ *626 S. Carrollton Ave., Uptown,* ☎ *504/866–9573. No credit cards.*

$ Progress Grocery and Central Grocery. These two old-fashioned Italian grocery stores in the French Quarter produce authentic muffulettas, one of the greatest gastronomic gifts of the city's Italian immigrants. They're good enough to challenge the po'boy as the local sandwich champ, and are made by filling soft round loaves of seeded bread with ham, salami, mozzarella, and a salad of marinated chopped green olives. Each sandwich, about 10 inches in diameter, is sold in quarters and halves. Central is better known, but Progress comes up with a sandwich that many neighborhood folks prefer because it's cheaper, more generous, and available in several varieties. You can eat your muffuletta at a counter in either place, but some prefer to take them out to a bench on Jackson Square or the Moon Walk along the Mississippi Riverfront, both just a few blocks away. ✕ *Progress: 915 Decatur St., French Quarter,* ☎ *504/525–6627.* ☉ *Mon.–Sat. 8 AM–5:30 PM. Central: 923 Decatur St.,* ☎ *504/523–1620.* ☉ *Daily 8 AM–5:30 PM.*

SEAFOOD

$ Acme Oyster and Seafood Restaurant. A rough-edged classic in every way, this no-nonsense eatery at the entrance to the French Quarter is a prime source of cool and salty raw oysters on the half shell; great shrimp, oyster, and roast-beef po-boys; and state-of-the-art red beans and rice. Table service is offered in the front dining room. If the tables are all taken, expect rather lengthy queues at the marble-topped oyster bar and cafeteria-style sandwich counter during peak lunch hours. Crowds are sparser in the late afternoon. And don't expect coddling. ✗ *724 Iberville St., French Quarter,* ☎ *504/522–5973. No reservations. AE, DC, MC, V. Closes at 10 PM Fri. and Sat., earlier on other nights.*

$ Mandina's. The interior of this white clapboard corner building is a study in 1940s nostalgia, with its functional bar facing a roomful of laminated tables set with sugar shakers, hot sauce, and salt and pepper. Regulars—a cross section of the population—endure a ¼-hour wait for a table under a 30-year-old newspaper clipping or the latest artwork from a St. Louis brewery. Butter, hearty seasonings, and tomato sauce are the staples. The shrimp rémoulade and old-fashioned gumbo are the logical appetizers. Broiled trout and shrimp, wading in seasoned butter, are tasty, as are the fried oysters and shrimp, the seafood or Italian sausage po-boys, and the super-sweet bread pudding. Service amounts to little more than taking and delivering orders. ✗ *3800 Canal St., Mid-City,* ☎ *504/482–9179. No reservations. No credit cards.*

STEAKS

$$$ Ruth's Chris Steak House. Ruth's Chris is sacred to New Orleans steak
★ lovers. The all-American menu fairly drips with butter, and the main draw is aged U.S. prime beef in he-man portions, charbroiled and served atop a sizzling seasoned butter sauce. Carefree locals often order a side of bordelaise sauce to add to the excess. The hefty filet mignon is often taller than it is wide, the New York strip is usually packed with flavor, and a monstrous porterhouse serves several. If the salads lack sparkle, the copious potato dishes are consistently first-rate, especially the julienne, shoestring, and lyonnaise. Lighter entrées (chicken breast, veal, seafoods) were added recently to mollify the health-conscious. The large plush, but unfussy dining rooms of the flagship Mid-City restaurant are lined in pale wood paneling and understated landscape paintings. Politicians, both actual and aspiring, are everywhere. The drinks are generous, and the energetic waitresses rarely falter. ✗ *711 N. Broad St., Mid-City,* ☎ *504/486–0810; 3633 Veterans Blvd., Metairie,* ☎ *504/888–3600. Reservations strongly advised, especially on weekends. AE, D, DC, MC, V.*

Lodging

Visitors to New Orleans have a wide variety of accommodations to choose from: posh high-rise hotels, antiques-filled antebellum homes, Creole cottages, or old slave quarters.

Always try to reserve well ahead, especially during Mardi Gras or other seasonal events (the Super Bowl will be played here in 1997). Frequently, hotels offer special packages at reduced rates, but never during Mardi Gras, when almost every accommodation doubles its rates and many require a 3- to 5-day minimum stay.

CATEGORY	COST*
$$$$	over $120
$$$	$90–$120
$$	$50–$90
$	under $50

All prices are for a standard double room, excluding 11% tax and a $1–$3 per room per night surcharge

Hotels

CENTRAL BUSINESS DISTRICT

Staying in the Central Business District will appeal to visitors who prefer accommodations in luxurious high-rise hotels. Hotels listed here are within walking distance of the French Quarter, but shuttles, taxis, buses, and the streetcar are available. *Walking in this area after dark is not recommended.*

$$$$ **Fairmont Hotel.** The Fairmont, which celebrated its 100th birthday in 1993 with a $22-million renovation, is one of the oldest grand hotels in America. The blue and gold Victorian splendor of the massive lobby evokes a more elegant and gracious era. The hotel is composed of three connected historic buildings. Special touches in every room include four down pillows, electric shoe-buffers, and bathroom scales. Suites have fax machines. Impressive murals depicting life in the South enliven the walls of the famed Sazerac Bar. The Sazerac Restaurant has an old-fashioned look. ⊞ *123 Burrone St., 70140,* ☎ *504/529–7111 or 800/527–4727,* ℻ *504/529–4775. 685 rooms, 50 suites. 4 restaurants, 4 bars, room service, pool, beauty salon, health club, 2 tennis courts, parking. AE, D, DC, MC, V.*

$$$$
★ **Lafayette Hotel.** This small brick dwelling has housed a Lafayette Hotel since it was built in 1916. The original hotel became seedy during the 1950s and eventually closed in 1985. After a $7.5 million renovation, however, it reopened in late 1991 to rave reviews. Special features are the handsome millwork, brass fittings, and marble baths throughout. The lobby is tiny but chic; rooms are spacious and sunny. Some have four-posters; each has cushy easy chairs and ottomans, in-room safes, terry-cloth robes, and closets with full-length mirrors—there are even books on the bookshelves. Though there's no pool, guests receive reduced admission to a nearby health club. ⊞ *600 St. Charles Ave., 70130,* ☎ *504/524–4441 or 800/733–4754,* ℻ *504/523–7327. 24 rooms, 20 suites with bath. Restaurant, no-smoking rooms, laundry service and dry cleaning, concierge, meeting rooms, parking. AE, D, DC, MC, V.*

$$$$
★ **Windsor Court Hotel.** Exquisite, gracious, elegant, eminently civilized—these words are frequently used to describe Windsor Court, but all fail to capture its wonderful quality. Le Salon's scrumptious high tea is served each afternoon in the lobby. Plush carpeting, canopy and four-poster beds, stocked wet bars, marble vanities, oversize mirrors, dressing areas—all contribute to the elegance and luxury of the Windsor Court. The hotel is across from the new Harrah's casino site and four blocks from the French Quarter. ⊞ *300 Gravier St., 70130,* ☎ *504/523–6000 or 800/262–2662,* ℻ *504/596–4513. 58 rooms, 266 suites. 2 restaurants, lounge, pool, hot tub, sauna, steam room, health club, laundry service, parking. AE, DC, MC, V.*

$$–$$$$ **New Orleans Hilton Riverside & Towers.** It's on the banks of the Mississippi, with Riverwalk sprawled out around it, the *Flamingo* riverboat casino (*see* Nightlife, *below*) docked almost on its doorstep, and the New Orleans Convention Center just down the street. Pete Fountain's Club (*see* Nightlife, *below*) is here. The River Center Tennis & Racquetball Club is a handy spot for working off calories. VIPs check into the Tower suites, where a concierge looks after things, but the best views of the river are in the appropriately named Riverside section. ⊞ *2 Poydras St., 70140,* ☎ *504/561–0500 or 800/445–8667,* ℻ *504/525–8636. 1,602 rooms, 86 suites. 3 restaurants, 6 lounges, 2 pools, tennis and racquetball club, business services. AE, D, DC, MC, V.*

$$–$$$$
★ **Sheraton New Orleans.** On Canal Street, across from the French Quarter, the Sheraton has an impressive lobby, decked out with a spiral stair-

case and player grand piano. A tropical atmosphere permeates its Gazebo Lounge, which features jazz nightly. Café Promenade encircles the second level. Executive rooms on the top floors come with many special amenities. The Waterbury Health Club is a superb facility. Usually bustling with conventioneers, this upscale Sheraton gets high marks for above-average rooms and top-quality service. ☎ *500 Canal St., 70130,* ☎ *504/525–2500 or 800/325–3535,* FAX *504/492–5615. 1,100 rooms, 72 suites. 3 restaurants, 2 lounges, no-smoking rooms, pool, health club, gift shop, valet service, parking. AE, D, DC, MC, V.*

$$ **Quality Inn–Midtown.** Too far to walk but only a short drive from the French Quarter. Rooms are motel-modern, as you would expect of a Quality Inn. ☎ *3900 Tulane Ave., 70119,* ☎ *504/486–5541 or 800/228–5151,* FAX *504/561–5858. 102 rooms. Restaurant, lounge, no-smoking rooms, pool, whirlpool, airport shuttle. AE, D, DC, MC, V.*

FRENCH QUARTER

Since most people who visit New Orleans stay in the Quarter, the 96-square-block area abounds with every type of guest accommodation. The selections that follow are all quality establishments chosen to provide variety in location, atmosphere, and price. Reservations are usually a must.

$$$$ **Monteleone Hotel.** The grande dame—and oldest hotel—of the Quar-★ ter, with its ornate Baroque facade, liveried doormen, and shimmering lobby chandeliers, was built in 1886. Rooms are extra large and luxurious, each decorated differently. Fabrics are rich, and there is a mix of four-posters, brass-frame beds, and beds with traditional headboards. Junior suites have a spacious combo bedroom and living room; some have four-posters with mirrored testers. Some bathrooms are too small, but many have phones. For extra pampering, stay in one of the opulent VIP suites. The exercise room and pool are on the roof. A slowly revolving Carousel Bar in the lobby is a New Orleans landmark. ☎ *214 Royal St., 70140,* ☎ *504/523–3341 or 800/535–9595,* FAX *504/528–1019. 600 rooms, 35 suites. 3 restaurants, 2 bars, pool, barbershop/beauty salon, exercise room, concierge, business services, meeting rooms. AE, DC, MC, V.*

$$$–$$$$ **Hotel Maison de Ville.** This small, romantic hotel lies in seclusion amid ★ the hustle and bustle of the French Quarter. Tapestry-covered chairs, a fire burning in the sitting room, and antiques-furnished rooms all contribute to a 19th-century atmosphere. Some rooms are in former slave quarters in the courtyard; others are on the upper floors of the main house. The Continental breakfast is served with a rose on a silver tray, either in your room, in the parlor, or on the patio. Other meals can be enjoyed at Le Bistro. Visitors who seek a special hideaway will love the Audubon housekeeping cottages—in a private, enclosed area, with statuary and individual patios—two blocks from the hotel. ☎ *727 Toulouse St., 70130,* ☎ *504/561–5858 or 800/634–1600,* FAX *504/528–9939. 14 rooms, 2 suites, 7 cottages. Restaurant, pool at cottage location, valet service, parking. AE, D, MC, V.*

$$$–$$$$ **Royal Orleans Hotel (Omni).** This elegant, white-marble hotel, built in ★ 1960, re-creates an aura that reigned in New Orleans more than a century ago. Rooms, though not large, are well appointed with marble baths (telephone in each) and more marble on dressers and tabletops. Balcony rooms cost the most. The well-known Rib Room Restaurant makes its home on the lobby level. ☎ *621 St. Louis St., 70140,* ☎ *504/529–5333 or 800/843–6664,* FAX *504/529–7089. 350 rooms, 16*

suites. Restaurant, 3 lounges, pool, barber shop, beauty salon, exercise room, valet service, parking. AE, D, DC, MC, V.

$$–$$$$ **Le Richelieu.** Here the friendly, personal atmosphere of a small hotel is accented with such luxury touches as generous bath-amenity packages and hair driers—and mostly at a moderate rate. Some rooms have mirrored walls and walk-in closets, many have refrigerators, and all have brass ceiling fans. Luxury suites (like the one Paul McCartney stayed in while cutting a record in New Orleans) are also available. An intimate bar and café off the courtyard has tables on the terrace by the pool. ☎ *1234 Chartres St., 70116, ☎ 504/529–2492 or 800/535–9653, FAX 504/524–8179. 69 rooms, 17 suites. Restaurant, lounge, pool, valet service, free parking. AE, D, DC, MC, V.*

$$–$$$$ **Olivier House.** The entrance of this small hotel, in two 1836 town houses, contains an enormous mirror in a carved frame and chandeliers that are original to the house. Room design and decor vary; some rooms have lofts, many have complete kitchens with microwaves; gas-burning fireplaces are found throughout. Most rooms are a comfortable mix of antiques and traditional decor; some have a tropical feeling, with wicker furnishings and sunny colors. Pets are welcome. Noisy birds inhabit the two pretty courtyards filled with tropical plants. Don't expect a spic-and-span luxury hotel; in this family-owned and operated charmer, the homey, casual atmosphere is the thing. ☎ *828 Toulouse St., 70112, ☎ 504/525–8456, FAX 504/529–2006. 42 rooms. Pool. AE, D, DC, MC, V.*

$$–$$$ ★ **Holiday Inn Château Le Moyne.** Old World atmosphere and decor pervades; eight suites occupy Creole cottages off a tropical courtyard. Here you'll find the familiar Holiday Inn standards, basic and clean, along with a good dose of French Quarter ambience in the structural decor. ☎ *301 Dauphine St., 70112, ☎ 504/581–1303 or 800/465–4329, FAX 504/523–5709. 160 rooms, 11 suites. Restaurant, lounge, pool. AE, D, DC, MC, V.*

$$–$$$ **Rue Royal Inn.** This circa 1850 home has balcony rooms overlooking a courtyard and Royal Street; one suite has a Jacuzzi. Each room has a coffeemaker. Great location is the main appeal here. ☎ *1006 Royal Street, 70116, ☎ 504/524–3900 or 800/776–3901, FAX 504/947–7454. 17 rooms, some with kitchenettes. AE, D, DC, MC, V.*

GARDEN DISTRICT/UPTOWN

$$–$$$$ ★ **Pontchartrain Hotel.** Maintaining the grand tradition is the hallmark of this quiet, elegant European-style hotel that has reigned on St. Charles Avenue for more than 60 years. Accommodations range from lavish sun-filled suites to small pensione-style rooms with showers. The internationally known Caribbean Room restaurant provides memorable dining. ☎ *2031 St. Charles Ave., 70140, ☎ 504/524–0581 or 800/777–6193, FAX 504/529–1165. 60 rooms, 42 suites. 2 restaurants, piano bar, valet service, concierge, parking. AE, D, DC, MC, V.*

$$ ★ **Josephine Guest House.** In this restored Italianate mansion, built in 1870, European antiques fill the rooms, and Oriental rugs cover gleaming hardwood floors. Four rooms and a parlor are in the main house; there are two smaller but still spacious rooms in the *garçonnière* (quarters where the original owners' sons stayed). The bathrooms are impressive in both size and decor. A complimentary Creole breakfast of orange juice, café au lait, and homemade biscuits can be brought to your room (Wedgwood china on a silver tray) or served on the secluded patio. The Josephine had a face-lift in 1994 that included upgrading the plumbing and installing phones in guest rooms. ☎ *1450 Josephine St., 70130, 1 block from St. Charles Ave., ☎ 504/524–6361 or 800/779–6361, FAX 504/523–6484. 6 rooms. AE, D, DC, MC, V.*

$$ **Quality Inn–Maison St. Charles.** This lovely property consists of five
★ historic buildings along St. Charles Avenue set amid well-kept grounds.
Rooms here are larger than average, and the hotel is conveniently lo-
cated on the St. Charles Streetcar line. ☎ *1319 St. Charles Ave., 70130,
☎ 504/522–0187 or 800/831–1783, FAX 504/525–2218. 112 rooms,
20 suites. Restaurant, lounge, no-smoking rooms, pool, hot tub, park-
ing (fee). AE, D, DC, MC, V.*

KENNER/AIRPORT

$$–$$$ **New Orleans Airport Hilton & Conference Center.** This sleek, modern
facility is directly opposite the New Orleans International Airport. ☎
*901 Airline Hwy., Kenner 70062, ☎ 504/469–5000 or 800/445–
8667, FAX 504/466–5473. 317 rooms, 2 suites. Restaurant, lounge, pool,
tennis court, exercise room, valet service, business services, airport shut-
tle, free parking. AE, DC, MC, V.*

$$ **Holiday Inn–Airport Holidome.** Some of the motel-modern rooms here
face the dome-covered pool area, and there are plenty of other recre-
ational activities found on the sprawling grounds. This is a good choice
for families. ☎ *2929 Williams Blvd., Kenner 70062, ☎ 504/467–5611
or 800/465–4329, FAX 504/469–4915. 302 rooms, 1 suite. Restaurant,
lounge, indoor pool, hot tub, sauna, exercise room, airport shuttle, free
parking. AE, D, DC, MC, V.*

Bed-and-Breakfasts

Bed-and-breakfast means overnight lodging and breakfast in a private
residence. Begin by writing or calling a reservation service and discussing
price range, type of residence, location, and length of stay. The service
in turn will provide you with descriptions of several B&Bs that meet
your criteria. From these choices you'll make a decision and send a 20%
deposit. You'll receive the address and other pertinent details before
you arrive.

$–$$$$ **Bed & Breakfast, Inc.—Reservations Service.** This service offers a va-
riety of accommodations in all areas of New Orleans. Some are 19th-
century historic homes. Guest cottages, rooms, and suites are also
available. Prices range from $40 to $150. ☎ *Write or call Hazel Boyce,
1021 Moss St., Box 52257, New Orleans 70152, ☎ 504/488–4640
or 800/729–4640, FAX 504/488–4639. No credit cards.*

$–$$$$ **New Orleans Bed & Breakfast.** Among 300 properties citywide are pri-
vate homes, apartments, and condos. Prices range from $45 to $250.
☎ *Contact Sarah-Margaret Brown, Box 8163, New Orleans 70182,
☎ 504/838–0071 or 504/838–0072, FAX 504/838–0140. AE, D, MC,
V.*

Hostels

$ **International Center YMCA.** Spartan accommodations are for both men
and women. Rooms have color TVs. The St. Charles Streetcar line is
nearby, convenient for sightseeing around town. ☎ *920 St. Charles Ave.,
70130, ☎ 504/568–9622, FAX 504/568–9622, ext. 268. 50 rooms
with shared baths. Restaurant, indoor pool, health club, parking (fee).
MC, V.*

$ **Marquette House, New Orleans International Hostel.** This is the fourth-
largest youth hostel in the country, run by Steve and Alma Cross. Bud-
get-priced rooms are very simple but clean. There are two equipped
community kitchens open to guest use, lockers, and a garden patio with
picnic tables. ☎ *2253 Carondelet St., 70130, ☎ 504/523–3014, FAX
504/529–5933. 160 dorm beds, 5 private rooms with shared bath, 12
apartments. Dining room, 2 lounges, coin laundry. AE, MC, V.*

The Arts

Comprehensive listings of events can be found in the weekly newspaper *Gambit,* which is distributed free at newsstands, supermarkets, and bookstores. The Friday edition of the daily *Times-Picayune* carries a "Lagniappe" tabloid that lists weekend events. The monthly *New Orleans Magazine* also has a Calendar section. Credit-card purchases of tickets for events at the Saenger Performing Arts Center, the Orpheum Theater, and Kiefer UNO Lakefront Arena can be made through TicketMaster (☎ 504/888–8181).

Concerts

Free jazz concerts are held on weekends in **Dutch Alley.** Pick up a schedule at the information kiosk (French Market at St. Philip St., ☎ 504/522–2621). The Louisiana Philharmonic Orchestra (☎ 504/523–6530) performs at the **Orpheum Theatre** (129 University Pl.).

Theater

The avant-garde, the offbeat, and the satirical are among the theatrical offerings at **Contemporary Arts Center** (900 Camp St., ☎ 504/523–1216). At **Le Petit Théâtre du Vieux Carré** (616 St. Peter St., ☎ 504/522–9958), classics, contemporary drama, children's theater, and musicals are presented. Touring Broadway shows, dance companies, and top-name talent appear at the **Saenger Performing Arts Center** (143 N. Rampart St., ☎ 504/524–2490). The **Kiefer UNO Lakefront Arena** (6801 Franklin Ave., ☎ 504/286–7222) is also a venue for major concerts.

Nightlife

Jazz was born in New Orleans, and the music refuses to be confined to nighttime. Weekend jazz brunches are enormously popular and pop up all over town. But a stroll down Bourbon Street will give you a taste of the city's eclectic rhythms. You'll hear Cajun, gutbucket, R&B, rock, ragtime, New Wave: You name it, and you'll hear it almost around the clock. During the annual Jazz and Heritage Festival, held from the last weekend in April through the first weekend in May, musicians pour in from all over the world to mix it up with local talent, and the music never misses a beat.

New Orleans is a 24-hour town, meaning that there are no legal closing times and it ain't over till it's over. Closing times, especially on Bourbon Street, depend on how business is. Your best bet is to call and ask before tooling out to bar-hop at 2 AM. It is also a superb idea to call and ask about current credit-card policy, cover, and minimum.

Gambit, the free weekly newspaper, has a complete listing of who's doing what where. Things can change between press and performance times, so if there's an artist you're especially eager to hear, it's wise to call and confirm before turning up.

Bars

One of the world's best-known bars and home of the Hurricane (a sweetly potent concoction of rum and fruit juices) is **Pat O'Brien's** (718 St. Peter St., ☎ 504/525–4823). There are three bars, including a lively piano bar and a large courtyard bar, and mobs of collegians and tourists line up to get in. Very lively, very loud, very late.

Casinos

At long last work has begun on a land-based casino at the foot of Canal Street. At press time, the Rivergate Exhibition Center was being demolished and on its site **Harrah's Casino New Orleans** will be built. The $790 million facility will be the world's largest casino, with 250,000 square feet. It is scheduled to be complete in April 1996. Renovation has also begun on Municipal Auditorium in Armstrong Park, which will house Harrah's temporary casino until the permanent venue is completed. The auditorium is to be ready for occupancy by July 1995. Virtually everything regarding gambling in New Orleans is a crapshoot, and the situation changes almost moment-to-moment. At press time the riverboat casinos listed below were operating; each is open 24 hours daily, and has a lounge and/or grill, live music, plus slots, video poker, and gaming tables for roulette, craps, blackjack, and big six:

Star Casino (1 Star Casino Blvd., on Lake Pontchartrain adjacent to Lakefront Airport, ☎ 504/243–0400 or, outside New Orleans, 800/504–7827).

Flamingo (Poydras Street Wharf, behind the Hilton Hotel, ☎ 504/587–7777 or, outside New Orleans, 800/587–5825) replaced the smaller *Queen of New Orleans.*

Boomtown Belle Casino (4132 Peters Rd., on the Harvey Canal, Westbank, ☎ 504/366–7711 or 800/366–7711) has a wild-west theme.

Treasure Chest (5050 Williams Blvd., Kenner, ☎ 504/443–8000 or 800/298–0711) is docked on Lake Pontchartrain, across from the Pontchartrain Center.

Dancing

This is New Orleans, so it shouldn't surprise you that even a bowling alley has live music. Locals flock to the **Mid-City Bowling Lanes** (4133 S. Carrollton Ave., ☎ 504/482–3133) to dance to homegrown bands.

Two-stepping to a Cajun band is billed as the "spécialité de la maison," but the **Maple Leaf Bar** (8316 Oak St., ☎ 504/866–9359) moves with rock, R&B, reggae, and gospel as well. (Cajun nights are special.) There's a $2–$5 cover, depending on what's up.

City Lights (310 Howard Ave., Warehouse District, ☎ 504/568–1700) draws a chic crowd for DJ music and 6-foot video screens. They're open Thurs.–Sat. from 8.

Jazz

Aboard the *Creole Queen* (Poydras St. Wharf, ☎ 504/524–0814) you'll cruise on the river with a Dixieland jazz band and there's a buffet to boot. If you've an ounce of romance racing through your veins, do it.

There's live music five nights a week at the **Palm Court Jazz Cafe.** Traditional jazz is the rule, with blues thrown in on Wednesday. The fine Creole and international kitchen stays open until the music stops. There's a $4 cover to sit at the tables, but not to hang out at the bar. *1204 Decatur St., ☎ 504/525–0200. ☉ 7–11 PM. Live music starts Wed., Thurs., and Sun. 8 PM; Fri. and Sat. 7 PM. Closed Mon. and Tues.*

Pete Fountain's Club (2 Poydras St., ☎ 504/523–4374) is a New Orleans legend with his clarinet and his band that plays in a plush 500-seat room on the third floor of the Hilton Hotel. This is Pete's home base, and the man's on the stand Tuesday, Wednesday, Friday, and Saturday when he's in town. But he makes frequent appearances around the country, so it's wise to call first.

Speaking of legends, the old-time jazz greats lay out the best traditional jazz in the world in a musty, funky hall that's short on comfort, long on talent. **Preservation Hall** (726 St. Peter St., ☎ 504/522–2238) is *the* place for traditional jazz, and it costs you a mere $3 at the door. You may have to stand in line to get in (and it's often standing-room-only inside), but it will help if you get here about 7:30.

Rambling, rustic, and raucous **Snug Harbor** (626 Frenchmen St., ☎ 504/949–0696) is where graybeards and undergrads get a big bang out of the likes of the Dirty Dozen, Charmaine Neville, the David Torkanowsky Trio, and Maria Muldaur.

R&B, Cajun, Rock, New Wave

Industrial-strength rock rolls out of the sound system at the **Hard Rock Café** (440 N. Peters St., ☎ 504/529–8617). Hard Rock Hurricanes are dispensed at a guitar-shaped bar, and the place is filled with rock 'n' roll memorabilia. Hamburgers, salads, and steaks are served.

Isaac Tigrett, co-founder of the Hard Rock Cafés, and Dan Ackroyd were among the heavy hitters behind the **House of Blues** (225 Decatur St., ☎ 504/529–2624), a $7 million music venue with an awesome sound system where local and nationally known artists perform. There's also a recording studio, restaurant, and a shop.

The college crowd raises the rafters at **Jimmy's Music Club** (8200 Willow St., ☎ 504/861–8200). The music, by national as well as local groups, is rock, New Wave, reggae, R&B . . . whatever. Fans of Jimmy Buffett flock to **Margaritaville Café** (1104 Decatur St., ☎ 504/592–2565), where local funk and R&B acts perform and occasionally Buffett himself appears. An institution, **Tipitina's** (501 Napoleon Ave., ☎ 504/897–3943) is sort of a microcosm of the Jazz Fest, featuring progressive jazz, reggae, R&B, rock, New Wave, and blues. Its name comes from a song by Professor Longhair, who was posthumously awarded a Grammy for Best Traditional Blues Recording, and the place is dedicated to his memory. Funky, mellow, loaded with laid-back locals. There's a $3–$10 cover.

New Orleans Essentials

Arriving and Departing

BY BUS

Greyhound (☎ 800/231–2222) operates out of Union Passenger Terminal (*see* By Train, *below*).

BY CAR

I–10 runs from Florida through New Orleans and on to California. I–55 is the north–south route, connecting with I–12 west of Ponchatoula and with I–10 a touch west of New Orleans; I–59 runs northeast into Mississippi and Alabama. U.S. 61, from the west, and U.S. 90, from the east, also run through New Orleans.

BY PLANE

New Orleans International Airport (Moisant Field), 15 miles west of New Orleans in Kenner, is served by American, Continental, Delta, Northwest, Southwest, TWA, United, and USAir. Foreign carriers serving the city include Aeromexico, Aviateca, Lacsa, Sahsa, and Taca.

Buses operated by **Louisiana Transit** (☎ 504/737–9611) run every 22 minutes between the airport and Elk Place in the Central Business District (CBD). Hours of operation are 6 AM to 6:20 PM; the last bus leaves the airport at 5:40 PM. The $1.10 trip downtown takes about an hour.

The **Airport Shuttle** (☎ 504/522–3500 or 800/543–6332) leaves the airport every 5–10 minutes, 24 hours a day, for the 20- to 30-minute trip into town. Small vans drop passengers off at their hotels, so arrival time at your destination depends upon the van's number of stops. The fare is $10 per person.

Taxi fare is $21 for one or two passengers, $8 per additional person. The driver may offer three or four strangers together a rate comparable to the airport shuttle.

You **drive** to New Orleans from Kenner via Airline Highway (U.S. 61) or I–10. Hertz, Avis, Budget, and other major car-rental agencies have airport outlets.

BY TRAIN
Amtrak (☎ 800/872–7245) trains pull into the CBD's Union Passenger Terminal (1001 Loyola Ave., ☎ 504/528–1610).

Getting Around
The French Quarter, laid out in a perfect grid, covers about a square mile and is best explored on foot. Should your feet fail you, look for the Vieux Carré shuttle that loops around the Quarter. Several of the CBD sights are clustered together near the river and can also be seen on a walking tour.

BY BUS
Buses require $1 exact change or a token (sold only in banks). Transfers are 10¢ extra. The Vieux Carré shuttle operates weekdays from 5 AM to 7:30 PM. The **Regional Transit Authority** (RTA) has a 24-hour information service (☎ 504/569–2700; TTY 504/243–3838). One- and three-day visitor passes cost $4 and $8 respectively and allow unlimited travel on buses and streetcars.

BY FERRY
A ferry will take you across the Mississippi from the Canal Street Wharf to Algiers Ferry Landing. The 25-minute round-trip excursion is free to pedestrians; motorists pay $1 for the return to the Canal Street Wharf. The **Canal Street Ferry** (☎ 504/364–8114) operates from 5:30 AM–9:30 PM.

BY STREETCAR
The **St. Charles Streetcar,** New Orleans's mobile Historic Landmark, clangs up St. Charles Avenue through the Garden District, past the Audubon Park and Zoo and other Uptown sights. The streetcar can be boarded in the CBD at Canal and Carondelet Streets ($1). A round-trip self-guided sightseeing jaunt covers just over 13 miles and takes 90 minutes. The streetcar operates daily, every five minutes 7:30 AM to 6 PM, every 15–20 minutes 6 PM to midnight, and hourly midnight to 7 AM.

The **Riverfront Streetcar** follows the river between Esplanade Avenue and the Robin Street Wharf. It makes 10 stops, five above and five below Canal Street. The fare is $1.25, and it operates weekdays 6 AM–midnight; weekends 8 AM–midnight.

Taxi fares start at $1.70, plus 50¢ per additional passenger and $1 per mile or 40 seconds stopped in traffic. For trips to special events, such as a ride to the Fair Grounds during Jazz Fest, cabs charge $3 per person. Try **United Cabs** (☏ 504/522–9771) or **Yellow-Checker Cabs** (☏ 504/525–3311).

Guided Tours

ORIENTATION
If you prefer a "known" in an unknown city, hop aboard an air-conditioned, 45-passenger **Gray Line** bus (☏ 504/587–0861) for a two-hour tour of New Orleans's major sights. Gray Line also offers a Loop Tour in small vans, with unlimited on-and-off privileges for an entire day. Pickups are every other hour at twelve spots in the French Quarter, CBD, and Garden District. Cost: $15 adults, $8 children. **Tours by Isabelle** (☏ 504/391–3544) uses air-conditioned, 14-passenger vans for a multilingual and more intimate three-hour tool around town. Both companies provide hotel pickup, and reservations can be made through your hotel.

SPECIAL-INTEREST
Heritage Tours (☏ 504/949–9805) conducts literary and historical walking tours of the French Quarter. **Classic Tours** (☏ 504/899–1862) is operated by two native New Orleanians who are in love with the city. Their chatty tours cover art, antiques, architecture, and history. **Le 'Ob's Tours** (☏ 504/288–3478) runs a daily African-American heritage/city tour highlighting sites and history important to the African-American experience. **Save Our Cemeteries** (☏ 504/588–9357) conducts lively guided tours of some of the city's aboveground graveyards. Statistics for the **Superdome** (☏ 504/587–3810) are staggering and you can learn all about the huge facility during daily tours. **Tours by Isabelle** (☏ 504/391–3544) takes you to the bayous for a visit with a Cajun alligator hunter. On the flatboats of **Wagner's Honey Island Swamp Tours** (☏ 504/641–1769), steered by a professional wetland ecologist, you can tour one of the country's best-preserved river swamps.

Important Addresses and Numbers

EMERGENCIES
Dial 911 for **police** or **ambulance** in an emergency. The following hospital emergency rooms are open all night: **Tulane Medical Center** (220 Lasalle St., ☏ 504/588–5711), in the CBD near the French Quarter; **Touro Infirmary** (1401 Foucher St., ☏ 504/897–8250), near the Garden District.

RADIO STATIONS
AM: WWL 870, talk, news; KGLA 1540, Spanish language; WNOE 101.1, country music, news, weather; WGSO 990, CNN radio; WWNO 89.9, NPR, classical music, jazz; WCKW 1010, classic rock; WQUE 1280, talk. **FM:** WCKW 92.3, classic rock; KWLD 106.7, oldies; WWOZ 90.7, community radio, New Orleans jazz; WNOE 101.1, country music, news, weather.

24-HOUR PHARMACY
Eckerd's (3400 Canal St., ☏ 504/488–6661); **Walgreen's** (3057 Gentilly Blvd., ☏ 504/282–2621; Lake Forest Ave., ☏ 504/242–0981).

VISITOR INFORMATION
Write to the **Greater New Orleans Tourist and Convention Commission** (1520 Sugar Bowl Dr., New Orleans 70112, ☏ 504/566–5011). The

Tourist Commission staffs a desk near the customs desk at New Orleans International Airport, but its main outlet is the **New Orleans Welcome Center.** *529 St. Ann St. in French Quarter,* ☎ *504/566–5068.* ☉ *Daily 9–5. Closed major holidays.*

SOUTH LOUISIANA

Just as the state has two distinct regions, so, too, does South Louisiana. You'll make two separate tours of South Louisiana, beginning with Acadiana. Also called French Louisiana, the region is the cradle of the Cajun craze that's swept the nation. The second tour will cover Baton Rouge, the state capital, and continue to plantation country—the only Southern section of South Louisiana.

Cajuns are descendants of 17th-century French settlers who established a colony they called l'Acadie in the present-day Canadian provinces of Nova Scotia and New Brunswick. The Acadians—"Cajun" is a corruption of "Acadian"—were expelled by the British in the mid-18th century. Their exile was described by Henry Wadsworth Longfellow in his epic poem *Evangeline.* They eventually found a home in South Louisiana, and there they have been since 1762, imbuing the region, the state, and the nation with their unique cuisine and culture. The flavor of the region is summed up in the Cajun phrase *Laissez les bons temps rouler!* (Let the good times roll!).

Cajun Country is made for meandering. You're going to take some scenic routes and state highways, and you're encouraged to take to the country roads along the way to further explore the backroads and byways of bayou country.

Exploring

Numbers in the margin correspond to points of interest on the South Louisiana map.

U.S. 90 drops down from New Orleans into the marshlands of Houma, an area that abounds with campgrounds and charter fresh- and saltwater fishing boats. This route will take you through Morgan City, where the first Tarzan film was made; Franklin, an official Main Street USA town; and one of the state's Native American reservations. We'll follow the rambling Bayou Teche (pronounced "tesh") into St. Martinville in Evangeline Country, and next you'll head for Lafayette, which proudly calls itself, with some justification, the capital of French Louisiana. LA 14 is the scenic route to Lake Charles, which is fishing, camping, and bird-watching territory. Looping back toward Baton Rouge, you'll go through the area famed for the *Courir du Mardi Gras,* or Mardi Gras Run, during which masked and costumed horseback riders make a mad dash through the countryside. The trip ends near Baton Rouge on the Mississippi River, where you'll begin our second tour.

❶ **Houma,** in Terrebonne Parish, dates from 1795 and is in the heart of the old Hache Spanish Land Grant. The town is named for the Houmas Indians (the stressed first syllable of Houma sounds like "home"). Terrebonne Parish is a major center for shrimp and oyster fisheries, and the blessing of the shrimp fleets in Chauvin and Dulac is a colorful April event.

To get a real feel for the area, head west of Houma on U.S. 90 to take the guided walking tour through the 30-acre **Wildlife Gardens.** All sorts of critters slither, slink, and fly in the natural-habitat facility. There is

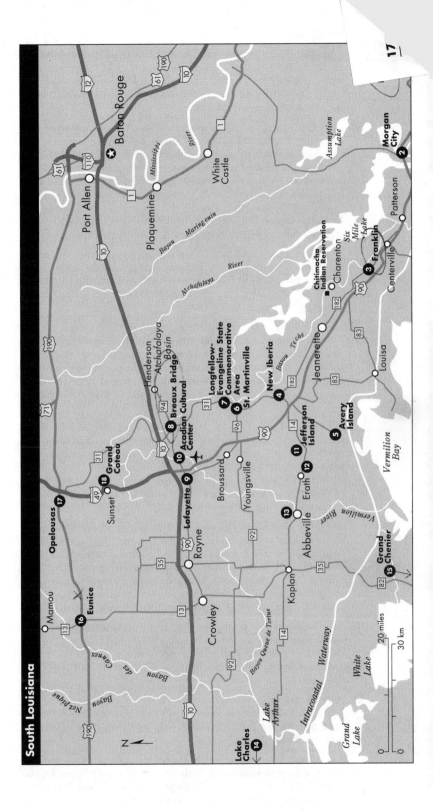

South Louisiana

a working alligator farm and a snack bar (though the two are unrelated). Guided tours are conducted at 10, 1, and 3:30, and there is an occasional twilight tour. Nature-lovers can B&B in a trapper's cabin. *14 mi west of Houma on U.S. 90 in Gibson, ☎ 504/575–3676. ☞ $8 adults, $6 children. Closed Sun.*

② Traveling northwesterly now on U.S. 90, you'll come to **Morgan City,** smack on the Atchafalaya River. This city struck it rich when the first oil-producing offshore well was completed on November 14, 1947, and the Kerr-McGee Rig No. 16 ushered in the "black gold rush." Front Street runs alongside the 22-mile-long floodwall. Atop the **Great Wall,** Moonwalk is a lookout with a great view of the Atchafalaya, as well as displays depicting the history of the region. At the **Morgan City Information Center** (725 Myrtle St., ☎ 504/384–3343, ⊘ daily 8–4) you can see a video of the first Tarzan movie, which was filmed here in 1917.

Across from the information center, you can take a guided tour of 3½-acre **Swamp Gardens,** a heritage park that depicts the settlement of Atchafalaya Basin; displays include pirogues and other aspects of bayou life. *725 Myrtle St., ☎ 504/384–3343. ☞ $2 adults, $1 children, under 5 free. ⊘ Daily 8–4.*

③ The little town of **Franklin** lies 20 miles northwest of Morgan City on U.S. 90. However, it is recommend that you get there via LA 182, which you pick up just outside of Patterson. This is Bayou Teche country, and the state highways follow the writhing bayou along some stretches. Teche is a Native American word meaning snake. According to an ancient Indian legend, the death throes of a giant snake carved the bayou.

If you're of a nostalgic bent, Franklin's Main Street may bring tears of joy to your eyes. The official Main Street USA status was bestowed on it by the National Trust for Historic Preservation. The street rolls out beneath an arcade of live oaks, and old-fashioned street lamps with NO HITCHING signs line the boulevard. Franklin is nestled along a bend in the bayou, and there is a splendid view of it from **Parc sur le Teche.** (To reach the park as you drive north through town, turn right on Willow Street by the courthouse square.)

The **Chitimacha Indian Reservation,** three miles northeast of Franklin, is one of three state Indian reservations. For centuries the Chitimacha flourished along the shores of Bayou Atchafalaya. The tribe's main settlement was in Charenton, site of the present reservation. The tribe is famous for its weaving, and Chitimacha baskets, as well as other small crafts items, are sold in the reservation's crafts shop. *LA 326, Charenton, ☎ 318/923–4830. ☞ Free. ⊘ Daily 8–4:30.*

The Chitimacha's main attraction these days is the **Cypress Bayou Casino,** which does a land-office business around the clock. The large and seemingly ever-expanding facility is awash with slots, video poker, and gaming tables. *832 Martin Luther King Rd., Charenton, ☎ 800/284–4386.*

④ **New Iberia**—the "Queen City of the Teche"—is the next stop along LA 182. New Iberia was founded in 1779 by Spanish settlers, who named the town after the Iberian Peninsula. The town is a blend of Spanish, French, and Acadian cultures.

Set in 2 lush acres on the bank of the bayou, in the shadows of moss-draped oaks, **Shadows-on-the-Teche** is one of the South's best-known plantation homes. Built in 1834 for sugar planter David Weeks, this fine old home epitomizes what went with the wind. *317 E. Main St.,*

New Iberia, ☎ *318/369–6446.* ☛ *$6 adults, $5.50 senior c̶* *children 6–11, under 6 free.* ☉ *Daily 9–4:30.*

TIME OUT Just one block from Shadow-on-the-Teche is Elaine and Al Landry's charming, affordable **Cafe Lagniappe Too.** Not only does Elaine do the cooking, she also makes the huggable, oversize stuffed dolls with funny faces that perch here and there; Al creates the colorful paintings that hang on the walls. For lunch there are salads, soups, and sandwiches, as well as stuffed eggplant and mirliton stuffed with shrimp and beef; the cuisine moves haute for dinner, with the likes of crab-and-corn bisque, excellent steaks, panéed catfish served with red bell pepper sauce, and grilled quail. *204 E. Main St., New Iberia,* ☎ *318/365-9419. AE, MC, V. No dinner Mon.–Thurs.; no lunch Sat. Closed Sun.*

City Park is a 45-acre grassy playground across the Teche from Main Street, with tennis courts, playgrounds, baseball and softball fields, a fishing pond, boat ramps, and picnic shelters with barbecue facilities. ☛ *Free.* ☉ *Weekdays 8 AM–9 PM, Sat. 1–9, Sun. 1–5.*

❺ Make a short detour, 9 miles south of New Iberia, to see **Avery Island.** The factory on the "island" (it's actually a salt dome) is the birthplace of Tabasco sauce, and descendants of Edmund McIlhenny continue making the hot sauce he invented in the mid-1800s. Other attractions are the 200-acre Jungle Gardens, lush with tropical plants, and Bird City, a sanctuary with flurries of snow-white egrets. *Off LA 329,* ☎ *318/369-6243 (Jungle Gardens) or 318/365-8173 (Tabasco factory).* ☛ *To gardens and sanctuary: $5.25 adults; $3.75 children 6–12, under 6 free.* ☛ *To Tabasco factory is free.* ☉ *Gardens daily 8–5, factory weekdays 9–4, Sat. 9–noon.*

❻ LA 31 hugs, as best it can, the Teche from New Iberia north to **St. Martinville** in the heart of Evangeline Country. This little town is awash with legends. Longfellow's poem was based on the story of Emmeline Labiche and Louis Arceneaux, two young lovers separated for years during Canada's Acadian exile. St. Martinville was a major entry point of Acadian refugees in the mid-18th century. Louis arrived in the town first and waited many long years hoping to find Emmeline. He eventually despaired of ever seeing her again and became engaged to another woman. Emmeline finally did reach St. Martinville, and, the story is told, Louis saw her by chance as she stepped ashore. Pale with shock, he told her that he was betrothed to another, turned on his heel, and disappeared. Their last, unhappy meeting place was beneath the **Evangeline Oak** (Evangeline Blvd. at Bayou Teche).

The Romance of Evangeline was filmed in St. Martinville in 1929. Dolores Del Rio starred as Evangeline, and posed for the bronze statue that the cast and crew donated to the town. You can see the statue in the cemetery behind the church of **St. Martin de Tours** (123 S. Main St.), near the grave of Emmeline Labiche. St. Martin de Tours, Mother Church of the Acadians, is one of the oldest Catholic churches (circa early 18th century) in the country. Inside there is a replica of the Lourdes Grotto and a baptismal font said to have been a gift from Louis XVI. In the late 18th century, St. Martinville was known as Petit Paris because it was a major refuge for royalists who fled the French Revolution. "Little Paris" was the scene of many regal balls, soirees, and operas.

The **St. Martinville Visitor Center** is in **La Maison Duchamp,** a Classic Revival structure built as a private home in 1876. Here you can pick up information about the area and also see a bedroom furnished with

antiques and turn-of-the-century photographs of the town.
at Evangeline Blvd., ☎ *318/394–2233.* ☛ *Free.* ⊙ *Daily 10–*

of the city limits, on LA 31 and the banks of the Teche, the
ow–Evangeline State Commemorative Area is a 157-acre park
shaded by majestic, moss-draped live oaks. The park contains picnic
tables and pavilions, a boat launch, and early Acadian houses. ☎
318/394–3754. ☛ *To grounds: $2 adults, senior citizens and children
under 12 free.* ⊙ *Daily 9–5.*

8 Continue northward on LA 31 for a look at the little town of **Breaux
Bridge,** home of world-famous **Mulate's** (*see* Dining, *below*) and the
self-proclaimed Crawfish Capital of the World. The **Crawfish Festival,**
held in May, draws upwards of 100,000 people.

9 About 15 minutes from Breaux Bridge on LA 94 is **Lafayette,** a major
center of Cajun lore and life. Stop in at the **Lafayette Convention and
Visitors Bureau** (Willow St. and Evangeline Thruway) and load up your
tote bag with maps and brochures.

The **Acadian Village,** nestled in 10 wooded acres, is a re-creation of
an early 19th-century bayou settlement. There is a general store, a blacksmith shop, a chapel, and houses representing different styles of Acadian architecture. *200 Greenleaf Rd. (LA 342),* ☎ *318/981–2364.* ☛
$5.50 adults, $4.50 senior citizens, $2 children 6–14. ⊙ *Daily 10–5.*

TIME OUT Affordable **Dwyer's Café** serves Cajun plate lunches, burgers, and sandwiches. *323 Jefferson St.,* ☎ *318/235-9364.* ⊙ *Weekdays 5 AM–4
PM, Sat. 5 AM–2 PM. No credit cards.*

The Louisiana Live Oak Society was founded in Lafayette more than
50 years ago. A charter member of that silent but leafy set dominates
the 900 block of St. John Street. The **St. John Oak** is 400 years old and
has a matronly waistline of about 19 feet. It is on the grounds of the
Cathedral of St. John the Evangelist (914 St. John St.), a Romanesque
church with Byzantine touches.

The Lafayette Natural History Museum is a busy place, with workshops,
movies, concerts, and planetarium programs. It's also the venue for the
annual September Louisiana Native Crafts Festival. *116 Polk St.,
Lafayette,* ☎ *318/268–5544.* ☛ *Free.* ⊙ *Mon. and Wed.–Fri. 9–5, Tues.
9–9, weekends 1–5.*

The museum's sister facility is the **Acadiana Park Nature Station,** a three-
story cypress pole structure with an interpretive center and discovery
boxes to help children get acquainted with the wildflowers, birds, and
other things they'll see along a 3½-mile trail. *E. Alexandre St., Lafayette,*
☎ *318/261–8448.* ☛ *Free.* ⊙ *Weekdays 9–5, weekends 11–3.*

The **Lafayette Art Gallery** gives visitors a close look at local arts and
crafts. *700 Lee Ave.,* ☎ *318/269–0363.* ☛ *Free.* ⊙ *Weekdays 10–4:30.*

10 The **Acadian Cultural Center,** a unit of the Jean Lafitte National Historical Park and Preserve opened in March 1994, traces the history of
the Acadians through numerous audiovisual exhibits of Cajun music,
food, and folklore. An excellent introductory film dramatizes the Acadian exile. *501 Fisher Rd.,* ☎ *318/232–0789 or 318/232–0961.* ☛
Free. ⊙ *Daily 8–5.*

Hook up with U.S. 90 now and go 15 miles south to the junction with
LA 675, where a right turn will take you to **Live Oak Gardens.** American actor Joseph Jefferson, who toured the country in the 19th cen-

tury portraying Rip Van Winkle, bought several thousand acres of ~ in South Louisiana and built his winter home on what came to be calleu **Jefferson Island.** In 1980, the salt dome on which the "island" rested collapsed, causing severe damage. The area, now called Live Oak Gardens, has been completely restored, with formal and informal gardens and groves of live oaks. Jefferson's house is a three-story, comfortably opulent, Southern Gothic home with Moorish touches. A café in the reception area overlooks Lake Peigneur. *5505 Rip Van Winkle Rd., off LA 14,* ☎ *318/365–3332.* ☛ *$10 adults, $9 senior citizens, $5.50 children 5–16.* ☉ *Daily 9–5 during daylight savings time, 9–4 during winter.*

At this point take LA 14 and head west toward Lake Charles. En route, about 10 or 15 minutes from Jefferson Island, you'll pass through two tiny Cajun villages, both of which are worth a stop. In **Erath,** you can poke through all sorts of Acadiana at the **Acadian Museum.** The several rooms are filled to the rafters with memorabilia donated by local folks—everything from antique radios and butter churns to patchwork quilts and yellowed newspaper clippings. There's even a costume worn by Armand Assante in the film *Belizaire, the Cajun,* which was filmed in these parts. *203 S. Broadway,* ☎ *318/233–5832 or 318/937–5468.* ☛ *Free, but donations are welcome.* ☉ *Weekdays 1–4.*

A few minutes west of Erath on LA 14, **Abbeville** is a charming town whose picturesque village square boasts a gazebo and moss-hung live oak trees. The vicinity of the square is the scene of the annual Giant Omelette Festival each November, when some 5,000 eggs go into the concoction. Pick up a self-guided walking tour brochure at the **Abbeville Main Street Program Office** in City Hall (101 N. State St., ☎ 318/898–4110). Many buildings in the 20-block Main Street district are on the National Register of Historic Places. **St. Mary Magdalen Catholic Church,** adjacent to the square, is a fine Romanesque Revival building with stunning stained glass windows.

On an earthier note, Abbeville is home to **Cajun Downs,** a "bush" track cut smack through a cane field where all manner of critters race—horses, mules, maybe even pigs or chickens. The track is more than 100 years old, and draws a Cajun Runyonesque crowd that cheers on the favorite with great enthusiasm. The track is only open on Sunday, when a half-dozen or so races are run. Call first to see if the races are on; schedules tend to be pretty informal here. *On LA 338 off the LA 14 bypass,* ☎ *318/893–8160 or 318/893–0421.*

Back on LA 14, head for **Lake Charles,** the state's third largest seaport. The city dates from the 1760s, when the first French settlers arrived. The first home was built by Charles Sallier on the shell beach by the lake, and the town was originally called Charlie's Lake. The city is blessed with more than 50 miles of rivers, lakes, canals, and bayous, making it a paradise for sailing, fishing, canoeing, shrimping, and crabbing. **North Beach** (☛ $1 per vehicle June–Aug.; free other times) is a white-sand beach on the north shore of the lake, where you can loll in the sun, swim, or rent a wave runner during summer months. Twelve miles north of the city on LA 378, **Sam Houston Jones State Park** (☎ 318/855–2665, ☛ $2 per vehicle) is a 1,068-acre recreation area that beckons sports and nature enthusiasts.

The **Imperial Calcasieu Museum,** on the site of Charles Sallier's home, has an extensive collection pertaining to Lake Charles and Calcasieu Parish. The museum includes an old-fashioned pharmacy, an Audubon collection, a Gay Nineties barbershop, and a modern fine-arts gallery.

204 W. Sallier St., Lake Charles, ☎ 318/439–3797. ☛ $1 adults, 50¢ students, children under 6 free. ☉ Tues.–Fri. 10–5, weekends 1–5.

★ The **Creole Nature Trail** is a 105-mile loop beginning on LA 27 in Sulphur, dipping down along the Gulf of Mexico on LA 82, and winding up back in Lake Charles. Beautiful in the spring, this drive takes you to the Sabine Wildlife Refuge (☛ Free), where interpretive displays include a diorama featuring the Cajun Man, an animated talking mannequin. Three miles south of the center, a 1½-mile marsh trail leads right into the wilds, and at its end an observation tower affords excellent views of the wilderness. (Bring along some insect repellent!)

East of the Creole Nature Trail on LA 82 (Hug-the-Coast Highway), which whips along the windswept coastal marshes, and southwest of ⑮ Grand Lake via LA 35 (if you're coming from Lafayette), is **Grand Chenier,** where you'll find the **Rockefeller Wildlife Refuge,** an 84,000-acre tract where thousands of ducks, geese, gators, wading birds, otters, and others while away the winter months.

Leave Lake Charles on I–10E, and exit on U.S. 165 headed north. An 18-mile drive will put you at the intersection of U.S. 190, where you'll head east again.

★ ⑯ This route will take you through the tiny town of **Eunice,** home of the Cajun radio show, *Rendez Vous des Cajuns* (*see* Nightlife, *below*), and the **Eunice Museum.** The museum is in a former railroad depot and contains displays on Cajun culture, including Cajun music and Cajun Mardi Gras. *220 S. C.C. Duson Dr., Eunice, ☎ 318/457–6540. ☛ Free. ☉ Tues.–Sat. 8–noon and 1–5.*

The **Prairie Acadian Cultural Center** in Eunice is a unit of the Jean Lafitte National Historical Park. The large facility traces the history and culture of the Prairie Acadians, whose lore and mores differ from those of the Bayou Acadians around Lafayette. Food, craft, and music demonstrations are held from time to time. *250 W. Park Ave., Eunice, ☎ 318/457–8490 or 318/457–8499. ☛ Free. ☉ Daily 8–5.*

The area surrounding Eunice is the major stomping grounds for the annual Courir du Mardi Gras, which takes place the Sunday before Fat Tuesday (Mardi Gras Day). *Le Capitain* leads a band of masked and costumed horseback riders on a mad dash through the countryside, stopping at farmhouses along the way to shout, *"Voulez-vous recevoir cette bande de Mardi Gras?"* (Do you wish to receive the Mardi Gras?) The answer is always Yes, and the group enlarges and continues, gathering food for the street festivals that wind things up.

⑰ Farther east on U.S. 190 is **Opelousas,** the third-oldest town in the state. Poste de Opelousas was founded in 1720 by the French as a trading post. The town is named for the Appalousa Indians, who lived in the area centuries before the French and Spanish arrived. For a brief period during the Civil War, Opelousas served as the state capital.

At the intersection of I–49 and U.S. 190, look for the **Acadiana Tourist Center** (☎ 318/948–6263), where you can get plenty of information, arrange for tours of historic homes, and see memorabilia pertaining to Jim Bowie, the Alamo hero who spent his early years in Opelousas.

The **Opelousas Museum and Interpretive Center** has among its eclectic exhibits a washbasin in which celebrity chef (and native son) Paul Prudhomme bathed as a babe, a Civil War Room, adorable dollhouses, and an old-time barber shop replete with antique accoutrements. *329 N. Main St., ☎ 318/948–2589. ☛ Free. ☉ Wed.–Sun. 9–5.*

⓲ A 15-minute drive south of Opelousas on I–49, exiting on LA 93, will put you on Main Street in peaceful little **Grand Coteau,** a religious and educational center. Virtually every structure in the village is on the National Register of Historic Places. Of particular note here are the **Church of St. Charles Borromeo** and the **Academy of the Sacred Heart.** The Church is a simple wooden structure with an ornate high-baroque interior. There are 36 works of art inside, most of which were done by Erasmus Humbrecht, whose works can also be seen in St. Louis Cathedral in New Orleans. The church's unusual bell tower is one of the area's most-photographed sights. Tours are given on weekdays (for a $1 donation per person), but you must call (☎ 318/662–5279) to make arrangements in advance.

Established in 1821, the Academy of the Sacred Heart is the second-oldest institution of learning west of the Mississippi, remaining in operation through fire, epidemics, and war. The academy contains the Shrine of Saint John Berchmans, in which occurred the Miracle of Grand Coteau. You'll hear all about the miracle on a guided tour. *For tour information, contact Wendy Ortego,* ☎ *318/662–5275.* ☛ *$5 adults, $3.50 senior citizens and children over 12, children under 12 free.*

Chretien Point Plantation, not far away, is noted not only for its grandeur but also for the role it played in *Gone With the Wind.* In the 1930s, a photographer infatuated with the house took pictures of it and sent them to Hollywood. As a result, its staircase was the model for the one in Scarlett O'Hara's Tara. The house takes bed-and-breakfast guests. *About 4 mi from Sunset on the Bristol/Bosco Rd.,* ☎ *318/662–5876.* ☛ *$5.50 adults, $5 senior citizens, $2.75 children 5–12, under 4 free.* ☉ *Daily 10–5, last tour at 4.*

You can continue on to Baton Rouge via either U.S. 190 or I–10, as Grand Coteau is cradled in between the two thoroughfares. The tour will begin in Baton Rouge and continue into plantation country.

What to See and Do with Children

Acadian Village, Lafayette (*see* Exploring, *above*).

Annie Miller's Terrebonne Swamp & Marsh Tours (*see* Guided Tours, *below*).

Atchafalaya Basin Backwater Adventure (*see* Guided Tours, *below*).

Avery Island (*see* Exploring, *above*).

Children's Museum. Interactive computers; a brass-rubbing station; child-sized courtroom, TV station, and grocery store; and other hands-on exhibits keep the young ones busy. *925 Enterprise Blvd., Lake Charles,* ☎ *318/433–9420 or 318/433–9421.* ☛ *$3.* ☉ *Tues.–Sat. 10–5, Sun. by appointment.*

Chitimacha Indian Reservation, Charenton (*see* Exploring, *above*).

City Park, New Iberia (*see* Exploring, *above*).

Creole Nature Trail, Lake Charles (*see* Exploring, *above*).

Hammond's Flying Service, Air Tours, Houma (*see* Guided Tours, *below*).

Lafayette Natural History Museum & Nature Station (*see* Exploring, *above*).

Live Oak Gardens (*see* Exploring, *above*).

McGee's Landing, Atchafalaya Basin Tours (*see* Guided Tours, *below*).

North Beach, Lake Charles (*see* Exploring, *above*).

Zoo of Acadiana. Wooden walkways lace through the 25-acre park, where more than 400 critters slink, slither, or fly in their natural habitats. There's a petting zoo for children. *Rte. 182 (4 mi south of Broussard),* ☎ *318/837–4325.* ☛ *$6 adults, $3 children.* ⊙ *Daily 9–5.*

Off the Beaten Path

People all over the world have a hankering for Cajun chank-a-chanking (dancing). To make Cajun music, musicians need those special triangles, accordions, and fiddles. A number of places in Cajun Country make not only music but musical instruments as well. Among them is the **Savoy Music Center Accordion Factory** in Eunice. The front half of the building is a music store, and behind it, Cajun accordions are made from scratch. Proprietor Marc Savoy says his factory turns out about five accordions a month and fills orders all the way from Alaska to New Zealand. On Saturday mornings, accordions and other instruments tune up and take off during the weekly jam sessions held in the shop. There's beer to drink, two-stepping to do, and musicians from all over the area dropping over to sit in on the informal sessions. *U.S. 190, 3 mi east of Eunice,* ☎ *318/457–9563.* ☛ *Free.* ⊙ *Tues.–Fri. 9–5, Sat. 9–noon.*

Participant Sports

Louisiana is not called Sportsman's Paradise for nothing. Hunting and fishing are a way of life in this state. There are approximately 1.7 million acres of publicly owned or managed lands open to hunting. For information on permits, limits, and seasons, contact the **Louisiana Department of Wildlife & Fisheries** (Box 15570, Baton Rouge 70895, ☎ 504/342–5868).

Biking
These flatlands and lush parks make for easy riding. There are 60 miles of marked bike trails in Lafayette. Guides, rental bikes, and maps are available at **Pack & Paddle** (601 E. Pinhook Rd., Lafayette, ☎ 318/232–5854).

Canoeing
Paddling is almost a breeze on the easy-going Whisky Chitto Creek. Canoes can be rented at **Arrowhead Canoe Rentals** (☎ 318/639–2086 or 800/637–2086) and at **White Sand Canoe Rental** (☎ 800/621–9306). Both are in the Lake Charles area.

Fishing
Trips to fish, sightsee, bird-watch, or hunt can be arranged at **Gator Guide Service** (Box 9224, New Iberia, ☎ 318/365–6400). **Sportsman's Paradise** (☎ 504/594–2414) is a charter fishing facility 20 miles south of Houma, with eight boats available year-round. **Salt, Inc. Charter Fishing Service** (Coco Marina, LA56 south of Houma, ☎ 504/594–6626 or 504/594–7581) offers fishing trips in the bays and barrier islands of lower Terrebonne Parish, as well as into the Gulf of Mexico.

In the far southwestern part of the state, **Burgess Offshore, Inc.** (☎ 800/932–5077) conducts offshore fishing trips, and **Hackberry Rod & Gun Club** (☎ 318/762–3391) is a charter saltwater fishing service.

Golf

You can tee off at **Pine Shadows Golf Center** (750 Goodman Rd., Lake Charles, ☎ 318/433–8681), **Mallard Cove** (Chennault Airpark, Lake Charles, ☎ 318/491–1241); **City Park Golf Course** (Mudd Ave. and Eighth St., Lafayette, ☎ 318/268–5557), and **Vieux Chene Golf Course** (Youngsville Hwy., Broussard, ☎ 318/837–1159).

Hiking/Nature Trails

The Old Stagecoach Road in **Sam Houston Jones State Park** (12 mi north of Lake Charles on LA 378, ☎ 318/855–2665) is a favorite for hikers who want to explore the park and the various tributaries of the Calcasieu River. The **Louisiana State Arboretum** (Ville Platte, ☎ 318/363–2503) is a 600-acre facility with 4 miles of nature trails.

Horseback Riding

There are trail rides, pony rides, and even hayrides at **Broken Arrow Stables** (3505 Broken Arrow Rd., New Iberia, ☎ 318/369–7669).

Dining and Lodging

Dining

Graced as the state is with waterways, Louisiana tables are laden with seafood in every imaginable and innovative variety. In South Louisiana, sea creatures are prepared with a Cajun flair, which usually means hot and spicy. Dress is informal unless otherwise noted.

CATEGORY	COST*
$$$$	over $35
$$$	$25–$35
$$	$15–$25
$	under $15

per person for a three-course meal, excluding drinks, service, and 7.5% sales tax

Lodging

Sleeping accommodations run from homey bed-and-breakfasts to chain motels to luxury hotels to elegant antebellum mansions open for overnighters.

CATEGORY	COST*
$$$$	over $120
$$$	$90–$120
$$	$50–$90
$	under $50

All prices are for a standard double room, excluding 6% tax.

Breaux Bridge

DINING

$$ **Mulate's.** A roadhouse with flashing yellow lights outside and plastic checkered cloths inside, Mulate's is an eatery, a dance hall, an age-old family gathering spot, and a celebrity, having been featured on the *Today* show and *Good Morning, America*, among other airings. A dressed-down crowd digs into the likes of stuffed crabs and the Super Seafood Platters. There's live music at lunch and dinner. ✕ 325 Mills Ave., in LA, ☎ 800/634–9880; outside LA, ☎ 800/422–2586. Reservations accepted. AE, MC, V.

Open New Years Eve. Go early Music starts ≈7 pm

Carencro

DINING

$$ **Prudhomme's Cajun Café.** In a suburb of Lafayette, celebrity chef Paul
★ Prudhomme's sister Enola—a major contributor to the *Prudhomme Family Cookbook*—has her country kitchen in a cypress cottage. Her specialties are blackened fish dishes, eggplant pirogue, and panfried rabbit in cream sauce—plus homemade jalapeño-and-cheese bread. ✕ *4676 N.E. Evangeline Thruway,* ☎ *318/896–7964. Reservations advised. AE, MC, V. Closed Mon.*

Lafayette

DINING

$$ **Cafe Vermilionville.** This 19th-century inn with crisp white napery, old-brick fireplaces, and a casual elegance serves French and Cajun cuisine. Among the specialties are fried soft-shell crab with crawfish fettuccine, smoked turkey and andouille gumbo, and Kahlua grilled shrimp. ✕ *1304 W. Pinhook Rd.,* ☎ *318/237–0100. Reservations advised. AE, MC, V.*

$$ **Prejean's.** Housed in a cypress cottage, this local favorite has a cozy oyster bar, red-checkered cloths, and live music nightly. Specialties include Prejean's Platter (seafood gumbo, fried shrimp, oysters, catfish, and seafood-stuffed bell peppers), as well as Cajun rack of elk, American buffalo au poivre, and steak and chicken in various costumes. ✕ *3480 U.S. 167N, next to Evangeline Downs,* ☎ *318/896–3247. Reservations accepted. AE, DC, MC, V.*

LODGING

$$–$$$$ **Holiday Inn Central–Holidome.** Seventeen acres containing virtually everything you'd ever need for a long and yuppie life. Rooms with modern furnishings surround the large entertainment area. ☎ *2032 N.E. Evangeline Thruway, 70509,* ☎ *318/233–6815 or 800/942–4868,* FAX *318/225–1954. 244 rooms, 6 suites. Restaurant, lounge, indoor pool, hot tub, sauna, 2 tennis courts, jogging, recreation rooms, airport shuttle. AE, D, DC, MC, V.*

$–$$ **Best Western Hotel Acadiana.** In 1993 the Hotel Acadiana was bought
★ by the Best Western chain and completely refurbished. Standard rooms now have marble-top dressers, minirefrigerators, and wet bars, and rooms on the concierge floor offer such perks as Continental breakfast, evening hors d'oeuvres, and turn-down service. The hotel has rooms equipped for people with disabilities. Even-numbered rooms face the pool. ☎ *1801 W. Pinhook Rd., 70508,* ☎ *318/233–8120 or 800/826–8386; in LA, 800/874–4664;* FAX *318/234–9667. 301 rooms, 3 suites. Restaurant, lounge, pool, 2 hot tubs, airport shuttle, free parking. AE, D, DC, MC, V.*

Lake Charles

DINING

$$–$$$ **Café Margaux.** Candlelight, soft pinks, white linens, tuxedoed wait-
★ ers, and a 5,000-bottle mahogany wine cellar. Specialties include a marvelous lobster bisque, rack of lamb *en croute,* good steaks, and fillet of flounder with lump crabmeat and brown meunière sauce. ✕ *765 Bayou Pines East,* ☎ *318/433–2902. Reservations advised. Jacket and tie. AE, D, MC, V. Closed Sun.*

LODGING

$$ **Holiday Inn, Lake Charles.** Between the lake and the interstate, the Holiday Inn has traditional furnishings in rooms done in soothing earth tones. The four-story structure offers 10 rooms for nonsmokers and five for guests with disabilities. Hotel guests can stroll through a "casinowalk" to board the Players Riverboat Casino, which docks next door. ⌑ *505 N. Lakeshore Dr., 70601, ☎ 318/433–7121 or 800/367–1814; in LA, 800/433–8809. 262 rooms, 7 suites. Restaurant, coffee shop, room service, pool, video poker machines, gift shop, airport shuttle, free parking. AE, D, DC, MC, V.*

$–$$ **Chateau Charles Hotel and Conference Center.** A New Orleans–style structure with wrought-iron trim and beamed ceilings, the hotel is on 25 acres, three minutes from downtown. There are two-bedroom suites with wet bars, microwaves, minirefrigerators; six apartments; and rooms for people with disabilities in the all-ground-level hotel. ⌑ *Box 1269, 70602, ☎ 318/882–6130 or 800/324–7647, FAX 318/882–6601. 212 rooms, 13 suites. Restaurant, lounge, no-smoking rooms, laundry, meeting rooms, airport shuttle. AE, D, DC, MC, V.*

$ **Players Riverboat Casino Hotel.** Formerly the Downtowner Motor Inn, this hotel, which opened in 1993, is virtually an extension of the floating casino (the riverboat docks at the hotel's dock on Lake Charles). This one is for folks who want plenty of gambling action. ⌑ *507 N. Lakeshore Dr., 70601, ☎ 318/433–0541 or 800/871–7666. 132 rooms, 2 suites. Restaurant, lounge, room service, free airport shuttle. AE, DC, MC, V.*

Opelousas

DINING

$ **Palace Café.** A down-home coffee shop on the town square, operated by the same family since 1927. Locals flock here for the café's famous homemade baklava. Among the eclectic specialties are cold fried chicken salad, baked eggplant stuffed with Alaskan king crabmeat dressing, and Greek salad with feta cheese, black and green olives, and anchovies. There are also steaks, fried chicken, sandwiches, burgers, and seafood. ✕ *167 W. Landry St., ☎ 318/942–2142. No reservations. MC, V.*

St. Martinville

DINING

$$ **La Place d'Evangeline.** In the historic redbrick Old Castillo Hotel, on
★ the banks of the Bayou Teche beneath the branches of the Evangeline Oak, dine in high-ceiling rooms where 18th-century royalists once held lavish balls and operas. Seafood is king here, with the menu listing the likes of crawfish pie, corn and crab bisque, red snapper (broiled, fried, stuffed, and blackened), and frog legs. The Evangeline Special is a dinner for two featuring steak and seafood and a complimentary bottle of wine. Do not pass up the homemade bread. Proprietors Peggy and Gerald Hulin have renovated the upstairs part of the old hotel, and five antiques-filled, high-ceilinged rooms are open for guests. ✕ *220 Evangeline Blvd., ☎ 318/394–4010. Reservations advised. AE, MC, V.*

The Arts

Concerts

Major concerts are held at the **Cajundome** in Lafayette (444 Cajundome Blvd., ☎ 318/265–2100) and the **Lake Charles Civic Center** (900 Lakeshore Dr., ☎ 318/491–1256).

Theater

The **Lake Charles Little Theater** (813 Enterprise Blvd., Lake Charles, ☎ 318/433–7988) puts on a variety of plays and musicals. The **The-**

atre 'Cadien (☎ 318/893–5655) performs plays in French in various venues. **Lafayette Community Theatre** (529 Jefferson St., ☎ 318/235–1532) offers contemporary plays with a Cajun flair.

Nightlife

Cajun Music

Louisiana is alive with all kinds of music, but while we're in Cajun Country our focus will be on the music of the Cajuns. And we'll introduce you to chank-a-chanking at a fais do-do. Translation? The little iron triangles in most Cajun bands make a rhythmic "chank-a-chank" sound, and most folks call dancing to the rhythm chank-a-chanking. As for fais do-do (pronounced "fay doh-doh"), that's the dance, or party, where you go to chank-a-chank. Fais do-dos crop up all over Cajun Country, sometimes in the town square, sometimes at somebody's house. There are also restaurants, dance halls, and lounges that regularly feature live Cajun music. The *Times of Acadiana* is a free newspaper that comes out every Wednesday and is available in hotels, restaurants, and shops. Check the "On the Town" section to see what's doing in the area.

The following restaurants and lounges regularly feature music for two-stepping, waltzing, and chank-a-chanking. ("Regularly" does not necessarily mean every night.) Sunday afternoon (all afternoon) is often devoted to dancing. Be sure to call to find out what the schedule is.

Mulate's (*see* Beaux Bridge Dining, *above*).

Prejean's (*see* Lafayette Dining, *above*).

Randol's (2320 Kaliste Saloom Rd., Lafayette, ☎ 318/981–7080). Hot dancing in a greenhouse setting.

La Poussière (1301 Grand Pointe Rd., Breaux Bridge, ☎ 318/332–1721). One of the oldest dance halls around.

Belizaire's (2307 N. Parkerson Ave., Crowley, ☎ 318/788–2501). Greybeards and babies and everyone else in between all take to the floor in this great restaurant/dance hall.

Slim's Y-Ki-Ki (LA 167, Washington Rd., Opelousas., ☎ 318/942–9980). *Louisiana Life* magazine rated this black zydeco club the best zydeco dancing place in the state.

Fred's Lounge (420 Sixth St., Mamou, ☎ 318/468–5411). The late Fred Tate (he died in 1992) opened his bar in 1946; in 1967, he began airing live Saturday morning radio broadcasts, complete with music and dancing, weather reports, and news. It starts at 8 AM and goes on till 2 PM.

Rendez Vous des Cajuns. This live radio show, mostly in French, has been described as a combination of the "Grand Ole Opry," the "Louisiana Hayride," and the "Prairie Home Companion." *Eunice,* ☎ 318/457–6575. ☞ *$2 adults, children under 6 free. Saturday nights from 6 to 8 in the Liberty Theatre, Park Ave. at Second St.*

Casinos

In addition to the **Cypress Bayou Casino** in Charenton (*see* Exploring, *above*), there are two other casinos on Louisiana Indian reservations. All three opened in 1994 and are wildly successful. The **Grand Casino Coushatta** (20 min north of I–10 on U.S. 165, ☎ 800/584–7263) is on the Coushatta Indian Reservation near Lake Charles. On the reservation of the Tunica-Biloxi tribe, the **Grand Casino Avoyelles** (711 E. Tunica Dr., Marksville, ☎ 800/946–1946) is one of the biggest success stories in the state. In addition to the usual gaming paraphernalia, the casino has two restaurants, a child-care center, and a vide cade. It's in central Louisiana, east of Alexandria.

Riverboat Casino

The 1,700-passenger, 28,000-square-foot paddlewheeler *Players* Riverboat Casino has blackjack, big six, roulette, craps, and more than 800 one-armed bandit machines. There's also a bar and grill and a buffet. *507 N. Lakeshore Dr., Lake Charles,* ☎ *800/275–6378. 6 3-hour cruises daily.*

South Louisiana Essentials

Arriving and Departing, Getting Around

BY BUS

Greyhound Southeast Lines (☎ 800/231–2222) has frequent daily departures to Franklin, Houma, Lafayette, Lake Charles, Morgan City, New Iberia, Opelousas, and Thibodaux.

BY CAR

The fastest route from New Orleans through Cajun Country to Lafayette and Lake Charles is via I–10, which cuts coast-to-coast across the southern United States. However, if you've time, do take the leisurely scenic drives for exploring.

Great Drives: LA 56 to LA 57 is a circular drive out of Houma, along which you can see shrimp and oyster boats docked along the bayous from May to December. Another circular drive is the Creole Nature Trail (LA 27) out of Lake Charles. LA 82 (Hug-the-Coast Highway) runs through the coastal marshes along the Gulf of Mexico.

BY PLANE

Lafayette Regional Airport (☎ 318/232–2808) is served by American Eagle, Continental, Atlantic Southeast (a Delta connection), and Northwest Airlink; **Lake Charles Regional Airport** (☎ 318/477–6051) is served by American Eagle and Continental.

BY TRAIN

Amtrak (☎ 800/872–7245) serves Franklin, Schriever (12 mi from Houma), Lafayette, New Iberia, and Lake Charles.

Guided Tours

Acadiana to Go (☎ 318/981–3918) gives guided tours of Acadiana, as well as the rest of Louisiana. **Allons à Lafayette** (☎ 318/269–9607) offers customized tours, with bilingual guides and itinerary planning for Lafayette and Cajun Country. **Annie Miller's Terrebonne Swamp & Marsh Tours** (☎ 504/879–3934) is especially popular with the kids. The lady who gets along great with gators does daily tours March 1– November 1 out of Houma into the swamps. **Coerte Voorhies** (☎ 318/233–7816), based in Lafayette, conducts tours into the 800,000-acre Atchafalaya Basin for photographers, ornithologists, and all nature lovers. **Hammond's Flying Service** (☎ 504/876–0584) has air tours, which soar out of Houma over the swamps, marshlands, and the Gulf of Mexico. **McGee's Landing** (☎ 318/228–2384) conducts pontoon-boat tours from the levee in Henderson into the Atchafalaya Basin. **Airboat Tours** (☎ 318/229–4457) skims through the remote swamps, bayous, and sloughs of Lake Fausse Pointe.

Important Addresses and Numbers

EMERGENCIES

Dial 911 for assistance, or try the emergency room at the **Medical Center of Southwest Louisiana** (2810 Ambassador Caffery Pkwy, Lafayette, ☎ 318/981–2949); in Lake Charles, **Lake Charles Area Medical Center** (4200 Nelson Rd., ☎ 318/474–6370).

RADIO STATIONS

AM: KROF 960, French/Cajun; KPEL 1420, news/talk; KLCL 1470, sports; KEUN 1490, country/news/sports. **FM:** KROF 105.1, oldies; KTDY 99.9, adult contemporary; KYKZ 96.1, country; KJJB 105.5, oldies.

24-HOUR PHARMACIES

In Lafayette, **Eckerd's** (3601 Johnston St., ☎ 318/984–5220); in Lake Charles, **Walgreen's** (300 18th St., ☎ 318/433–4178).

VISITOR INFORMATION

The **Iberia Parish Tourist Commission** (2690 Centre St., New Iberia, ☎ 318/365–1540; ☉ Daily 9–5). The **Lafayette Convention and Visitors Commission** (1400 N.W. Evangeline Thruway, ☎ 318/232–3808 or 800/346–1958; in Canada, 800/543–5340; 𝔽𝔸𝕏 318/232–0161; ☉ Weekdays 8:30–5, weekends 9–5). For information from the visitors commission via fax, call 800/884–7329, main menu ext. 610. The **Southwest Louisiana Convention & Visitors Bureau** (1211 N. Lakeshore Dr., Lake Charles, ☎ 318/436–9588 or 800/456–7952, 𝔽𝔸𝕏 318/494–7952; ☉ Weekdays 8–5, weekends 9–3).

BATON ROUGE AND PLANTATION COUNTRY

Your meander through South Louisiana brings you now to Baton Rouge, the state capital. Legend has it that in 1699 French explorers observed that a red stick planted in the ground on a high bluff overlooking the Mississippi served as a boundary between two Indian tribes. Sieur d'Iberville, leader of the expedition, noted *le baton rouge*—the red stick—in his journal, and *voila!* Baton Rouge.

This is the city from which Huey P. Long ruled the state; it is also the site of his assassination. Even today, more than half a century after Long's death, legends abound of the colorful, cunning, and controversial governor and U.S. senator.

The parishes to the north of Baton Rouge are quiet and bucolic, with gently rolling hills, high bluffs, and historic districts. John James Audubon lived in West Feliciana Parish in 1821, tutoring local children and painting 80 of his famous bird studies. In both terrain and traits, this region is more akin to North Louisiana than to South Louisiana—which is to say, the area is very Southern.

As you are by now aware, Louisiana is graced with many stately mansions. But the area designated Plantation Country begins with a reservoir of fine old homes north of Baton Rouge that cascades all the way down the Great River Road to New Orleans.

Exploring

Numbers in the margin correspond to points of interest on the Baton Rouge and Plantation Country map.

After touring the state capital, take LA 61 to see the historic districts and plantations in the parishes north of Baton Rouge. An overnight stay in one of the plantation bed-and-breakfasts is recommended. From St. Francisville, take the free ferry at the tip of town and start south on LA 1 to see the antebellum gems that decorate the Great River Road between Baton Rouge and New Orleans.

❶ Start your tour of **Baton Rouge** at the Visitor Information Center in the lobby of the **State Capitol Building.** Armed with maps and brochures, you can take a tour of the first floor, which includes the spot where Huey Long was shot. This building is America's tallest state capitol, standing 34 stories tall. There is an observation deck on the 27th floor that affords a spectacular view of the Mississippi River and the city. *State Capitol Dr.,* ☎ *504/342–7317.* ☛ *Free.* ⊙ *Daily 8–4:30; last tour at 4* PM.

A museum in the **Pentagon Barracks** has exhibits that acquaint visitors with the Capitol complex. The barracks were originally built in 1823–24 to quarter U.S. Army personnel, and when Louisiana State University moved from Pineville to Baton Rouge in 1869, it was to these buildings. *959 3rd St., on the State Capitol grounds,* ☎ *504/342–1866.* ☛ *Free.* ⊙ *Tues.–Sat. 10–4, Sun. 1–4.*

Only one battle of the American Revolution was fought outside the 13 original colonies, and it was fought on these capitol grounds. One of the historic buildings, the **Old Arsenal Museum,** a restored heavy-duty structure dating from about 1838, now houses a museum. A terrific place for children, the museum has hands-on exhibits set up inside powder kegs, displays on Louisiana's Native American history, and a giant jigsaw meant to compare the capitol grounds as they appear both today and in 1865. *State Capitol Grounds,* ☎ *504/342–0401.* ☛ *$1 adults, 50¢ children 6–17, senior citizens and children under 6 free.* ⊙ *Weekdays 9–4, Sat. 10–4, Sun. 1–4.*

★ In 1994, a $17 million renovation was completed at the castlelike, Gothic Revival **Old State Capitol,** restoring the building to its original grandeur. When it was built in 1849, the structure was considered by some to be a masterpiece, by others a monstrosity. No one can deny that it's colorful and dramatic. In the entrance hall a stunning purple, gold, and green spiral staircase winds toward a stained–glass atrium. The building now houses the Louisiana Center for Political and Government History, an education and research facility with audiovisual exhibits. In the House chamber a multimedia show plays every hour beginning at 10:15, with the last show at 4. *110 North Blvd. at River Rd.,* ☎ *504/342–0500.* ☛ *$5 adults, $3 senior citizens, $2 students.* ⊙ *Tues.–Sat. 10–4, Sun. noon–4.*

Across the street from the Old State Capitol is the **Louisiana Arts & Science Center Riverside Museum,** housed in a 1925 Illinois Central railroad station. There is a fine arts museum with changing exhibits, an Egyptian tomb exhibit, restored trains from the 1890s to the 1950s, and a Discovery Depot with a children's art gallery and workshop. Once a month the museum presents a hands-on Challenger simulated space flight, replete with interactive computers. Call for specific times. *100 S. River Rd.,* ☎ *504/344–5272.* ☛ *$2 adults, $1 senior citizens and children; free Sun. 1–4.* ⊙ *Tues.–Sat. 10–4, Sun. 1–4.*

Another unit of the **Louisiana Arts & Science Center** is housed in the restored Old Governor's Mansion, which was built in 1930 during Huey Long's administration. Rooms in the antiques-filled house are dedicated to the memories of Louisiana governors. *502 North Blvd.,* ☎ *504/344–*

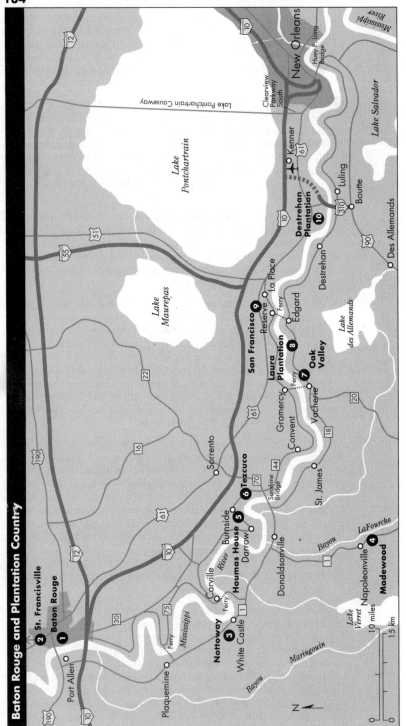

Baton Rouge and Plantation Country

5272. ☛ *$2 adults, $1 senior citizens and children 2–12; free Sun. 1–4.* ☽ *Sat. 10–4, Sun. 1–4.*

★ The **USS Kidd,** a Fletcher Class Destroyer, is a WWII survivor restored to its V–J Day configuration. Visitors are provided with a brochure detailing a self-guided tour that takes in more than 50 inner spaces of this ship, including one set up as a Nautical History Museum. Among its exhibits are articles from the 175 Fletcher-class ships that sailed for the United States, a collection of ship models, and a restored P-40 fighter plane hanging from the ceiling. Movies, such as Eagles over the Gulf and Victory at Sea, are screened in a 120-seat theater. *305 S. River Rd. (Government St. at the levee),* ☎ *504/342–1942.* ☛ *$5 adults, $3.50 children 5–18, children under 5 free.* ☽ *Daily 9–5.*

TIME OUT Downtown business people flock to **Maggio's** for hearty, inexpensive breakfasts (two-fisted biscuits, pancakes, and the like) and lunches (spaghetti and meatballs is usually one of the specials). The atmosphere couldn't be more casual, and the most expensive item on the menu is $6.50. *320 St. Charles St.,* ☎ *504/336-9512.* ☽ *Mon.–Sat. 6 AM–3 PM. No credit cards.*

About 1½ miles from the center of town, **Magnolia Mound Plantation** (circa 1791) is a raised cottage furnished with American Federal antiques and Louisiana artifacts. On Tuesday and Thursday from October through May cooking demonstrations are conducted in the outbuildings. *2161 Nicholson Dr.,* ☎ *504/343–4955.* ☛ *$3.50 adults, $2.50 senior citizens, $1.50 students, 75¢ children.* ☽ *Tues.–Sat. 10–4, Sun. 1–4.*

Continuing south on Nicholson Drive you'll come to **Louisiana State University.** LSU was founded in Pineville in 1860 as the Louisiana State Seminary of Learning and Military Academy. Its president was William Tecumseh Sherman, who resigned when war broke out and four years later made his famous march through Georgia. The 200-acre campus has several museums of interest, as well as Indian burial mounds that are of particular interest to archaeologists and archaeology buffs.

Baton Rouge's other major institution of higher learning is **Southern University,** about 5 miles north of town on U.S. 61. Founded in 1880, Southern U. is the nation's largest predominantly black university.

Fourteen miles north of Baton Rouge on U.S. 61, you'll come to the **Port Hudson State Commemorative Area.** The 650-acre park is the site of a fiercely fought Civil War battle, and the longest siege in American military history. There are high viewing towers, gun trenches, and, on the first Sunday of each month, small arms demonstrations. On a more peaceful note, there are 7 miles of hiking trails. *756 W. Plains-Port Hudson Rd. (U.S. 61),* ☎ *504/654–3775.* ☛ *$2.* ☽ *Wed.–Sun. 9–5.*

❷ About 10 miles farther brings you to **St. Francisville,** which has been described as a town 2 miles long and 2 yards wide. Much of the long, skinny town is listed on the National Register of Historic Places. Allow plenty of time for your visit to ★**Rosedown Plantation and Gardens.** This house and its surroundings bring on a bad attack of hyperbole. Suffice it to say that the opulent house dates from 1835, is beautifully restored, and nestles in 28 acres of exquisite formal gardens. Rosedown offers bed-and-breakfast accommodations, though not in the main mansion. *12501 LA 10, just off U.S. 61,* ☎ *504/635-3332.* ☛ *$10.* ☽ *Mar.–Oct., daily 9–5; Nov.–Feb., daily 10–4.*

A few miles south of St. Francisville, off U.S. 61, you'll find the 100-acre **Audubon State Commemorative Area,** where Audubon did a major portion of his "Birds of America" studies. The three-story Oakley Plantation House on the grounds is where Audubon tutored the young Eliza Pirrie. *LA 956, ☎ 504/635–3739. ☛ To the park and plantation: $2 per car. ⊙ Daily 9–5.*

The **Myrtles** bills itself as America's Most Haunted House and, to prove it, does mystery tours on Friday and Saturday nights. The Myrtles is also noted for its 110-foot gallery with Wedgwood blue cast-iron grillwork. The house was built around 1796, and has elegant formal parlors with rich molding and faux marble paneling. Rooms in the main house and the cottages are let for B&B, and the Carriage House Restaurant is a fine place for lunch or a candlelit dinner. *7747 U.S. 61, about 1 mi north of downtown St. Francisville on U.S. 61, ☎ 504/635–6277. ☛ Daily tour $6 adults, $3 children under 13. ☛ Mystery tour $8 adults, $4 children. ⊙ Daily 9–5; mystery tours Fri. and Sat. nights.*

Drive aboard the ferry ($1 per car) just outside St. Francisville for a breezy ride across the Mississippi. Pick up LA 1 in New Roads and head south. You'll be driving right alongside **False River,** which was an abandoned riverbed that became a lake. In contrast to the muddy Mississippi, the waters of False River are dark blue. This is an excellent fishing area, and you'll see long piers and fishing boats tied up all along the route.

❸ Sixteen miles south of Baton Rouge is **Nottoway,** the South's largest plantation home, built in 1859 by famed architect Henry Howard. The Greek Revival/Italianate mansion has 64 rooms filled with antiques and is especially noted for its white ballroom, which has original crystal chandeliers and hand-carved Corinthian columns. Several of the rooms are open for overnighters (*see* White Castle Lodging, *below*). Before you leave the lush grounds of Nottoway, walk across the road and go up on the levee for a splendid view of Old Man River. *30970 LA 405, 2 mi north of White Castle, ☎ 504/545–2730. ☛ $8 adults, $3 children under 12. ⊙ Daily 9–5.*

★ ❹ Henry Howard was also the architect for **Madewood,** a magnificent 21-room Greek Revival mansion with double galleries and white columns. *A Woman Called Moses,* starring Cicely Tyson, was filmed in the house. This, too, is an elegant antebellum bed-and-breakfast (*see* Napoleonvillle Lodging, *below*). *4250 LA 308, 2 mi south of Napoleonville, ☎ 504/369–7151. ☛ $5 adults, $4 students, $3 children under 12; 10% discount for senior citizens. ⊙ Daily 10–5.*

❺ On the East Bank of the River, docents in antebellum garb guide you through **Houmas House,** a Greek Revival masterpiece famed for its three-story spiral staircase. *Hush Hush, Sweet Charlotte,* with Bette Davis and Olivia de Haviland, was filmed here. *LA 942, ½ mi off LA 44 in Burnside, ☎ 504/522–2262. ☛ $7 adults, $5 children 13–17, $3.50 children 6–12. ⊙ Feb.–Oct., daily 10–5; Nov.–Jan., daily 10–4.*

❻ Built in 1835, **Tezcuco** is a graceful raised cottage with delicate wrought-iron galleries, ornate friezes, an antiques shop, a restaurant, and overnight cottages. *LA 44, about 7 mi above Sunshine Bridge, ☎ 504/562–3929. ☛ $6 adults, $5.50 senior citizens, $3.25 children 4–12; $4 to tour grounds only. ⊙ Mar.–Oct., daily 10–5; Nov.–Feb., daily 10–4.*

❼ **Oak Alley** is also a movie star, having served as the setting for the Don Johnson–Cybil Shepherd TV remake of *The Long Hot Summer* and more recently for scenes in the Tom Cruise film, *Interview with a Vampire*. The house dates from 1839, and the 28 gnarled and arching live oaks trees that give the house its name were planted in the early 1700s. There is a splendid view of those trees from the upper gallery. *LA 18, 6 mi upriver of the Gramercy-Vacherie ferry, ☎ 504/523–4351.* ☛ *$6.50 adults, $3.50 children 13–18, $2 children 6–12, under 6 free.* ☉ *Daily 9–5.*

❽ Different from the dressed-up River Road mansions, **Laura Plantation** is an in-progress restoration of the main house and six slave cabins of a former sugar plantation. Opened for tours in 1994, it is named for the 1805 owner/manager Laura Locoul, and the restoration is based on historical documents that include 100 pages of her diary. The story of the plantation is told by costumed docents who portray past residents. The *Br'er Rabbit* stories are said to have first been told here by Senegalese slaves. The $1.3 million project, scheduled for completion in 2005, will include bed-and-breakfast accommodations. *2247 Hwy. 18, Vacherie, ☎ 504/265–7690.* ☛ *$5 adults, $3.50 students 13–18, under 12 free.* ☉ *Daily 9–5.*

❾ **San Francisco,** completed in 1856, is an elaborate Steamboat Gothic house noted for its ornate millwork and ceiling frescoes. *LA 44 near Reserve, ☎ 504/535–2341.* ☛ *$7 adults, $4 students, $2.75 children 6–11.* ☉ *Daily 10–4.*

❿ **Destrehan Plantation** is the oldest plantation left intact in the lower Mississippi Valley. The simple West Indies–style house, dating from 1787, is typical of the homes built by the earliest planters in the region. *9999 River Rd., ☎ 504/764–9315.* ☛ *$6 adults, $3 children 13–18, $2 children 6–12, discount for AAA members.* ☉ *Daily 9:30–4.*

Destrehan is about an hour's drive from New Orleans, and U.S. 61 will take you right into the city.

What to See and Do with Children

Blue Bayou Water Park (*see* Participant Sports, *below*).

Samuel Clemens Riverboat. One-hour narrated cruises on the Mississippi River take in Baton Rouge harbor. *Departures are from South Blvd. at the river, ☎ 504/381–9606.* ☛ *$6 adults, $4 children under 13. Cruises offered Apr.–Nov., winter schedule varies.*

Louisiana Arts & Science Center Riverside Museum (*see* Exploring, *above*).

Off the Beaten Path

Spread over five acres of the 450-acre Burden Research Plantation, the **LSU Rural Life Museum** is an outdoor teaching and research facility. With three major areas (the Barn, the Working Plantation, and Folk Architecture), the compound's 20 or so rustic 19th-century structures represent the rural life of early Louisianians. Hundreds of items are displayed in the enormous barn, including a "prairie schooner", ancient surreys and sulkies, antique cars, tools and dental implements, and African artifacts and masks. The working plantation's several buildings include a grist mill, a blacksmith's shop, and several outbuildings. Folk architecture is represented by a country church, a dogtrot house, an Acadian house, and other buildings. All, except the simulated cemetery, are furnished with ancient items. *In Baton Rouge on Essen Lane, just off I-10, ☎ 504/765–2437.* ☛ *$5 adults, $2 children 3–12.* ☉ *Daily 8:30–5.*

Participant Sports

Golf

Baton Rouge has two 18-hole championship golf courses that are open to the public: **Santa Maria** (1930 Perkins Rd., ☎ 504/752–9667) and **Webb Park** (1351 Country Club Dr., ☎ 504/383–4919), which is close to most hotels. In St. Francisville you'll find the **Bluffs** (LA 965, 6 mi east of U.S. 61, ☎ 504/634–5222), an 18-hole Arnold Palmer course that visitors are welcome to play.

Hiking

There are 7 miles of hiking trails in the **Port Hudson State Commemorative Area** (756 W. Plains–Port Hudson Rd., Hwy. 61, ☎ 504/654–3775).

Swimming

Blue Bayou Water Park has all sorts of flumes, sleds, and slides—including a corkscrew critter, a wave pool, and a seven-story slide. For the little ones there's a 7,000-square-foot Pollywog pool. There's also a restaurant and a fast-food facility. *18142 Perkins Rd. off I–10, Baton Rouge,* ☎ *504/753–3333.* ☛ *$13.99 for anyone over 4′, $10.95 for anyone under 4′.* ⊙ *June 1–Labor Day, daily 10–6.*

Tennis

In Baton Rouge, you can lob and volley at **City Park** (1440 City Park Ave., ☎ 504/344–4501 or 923–2792); **Highland Road Park** (Highland and Amiss Rd., ☎ 504/766–0247); and **Independence Park** (549 Lobdell Ave., ☎ 504/923–1792).

Dining and Lodging

Dining

Dress is casual unless otherwise noted.

CATEGORY	COST*
$$$$	over $35
$$$	$25–$35
$$	$15–$25
$	under $15

per person for a three-course meal, excluding drinks, service, and 7% tax

Lodging

Staying on the plantation is your best bet for lodging in South Louisiana, but if you are stuck in the city or are budget conscious, you'll have no problem finding suitable accommodations.

CATEGORY	COST*
$$$$	over $120
$$$	$90–$120
$$	$50–$90
$	under $50

All prices are for a standard double room, excluding 5%–7% tax

Baton Rouge

DINING

$$ Drusilla's. The several large rooms that comprise this rambling restaurant are decorated with murals and paintings of sea scenes and sea creatures, setting the mood for the seafood served here. Munch on plump, seasoned hush puppies while you study the extensive menu. Standout appetizers include escargot in mushroom caps, fried crab fingers, and oysters on the half shell. "A Taste of Louisiana"—a sampling of seafood gumbo, seafood eggplant casserole, shrimp au gratin, fried shrimp, fried catfish, french fries, and salad—is a good choice. There are several Cajun fried sea critters and a lengthy list of broiled dishes. The steaks are well prepared. Save room for the Choc-A-Holic Delite. ✕ *3482 Drusilla La. (Drusilla Shopping Center),* ☎ *504/923–0896. Reservations advised for dinner. AE, DC, MC, V.*

$$ **Juban's.** An upscale bistro with a lush courtyard and walls adorned
★ with art, Juban's is a family owned and operated restaurant that proudly presents its house specialty—hallelulah crabs, a delectable concoction of stuffed softshell crabs dressed in a creole sauce. The sophisticated menu lists, among the starters, oysters Rockefeller and Bienville, and for the main course a tempting assortment of seafood, beef, and veal dishes, as well as roasted duck, rabbit, and quail. Vegetables are exceptionally tasty here, and Juban's own mango tea is delicious. The warm bread pudding is something to write home about. ✕ *3739 Perkins Rd. (Acadiana Shopping Center),* ☎ *504/346–8422. Reservations advised for dinner. AE, DC, MC, V. No lunch Sat. Closed Sun.*

$ **Mamacita's.** Gussied up with splashy murals of Mexican scenes, bright hues of pink and green, and sombreros hanging here and there, Mamacita's is very popular with locals. A whole raft of combination platters, fajitas, burritos, tacos, and enchiladas are on the list, and portions are huge. Gringos can get mesquite-grilled burgers, a grilled red snapper, or a pound and a half of barbecue pork ribs. ✕ *7524 Bluebonnet Blvd. (Bluebonnet Village),* ☎ *504/769–3850. Reservations advised for dinner. AE, D, DC, MC, V.*

LODGING

$$$ **Crown Sterling Suites.** This centrally located property has a southwestern motif. Each two-room suite, with complexions of peaches and greens, has a galley kitchen with microwave and coffeemaker, and custom-made mahogany furniture. The complimentary full breakfast is cooked to order. 🏨 *4914 Constitution Ave., 70808,* ☎ *504/924–6566 or 800/433–4600,* ℻ *504/923–3712. 224 suites. Restaurant, lounge, room service, indoor pool, sauna, steam room, gift shop, laundry service, free airport shuttle, free parking. AE, D, DC, MC, V.*

$$–$$$ **Baton Rouge Hilton.** Centrally located at I–10 and College Drive, this high-rise hotel underwent a $4.5 million top-to-bottom renovation in 1993. Rooms and public spaces have a somewhat formal feel, with traditional furnishings. Of the six suites, two are split-level; the top two floors offer VIP perks such as Continental breakfast and afternoon hors d'oeuvres and cocktails. 🏨 *5500 Hilton Ave., 70808,* ☎ *504/924–5000 or 800/621–5116; in LA, 800/221–2584;* ℻ *504/925–1330. 292 rooms, 6 suites. Restaurant, coffee shop, lounge, no-smoking rooms, room service, sauna, 2 lighted tennis courts, health club, jogging, gift shop, laundry service, concierge, business services, free airport shuttle, free parking. AE, D, DC, MC, V.*

$$ **Marriott's Residence Inn.** One- and two-bedroom suites in this centrally
★ located hotel come with dens, wood-burning fireplaces, dining rooms, and fully equipped kitchens. The two-bedroom suites have whirlpool tubs. Rooms have traditional furnishings. 🏨 *5522 Corporate Blvd., 70808,* ☎ *504/927–5630 or 800/331–3131,* ℻ *504/926–2317. 80 suites. Pool, laundry service, concierge, free parking. AE, D, DC, MC, V.*

Cheneyville

LODGING

$$ **Loyd Hall Plantation.** This is the perfect place for a quiet getaway. Ad-
★ jacent to a historic plantation mansion, accommodations are in a rus-
tic replica of a 19th-century farmhouse; a 3-room cottage that once
housed the comissary; or two suites in the restored kitchens over-
looking the pool. All units are furnished with a blend of antiques and
modern comforts: wood-burning fireplaces, rockers on the porches, four-
poster or tester beds, air-conditioning, TV, and modern kitchens stocked
with breakfast fixings. ▦ *292 Loyd Bridge Rd., 71325,* ☎ *318/776–
5641 or 800/749–1928,* FAX *318/279–2335. Housekeeping cottage (2
bedrooms share bath), housekeeping cottage with private bath, 2 suites
with private bath. Stocked kitchen, pool. AE, MC, V.*

Donaldsonville

DINING

$$$ **Lafitte's Landing.** Pirate Jean Lafitte is said to have frequented this raised
★ Acadian cottage, which dates from 1797. Chef John Folse, who is
renowned the world over in culinary circles, prepares such delicacies
as shrimp Anne (pecan-smoked shrimp served on fried zucchini) and
pecan-smoked tournedos finished with a pecan tasso glace. ✗ *Sunshine
Bridge Access Rd.,* ☎ *504/473–1232. Reservations advised. Jacket required. D, MC, V.*

Livonia

DINING

$$ **Joe's "Dreyfus Store".** This restaurant—off the beaten track, 35 miles
★ west of Baton Rouge—is simply one of Louisiana's best. The rustic frame
house contained the Dreyfus Store from 1920 until 1989; shelves along
the wall are still lined with relics from its general store days, and the
restaurant still uses many of the store's original chairs and cabinets.
The atmosphere is quite casual. The highly creative cuisine includes
sherry-spiked turtle soup; charbroiled, bacon-wrapped quail; oysters
en brochette; and a superb pork tenderloin, charbroiled, marinated,
and served on a bed of braised red cabbage. B&B accommodations are
available in the nearby Dreyfus House, a quaint Victorian cottage
brimming with antiques. ▦ *2731 Maringouin Dr. (Rte. 77S),* ☎
*504/637–2625. No reservations. No credit cards. No dinner Sun.
Closed Mon.*

Napoleonville

LODGING

$$$$ **Madewood.** Expect gracious Southern hospitality in this antiques-
filled Greek Revival mansion, which is both elegant and cozy. There
are five rooms in the main mansion, and three suites in a cottage be-
hind it. The $165 price for a room or a suite includes not only a full
breakfast but wine and cheeses in the parlor, followed by a candlelit
Southern dinner in the stately dining room. ▦ *4250 LA 308 (2 mi south
of Napoleonville), 70390,* ☎ *504/369–7151 or 800/749–7151; in LA,
800/375–7151. 5 rooms with private bath, 3 suites. AE, D, MC, V.*

White Castle

LODGING

$$$–$$$$ **Nottoway.** A massive Italianate mansion with 64 rooms filled with an-
tique treasures, this is reputed to be one of the most stunning B&Bs
in the nation. Thirteen of its elegant rooms are let to overnight guests,
who are welcomed with complimentary sherry upon arrival. Your first

breakfast of croissants, juice, and coffee is served in your room; the second breakfast a short while later is a full feast in the Magnolia Room. 🏠 *30970 LA 405, 2 mi north of White Castle, 70788,* ☎ *504/545–2730. 64 rooms with baths. AE, D, MC, V.*

The Arts

Concerts

Top-name stars such as Alabama and Neil Diamond are booked into the **Centroplex Theatre for the Performing Arts** (☎ 504/389–3030).

Guest soloists perform frequently with the **Baton Rouge Symphony Orchestra** (Centroplex Theatre for the Performing Arts, ☎ 504/387–6166). LSU's annual **Festival of Contemporary Music** (☎ 504/388–5118), which takes place in February, is more than 40 years old.

Theater

The **Swine Palace Theatre** (LSU Theater on Dalrymple Dr., LSU campus, ☎ 504/388–5128) is an Equity theatre whose director is the estimable Barry Kyle.

The **Baton Rouge Little Theatre** (7155 Florida Blvd., ☎ 504/924–6496) has been presenting musicals, comedies, and dramas for more than 40 years.

Cabaret Theatre (3116 College Dr., ☎ 504/927–7529) presents productions by local groups affiliated with the LSU dramatic arts program or the Baton Rouge Little Theatre.

Nightlife

Baton Rouge

BARS AND NIGHTCLUBS

Housed in an old movie house, the **Varsity Theatre** (3353 Highland Rd., ☎ 504/343–5267 or 504/383–7018) features live shows, live music, and dancing. The same, along with pool tables, attracts a younger crowd to the **Caterie** (Acadian Perkins Plaza, 3617 Perkins Rd., ☎ 504/383–4178). The **Chimes** (3357 Highland Rd., next to the Varsity Theatre, ☎ 504/383–1754) is a popular gathering place for the young crowd. **Gino's Restaurant** (4542 Bennington Ave., ☎ 504/927–7156) has a piano bar and occasionally a jazz trio. The young and not so young dance in a tropical setting at **TD's** (Baton Rouge Hilton Hotel, ☎ 504/924–5000). And there's live jazz at **Rick's Café Americain** (2363 College Dr., ☎ 504/924–9042).

CAJUN CLUBS

Mulate's (8322 Bluebonnet Rd., ☎ 504/767–4794) in Baton Rouge is a chip off the famed old Breaux Bridge block.

COUNTRY/WESTERN

The **Texas Club** (456 N. Donmoor Ave., ☎ 504/928–4655) is the hot spot for top-name country artists.

RIVERBOAT CASINOS

There are two floating casinos on the Mississippi River at Baton Rouge. Both are loaded up with games of chance and other lively entertainment. Carnival's **Casino Rouge** (☎ 800/447–6843) docks across from the capitol, and **Argosy's Belle of Baton Rouge** (☎ 800/266–2692) is berthed at Catfish Town, Front and Government Streets.

Baton Rouge and Plantation Country Essentials

Arriving and Departing, Getting Around

BY BUS
Greyhound Southeast Lines (☎ 800/231–2222) has frequent daily service to Baton Rouge and surrounding towns.

BY CAR
I–10 and U.S. 190 run east–west through Baton Rouge. I–12 heads east, connecting with north–south I–55 and I–59. U.S. 61 leads from New Orleans to Baton Rouge and north. Ferries across the Mississippi cost $1 per car; most bridges are free.

Great Drives: LA 1 travels along False River, which is a blue "oxbow lake" created ages ago when the mischievous, muddy Mississippi changed its course. Water lazily nudges the shore along the route, which wanders past gracious homes and small lake houses.

BY PLANE
Baton Rouge Metropolitan Airport (☎ 504/355–0333), 12 miles north of downtown, is served by American, Continental, Delta, and Northwest.

Guided Tours
Tiger Taxi & Tours (☎ 504/921–9199 or 504/635–4641) runs Baton Rouge city tours, tours of plantation country, and swamp tours. **Rachel Hall's St. Francisville Tours** (☎ 504/635–6283) conducts van tours of the Feliciana parishes north of Baton Rouge.

Important Addresses and Numbers

EMERGENCIES
Dial 911 for assistance. Hospital emergency rooms are open 24 hours a day. **Baton Rouge General Medical Center** (3600 Florida Blvd., ☎ 504/387–7000); **Our Lady of the Lake Medical Center** (5000 Hennessy Blvd., ☎ 504/765–6565).

RADIO STATIONS
AM: KBRH 1260, CNN news/talk; WIBR 1300, news/talk/sports. **FM:** WYNK 101.5, country; WBRH 90.3, jazz/alternative; WGGZ 98.1D, oldies.

24-HOUR PHARMACY
Eckerd's (3651 Perkins Rd., ☎ 504/344–9459; 14455 Greenwell Springs Rd., ☎ 504/261–6541).

VISITOR INFORMATION
The **Louisiana Visitor Information Center** (Louisiana State Capitol Bldg., State Capitol Dr., Box 94291, Baton Rouge 70808-9291, ☎ 504/342–7317). The **Baton Rouge Area Convention & Visitors Bureau** (730 North Blvd., Box 4149, Baton Rouge 70804, ☎ 504/383–1825 or 800/527–6843).

West Feliciana Historical Society Information Center (364 Ferdinand St., St. Francisville, ☎ 504/635–6330) is another useful stop for advice and information.

NATCHITOCHES AND NORTH CENTRAL LOUISIANA

Exploring

The earliest permanent European settlement in the Louisiana Purchase territory was not New Orleans but the little town of **Natchitoches** (pronounced *Nak*-uh-tish), which predates the Crescent City by four years. Nestled in rolling green hills and thick pine forests, Natchitoches has two other claims to fame. The town hosts a sparkling Christmas Festival of Lights, which was featured in the film *Steel Magnolias,* and it's the hometown of that film's screenwriter, Robert Harling. The friendly residents are happy to point out where Dolly Parton, Sally Field, Julia Roberts, and the other magnolias hung out during filming.

Front Street, which is lined with small, wrought iron–face buildings, lies alongside pretty Cane River Lake. The lake's sloping grass-green banks are shaded by giant weeping willow trees. The downtown area is part of a 33-block historic district, which contains a number of homes open to the public. Trolley, boat, and minibus tours, all of which focus on *Steel Magnolias* sites, are available (Cane River Cruises, ☎ 318/352–7093).

The **Museum of Historic Natchitoches** examines the colorful history of the area. Rooms are devoted to the 1803 Louisiana Purchase, the prehistoric Caddo Indians (with artifacts from 5000 BC), the French and Spanish influence of the 1700s, and to the movies *Steel Magnolias* and *The Horse Soldiers,* both of which were filmed in Natchitoches. *840 Washington St., ☎ 318/357–0700.* ☛ *$2 adults, $1 children, children under 5 free.* ☼ *Daily 9–5.*

Fort St. Jean Baptiste is a reconstruction of the outpost that stood near this site in 1716. The several replica buildings were constructed using 18th-century hardware, including handmade door latches and hinges. Structures include a church, powder magazine, warehouse, and kitchen. *Corner Mill and Jefferson Sts., ☎ 318/357–3101.* ☛ *$2 adults, children under 12 free.* ☼ *Daily 9–5.*

Natchitoches is on the fringe of the 100,000-acre **Kisatchie National Forest** (☎ 318/352–2568). In addition to its hardwood and pine forests, it offers equestrian, hiking, and nature trails; picnic and camping sites; and splendid vistas.

The Cane River Lake drifts southward from Natchitoches, lined by tall trees, stately plantations, and humble cottages. Several plantation homes are open for tours in "Cane River Country." ★**Melrose Plantation** was the home of the late primitive artist Clementine Hunter, who was known as the "black Grandma Moses." The first owner of Melrose was a black freed slave who, with her family, began construction of the seven buildings in 1796. In this century, Melrose was the home of a patron of the arts whose guests included Erskine Caldwell, Lyle Saxon, and Alexander Woollcott. The African House, an unusual Congo-style structure the second floor of which is decorated with Hunter's murals, is of particular interest. *Rte. 119, Melrose, ☎ 318/379–0055.* ☛ *$5 adults, $2 children 13–18, $1 children 6–12.* ☼ *Daily noon–4.*

Handmade brick, heart cypress, and wood pegs were used to build the Kate Chopin House, which houses the **Bayou Folk Museum.** Completed in 1813, in the 1880s this raised cottage was the home of Kate Chopin, author of *The Awakening*. The house is cluttered with an eclectic collection of treasures and trifles donated by locals. The museum contains photographs and memorabilia and a first edition of *Bayou Folk*, a collection of Chopin's short stories about Cane River Country. *Cloutierville,* ☏ *318/379–2233.* ☞ *$5 adults, $2.50 children.* ☉ *Mon–Sat. 9–5, Sun. 1–5.*

The still-working **Magnolia Plantation** is a National Bicentennial Farm, one of only two west of the Mississippi. The mansion's 27 rooms are furnished with an extensive collection of Louisiana and Southern Empire antiques. The outbuildings, which include brick cabins and a barn containing the only cotton press in the United States still in its original location, will become part of the projected Cane River Creole National Historical Park. *Hwy. 119 near Derry, 22 mi south of Natchitoches,* ☏ *318/379–2221.* ☞ *$5 adults, $3 students, $2 children.* ☉ *Daily 1–4 by appointment.*

What To See and Do with Children

Kisatchie National Forest (*see* Exploring, *above*)

Cane River Cruises (☏ 318/352–7093) offers tours by boat and bus, but it's tours on the little trolley that excite the kids.

Dining and Lodging

Dining
Dress is casual unless otherwise noted.

CATEGORY	COST*
$$$$	over $35
$$$	$25–$35
$$	$15–$25
$	under $15

per person for a three-course meal, excluding drinks, service, and 7% sales tax

$$ **Landing.** This large, noisy bistro with white tablecloths is one of the
★ town's most popular restaurants. The extensive menu includes such starters as shrimp remoulade, potato skins, and fried cheese sticks. Pasta, steak, chicken, and seafood are prepared a number of different ways. The spicy, country-fried steak is distinctive; the garlic bread is superb, as is the bread pudding. ✗ *530 Front St.,* ☏ *318/352–1579. Reservations advised for dinner. AE, MC, V. Closed Mon.*

$ **Lasyone's Meat Pie Kitchen.** Natchitoches is famed for its succulent meat pies, and the best place to sample them is this ultracasual country-kitchen café. Other offerings include meat, chicken, and seafood; for dessert, select from a display of Cane River cream pies. ✗ *622 2nd St.,* ☏ *318/352–3353. No reservations. No credit cards. Closed Sun.*

$ **Lea's Lunch Room.** Louisianans who frequently make the trek from north to south Louisiana often plan to arrive in Lecompte (pronounced le-*count*) at lunch time. There's nothing fancy here: just a huge sun-and noise-filled room, where country food has been served since 1928. The cornbread and homemade pies are legendary. Expect brusque service and plate lunches of prodigious proportions. ✗ *U.S. 71S, Lecompte,* ☏ *318/776–5178. No reservations. No credit cards. Closed Mon.*

$ **Open Hearth.** On the ground floor of the Cloutier Townhouse, this deli and market features products of celebrity Chef John Folse of Lafitte's Landing. Cajun and creole soups, po'boys, Folse's chef salad, and a variety of deli sandwiches are on the menu. You can call in orders for take-out, or dine in the casual eatery. ✕ *8 Ducournau Sq., Front St.,* ☏ *318/352–3197. No reservations. AE, DC, MC, V.*

Lodging

CATEGORY	COST*
$$$$	over $120
$$$	$90–$120
$$	$50–$90
$	under $50

All prices are for a standard double room, excluding 3% tax

$$ **Cloutier Townhouse.** On Front Street, overlooking Cane River Lake, this elegant three-story town house offers B&B accommodations. The exterior is adorned with filigreed cast-iron galleries, and the interior has high ceilings, hardwood floors, and Louisiana Empire antiques. The larger and quieter of the two bedrooms is the master bedroom, which has a tester bed, gas fireplace, wing chairs, and a settee. The master bath has a Jacuzzi and lighted shower stall. Breakfast includes homemade multigrain bread, fresh fruit, and traditional Natchitoches meat pies. ⌨ *8 Ducournau Sq., 71457,* ☏ *318/352–5242. 2 double rooms with bath. Deli. MC, V.*

$$ **Holiday Inn.** Comfortable and predictable rooms are available in this link of the familiar chain. On the outskirts of town, it offers a restaurant, outdoor pool, and cable TV. ⌨ *Hwy. 1 South Bypass,* ☏ *318/357–8281 or 800/465–4329,* 🖷 *318/357–8281, ext. 286. 143 rooms, 2 suites. Restaurant, lounge, pool. AE, D, DC, MC, V.*

$$ **Jefferson House.** A B&B within walking distance of the historic district, Jefferson House is a split-level frame structure in a serene setting. Guests occupy the entire first floor, which is decorated in a tasteful blend of traditional furnishings and East Asian objets d'art. A large stately parlor has a high beamed ceiling, brick fireplace, and doors opening to a veranda with rocking chairs and a view of Cane River Lake. Bedrooms have quilted spreads and matching drapes; baths are large and modern. ⌨ *229 Jefferson St., 71457,* ☏ *318/352–3957 or 318/352–5756. 2 rooms with bath. MC, V.*

$ **Fleur-de-Lis.** The granddaddy of local B&Bs is an unpretentious turn-of-the-century house with a front porch and swing. The downstairs family room looks and feels lived-in. Full breakfast is served family-style in an adjacent dining room. Guest rooms have a four-poster or a brass bed and wicker furnishings; baths are small but modern. ⌨ *336 2nd St., 71457,* ☏ *318/352–6621 or 800/489–6621. 5 rooms with bath. AE, MC, V.*

The Arts

The **Melrose Plantation Arts and Crafts Festival,** an annual event held the second weekend in June, showcases 135–150 regional craftsmen and craftswomen displaying their arts beneath the canopy of live oaks on the picturesque grounds of Melrose Plantation (*see* Exploring, *above*). There are also food booths galore featuring Nachitoches meat pies and oodles of homemade desserts. Call the Chamber of Commerce at 318/352–4411 for more information.

Natchitoches and North Central Louisiana Essentials

Arriving and Departing, Getting Around

BY BUS

Natchitoches is served by **Greyhound** (☏ 800/231–2222).

Route 1 and I–49, which cut north–south through the state's midsection, bisect Natchitoches.

Guided Tours

Tours by Jan (☏ 318/352–2324 or 318/352–3802, ℻ 318/352–0666), **Ducournau Square, Inc.** (☏ 318/352–5242), and **Unique Tours of Natchhitoches** (☏ 318/357–8698) all offer walking and driving tours of Natchitoches and the Cane River region.

Important Address and Numbers

EMERGENCIES

Dial 911 for **police** and **ambulance** in an emergency. The **Natchitoches Parish Hospital** (501 Keyser, ☏ 318/352–1200) offers help in medical emergencies.

RADIO STATION

FM: KNWD 91.7, rock and alternative.

VISITOR INFORMATION

The **Natchitoches Parish Tourist Office** (781 Front St., ☏ 318/352–8072) provides information about the region, including self-guided walking/driving-tour brochures.

5 Mississippi

Dotted with Civil War battlegrounds, Mississippi is a gold mine for history buffs and offers some of the best preserved examples of antebellum architecture in the South. The Natchez Trace, a string of magnolias and hilltop vistas, cuts across the heart of Dixie passing through Tupelo, Jackson, and antebellum Natchez. The mighty Mississippi provides the natural western border of the state, winding slowly through the delta past the port towns of Greenville and Vicksburg. Even the riverboat casinos along the Gulf Coast evoke a sense of the past.

Updated by
Patti Nickell

AS YOU ENTER THE LUSH AND LOVELY Magnolia State, slow down, look around, and listen carefully so as not to miss a single one of the South's great treasures. Mississippi is, indeed, deep in the heart of Dixie, and Dixieland is steeped in legend and lore.

Listen, and hear the soft, gentle drawl of an authentic Southern welcome. Stop in small towns, rich with historic houses and museums, busy with locals eager to regale you with slightly partisan tales of the Civil War. Sit still and catch snippets of the gossip that permeates the air of any eatery redolent with country cooking. Gossip and good food get on famously down South.

Mississippians eat, sleep, and breathe history—so much so that they subconsciously perpetuate the presence of ancestors. Dyed-in-the-wool Mississippians honor tradition, which manifests itself in everything from the meticulous upkeep of stately old homes to the painstaking preservation of colorful front-porch stories passed down from generation to generation.

You'll feel exalted reading William Faulkner's Nobel Prize address, you'll laugh at the characters in Eudora Welty's short stories, and find pathos aplenty in Tennessee Williams's plays. Hear the Delta Blues music of Robert Johnson and B. B. King, and roll to the rock of Tupelo native Elvis Presley. Mississippians all, they've contributed to a mystique no other state can touch.

Stick around for the weekend, and you'll surely stumble upon a festival or two. Mississippi celebrates all year, from pilgrimages to antebellum mansions to possums and pig fests. The Mississippi Division of Tourism (Box 1705, Ocean Springs, MS 39566, ☎ 601/359–3297 or 800/927–6378) will gladly send you a travel planner. A sampling of what's in store: Kosciusko's Natchez Trace Festival in April, Biloxi's Blessing of the Fleet and Jackson's Jubilee! JAM in May. Long steamy summers are endured thanks in part to the Choctaw Indian Fair near Philadelphia, followed by the Neshoba County Fair—America's giant house party. Fall brings historic house tours and antiques browsing in Natchez, as well as the Great Mississippi River Balloon Race. Jackson's big Mistletoe Marketplace culls holiday shoppers in November, and many communities present crafts shows and fairs in time for gift buying. Almost every town throws some sort of memorable Christmas celebration.

Prepare for the weather—Mississippi's fairly fickle. Spring and fall are glorious, while lazy summer days call for cool drinks on the shady veranda. Now and then, a winter cold snap sends porchsitters scurrying inside. Locals say it's tolerable here year-round, but be prepared for a few mood swings.

Any time of year, explore Mississippi's precious string of magnolias and hilltop vistas: the Natchez Trace. As you drive along sampling this gorgeous countryside, you may come to understand the sentiments of Blanche DuBois, that unforgettable Mississippi belle and Tennessee Williams heroine who declared in *A Streetcar Named Desire,* "I've always depended on the kindness of strangers."

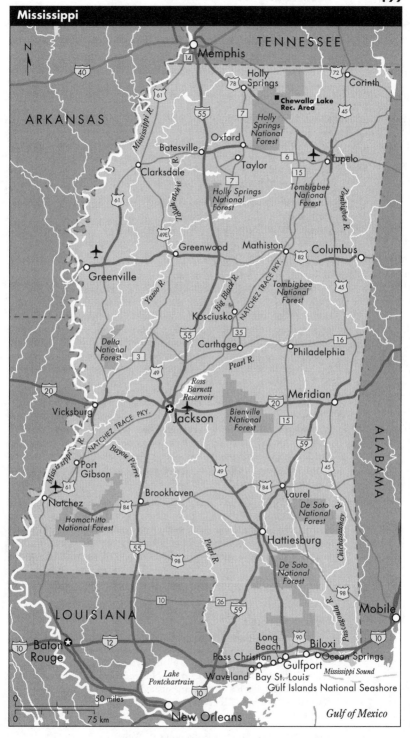

Mississippi

THE GULF COAST

The Mississippi Gulf Coast runs along U.S. 90 from Alabama to Louisiana. The traveler seeking a boisterous good time will find it in the restaurants, bars, hotels, motels, and souvenir shops that jostle for space along U.S. 90's busy four lanes, and in the riverboat casinos permanently docked at the water's edge.

Don't let the clamor of this neon strip hide the coast's quieter treasures: the ancient land, sculpted by wind and water, continually changing; serene beachfront houses set on green and shady lawns; the teeming wildlife of the Mississippi Sound and its adjacent bayous and marshes; the unspoiled natural beauty of the seven barrier islands that separate the Gulf of Mexico from the Mississippi Sound.

On a clear day, if you have good eyesight or a good imagination, you can see these islands. Their names (from east to west) are Petit Bois (anglicized as "Petty Boy"), Horn, East and West Ship, and Cat. Two others, Round and Deer, lie within the Mississippi Sound.

Three hundred years ago, France, England, and Spain ruled the area, according to their fortunes in international wars. Street names, family names, and traditions still reflect this colorful heritage. In the late 19th and early 20th centuries, the coast became a fashionable vacation spot for wealthy New Orleanians and Delta planters eager to escape yellow fever epidemics. Elegant hotels, imposing beachfront mansions, and smaller summer homes sprang up. Today the homes that have endured the vagaries of time and hurricanes stand along the beach—brave and beautiful survivors. Many are not open to the public, but are worth a visit to view their architectural style.

The coast's people today are known as easygoing and tolerant, artistic and hardy. Add the local love of fun and frolic, and you'll understand why Las Vegas–style gaming has been a major coastal to-do since its inception in August 1992. Dockside gambling's replica ships recall the days of riverboat gambling once rampant along the mighty Mississippi. Casino vessels today, however, are permanently moored and open round the clock. Restaurants, dockside cafés, and Southern hospitality are among the offerings.

Enjoy wondrous walks along the water, but take your cue from the natives and ignore any urge to swim in the sound. It's too murky (at best). Instead, admire the stately live oaks and accept the salutes of crabs. Go floundering and spear your supper. Above all, slow down. On the Mississippi Coast only the traffic on U.S. 90 moves quickly.

Exploring

Ocean Springs

To begin at the beginning, at least as far as Mississippi is concerned, start in **Ocean Springs.** Here, in 1699, the French commander Pierre LeMoyne Sieur D'Iberville established Fort Maurepas to shore up France's claim to the central part of North America. This first colony was temporary, but it's fondly remembered by Ocean Springs in its spring festival celebrating D'Iberville's landing. Magnificent oaks shade the sleepy town center, a pleasant area of small shops to explore on foot.

Ocean Springs is famous as the home of Walter Anderson (1903–65), an artist of genius and grand eccentricity who enjoyed an ecstatic communion with nature, which he revealed in thousands of drawings and watercolors, most of them kept secret until his death. You can discover his work at the **Walter Anderson Museum of Art,** to which murals from the **Anderson Cottage** were moved, and the adjoining **Old Community Center.** Anderson painted the intricate murals in the Community Center for a fee of $1; they are appraised at $1 million. *510 Washington Ave., ☎ 601/872–3164. ☛ $3 adults, $1 children under 13. ☉ Tues.–Sat. 10–5, Sun. 1–5.*

The nearby **Shearwater Pottery and Showroom** offers a wide selection of original and reproduction Anderson family hand-thrown and cast pottery. Visitors can watch the pottery being made in the workshop. *102 Shearwater Dr., ☎ 601/875–7320. Showroom open Mon.–Sat. 9–5:30, Sun. 1–5:30. ☉ Workshop weekdays 9–noon, 1–4.*

A brochure from the **Ocean Springs Chamber of Commerce** (1000 Washington Ave., ☎ 601/875–4424) will guide you on a driving tour of the D'Iberville Trail, shaded by moss-draped trees and bordered by weathered but lovely summer houses.

★ **Gulf Islands National Seashore**—which includes Ship, Horn, and Petit Bois islands—has its headquarters on Ocean Springs's Davis Bayou. When heat and humidity allow, picnic here and explore the nature trails. *3500 Park Rd., Ocean Springs, ☎ 601/875–9057.*

Biloxi

From Ocean Springs, cross the Biloxi–Ocean Springs bridge to **Biloxi,** practicing the correct pronunciation, "Bi-LUX-i," as you go. Biloxi is the oldest continuous settlement on the Gulf Coast and the third-largest city in Mississippi. When Pierre LeMoyne Sieur D'Iberville met the Indians who called themselves Biloxi, or "first people," he gave their name to the area and to the bay. The French constructed Fort Louis here; it served as the capital of the Louisiana Territory from 1720 to 1722, when the capital was moved to New Orleans.

Along the water, you can glimpse distant islands from the telescopes on Biloxi–Ocean Springs Bridge and visit the **J. L. Scott Marine Education Center and Aquarium,** which features 41 live exhibits and aquariums brimming with turtles, alligators, snakes, eels—the centerpiece is a spectacular 42,000-gallon tank. *115 Beach Blvd., Biloxi, ☎ 601/374–5550. ☛ $3 adults, $2 senior citizens, $1.50 children. ☉ Mon.–Sat. 9–4.*

Across U.S. 90 is **Point Cadet Plaza,** a waterfront complex with a marina and the **Seafood Industry Museum.** In the 1880s Point Cadet was home to European immigrants who flocked to Biloxi to work in the seafood canneries. Exhibits depict the growth and development of the Gulf Coast seafood industry. And a re-created schooner is available here for short trips and charters; call for fees and schedules. *Point Cadet Plaza, Hwy. 90 and 1st St., ☎ 601/435–6320. Museum ☛ $2.50 adults, $1.50 children and senior citizens. ☉ Mon.–Sat. 9–5.*

Biloxi's **Small Craft Harbor,** off U.S. 90 on the sound, captures the atmosphere of a lazy fishing village. Catch the **Sailfish Shrimp Tour** boat here to experience 80 minutes as a shrimper. Cast your nets upon the waters and let the crew identify your catch, however bizarre, for you. *Biloxi Small Craft Harbor, ☎ 601/385–1182. ☛ $9 adults, $5 children 4–12, under 4 free. Call for schedule.*

Biloxi's landmark 65-foot-tall **lighthouse** on U.S. 90 was erected in 1848. During the Civil War, Federal forces, operating from Ship Island, blockaded the Mississippi Sound and cut Biloxi off from much-needed supplies. When the Yankees demanded that Biloxi submit or starve, the reply was that the Union would have to "blockade the mullet" first. Ever since, mullet has been known as "Biloxi bacon" and honored with its own festival each October. The city defended itself with what appeared to be a formidable cannon array near the lighthouse but what was actually only two cannons and many logs painted black! *U.S. 90 at Porter Ave.,* ☎ *601/435–6293. Donations accepted.* ⊘ *By appointment.*

Mardi Gras is almost as grand a celebration in Biloxi as in nearby New Orleans, and the Krewe costumes are equally festive. See costumes and crowns at the Mardi Gras Museum, housed in the old Magnolia Hotel, an 1847 structure listed on the National Register of Historic Places. *119 Rue Magnolia,* ☎ *601/432–8806. Donations accepted.* ⊘ *Weekdays 10–4.*

TIME OUT The late Mary Mahoney's **Old French House Restaurant** is in a renovated 1737 mansion with several elegant dining rooms and enclosed patios. Locals swear by it, perhaps more for the comfort of its old brick and age-darkened wood and for the memory of Mary herself (who always went from table to table, chatting with customers) than for the food. Come for drinks in the Old Slave Quarter (11–11) and for Le Café's beignets, coffee, gumbo, and po'boys served 'round the clock (there's take-out, too). Afterward, walk across the street to the George Ohr Arts & Cultural Center (136 G.E. Ohr St., ☎ 601/374–5547) to see the collection of pottery by the eccentric Ohr, known as "the mad potter of Biloxi." *116 Rue Magnolia,* ☎ *601/374–0163. AE, DC, MC, V.*

Heading on U.S. 90 toward Gulfport is **Beauvoir,** the antebellum beachfront mansion that was the last home of Jefferson Davis. Here the president of the Confederacy wrote his memoirs and his book *The Rise and Fall of the Confederate Government.* The serene, raised cottage-style house, with its sweeping front stairs, is flanked by pavilions and set on a broad lawn shaded by ancient live oaks. A Confederate cemetery on the grounds includes the Tomb of the Unknown Soldier of the Confederacy. The gift shop is well stocked with history books and CSA material. *2244 Beach Blvd.,* ☎ *601/388–1313.* ☛ *$4.75 adults, $2.50 children 6–15, $4.25 senior citizens and military personnel, children under 6 free.* ⊘ *Daily 9–5.*

Gulfport

Gulfport merges seamlessly with Biloxi along U.S. 90. If you have time for only one activity on the coast, make it a getaway to **Ship Island** on the passenger ferry from the Gulfport Harbor (ferry runs Mar.–Oct.). At Ship Island, a part of Gulf Islands National Seashore, a U.S. Park Ranger will guide you through Fort Massachusetts, built in 1859 and used by Federal troops to blockade the sound during the Civil War. The rangers will treat you to tales of the island's colorful past, including the story of the *filles aux casquettes*—young women sent by the French government as brides for the lonely early colonists. Each girl (*fille*) carried a small hope chest (*casquette*). Spend the day sunning, swimming in the clear green water, and beachcombing for treasures washed up by the surf. You'll feel a world away (just remember to return on the last boat). *Ticket office at Gulfport Harbor in Joseph T. Jones Memorial Park, east of intersection of U.S. 49 and U.S. 90,* ☎ *601/864–3797. Fees vary; call ahead.*

West of Gulfport the landscape grows increasingly broad, wild, and lovely. The highway runs between stately homes on the north and shimmering water on the south from Long Beach through Pass Christian and from Bay St. Louis to Waveland.

Pass Christian (Chris-chi-ANN) suffered the full fury of Hurricane Camille on August 17, 1969, but not even Camille could erase its history. Here sailboat racing began in the South, and here the second yacht club in the country was formed (it still exists today). Louisiana landowner Zachary Taylor was at the yacht club when he was persuaded to run for the presidency. In 1913, President Woodrow Wilson and his family spent a Christmas vacation here, but his Dixie White House, the Herndon Home, was destroyed by Camille.

Off the Beaten Path

Crosby Arboretum. Well worth a detour to nearby Picayune, the arboretum, with its 64-acre Interpretive Center Pinecote, focuses exclusively on the ecosystems of the 16,000-square-mile Pearl River Drainage Basin of southern Mississippi and Louisiana. *I–59, exit 4 at Picayune, 1986 Ridge Rd.,* ☎ *601/799–2311.* ☉ *Wed.–Sun. 10–5.* ☛ *$3 adults, $1 children under 12.*

What to See and Do with Children

Boating (*see* Participant Sports, *below*).

The **Doll House** accommodates a collection of contemporary and antique dolls and stuffed animals. *1201 Bienville Blvd. (U.S. 90), Ocean Springs,* ☎ *601/872–3971. Donation requested for YMCA Pet Shelter.* ☉ *Tues.–Sun. 1–5.*

Fishing (*see* Participant Sports, *below*).

Funtime USA will entertain children for hours, with its water slides, playground, bumper boats and cars, and more than 100 arcade games. *U.S. 90 and Cowan Rd., Gulfport,* ☎ *601/896–7315.* ☛ *Grounds free; fee for rides and games.* ☉ *Summer months, daily 9 AM–midnight; rest of year, daily 9–4.*

Gulf Islands National Seashore (*see* Exploring, *above*).

J.L. Scott Marine Education Center and Aquarium (*see* Exploring, *above*).

Marine Life Oceanarium offers continuous shows with performing dolphins, sea lions, and macaws. *Joseph T. Jones Memorial Park, east of intersection of U.S. 49 and U.S. 90, Gulfport,* ☎ *601/863–0651.* ☛ *$9.25 adults, $5.95 children 3–11, children under 3 free.* ☉ *Daily 9 AM–sunset.*

Shopping

At **Ballard's Pewter** (1110 Government St., Ocean Springs, ☎ 601/875–7550) you can find necklaces and earrings made from sand dollars and crabs, or have the pewtersmith fashion a "bespoke" (custom-made) piece.

Hillyer House (207 East Scenic Dr., Pass Christian, ☎ 601/452–4810) sells handmade jewelry, pottery, glass, and brass made by local and regional artists, plus packaged southern gourmet foods.

Beaches

Twenty-six miles of man-made beach extend from Biloxi to Pass Christian. Toward the west the beaches become less commercialized and crowded; **Pass Christian's** is the best of all. Tan, sail, jet ski, or beach-comb, but *don't swim;* it's shallow and murky.

Participant Sports and Outdoor Activities

Boating

Sailboats, sailboards, Jet Skis, and catamarans may be rented from the many vendors who station themselves along the beach.

Camping

Take U.S. 90 to Waveland, turn south on Nicholson, and follow the signs to **Buccaneer State Park** (☎ 601/467–3822), which conceals 129 campsites in a grove of live oaks streaming with moss. An Olympic-size wave pool may lure you from the nature trail and picnic sites. There are no cabins, but toilet and shower facilities are available. **Gulf Islands National Seashore** (*see* Exploring, *above*) offers campsites for trailers and RVs.

Crabbing and Fishing

For **floundering** you'll need nighttime, a light, and a gig. Head for the sound, roll up your jeans, and spear your supper! A chicken neck and a string will put you in the **crabbing** business at any public pier. If you're feeling lazy, substitute a crab trap for the string.

Charter boats for half-day, full-day, or overnight **deep-sea fishing** can be found at marinas and harbors all along the Gulf Coast. Prices start around $30 per person; group rates are usually available. The Mississippi Beach Convention and Visitors Bureau (☎ 601/896–6699 or 800/237–9493) can assist you.

Golf

The coast's climate allows for year-round golfing, and golf packages are offered by many coast hotels and motels. Diamondhead's **Pine** and **Cardinal courses** (7600 Country Club Circle, ☎ 601/255–3910) offer 36 holes that challenge even the pros. Wooded, gently rolling, and well-kept, they are ringed by the large, elegant houses and condominiums of Diamondhead resort community. **Mississippi National Golf Club** (900 Hickory Hill Dr., Gautier, ☎ 601/497–5150 or 800/538–3155) offers visitors fairways lined with whispering pines, tall oaks, magnolias, and dogwoods. Flowers surround the teeing areas. **Pine Island Golf Course** (Gulf Park Estates, 2¼ mi east of Ocean Springs, 3 mi south of U.S. 90, ☎ 601/875–1674) was designed by Pete Dye, who created the tournament players course in Jacksonville. This course spans three islands, and its abundant wildlife, beautiful setting, and clubhouse can console you for any double bogeys. **Windance Country Club** (19385 Champion Circle, Gulfport, ☎ 601/832–4871) has a golf course ranked by *Golf Digest* among the top 100 in the United States; non-members can play here through hotel golf packages. Rates are $18–$55.

Dining and Lodging

Dining

Fresh Gulf seafood, particularly redfish, flounder, and speckled trout dishes, stars in coast restaurants. Soft-shell crab is a coast specialty, and crab claws are a traditional appetizer. Coast natives are fond of quaffing Barq's root beer with their seafood. Dress is casual unless otherwise noted.

CATEGORY	COST*
$$$$	over $20
$$$	$15–$20
$$	$10–$15
$	$5–$10

per person for a three-course meal, excluding drinks, service, and 8% sales tax

Lodging

With the 1993 advent of dockside casinos, the hotel business is booming. Reserve a couple of weeks ahead—gambling aficionados say the "coast is cookin'."

CATEGORY	COST*
$$$$	over $70
$$$	$50–$70
$$	$30–$50
$	$20–$30

All prices are for a standard double room, excluding 9% tax

Biloxi

DINING

$$–$$$ Fisherman's Wharf. A neighboring shrimp factory perfumes the parking lot here, but race inside to fresher air and views of oyster shuckers at work on the pier. You'll find soft-shell crab, gumbo, and oyster po'boys among the lunch specials; broiled catch-of-the-day for dinner; and always, the only dessert, the mysterious Fisherman's Wharf pie. ✕ *315 E. Beach Blvd.,* ☎ *601/436–4513. No reservations. AE, D, DC, MC, V.*

$ McElroy's Harbor House Restaurant. Biloxi natives and real shrimpers eat hearty breakfasts, lunches, and dinners here in functional surroundings. Notable are the po'boys, oysters on the half shell, broiled stuffed flounder, and stuffed crabs. You can also try "Biloxi bacon." ✕ *Biloxi Small Craft Harbor, 695 Beach Blvd.,* ☎ *601/435–5001. No reservations. AE, DC, MC, V.*

$ Ole Biloxi Schooner. Coast residents flock to this family-run restaurant on Biloxi's serene back bay. It's tiny—little more than a shack—but the food is good, especially the gumbo and the po'boys, which come "dressed" and wrapped in paper. ✕ *159 E. Howard,* ☎ *601/374–8071. No reservations. No credit cards.*

LODGING

$$$–$$$$ Treasure Bay. Formerly the Royal d'Iberville, the hotel has been spruced up by a recent renovation: The spacious rooms are now bright with chintz, and there's a new casino. Furniture is hotel-functional; the large public areas are comfortably contemporary. ⌸ *1980 W. Beach Blvd., Biloxi 39530,* ☎ *601/385–6000 or 800/388–3955. 254 rooms. Restaurant, lounge, 2 pools, 3 tennis courts, casino, meeting rooms. AE, DC, MC, V.*

$$$ Broadwater Beach Resort Hotels. This sprawling property is the South's largest resort and casino, and it comes complete with golf courses, tennis courts, a marina, and, of course, a casino. Accommodations vary depending on which of the three hotels in the resort you choose, and rates vary according to room size and location. ⌸ *2110 Beach Blvd., 39533,* ☎ *601/388–2211 or 800/647–3964,* ℻ *601/385–1801. 830 rooms, 20 suites. 4 restaurants, lounge, 4 pools, 2 18-hole golf courses, 6 tennis courts, boating marina, casino. AE, MC, V.*

Diamondhead

LODGING

$$$ **Diamondhead Days Inn.** This standard-issue motel attracts golfers who play the nearby Diamondhead Pine and Cardinal courses (*see* Participant Sports, *above*). ▦ *103 Live Oak Dr., 39525,* ☎ *601/255–1300 or 800/497–3685,* ℻ *601/255–9848. 153 rooms. Restaurant, lounge. AE, MC, V.*

Gulfport

DINING

$$–$$$ **Vrazel's.** In 1969, Hurricane Camille blew away the restaurant that had long stood here; the brick building that replaced it gets its charm from soft lighting and dining nooks with large windows facing the beach. Added attractions include the red snapper, Gulf trout, flounder, and shrimp prepared every which way: étouffée, au gratin, à la Cajun, almandine, à la Vrazel, blackened, Pontchartrain, meunière. For the best of land and sea, try veal Aaron (crabmeat, mushrooms, and lemon sauce combined with tender veal medallions). ✕ *3206 W. Beach Blvd. (U.S. 90),* ☎ *601/863–2229. Dinner reservations advised. AE, D, DC, MC, V.*

Long Beach

DINING

$$$ **Chappy's.** Special-occasion dining for Coast residents often means a visit to this pleasant restaurant with its twinkling white lights outside, its attentive waiters inside. Specialties include rich gumbo, redfish pan-fried Cajun style, and barbecued shrimp. The fish, fresh from the Gulf, is cooked by Chappy himself. ✕ *624 E. Beach,* ☎ *601/865–9755. Reservations advised. AE, D, DC, MC, V.*

Ocean Springs

DINING

$$$ **Germaine's.** Formerly Trilby's, this little house surrounded by live oaks has served many a great meal to its faithful clientele. The atmosphere is reminiscent of New Orleans, with unadorned wooden floors, walls decked in local art-for-sale, fireplaces, and attentive service. Specialties include mushrooms *le marin*, crabmeat au gratin, trout *desoto*, veal Angela, and chicken Chardonnay. ✕ *1203 Bienville Blvd., U.S. 90E,* ☎ *601/875–4426. Reservations advised. Jacket and tie. AE, DC, MC, V.*

$$–$$$ **Jocelyn's Restaurant.** Jocelyn scandalized Mississippians when she left
★ Trilby's kitchen (now Germaine's, *see above*), but they love her cooking just as much in this old frame house. This is as good as coast seafood gets. The specialty is the day's catch of flounder, trout, and snapper subtly seasoned and served with garnishes as bright and original as modern art. Stuffed eggplant is another specialty. ✕ *U.S. 90E, opposite Sunburst Bank,* ☎ *601/875–1925. No reservations. No credit cards.*

Pass Christian

DINING

$$$ **Blue Rose Restaurant & Lounge.** This antiques-filled West Indian–style
★ house (circa 1848), with a wonderful view of the Pass Christian Yacht Harbor and the Gulf of Mexico, is known in these parts for its Sunday Champagne Brunch featuring eggs Benedict and Creole platter (redfish, crab cakes, and barbecued shrimp). Other times, the kitchen turns out beautifully prepared and presented traditional New Orleans cuisine including a thick gumbo, pasta Orleans with oyster sauce, and trout

roulades with crab meat dressing and cayenne cream. ✕ *120 W. Scenic Dr.,* ☎ *601/452–9402. Reservations advised. AE, DC, MC, V.*

Waveland

DINING

$ **Lil Ray's.** The appointments are limited to trestle tables and benches. This is a place to dream about when you're hungry for seafood platters and po'boys. A waitress, asked by a customer for a diet drink, said it best: "Mister, this ain't no diet place." ✕ *613 Hwy. 90,* ☎ *601/467–4566. Reservations accepted. D, MC, V.*

Nightlife

Bars

Sip a cocktail at any of the 13 splashy, Las Vegas–style casinos permanently docked along the waterfront in Gulfport, Biloxi, Bay St. Louis, and Waveland. The casinos, with their numerous bars, lounges, and restaurants, are open 24 hours a day.

Live Entertainment

With the advent of casinos and all the accoutrements of dockside gambling, Coast nightlife is plentiful. To partake of the inimitable laid-back lifestyle, locals flock to **Dock of the Bay** (119 N. Beach Blvd., Bay St. Louis, ☎ 601/467–9940), where you'll hear great live easy rock music in the lounge and savor good grub in the restaurant.

Gulf Coast Essentials

Arriving and Departing, Getting Around

BY BUS

Coast Area Transit (333 DeBuys Rd., Gulfport, ☎ 601/896–8080) provides a coastwide public transportation system. **Greyhound** (☎ 800/231–2222) connects the coast with Jackson, New Orleans, and Mobile (Biloxi: 502 W. Railroad Ave., ☎ 601/436–4335; Gulfport: 11205 25th Ave., ☎ 601/863–1022; Bay St. Louis: 512 Ulman Ave., ☎ 601/467–4272).

BY CAR

You can drive across the entire coast in 1½ hours on I–10 and U.S. 90, reaching New Orleans in just over an hour from Gulfport. Jackson is fewer than three hours straight up U.S. 49, north from Gulfport.

BY PLANE

Fly into **Gulfport-Biloxi Regional Airport** (Airport Rd., off Washington Ave., Gulfport) and you can be on the beach in 15 minutes. Try American Eagle, ASA/The Delta Connection, Continental Express, or Northwest Airlink.

Guided Tours

Celebrity Limousine and Tours Service (2421 South Shore Dr., Biloxi, ☎ 601/388–1384) charters bus tours of the coastal area and New Orleans. **Magnolia Tours & Transportation** (111 Rue Magnolia, Suite 202, Biloxi 39530, ☎ 601/374–7423 or 800/642–4684) custom-plans group tours in buses or vans. **Riviera Holidays** (1042 Beach Blvd., Biloxi 39530, ☎ 601/432–8080 or 800/362–7350) arranges tours along the Mississippi coast.

Important Addresses and Numbers

EMERGENCIES

Dial 911, call the **Mississippi Highway Patrol** (☎ 601/864–1314), or go to the emergency room at **Gulf Coast Medical Center** (180 DeBuys Rd., Biloxi, ☎ 601/388–6711).

PHARMACY

Talvert Gamble (2561 Pass Rd., Biloxi, ☎ 601/388–1411).

RADIO STATIONS

FM: KNN 99.1, country; WMJY 93.7, adult contemporary.

VISITOR INFORMATION

Get a free *Attractions and Accommodations* guide to the Gulf Coast area at the **Mississippi Beach Convention and Visitors Bureau** (Box 6128, Gulfport 39506, ☎ 601/896–6699 or 800/237–9493. ☺ Weekdays 8–5).

THE NATCHEZ TRACE

The flower-sprigged and forested **Natchez Trace Parkway** is a vast and verdant history lesson. This enchanted path between Nashville and Natchez is said to be about 8,000 years old. It follows the early paths worn by Choctaw and Chickasaw Indians, flatboatmen, outlaws, itinerant preachers, postriders, soldiers, and settlers. Landscaped by the National Park Service, the Trace is meticulously manicured to show off the straightest pines and spookiest cypresses, to alternate peaceful vistas of reeds and still waters with dense woodlands where the dogwood stars shine. The Trace grows increasingly wild and mysterious as it nears Natchez; the outlaws who frequented the early trails come unwanted to mind.

Now virtually completed, the Trace is almost 450 miles long, with 313 miles in Mississippi. There are no billboards along its route, and commercial vehicles are forbidden to use it. Park rangers are serious about the 50 mph speed limit; you'll probably get acquainted with one if you drive any faster.

You can make the drive in seven hours from Tupelo to Natchez by driving diagonally across the state. However, to fully appreciate the beauty and history of the Trace requires a more leisurely approach, perhaps a weeklong odyssey.

Exploring

Numbers in the margin correspond to points of interest on the Natchez Trace map.

The Mississippi segment of the Natchez Trace begins as you enter the state's northeast corner, between Iuka and Belmont. It wanders through a hilly landscape of dense forests, sparkling streams, and well-maintained state parks.

Named for J. P. Coleman, Mississippi's governor from 1955 to 1959, ❶ **J. P. Coleman State Park** (613 County Rd. 321, 13 mi north of Iuka off U.S. 25, Iuka 38852, ☎ 601/423–6515) vies with Tishomingo State Park for the title of most spectacular Mississippi state park. There are wooded campsites for tents and RVs, and 10 secluded cabins, some of them old and rustic, others from the 1970s with fireplaces and central air and heat. Rooms at the balconied lodge overlook the shale beaches

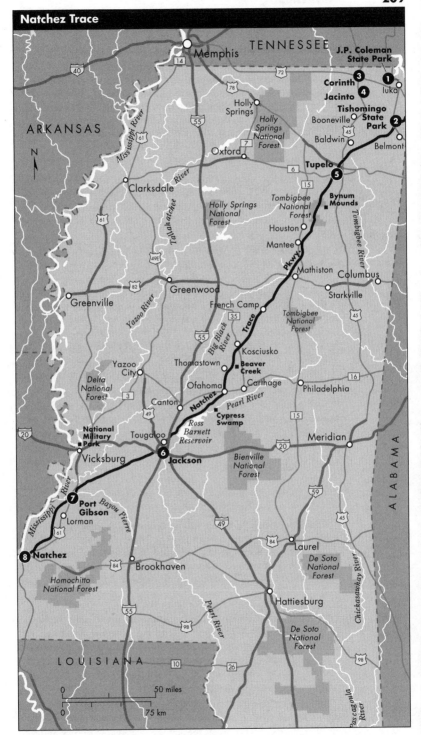

Natchez Trace

of serene Pickwick Lake. Visitors explore nature trails, rent canoes and boats, fish, swim, and waterski.

❷ **Tishomingo State Park** (Natchez Trace MM 304, Box 880, Tishomingo 38873, ☎ 601/438–6914) lies in the Appalachian foothills, making its terrain unique in Mississippi. If you're feeling peppy, a 13-mile nature trail winds through a canyon along steep hills by waterfalls, granite outcrops, and a swinging bridge; otherwise, take the winding roads through forests so leafy they can hide the brightest day in shadow. Eight-mile canoe trips and float trips are offered from mid-March to October. Around Haynes Lake are primitive campsites and hookups. Rustic cabins can also be found in the park. Bring your own food.

❸ **Corinth** is a town of special interest for Civil War enthusiasts. The Battles of Shiloh and Corinth are commemorated with markers and displays throughout the area. Corinth was settled just seven years before the war and assumed military importance because of its two railroad lines.

In April 1862, after the bloody battle of Shiloh, near Shiloh Church in Tennessee, 21 miles to the north, the Confederates turned Corinth into a vast medical center. In May 1862, the Confederates, under General P. G. T. Beauregard, were forced to withdraw further; their retreat involved the most ingenious hoax of the war: To fool the Federal forces, campfires were lighted, dummy cannoneers were placed at fake cannons, empty trains were cheered as if they brought reinforcements, and buglers moved along the deserted works, playing taps. Union forces occupied the town and, in October 1862, a Confederate attempt to recapture the town failed.

To visit all of Corinth's Civil War sites, follow the street markers, using the self-guided tour brochure available free at the **Northeast Mississippi Museum.** *4th St. at Washington St.,* ☎ *601/287–3120.* ☛ *Free.* ☼ *Daily 1–4.*

❹ Between Corinth and Tupelo is **Jacinto,** a ghost town with a restored Federal-style courthouse (1854) surrounded by pre-1870 buildings that are slowly being restored. Jacinto also has nature trails that lead to mineral springs, and a swinging bridge. *On MS 356, 9 mi east of U.S. 45,* ☎ *601/286–8662.* ☛ *Free. Opening times vary; call ahead.*

The **Natchez Trace Parkway Visitor Center** (*see* Visitor Information, *below*) is 6 miles north of Tupelo on the Trace. The Visitor Center offers exhibits, a 12-minute film, a hands-on area for children, and the *Official Map and Guide,* which opens to a 4-foot length to give detailed, mile-by-mile information from Nashville to Natchez.

Tupelo

❺ The largest city in north Mississippi, **Tupelo** (named after the tupelo gum tree), was founded in 1859 and is a city of accomplishment. Progressive leaders have successfully lured business and industry to an area that only 30 years ago was predominantly agricultural. The arts flourish here, and the medical center is among the largest in the state. The scenic hill country provides beautiful places to camp, swim, fish, jog, and bike.

Why do so many tourists flock here? Because this is a city of destiny: the birthplace of Elvis Presley, the acknowledged king of rock and roll. The **Tupelo Convention and Visitors Bureau** is a good place to start your tour (*see* Visitor Information, *below*). From here, head to ★**Elvis Presley's birthplace,** a tiny, two-room "shotgun" house built by his father,

Vernon Presley, for $180. Elvis Aaron Presley was born here on January 8, 1935. The home has been restored and furnished much as it was when the Presleys lived in it. The house is now surrounded by **Elvis Presley Park,** land purchased with proceeds from Elvis's 1956 concert at the Mississippi–Alabama Fair. The park includes a swimming pool, tennis courts, playground, and a gift shop (for Elvis souvenirs) in the Youth Center, and the **Elvis Presley Museum,** opened in August 1992, with more than 3,000 pieces of previously unseen Elvis memorabilia. The **Elvis Presley Memorial Chapel,** suggested by the singer in 1971 as a place for his fans to meditate, was dedicated in 1979, two years after Presley's death. *Off Old Hwy. 78, at 306 Elvis Presley Dr.,* ☎ *601/841– 1245.* ☛ *Birthplace $1 adults, 50¢ children.* ☛ *Museum $4 adults, $2 children.* ☉ *May–Sept., Mon.–Sat. 9–5:30, Sun. 1–5; Oct.–Apr., Mon.–Sat. 9–5, Sun. 1–5.*

Five miles north of the Presley birthplace is **Elvis Presley Lake and Campground,** where you can ski, sun, and fish—and think about Elvis. *Off Canal St. extended,* ☎ *601/841–1304. Primitive and full-service campsites.* ☛ *Free; separate fees for camping and boat launching.*

The **Tupelo Museum** displays further Presley memorabilia along with other exhibits, including a turn-of-the-century Western Union office, a working sorghum mill, a train depot and caboose, and an old-time country store. *James J. Ballard Park, off MS 6W,* ☎ *601/841–6438.* ☛ *$1 adults, 50¢ children 3–12 , children under 3 free.* ☉ *Tues.–Fri. 8–4, weekends 1–5.*

Once you've satisfied your Elvis mania, turn your thoughts to the Civil War Battle of Tupelo. In 1864, Union General A. J. Smith marched 14,000 troops against Nathan Bedford Forrest's forces near Tupelo. Smith's goal was to end the constant Southern harrassment of supply lines to Sherman's army besieging Atlanta. The battle, on July 14, 1864, was the last major battle in Mississippi and one of the bloodiest. A **National Battlefield** site on West Main Street (MS 6), inside the city limits, commemorates the battle with monuments and displays.

From Tupelo, the trip to Jackson takes three hours if you don't stop. It can easily take an entire day, however, if you stop to read the brown wooden markers, explore nature trails, and admire the neat fields, trees, and wildflower meadows.

Bynum Mounds (mile marker 232.4) are ceremonial hills that were constructed between 100 BC and AD 200 by prehistoric people. Exhibits describe their daily existence.

At **French Camp** (mile marker 180.7), where Frenchman Louis LeFleur established a stand (or inn) in 1812, you can watch sorghum molasses being made on Saturday in late September and October. And you can see Native American and French artifacts inside the authentic "dogtrot-style" cabin.

At **Beaver Creek** (mile marker 145.1), a short (5- to 10-minute), self-guided nature trail explains beavers' habits.

Cypress Swamp (mile marker 122.0), a pleasure today, was once a treacherous, mosquito-infested morass for early travelers. A 20-minute self-guided nature walk takes you through the tree-canopied tupelo/bald cypress swamp.

The **Mississippi Crafts Center at Ridgeland** displays and sells high quality crafts in a dogtrot log cabin. Members of the Craftsman's Guild of Mississippi have created pewter and silver jewelry, pottery, handwoven and handscreened clothing, whimsical wooden toys, highly prized Choctaw Indian baskets, and other interesting items. The Center sponsors free demonstrations (usually on weekends) of basketweaving, wood carving, pottery, and quilting. *Natchez Trace at Ridgeland (MM 102.4),* ☎ *601/856–7546.* ☛ *Free.* ⊙ *Daily 9–5. Facilities: rest rooms, picnic tables.*

The parkway is incomplete from mile marker 101.5 to 87.0. I–55, I–20, and I–220 are connecting routes. To reach Jackson, follow I–55 south from the Trace.

Jackson

6 At its spangled edges, **Jackson** has little to distinguish it, but the state capital becomes increasingly original toward its shady heart. The downtown area has many small museums and most of the city's notable architecture.

The city is named for Andrew Jackson, who was popular with Mississippians long before he became president. As Major General Jackson, he helped negotiate the Treaty of Doak's Stand by which the Choctaw Indians ceded large chunks of Mississippi to the United States, on October 18, 1820. The City of Jackson is the county seat of Hinds County, named for another negotiator, Major General Thomas Hinds, an enterprising and daring hero of the Battle of New Orleans in the War of 1812.

The **Jackson Visitor Information Center** (*see* Visitor Information, *below*) is located in the Chimneyville Crafts Building on the grounds of the **Jim Buck Ross Mississippi Agriculture and Forestry Museum,** which looks like an old farm marooned in the midst of expanding suburbs, but the city was actually here first. The 10 farm buildings were brought here to stand exactly as they once did in Jefferson Davis County, Mississippi. A crossroads town, similar to small Mississippi towns in the 1920s, has been assembled. Work goes on in a blacksmith's shop and a cotton gin, meetings are held in the old Masonic Lodge, and the 1897 Epiphany Episcopal church building can be rented for weddings. The General Store sells soft drinks, snacks, and souvenirs. A complete tour of the museum, which has fine exhibits on agriculture, forestry, and farm-related aviation, takes about 90 minutes. *1150 Lakeland Dr., Jackson 39216,* ☎ *601/354–6113 or 800/844–8687.* ☛ *$3 adults, $2.75 senior citizens, $1 children 6–18, children under 6 free.* ⊙ *Mon.–Sat. 9–5, Sun. 1–5.*

The **Old Capitol Building** sits serenely on Capitol Green, with the **War Memorial Building** (1940) to the north and the **Mississippi Archives Building** (1971) to the south. Begun in 1833 and completed in 1838 , the Old Capitol, with its simple columns and elegant proportions, is an excellent example of Greek Revival architecture. The building was restored in 1959–61 for use as the **State Historical Museum.** Capitol Green is a leafy reminder of the checkerboard pattern of alternating squares of buildings and parks recommended by President Thomas Jefferson and proposed for Jackson by Peter A. Vandorn. Vandorn submitted a map and plan for the new city in April 1822. The Vandorn map and other exhibits depicting Mississippi's history are on display in the museum. *100 S. State St.,* ☎ *601/359–6920.* ☛ *Free.* ⊙ *Weekdays 8–5, Sat. 9:30–4:30, Sun. 12:30–4:30. Guided tours available.*

The **Jackson Zoological Park** uses more than 100 acres to re-create a natural habitat for about 500 animals. The zoo also contains a children's zoo, complete with hands-on exhibits and a miniature train. *2918*

W. Capitol St., ☎ *601/352–2580.* ☛ *$4 adults, $2 children 3–12.* ☾ *Daily 9–5.*

Baseball fans, venture off I–55 onto Lakeland Drive to see the **Dizzy Dean Museum.** Here you'll see artifacts and personal effects of the late, colorful Hall of Fame pitcher for the St. Louis Cardinals and amusing sportscaster. *1202 Lakeland Dr.,* ☎ *601/960–2404.* ☛ *$1.* ☾ *Apr.–Sept. 1, Tues.–Sat. 11–6, Sun. 1–5.*

City Hall (219 S. President St., ☎ 601/960–1035) is a white Greek Revival building that has served continuously as Jackson's center of government since its opening in 1847. A Masonic Hall originally occupied the third floor. During the Civil War, City Hall was used as a hospital. Look into the tiny City Council chamber with its black-and-white floors and heavy red velvet curtains. On the west side of the building is the formal Josh Halbert Garden, with a 1968 statue of Andrew Jackson.

In the **Mississippi Arts Center** you will find the **Mississippi Museum of Art** and the **Impressions Gallery.** The museum, *dedicated to preserving Mississippi's artistic heritage,* has changing exhibits and a permanent collection of regional paintings. In the high-tech, hands-on Impressions Gallery, you can create music by walking through beams of light, wave your arms to send colors rippling from your shadow, and more—all in the name of education and art. *201 E. Pascagoula St.,* ☎ *601/960–1515.* ☛ *$3 adults, $2 children;* ☛ *Impressions Gallery free.* ☾ *Tues.–Sat. 10–5.*

Davis Planetarium is the largest planetarium in the Southeast and one of the world's best equipped, but its shows vary wildly in quality and scope. *201 E. Pascagoula St.,* ☎ *601/960–1550.* ☛ *$4 adults, $2.50 children under 12 and senior citizens. Hours vary; call ahead.*

The **U.S. Federal Courthouse** (245 E. Capitol St.) is a good example in concrete and sandstone of the streamlined art deco–style that was popular between the world wars, a time when many Jackson buildings were constructed. This building was completed in 1934 and served as Jackson's post office and as a federal court building until 1988, when a new post office was built. The motifs of eagles, stars, and geometric designs on the exterior are repeated throughout the interior and on the freestanding aluminum light fixtures around the building.

St. Andrew's Episcopal Cathedral is an important example of Gothic Revival architecture enhanced by fine stained-glass windows. *305 E. Capitol St.,* ☎ *601/354–1535.* ☾ *Weekdays.*

Lamar Life Building, adjacent to St. Andrew's, was designed to complement the cathedral. Although it has lost the alligators that once flanked its doors, it still exhibits other Gothic designs and a crenellated clock tower. The president of Lamar Life during the building's construction (1924–25) was C. W. Welty, father of Eudora Welty, Pulitzer Prize–winning author and lifelong Jackson resident.

The **Mississippi Governor's Mansion** has been continuously in use as the official home of the state's first family since its completion in 1842. At that time, Jackson was a tiny city and this grand Greek Revival dwelling was an optimistic statement. General Sherman presumably lived here during his occupation of Jackson in 1863. The mansion is one of only two executive residences to be designated a National Historic Landmark. Invest 30 minutes in the lively tours, strong on legend as well as fact. *300 E. Capitol St., ☎ 601/359–6421. ☛ Free. Tours Tues.–Fri. 9:30–11:30.*

Smith Park is the only public square that remains from the 1822 checkerboard plan of the city. It is the center of the Smith Park Historic District. The park was a grazing area for animals until 1884, when James Smith of Glasgow, Scotland, a former Jacksonian, donated $100 to fence and beautify it, and the park was named for him. It is the setting for a famous short story, "The Winds," by Eudora Welty. The park hosts frequent concerts, festivals, picnics, and art exhibits. A popular "Fridays in Smith Park" program offers noontime entertainment in April and October.

The **Cathedral of St. Peter the Apostle** (203 N. West St.), built 1897–1900, is the third building of the congregation, which organized in 1846. Their first building was burned by Federal troops in 1863, as were many others in the city. Their second church, now in the very center of the downtown area, at the site of the present rectory (123 N. West St.), was criticized for its remoteness from town. It is only open to the public for church services.

Mynelle Gardens is a 7-acre botanical showplace, where you're invited to stroll leisurely along colorful paths where Southern flora and sparkling streams recall gentler times. It was in need of some sprucing up on a recent visit. *4736 Clinton Blvd., ☎ 601/960–1894. ☛ $2 adults, 50¢ children. ⊙ Mar.–Oct., daily 9–6; Nov.–Feb., daily 8–5.*

The **Galloway House** (304 N. Congress St.) is a two-story Second Empire house. Completed in 1889, this house was built for Methodist Bishop Charles Galloway, a distinguished churchman of international renown. In 1983 it was renovated for use as a law office.

The **New Capitol** sits in Beaux Arts splendor at the junction of Mississippi and North Congress streets, its dome surmounted by a gold-plated copper eagle with a 15-foot wingspan. Completed in 1903 at a cost of $1 million, the Capitol enjoyed a $19-million renovation from 1979 to 1983. It was designed by the German architect Theodore C. Link, who was strongly influenced by the Capitol in Washington, DC. Elaborate architectural details inside the building include a Tiffany window. *400 High St., ☎ 601/359–3114. ☛ Free. ⊙ Weekdays 8–5, Sat. 10–4, Sun. 1–4. Guided tours: weekdays 9, 10, 11, 1:30, 2:30, 3:30.*

Eudora Welty Library, the largest public library in Mississippi, is named in honor of the city's famed short-story writer and novelist (*The Ponder Heart, Losing Battles, The Optimist's Daughter*). The library opened in 1986; it has a 42-foot-long circulation desk, handcrafted of African rosewood and curly maple by local craftsman Fletcher Cox. It houses the Mississippi Writer's Room exhibit on Miss Welty, William Faulkner, Tennessee Williams, Margaret Walker Alexander, Ellen Douglas, and many others. *300 N. State St., ☎ 601/968–5811. ⊙ June–Aug., Mon.–Thurs. 10–9, Fri. and Sat. 10–6; Sept.–May, Mon.–Thurs. 10–9, Fri. and Sat. 10–6, Sun. 1–5.*

A few Victorian homes stand on North State Street between College and Fortification streets, the survivors of the many large houses that lined this street in its heyday as Jackson's best address. The **Morris House** (505 N. State St.) is a Classic Revival house built about 1900. The **Virden-Patton House** (512 N. State St.), built about 1849, was undamaged in the Civil War, suggesting that Union officers may have used it as headquarters. The **Millsaps-Buie House** (628 N. State St.), built in 1888, has been restored as a bed-and-breakfast inn (*see* Lodging, *below*). It was built by Major Reuben Webster Millsaps, the founder of Millsaps College in Jackson. Two doors north is the **Garner Green House** (1910), with an imposing portico of Corinthian columns. This house was moved across the street from its original location and restored in 1988 to become an office building. **Greenbrook Flowers** (circa 1895–97; 705 N. State St.) occupies the former St. Andrew's Episcopal rectory; it has been greatly altered. With the exception of the bed and breakfast, none of these homes are open to the public.

The **Manship House** was built about 1857 by Charles H. Manship, the Jackson mayor who surrendered the city to General William Tecumseh Sherman on July 16, 1863. The museum is a careful restoration of a small Gothic Revival–style home with examples of wood graining painted by Manship himself. *420 E. Fortification St. (enter parking area from Congress St.),* ☎ *601/961–4724.* ☛ *Free. Tours: Tues.–Fri. 9–4, weekends 1–4.*

C. W. Welty and his wife, Chestina, built the house at **741 North Congress Street** in 1907. Their daughter Eudora was born here in 1909 in the master bedroom on the second floor. Welty used images of this house and neighborhood in many of her literary works, including *The Golden Apples.* It has been restored for use as a law office.

The **Smith Robertson Museum** has African-American artifacts and exhibits focusing on black life in Mississippi throughout its history. The building, which was the first public school for black children in Jackson, has been creatively adapted for use as a museum and meeting place. *528 Bloom St.,* ☎ *601/960–1457.* ☛ *$1 adults, 50¢ children.* ☺ *Weekdays 9–8, Sat. 9–noon, Sun. 2–5.*

Jackson's oldest house, the **Oaks,** was built by James Hervey Boyd, mayor of Jackson between 1853 and 1858. *823 N. Jefferson St.,* ☎ *601/353–1742.* ☛ *$2 adults, $1.25 children.* ☺ *Tues.–Sun. 10–3.*

Jackson is a city of neat, tree-shaded neighborhoods, excellent for walking, jogging, or Sunday driving, especially the **Belhaven area** bounded by Riverside Drive, I–55, Fortification Street, and North State Street. **Carlisle, Poplar, Peachtree,** and **Fairview streets** are distinguished by fine homes.

Return to the Natchez Trace on I–20 (west), then head south to **Rocky Springs** (mile marker 54.8), where post riders stopped during the early 1800s, and General Grant's army camped on its march to Jackson and Vicksburg during the Civil War. You can camp here, too. It's a first-come, first-served race, especially on weekends, but at least you needn't worry about Confederate sharpshooters. Overhung by ancient trees, the stream ripples and sings like mountain waters. Trails meander through the woods and up a steep hill to a tiny old cemetery and **Rocky Springs Methodist Church** (1837), where services are still held Sunday.

At mile marker 41.5 is a portion of the **Old Trace,** a short section of the original Indian Trace of loess soil (easily eroded and compacted earth). You can park and walk along it for a short way.

❼ **Port Gibson** is the earliest still-existent town on the Trace. Aptly named Church Street is a shady main thoroughfare lined with churches and stately homes. You won't miss the **First Presbyterian Church** (1859), with its spire topped by a 10-foot hand pointing heavenward. The church chandeliers came from the old steamboat *Robert E. Lee.* Among the old churches and houses along Church Street are **Gage House** (602 Church St.), 1830, with double galleries and a handsome brick de-

pendency; **Temple Gemiluth Chassed** (706 Church St.), 1892, a syna-
gogue with Moorish Byzantine architecture unique in Mississippi; **St.
James Episcopal Church** (808 Church St.), circa 1897, a high Victo-
rian Gothic structure designed by a Boston architect, thus reflecting
Massachusetts architecture; **Port Gibson Methodist Church** (901 Church
St.), 1860, Romanesque Revival in style; the **Hughes Home** (907 Church
St.), 1825, once owned by Henry Hughes, author of the first sociol-
ogy textbook, and once the residence of poet Irvin Russell; and **St.
Joseph's Catholic Church** (909 Church St.), 1849, Gothic in style, with
pointed arches and buttresses. **Gibson's Landing** (1002 Church St.) is
called the "Disharoon House" by locals. Built in the 1830s, it's now
a bed-and-breakfast, as is the palatial mid-19th century, 30-room mansion, **Oak Square** (*see* Lodging, *below*). This classic Greek Revival treasure is open for tours by appointment. **Mississippi Cultural Crossroads**
(507 Market St., ☎ 601/437–8905, ☉ Weekdays 8–5) has an enviable collection of quilts on display and for sale. The **Chamber of Commerce,** where you can get maps to local historic sites, is housed in a
small 1805 home built by Port Gibson's founder Samuel Gibson and
moved to this site in 1980. *South end of Church St.,* ☎ *601/437–4351.*
☉ *Feb.–Nov., weekdays 8–4, Sat. 9–4, Sun. noon–4; Dec.–Jan., weekdays 8–4.*

Grand Gulf Military Monument commemorates the once-thriving town
of Grand Gulf, site of an 1862 Civil War naval battle. On a steep hill,
the old town site has become a museum with an 1863 cannon, a collection of carriages, an 1820s dogtrot cabin, an old Catholic church,
and a Spanish house from the 1790s. *North of Port Gibson off U.S.
61., Rte. 2, Port Gibson,* ☎ *601/437–5911.* ☛ *$1.50 adults, 75¢ chil-
dren.* ☉ *Mon.–Sat. 8–noon, 1–5; Sun. 9–noon, 1–6.*

TIME OUT Handmade bonnets swing in the breeze on the porch of the **Old Country
Store,** which was a plantation store built in 1875. Its longleaf-pine flooring is jammed with display cases, most installed when the store was
built, and you can buy souvenirs, soft drinks, and snacks, including mellow hoop cheese. *U.S. 61, in Lorman,* ☎ *601/437–3661.*

Ask directions at the Old Country Store to the restored **Rodney Presbyterian Church** (about 12 mi southwest of Lorman). The town of Rodney, once home to wealthy plantation owners and river merchants,
became a ghost town when the Mississippi River shifted its course. Your
visit to Rodney will be enhanced by reading Eudora Welty's powerful
essay "Some Notes on River Country" and her short story "At the Landing."

Northwest of Lorman, on MS 552, are 23 vine-clad columns that are
the romantic ruins of **Windsor,** a huge Greek Revival mansion that was
built in 1861 and burned down in 1890. The ruins were featured in
Raintree County, a late '50s film starring Elizabeth Taylor.

Emerald Mound (mile marker 10.3) is the second-largest Indian mound
in the country, covering almost 8 acres. It was built around 1300 for
religious ceremonies practiced by ancestors of the Natchez Indians. It's
a good place to picnic or view a sunset.

The Parkway abruptly ends, putting you on U.S. 61 as you near
Natchez. You'll pass through the little town of **Washington,** with the
buildings of historic Jefferson College meticulously restored. Washington
was the capital of the Mississippi Territory from 1802 to 1817, and
Jefferson College was chartered in 1802 as the territory's first educational institution. Here Aaron Burr, who served as Thomas Jefferson's

vice president, was arraigned for treason in 1807. Burr was lionized by Natchez society while he awaited trial. *U.S. 61, Natchez,* ☎ *601/442–2901.* ☛ *Free.* ☉ *Buildings Mon.–Sat. 9–5, Sun. 1–5.*

Natchez

★ ❽ Antebellum **Natchez** is named for the mound-building, sun-worshiping Natchez Indians who lived here, undisturbed, in small villages before the French built Fort Rosalie in 1716. Later the city came under British rule (1763–79), and the district known today as **Natchez-under-the-Hill** grew up at the Mississippi River landing beneath the bluff. The Spanish took control in 1779; they left their mark on the city by establishing straight streets—which intersect at right angles, atop the bluff—and green parkland that overlooks the river. The United States claimed Natchez by treaty and the U.S. flag first flew over Natchez in March of 1798. The city gave its name to the Natchez Trace and prospered as travelers heading for Nashville passed through with money in their pockets and a willingness to spend it on a rowdy good time.

The real glory days came between 1819 and 1860, when cotton plantations and the bustling river port poured riches into Natchez. Wealthy planters built stylish town houses and ringed the city with opulent plantation homes. Because the city had little military significance, it survived the Civil War almost untouched, though its economy suffered. The city entered a decline that actually saved its architectural treasures. No one could afford to tear houses down or even to remodel them. In 1932, the women of Natchez originated the idea of a pilgrimage, which would raise money for preservation. The Natchez Pilgrimage is now held twice a year, three weeks in October and four weeks in March and April. Many houses are open only during Pilgrimage weeks, when crowds flock to see them, but others are open year-round.

These days, Natchez relives its colorful past in the form of dockside gambling, held on the river Under the Hill. *Lady Luck* is a riverboat casino docked permanently on the mighty Mississippi, and she offers two restaurants, numerous lounges, and Las Vegas–style gambling for anyone over 21 with money to burn.

Begin your sightseeing at one of the tourist information centers (*see* Important Addresses and Numbers, *below*). The chamber of commerce offers a free self-guided walking tour. At the **Pilgrimage Tour Headquarters** (Canal and State Sts., ☎ 601/446–6631 or 800/647–6742) you can purchase *Natchez: Walking Guide to the Old Town* and a plethora of additional books and maps of this fascinating city. New in Natchez is an authentic double-decker London bus offering scheduled tours throughout the day. *416 Main St.,* ☎ *601/445–9300.* ☛ *$10 adults, $5 children 12–4, under 4 free.*

Stanton Hall (1857) is one of the most palatial and most photographed houses in America. Four giant fluted columns surmount double porticos enclosed by delicate, lacy wrought-iron railings. This magnificent preservation project of the Pilgrimage Garden Club is furnished with important Natchez antiques and objets d'art. *401 High St.,* ☎ *601/442–6282 or 800/647–6742.* ☛ *$5 adults, $2.50 children.* ☉ *Daily 9–5.*

Rosalie (circa 1823) established the ideal form of the "Southern mansion" with its white columns, hipped roof, and red bricks. Furnishings purchased for the house in 1858 include a famous Belter parlor set. *100 Orleans St.,* ☎ *601/445–4555.* ☛ *$5 adults, $2.50 children over 10.* ☉ *Daily 9–5.*

Magnolia Hall (circa 1858) was shelled by the Union gunboat *Essex* during the Civil War. The shell reportedly exploded in a soup tureen, scalding several diners. The Greek Revival mansion has stucco walls and fluted columns topped with curving Ionic capitals. Note the plaster magnolia blossoms on the parlor ceiling. There is a costume museum on the second floor. *215 S. Pearl St.,* ☎ *601/442–6672.* ☛ *$5 adults, $2.50 children. Tours daily 9–5.*

Natchez National Historical Park was established in 1988 to help preserve and interpret this city so historically significant to the development of the American South. Currently, two properties are featured: **Melrose** (circa 1845), a mansion that symbolizes the era when cotton ruled, and the **William Johnson House** (circa 1841). Johnson was a prominent "free man of color," and his house, currently being restored, will eventually open as a museum of African-American history; at press time it could only be viewed from the outside. *Melrose: 1 Melrose–Montebello Pkwy.,* ☎ *601/446–5790. William Johnson House: 210 State St.,* ☎ *601/442–7047.* ☛ *To Melrose: $4 adults, $2 children under 16.* ⊙ *Daily 9–5.*

Longwood (circa 1860–61) is the largest octagonal house in the United States. When the Civil War broke out, Northern workers fled to their homes, preventing the immensely wealthy Dr. Haller Nutt from completing the mansion. Hoping to finish the house at the war's end, Nutt moved his family into the basement, but he died in 1864. Still unfinished, Longwood is now a museum for the Pilgrimage Garden Club and a National Historic Landmark. *140 Lower Woodville Rd.,* ☎ *601/442–5193.* ☛ *$5 adults, $2.50 children.* ⊙ *Daily 9–5; hours for Spring and Fall Pilgrimages vary, so call ahead.*

What to See and Do with Children

Columbus

A short drive south of Columbus (*see* Off the Beaten Path, *below*) will land you at **Sunshine Farms,** where fainting goats, miniature horses, and a plethora of farm animals will delight the kids. *Off Hwy. 45,* ☎ *601/726–2264.* ☛ *$3.50 for adults and children.* ⊙ *Mon.–Sat. 10–5.*

Jackson

Chuck E. Cheese's Pizza Time Theatre. Arcade and entertainment for the under-12 set. *5465 I–55N,* ☎ *601/956–5252.* ⊙ *Mon.–Thurs. 11–9:30, Fri. and Sat. 11–11, Sun. noon–9:30.*

Impressions Gallery (*see* Exploring, *above*).

Jim Buck Ross Mississippi Agriculture and Forestry Museum (*see* Exploring, *above*).

The **New Capitol** is awe-inspiring enough in its decorations (4,500 bare light bulbs, and plenty of gilt) to interest even young children (*see* Exploring, *above*).

Space Port. Large video arcade. *N. Park Mall, 1200 E. County Line Rd.,* ☎ *601/956–7315.* ⊙ *Mon.–Sat. 10–9:30, Sun. 1–6.*

Zoological Park. This family recreational spot features animals in natural settings, including many endangered species. (*see* Exploring, *above*).

Natchez

Carriage rides are a fun way to see downtown Natchez. Tours begin at Natchez Pilgrimage Tour Headquarters (Canal St. at State St.) or the Eola Hotel (110 N. Pearl St.). A tour lasts about 30 minutes and costs $8 adults, $4 children under 13.

Grand Village of the Natchez Indians. The archaeological park and museum depicts the culture of the Natchez Indians, which reached its zenith in the 1500s. *400 Jefferson Davis Blvd.,* ☎ *601/446–6502.* ☛ *Free.* ☉ *Mon.–Sat. 9–5, Sun. 1:30–5.*

Longwood. An air of mystery surrounds this uncompleted octagonal house, making it perhaps the only Natchez mansion guaranteed to interest children (*see* Exploring, *above*).

Port Gibson

Grand Gulf Military Monument. Children love the steep trail, the observation tower, the old waterwheel, and the blood-stained uniforms (*see* Exploring, *above*).

Off the Beaten Path

Columbus, 45 miles east of the Natchez Trace on U.S. 82, is one of Mississippi's most undisturbed antebellum towns, and one that claimed the moniker "Possumtown" until the city was chartered in 1821 and a more dignified name was chosen. This river city (on the Tombigbee) contains 100 pre–Civil War mansions—some of which are open to the public as bed-and-breakfasts or for tours—and many historic sites. Columbus is called the town "where flowers healed a nation" because of a group of gracious women who, in 1866, placed flowers on the graves of both Confederate and Union soldiers. The gesture inspired the poem "The Blue and the Gray," and Columbus's Decoration Day at Friendship Cemetery is now observed as the nation's Memorial Day. The **Convention and Visitors Bureau** (321 7th St., Box 789, Columbus 39703, ☎ 601/329–1191 or 800/327–2686) has additional information.

Magnificent **Waverley Mansion** (1852) is a genuine Mississippi showplace. Privately owned, it's immaculately restored: Outstanding antiques adorn each spacious room. *10 mi northwest of Columbus, off MS 50, Rte. 2, West Point,* ☎ *601/494–1399.* ☛ *$7.50, children under 6 free.* ☉ *Daily 8–sunset.*

Shopping in Jackson

Antiques

Bobbie King's (Woodland Hills Shopping Center, Old Canton Rd. at Duling Ave., ☎ 601/362–9803) specializes in new and heirloom textiles and exhibits them in lavish displays with one-of-a-kind accessories. **C. W. Fewel III & Co., Antiquarians** (840 N. State St., ☎ 601/355–5375) specializes in fine 18th- and 19th-century furnishings and accessories.

Books

Books by Mississippi authors and about Mississippi are available from knowledgeable booksellers at **Lemuria** (202 Banner Hall, 4465 I–55N, ☎ 601/366–7619). **Choctaw Books** (926 North St., ☎ 601/352–7281) stocks first editions of Southern writers' works.

Flea Market

If you're in the mood for a treasure hunt, the **Fairground Antique & Flea Market,** with 220 dealers, often harbors some fine pieces among the simply fun stuff. *900 High St.,* ☎ *601/353–5327.* ◎ *Sat. 8–5, Sun. 10–5.*

Gifts

The members of the Craftsman's Guild of Mississippi have raised crafts from their "arts and crafts" status to "craft as art." Their work is sold in the Jackson area at **Mississippi Crafts Center** (*see* Exploring, *above*), the **Old Capitol Museum** shop (*see* Exploring, *above*), and the **Chimneyville Crafts Gallery** (1150 Lakeland Dr., ☎ 601/981–2499).

The **Everyday Gourmet** (2905 Old Canton Rd., ☎ 601/362–0723; 1625 County Line Rd., ☎ 601/977–9258) stocks state products, including pecan pie, bread, and biscuit mixes; muscadine jelly; jams and chutneys; cookbooks; fine ceramic tableware; and a complete stock of kitchenware and gourmet foods.

Participant Sports

Golf

JACKSON

Semiprivate **Lefleur's Bluff State Park** features 18 holes (Highland Dr. at Lakeland Dr., ☎ 601/987–3998) and has a reciprocity agreement with nearby clubs.

Jogging

JACKSON

Jog on paths that curve under tall pines and stretch down to a sunny meadow in **Parham Bridges Park** (5055 Old Canton Rd.).

NATCHEZ

An asphalt road runs about 1½ miles through **Duncan Park** (Duncan St. at Auburn Ave.).

Tennis

JACKSON

Lob and volley at **Tennis Center South** (2827 Oak Forest Dr., off Mc-Dowell Rd., ☎ 601/960–1712) and **Parham Bridges Park** (5055 Old Canton Rd., ☎ 601/956–1105).

NATCHEZ

There are courts in **Duncan Park** (Duncan St. at Auburn Ave., ☎ 601/442–1589)

Dining and Lodging

Dining

In Tupelo, Jackson, and Natchez you can find everything from caviar to chitlins. Fine food often comes in casual surroundings. Jackson has several elegant restaurants. Natchez has its share of fine dining, and also serves up plantation breakfasts in antebellum opulence. Tupelo offers a wide variety, but specializes in down-home cooking. If you're eating on the run, Jackson's County Line Road east of I–55 and the East Frontage roads along I–55N are jammed with fast-food joints. Blue plate dinners of fresh Mississippi vegetables are a widely available alternative. Dress is casual unless otherwise noted.

CATEGORY	COST*
$$$$	over $20
$$$	$15–$20
$$	$10–$15
$	under $10

*per person for a three-course meal, excluding drinks, service, and 8% sales tax

Lodging

National hotel and motel chains are found throughout the region, though the choice is greater in Jackson. In Natchez, travelers will find plantation homes that open their doors in bed-and-breakfast courtesy.

CATEGORY	COST*
$$$$	over $70
$$$	$50–$70
$$	$30–$50
$	under $30

*All prices are for a standard double room, excluding 7% tax

Jackson

DINING

$$$
★ **Nick's.** Seafood—grilled, panéed, or sautéed—is served at this casually elegant restaurant. Grilled blackfish with crabmeat is one of the many luncheon specials, while dinner brings out more elaborate seafood masterpieces. Soup, pasta or salad, and vegetable du jour are included with the entrée. Desserts are wonderful, too, especially the white-chocolate mousse with raspberry sauce. Nick's has the most extensive wine list in Mississippi. ✕ 1501 Lakeland Dr., ☎ 601/981–8017. Reservations accepted. AE, DC, MC, V.

$$$
★ **Ralph & Kacoo's.** Ralph & Kacoo's originated in South Louisiana, so Cajun fare is naturally de rigueur. Crawfish étouffée is prepared to perfection, cher! ✕ 100 Dyess Rd. (County Line Rd. and I–55), ☎ 601/957–0702. AE, MC, V.

$$ Iron Horse Bar & Grill. Near downtown, this fern-filled restaurant in a converted factory features Southwestern fare, including fajitas and mesquite-grilled seafood or steak. Folks who order the juicy prime rib give it rave reviews, too. ✕ 320 W. Pearl St., ☎ 601/355–8419. Reservations advised. AE, MC, V.

$$ Primos. Opening in this spot in 1944, after spending its first 15 years in another Jackson location, this cozy and comfy eatery has much experience pleasing local palates. The main dining room recalls a French country inn, while the patio is pure American South. House specialties are fresh seafood and prime ribs. ✕ 4330 State St., ☎ 601/982–2064. Reservations accepted. AE, DC, MC, V.

$–$$ Palette. This restaurant, in a gallery in the Mississippi Museum of Art, is one of the state's finest lunch spots. Everybody likes the large, light-filled spaces, the art on the white walls, the friendly bustle of the arts community and businesspeople, the piano music, and, most of all, the food—carefully prepared and beautifully presented. You may find Mississippi catfish sautéed in pecan butter; fresh vegetable lasagne; or chicken with penne in garlic brie sauce; but the delicacies change frequently. ✕ 201 E. Pascagoula St., ☎ 601/960–2003. No reservations. MC, V. Closed Mon.

$ Gridley's. Mexican tile tables and floors enhance small, sunny dining areas. Gridley's is famous for its spicy barbecued pork and ribs served with all the trimmings—coleslaw, baked beans, and potatoes. ✕ 1428 Old Square Rd., ☎ 601/362–8600. No reservations. AE, MC, V.

LODGING

$$$$ **Fairview.** Listed on the National Register of Historic Places, this seven-room Colonial Revival mansion is located in Jackson's prestigious Belhaven section, conveniently situated near many of the major attractions, yet secluded enough to suggest a country retreat. Period antiques fill the public rooms, and the guest rooms are decked out in chintz and Laura Ashley fabrics. A full breakfast is included in the tariff. ☎ *734 Fairview St., 39202, 601/948–3429. 7 rooms with bath. AE, MC, V.*

$$$–$$$$ **Millsaps-Buie House.** This Queen Anne–style home, with its corner tur-
★ ret and tall-columned porch, was built in 1888 for Jackson financier and philanthropist Major Reuben Webster Millsaps, founder of Millsaps College in Jackson; it is listed on the National Register of Historic Places. Restored as a B&B in 1987, its guest rooms are individually decorated with antiques. An attentive staff serves morning coffee and pastries in your room or in the Victorian dining room. ☎ *628 N. State St., 39202,* ☎ ℻ *601/352–0221. 11 rooms with bath. AE, DC, MC, V.*

$$$ **Ramada Plaza Hotel.** This high-rise convention motel is sleekly contemporary and conveniently located just off I–55N. Rooms are comfortable and clean but nothing to write home about. ☎ *1001 County Line Rd., 39211,* ☎ *601/957–2800 or 800/228–9898,* ℻ *601/957–3191. 300 rooms. Restaurant, bar, barber shop, gift shop, airport shuttle. AE, DC, MC, V.*

$$–$$$ **Edison Walthall Hotel.** The cornerstone and huge brass mailbox near the elevators are almost all that remain of the original Walthall Hotel. The dismal motel that occupied the site next was transformed into the new hotel. The marble floors, gleaming brass, a paneled library/writing room, and cozy bar almost fool you into thinking this is a restoration. ☎ *225 E. Capitol St., 39201,* ☎ *601/948–6161 or 800/932–6161,* ℻ *601/948–0088. 202 rooms, 6 suites. Pool, hot tub, airport shuttle. AE, DC, MC, V.*

Natchez
DINING

$$$ **Liza's.** Opened in October 1993 in a historic house (circa 1852) with
★ a view of the Mississippi River, this restaurant quickly established a loyal following. The menu features regional New American cuisine not often found in a small Southern town; roast breast of duck with tart cherry sauce served with pecan wild rice and sautéed veal medallions with smoked garlic Alfredo are popular choices. ✗ *657 S. Canal St.,* ☎ *601/446–6368. Reservations advised. MC, V. No lunch.*

$$ **Carriage House Restaurant.** Located on the grounds of Stanton Hall (*see* Exploring, *above*), the restaurant specializes in southern fare—fried chicken, baked ham, and their famous mouth-watering miniature biscuits. The Victorian parlor ambience is delightful. ✗ *401 High St.,* ☎ *601/445–5151. Reservations recommended. Lunch daily; no dinner except during Pilgrimage (Oct.–Mar.). AE, MC, V.*

$$ **Natchez Landing.** The porch tables provide a view of the Mississippi
★ River, which is at its very best when both the *Delta Queen* and *Mississippi Queen* steamboats dock. Specialties are barbecue (pork ribs, chicken, beef) and fried and grilled catfish. ✗ *35 Silver St., Natchez-Under-the-Hill,* ☎ *601/442–6639. No reservations. AE, MC, V.*

$$ **Pearl Street Pasta.** This small, intimate restaurant with minimalist decor is known for its fresh pasta and daily specials. Favorites on the menu are the Cajun shrimp pasta, Italian chicken salad pasta, and pasta jambalaya. ✕ *105 S. Pearl St., 601/442–9284. Reservations advised. AE, MC, V.*

$$ Scrooge's. The old storefront-cum-restaurant has a pub atmosphere downstairs and a more subdued intimate ambience upstairs. The menu includes red beans and rice, and mesquite-grilled chicken or shrimp with angel-hair pasta. ✕ *315 Main St., ☎ 601/446–9922. No reservations. AE, MC, V.*

$ Cock of the Walk. The famous original of a regional franchise, this marvelous old train depot overlooking the Mississippi River specializes in fried catfish fillets, fried dill pickles, hush puppies, mustard greens, and coleslaw. There's also blackened or grilled catfish or chicken. ✕ *200 N. Broadway, on bluff, ☎ 601/446–8920. Reservations accepted. AE, MC, V.*

DINING AND LODGING

$$$–$$$$ Monmouth. This plantation mansion (circa 1818) was owned by Mis-
★ sissippi governor John A. Quitman from 1826 to his death in 1858. Guest rooms are decorated with tester beds and antiques. The grounds are tastefully landscaped, with a New Orleans–style courtyard, a pond, and a gazebo. The plantation dinner, featuring true-to-period foods served in the ornate dining room, is an unforgettable experience. ⊞ *36 Melrose Ave., 39120, ☎ 601/442–5852 or 800/828–4531. 17 rooms with bath, 2 suites. Reservations required for dinner. AE, MC, V.*

LODGING

This list includes the area's most popular bed-and-breakfast inns. **Natchez Pilgrimage Tours** (*see* Visitor Information, *below*) can answer questions and handle reservations.

$$$$ Briars. Once the home of Varina Howell, the wife of Jefferson Davis, the Briars sits on a promontory overlooking the Mississippi River. The 19 acres of landscaped grounds are a perfect place for peaceful strolling, and the 13 rooms are beautifully decorated with period furnishings imparting a gracious plantation feel. ⊞ *31 Irving La. (behind the Ramada Hilltop), ☎ 601/446–9654 or 800/634–1818. 13 rooms with bath. AE, MC, V.*

$$$$ The Burn. This elegant 1836 mansion offers a seated plantation breakfast, private tour of the home, and swimming pool. The inn is under new ownership, but the ambiance remains the same. Rooms are named for their individual decor and color schemes; the Blue Room was the favorite of actress Helen Hayes, who stayed often. ⊞ *712 N. Union St., 39120, ☎ 601/442–1344 or 800/654–8859, FAX 601/445–0606. 7 rooms with bath. AE, MC, V.*

$$$$ Dunleith. Stately, colonnaded Dunleith is a popular Natchez bed-and-breakfast inn. The elegant, plantation-style rooms are furnished with four-poster beds and antiques. Guests are served breakfast in the former poultry house, featuring old brick walls and a fireplace. Beautiful gardens enhance this Greek Revival mansion. ⊞ *84 Homochitto St., 39120, ☎ 601/446–8500 or 800/433–2445. 12 rooms with bath. AE, MC, V.*

$$$ Natchez Eola Hotel. This beautifully restored 1920s hotel has an ele-
★ gant, formal lobby and small guest rooms with antique reproduction furniture. The Natchez Eola is one of only 60 hotels in the United States to be selected by the National Trust for Historic Preservation as one in which architecture and historic integrity have been maintained. ⊞ *110 N. Pearl St., 39120, ☎ 601/445–6000 or 800/888–9140, FAX 601/446–5310. 125 rooms, 5 suites. Restaurant, lounge, gift shop. AE, DC, MC, V.*

$$ **Ramada Hilltop.** Renovated in 1992, this updated motel sits on a bluff overlooking the Mississippi River, and Louisiana to the west. Rooms are Ramada generic but functional. ⌕ *130 John R. Junkin Dr., 39120,* ☎ *601/446–6311 or 800/256–6311,* ℻ *601/446–6321. 162 rooms, 6 suites. Restaurant, lounge, pool. AE, DC, MC, V.*

Port Gibson
LODGING

$$$–$$$$ **Oak Square.** Constructed about 1850, this home, with its numerous outbuildings and lovely gardens, occupies an entire block on historic Church Street. Now a bed-and-breakfast inn, it offers a full southern breakfast. Rooms are comfortable and have a private bath and color TV. ⌕ *1207 Church St., 39150,* ☎ *601/437–4350 or 800/729–0240. 12 rooms. AE, MC, V.*

Tupelo
DINING

$$$ **Jefferson Place.** This austere 19th-century house is lively inside, with red-checked tablecloths and bric-a-brac. The place is popular with the college crowd; short orders and steaks are the specialties. ✕ *823 Jefferson St.,* ☎ *601/844–8696. No reservations. AE, MC, V. Closed Sun.*

$$ **Harvey's.** It's a favorite in four cities, and here's why: Harvey's restaurants have based their reputation on consistency and quality in food and service. Try the prime rib, seafood, steak, or, for lighter fare, the chicken Alpine or great garden salad. Lots of plants and warm wood tones add to the appeal. ✕ *424 S. Gloster St.,* ☎ *601/842–6763. AE, MC, V. Closed Sun.*

$ **Vanelli's.** Family pictures and scenes of Greece decorate the walls of this comfortably nondescript restaurant where tables wear traditional red-and-white checkered tablecloths. Specialties (all homemade) include pizza with 10 toppings, lasagna, moussaka, manicotti, and Greek salad. Vanelli's own bakery produces breads, strudels, and pastries. ✕ *1302 N. Gloster St.,* ☎ *601/844–4410. Reservations accepted. AE, D, MC, V.*

LODGING

$$–$$$ **Executive Inn.** Guest rooms in this large, contemporary hotel are plain and functional, yet clean. ⌕ *1011 N. Gloster St., 38801,* ☎ *601/841–2222 or 800/533–3220,* ℻ *601/844–7836. 115 rooms. Restaurant, lounge, indoor pool, hot tub, sauna. AE, DC, MC, V.*

$$ **Ramada Inn.** This modern hotel caters to business travelers and conventions as well as families. There is dancing nightly (except Sunday) in Bogart's Lounge. Breakfast and lunch buffets are served. ⌕ *854 N. Gloster, 38801,* ☎ *601/844–4111 or 800/228–2828. 230 rooms, 10 suites. Pool, barbershop, beauty shops. AE, DC, MC, V.*

$–$$ **Trace Inn.** This old motel on 15 acres near the Natchez Trace offers neat rooms and friendly service. ⌕ *3400 W. Main St., 38801,* ☎ *601/842–5555,* ℻ *601/844–3105. 134 rooms. Restaurant, pool, playground. AE, MC, V.*

Nightlife

Jackson

Rodeo's (6107 Ridgewood Rd., ☎ 601/957–9300) is the current "in" spot, where live music and dancing attract big crowds. **Hal and Mal's** (200 S. Commerce St., ☎ 601/948–0888) is another popular night spot. There's live entertainment at the **Dock** (Main Harbor Marina at Ross Barnett Reservoir, ☎ 601/856–7765) Thursday–Sunday, when some

2,000 people pass through. The restaurant, which sits on a pier, generally attracts a young crowd, but draws an older one on Sunday. The mood is set by the people who step off their boats to dine, drink, and listen to the rock and roll and rhythm and blues. **Poet's** (1855 Lakeland Dr., ☎ 601/982–9711) presents food, drink, and a jazz trio in an old-fashioned atmosphere, created by antiques, old signs, pressed-tin ceiling, and wooden floors.

Natchez

King's Tavern (619 Jefferson St., ☎ 601/446–8845) is in the oldest house in the Natchez Territory (1789). The lounge is rustic yet inviting, especially if you're an "Old Natchez" aficionado. **Under-the-Hill Saloon** (Silver St., ☎ 601/446–8023) features live entertainment on weekends in one of the few original buildings left in Natchez-Under-the-Hill.

Natchez Trace Essentials

Arriving and Departing, Getting Around

BY BUS

Greyhound (☎ 800/231–2222) offers daily service to Tupelo, Corinth, Columbus, Philadelphia, Jackson, Port Gibson, and Natchez. Stations are at 201 Commerce St., Tupelo, ☎ 601/842–4557; 904 Main St., Columbus, ☎ 601/328–4732; 204 U.S. 72E, Corinth, ☎ 601/287–1466; 201 S. Jefferson St., Jackson, ☎ 601/353–6342; and 103 Lower Woodville Rd., Natchez, ☎ 601/445–5291.

BY CAR

This is the only way to tour the Trace properly, though you can reach the major cities along the highway by plane and by bus. Corinth is at the intersection of U.S. 72 and U.S. 45, and Tupelo is 5 miles south of the Natchez Trace Parkway at the intersection of U.S. 45 and U.S. 78.

The Trace is incomplete at Jackson, connected by I–55 and I–20, which run through the city. Jackson is also on U.S. 49 and U.S. 51. Natchez, the beginning of the Natchez Trace Parkway (but the end of this tour), is also served by U.S. 61.

BY PLANE

Golden Triangle Regional Airport (U.S. 82, 10 mi west of Columbus) is served by Northwest Airlink, American Eagle, and Atlantic Southeast Airlines, with connections nationwide through Memphis and Atlanta.

American, Continental Express, Delta, and Northwest Airlines offer nonstop daily flights to Dallas, Atlanta, and New Orleans, with direct service available nationally. The airport, **Allen C. Thompson Field,** is east of Jackson off I–20, 10 minutes from downtown.

Tupelo Municipal Airport (631 Jackson Extended, 5 mi west of Tupelo, ☎ 601/841–6570), is served by Northwest Airlink and American Eagle.

Guided Tours

Jackson Tour & Travel (1801 Crane Ridge Dr., Jackson 39216, ☎ 601/981–8415 or 800/873–8572) offers independent departures to the state's prime attractions. Natchez and New Orleans are popular destinations, whether for antebellum house touring or antiquing. JT&T is one of the South's premier tour operators.

In Natchez, **Natchez Pilgrimage Tours, Inc.** (Box 347, Natchez 39121, ☎ 601/446–6631 or 800/647–6742) takes groups of 20 or more to tour about a dozen antebellum homes year-round (during Pilgrimage, between 24 and 30 homes are open). Tours are conducted mornings and afternoons, and bus tickets can be bought at six of the area's hotels (for spring and fall tours only.) Tour tickets can be bought at the Pilgrimage Tour office on the corner of Canal and State streets or the individual homes (no individual tickets during pilgrimage.)

Important Addresses and Numbers

EMERGENCIES

In towns and cities, dial 911 for **police** or **ambulance.** For help on the Natchez Trace, dial 0 and ask for the nearest Park Ranger. Seek medical help at **North Mississippi Regional Medical Center** (830 S. Gloster St., Tupelo, ☎ 601/841–3000), **Mississippi Baptist Medical Center** (1225 N. State St., Jackson, ☎ 601/968–1776), and **Jefferson Davis Hospital** (Sgt. Prentiss Dr., Natchez, ☎ 601/442–2871).

RADIO STATIONS

AM: WKTS 95.5, country; WTUP 1490, all-sports talk. **FM:** WJMI 99.7, urban contemporary; WQNZ, 95.1, country; WTRC 97.3, adult contemporary/news/sports.

24-HOUR PHARMACIES

In Jackson, **Eckerd's** (DeVille Plaza, I–55N, E. Frontage Rd., ☎ 601/956–5143) and **Super D Drugs** (327 Meadowbrook, Meadowbrook Shopping Center, Jackson, ☎ 601/366–1449).

VISITOR INFORMATION

The **Alliance** (810 Tate St., Corinth 38834, ☎ 601/287–5269 or 800/748–9048, ☉ Weekdays 8–5). **Metro Jackson Convention and Visitors Bureau** (Box 1450, Jackson 39215 , ☎ 601/960–1891 or 800/354–7695, ☉ Weekdays 8:30–5). **Jackson Visitor Information Center** (by the Mississippi Agriculture and Forestry Museum, 1150 Lakeland Dr., east of I–55, 39215, ☎ 601/960–1800, ☉ Weekdays 8:30–4:30). **Natchez Trace Parkway Visitor Center** (Rte. 1, NT-143, Tupelo 38801; on the Natchez Trace Pkwy., mile marker 266, ☎ 601/680–4025, ☉ Daily 8–5). **Natchez Convention & Visitors Bureau** (311 Liberty Rd., Natchez 39120, ☎ 601/446–6345 or 800/647–6724, ☉ Weekdays 8–5). **Natchez Pilgrimage Tours** (to purchase tickets for Pilgrimage tours and activities, Canal St. at State St., Box 347, Natchez 39120, ☎ 601/446–6631 or 800/647–6742, ☉ Daily 8:30–5:30). **Tupelo Convention and Visitors Bureau** (399 E. Main St., Box 1485, Tupelo 38801, ☎ 601/841–6521 or 800/533–0611, ☉ Weekdays 8–5, Sat. 9–5, Sun. 1–5).

HOLLY SPRINGS AND OXFORD

Holly Springs and Oxford, just east of I–55 in north Mississippi, are sophisticated versions of the Mississippi small town; both are courthouse towns incorporated in 1837. They offer visitors historic architecture, arts and crafts, literary associations, a warm welcome, and those unhurried pleasures of Southern life that remain constant from generation to generation—entertaining conversation, good food, and nostalgic walks at twilight.

Exploring

Holly Springs

Holly Springs arose from a crossroads of old Indian trails originally called Spring Hollow. Here Chickasaw Indians and travelers stopped to rest and bathe in the medicinal waters of springs in glades of holly trees. After the Chickasaw Cession in 1832, settlers came from the Carolinas, Virginia, and Georgia. Holly Springs became an educational, business, and cultural center as the newly arrived planters gained great wealth. Cotton barons built palatial mansions and handsome commercial buildings. Today Holly Springs has more than 200 structures (61 of which are antebellum homes) listed on the National Register of Historic Places.

Holly Springs survived at least 50 raids during the Civil War. In December 1862, the Confederate army under General Earl Van Dorn destroyed $1 million worth of Union supplies intended for General Grant's use in his march against Vicksburg. Bent on reprisals against the city, Grant ordered General Benjamin Harrison Grierson to burn it in 1864. A clever Holly Springs matron, Maria Mason, invited the general into her home to chat. They discovered that they shared a love of music and that they had studied piano under the same teacher; so instead of destroying Holly Springs, Grierson enjoyed its hospitality at a series of afternoon gatherings and piano concerts. Many of Holly Springs's historic homes are open only during Pilgrimage (the last weekend in April), but the following landmarks are open daily.

Montrose (1858) was built by Alfred Brooks as a wedding present for his daughter. Now owned by the Holly Springs Garden Club, this mansion has an elegant spiral staircase as well as elaborate cornices and plaster ceiling medallions. *307 E. Salem Ave.* ☛ *$5 adults, children under 12 free.* ⊙ *By appointment with the Chamber of Commerce,* ☎ *601/234–4651.*

Rust College (N. Memphis St., ☎ 601/252–4661), founded in 1868, contains **Oak View** (circa 1860), one of the oldest buildings in the state associated with black education. Metropolitan Opera star Leontyne Price, a native of Laurel, Mississippi, graduated from Rust. The **Yellow Fever House** (104 E. Gholson Ave.), built in 1836, was Holly Springs's first brick building. It was used as a hospital during the 1878 yellow fever epidemic. At press time it was under renovation and scheduled to open as a museum, but for now you can view only the exterior. **Hillcrest Cemetery** (380 S. Maury St.) contains graves of 13 Confederate generals. Many of the iron fences surrounding the graves were made locally before the Civil War.

The **Kate Freeman Clark Art Gallery** is dedicated solely to the work of Holly Springs resident Kate Freeman Clark, who was trained in New York City during the 1890s. Clark completed more than 1,000 works on canvas and paper, including landscapes and portraits. She returned to Holly Springs in the 1920s and never painted again. Many of her friends did not know of her talent until her paintings were discovered after her death. In her will she left funds to establish a museum. *292 E. College Ave.,* ☎ *601/252–4211.* ☛ *$2 adults, $1 children.* ⊙ *By appointment.*

Even the briefest visit to Holly Springs should include a look at the exteriors of several homes that are not usually open to the public. **Oakleigh,** on Salem Avenue across the street from Montrose, is a mansion with fine details. Also on Salem Avenue are **Cedarhurst** and **Airliewood,** brick houses constructed in the Gothic style popularized in the 1850s by Andrew Jackson Downing. General Grant used Airliewood as his headquarters during his occupation of Holly Springs.

Oxford

Oxford and Lafayette County were immortalized as "Jefferson" and "Yoknapatawpha County" in the novels of Oxford native William Faulkner, but even if you're not a Faulkner fan, this is a great place to experience small town living. You won't be bored; the characters who fascinated Faulkner still live here, and the University of Mississippi keeps things lively.

Faulkner received the Nobel Prize for Literature in 1949, and his readers will enjoy exploring the town that inspired *The Hamlet, The Town,* and *The Mansion.* "I discovered that my own little postage stamp of native soil was worth writing about, and that I would never live long enough to exhaust it," said Faulkner. "I created a cosmos of my own."

Many people who knew the eccentric Mr. Bill still live in Oxford and are willing to share stories about him. You may encounter them around **Courthouse Square** in the center of town. The Square is a National Historic Landmark, and at its center is the white sandstone **Lafayette** (pronounced "Luh-FAY-it") **County Courthouse,** named for the French Revolutionary War hero the Marquis de Lafayette. The courthouse was rebuilt in 1873 after Union troops burned it; on its south side is the monument to Confederate soldiers. The courtroom on the second floor is original.

TIME OUT At **Square Books** the knowledgeable staff can tell you about Oxford's "writers in residence." While enjoying cappuccino, espresso, or delicious desserts, keep an eye out for well-known writers who may stroll over from the university, among them Barry Hannah (*Geronimo Rex*) or John Grisham (*The Firm*). *160 Courthouse Sq.,* ☎ *601/236-2262.* ۞ *Mon.–Thurs. 9–9, Fri. and Sat. 9 AM–10 PM, Sun. 10–6.*

University Avenue from South Lamar Boulevard just south of the Courthouse Square to the University of Mississippi is one of the state's most beautiful sights when the trees flame orange and gold in the fall, or when the dogwoods blossom in the spring.

The **University Museums** display the brightly colored primitive paintings of local artist Theora Hamblett. Hamblett gained international fame for her works depicting dreams and visions, children's games, Mississippi landscapes, and scenes from her childhood. Here, too, is an outstanding antiquities collection and what may perhaps be the country's quirkiest exhibit—a collection of fully dressed fleas! *University Ave. at 5th St.,* ☎ *601/232-7073.* ☛ *Free.* ۞ *Tues.–Sat. 10–4:30, Sun. 1–4.*

Just beyond the museum is the **University of Mississippi,** the state's beloved "Ole Miss," which opened in 1848 with 80 students. The **Grove,** the tree-shaded heart of the campus, is almost as important a meeting place as Courthouse Square. (It was supposedly here that Faulkner, just fired from his job as postmaster for writing novels on the job, said, "Never again will I be at the beck and call of every son-of-a-bitch who's got two cents to buy a stamp.") Contact the school's **Public Relations Department** (☎ 601/232–7236) for information about university plays, lectures, sporting events, and special events.

Facing the Grove, antebellum **Barnard Observatory** houses the **Center for the Study of Southern Culture,** with exhibits on Southern music, folklore, and literature, and the world's largest blues archive (40,000 records). The center's annual Faulkner seminar attracts Faulkner scholars from around the world (*see* The Arts, *below*), and the Oxford Conference for the Book, held each April, attracts book lovers from across the United States. The center's remarkable *Encyclopedia of Southern Culture* is for sale here. *Barnard Observatory, University of Mississippi,* ☎ *601/232–5993.* ☛ *Free.* ⊙ *Weekdays 8–5.*

The **Mississippi Room** in the John Davis Williams Library contains both a permanent exhibit on Faulkner, including his Nobel Prize medal, and first editions of other Mississippi authors. *On campus,* ☎ *601/232– 7408.* ☛ *Free.* ⊙ *Weekdays 8:30–5.*

★ **Rowan Oak** was the home of William Faulkner from 1930 until his death in 1962. Although this is one of Mississippi's most famous attractions, there are no signs to direct you to the home and only an unobtrusive historic marker at the site. The house and its surrounding 32 acres are as serene and private as they were when Faulkner lived and wrote here. Built about 1848 by Colonel Robert Sheegog, the two-story, white-frame house with square columns represents the primitive Greek Revival style of architecture common to many Mississippi antebellum homes. After the Civil War it fell into disrepair and, in 1930, was purchased by Faulkner and his bride of one year, Estelle Oldham Franklin. The house was both a sanctuary and a financial burden to the author; it is now a National Historic Landmark owned by the University of Mississippi. Faulkner made improvements and additions to the house, including a brick wall to shield him from curious strangers. After winning the Nobel Prize, he added the study where his bed, typewriter, desk, and other personal items, such as his sunglasses, a Colgate shave stick refill, an ink bottle, and a can of dog repellent, still evoke his presence. Faulkner wrote an outline for his novel *The Fable* on the walls of the study, which is reputed to be the most photographed room in the state. The days of the week are neatly printed over the head and length of the bed, and to the right of the door leading into the room is the notation, "Tomorrow." *Old Taylor Rd.,* ☎ *601/234–3284.* ☛ *Free.* ⊙ *Tues.–Sat. 10–noon and 2–4, Sun. 2–4.*

Faulkner's funeral was held at Rowan Oak, and he was buried in the family plot in **St. Peter's Cemetery** at Jefferson and North 16th streets, beside his relatives. Also buried here is Caroline Barr, "Mammy Callie," Faulkner's childhood nurse. The tomb of the author's brother, Dean Faulkner, who was killed in an airplane crash, bears the same epitaph as the one Faulkner had given to John Sartoris in the novel *Pylon.*

What to See and Do with Children

Holly Springs
Chewalla Lake and Recreation Area (*see* Participant Sports, *below*).

Oxford
Avent Park (*see* Participant Sports, *below*).

Square Books has a large collection of children's books (*see* Time Out in Exploring, *above*).

Off the Beaten Path

William Faulkner was married in little **College Hill Presbyterian Church** (8 mi northwest of Oxford on College Hill Rd.) on June 20, 1929. The slave gallery doors and original pews are intact, although it's believed that Sherman stabled horses here during his occupation of College Hill in 1862. Behind the church is one of north Mississippi's oldest cemeteries.

From Oxford take Old Taylor Road to reach **Taylor.** Downtown **Taylor** sports three buildings, of which two are grocery stores and one is a potter's shop. The old Taylor Grocery has a restaurant in back where catfish and trimmins' are served Thursday through Sunday nights (☎ 601/236–1716). In sculptor **William Beckwith's studio** you can see his statue of Temple Drake, the character who waited for the train in Taylor in Faulkner's novel *Sanctuary*. Small as it is, Taylor is achieving cult status; it's proper to brag about coming here!

Participant Sports

Holly Springs's **Chewalla Lake and Recreation Area** are part of Holly Springs National Forest and have nature trails, picnic areas, swimming, boating, camping, and fishing (license required). *MS 4 to Higdon Rd. then turn east; drive 7 mi to entrance. Information: National Forests Mississippi, 100 W. Capitol St., Suite 1141, Jackson 39269, ☎ 601/960–4391.*

Oxford's Avent Park (Park Dr., the continuation of Bramlett Rd., which runs north of E. Jackson Ave.) has tennis courts, a playground, picnic areas, and a jogging trail.

Dining and Lodging

Dining
You don't have to travel far in these small towns to find one-of-a-kind dining experiences. Food, not decor, is usually the focus, and you can dress informally.

CATEGORY	COST*
$$$$	over $20
$$$	$15–$20
$$	$10–$15
$	under $10

per person for a three-course meal, excluding drinks, service, and 8% sales tax

Lodging
When staying overnight in Oxford try the Oliver-Britt House or Puddin Place, especially if you'd like to hear town gossip from your innkeeper. For more conventional lodgings, try the Alumni House on the University of Mississippi campus or, more conventional yet, the Holiday Inn.

CATEGORY	COST*
$$$$	over $70
$$$	$50–$70
$$	$30–$50
$	$20–$30

All prices are for a standard double room, excluding 8% tax

Holly Springs
DINING
$ **Phillips Grocery.** The building was constructed in 1882 as a saloon for railroad workers. Today it's decorated with antiques and crafts, and serves big, old-fashioned hamburgers. ✕ *541A Van Dorn St., across from old depot,* ☎ *601/252–4671. No reservations. No credit cards. Closed Sun.*

Oxford

DINING

$$$–$$$$ **City Grocery Store.** What was once a grocery store is now a trendy bistro
★ on Oxford's historic square with ambiance to spare. The chef's inno-
vative menu is more suggestive of New Orleans than north Mississippi.
The crab ravigotte with roasted corn and sweet peppers, grilled Jamaican
pork loin, and bread pudding with butter-rum sauce are show stop-
pers. ✕ *1118 Van Buren Ave.,* ☎ *601/232–8080. AE, MC, V.*

$$ **Downtown Grill.** With its comfortable plaid chairs and dark walls, the
Grill's bar could be a club in Oxford, England. But then there's the
light and airy balcony overlooking the square—pure Oxford, Mississippi. Downstairs in the restaurant, specialties include famous seafood
gumbo; Mississippi catfish either grilled or Lafitte (topped with shrimp,
julienned ham, and a savory cream sauce); and an array of rich desserts.
✕ *1115 Jackson Ave.,* ☎ *601/234–2659. Reservations advised. AE,
MC, V.*

$ **Smitty's.** Homestyle cooking features red-eye gravy and grits, biscuits
with blackberry preserves, fried catfish, chicken and dumplings, cornbread, and black-eyed peas. The menu says, "If'n You Need Anything
That Ain't on Here, Holler at the Cook." ✕ *208 S. Lamar Blvd., south
of square,* ☎ *601/234–9111. MC, V.*

LODGING

$$$$ **Puddin Place.** Near the Ole Miss campus, this Victorian house has a
wonderful back porch with swings and rockers. The two suites are
thoughtfully furnished with antiques and collectibles. The downstairs
suite has its own washer and dryer as well as two working fireplaces;
the upstairs suite has four working fireplaces—including one in the bathroom. ▦ *1008 University Ave., 38655,* ☎ *601/234–1250. 2 suites.
No credit cards.*

$$ **Holiday Inn.** These functional rooms have no surprises. The restaurant,
however, can do a surprisingly good breakfast, though you'll proba-
bly choose Smitty's for the biscuits (*see* Dining, *above*). ▦ *400 N. Lamar,
38655,* ☎ *601/234–3031,* ℻ *601/234–2834. 100 rooms. Lounge, pool.
AE, DC, MC, V.*

$$ **Oliver-Britt House.** There are five comfortable, pleasant rooms, each
with bath and color TV, in a restored home built about 1900 and run
as a casual B&B. The location, midway between the university and Courthouse Square, is convenient. ▦ *512 Van Buren Ave., 38655,* ☎
601/234–8043. 5 rooms. AE, MC, V.

$–$$ **Alumni House.** The hotel-style rooms are plain and clean; the only real
plus is their location on the Ole Miss campus. ▦ *University of Mississippi, 38677,* ☎ *601/234–2331. 35 rooms. MC, V.*

The Arts

Faulkner and Yoknapatawpha Conference. This event, held the first
week in August, includes lectures by Faulkner scholars and field trips
in "Yoknapatawpha County." The annual **Elvis Conference** is also held
here in August. For information, contact the Center for the Study of
Southern Culture, University of Mississippi, Oxford 38677, ☎ 601/232–
5993.

Nightlife

Local Oxford bands play Cajun, country, reggae, and motown Tuesday–Saturday at the **Gin** (E. Harrison St. and S. 14th St., ☎ 601/234–
0024). The **Hoka** (304 S. 14th St., ☎ 601/234–3057), a warehouse-
turned-movie theater-restaurant, has been called the "only Bohemian

café in Mississippi" by author Barry Hannah. It has hard wooden booths, a jukebox, and is unbelievably cluttered. BYOB to enjoy arty movies and short-order food, especially the cheesecake.

Holly Springs and Oxford Essentials

Arriving and Departing, Getting Around

BY BUS
Greyhound (☎ 800/231–2222) has a station in Holly Springs (490 Craft St., ☎ 601/252–1353).

BY CAR
A 30-minute drive from Memphis, Holly Springs is in north Mississippi near the Tennessee state line on U.S. 78 and MS 4, MS 7, and MS 311. Oxford is 29 miles south of Holly Springs on MS 7. Oxford is also accessible from I–55, 23 miles east of Batesville on MS 6.

Guided Tours
Guided tours of the University of Mississippi (Ole Miss) campus are available upon request from the admissions office (☎ 601/232–7378).

Important Addresses and Numbers

EMERGENCIES
In Holly Springs, dial 0 for assistance. In Oxford, dial 911. Medical help is available at **Baptist Memorial North Mississippi Hospital** (U.S. 75, 1 mi south of the Oxford Sq. on S. Lamar Ave., ☎ 601/232–8100).

RADIO STATIONS
AM: WSUH 1420, news/talk. **FM:** WOXD 95.5, oldies; WWMS 97.5, contemporary and country.

VISITOR INFORMATION
Holly Springs Chamber of Commerce (154 S. Memphis St., ☎ 601/252–2943, ☉ Weekdays 9–5). **Oxford Information Center** (cottage next to City Hall, ☎ 601/232–2419, ☉ Daily 9–5). **Oxford Tourism Council** (115 Courthouse Square, Box 965, Oxford 38655, ☎ 601/234–4680, ☉ Weekdays 9–5). **Oxford-Lafayette County Chamber of Commerce** (299 W. Jackson Ave., ☎ 601/234–4651, ☉ Weekdays 8:30–4).

THE DELTA

"The Delta begins in the lobby of the Peabody Hotel in Memphis and ends on Catfish Row in Vicksburg," said Greenville journalist David Cohn. In between is an intimate set of personal relationships and a vast agricultural plain created by the Mississippi River. If life should give you only one day in the Delta, use it to cruise down U.S. 61 and the Great River Road (MS 1) from Memphis to Vicksburg. Time it right for lunch in Clarksdale, Merigold, or Boyle, and dinner at Doe's in Greenville. Then on a Saturday night you'll be able to pick up public radio's "Highway 61" with host Bill Ferris, creator and director of the Center for the Study of Southern Culture at the University of Mississippi in Oxford. He'll be playing the blues about the time you glimpse the first kudzu near Vicksburg.

Exploring

Numbers in the margin correspond to points of interest on the Mississippi Delta map.

Head down U.S. 61 from Memphis through the Mississippi Delta. Fifty miles south you'll enter **Coahoma County** (from the Choctaw word "Co-i-humma," meaning "red panther"). At **Rich,** swing west on U.S. 49 for a spectacular view of the Mississippi River from the **Mississippi–Arkansas Bridge.** Continue south on MS 1 to skirt serene **Moon Lake** and **Friars Point.** The levee parallels MS 1 for most of the southbound trip; park and climb up for a look at the "Father of Waters."

At **Rena Lara,** turn west to **Sunflower Landing** on Desoto Lake. Near here, in May 1541, Hernando DeSoto "discovered" the Mississippi River.

Return to Rena Lara, backtrack to **Sherard,** and head east on MS 322 to **Clarksdale.** As a child, author Tennessee Williams spent time here, visiting his grandfather, the rector of St. George's Episcopal Church. (In Williams's *Cat on a Hot Tin Roof,* Brick was running high hurdles at nearby Friars Point when he broke his leg.) The **Delta Blues Museum** is a testament to the important role played by Clarksdale and Coahoma County in the history of the blues. The museum features exhibits and programs highlighting the history of the blues, tracing its influence on rock, jazz, and pop music through videotapes, slides, records, and books. *Carnegie Public Library,* ☎ 601/624–4461. ☛ *Free.* ⊙ *Weekdays 9–5.*

Continue to **Merigold** on U.S. 61. The **McCartys of Merigold** are famous throughout the state for their pale stoneware. Their shop features their pottery and handcrafted jewelry; in the spring and summer you may get a peek at their gardens. *Corner Goff and St. Mary Sts.,* ☎ 601/748–2293. ⊙ *Feb.–Dec., Tues.–Sat. 10–4.*

From Merigold continue through Cleveland to Boyle if you're planning to lunch at the Sweet Olive (*see* Dining and Lodging, *below*), or turn west on MS 8 to pastoral **Rosedale** for sweeping views of the Mississippi River. The **Great River Road State Park** has a 75-foot-high overlook tower. *Off MS 1 in Rosedale, Box 292, Rosedale, 38769,* ☎ 601/759–6762. ⊙ *Daily 8–5.*

From Rosedale, follow MS 1 into **Greenville,** the seat of Washington County. The city is named for Revolutionary War hero General Nathaniel Greene, a close friend of George Washington, for whom the county is named. The city's history has been dominated by the Mississippi River. The river created the rich soil in which cotton flourished, and Greenville was—and is—the port used by the massive Delta plantations to ship their bales to market. During the Civil War battle for Vicksburg, Union troops burned Greenville to the ground. The citizens rebuilt the town only to suffer a yellow fever epidemic in 1877. Then, in 1890, the city suffered disastrous flooding; levees finally solved the problem after the great flood of 1927. At the turn of the century Greenville developed into a major river port.

Greenville probably has produced more writers than any other city of its size in the country. These include William Alexander Percy (*Lanterns on the Levee*), his nephew Walker Percy (*The Last Gentleman, The Moviegoer*), Ellen Douglas (*A Family's Affair, The Magic Carpet*), Hodding Carter (Pulitzer Prize–winning, crusading journalist), Shelby Foote (*The Civil War, Love in a Dry Season*), and Hodding Carter III (television news commentator and journalist). The best reason to visit Greenville, however, is to eat at **Doe's** (*see* Dining, *below*).

Follow MS 1 south. At MS 436, go west 2 miles to photograph the vine-covered ruins of **St. John's Episcopal Church.** Only its walls and

Mississippi Delta

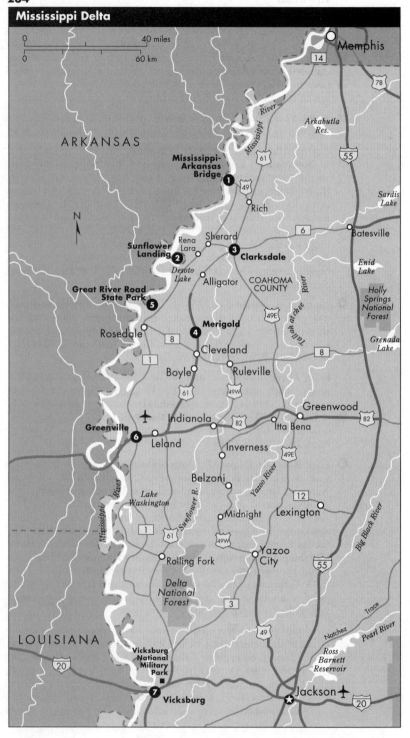

0 _____ 40 miles
0 _____ 60 km

Memphis
14
78

ARKANSAS

Mississippi River

55

Arkabutla Res.

61

Mississippi-Arkansas Bridge ❶
49

Rich ○

Sherard ○
6
Batesville ○

Sardis Lake

Rena Lara ○
Sunflower Landing ❷
Desoto Lake
❸ **Clarksdale**

Alligator ○
COAHOMA COUNTY

Enid Lake

Holly Springs National Forest

Great River Road State Park ❺
49E

❹ **Merigold**

Tallahatchee River

Rosedale ○
8
Cleveland ○
8

Grenada Lake

1
Boyle ○
Ruleville ○

61
49W

Greenwood
82

Indianola ○
82
Itta Bena ○

Greenville ❻ ○
Leland

Inverness ○
49E

Belzoni ○

Lake Washington

Sunflower R.

Yazoo River

12

Midnight ○
Lexington ○

1
61
49W

Rolling Fork ○
Yazoo City ○
55

Delta National Forest

3

49

Big Black River

LOUISIANA

Vicksburg National Military Park ■

Natchez Trace

Pearl River

Ross Barnett Reservoir

20

❼ **Vicksburg**

Jackson ✈
20

bell tower remain; its windows were removed during the Civil War so that the leading could be melted to make bullets.

At MS 14, go east to Rolling Fork, then south on U.S. 61 through fields and wildlife areas to Vicksburg.

❼ Near the site of present-day **Vicksburg**, the Spanish established Fort Nogales in 1790. Vicksburg itself began as a mission founded by the Reverend Newitt Vick in 1814. He chose a spot high on the bluffs above a bend in the Mississippi River, a location that would have important consequences for the young city and for the nation not 50 years later.

During the War Between the States, the Confederacy and the Union vied for control of this strategic location. U.S. Grant's men doggedly slogged through canals and bayous in five futile attempts to capture the city, which was called the Gibraltar of the Confederacy because of its almost impregnable defenses. Then, in a series of raids and battles, Grant laid waste the area between Vicksburg and Jackson to the east and Port Gibson to the south. Grant's attacks on Vicksburg were repulsed once again; he then laid siege to the city for 47 days. On July 4, 1863, the city surrendered, giving the Union control of the river and sounding the death knell for the Confederacy.

The suffering at Vicksburg was profound. The land was devastated; today's green and serene countryside was a region of blasted trees and ★ blackened hills. Vicksburg's **National Military Park** marks the spot where the town was under siege. Battle positions are marked, and monuments line the park's 16-mile drive. The Visitor Center offers orientation programs and exhibits. A guided tour is a good investment, should time and money ($20 for 2 hours) permit. The self-guided driving tour is well marked, however, and a cassette tape may be rented for $4.50. *Entrance and visitor center on Clay St. (U.S. 80), directly off I–20, Exit 4B, ☎ 601/636–0583. ☞ $4 per car. ☉ Fall–spring, daily 8–5; summer, daily 8–6.*

The Union gunboat, the **USS Cairo,** was the first ironclad ever sunk by an electrically detonated mine. It has been raised from the Yazoo River and restored. A small museum adjacent to it displays Civil War artifacts recovered from the *Cairo. 3201 Clay St., Vicksburg Military Park, ☎ 601/636–0583. ☞ Free. ☉ Fall–spring, daily 9–5; summer, daily 9–6.*

The Vanishing Glory is a multimedia, 15-projector show portraying the sights and sounds of Vicksburg under siege. *717 Clay St., ☎ 601/634– 1863. ☞ $3.50 adults, $2 children 6–18, children under 6 free. ☉ Daily 10–5.*

Vicksburg's historic homes may have cannonballs imbedded in their walls, but they have been beautifully restored. Worth a visit are **Cedar Grove** (2200 Oak St., *see* also Lodging, *below*), **Balfour House** (Crawford and Cherry Sts.), and the **Martha Vick House** (1300 Grove St.).

Mississippi River adventures await those who wish to travel aboard a 40-foot tour boat as it jets down the river. March 1–November 15 (daily at 10, 2, and 5), **Hydro-Jet Boat Tours** depart Vicksburg on a narrated, one-hour tour. ☎ 601/638–5443 or 800/521–4363. ☞ *$16 adults, $8 children 6–12, under 6 free.*

In 1894 Coca-Cola was first bottled at the **Biedenharn Candy Company,** which is now a Coke museum. *1107 Washington St., ☎ 601/638– 6514. ☞ $1.75 adults, $1.25 children under 12. ☉ Mon.–Sat. 9–5, Sun. 1:30–4:30.*

What to See and Do with Children

Biedenharn Candy Company (*see* Exploring, *above*).

Hydro-Jet Boat Tours (*see* Exploring, *above*).

Jim Henson/Muppets Museum in Leland (S. Deer Creek Dr. E, ☎ 601/686–2687) is open daily; ☛ Free.

Toys and Soldiers Museum. More than 30,000 toy soldiers, a miniature circus, antique trains, and old toys are on display. *1100 Cherry St., Vicksburg, ☎ 601/638–1986. ☛ $2 adults, $1.50 grades 1–12, preschoolers free. ☉ Mon.–Sat. 9–4:30, Sun. 1:30–4:30.*

USS *Cairo* and the ***Cairo*** Museum (*see* Exploring, *above*).

Vicksburg National Military Park (*see* Exploring, *above*).

Off the Beaten Path

The **Ethel Wright Mohamed Stitchery Museum** in Belzoni contains pictures embroidered by the late Mrs. Mohamed, who took up needlework in her 60s to record her life in the Delta with her storekeeper husband and eight children. Some of Mrs. Mohamed's work is in the Smithsonian's permanent collection. The gallery is in the Mohamed family home, and the pictures cover every wall. *307 Central St., ☎ 601/247–1433. ☛ $2. ☉ By appointment.*

In Indianola, the **Crown Restaurant** in the **Antique Mall** serves lunch in a setting reminiscent of an English pub. You can buy your plate, chair, or table, or the antique English furnishings and accessories that fill the large restaurant/shop. If you come here on U. S. 82 from Greenville, you'll pass through prime antiquing territory. *MS 448, Crown Restaurant, ☎ 601/887–2522. ☉ Tues.–Sat. 9–5.*

Near Greenwood, **Florewood River Plantation State Park** is an exact replica of an 1850s working plantation, complete with reenactments in the school, blacksmith shop, plantation store, and more. This living history park is well worth the trip. *Box 680 (2 mi west of Greenwood on Hwy. 82), Greenwood, 38930, ☎ 601/455–3821. ☛ $3.50 adults, $3 senior citizens, $2.50 children. ☉ Tues.–Sat. 9–5, Sun. 1–5.*

Shopping

Climb up into the **Attic Gallery** (1406 Washington St., Vicksburg, ☎ 601/638–9221) to see regional art and fine crafts chosen with a discriminating eye—a Southern rival to New York galleries.

Participant Sports

Jogging
The hilly roads in the **Vicksburg National Military Park** (I–20, Exit 4-B, Clay St.) are a challenging course for joggers.

Tennis
Carrie Stern Courts (Eureka St., Greenville), **Ward Park** (MS 1S, Greenville), and **Clear Creek** (I–20, Bovina exit 7, Vicksburg).

Dining and Lodging

Dining

Whether they need to celebrate the cotton crop or bemoan it, Delta folks love to get together and will drive for hours to party or eat out. Good food and drink are required; fancy surroundings aren't. Dress is casual unless otherwise noted.

CATEGORY	COST*
$$$$	over $20
$$$	$15–$20
$$	$10–$15
$	under $10

per person for a three-course meal, excluding drinks, service and 7% sales tax

Lodging

CATEGORY	COST*
$$$$	over $70
$$$	$50–$70
$$	$30–$50
$	under $30

All prices are for a standard double room, excluding 7% tax

Boyle

DINING

$ Sweet Olive. Lunch is served in the living and dining rooms of this restored Victorian home. The menu varies with the chef's whim—chicken in a sour-cream sauce with fruit salad, perhaps, or for dessert, praline cheesecake or ice cream pie. ✗ *328 N. Bayou Ave., off U.S. 61 about 1 mi from Cleveland,* ☎ *601/846–1100. Reservations advised. No credit cards. No dinner. Closed Sun. and Mon.*

Clarksdale

DINING

$ Rest Haven. The Delta's large Lebanese community influences the food, which is considered regional fare. Among the favorites: *kibbie* (seasoned lean ground steak with cracked wheat); spinach and meat pies; and cabbage rolls. Daily plate lunch specials include chicken and dumplings, and red beans and sausage over rice. ✗ *419 State St. (Hwy. 61),* ☎ *601/624–8601. No credit cards. Closed Sun.*

Greenville

DINING

$ Doe's. This is a tumbledown building, visually as uninspiring as any restaurant you'll find—Formica-top tables, mismatched chairs, mismatched cutlery, mismatched plates—and you're practically eating in the kitchen. But when you see that huge steak hanging off your plate, you'll know why this place is famous. Hot tamales (a popular takeout item) and the house salad dressing (olive oil, lemon juice, garlic) are specialties. ✗ *502 Nelson St.,* ☎ *601/334–3315. Reservations advised. MC, V.*

Vicksburg

DINING

$$$–$$$$ **Tuminello's.** Since 1899 Vicksburg residents and visitors have come here
★ for fresh seafood and Italian fare. The old brick building, once Tuminello's Grocery, now with sparkling chandeliers and paneling made

from willow trees along the Mississippi, is a pleasant atmosphere for dining. Specialties include veal sautéed with crabmeat and asparagus spears; baked stuffed redfish; and shrimp *francesca* (sautéed in Imperiale sauce and flamed with brandy). ✘ *500 Speed St.,* ☎ *601/634–0507. Reservations accepted. AE, MC, V.*

$$$ **Delta Point.** This large, elegant restaurant sits high on the bluff, and
★ its picture windows provide excellent views of the Mississippi River. Service is impeccable, the menu varied and ambitious, and the food superb. China, crystal, and flowers contribute to the gracious mood. Specialties are beef tenderloin stuffed with marinated Bing cherries; shrimp and fettuccine; and cherries jubilee and bananas Foster. ✘ *4144 Washington St.,* ☎ *601/636–5317. Reservations advised. AE, DC, MC, V.*

$ **Walnut Hills.** If you're yearning for authentic regional cooking, this restaurant is a must. Don't miss the outstanding fried chicken, served with such vegetables as fresh snap beans or purple-hull peas. For dessert, try the blackberry cobbler. ✘ *1214 Adams St., at Clay St.,* ☎ *601/638–4910. Reservations required for large groups. MC, V.*

LODGING

$$$$ **Cedar Grove.** This 1840s mansion and its grounds cover an entire city block. Guest rooms and the entire house are furnished with period antiques, including Union cannon balls still visible in the walls. Hear nearby river traffic from the quiet, gaslit grounds. A house tour and hearty plantation breakfast are included. 🖭 *2200 Oak St.,* ☎ *601/636–1000 or 800/862–1300,* ℻ *601/634–6126. 35 rooms with bath. Pool. AE, MC, V.*

$$$$ **Duff Green Mansion.** This 1856 mansion was used as a hospital during the Civil War. Each guest room is decorated with antiques, including half-tester beds. A large, Southern-style breakfast and a tour of the home are included. 🖭 *1114 1st East St., 39180,* ☎ *601/638–6662 or 800/992–0037. 5 rooms with bath, 1 suite. Pool. AE, MC, V.*

$$ **Delta Point Inn.** A good location, clean rooms, and free continental breakfast make this a solid choice if you're not up for staying in an antebellum home. Owned by the Ameristar Casino, the hotel provides free transport to the casino for guests (who are gamblers for the most part). 🖭 *4155 Washington St.,* ☎ *601/636–5145,* ℻ *601/636–5314. 54 rooms. AE, D, DC, MC, V.*

Nightlife

In Vicksburg, **Maxwell's** (4702 Clay St., ☎ 601/636–1344 or 800/418–7379) offers live entertainment in its lounge each weekend. **Miller's Still,** in the River Road Restaurant (1101 Washington St., ☎ 601/638–8661), is open daily with live entertainment Thursday–Saturday. **Beechwood Restaurant & Lounge** (4449 Hwy. 80E, ☎ 601/636–3761) is a hot spot for Monday Night Football fans. Live entertainment nightly. Four Vegas-style casinos, **Harrah's Casino** (☎ 800/427–7247), **Rainbow Casino** (☎ 800/503–3777), **Ameristar** (☎ 800/700–7770), and **Isle of Capri Casino** (☎ 800/843–4753), open 24 hours a day, are permanently docked on the Mississippi River near downtown. "Viva Las Vicksburg!"

Delta Essentials

Arriving and Departing, Getting Around

BY BUS

Greyhound (☎ 800/231–2222) stops in Belzoni (West Side Grocery, 711 Francis St., ☎ 601/247–2150), Clarksdale (1604 State St., ☎ 601/627–7893), Cleveland (U.S. 61N, ☎ 601/843–5113), Greenville

(1849 U.S. 82E, ☎ 601/335–2633), and Vicksburg (1511 Walnut St., ☎ 601/638–8389).

BY CAR
U.S. 61 runs from Memphis through the Delta to Vicksburg, Natchez, and Baton Rouge, LA. The Great River Road (MS 1) parallels U.S. 61 and the river through part of this route.

BY PLANE
The **Greenville Municipal Airport** (☎ 601/334–3121) on Air Base Road is served by Northwest Airlink (☎ 601/335–5362).

Important Addresses and Numbers

EMERGENCIES
In Greenville and Vicksburg, dial 911 for **police** and **ambulance** in emergencies. Seek medical help at **Delta Regional Medical Center** (1400 E. Union Ave., Greenville, ☎ 601/378–3783) and at **Vicksburg Medical Center** (3311 I–20 Frontage Rd., ☎ 601/636–2611).

RADIO STATIONS
FM: WAID 106.5, urban contemporary; WBBV 101.1, country.

VISITOR INFORMATION
Clarksdale-Coahoma County Chamber of Commerce (1540 De Soto Ave., Box 160, Clarksdale 38614, ☎ 601/627–7337, ☉ Weekdays 8:30–5). **Cleveland–Bolivar County Chamber of Commerce** (600 3rd St., Box 490, Cleveland 38732, ☎ 601/843–2712, ☉ Weekdays 8:30–noon, 1–5). **Greenville–Washington County CVB** (410 Washington Ave., Greenville 38701, ☎ 601/334–2711 or 800/467–3582, ☉ Weekdays 9–5). **Greenwood Convention & Visitors Bureau** (1904 Le Flore Ave., Box 739, Greenwood 38930, ☎ 601/453–9197 or 800/748–9064, ☉ Weekdays 9–5). **Mississippi Welcome Center** (4210 Washington St., Vicksburg 39180, ☎ 601/638–4269, ☉ Daily 8–5). **Vicksburg Convention & Visitors Bureau** (Clay St. and Old Hwy. 27, Box 110, Vicksburg 39181, ☎ 601/636–9421 or 800/221–3536, ☉ Daily 8–5). **Washington County Welcome Center** (U.S. 82 at Reed Rd., Box 6022, Greenville 38701, ☎ 601/332–2378, ☉ Daily 8–5).

6 North Carolina

Historic sights and natural wonders galore accent North Carolina, from Old Salem, where the 1700s spring to life today, to the Great Smoky and Blue Ridge Mountains, where waterfalls cascade over high cliffs into gorges thick with evergreens, to the Cape Hatteras and Cape Lookout national seashores, where tides wash over shipwrecks and lighthouses stand as they have for 200 years. Here, too, you'll find sophisticated cities like Charlotte, first-class golf in the Pinehurst Sandhills, and fields of tobacco in the Piedmont.

By Carol
Timblin

Updated by
Susan Ladd

NORTH CAROLINA MAY NOT HAVE IT ALL, but don't try telling that to a North Carolinian. Any native will point to its mountains, some of the tallest in the east, which are laced with waterfalls cascading over rocky cliffs into gorges thick with evergreens. He or she will tell you about Cape Hatteras and Cape Lookout national seashores, where tides wash over the wooden beams of ancient shipwrecks, and lighthouses have stood for 200 years. You'll be invited to Charlotte, the state's largest city, where banking and professional basketball draw national attention, and to the Research Triangle Park, at which the technology of virtual reality got a trial run.

North Carolina geography has carved out three distinct regions: The mountains, the Piedmont, and the coast. The Great Smoky and Blue Ridge mountain ranges create the rough, slanted border of western North Carolina. The mountains taper off into foothills and then into the Piedmont, a gently rolling landscape characterized by rich farmlands to the north, red clay soil in the center, and sandy pine forests to the south. Most major cities have grown up in the center of the state, built primarily by the textile, furniture, and tobacco industries. The rolling hills of the Piedmont level off into the rich soil of the coastal plain. Much of eastern North Carolina remains agricultural and rural. Wilmington is a bustling port city, in sharp contrast to the tranquil villages along the Outer Banks.

Golf is the recreational focus in the Sandhills, while skiing has taken hold in the High Country (Alleghany, Ashe, Avery, Mitchell, and Watauga counties). Asheville has maintained its status as a resort city for more than 100 years and continues to grow in popularity.

North Carolina has courted visitors since the first English settlers arrived in 1584. Since the Depression of the 1930s, when the state began to realize the importance of tourism, the welcome mat has been out. The Blue Ridge Parkway was built largely by the CCC (Civilian Conservation Corps), as were many state park facilities. Cape Hatteras was declared a national seashore—the country's first—in 1953. A good highway system and several airports were built, and now eight welcome centers greet visitors at state borders. People come to North Carolina for its historic sites and natural wonders, its sports, resorts, and down-home cooking, not to mention its legendary barbecue. And tourism today, after tobacco and textiles, is the state's largest industry.

CHARLOTTE

Charlotte, once a sleepy Southern crossroads, has grown up to be quite a sophisticated city—with luxury hotels, excellent restaurants, sporting events, and varied cultural activities. The acquisition of a professional football franchise is the city's most recent achievement, and Carolina Panthers mania is already sweeping the state. The Charlotte Hornets basketball team has been setting NBA attendance and merchandise sales records since the team was formed in 1988.

Though Charlotte dates to Revolutionary War times (it is named for King George III's wife, Queen Charlotte), its Uptown is distinctively New South. The NationsBank Corporate Center, a 60-story skyscraper designed by Cesar Pelli, dominates the skyline. The Queen City is the largest city in the Carolinas, the third largest banking center in the nation, and a major trade and distribution center.

North Carolina

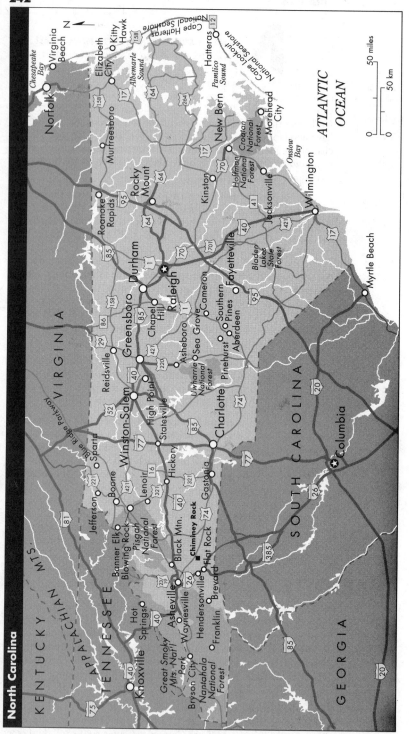

Heavy development has created some typical urban problems. Outdated road systems make traffic a nightmare during rush hour, and virtually all the city's restaurants are packed on weekends. But the southern courtesy of the locals is contagious, and people still love the traditional pleasure of picnicking in Freedom Park.

Exploring

Uptown Charlotte Walking Tour

Numbers in the margin correspond to points of interest on the Charlotte map.

Uptown Charlotte is ideal for walking, and buses are adequate for getting around within the city limits; otherwise, you will need a car. The city was laid out in four wards from the Square, at Trade and Tryon streets. Stop first at **Info Charlotte** on South Tryon Street (*see* Visitor Information, *below*) for information on a self-guided walking tour of Fourth Ward (*see below*) and a historic tour of Uptown, as well as maps and brochures. You can park your car in an open lot a few blocks east of the Square, where Trade and Tryon intersect.

Take a stroll down **Tryon Street** and enjoy the ambience of this revitalized area, noting the outdoor sculptures on the plazas and the creative architecture of some of the newer buildings, among them the
❶ **NationsBank Corporate Center,** a 60-story structure with a crownlike top designed by Pelli, which opened in late 1992. Its main attraction is three philosophical frescoes by Ben Long that symbolize the city's past, present, and future. Also housed in the tower are the **North Carolina Blumenthal Performing Arts Center** and **Founders Hall,** a complex of restaurants and shops.

❷ From the bank, head north on North Tryon Street to **Discovery Place,** the city's premier attraction. Make the wonderful hands-on Science Museum a priority, and allow at least two hours for the aquariums, the rain forest, the Omnimax theater, and Kelly Space Voyager Planetarium. Check the schedule for special exhibits. *301 N. Tryon St.,* ☎ *704/372–6261 or 800/935–0553.* ☛ *$5.50–$8.50 adults, $4.50–$7.50 senior citizens and students, $2.75–$5.50 children 3–5.* ☉ *Mon.–Sat. 9–6, Sun. 1–6.*

❸ **Fourth Ward,** Charlotte's new "old" city, which lies just north of Discovery Place, offers a refreshing change from the newly developed parts of town. The self-guided tour brochure available at Info Charlotte (330 S. Tryon St.) that includes house numbers, points to 18 historic sites in the area. Be sure to stop by **Old Settlers Cemetery,** behind the **First Presbyterian Church,** which contains stones that date to the 1700s. The church, which takes up a city block and faces West Trade Street, reflects the prosperity of the early settlers and their descendants. By the turn of the last century, they had built this Gothic Revival complex with stained glass to replace a much simpler meeting house. **Fourth Ward Park** is an oasis in the middle of the city. **Alexander Michael's** (401 W. Ninth St., ☎ 704/332–6789) is a favorite eatery. **Poplar Street Books** is housed in the Victorian Young-Morrison House (226 W. Tenth St.). U.S. President Taft spent the night in the **Liddell-McNinch House** (511 N. Church St.), now a restaurant, when he visited Charlotte in 1909. **Spirit Square** (345 N. College St.), in a former church, includes galleries, a performing arts center, and classrooms that used to be the sanctuary for the First Baptist Church. The **public library** (310 N. Tryon St.), which contains a mural reproducing a Romare Bearden painting, is open weekdays 9–9, Saturday 9–6, and Sunday 2–6.

Charlotte

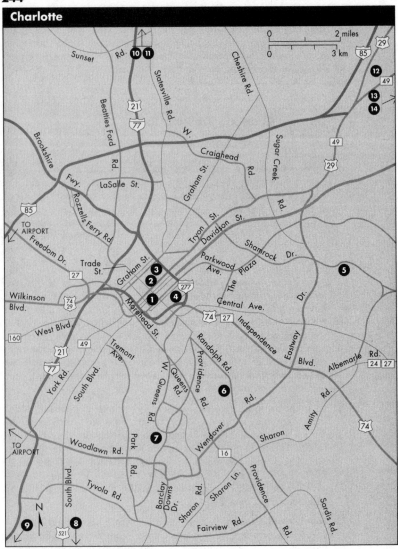

Afro-American
Cultural Center, **4**

Backing Up Classics
Memory Lane Motor
Car Museum, **14**

Charlotte Motor
Speedway, **13**

Discovery Place, **2**

Energy Explorium, **11**

Fourth Ward, **3**

Hezekiah Alexander
Homesite and History
Museum, **5**

James K. Polk
Memorial, **8**

Latta Plantation
Park, **10**

Mint Museum of Art, **6**

NationsBank
Corporate Center, **1**

New Heritage USA, **9**

UNC Charlotte
Botanical Garden and
Sculpture Garden, **12**

Wing Haven Gardens
and Bird Sanctuary, **7**

Other Area Attractions

You can reach the Afro-American Cultural Center, Hezekiah Alexander Homesite, Mint Museum, and Charlotte Nature Museum by city bus; for visits elsewhere, a car is needed.

❹ From Uptown Charlotte, follow Seventh Street east to North Myers Street. The **Afro-American Cultural Center,** an arts center that has galleries and a theater, is housed in the former Little Rock AME Zion Church. *401 N. Meyers St.,* ☎ *704/374–1565.* ☛ *Free.* ☉ *Tues.–Sat. 10–6, Sun. 1–5.*

❺ From Seventh Street, go east on Central Avenue to Eastway Drive, north to Shamrock Drive, and east to the **Hezekiah Alexander Homesite and Charlotte History Museum.** The stone house, built in 1774, is the oldest dwelling in the county. Here, Alexander and his wife, Mary, reared 10 children and farmed the land. Costumed docents give guided tours, and seasonal events commemorate the early days. *3500 Shamrock Dr.,* ☎ *704/568–1774.* ☛ *$4 adults, $3 senior citizens, $2 children 6–12.* ☉ *Tues.–Fri. 10–5, weekends 2–5.*

★ ❻ Follow Eastway Drive (Charlotte 4) south to Randolph Road and turn right to the **Mint Museum of Art.** Built in 1837 as a U.S. Mint, it has served as a home for art since 1936, attracting such visiting exhibits as "Classical Taste in America." *2730 Randolph Rd.,* ☎ *704/337–2000.* ☛ *$4 adults, $3 senior citizens, $2 students 13 and older, children under 12 free.* ☉ *Tues. 10–10, Wed.–Sat. 10–5, Sun. noon–5. Closed major holidays.*

❼ Continue on Charlotte 4 (Wendover Rd.) for a visit to **Wing Haven Gardens and Bird Sanctuary** in Myers Park, one of Charlotte's loveliest neighborhoods. The 3-acre garden, developed by the Clarkson family, is home to more than 135 species of birds. *248 Ridgewood Ave.,* ☎ *704/331–0664.* ☛ *Free.* ☉ *Sun. 2–5, Tues.–Wed. 3–5 or by appointment.*

❽ The **James K. Polk Memorial,** now a state historic site, marks the humble 1795 birthplace of the 11th president. Guided tours of the log cabins are available, and exhibits in the center depict early life in Mecklenburg County. *U.S. 521, Pineville,* ☎ *704/889–7145.* ☛ *Free.* ☉ *Apr.–Oct., Mon.–Sat. 9–5, Sun. 1–5; Nov.–Mar., Tues.–Sat. 10–4, Sun. 1–4.*

❾ Head south on I–77 for about 12 miles to **New Heritage USA,** on the South Carolina line, the 2,200-acre Christian theme park once owned by Jim and Tammy Bakker's PTL television ministry. It's a very pleasant place, with an elaborate water park (open mid-May–Labor Day), paddle boats, farm animals, bike rentals, horseback riding, and shops. You can also visit Billy Graham's boyhood home, which was moved to the site. *3000 Heritage Pkwy., Fort Mill, SC,* ☎ *803/548–7800 or 800/374–1234.* ☛ *Free to the park and Graham house; attractions cost $1–$13.*

❿ **Latta Plantation Park,** northwest of town (off I–77, near Huntersville), centers on Latta Place, a Catawba River plantation house built by merchant James Latta in the early 1800s. Costumed guides give tours of the house. The park also has farm animals, an equestrian center, and the Carolina Raptor Center, a unique nonprofit facility where injured raptors are rehabilitated and then released. Those unable to return to the wild are cared for and used to educate visitors about the importance of bald eagles, owls, and other birds of prey. *5225 Sample Rd., Huntersville,* ☎ *704/875–2312 (Latta Place), 704/875–1391 (park),* or 704/875–6521 *(Carolina Raptor Center).* ☛ *House tour $2 adults, $1.50 senior citizens, $1 children.* ☛ *Raptor Center $2 adults, $1 students 6 and older. Park* ☉ *Daily 7 AM–dark; Carolina Raptor Center* ☉ *Tues.–Sun. 10–5; house tours Tues.–Fri. at 1:30 and 3:30, weekends at 1:30, 2:30, 3:30.*

⑪ Continue on I–77N to the **Energy Explorium,** operated by Duke Power Company on Lake Norman. Hands-on exhibits let you simulate the creation of nuclear power and other kinds of energy. A wildflower garden and picnic area offer diversion of a different kind. *McGuire Nuclear Site, off I–77 and NC 73, Huntersville,* ☎ *704/875–5600 or 800/777–0003.* ☛ *Free.* ☉ *Mon.–Sat. 9–5, Sun. noon–5. Closed major holidays.*

⑫ The **UNC Charlotte Botanical Garden and Sculpture Garden,** on Route 49 off I–85, has a rhododendron garden and greenhouse with a rain forest, orchids, carnivorous plants, and cacti. Sculptures are constantly being added to the adjoining Sculpture Garden. *Rte. 49,* ☎ *704/547–4286.* ☛ *Free.* ☉ *Gardens daylight–dark, greenhouse weekdays 8–5 and weekends by appointment.*

⑬ Northeast of town on Route 29, you'll come to the **Charlotte Motor Speedway.** Learn all about racing at this state-of-the-art facility (which has condos overlooking the first turn), browse through the gift shop, or even take a lesson at the track through the Richard Petty Driving School (☎ 704/455–9443) or Fast Track Driving School (☎ 704/455–1700). *Rte. 29 at Concord,* ☎ *704/455–3200.* ☛ *Tour $3, children under 3 free.* ☉ *Mon.–Sat. 9–4, Sun. 1–4.*

⑭ At the **Backing Up Classics Memory Lane Museum** (we're not making this up), you can see up close some of the '50s race and muscle cars that have been the workhorses of stock-car racing. *4545 Hwy. 29, Harrisburg,* ☎ *704/788–9494.* ☛ *$4.50 adults, $4 senior citizens and students, children 6 and under free.* ☉ *Weekdays 9–5:30, Sat. 9–5, Sun. noon–5.*

What to See and Do with Children

At **Celebration Station,** a commercial park, you can play miniature golf, ride in go-carts and bumper boats, try your skill at arcade games, stuff yourself, and watch mechanical cartoon characters entertain you. *10400 Cadillac St., Pineville,* ☎ *704/552–7888.* ☛ *$3–$4 per attraction.* ☉ *Mon.–Thurs. 4–9, Fri. 4–11, Sat. 10 AM–11 PM, Sun. 10–9. Closed Thanksgiving and Dec. 25.*

Paramount's Carowinds, off I–77, a 91-acre theme amusement park on the South Carolina state line, has taken on a new image since its acquisition by the movie studio and the addition of new attractions based on films. Costumed movie characters and actors greet visitors to the park, and the Paladium offers musical concerts with star entertainers. *Carowinds Blvd.,* ☎ *704/588–2600 or 800/888–4386.* ☛ *$25.95 adults, $13.50 senior citizens over 60 and children 4–6.* ☉ *June–Aug., daily; mid-Mar.–May. and Sept.–mid-Oct., weekends only; the park usually opens around 10 AM, closing hours vary.*

The **Charlotte Nature Museum** has live animals, nature trails, hands-on exhibits, and nature films. *1658 Sterling Rd. (next to Freedom Park),* ☎ *704/337–2660.* ☛ *$1, under 3 free.* ☉ *Weekdays 9–5, Sat. 10–5, Sun. 1–5. Closed major holidays.*

Reed Gold Mine, east of Charlotte in Cabarrus County, is where America's first gold rush began following Conrad Reed's discovery of a 17-

pound nugget in 1799. Visitors may explore the underground mine shaft and gold holes, pan for gold during the summer months, learn about the history of gold mining, or enjoy a picnic. *Take NC 24/27 to Locust and follow the signs,* ☎ *704/786–8337.* ☛ *Free, but gold panning is $3 (group rate $1 per person).* ☺ *Apr.–Oct., Mon.–Sat. 9–5, Sun. 1–5; Nov.–Mar., Tues.–Sat. 10–4, Sun. 1–4.*

At the **N.C. Transportation Museum,** north of Salisbury, once a railway repair facility, a restored train takes passengers on a 45-minute ride over the 57-acre complex, with a stop at the round house. The museum, a state historic site, traces the development of transportation in North Carolina from Indian times to the present. The gift shop sells some unique train memorabilia. *Off I–85 at Spencer,* ☎ *704/636–2889.* ☛ *Free, train rides $2.50–$3.50.* ☺ *Apr.–Oct., Mon.–Sat. 9–5, Sun. 1–5; Nov.–Mar., Tues.–Sat. 10–4, Sun. 1–4.*

Shopping

Charlotte is the largest retail center in the Carolinas, with the majority of stores in suburban malls. Villages and towns in outlying areas offer some regional specialties. Uptown shops are open 10–5:30 daily except Sunday. Malls are open Monday–Saturday 10–9 and Sunday 1–6. Sales tax is 6%.

Shopping Districts

You can buy well-known brands at a discount in outlets in **Midtown Square** (401 S. Independence Blvd.) near Uptown, **Windsor Square** (9915 E. Independence Blvd.) near Matthews, or **Outlet Marketplace,** (off I–77, Ft. Mill, SC).

Carolina Place Mall (11025 Carolina Place Pkwy., off I–277 at Pineville; 704/543–9300) is the newest mall in the area, with Belk, Dillard's, Hecht's, and JC Penney as anchors. **SouthPark Mall** (4400 Sharon Rd., ☎ 704/364–4411) in the most affluent section of the city, caters to upscale customers. Belk, Dillard's, Hecht's, Montaldo's, and Sears are here. The main attraction at **Eastland Mall** (5431 Central Ave., ☎ 704/537–2626), on the east side of town, is an ice-skating rink. Dillard's, Belk, JC Penney, Sears, and other retail stores are also located here.

Specialty Stores

ANTIQUES

The towns of Waxhaw, Pineville, and Matthews are the best places to find antiques. Each has a number of shops, and Waxhaw sponsors an annual antiques fair each February. Shops are usually open Monday through Saturday in Pineville and Matthews. In Waxhaw, some shops are open on Sunday but closed on Monday. You can find a good selection of antiques at the **Metrolina Expo** (off I–77N at 7100 Statesville Rd.) on the first and third weekends of the month.

BOOKS

There are some excellent bookshops in Charlotte. **Little Professor Book Center** (Park Road Shopping Center, ☎ 704/525–9239; South Lake Shopping Center, Lake Norman, ☎ 704/896–7323) has a nice selection of contemporary fiction and classics. **Barnes & Noble Bookstore** (5837 E. Independence Blvd., ☎ 704/535–9810; 10701 Centrum Pkwy., Pineville, ☎ 704/541–1425) is an upscale chain with more than 100,000 titles. The **Intimate Bookshop** (South Park Mall, ☎ 704/366–6400; Eastland Mall, ☎ 704/568–3600; University Place, ☎ 704/547–7400) is a locally based chain with a fine selection and warm atmosphere.

Borders Books & Music (4500 Sharon Rd., ☎ 704/365–6261), the newest contender in the Charlotte book market, has 100,000 titles and a built-in espresso bar where you can mull over the choices. **Newsstand International** (5636 E. Independence Blvd., ☎ 704/365–0910) carries 5,000 newspapers, maps, and magazines from around the world.

CRAFTS
The best buys are in the **Metrolina Expo** (*see* Antiques, *above*). At the **Carolina Craft Shows,** held in the fall and spring at the Convention Center, as well as the **Southern Christmas Show** and the **Southern Spring Show** at the Merchandise Mart, you can buy a wide variety.

FOOD AND PLANTS
Try the **Charlotte Regional Farmers Market** (1715 Yorkmount Rd.) for fresh produce and fish, plants, and crafts. The **Harris-Teeter** grocery store in Morrocroft Village (6701 Morrison Blvd., ☎ 704/364–1245) is a white-columned showplace with a staff chef who oversees an elaborate dine-in deli and the two other stores.

Participant Sports and Outdoor Activities

Bicycling
North Carolina has designated bike tour routes stretching from the coast to the mountains. There is one between Southpark and Uptown Charlotte. Route maps are available from the NC Department of Transportation (Box 25201, Raleigh 27611).

Camping
Near Charlotte, try McDowell Park and Nature Reserve (15222 York Rd., ☎ 704/588–5224), Carowinds (*see above*), and Duke Power State Park(Rte. 2, Box 224–M, Troutman, ☎ 704/528–6350).

Canoeing
Inlets on Lake Norman and Lake Wylie are ideal for canoeing, as are some spots of the Catawba River. The Pee Dee River east of Charlotte and the New River in the mountains offer other options.

Fishing
There's good fishing in Charlotte's neighboring lakes and streams. A mandatory state license can be bought at local bait and tackle shops or over the phone (with a credit card) from the North Carolina Wildlife Commission (☎ 919/715–4091).

Golf
There are 23 public and 31 private courses in the Charlotte area. The *Metrolina Golf Guide,* a free publication available at the visitor center, has a complete list. **Crystal Springs Golf Club** (NC 51, Pineville, ☎ 704/588–2640) is an 18-hole championship course with restaurant and lounge. **Highland Creek Golf Club** (7001 Highland Creek Pkwy., ☎ 704/875–9000), an 18-hole course with a driving range, is considered by some to be the best public course in Charlotte. **Larkhaven Golf Club** (4801 Camp Stewart Rd., ☎ 704/545–4653) is an 18-hole championship course with club house and pro shop. **Paradise Valley Golf Center** (9309 N. Tryon St., ☎ 704/547–0222), in the University area, has a 9-hole regulation course and a 9-hole par-three course. The driving range is down the street (9615 N. Tryon St., ☎ 704/548–8114). The **Peninsula Club** (19101 Peninsula Club Dr., Davidson, ☎ 704/896–7080) recently hosted the Carolinas LPGA. **Woodbridge Golf Links** (922 New

Camp Creek Church Rd., Kings Mountain., ☎ 704/482–0353), an attractive course featuring covered cart bridges, has 18 holes and a driving range.

Hiking

Crowder's Mountain and Kings Mountain near Gastonia and the Uwharrie Mountains east of Charlotte offer plenty of varied terrain and challenge for hikers.

Jogging

Jogging trails and tracks can be found in most city and county parks and at many local schools. Contact the Mecklenburg County Parks and Recreation Department (☎ 704/336–3854). The **Charlotte Track Club** (☎ 704/358–0713) meets monthly and holds regular group runs Sundays at 7:30 AM at McAlpine Creek Park.

Swimming

The **Mecklenburg County Aquatic Center** (800 E. 2nd St., ☎ 704/336–3483) has a 50-meter lap pool, hydrotherapy pool, fitness room, and whirlpool. It is open daily to local residents and visitors. ☛ *$4 nonresident adults, $3 children under 19.*

Tennis

Courts are available in several city parks, including Freedom, Hornet's Nest, Park Road, and Veterans. A growing number of hotels and motels provide courts as well. For details, call the Charlotte Park and Recreation Department (☎ 704/336–3854).

Spectator Sports

Baseball

The **Charlotte Knights** play from April through August at Knights Castle (I–77 and Gold Hill Rd., SC, ☎ 704/357–8071 or 803/548–8050).

Basketball

The **Charlotte Hornets** play from November to April at the Charlotte Coliseum (Tyvola Rd., off the Billy Graham Pkwy., ☎ 704/357–0489).

Football

The **Carolina Panthers** NFL team plays September–January at the new Carolinas Stadium downtown (S. Tryon St., ☎ 704/358–7800).

Hockey

The **Charlotte Checkers** play from mid-October to mid-March at Independence Arena (2700 E. Independence Blvd., ☎ 704/342–4423).

Racing

NASCAR races, such as the **Coca-Cola 600** and **Mello Yello 500,** draw huge crowds at the Charlotte Motor Speedway near Concord. For tickets, call 704/455–3200.

Dining

If there is one sure indication of Charlotte's transformation from Southern town to big city, it's the restaurant scene. Risotto and dim sum are becoming as common as grits and cornbread. These days, it's probably easier to find a good Thai restaurant than it is to find barbecue. Ethnic specialties of all kinds are available, as well as American nouvelle cuisine and various upscale chain restaurants. But if it's good old-fashioned Southern cooking you want, you can still find that, too. Dress is casual unless otherwise noted.

CATEGORY	COST*
$$$$	over $20
$$$	$15–$20
$$	$10–$15
$	under $10

*per person for a three-course meal, excluding drinks, service, and 6% sales tax

American

$$$–$$$$ **Townhouse.** American cuisine with a French twist is exquisitely prepared and served in an atmosphere of casual elegance. Choose from appetizers such as spinach lasagna with snails and garlic cream and entrées such as carmelized salmon, or let the chef compose a five-course "chef's choice" menu for $45 per person. ✕ *1011 Providence Rd.,* ☎ *704/335–1546. Reservations accepted. AE, DC, MC, V. Closed Sun.*

$$–$$$ **Newmarket Grille.** You can enjoy a variety of moderately priced dishes, including soups, sandwiches, salads, pastas, steak, and fish, within the rich mahogany walls of this restaurant in the Arboretum Shopping Center on the south side. Outdoor dining is also an option, and there's a cozy, dark bar for getting together with friends. ✕ *8136 Providence Rd.,* ☎ *704/543–4656. No reservations. AE, DC, MC, V.*

$$–$$$ **Providence Café.** Many of the dishes (especially the sandwiches) served in this chic, contemporary eatery decorated with neon and original art center around the foccacia that is baked daily on the premises. The eclectic menu also includes chicken, steaks, and seafood grilled over green hickory wood. It's a great place for Sunday brunch and after-hours desserts with cappuccino or espresso. ✕ *110 Perrin Pl.,* ☎ *704/376–2008. No reservations on weekends. AE, D, MC, V.*

$–$$ **Grady's American Grill.** Packed every night of the week, this restaurant has earned praise from patrons for its friendly service and excellent food. Favorites are the greenhouse salad served with honey-mustard dressing, the mesquite-grilled chicken or fish, and the hot chocolate bar cake. There's usually a wait of 30 minutes to an hour, but the time passes quickly at the lively bar. ✕ *5546 Albemarle Rd.,* ☎ *704/537–4663. No reservations. AE, DC, MC, V.*

$ **Landmark Restaurant-Diner.** This New York–style eatery in the Eastland Mall neighborhood is a cut above most inexpensive restaurants, and it's open until 3 AM on weeknights and 24 hours on weekends. Decorated in contemporary colors, this spacious restaurant is a good place for an informal breakfast, lunch, dinner, or after-hours dessert. (Ask for the New York–style cheesecake from the in-house bakery.) ✕ *4429 Central Ave.,* ☎ *704/532–1153. Reservations accepted for parties of 8 or more. AE, MC, V. Closed Dec. 25.*

Chinese

$$ **Ginger Root.** Relaxation is guaranteed the moment you step into the quiet, peaceful atmosphere of this Uptown restaurant, convenient to the art centers and galleries. Ideal for lunch or dinner, the restaurant offers pork, chicken, beef, and seafood dishes, served Hunan, Szechuan, Yu Shawn, or Kao Pao style. There's also a comfortable bar. ✕ *201 E. 5th St.,* ☎ *704/377–9429. Reservations advised. AE, DC, MC, V.*

Continental

$$$$ **Lamplighter.** You don't have to go abroad to find gourmet cuisine served
★ in an elegant setting. Just step into the softly lit, sophisticated atmosphere of the Lamplighter, in an old Dilworth home. The trio combination entrées (beef, veal, and lamb, or different seafoods) are
exceptional, and the wine list is extensive. There's a quiet, intimate lounge
for cocktails. ✕ *1065 E. Morehead St.,* ☎ *704/372–5343. Reservations advised. Jacket required. AE, DC, MC, V.*

$$ **Pewter Rose Bistro.** In a renovated textile mill in historic Dilworth, 5
★ minutes from Uptown, the Pewter Rose Bistro is a favorite hangout
for Charlotte's young professionals. Lace curtains and plants decorate
the dining room, and the kitchen specializes in fresh seasonal foods,
plus a variety of chicken and seafood dishes. You can order pasta with
feta cheese, sun-dried tomatoes and olives vegetarian or add chicken
for a heartier meal. A nice place to go for Sunday brunch. ✕ *1820 South
Blvd.,* ☎ *704/332–8149. Reservations for parties of 6 or more. AE,
D, MC, V. Closed Mon.*

Italian

$$$$ **Bravo!** Authentic classic Italian cuisine is served in a Mediterranean-
style atmosphere at this hotel restaurant, the "in" place for special cel-
ebrations and Sunday brunches. The professionally trained singing
waitresses and waiters never seem to tire of performing or graciously
serving. ✕ *Adams Mark Hotel, 555 S. McDowell St.,* ☎ *704/372–5440.
Reservations advised. Jacket required. AE, D, MC, V.*

$$–$$$ **Cafe 521.** Put on your Doc Maartens and join the Generation Xers for
excellent Northern Italian cuisine at one of the city's coolest restau-
rants. Don't miss the zesty minestrone. Industrial looking on the out-
side, the restaurant is painted with funky murals on the inside. ✕ *521
N. College St.,* ☎ *704/377–9100. Reservations accepted. AE, D, MC,
V.*

$–$$ **PizZarrelli Trattoria.** The secret to the unique flavor of the made-from-
scratch pizzas is in the wood-burning brick ovens, built by Italian ma-
sons. The menu also features calzone, lasagna, spaghetti, and other
Southern Italian dishes—all family recipes and especially good when
served with the mellow house wine. The tables are covered with red-
checked gingham, and the walls are adorned with posters and photographs that chronicle the professional singing career of owner Neal
Zarrelli, a former opera star who often sings for his customers. ✕ *9101
Pineville-Matthews Rd., Pineville,* ☎ *704/543–0647. Reservations
accepted. MC, V.*

Thai

$$–$$$ **Thai House.** Fiery pleasure awaits the adventurous diner who samples
from a selection of vegetarian, seafood, and classic Thai dishes. Regarded by many as the best Thai food in town, this restaurant is open
daily for lunch and dinner. The satay and Phad Thai noodles are mild
enough for any taste buds, but many other classic dishes are prepared
as firey as you request. ✕ *3210 N. Sharon Amity Rd.,* ☎ *704/532–
6868. Reservations advised for parties of 6 or more. AE, D, MC, V.*

Lodging

Approximately 14,000 hotel rooms are available in the Charlotte area,
from economy motels to convention hotels or bed-and-breakfast houses.
Most of the major chains are represented, from Hilton, Hyatt, and Sheraton, to EconoLodge, Days Inn, and Motel 6. Some hotels offer great
weekend packages. A 6% accommodations tax and 6% sales tax are

added to every room charge. Pick up the "Charlotte Visitors Guide" for a more comprehensive list.

CATEGORY	COST*
$$$$	over $100
$$$	$60–$100
$$	$30–$60
$	under $30

All prices are for a standard double room, excluding 12% tax

Hotels

$$$ Dunhill. Charlotte's oldest and most historic hotel (built in 1929) fea-
★ tures artwork by Philip Moose and 18th- and 19th-century reproduc-
tion furniture in the lobby, restaurant, and guest rooms. The restaurant,
Monticello's, gets rave reviews for its beautifully presented American
cuisine. ☎ 237 N. Tryon St., 28202, ☎ 704/332–4141 or 800/354–
4141, FAX 704/376–4117. 59 rooms and 1 penthouse with Jacuzzi.
Restaurant, lounge. AE, D, DC, MC, V.

$$$ Embassy Suites. An eight-story atrium and three glass elevators dis-
tinguish this all-suite hotel, near the airport and the Coliseum. Guests
have the option of regular suites (which have two rooms, plus a cof-
feemaker, refrigerator, microwave, and regular amenities) or 12 executive suites, four of which have Jacuzzis. Guests are served a
cooked-to-order full breakfast and are treated to an afternoon reception. ☎ 4800 S. Tryon St., 28217, ☎ 704/527–8400 or 800/362–2779,
FAX 704/527–7035. 274 suites. Restaurant, lounge, indoor pool, hot
tub, sauna, health club, meeting rooms, airport shuttle. AE, D, DC,
MC, V.

$$$ Hilton at University Place. This high-rise with a three-story atrium
dominates the European-style shopping and entertainment village near
the University of North Carolina at Charlotte. Movies, restaurants, shops,
a bank, and even a hospital are just a few steps from the hotel door.
Dining is offered in the Lakefront Café. ☎ 8629 J.M. Keynes Blvd.,
28262, ☎ 704/547–7444 or 800/445–8667, FAX 704/548–1081. 240
rooms, 3 suites. Restaurant, bar, pool, exercise room, beach, meeting
rooms. AE, D, DC, MC, V.

$$$ Hyatt Charlotte SouthPark. The focal point of the four-story atrium is
a Mexican water fountain surrounded by 25-foot olive trees. Guest rooms
are equipped with data ports for laptop computers and fax machines.
Meeting rooms and the lower lobby give onto the open-air courtyard.
Scalini's restaurant serves Northern Italian cuisine; the Club piano bar
is a favorite with the after-hours crowd. ☎ 5501 Carnegie Blvd.,
28209-3462, ☎ 704/554–1234 or 800/233–1234, FAX 704/554–8319.
258 rooms, 4 suites. Restaurant, indoor pool, hot tub, sauna, health
club, meeting rooms, airport shuttle. AE, D, DC, MC, V.

$$$ Omni Charlotte Hotel. The pink marble used in the public rooms
makes this one of Charlotte's classiest Uptown hotels. Guests can
enjoy the ambience of C. Banknight's Bistro and Bar and then work
out with Charlotte's movers and shakers in the adjoining 50,000-
square-foot YMCA, which includes an indoor track and a lap pool.
For special pampering, stay on the Club levels or in the Presidential
Suite. ☎ 222 E. 3rd St., 28202, ☎ 704/377–6664 or 800/843–6664,
FAX 704/377–4143. 392 rooms, 18 suites. Restaurant, bar, indoor pool,
health club, meeting rooms. AE, D, DC, MC, V.

$$$ Radisson Plaza Hotel. Convenience and contemporary elegance are
yours at this property just steps from the Square and the center of Up-
town. It's also connected to the Overstreet Mall, a complex of shops
and restaurants. Try dining at the Azaleas American Grill. All guests

get complimentary newspapers and free parking. ⊞ *1 Radisson Plaza, 101 S. Tryon St., 28280,* ☎ *704/377–0400 or 800/333–3333,* ℻ *704/347–0649. 361 rooms, 4 suites. Restaurant, bar, pool, sauna, health club, meeting rooms, airport shuttle. AE, D, DC, MC, V.*

$ **Comfort Inn–Lake Norman.** This economy motel, north of Charlotte on I–77 near Lake Norman, offers complimentary breakfast and rooms with refrigerators and coffeemakers. Some rooms also have VCRs, microwaves, and whirlpool baths. ⊞ *20740 Torrence Chapel Rd., Davidson 28036,* ☎ *704/892–3500 or 800/484–9751,* ℻ *704/892–6473. 90 rooms. Pool, coin laundry. AE, D, DC, MC, V.*

Bed-and-Breakfasts

$$$–$$$$ **Inn Uptown.** This 1891 brick château on the edge of the historic 4th Ward neighborhood is popular with business and leisure travelers because of its proximity to Uptown businesses and attractions. Deep green wallpaper and a green-and-white-striped bedspread lend formal elegance to one room; some rooms have whirlpools and fireplaces. A complimentary full breakfast is served, and there is turn-down service. ⊞ *129 Poplar and 5th St., 28202,* ☎ *704/342–2800 or 800/959–1990,* ℻ *704/342–2222. 6 rooms. In-room modem lines. AE, D, DC, MC, V.*

$$$ **Homeplace.** This spotless turn-of-the-century Victorian gem is now a
★ bed-and-breakfast inn filled with antiques and memorabilia from yesteryear. The inn's guest rooms all have private baths, and breakfast is prepared by owners Peggy and Frank Darien. The Homeplace is in a residential neighborhood. ⊞ *5901 Sardis Rd., 28270,* ☎ *704/365–1936. 2 rooms and 1 2-bedroom suite. AE, MC, V.*

$$$ **Morehead Inn.** Though it's a commercial venture catering to corporate clients, this Dilworth inn has all the comforts of a beautiful home. Wedding parties find it ideal. A Continental breakfast comes with the room. ⊞ *1122 E. Morehead St., 28204,* ☎ *704/376–3357,* ℻ *704/335–1110. 11 rooms. Meeting rooms. AE, DC, MC, V.*

Nightlife

Bailey's Sports Bar & Grille. (5873 Albemarle Rd., ☎ 704/532–1005; 8500 Pineville-Matthews Rd., ☎ 704/541–0794) offers billiards in an upscale setting, big screen TV, and deli-style food.

Blockbuster Pavilion (707 Blockbuster Blvd., ☎ 704/549–1292) and the **Paladium Amphitheater** at Paramount's Carowinds (14523 Carowinds Blvd., ☎ 704/588–2600 or 800/888–4386) present stars in concert mid-spring through mid-fall. Ticket prices vary.

Comedy Zone (5317 E. Independence Blvd., ☎ 704/568–4242) showcases live comedy nightly except Monday, with two shows nightly Friday and Saturday.

Dilworth Brewing Company (1301 East Blvd., ☎ 704/377–2739) features rock bands on Friday and Saturday nights, plus several varieties of excellent beer made on the premises.

Edge Nitelife (4369 South Tryon St., ☎ 704/525–3343) is a progressive dance club for the younger set.

Lizzie's (4809 S. Tryon St., ☎ 704/527–3064), a restaurant on the south side, is best known for its piano bar, occasionally featuring owner Liz King.

Charlotte Essentials

Arriving and Departing

BY BUS
Greyhound Lines (601 W. Trade St., ☎ 800/231–2222) serves the Charlotte area.

BY CAR
Charlotte is a transportation hub; I–85 and I–77, north–south routes, run through, and I–40, east–west, is 40 miles to the north. U.S. 74, a major east–west route, also serves the city. I–277 and Charlotte 4 are inner-city loops. I–485, a planned outer loop, has one completed link between I–77 and Elm Street south of Charlotte.

BY PLANE
Charlotte-Douglas International Airport (☎ 704/359–4013) is west of the city off I–85. Carriers include American, British Airways, Delta, Northwest, TWA, United, USAir, and their local affiliates. Direct service is available to London, Frankfurt, Nassau, Grand Cayman, Montego Bay, and Puerto Rico.

Taxis cost about $12 ($2 each additional person), and airport vans are approximately $5 per person. Most major hotels provide complimentary transportation. By car, take the Billy Graham Parkway, then Wilkinson Boulevard (U.S. 74) east to I–277, which leads to the heart of Uptown.

BY TRAIN
Amtrak (1914 N. Tryon St., ☎ 704/376–4416 or 800/872–7245) offers daily service to Washington, DC, Atlanta, GA, and points beyond, and there's daily service to Raleigh.

Getting Around

BY BUS
Charlotte Transit (☎ 704/336–3366) provides public transportation throughout the city. The Transit Mall has bus shelters on Trade and Tryon streets in Uptown. Fares are 80¢ for local rides and $1.15 for express service; senior citizens with ID cards pay 30¢ between 9 and 3, after 6, and on weekends. Free bus service is available between Mint and Kings Drive on Trade and between Stonewall and 11th on Tryon weekdays 9–3.

BY TAXI
Yellow Cab (☎ 704/332–6161) has cars and airport vans. The **University Shuttle** (☎ 704/553–2424) caters to business travelers. Passengers pay a set flat rate.

Guided Tours

Guided tours are given by **Gray Line** (☎ 704/359–8687), **Adam's Stage Lines** (☎ 704/537–5342), and **Queens Carriages** (☎ 704/391–1232). The *Catawba Queen* paddle wheeler (☎ 704/663–2628) gives dinner cruises and tours on Lake Norman.

Several balloon companies give aerial tours, which end with champagne: **Balloons Over Charlotte** (☎ 704/541–7058), **Adventures Aloft of Charlotte** (☎ 704/545–6418), and **Fantasy Flights** (☎ 704/552–0469).

Important Addresses and Numbers

EMERGENCIES
Dial 911 for **police** and **ambulance** in an emergency.

PHYSICIANS
Care Connection, operated by Presbyterian Hospital, will give physician referrals and make appointments (☎ 704/384–4111, open weekdays 8:30–4:30). **Healthfinder,** run by Mercy Hospital, is a similar operation offering recorded information (☎ 704/379–6100). The **Mecklenburg County Medical Society** also gives physician referrals (☎ 704/376–3688, ⊙ Weekdays 9–1).

RADIO STATIONS
AM: WAQS 610, sports, talk; WBT 1110, sports, talk, country; WGSP 1310, Christian. **FM:** WSOC 103.7, country; WFAE 90.7, National Public Radio; WWMG 96, oldies; WXRC 95.7, rock; WMXC 104.7, adult contemporary.

24-HOUR PHARMACY
Eckerd Drugs (Park Road Shopping Center, ☎ 704/523–3031; 3740 E. Independence Blvd., ☎ 704/536–3600).

VISITOR INFORMATION
Info Charlotte (330 S. Tryon St., ☎ 704/331–2700 or 800/231–4636) is open weekdays 8:30–5, Sat. 10–4, and Sun. 1–4. Parking is available. The **N.C. Welcome Center** (on I–77 northbound at the South Carolina line, ☎ 704/588–2660) is open daily 8–5 except Christmas Eve, Christmas Day, New Year's Day, and Thanksgiving. The **Charlotte-Douglas International Airport** has a welcome center in the baggage claim area that's open daily, 7 AM–11 PM.

THE TRIANGLE

The cities of Raleigh, Durham, and Chapel Hill make up "The Triangle," so called because together they form a triangle, with Raleigh to the east, Durham to the north, and Chapel Hill to the west, and because of the Research Triangle Park—a complex of public and private research facilities between the three cities that attracts scientists from all over the world. Although the cities lie within 30 miles of each other and all three can be cursorily visited in one day, plan to spend at least a day in each because of their unique character.

Raleigh is Old South and New South, down-home and upscale, all in one. Named for Sir Walter Raleigh (who established the first English colony on the coast in 1585), Raleigh is the state capital and the largest and busiest of the three cities. The state's largest and best museums are here, as are North Carolina State University and six other universities and colleges.

Durham, a tobacco town for decades (and once called Bull Durham, after one of the many brands of tobacco manufactured here), is now known as the City of Medicine, for the nationally known medical and research centers at Duke University. With more than 20,000 employees, Duke is not only the largest employer in Durham, it's one of the largest employers in the state.

Chapel Hill may be the smallest city in The Triangle, but its reputation as a seat of learning—and of liberalism—looms large indeed. The home of the nation's first state university, the University of North Carolina, Chapel Hill remains a quiet, tree-shaded small town that is crowded with students and retirees.

Politics and basketball are always hot topics throughout The Triangle. The NCAA basketball championship has traded hands among the area's three schools often in the last decade.

Exploring

Raleigh

Raleigh is spread out, so a car is almost a necessity unless you limit your sightseeing to downtown, where the streets are laid out in an orderly grid fashion with the State Capitol as the hub. Most of the attractions in the downtown Raleigh walking tour are state government and historic buildings and are free to the public. You'll need several hours just to hit the high spots, even more time if you tend to get hooked on museums (which are also free).

STATE CAPITOL WALKING TOUR

After stopping in at the Capital Area Visitor Center to pick up maps and brochures, begin your tour at the **State Capitol,** a beautifully preserved example of Greek Revival architecture, which once housed all the functions of state government. Finished in 1840 and restored during the 1976 Bicentennial, its rich wood furnishings and elaborate decoration give it a special warmth not found in the more contemporary 1960s State Legislative Building. *Capitol Sq.,* ☎ *919/733–4994.* ☉ *Weekdays 8–5, Sat. 9–5, Sun. 1–5. Closed certain holidays.*

The **State Legislative Building,** on the corner of Salisbury and Jones streets, sits one block north of the Capitol building. When the legislature is in session, it hums with lawmakers and lobbyists, and it's fun to watch from the gallery. A free guided tour is available through the Visitor Center (*see below*). *Salisbury and Jones Sts.,* ☎ *919/733–7928.* ☉ *Weekdays 8–5, Sat. 9–5, Sun. 1–5.*

A half block away is the **North Carolina Museum of Natural Sciences,** where you can check out the massive skeletons of whales and dinosaurs or watch volunteers cleaning fossil bones. The gift shop sells some unusual souvenirs. *102 N. Salisbury St.,* ☎ *919/733–7450.* ☉ *Mon.–Sat. 9–5, Sun. 1–5.*

Adjacent to the Museum of Natural Sciences, on Bicentennial Plaza, is the **North Carolina Museum of History.** Founded in 1898, the museum recently opened a new, state-of-the-art facility that combines artifacts, audiovisual programs, and interactive exhibits to bring the state's history to life. Exhibits include the N.C. Sports Hall of Fame, N.C. Folklife, and Women Making History. *1 East Edenton St.,* ☎ *919/715–0200.* ☉ *Tues.–Sat. 9–5, Sun. 1–6.*

The **Executive Mansion** (200 N. Blount St., ☎ 919/733–3456) is a brick turn-of-the-century Queen Anne cottage-style structure with gingerbread trim. Tour hours vary; check with the Capital Area Visitor Center. A stroll through the nearby **Oakwood Historic District** will introduce you to more fine examples of Victorian architecture.

The revitalized **City Market** (Martin St. and Moore Sq.) is home to specialty shops, art galleries, restaurants, and **Playspace,** a children's educational play center. Trolleys shuttle between downtown and the market at lunchtime; the fare is only 10¢. ☎ *919/828–4555.* ☉ *Stores Mon.–Sat. 10–5:30; restaurants, Mon.–Sat. 7 AM–1 AM and Sun. 11:30–10.*

Fayetteville Street Mall extends from the State Capitol to the Raleigh Civic and Convention Center. Open to pedestrians only, it has a variety of shops, a couple of restaurants, and a bronze statue of Sir Walter Raleigh.

The **North Carolina Museum of Art** (Hillsborough St. W) exhibits art from ancient Egyptian times to the present, from the Old World and the New. The **Museum Café** is open for lunch Tuesday–Sunday, with live entertainment Friday evening. *2110 Blue Ridge Blvd., ☎ 919/833–1935 (restaurant ☎ 919/833–3548). Free guided tours daily at 1:30 PM. ☺ Tues.–Thurs. and Sat. 9–5, Fri. 9–9, Sun. 11–6.*

From downtown, follow Hargett St. east to the **Wakefield/Joel Lane House.** The oldest dwelling in Raleigh and the home of the landowner "father of Raleigh" dates to the 1760s. *720 W. Hargett at St. Mary's St., ☎ 919/833–3431. ☛ Free. ☺ Mar.–mid-Dec., Tues., Thurs., and Fri. 10–2.*

Return on Hargett Street through downtown to Person Street and then take it north to **Mordecai Historic Park** to see some early buildings that were moved within the park, including a house dating to 1785 and the house where President Andrew Johnson was born. One-hour guided tours are given. *One Mimosa St., ☎ 919/834–4844. Tour: $3 adults, $1 children 7–17. ☺ Weekdays 10–3, weekends 1:30–3:30.*

Durham

From Raleigh, take I–40 west to the Durham Freeway (NC 147), which brings you into downtown Durham and **Duke University.** A stroll along the beautiful tree-lined streets of the campus, which are dominated by Gothic-style buildings, is a lovely way to spend a few hours.

A right onto Anderson Street from the Durham Freeway brings you to the 55-acre **Sarah P. Duke Gardens,** complete with a wisteria-draped gazebo and a Japanese garden with a lily pond teeming with fat goldfish. *Main entrance on Anderson St., West Campus, ☎ 919/684–3698. ☺ Daily 8 AM to dusk.*

Head west on Campus Drive to Chapel Drive. The Gothic-style **Duke Chapel,** built in the early 1930s, is the centerpiece of the campus. Modeled after Canterbury Cathedral, it has 77 stained glass windows and a 210-foot bell tower. *West Campus, ☎ 919/681–1704. ☺ During daylight hours.*

TIME OUT Return to Anderson Street, head north on Anderson to Hillsborough Road, and take Hillsborough east to 9th Street. At **McDonald's Drug Store** (732 9th St., ☎ 919/286–2770), an old-fashioned soda fountain serves up the best milkshakes in town.

African-American art is showcased at the **North Carolina Central University Art Museum,** south of the Durham Freeway on Fayetteville Street. *1801 Fayetteville St., ☎ 919/560–6211. ☛ Free. ☺ Tues.–Fri. 9–5, Sun. 2–5.*

From the Durham Freeway, take U.S. 501N (Roxboro Rd.) to **West Point on the Eno.** On the banks of the Eno River, this city park has a 19th-century blacksmith shop, 1880s home, and a restored mill dating from 1778. *5101 N. Roxboro Rd., ☎ 919/471–1623. ☛ Free. ☺ Daily 8 AM–sunset (historic buildings open weekends only).*

West of the park on Cole Mill Road, the 2,064-acre **Eno River State Park** has hiking trails, historic homes and mills, and Class II rapids. *Rte. 2, Box 436-C, 27705, ☎ 919/383–1686. ☛ Free. ☺ Daily 8 AM–sunset.*

Chapel Hill

U.S. 15–501 takes you from Durham into Chapel Hill. **Morehead Planetarium,** where the original Apollo astronauts and many since have trained, was the first planetarium in the state. Visitors can learn about the constellations and take in laser light shows. *E. Franklin St.,* ☎ *919/549–6863 or 919/962–1247.* ☛ *$3 adults, $2.50 children, students, and senior citizens.* ☉ *Sun.–Fri. 12:30–5 and 7 PM–9:45 PM, Sat. 10–5 and 7 PM–9:45 PM. Closed Dec. 24–25.*

After leaving the planetarium, walk left on E. Franklin Street a couple of blocks, into the heart of downtown Chapel Hill. **Franklin Street,** lined with bicycle shops, bookstores, clothing stores, restaurants and coffee shops, and flower vendors on the sidewalk, runs along the northern edge of the **University of North Carolina** campus, which is dotted with oak-shaded courtyards and stately old buildings.

Follow U.S. 15–501 Bypass south to the **N.C. Botanical Garden,** known as the largest natural botanical garden in the Southeast. Two miles of nature trails wind through a 300-acre Piedmont forest; there's also a legendary herb garden and carnivorous plant collection. *Old Mason Farm Rd., 27599,* ☎ *919/962–0522.* ☛ *Free.* ☉ *Mar.–mid-Nov., daily 8–5; mid-Nov.–Feb., weekdays 8–5.*

What to See and Do with Children

Pullen Park (520 Ashe Ave., near NCSU, ☎ 919/831–6468 or 919/831–6640) attracts large crowds during the summer to its 1911 Dentzel carousel and train ride. You can swim here, too, and enjoy an arts and crafts center and the Theater in the Park.

The **ArtsCenter** (300G E. Main St. in Carrboro near Chapel Hill, ☎ 919/929–2787) offers classes of all kinds for children, as well as entertainment.

At the **North Carolina Museum of Life and Science,** you can create a 15-foot tornado, pilot an Apollo capsule, encounter near life-size models of dinosaurs on the nature trail, and ride a train through a 78-acre wildlife sanctuary. The nature center has such native North Carolina animals as flying squirrels. *433 Murray Ave., off I–85 in Durham,* ☎ *919/220–5429.* ☛ *$5.50 adults, $3.50 senior citizens and children 3–12, under 3 free.* ☉ *Mon.–Sat. 10–5, Sun. 1–5.*

Off the Beaten Path

Bennett Place State Historic Site. In this farmhouse in Durham in April 1865, Confederate General Joseph E. Johnston surrendered to U.S. General William T. Sherman. The two generals then set forth the terms for a "permanent peace" between the South and the North. Historic reenactments are held annually. *4409 Bennett Memorial Rd., Durham 27705,* ☎ *919/383–4345.* ☛ *Free.* ☉ *Apr.–Oct., Mon.–Sat. 9–5, Sun. 1–5; Nov.–Mar., Tues.–Sat. 10–4, Sun. 1–4.*

Shopping

Shopping Districts

Fearrington Village, a planned community 8 miles south of Chapel Hill on U.S. 15–501, has a number of upscale shops selling art, garden items, handmade jewelry, and more. **Franklin Street** in Chapel Hill has a wonderful collection of shops, including bookstores, art galleries,

No matter where you go, travel is easier when you know the code.^{SM}

dial 1 8 0 0
C A L L
A T T®

Dial 1 800 CALL ATT and you'll always get through from any phone with any card* and you'll always get AT&T's best deal.** It's the one number to remember when calling away from home.

*Other long distance company calling cards excluded.
**Additional discounts available.

AT&T
Your True Choice

crafts shops, and clothing stores. Durham's **9th Street** has funky shops and restaurants that cater to the hip student crowd.

Shopping Malls

Brightleaf Square (905 W. Main St., Durham) is an upscale shopping-entertainment complex housed in old tobacco warehouses in the heart of downtown.

Cameron Village Shopping Center (1900 Cameron St.), Raleigh's oldest shopping center and one of the first in the Southeast, features specialty shops and upscale boutiques.

Cary Towne Center (1105 Walnut St., Cary), located in a suburb of Raleigh just off I–40, features five department stores as well as 125 specialty shops and restaurants.

Crabtree Valley Mall (Glenwood Ave.; U.S. 70) is Raleigh's largest enclosed mall. Stores include Belk, Sears, and Hecht's.

North Hills Mall (Six Forks Rd. and Beltline) offers the latest in high fashion. Stores include Montaldo's, Tyler House, and Dillard's.

Specialty Stores

ART AND ANTIQUES

City Market (Martin St. at Moore Sq., ☎ 919/828–4555) is a revitalized shopping area with a number of shops selling antiques and art. Check out Artspace, a gallery where you can watch artists at work in their glassed-in studios.

BOOKS

The **Intimate Bookshop** (119 E. Franklin St., Chapel Hill, ☎ 919/929–0411), a town mainstay for years, has now spawned a regional chain. This is the original store owned by Wallace Kuralt (brother of former CBS commentator Charles Kuralt, one of UNC's most famous graduates).

At **McIntyre's Fine Books** (Fearrington Village, ☎ 919/542–3030), you can curl up and read in an armchair by the fire in one of the cozy library rooms.

FLEA MARKETS

The **Raleigh Flea Market Mall** offers antiques, knickknacks, and more. *1924 Capital Blvd.,* ☎ *919/839–0038.* ⊘ *Weekends 9–5.*

FOOD

State Farmer's Market. This 60-acre market includes a garden center and a down-home-style restaurant. *Lake Wheeler Rd. and I–40,* ☎ *919/733–7417 (market) or 919/833–7973 (restaurant).* ⊘ *June–Sept., daily 8–7:30; Oct.–May, daily 8–6.*

9th Street Bakery (776 9th St., Durham, ☎ 919/286–0303) is earning a reputation throughout the state for its baked goods.

A Southern Season (Eastgate Mall, Chapel Hill, ☎ 919/929–7133 or 800/253–3663) offers such Tar Heel treats as cheese, wine, barbecue sauces, peanuts, turkeys, and hams.

Wellspring Grocery (737 9th St., Durham, ☎ 919/286–2290; 81 S. Elliott Rd., Chapel Hill, ☎ 919/968–1983; 3540 Wade Ave., Raleigh, ☎ 919/828–5805) has outstanding fresh produce and the widest selection of health foods in town.

Julian's College Shop (140 E. Franklin St., Chapel Hill, ☎ 919/942–4563) is owned by the mother of designer Alexander Julian, a Chapel Hill native.

Participant Sports and Outdoor Activities

Bicycling
Raleigh has more than 25 miles of greenways for biking, and maps are available at Raleigh Parks and Recreation (☎ 919/831–6640). Chapel Hill is a great town for biking; for a bicycling map, contact the Chapel Hill/Orange County Visitors Bureau (*see* Visitor Information, *below*).

Camping
Try the North Carolina State Fairgrounds, William B. Umstead State Park, Eno River State Park at Durham, Clemmons State Forest near Clayton, or Jordan Lake between Apex and Pittsboro. Other options are Lake Gaston and Kerr Lake near the Virginia line. *For details, call the Greater Raleigh Convention and Visitors Bureau, ☎ 919/834–5900 or 800/849–8499, or the North Carolina Division of Travel and Tourism, ☎ 919/733–4171 or 800/847–4862.*

Canoeing
Lake Wheeler and Shelley Lake are the best places for canoeing. The Eno River State Park near Durham is another option. The Haw River is popular as well, but can be treacherous after a heavy rain.

Fishing
Jordan Lake, a 13,900-acre reservoir in Apex, is a favorite fishing spot. Others are Lake Wheeler in Raleigh and the Falls Lake State Recreation Area in Wake Forest. You can buy a fishing license at local bait-and-tackle shops or over the phone (with a credit card) from the North Carolina Wildlife Commission (☎ 919/715–4091).

Fitness
The **YMCA** (1601 Hillsborough St., ☎ 919/832–6601) will permit visitors to use their facilities for $3–$10, provided they have a YMCA membership elsewhere. The Y also accepts guests staying at certain local hotels. Hotels with fitness centers are noted in the accommodations listings.

Golf
There are 14 golf courses within a half-hour drive of downtown Raleigh. Durham has four public courses, and Chapel Hill has one. **Cheviott Hills Golf Course** (7301 Capitol Blvd., Raleigh, ☎ 919/876–9920) is an 18-hole championship course. **Devil's Ridge Golf Club** (Holly Springs Rd., Cary, ☎ 919/557–6100), about 15 miles from Raleigh, is a challenging course with large, rolling greens. **Duke University Golf Course** (Cameron Blvd. and Science Dr., Durham, ☎ 919/681–2288) has a newly renovated Robert Trent Jones course. **Finley Golf Course** (Finley Golf Course Rd., Chapel Hill, ☎ 919/962–2349), on the UNC campus, has an 18-hole course, driving range, putting green, and lessons. **Hillandale Golf Course** (Hillandale Rd., Durham, ☎ 919/286–4211) has an 18-hole George Cobb course. The **Neuse Golf Club** (Hwy. 42E, Clayton, ☎ 919/550–0550) is an attractive course located on the banks of the Neuse River. **Lochmere Golf Club** (Kildare

Farms Rd., Cary, ☎ 919/851–0611) provides a friendly atmosphere and good value.

Hiking

Jordan Lake, Lake Wheeler, and William B. Umstead State Park in Raleigh, and Eno River State Park and Duke Forest in Durham, offer thousands of acres for hiking. For trail information, call the North Carolina Division of Travel and Tourism (☎ 919/733–4171 or 800/847–4862).

Jogging

Runners frequent Shelley Lake, the track at NCSU, and the Capitol Area Greenway system.

River Rafting

You can shoot the rapids at Eno River State Park (*see* Exploring Durham, *above*).

Tennis

More than 80 courts in Raleigh city parks are available for use. Millbrook Exchange Park (1905 Spring Forest Rd.) holds city tournaments. (For more details on tennis courts in Raleigh, call 919/876–2616.) For information on Durham's six public courts, call the Parks and Recreation Department (☎ 919/560–4355). For information on Chapel Hill tennis courts, call the Chapel Hill Parks and Recreation Department (☎ 919/968–2784) or the Orange County Parks and Recreation Department (☎ 919/732–8181).

Spectator Sports

Baseball

The **Carolina Mudcats** play at Five County Stadium in Zebulon, east of Raleigh (☎ 919/269–2287).

The **Durham Bulls** play at their brand new stadium near downtown Durham (200 Willard St., ☎ 919/688–8211).

Basketball

The Triangle is basketball heaven, with three Atlantic Coast Conference teams: Duke's **Blue Devils** (☎ 919/681–2583), the University of North Carolina's **Tarheels** (☎ 919/962–2296), and North Carolina State University's **Wolfpack** (☎ 919/515–2106).

Ice Hockey

The **Raleigh Icecaps** compete in Dorton Arena at the NC State Fairgrounds (☎ 919/755–0022).

Soccer

The **Raleigh Flyers,** the city's first professional soccer team, competes in the Interregional Soccer League (☎ 919/890–6026).

Dining

Dining in the Triangle is both sophisticated and down-home. There are many upscale restaurants, as well as informal places where barbecue, Brunswick stew, fried chicken, and lots of country vegetables are served in great quantities for very low prices. Dress is usually casual.

CATEGORY	COST*
$$$$	over $25
$$$	$15–$25
$$	$8–$15
$	under $8

*per person for a three-course meal, excluding drinks, service, and 6% sales tax

Chapel Hill

$$-$$$ Aurora. In a historic textile mill in nearby Carrboro, Aurora specializes in northern Italian cuisine. The changing menu sometimes includes succulent sea scallops and shiitake mushrooms sautéed in rosemary and white wine, fresh chive pasta stuffed with four cheeses and tossed with walnut sauce, and veal sautéed with Golden Delicious apples. ✗ *Carr Mill Mall, Carrboro,* ☎ *919/942–2400. Reservations accepted. AE, MC, V.*

$$-$$$ Pyewacket Restaurant. What began as a hole-in-the-wall vegetarian restaurant in 1977 has become one of Chapel Hill's most popular restaurants. Now in bigger digs and offering courtyard dining, Pyewacket has added seafood and pasta specialties to its former vegetarian repertoire. Appetizers include smoked trout paté; entrées range from Southwest grilled seafood to spinach lasagna. ✗ *431 West Franklin St.,* ☎ *919/929–0297. Reservations accepted. AE, DC, MC, V.*

$$ Crook's Corner. If there's such a thing as chic Southern cooking, Crook's produces it. Particularly famous for its barbecue, the restaurant also turns out such regional Southern specialties as hoppin' John, hot pepper jelly, collards, crab gumbo, cheese grits, and buttermilk pie. One of the joys of summer is lunching on Crook's patio, under the huge pig sculpture that sparked a local debate when erected but is now a beloved local landmark. ✗ *610 West Franklin St.,* ☎ *919/929–7643. Reservations accepted. AE, MC, V.*

Durham

$$ Bullock's Bar-B-Cue. If you want to experience local cuisine, try the Brunswick stew, barbecue, southern fried chicken, and hush puppies at this casual eatery that offers eat-in or carry-out service. It's first-come, first-served, so come early. ✗ *3330 Wortham St.,* ☎ *919/383–3211. No credit cards. Closed Sun.*

$$ Cafe Parizäde. This Erwin Square Mediterranean restaurant gets high marks for its food, service, and atmosphere (soft lighting and white tablecloths give the place an elegant feel, even at lunch). Start with grilled bread soaked in garlic oil, fresh tomatoes and eggplant relish, or fried calamari with jalapeno-tomato salsa. Then choose among such entreés as fettucine with fresh salmon and black pepper dill cream, sesame pasta with scallops, and roasted duck with fresh vegetables. ✗ *2200 West Main St.,* ☎ *919/286–9712. Reservations accepted. Closed Sun. AE, MC, V.*

Raleigh

$$$ Angus Barn, Ltd. This Raleigh tradition is housed in a huge rustic barn. Gingham- and denim-clad waiters and waitresses add authenticity to the farmlike scene. The astonishing wine and beer list covers 35 pages of the menu. The restaurant serves the best steaks, baby back ribs, and prime rib, plus fresh seafood, for miles around. Desserts are heavenly. ✗ *U.S. 70W at Airport Rd.,* ☎ *919/781–2444. Reservations advised. AE, DC, MC, V.*

$$$ **42nd St. Oyster Bar.** This much talked-about restaurant is the place to see and be seen in Raleigh. Politicians, businessmen, and laborers sit side by side downing succulent oysters and other seafood. There's live jazz on Friday and Saturday evenings. ✕ *508 W. Jones St., ☎ 919/831–2811. No reservations. AE, DC, MC, V.*

$$–$$$ **Jean Claude's Café.** Casual and chic, this restaurant on the north side features authentic French cuisine, including such specials as veal sweetbreads, braised scallops, and smoked salmon. ✕ *6111 Falls of Neuse Rd., ☎ 919/872–6224. Reservations accepted. MC, V. Closed Mon.*

$$ **Est Est Est Trattoria.** The best place in town for authentic northern Italian pasta. ✕ *19 W. Hargett St., ☎ 919/832–8899. Reservations accepted for parties of 6 or more. AE, MC, V. Closed Sun.*

$ **Big Ed's City Market Restaurant.** A must for breakfast, this Raleigh favorite in the City Market serves three home-cooked meals. ✕ *220 Wolfe St., ☎ 919/836–9909. Reservations not required. No credit cards. Closed Sun.*

$ **Greenshields Brewery & Pub.** Enjoy beer and ale brewed on the spot with your soups, salads, sandwiches, and such entrées as fish and chips, shepherd's pie, and steak in this English-type pub in the City Market. ✕ *214 E. Martin St., City Market, ☎ 919/829–0214. Reservations accepted. AE, D, MC, V.*

Lodging

The Triangle has lodgings in all price ranges—from convention hotels to bed-and-breakfast houses to economy chains. Major hotel chains represented here are Holiday Inn, Hilton, Radisson, Marriott, Embassy Suites, and Sheraton. Inexpensive lodging is offered by Comfort Inn, EconoLodge, Crickett Inn, Days Inn, and Hampton Inn. Since Raleigh is a business town, many hotels and motels advertise special weekend rates.

CATEGORY	COST*
$$$$	over $100
$$$	$60–$100
$$	$30–$60
$	under $30

All prices are for a standard double room, excluding 8% tax

Chapel Hill

$$$$ **Fearrington House.** This French-style country inn is a member of the
★ prestigious Relais & Chateaux group. The 200-year-old farm has been remade into a residential community that looks like an English country village. Modern guest rooms, furnished in English pine, floral print fabrics, and dried flower arrangements, are situated around a garden courtyard. The farmhouse restaurant, done up in green ivy and delicate peach prints, serves regional food prepared in a classic manner; Carolina crab cakes with mustard mayonnaise and beef tenderloin with merlot and peppercorn sauce are favorites here. Afternoon tea and breakfast are included in the rate. ⌕ *8 mi south of Chapel Hill on U.S. 15–501 (postal address: Fearrington Village Center, Pittsboro 27312), ☎ 919/542–2121, ℻ 919/542–4202. 15 double rooms with baths, 9 suites. AE, MC, V.*

Durham

$$$$ **Washington Duke Hotel & Golf Club.** On the campus of Duke University, this luxurious inn overlooks the Robert Trent Jones golf course. On display in the public rooms are memorabilia belonging to the Duke family for whom the hotel and university are named. The bar is called

the Bull Durham. ☎ *3001 Cameron Blvd., 27706,* ☎ *919/490–0999 or 800/443–3853,* FAX *919/688–0105. 171 rooms, 7 suites. Restaurant, bar, pool, 18-hole golf course, jogging. AE, DC, MC, V.*

$$$–$$$$ **Arrowhead Inn.** This bed-and-breakfast inn, in an 18th-century white clapboard farmhouse with black shutters, has brick chimneys and tall Doric columns. It's a few miles outside Durham and offers a homelike setting with antiques, old plantings, and a log cabin in the garden. Guests are served a hearty breakfast. ☎ *106 Mason Rd., 27712,* ☎ FAX *919/477–8430. 8 rooms, 6 with private bath. AE, D, DC, MC, V.*

$$$–$$$$ **Blooming Garden Inn.** This B&B is truly a bright spot in the Holloway
★ Historic District. With yellow paint on the exterior, the inn explodes inside with color and warmth, thanks to exuberant hosts Dolly and Frank Pokrass. For breakfast you might have walnut crepes with ricotta cheese and warm raspberry sauce. ☎ *513 Holloway St., 27701,* ☎ *919/687–0801. 5 rooms with private baths. AE, D, DC, MC, V.*

Raleigh

$$$ **Courtyard by Marriott–Airport.** Convenient to the airport and the Research Triangle Park, this chain offers many luxuries, including a Continental breakfast, without hefty rates. Rooms are predictably modern, as you would expect from this chain, and some have refrigerators. ☎ *2001 Hospitality Ct., 27560,* ☎ *919/467–9444 or 800/321–2211,* FAX *919/467–9332. 152 rooms. Facilities: dining room, pool, hot tub, exercise room, coin laundry, airport shuttle. AE, D, DC, MC, V.*

$$$ **North Raleigh Hilton.** This is a favorite capital city spot for corporate meetings. The Tower Suites offer a complimentary Continental breakfast, free hors d'oeuvres, concierge, newspapers, and secretarial service if wanted. Guests enjoy dining in Lofton's restaurant and listening to the piano afterward in the lobby bar. Bowties is one of the city's hottest nightspots. ☎ *3415 Wake Forest Rd., 27609,* ☎ *919/872–2323 or 800/445–8667,* FAX *919/876–0890. 330 rooms, 7 suites. Restaurant, indoor pool, health club, nightclub, meeting rooms, airport shuttle. AE, D, DC, MC, V.*

$$$ **Oakwood Inn.** In Historic Oakwood, one of the city's oldest downtown neighborhoods, this is an alternative to hotel/motel living. Built in 1871 and now on the National Register of Historic Places, the inn is furnished with Victorian period pieces. Guests are served a sumptuous complimentary breakfast and assisted with dinner reservations and evening entertainment plans. ☎ *411 N. Bloodworth St., 27604,* ☎ *919/832–9712 or 800/267–9712,* FAX *919/836–9263. 6 rooms with bath. AE, D, DC, MC, V.*

$$$ **Raleigh Marriott Crabtree Valley.** This is one of the city's most luxurious hotels. Fresh floral arrangements adorn the elegantly decorated public rooms. Guests enjoy the intimacy of the Scotch Bonnets restaurant, the family atmosphere of Allie's, and Champions Sports Bar. The concierge floor offers complimentary Continental breakfast and hors d'oeuvres. ☎ *4500 Marriott Dr. (U.S. 70W near Crabtree Valley Mall), 27612,* ☎ *919/781–7000 or 800/228–9290,* FAX *919/781–3059. 372 rooms, 3 suites. Restaurant, bar, indoor/outdoor pool, hot tub, exercise room, recreation room, airport shuttle. AE, D, DC, MC, V.*

$$$ **Velvet Cloak Inn.** This hotel is in a class of its own. Local brides have wedding receptions in the tropical garden around the enclosed pool, and politicians frequent the bar at Baron's Lounge. The Charter Room, an elegant restaurant, often has live entertainment. Afternoon tea and cookies are served in the lobby. Rooms in the brick structure, decorated with delicate wrought iron, are frequently refurbished. ☎ *1505 Hillsborough St., 27605,* ☎ *919/828–0333 or 800/334–4372; in NC,*

800/662–8829; FAX 919/828–2656. 168 rooms, 4 suites. 2 restaurants, lounge, meeting rooms, airport shuttle. AE, D, DC, MC, V.

$$–$$$ **Quality Suites Hotel.** Minutes from downtown, this hotel offers luxurious two-room suites equipped with VCRs, cassette stereos, microwaves, wet bars, and refrigerators. The manager's evening reception and the cooked-to-order breakfast are included in the rate. ⊞ *4400 Capital Blvd., 27604, ☎ 919/876–2211 or 800/543–5497, FAX 919/790–1352. 114 suites. Pool, exercise room, meeting rooms. AE, D, DC, MC, V.*

$$–$$$ **Ramada Inn Crabtree.** This hotel gets the award for being the friendliest motel in town, and rooms are comfortable and clean at this link in the familiar chain. It's also where football and basketball teams like to stay when they're here for a game, as evidenced by the helmet collection and other sports memorabilia in the Brass Bell Lounge. ⊞ *3920 Arrow Dr. (U.S. 70 and Beltline), 27612, ☎ 919/782–7525 or 800/441–4712. 174 rooms and suites. Restaurant, lounge, pool, jogging, meeting rooms, airport shuttle. AE, D, DC, MC, V.*

$$ **Hampton Inn North Raleigh.** This budget motel offers inexpensive rates without sacrificing quality. A Continental breakfast, local calls, and in-room movies are available at no extra charge. ⊞ *1001 Wake Towne Dr., 27609, ☎ 919/828–1813 or 800/426–7866, FAX 919/834–2672. 131 rooms. Pool, meeting rooms. AE, D, DC, MC, V.*

The Arts

The **North Carolina Theatre** (One E. South St., Raleigh, ☎ 919/831–6916), the state's only professional nonprofit theater, produces five Broadway shows a year. Durham's newly renovated, 1926 Beaux Arts **Carolina Theatre** (309 Morgan St., ☎ 919/560–3060) hosts the city's symphony and opera company, as well as the International Jazz Festival in March and the American Dance Festival in June. The **North Carolina Symphony** (2 E. South St., Raleigh, ☎ 919/733–2750) gives more than 200 concerts in the state annually.

Playmakers Repertory Company (CB 3235 Graham Memorial, Chapel Hill, ☎ 919/962–7529) performs six plays annually at the Paul Green Theatre. Jazz and folk music, dance and theater are all offered at the **ArtsCenter** (300G E. Main St., Carrboro, ☎ 919/929–2787).

Nightlife

Much of Raleigh's nightlife is centered in the larger hotels, such as the Hilton or the Marriott. **Bowties** (North Raleigh Hilton, 3415 Wake Forest Rd., ☎ 919/878–4917) is a popular after-hours spot. **Charlie Goodnight's Comedy Club** (861 W. Morgan St., ☎ 919/828–5233) combines dinner with a night of laughs. Another option is **Comedy Sportz** (204 Wolfe St., City Market, Raleigh, ☎ 919/829–0822; Omni Europa, U.S. 15–501, Chapel Hill, ☎ 919/968–4900). Chapel Hill is the place to hear live rock and alternative bands. **Cat's Cradle** (206 W. Franklin St., ☎ 919/967–9053) features entertainment nightly. **He's Not Here** (112½ W. Franklin St., ☎ 919/942–7939) features live music Friday and Saturday nights, with concerts outdoors in warm weather.

Triangle Essentials

Arriving and Departing
BY BUS

Carolina Trailways/Greyhound Lines (☎ 800/231–2222) serves Raleigh, Durham, and Chapel Hill.

BY CAR

I–440 forms a perimeter route around Raleigh. I–40 runs west of downtown (to Durham and Chapel Hill), joining I–85 on the west side and crossing I–95 on the east side. U.S. 1, which runs north and south, also links to I–85 going northeast. U.S. 64 and U.S. 70 run east–west through Raleigh.

BY PLANE

The **Raleigh–Durham International Airport** (RDU, ☎ 919/840–2123), between the two cities off I–40, is served by American, Delta, Northwest, TWA, United, USAir, and Midway, with flights to London, Cancun, Bermuda, Puerto Rico, Nassau, and the U.S. Virgin Islands. If you're driving to Raleigh, take I–40 east to Exit 285; for Chapel Hill, take I–40 west to exits 273, 270, and 266; for Durham, also take I–40 west to NC 147. It takes about 20 minutes to get to any of the three cities.

BY TRAIN

Amtrak (320 W. Cabarrus St., ☎ 919/833–7594 or 800/872–7245) has one daily train northbound and one southbound, with stops in Raleigh and Durham. Service to Charlotte is also offered daily.

Getting Around

BY BUS

Capital Area Transit (☎ 919/833–5701) is Raleigh's public transport system. Fares are 50¢. Children under 4 ride free.

Chapel Hill Transit (☎ 919/968–2769) buses serve the city as well as Research Triangle Park and Duke University.

Triangle Transit Authority (☎ 919/549–9999), which links downtown Raleigh with the Research Triangle Park, Durham, and Chapel Hill, runs weekdays except major holidays. Fares: $1 for a 10-mile trip, $1.50 for 15 miles, and $2 for 20 miles. Senior citizens and riders with disabilities pay half fare.

BY TAXI

Approximately 28 taxi companies serve The Triangle; contact City Taxi (Raleigh, ☎ 919/832–1489), **National Cab** (Raleigh–Durham Airport, ☎ 919/469–1333), or Orange Cab (Durham, ☎ 919/682–6111) for service. Fares are calculated by the mile.

BY TROLLEY

The **Trolley Through Raleigh** (☎ 919/833–5701) makes six stops around the city, including City Market and the Capital Area Visitor Center. Trolleys run weekdays 11:20–2 and the fare is 10¢. From noon to 4 PM on the third Saturday of each month, Mordecai Historic Park (*see above*) runs a **historic trolley tour** of Raleigh (fare: $3 adults, $1 children 7–17), with a pickup at the Amtrak station by advance arrangement.

Chapel Hill Trolley (☎ 919/968–2769) serves downtown Chapel Hill, UNC Hospitals and campus, plus Franklin and Rosemary Street businesses. Trolleys run weekdays 11:30–2:30, and the fare is 25¢. The **Historic Chapel Hill/UNC Trolley Tour** (☎ 919/942–7818) operates April–June and September–November, Wednesdays at 3 PM. The fare is $3 adults, $1 children under 12.

Guided Tours

Capital Area Visitor Center provides maps, brochures, and free tours of the executive mansion, state capitol, legislative building, and other government buildings. *301 N. Blount St.,* ☎ *919/733–3456.* ☉ *Weekdays 8–5, Sat. 9–5, Sun. 1–5.*

UNC Visitors Center offers information about the University, campus parking, and conducts tours of the campus, highlighting its many historic buildings and monuments. *Morehead Planetarium, Franklin St.,* ☎ *919/962–1630.* ☉ *Weekdays 10–5.*

Important Addresses and Numbers

EMERGENCIES

Dial 911 for **police** or **ambulance** in an emergency. Hospital emergency rooms are open 24 hours a day. For minor emergencies, go to one of the many urgent-care centers in Raleigh, Durham, and Chapel Hill. The **Wake County Medical Society** (☎ 919/821–2227) can refer you to a doctor.

PHARMACIES

Kerr Drug Store (Lake Boone Shopping Center, 2462 Wycliff Rd., Raleigh, ☎ 919/781–4070) is open 24 hours. **Eckerd Drugs** (3527 Hillsborough Rd., Durham, ☎ 919/383–5591) is open 7 AM–midnight.

RADIO STATIONS

AM: WPTF 680, news, talk; WKIX 850, country. **FM:** WCPE 89.7, classical; WQDR 94.7, country; WUNC 91.5, National Public Radio; WRAL 101.5, adult contemporary; WDUR 104, urban contemporary.

VISITOR INFORMATION

The **Greater Raleigh Convention and Visitors Bureau** offers information on the area. *225 Hillsborough St., Suite 400,* ☎ *919/834–5900 or 800/849–8499.*

The **Durham Convention & Visitors Bureau** (101 E. Morgan St., Durham 27701, ☎ 919/687–0288 or 800/446–8604) provides information on that city. The **Durham Bullhorn** provides 24-hour recorded information on events and activities (☎ 919/688–2855 or 800/772–2855).

Chapel Hill/Orange County Visitors Bureau (Box 600, Chapel Hill 27514, ☎ 919/968–2060). The **Downtown Chapel Hill Welcome Center** provides maps, brochures, and flyers on attractions, accommodations, and services. Volunteers are usually on hand to answer questions. *113 W. Franklin St.,* ☎ *919/929–9700.* ☉ *Tues.–Sat. 10–4.*

THE SOUTHERN PINES AND PINEHURST SANDHILLS

Because of their sandy soil—once the beaches of the Atlantic Ocean—the Sandhills weren't of much use to early farmers, most of whom switched to lumbering and making turpentine for a livelihood. Since the turn of the century, however, this area has proven ideal for golf and tennis. Today promoters call it the Golf Capital of the World; the Tufts Archives honors the sport and the founding of Pinehurst. First-class resorts are centered around more than three dozen golf courses, including the famed Pinehurst Number 2 and several spectacular new courses.

The Highland Scots, who settled the area, left a rich heritage perpetuated through festivals and gatherings. In Colonial times, English potters were attracted to the rich clay deposits in the soil, and today their descendants and others turn out beautiful wares that are sold in more than 40 local shops.

Exploring

Southern Pines

Southern Pines, the center of the Sandhills, is a good place to start a tour. The **Shaw House,** the oldest structure in town (circa 1840), serves as headquarters for the Moore County Historical Association. *S. W. Broad St. and Morganton Rd.,* ☎ *910/692–2051.* ☛ *Free.* ☉ *Wed.–Sun. 1–4.*

Weymouth Center, former home of author James Boyd, hosts numerous music, lecture, and holiday events. *E. Vermont Ext.,* ☎ *910/692–6261.* ☛ *Free. Call ahead to arrange tours.* ☉ *Weekdays 10–noon, 2–4.*

Weymouth Woods Nature Preserve, on the eastern outskirts of town, is a 571-acre wildlife preserve with 4 miles of hiking trails, a beaver pond, and a naturalist on staff. *400 N. Ft. Bragg Rd. (off U.S. 1),* ☎ *910/692–2167.* ☛ *Free.* ☉ *Mon.–Sat. 9–6, Sun. noon–5.*

PINEHURST

Pinehurst lies 8 miles west of Southern Pines via U.S. 15–501, or Midland Road. The New England–style village, with its quiet, shaded streets and immaculately kept cottages, was laid out in the late 1800s in a wagon-wheel fashion, by landscape genius Frederick Law Olmsted. It is a mecca for sports enthusiasts, retirees, and tourists.

Tufts Archives recounts the founding of Pinehurst in the letters, pictures, and news clippings, dating from 1895, of James Walker Tufts. Golf memorabilia is also on display. *Given Memorial Library, Pinehurst,* ☎ *910/295–6022 or 910/295–3642.* ☉ *Weekdays 9:30 AM–12:30 PM and 2–5 PM; Sat. 9:30 AM–12:30 PM.*

Aberdeen

In **Aberdeen,** a town of Scottish ancestry south of Pinehurst, there's a beautifully restored turn-of-the-century train station, and on Bethesda Road east of town, the **Bethesda Presbyterian Church,** founded in 1790. The present wooden structure, which is used for weddings, funerals, and reunions, was built in the 1860s, and has bullet holes from a Civil War battle. The cemetery, where many early settlers are buried, is always open. Continue on Bethesda Road to the **Malcolm Blue Farm,** featuring farm buildings and an old grist mill. A September festival recalls life here in the 1800s. *Bethesda Rd.,* ☎ *910/944–7558.* ☉ *By appointment only.*

Asheboro

Follow U.S. 220 north to NC 159, which leads to the ★**North Carolina Zoological Park** at Asheboro. This 1,400-acre natural habitat for animals is one of the up-and-coming zoos of the late 20th century. The park includes the African Pavilion, an aviary, a gorilla habitat, a Sonora Desert habitat, and a new North American habitat with polar bears and sea lions. ☎ *910/879–7000 or 800/488–0444.* ☛ *Including tram ride: $6 adults, $4 senior citizens and children 2–12.* ☉ *Daily 9–5.*

Shopping

Antiques

Shop for antiques in **Cameron,** which hasn't changed much since the 19th century. Approximately 60 antiques dealers operate out of several stores. The town itself has been declared a historic district. *Off U.S. 1, 10 mi north of Southern Pines,* ☎ *910/245–7001.* ⊙ *Most shops Wed.–Sat. 10–5, Sun. 1–5.*

Herbs and Wildflowers
Sandhill Farms, 12 miles east of Cameron off Highway 24, is a one-of-a-kind operation offering herbs, wildflowers, wreaths, crafts, and oils. ☎ *919/499–4753.* ⊙ *Weekdays 1–5. Closed Jan.–Feb. except by appointment.*

Pottery
Mugs, bowls, pitchers, platters, and sometimes clay voodoo heads can be found in about 60 shops scattered along and off Route 705 and U.S. 220 in Seagrove. The work of some local potters is exhibited in national museums, including the Smithsonian. A map locating the various pottery studios is available at most shops and at the guild headquarters in downtown Seagrove. *124 E. Main St.,* ☎ *910/873–7887.* ⊙ *Most shops Tues.–Sat. 10–5.*

Participant Sports

Golf
The Sandhills doesn't call itself the Golf Capitol of the World for nothing. More than three dozen courses await you in this golfers' paradise. Several of the area's courses host the biggest tournaments in the sport. A complete list of golf courses and their fee ranges is available from the Pinehurst Area Convention and Visitors Bureau (*see* Visitor Information, *below*).

Pinehurst Resort and Country Club (Carolina Vista, Pinehurst, ☎ 910/295–6811 or 800/487–4653) celebrated its 100th birthday in 1995. It boasts eight courses designed by masters like Donald Ross, including the famed Number 2, rated second-best resort course in America by *Golf Digest.* Number 7 is also highly ranked. The U.S. Open will be played here in 1999. **Pine Needles Resort** (Box 88, Southern Pines, ☎ 910/692–7111) has a Donald Ross–designed course that will host the 1996 U.S. Women's Open.

The **Pit Golf Links** (Hwy. 5, Box 5789, Pinehurst, ☎ 910/944–1600 or 800/574–4653) is ranked among America's 75 best public courses by *Golf Digest.* The eighth hole is ranked by *Golf Magazine* as one of the 50 best holes open to the public. **Mid-Pines Resort** (1010 Midland Rd., Southern Pines, ☎ 910/692–2114 or 800/323–2114) is a quieter golf getaway with a Donald Ross–designed course. **Legacy Golf Links** (U.S. 15–501 South, Aberdeen, ☎ 910/944–8825 or 800/344–8825) has the first American course designed by Jack Nicklaus Jr. **Club at Longleaf** (Box 5789, Pinehurst, ☎ 910/692–6100 or 800/889–5323) was built on a former horse farm. The front nine plays through posts, rails, and turns of the old race track. **Talamore at Pinehurst** (1595 Midland Rd., Southern Pines, ☎ 910/692–5884 or 800/552–6292), designed by Rees Jones, was ranked 14th in the state by *Golf Digest.* It's most unusual feature is llama caddies.

Horseback and Carriage Riding
Riding instruction and carriage rides are available by appointment at **Pinehurst Stables** (Hwy. 5, ☎ 910/295–8456).

Tennis

The **Lawn and Tennis Club of North Carolina** (☎ 910/692–7270) and **Pinehurst Resort and Country Club** (☎ 910/295–6811) are known for their clinics. Public courts can be found in **Aberdeen, Carthage, Pinebluff,** and **Southern Pines** and at **Sandhills Community College.** For details, contact the Pinehurst Area Convention and Visitors Bureau (*see* Visitor Information, *below*) or the Moore County Parks and Recreation Department (☎ 910/947–2504).

Dining and Lodging

Dining

No particular local cuisine typifies the Sandhills, but the area has a number of sophisticated restaurants. Casual but neat clothing and golf wear are suitable anywhere in the Sandhills.

CATEGORY	COST*
$$$$	over $25
$$$	$15–$25
$$	$8–$15
$	under $8

per person for a three-course meal, excluding drinks, service, and 6% sales tax

Lodging

Most lodging options in the Sandhills are in the luxury resort category, featuring full amenities and services. However, there are a few chain motels in Southern Pines, as well as several bed-and-breakfasts in the area.

CATEGORY	COST*
$$$$	over $100
$$$	$60–$100
$$	$30–$60
$	under $30

All prices are for a standard double room, excluding 8% tax

Aberdeen
LODGING

$$–$$$ **Inn at Bryant House.** Downtown, one block off U.S. 1, this charming B&B is like a home away from home. The inn offers golf packages and arranges tennis and horseback riding. 🖼 *214 N. Poplar St., 28315,* ☎ *910/944–3300 or 800/453–4019,* 𝔽𝔸𝕏 *910/944–8898. 9 rooms, most with private bath. AE, D, MC, V.*

Cameron
DINING

$ **Dewberry Deli.** Housed in the Old Hardware, this eatery is a wonderful place for a sandwich or salad after shopping for antiques. ✗ *Carthage St.,* ☎ *910/245–3697. No reservations. No credit cards.* ⊙ *Tues.–Sat. 11–4:30.*

Eagle Springs
LODGING

$$$ **Inn at Eagle Springs.** A private girls' school during the 1920s, this B&B, amid the pines in a remote area 15 miles from Pinehurst, is great for golfers who want rest and quiet. The action-oriented might be bored, however. A full breakfast is always provided, and other meals can be arranged ahead. ⌨ *1813 Samarcand Rd., Box 56, 27242,* ☎ *910/673–2722,* 𝔽𝔸𝕏 *910/673–7740. 6 rooms. No credit cards.*

Pinehurst
DINING
$ **Pinehurst Playhouse Restaurant.** This casual eatery housed in an old theater is in the heart of the village and is *the* place to meet for soups and sandwiches. ✕ *Theater Bldg., W. Village Green.,* ☎ *910/295–8873. No reservations. No credit cards.* ☉ *Weekdays 9–4, Sat. 11–4.*

DINING AND LODGING
$$$$ **Holly Inn.** This renovated wooden inn, built in 1895, is testimony to James Tufts' success as a hotelier. It was so popular that he was forced to build a bigger structure—now the Pinehurst Resort. ⌨ *Cherokee Rd., Box 2300, 28374,* ☎ *910/295–2300 or, in NC, 800/682–6901,* 𝔽𝔸𝕏 *910/295–0988. 77 rooms and suites. Restaurant, lounge, pool. AE, DC, MC, V.*

$$$$ **Magnolia Inn.** Once just a hangout for golfing buddies, this Old South inn is now tastefully decorated with fresh paint and unusual antiques. The inn's dining room serves superb grilled Norwegian salmon and roasted herb-crusted rack of lamb, among other delectables—there's also an English pub, where you can discuss your golf game. ⌨ *Magnolia and Chinquapin Rds., Box 818, 28374,* ☎ *910/295–6900 or 800/526–5562,* 𝔽𝔸𝕏 *910/215–0858. 12 double rooms. Restaurant, pub, pool. AE, MC, V.*

$$$$ **Pinehurst Resort and Country Club.** This venerable resort hotel, in operation for nearly a century, has never lost the charm that founder James Tufts intended it to have. Civilized decorum rules in the spacious public rooms, on the rocker-lined wide verandas, and amid the lush gardens of the surrounding grounds. Guests can play lawn croquet, shoot skeet, or tee off on one of seven premier golf courses. The Carolina Dining Room is known for its gourmet cuisine. ⌨ *Carolina Vista, Box 4000, 28374,* ☎ *910/295–6811 or 800/487–4653,* 𝔽𝔸𝕏 *910/295–8503. 310 rooms, 125 condos. Dining room, pool, 7 18-hole golf courses, 20 tennis courts, croquet, windsurfing, boating, fishing, bicycles, children's programs, meeting rooms, airport shuttle. AE, D, DC, MC, V.*

$$$ **Pine Crest Inn.** After an extensive remodeling, this small village inn, once owned by golfing great Donald Ross, sports chintz and mahogany in its rooms. Chefs Carl and Peter Jackson whip up some great dishes, including homemade soups; fresh seafood dishes; and the house special, stuffed pork chops. Mr. B's Bar is the liveliest nightspot in town. Guests have golf and tennis privileges at local clubs. Rates include two meals per day. ⌨ *Dogwood Rd., Box 879, 28374,* ☎ *910/295–6121,* 𝔽𝔸𝕏 *910/295–4880. 40 rooms, 3 suites. AE, D, DC, MC, V.*

Southern Pines
DINING
$$$ **Mannie's Dinner Theater.** Guests can see musicals here on Saturday evening, after a dinner of prime rib or shrimp scampi. ✕ *210 W. Penn. Ave.,* ☎ *910/692–8400. Reservations required for dinner theater. AE, MC, V. Closed Sun.*

$$–$$$ **Lob Steer Inn.** Come hungry for broiled seafood and prime rib dinners, complemented by salad and dessert bars. The restaurant is upscale. ✕ *U.S. 1, Southern Pines,* ☎ *910/692–3503. Reservations advised on weekends. AE, DC, MC, V. No lunch.*

$–$$ Silver Bucket Restaurant. You can order just about any kind of fish—plus steaks, ribs, barbecue, and some Italian dishes—for a tasty and satisfying meal. The atmosphere is très casual. ✕ *S.E. Broad St.,* ☎ *910/692–6227. Reservations accepted. MC, V. Closed Mon.*

$ Whiskey NcNeill's Restaurant. Diners fill up on soups, sandwiches, salads, and a variety of entrées (from grilled sirloin to pork chops) over what used to be a grease pit of a downtown filling station but is now a fabulous spot for lunch and dinner. Stare closely at the building, and you can practically imagine pulling up to the pump in your '57 Chevy. ✕ *181 N.E. Broad St.,* ☎ *910/692–5440. Reservations accepted. MC, V.*

LODGING

$$$–$$$$ Pine Needles Resort and Country Club. One of the bonuses of staying at this informal lodge is the chance to meet Peggy Kirk Bell, a champion golfer and golf instructor. She built the resort with her late husband, and she continues to help run it. The rooms of the spacious lodge are done in a rustic style, with exposed beams in many rooms. ▦ *1005 Midland Rd., Box 88, Southern Pines 28387,* ☎ *910/692–7111 or 800/747–7272,* ℻ *910/692–5349. 71 rooms. Restaurant, pool, hot tub, sauna, whirlpool, 18-hole golf course, 2 tennis courts, airport shuttle. AE, MC, V.*

$$$ Mid Pines Inn and Golf Club. This resort community includes an 18-hole golf course designed by Donald Ross that has been the site of numerous tournaments. ▦ *1010 Midland Rd., Southern Pines 28387,* ☎ *910/692–2114 or 800/323–2114,* ℻ *910/692–4615. 118 rooms. Restaurant, lounge, pool, 18-hole golf course, 4 tennis courts, game room, meeting rooms, airport shuttle. AE, DC, MC, V.*

Southern Pines and Pinehurst Sandhills Essentials

Arriving and Departing, Getting Around

BY CAR

U.S. 1 runs north–south through the Sandhills and is the recommended route from the Raleigh–Durham area, a distance of about 70 miles. Another alternate is U.S. 15–501 from Chapel Hill. U.S. 74 from Charlotte intersects U.S. 1 at Rockingham, about 25 miles south of Southern Pines.

BY PLANE

Visitors arrive via USAir Express (☎ 800/428–4322) from **Charlotte–Douglas International Airport** or they fly into the **Raleigh–Durham Airport** or the **Piedmont Triad International Airport** and rent a car.

BY TRAIN

Amtrak (☎ 910/692–6305 or 800/872–7245) southbound and northbound trains, one daily from each direction, stop in Southern Pines.

Important Addresses and Numbers

EMERGENCIES

Dial 911 for **police** or **ambulance** in an emergency. For medical care, go to the emergency room of the **Moore Regional Hospital** (Memorial Dr., Pinehurst, ☎ 910/215–1111).

RADIO STATIONS

AM: WQNX 1350, talk; WKHO 550, easy listening; WEEB 990, news, talk. **FM:** WIOZ 107, easy listening.

VISITOR INFORMATION
Pinehurst Area Convention and Visitors Bureau (1480 Hwy. 15–501 N, Box 2270, Southern Pines 28388, ☎ 910/692–3330 or 800/346–5362). For details on local events, call 910/692–1600.

WINSTON-SALEM

The manufacture of cigarettes, textiles, and furniture built a solid economic base in the Winston-Salem area; major area employers today also include USAir, Wachovia Bank, the Bowman Gray School of Medicine, and N.C. Baptist Hospital. Winston-Salem residents' donations to the arts are among the highest per capita in the nation, and the North Carolina School of the Arts commands international attention. Wake Forest University, where writer Maya Angelou teaches, is also here. Old Salem, a restored 18th-century Moravian town within the city of Winston-Salem, has been drawing tourists since the early 1950s.

Exploring

Begin your tour of the city at the **Winston-Salem Visitor Center** (*see* Visitor Information, *below*), where you'll see a 12-minute film on the area.

★ **Old Salem** is just a few blocks from downtown Winston-Salem and only a stone's throw from Business I–40 (take the Old Salem/Salem College exit). The 1700s live again in this village of 80 original brick and wooden structures. The aromas of freshly baked bread, sugar cakes, and ginger snaps mix with those of beeswax candles and newly dyed flax. Tradesmen work in their shops making pewterware, cooking utensils, and other items, while the womenfolk embroider and weave cloth. There are African-American interpretations at each site. The Moravians, a Protestant sect, fled to Georgia to find religious freedom; from there they went to Bethlehem, Pennsylvania, finally settling here. In 1753, they built Bethabara (on Bethabara Rd., off University Pkwy.) and in 1766 built Salem. Tour tickets will get you into several restored buildings at Old Salem, but you may wander through the streets free of charge. Old Salem will undergo expansion over the next few years. *600 S. Main St., 27101, ☎ 910/721–7300 or 800/441–5305. ☛ $12 adults, $6 children ages 6–14; combination ticket with MESDA (see below), $16 adults, $8 children. ☺ Mon.–Sat. 9:30–4:30, Sun. 1:30–4:30.*

TIME OUT **Winkler Bakery** will satisfy your craving for hot, freshly baked Moravian sugar cake. *525 S. Main St., ☎ 910/721-7302. ☺ Mon.–Sat. 9-5, Sun. 1:30-5.*

Another way to step back in time is to enter the **Museum of Early Southern Decorative Arts (MESDA).** Six galleries and 19 rooms decorated with period furnishings are augmented with a new discovery center. *924 S. Main St., ☎ 910/721–7360. ☛ $6 adults, $3 children, ages 6–14; combination ticket with Old Salem, $16 adults, $8 children. ☺ Mon.–Sat. 10:30–4:30, Sun. 1:30–4:30.*

Stroh Brewery, approximately 5 miles south of downtown via U.S. 52, rolls out 5.5 million barrels of beer a year as the second-largest brewery in the country. A single machine can fill and seal up to 1,500 12-ounce cans of beer per minute. You can see it made and enjoy a complimentary drink. *Schlitz Ave., U.S. 52S at S. Main St., ☎ 910/788–6710. ☛ Free. ☺ Weekdays 1–4, with tours conducted on the hour.*

R. J. Reynolds Whitaker Park is one of the world's largest and most modern cigarette manufacturing centers. On the guided tour you see how 8,000 are produced every minute. *1100 Reynolds Blvd.,* ☎ *910/741–5718.* ☛ *Free.* ☉ *Late Sept.–Apr., weekdays 8–6; late May–early Sept., weekdays 8–8.*

Historic **Bethabara Park** is another vision from the 1700s. You can explore the foundations of the town, as well as the three remaining buildings. Kids love the reconstructed Indian fort. A greenway now connects the park to another restoration of a 1700s mill, fort, and village. *2147 Bethabara Rd.,* ☎ *910/924–8191.* ☛ *Free.* ☉ *Weekdays 9:30–4:30, weekends 1:30–4:30. Guided tours Apr.–Nov. or by appointment. Brochures for a self-guided walking tour are available year-round at the visitor center.*

The **Museum of Anthropology,** the only one in the state, displays objects from cultures around the globe. *Wake Forest University,* ☎ *910/759–5282.* ☛ *Free.* ☉ *Tues.–Sat. 10–4:30.*

Reynolda House Museum of American Art, formerly the home of tobacco magnate R. J. Reynolds, contains an outstanding collection of American art, a costume collection, and clothing and toys used by the Reynolds children. In Reynolda Village, on the estate, there are shops and restaurants. *Reynolda Rd.,* ☎ *910/725–5325.* ☛ *$6 adults, $3 students, $5 senior citizens.* ☉ *Tues.–Sat. 9:30–4:30.*

The **Southeastern Center for Contemporary Art (SECCA),** near Reynolda House, is the place to see the latest in Southern painting, sculpture, and printmaking. *750 Marguerite Dr.,* ☎ *910/725–1904.* ☛ *$3 adults, $2 students and senior citizens, children under 12 free.* ☉ *Tues.–Sat. 10–5, Sun. 2–5.*

The manor house at **Tanglewood Park,** the former home of the late William and Kate Reynolds, has just been spruced up with antiques and furnishings of the 1920s and now takes overnight guests. The public park has riding, golf, tennis, boating, camping, and PGA golf. *Hwy. 158 off I–40, Clemmons,* ☎ *910/766–0591.* ☛ *$2 per car, plus separate fees for each activity.*

Chinqua–Penn Plantation, 40 miles north of Winston-Salem on NC 158, is a National Register English country mansion built by Jeff and Betsy Penn in 1925. The Penns were world travelers, and filled the house with an eclectic collection of artifacts representing 30 countries. The estate also has a Chinese pagoda, three-story clock tower, greenhouses, and formal gardens. *2138 Wentworth St., Reidsville 27320,* ☎ *910/349–4576.* ☛ *$7 adults, $6 seniors citizens, $2.50 students.* ☉ *Tues.–Sat. 10–6, Sun. 1–6. Closed Jan.–Feb.*

What to See and Do with Children

Bethabara Park (*see* Exploring, *above*).

SciWorks. Look at the stars, handle live starfish in the tidal pool, pet the lambs and goats, and make discoveries at this hands-on museum. The complex includes the museum, an outdoor park, and a planetarium. *400 W. Hanes Mill Rd., Winston-Salem 27105,* ☎ *910/767–6730.* ☛ *Museum $4 adults, $2.50 students and senior citizens, children under 5 free.* ☛ *The "Works" (planetarium, park, and museum): $7 adults, $5 students and senior citizens.* ☉ *Mon.–Sat. 10–5, Sun. 1–5.*

Shopping

Shopping Districts
Hanes Mall (Silas Creek Pkwy. and Hanes Mall Blvd.) is one of the finest malls in the region, with such major department stores as Hecht's and Dillards and specialty stores like the Nature Company and Banana Republic.

Outlets
This is a textile center, so there are many clothing outlets clustered along the interstates. **Marketplace Mall** (2101 Peters Creek Pkwy., ☎ 910/759–9889) has 36 outlet stores under one roof, including specialty shops, shoes, and apparel. The 100 stores in **Burlington Manufacturers Outlet Center** (☎ 910/227–2872) make the area off I–85 near Burlington a mecca for dedicated shoppers. ☉ *Most stores Mon.–Sat. 10–9, Sun. 1–6.*

Books
Rainbow News & Cafe (712 Brookstown Ave., ☎ 910/723–0858) is a wonderful place where book lovers can browse for days through several converted old homes filled to the rafters with new and used books, then read their choice over a bowl of the best homemade soup in the city.

Crafts
The *New York Times* called the **Piedmont Craftsmen's Shop and Gallery** a "showcase for Southern crafts." *1204 Reynolda Rd.,* ☎ *910/725–1516.* ☉ *Tues.–Sat. 10–6, Sun. 1–5.*

Participant Sports

Golf
Bryan Park and Golf Club (6275 Bryan Park Rd., Brown Summit, ☎ 910/375–2200) is a highly regarded course east of Winston-Salem. Its Champions Course was runner-up for best new public course of 1990 by *Golf Digest*. **Oak Hollow Park Golf Course** (1400 Oakview Rd., High Point, ☎ 910/883–3260), south of Winston-Salem, was ranked among America's 75 best public courses by *Golf Digest*. **Tanglewood Park Golf Club** (NC 158, Clemmons, ☎ 910/766–5082) has two fine 18-hole courses; the Reynolds Course and the Championship Course, where the Vantage Championship is played each year.

Dining

Traditional dining in these parts is Southern—fried chicken, ham, vegetables, biscuits, fruit cobblers, and the like. Chopped or sliced pork barbecue is also a big item. Nowadays, however, there's a growing number of gourmet restaurants. Unless otherwise noted, casual wear is acceptable throughout the region.

CATEGORY	COST*
$$$	$15–$25
$$	$8–$15
$	under $8

per person for a three-course meal, excluding drinks, service, and 6% tax

$$$ Leon's Café. This casual eatery in a renovated building near Old Salem serves some of the best gourmet food in town—fresh seafood, chicken breasts with raspberry sauce, lamb, and other specialties. The restaurant's dark colors are set off by artworks and lacy window treatments. ✗ *924 S. Marshall St.,* ☎ *910/725–9593. Reservations advised. AE, MC, V.*

$$–$$$ Noble's Grille. This upscale French restaurant serves a variety of entrées grilled or roasted over an oak-and-hickory fire, including braised rabbit with black-pepper fettuccine and Carolina *poussin* with polenta. Decorated in an airy style with tall windows and track lighting, the dining room affords a view of the kitchen's wood-burning grill. ✗ *380 Knollwood St.,* ☎ *910/777–8477. Reservations advised. Jacket and tie. AE, DC, MC, V.*

$$–$$$ Old Salem Tavern Dining Room. Eat Moravian food in a Moravian setting served by waiters in Moravian costumes. Standard menu items are chicken pie (excellent choice!), ragout of beef, and rack of lamb. From April through October you can dine outside under the arbor. ✗ *736 S. Main St.,* ☎ *910/748–8585. Reservations advised. AE, MC, V.*

$$ Café Piaf. Inside the Stevens Center, a restored Art Deco performing-arts space, the café offers pasta primavera, chicken Piaf (mushroom pâté and chicken breast in puff pastry with champagne or mushroom cream sauce), and other French entrées. Dessert and coffee follow performances. ✗ *401 W. 4th St.,* ☎ *910/750–0855. Reservations advised. AE, DC, MC, V.*

$$ Maze. Innovative American fare, such as chicken with black-eyed-pea salad or eggplant sandwiches draw diners to this restaurant in Reynolda Village. ✗ *120 Reynolda Rd.,* ☎ *910/748–0269. Reservations advised for parties of 6 or more. AE, MC, V.*

$$ Newmarket Grille. Fresh vegetables and meats, plus homemade breads and desserts, make this establishment a winner. The varied menu includes fresh grilled fish, poultry, beef, and pork dishes, as well as some stir-fry items, plus burgers and sandwiches. The bar is a popular gathering spot for the city's movers and shakers. ✗ *300 S. Stratford Rd., 27103,* ☎ *910/724–5220. No reservations. AE, DC, MC, V.*

Lodging

CATEGORY	COST*
$$$$	over $100
$$$	$60–$100
$$	$30–$60
$	under $30

All prices are for a standard double room, excluding 8% service charge.

$$$$ Brookstown Inn. Sleep under a comfy handmade quilt in front of the fireplace or enjoy wine and cheese in the spacious lobby of this unusual bed-and-breakfast hotel, built in 1837 as one of the first textile mills in the South. Some rooms have whirlpools. Breakfast is Continental. ▥ *200 Brookstown Ave., 27101,* ☎ *910/725–1120 or 800/845–4262,* FAX *910/773–0147. 71 rooms. Meeting rooms. AE, DC, MC, V.*

$$$–$$$$ Adam's Mark Winston Plaza Hotel. Centrally located off I–40, this elegant hotel, Winston's premier lodging, has a marble lobby, traditional furnishings, and almost 10,000 square feet of meeting space. ▥ *425 N. Cherry St., 27101,* ☎ *910/725–3500 or 800/444–2326,* FAX *910/721–2240. 317 rooms. 2 restaurants, bar, pool, sauna, steam room, gift shop, recreation room. AE, D, DC, MC, V.*

$$$–$$$$ **Henry F. Shaffner House.** Accessible to downtown and Old Salem, this B&B is a favorite with business travelers and honeymoon couples. The rooms in the restored English Tudor house are furnished in 19th-century Victorian elegance. In addition to a complimentary Continental breakfast, there's afternoon tea and evening wine and cheese. ⊞ *150 S. Marshall St., 27101,* ☎ *910/777–0052,* FAX *910/777–1188. 8 rooms with bath. AE, MC, V.*

$$$–$$$$ **Tanglewood Manor House.** This former home of a branch of the Reynolds family provides bed-and-breakfast guests with 10 rooms in the antiques-filled manor house, 18 lodge rooms, and four cottages on Mallard Lake in Tanglewood Park. Continental breakfast, admissions to the park, swimming, and fishing are included in the cost. ⊞ *Hwy. 158 off I–40, Clemmons 27012,* ☎ *910/766–0591,* FAX *910/766– 1571. 32 rooms. AE, DC, MC, V.*

$$$ **Comfort Inn–Cloverdale Place.** Off I–40 near downtown and Old Salem, this immaculately kept inn offers a free Continental breakfast. ⊞ *110 Miller St., 27103,* ☎ *910/721–0220 or 800/228–5150,* FAX *910/723– 2117. 122 rooms. Pool, health club, meeting room. AE, D, DC, MC, V.*

Winston-Salem Essentials

Arriving and Departing, Getting Around

BY BUS
Contact **Greyhound Lines** (☎ 910/723–3663 or 800/231–2222).

BY PLANE
Continental Airlines has a hub at **Piedmont Triad International Airport** (☎ 910/665–5666). It is also served by American, Delta, United, and USAir.

BY TRAIN
Amtrak serves Greensboro (☎ 910/855–3382 or 800/872–7245), about 25 miles away.

BY TROLLEY
Trolleys run throughout downtown. The fare is 10¢.

Guided Tours
Contact **Carolina Treasures and Tours** (1031 Burke St., Winston-Salem 27101, ☎ 910/631–9144) or **Margaret Glenn Tours** (Box 11342, Winston-Salem 27116, ☎ 910/724–6547).

Important Addresses and Numbers

EMERGENCIES
Dial 911 for **police** and **ambulance** in an emergency.

RADIO STATIONS
AM: WSJS 600, news, talk; WSMX 1500, gospel; WAAA 980, urban contemporary. **FM:** WXRA 94.6, alternative rock; WMAG 99.5, adult contemporary; WBFJ 89.3, Christian; WFDD 88.5, National Public Radio; WJMH 102, urban contemporary; WTQR 104.1, country.

VISITOR INFORMATION
Winston-Salem Convention & Visitors Bureau (Box 1408, Winston-Salem 27102, ☎ 910/725–2361 or 800/331–7018). A visitor's **reception center** in the City Market building (601 N. Cherry St., Suite 100, ☎ 910/777–3796) is open daily.

THE OUTER BANKS

North Carolina's Outer Banks, a series of barrier islands, stretch from the Virginia state line south to Cape Lookout. Throughout history the nemesis of shipping, these waters have been called the "Graveyard of the Atlantic"; a network of lighthouses and lifesaving stations was built, which draws visitors today, and the many submerged wrecks attract scuba divers. English settlers landed here in 1587 and attempted to colonize the region, but the colony—known today as "The Lost Colony"—disappeared without a trace. The islands' coves and inlets offered privacy to pirates—the notorious Blackbeard lived and died here. For many years the Outer Banks remained isolated, home only to a few families who made their living by fishing. Today the islands, linked by bridges and ferries, have become popular tourist destinations. Much of the area is included in the Cape Hatteras and Cape Lookout national seashores. The largest towns are Kitty Hawk, Kill Devil Hills, Nags Head, and Manteo.

On the inland side of the Outer Banks is the historic Albemarle region, a remote area of small villages and towns surrounding Albemarle Sound. Edenton was the Colonial capital for a while, and many of its early structures are preserved.

Exploring

Numbers in the margin correspond to points of interest on the Outer Banks map.

You can tour the Outer Banks from the southern end or, as in the following route, from the northern end. You can drive the 70-mile stretch in a day, but be sure to allow plenty of time in summer to wait for the ferry connecting the islands, and to explore the undeveloped beaches, historic lifesaving stations, and charming beach communities stretched

★ along the **Cape Hatteras** and **Cape Lookout National seashores.** Rentals are available from Corolla to Ocracoke, with the highest concentration of accommodations in the area from Kill Devil Hills to Nags Head. Be aware that during major storms and hurricanes the roads and bridges become clogged with traffic. In that case, follow the blue-and-white evacuation signs.

The small settlements of **Corolla** and **Duck** are largely seasonal residential enclaves full of summer rental condominiums with, in Duck, a growing number of restaurants and shopping outlets. Drive slowly in Corolla; wild ponies wander free here and always have the right of way. **Kitty Hawk,** with 1,672 permanent residents, is among the quieter of the beach communities, with fewer rental accommodations.

❶ **Kill Devil Hills,** on U.S. 158 Bypass, has been the site of rapid development over the last decade. Its population explodes in summer, and though many businesses are seasonal, you can find anything you need here year round. It's also the windswept site of man's first motorized

★ flight. The **Wright Brothers National Memorial,** a granite monument that resembles the tail of an airplane, stands as a tribute to Wilbur and Orville Wright, two bicycle mechanics from Ohio who took to the air on December 17, 1903. You can see a replica of *The Flyer* and stand on the exact spot where it made four takeoffs and landings, the longest being a distance of 852 feet. Exhibits and an entertaining, informative talk by a National Park Service ranger make the event come to life again. The Wrights had to bring in the unassembled airplane by boat and also all their food and supplies for building a camp. They made four trips to the site, beginning in 1900. The First Flight is commemorated annually. ☎ 919/441–7430. ☛ *$4 per carload or $2 per person, children under 16 free.* ⊙ *Daily 9–5; extended hours in summer. Closed Dec. 25.*

A few miles south of Kill Devil Hills, via U.S. 158 Bypass, is **Jockey's Ridge State Park,** the tallest sand dune in the East and a popular spot for hang gliding and kite flying. You can join in the activities and have a picnic here. *Rte. 158 Bypass, MM 12,* ☎ *919/441–7132.* ☛ *Free.* ⊙ *Daily 8 AM–sunset.*

Nags Head got its name because Outer Bankers hoping for shipwrecks would tie lanterns around the heads of their horses to deceive merchant ships about the location of the shoals, thus profiting from the cargo that washed ashore. It is the most commercial area, with restaurants, motels, and hotels.

Take U.S. 64/264 from U.S. 158 Bypass to reach the appealing town of **Manteo** on **Roanoke Island.** Clustered together on the other side of Manteo you'll find the lush **Elizabethan Gardens,** which were established as a memorial to the first English colonists. They are impeccably maintained by the Garden Club of North Carolina and are a fine site for a leisurely stroll. *U.S. 64, Manteo,* ☎ *919/473–3234.* ☛ *$2 adults, children under 12 free when accompanied by an adult.* ⊙ *Mar.–Nov., daily 9–5; Dec.–Jan., weekdays 9–4.*

Fort Raleigh National Historic Site is a reconstruction of what is thought to be the original fort of the first Carolinian colonists. Be sure to see the orientation film and then take a guided tour of the fort. A nature trail leads to an outlook over Roanoke Sound. On special occasions, musicians play 16th-century music in the visitor center. *U.S. 64/264, 3 mi north of Manteo,* ☎ *919/473–5772.* ☛ *Free.* ⊙ *Daily 9–5; extended hours in summer.*

The Lost Colony, an outdoor drama staged at the Waterside Amphitheatre, reenacts the story of the first colonists who settled here in 1587 and then disappeared. *1409 U.S. 64/264,* ☎ *919/473–3414 or 800/488–5012.* ☛ *$12 adults, $11 senior citizens, $6 children under 12. Reservations advised. Performances mid-June–late Aug., Sun.–Fri. at 8:30 PM.*

A short drive away (right next to the Dare County Regional Airport) is the **North Carolina Aquarium/Roanoke Island,** one of three in the state. The aquarium features a new shark exhibit, and children love the unusual hands-on exhibit that is the aquatic equivalent of a petting zoo. *Airport Rd. (off U.S. 64), Manteo,* ☎ *919/473–3493.* ☛ *$3 adults, $2 senior citizens and active military personnel, $1 children 6–17.* ⊙ *Mon.–Sat. 9–5, Sun. 1–5.*

Back in Manteo, across a short bridge next to the Tranquil House Inn, is the **Elizabeth II State Historic Site,** a 16th-century vessel re-created to commemorate the 400th anniversary of the landing of the first colonists on Roanoke Island. A visitor center has exhibits on exploration and shipboard life. Historical interpretations are given by costumed guides during the summer. *Downtown Manteo,* ☎ *919/473–1144.* ☛ *$3 adults, $2 senior citizens, $1.50 students (any age), children 5 and under free.* ⊙ *Nov.–Mar., Tues.–Sun. 10–4; Apr.–Oct., daily 10–6.*

Resume your journey southward on Route 12. On the way you will pass over **Herbert C. Bonner Bridge,** which arches for three miles over

The Outer Banks

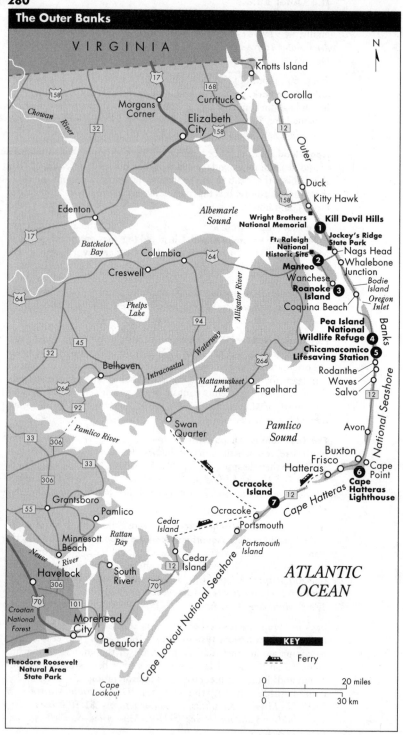

VIRGINIA

N

Knotts Island

[17]

[168]

[158]

Currituck

Corolla

Chowan

Morgans
Corner

[12]

Elizabeth
City

[32]

Duck

River

[158]

Kitty Hawk

Outer

[158]

Albemarle
Sound

Wright Brothers
National Memorial

Kill Devil Hills

①

Edenton

Jockey's Ridge
State Park

[17]

Ft. Raleigh
National
Historic Site

Nags Head

*Batchelor
Bay*

Columbia

[64]

Manteo

②

Whalebone
Junction

Creswell

Wanchese

*Bodie
Island*

[64]

**Roanoke
Island**

③

Coquina Beach

*Oregon
Inlet*

*Phelps
Lake*

[94]

**Pea Island
National
Wildlife Refuge** **④**

Banks

[32]

[45]

**Chicamacomico
Lifesaving Station** **⑤**

Rodanthe

Alligator River

[264]

Waves

Belhaven

Salvo

[12]

[264]

*Mattamuskeet
Lake*

Engelhard

National Seashore

[92]

Intracoastal

Avon

[33]

[306]

Pamlico River

Swan
Quarter

*Pamlico
Sound*

Buxton

[33]

Frisco

Cape
Point

[306]

Hatteras

⑥

Grantsboro

[55]

Pamlico

**Ocracoke
Island**

**Cape
Hatteras
Lighthouse**

Minnesott
Beach

*Rattan
Bay*

Ocracoke

⑦

[12]

Cape Hatteras

*Portsmouth
Island*

Neuse

*Cedar
Island*

Portsmouth

Havelock

River

South
River

[306]

Cedar
Island

[12]

*ATLANTIC
OCEAN*

[70]

*Croatan
National
Forest*

[101]

[70]

**Morehead
City**

Cape Lookout National Seashore

KEY

Beaufort

🚢 Ferry

**Theodore Roosevelt
Natural Area
State Park**

*Cape
Lookout*

0		20 miles

0		30 km

Oregon Inlet and carries traffic to Hatteras Island, the "Blue Marlin Capital of the World."

❹ Pea Island National Wildlife Refuge, between Oregon Inlet and Rodanthe, is made up of more than 5,000 acres of marsh. On the Atlantic Flyway, it's a birder's paradise: More than 265 species are spotted regularly, including endangered peregrine falcons and piping plovers. *Pea Island Refuge Headquarters,* ☎ *919/473–1131.* ☛ *Free.* ☼ *Apr.–Nov., weekdays 8–4.*

❺ Rodanthe is the site of the 1911 **Chicamacomico Lifesaving Station.** Now restored, the museum tells the story of the 24 stations that once lined the Outer Banks. Living-history reenactments are performed June–August. ☎ *919/987–2203.* ☛ *Free.* ☼ *May–Oct., Tues., Thurs., and Sat. 11–5.*

❻ Cape Hatteras Lighthouse, about 30 miles south of Rodanthe, sits as a beacon to ships offshore. The 208-foot lighthouse is the tallest in the East, and is open for climbing in summer months. Offshore lie the remains of the *Monitor,* a Confederate ironclad ship that sank in 1862. The visitor center offers information on the national seashore. *Hatteras Island Visitor Center,* ☎ *919/995–4474.* ☛ *Free.* ☼ *Daily 9–5.*

At Hatteras, board the free ferry to Ocracoke Island. Boats leave every **❼** half hour, and the journey takes 40 minutes. **Ocracoke Island** was cut off from the world for so long that native residents still speak in quasi-Elizabethan accents; today, however, the island is a refuge for tourists. There is a village of shops, motels, and restaurants around Silver Lake Harbor, which is where the infamous pirate Blackbeard met his death in 1718. The Ocracoke Lighthouse is a photographer's dream. *Ocracoke Visitor Center,* ☎ *919/928–4531.*

Cape Lookout National Seashore (☎ *919/728–2250*) extends for 55 miles from Portsmouth Island to Shackleford Banks. It includes 28,400 acres of uninhabited land and marsh, accessible only by boat or ferry. Portsmouth, a deserted village that was inhabited from 1753 until 1984, is being restored, and wild ponies roam the Shackleford Banks.

Off the Beaten Path

Merchants Millpond State Park. A 170-year-old millpond and an ancient Southern swamp comprise one of the state's rarest ecosystems. Cypress and gum trees hung with Spanish moss reach out of the still, dark waters, which are ideal for canoeing. Fishing, hiking, and camping are also available. *Rte. 1, Box 141-A, Gatesville 27938,* ☎ *919/357–1191.* ☛ *Free.* ☼ *Sept.–May, daily 8–8; June–Aug., daily 8 AM–9 PM.*

Somerset Place. The Collins family kept meticulous records on the 300 slaves that worked this plantation on Albemarle Sound (now a state historic site) in the 1800s. The slaves' descendants still hold family reunions here. *Off U.S. 64 at Creswell,* ☎ *919/797–4560.* ☛ *Free.* ☼ *Apr.–Oct., Mon.–Sat. 9–5, Sun. 1–5; Nov.–Mar., Tues.–Sat. 10–4, Sun. 1–4.*

Beaches

Kill Devil Hills has 5 miles of beach with 27 public access areas with limited parking off NC 12. Some have off-road vehicle access. Because of the large number of rental cottages and hotels, this beach tends to have a higher number of people, but it is seldom uncomfortably crowded, even at the height of the season.

Nags Head has 11 miles of beach with 33 public access areas, all with parking and some with rest rooms and showers. You'll usually have company on this beach as well. One point of interest is mile marker 11.5, site of the first North Carolina Historic Shipwreck Site. The USS *Huron* lies in 20 feet of water roughly even with the Nags Head pier.

Cape Hatteras National Seashore offers more than 70 miles of unspoiled beaches stretching from Nags Head to Ocracoke Island. Preserved as Cape Hatteras National Seashore, this coastal area is ideal for swimming, surfing, windsurfing, diving, boating, and any number of water activities. It's easy to find a slice of beach all your own as you drive south down NC 12, but park only in designated areas. If you want to swim, beware of strong tides and currents—there are no lifeguard stations. Fishing piers are located in Rodanthe, Avon, and Frisco.

Coquina Beach (off NC 12, 8 mi south of U.S. 158) on the Cape Hatteras National Seashore, is considered by some to be the best swimming hole on the Outer Banks. The wide-beamed ribs of the shipwreck *Laura Barnes* rest in the dunes here, and facilities include picnic shelters, rest rooms, showers, and bath houses.

Ocracoke Island beaches are among the least populated and most beautiful on the Cape Hatteras National Seashore. There are 4 public access areas with parking, as well as off-road vehicle access. Be sure to stop at the Ocracoke Pony Pen, where you can see direct descendants of Spanish mustangs that once roamed wild on the island.

Participant Sports and Outdoor Activities

Camping
Camping is permitted in designated areas all along the Cape Hatteras National Seashore (Rte. 1, Box 675, Manteo 27954, ☎ 919/473–2111). All campgrounds in the park have cold showers, drinking water, tables, grills, and rest rooms (except Ocracoke, which has pit toilets). Sanitary stations for recreational vehicles are at Oregon Inlet, Cape Point at Cape Hatteras, and Ocracoke. Oregon Inlet, Cape Point, and Ocracoke are open from mid-April through mid-October; Frisco, mid-June to late August. Be sure to take along extra-long tent stakes for sand, and don't forget the insect repellent. All sites are available on a first-come, first-served basis (except Ocracoke, where reservations are accepted). There are also many private campgrounds scattered along the Outer Banks. For information about these, contact the Dare County Tourist Bureau (☎ 919/473–2138).

Fishing
This area is a paradise for anglers who enjoy surf casting or deep-sea fishing. You can board a charter boat or head your own craft out of **Oregon Inlet Fishing Center** (☎ 919/441–6301 or 800/272–5199) or **Pirates Cove Yacht Club** (☎ 919/473–5577 or 800/367–4728) in Manteo. You don't need a license for saltwater fishing.

Hang Gliding
Only a few miles from where Wilbur and Orville Wright first took flight, you can try your hand at hang gliding. The giant sand dune at Jockey's Ridge State Park is where national champions gather every May for the Hang Gliding Spectacular. Lessons are given by **Kitty Hawk Kites** (U.S. 158 at MM 13, Nags Head, ☎ 919/441–4124 or 800/334–4777) and by **Corolla Flight** (Box 1021, Kitty Hawk 27949, ☎ 919/453–4800).

Golf

Nags Head Golf Links (MM 15, Nags Head, ☎ 919/441–8074 or 800/851–9404) offers ocean views and a Scottish feel. **Sea Scape Golf Course** (Kitty Hawk, ☎ 919/261–2158) is an authentic links course set amid the dunes.

Scuba Diving

With over 600 known shipwrecks off the coast of the Outer Banks, diving opportunities are virtually unlimited. The *Monitor* is off-limits, however. The **USS *Huron* Historic Shipwreck Preserve,** which lies offshore between mile markers 11 and 12, is a popular diving site. Dive shops include: **Hatteras Divers** (☎ 919/986–2557) and **Nags Head Pro Dive Shop** (☎ 919/441–7594).

Surfing and Windsurfing

The Outer Banks offer ideal conditions for these sports. Contact **Kitty Hawk Sports** (U.S. 158 at MM 13, ☎ 919/441–6800 or 800/334–4777) or **Bert's Surf Shop** (MM 10, Nags Head, ☎ 919/441–1939; MM 4, Kitty Hawk, ☎ 919/261–7584). A favorite spot for windsurfing on the Pamlico Sound between Buxton and Avon is known as **Canadian Hole** for all the northern visitors who congregate here to catch the wind.

Dining and Lodging

While you can find fancy restaurants catering to tourists in the major towns, by far the best fare around here is the fresh seafood. There are plenty of raw bars featuring oysters and clams on the half shell, and seafood houses offering fresh crabs (soft-shells in season, early in the summer) and whatever local fish—tuna, wahoo, dolphin (mahi-mahi, not Flipper)—has been hauled in that day. Competition keeps them on their toes, so the cooking is good. Dress is usually casual.

CATEGORY	COST*
$$$$	over $25
$$$	$15–$25
$$	$8–$15
$	under $8

per person for a three-course meal, excluding drinks, service, and 6% sales tax

The majority of motels and hotels are clustered in the Nags Head–Manteo area, with rental properties in all the towns that dot the Cape Hatteras National Seashore. There are 60 cottages for rent on Ocracoke Island, plus a dozen or so motels and inns. The Dare County Tourist Bureau (☎ 919/473–2138) can steer you in the direction of agencies to arrange weekly or monthly rentals.

CATEGORY	COST*
$$$$	over $100
$$$	$60–$100
$$	$30–$60
$	under $30

All prices are for a standard double room, excluding 8% tax

Buxton

DINING

$$$ **Great Salt Marsh.** A clean, well-lighted place with a black-and-white checkered art-deco look, the restaurant serves lunch and dinner to regulars and the passers-through. Among the imaginative appetizers are fresh green beans sautéed and served with Parmesan cheese, and such entrées as Pamlico crab cakes with "absolutely no filler" and soft crabs served on a bed of garlic-laced spinach. It has a splendid wine list. ✗ *Osprey Shopping Center, Hwy. 12,* ☎ *919/995–6200. Reservations strongly advised. AE, D, DC, MC, V.*

Duck

DINING AND LODGING

$$$$ **Sanderling Inn and Restaurant.** If you enjoy being pampered, come to this inn on a remote beach north of Duck. Guests are treated to afternoon tea. For recreation you can play tennis, go swimming, or take a nature walk through the Pine Island Sanctuary and then curl up with a good book from the inn's library—or enjoy a videotape. Though it was built in 1985 and has all the contemporary conveniences, the inn has the stately, mellow look of old Nags Head. Ceiling fans, wicker, and neutral tones give rooms a cool and casual feel. The ambitious but unexceptional restaurant is in a beautifully renovated lifesaving station. It serves three meals a day, and reservations are required for dinner. ⌨ *1461 Duck Rd., 27949,* ☎ *919/261–4111 or 800/701–4111. 60 rooms and 28 efficiencies. Restaurant, pool, hot tub, 2 tennis courts, health club, meeting rooms. AE, D, MC, V.*

Kill Devil Hills

DINING

$$–$$$ **Etheridge Seafood Restaurant.** The fish comes straight from the boat to the kitchen at this family-owned seafood house, in operation for over half a century. It's decorated with Etheridge family memorabilia, depicting their successful fishing and warehousing operation. ✗ *U.S. 158 Bypass at MM 9.5,* ☎ *919/441–2645. No reservations. MC, V. Closed Nov.–Feb.*

LODGING

$$$–$$$$ **Ramada Inn.** Rooms in this convention-style hotel have ocean views and come with refrigerators and microwave ovens. Peppercorns restaurant, overlooking the ocean, serves breakfast and dinner, and lunch is available on the sun deck next to the pool. ⌨ *U.S. 158, MM 9.5, Box 2716, 27948,* ☎ *919/441–2151 or 800/635–1824,* 🖷 *919/441–1830. 172 rooms. Pool, hot tub, meeting rooms. AE, D, DC, MC, V.*

Nags Head

DINING

$$$ **Owens' Restaurant.** Housed in an old Nags Head–style clapboard cottage, Owens' has been in the same family since 1946. The seafood is outstanding—especially the coconut shrimp and lobster bisque. Nightly entertainment is offered in the brass-and-glass Station Keeper's Lounge. ✗ *U.S. 158, MM 17,* ☎ *919/441–7309. Reservations accepted for large parties only. AE, DC, MC, V. No lunch. Closed Jan.–Mar.*

$$–$$$ **Lance's Seafood Bar & Market.** You can contemplate the fishing and hunting memorabilia while you dine on steamed or raw seafood and then drop the shells through the hole in the table. ✗ *U.S. 158 Bypass, MM 14,* ☎ *919/441–7501. AE, MC, V. Closed Dec. 25.*

LODGING

$$$–$$$$ **First Colony Inn.** The rooms in this historic inn near the ocean are fur-
★   nished with four-poster and canopied beds, hand-crafted armoires, and English antiques. The suites have wet bars, kitchenettes, and Jacuzzis. A Continental breakfast and afternoon tea come with the room. ⌨ *6720 S. Virginia Dare Trail, 27959,* ☎ *919/441–2343 or 800/368–9390. 26 rooms. Refrigerators, pool, coin laundry. D, MC, V.*

Ocracoke

DINING AND LODGING

$$–$$$ **Island Inn and Dining Room.** The inn was built as a private lodge back in 1901. It shows its age a bit, but is full of Outer Banks character and is being upgraded a step at a time. The large rooms in the Crow's Nest on the third floor are the best; they have cathedral ceilings and look out over the island. The dining room is known for its oyster omelet, crab cakes, and hush puppies. Reservations are advised, particularly for dinner. ⊞ *Rte. 12, Box 9, 27960,* ☎ *919/928–4351 (inn) or 919/928–7821 (dining room). 35 rooms. Pool. D, MC, V.*

Roanoke Island

DINING

$$$ **Queen Anne's Revenge.** This stately old home expanded into a restaurant serves some of the best seafood on the coast from a secluded location in the woods of Wanchese. Nightly specials, like marinated grilled tuna, are always fresh and well-prepared; even the side dishes are impressive. ✕ *4 mi off U.S. 64, Wanchese,* ☎ *919/473–5466. Reservations accepted for parties of 8 or more. AE, D, DC, MC, V. Closed Tues. Nov.–Mar.*

$$ **Weeping Radish Brewery and Restaurant.** Waiters dressed in Bavarian costumes serve German dishes while German music plays in the background. Tours of the brewery are given upon request. The beer is superb, but this isn't the place for seafood. ✕ *U.S. 64, Manteo,* ☎ *919/473–1157. Reservations advised for parties of 6 or more. MC, V. Closed major holidays.*

DINING AND LODGING

$$$$ **Tranquil House Inn.** This 19th-century-style waterfront inn is only a few steps from shops, restaurants, and the Elizabeth II State Historic Site, but bikes are provided for adventures beyond. Handmade comforters in designer fabrics give rooms a cozy feel. Some of the bathroom mirrors are hand-stenciled to match the flowers in the wallpaper. A Continental breakfast and wine and cheese each evening is on the house. The new restaurant, 1587, serves inventive entrées like sesame-crusted tuna with wasabi vinaigrette and shiitake mushrooms. ⊞ *Queen Elizabeth Ave., the Waterfront, Box 2045, Manteo 27954,* ☎ *919/473–1404 or 800/458–7069,* FAX *919/473–1526. 25 rooms. AE, D, MC, V.*

Outer Bank Essentials

Arriving and Departing, Getting Around

BY BOAT

Seagoing visitors travel the Intracoastal Waterway through the Outer Banks and Albemarle region. Boats may dock at Elizabeth City (☎ 919/338–2886), Manteo Waterfront Docks (☎ 919/473–3320), Park Service Docks at Ocracoke (☎ 919/928–5111), and other ports. For a complete list of facilities, see the North Carolina Coastal Boating Guide compiled by the North Carolina Department of Transportation (☎ 919/733–2520).

BY CAR

U.S. 158 links the Outer Banks with U.S. 17 leading to Norfolk and other places north. U.S. 64, 70, and 264 are western routes. Route 12 goes south toward Ocracoke Island and north toward Corolla. Toll ferries connect Ocracoke to Cedar Island and Swan Quarter. For reservations, call 800/293–3779). There is a free ferry across Hatteras

Inlet. On summer weekends, traffic waiting for the Hatteras Inlet ferry can be backed up for hours.

BY PLANE

The closest commercial airports are the **Raleigh–Durham International Airport** (☎ 919/840–2123) and **Norfolk International** (☎ 804/857–3340), both of which are served by major carriers, including American, Continental, Delta, and USAir. Southeast Airlines (☎ 919/473–3222) provides charter service between the **Dare County Regional Airport** (919/473–2600) at Manteo and major cities along the East Coast.

BY TAXI

Beach Cabs (☎ 919/441–2500), based in Nags Head, offers 24-hour service from Norfolk to Ocracoke and towns in between. Another option is **Outer Banks Limousine Service** (☎ 919/261–3133).

BY TRAIN

Amtrak service (☎ 800/872–7245) is available to Norfolk, VA, about 75 miles to the north.

Guided Tours

Historic Albemarle Tour, Inc. (Box 759, Edenton 27932, ☎ 919/482–4747) offers guided tours of Edenton and publishes a brochure on a self-guided tour of the Albemarle Region.

Kitty Hawk AeroTours leave from the First Flight Airstrip or from Manteo for Kitty Hawk, Corolla, Cape Hatteras, Ocracoke, Portsmouth Island, and other areas along the Outer Banks. ☎ *919/441–4460. Tours run Mar.–Labor Day.*

The **North Carolina Aquarium/Roanoke Island** (Box 967, Airport Rd., Manteo 27954, ☎ 919/473–3493) sponsors summer boat tours of the estuary and the sound.

Ocracoke Trolley Tours (of Ocracoke Island) depart from Trolley Stop One in Ocracoke. *NC 12, Ocracoke, ☎ 919/928–6711. Tours run Easter–Labor Day, Mon.–Sat.*

Important Addresses and Numbers

EMERGENCIES

Dial 911 for Oregon Inlet, Roanoke Island, Hatteras Island, and Ocracoke Island. For non-emergency care, contact **Ocracoke Health Center** (☎ 919/928–1511). The **Outer Banks Medical Center** (☎ 919/441–7111) at Nags Head is open 24 hours a day. For Coast Guard assistance, dial ☎ 919/995–6411.

RADIO STATIONS

AM: WOBR 1530, vacation information, news, weather; WGAI 560, adult contemporary. **FM:** WNHW 92, country; WOBR 95.3, adult contemporary; WRSF 105.7, country; WVOD 99.1, beach, Top 40; WCXL 104.1, adult contemporary.

VISITOR INFORMATION

Dare County Tourist Bureau (Box 399, Manteo, 27954, ☎ 919/473–2138). **Historic Albemarle Tour, Inc.** (Box 759, Edenton 27932, ☎ 919/482–7325).

WILMINGTON AND THE CAPE FEAR COAST

The old seaport town of Wilmington has much to celebrate these days. Thanks to efforts led by the Downtown Area Revitalization Effort (DARE), the once-decadent downtown has been reborn. *Henrietta II*, a paddle wheeler similar to those that used to ply the waters of the Cape Fear River, has been put into service as a tourist vessel. Visitors are drawn to the Coast Line Convention Center complex, reminiscent of old railroad days, and to the charms of Chandler's, the Cotton Exchange, and Water Street Market, now shopping and entertainment centers. They also come to Wilmington for special annual events such as the Azalea Festival, North Carolina Jazz Festival, Christmas candlelight tours, and fishing tournaments. And on the surrounding Cape Fear Coast visitors tour old plantation houses and azalea gardens, study sea life at the state aquarium, and bask in the sun at nearby beaches.

Exploring

Wilmington

USS *North Carolina* Battleship Memorial, a top tourist priority, can be reached by car or by taking the river taxi from Riverfront Park. The ship participated in every major naval offensive in the Pacific during World War II. The self-guided tour takes about two hours, and a 10-minute film is shown throughout the day. Narrated tours on cassette are available for rent, and a 70-minute sound-and-light spectacular, "The Immortal Showboat," is presented nightly at 9 from early June until Labor Day. *Box 480, Wilmington 28402,* ☎ *910/251–5797.* ☛ *$6 adults, $3 children 6–11; sound-and-light show $3.50 adults, $1.75 children.* ⊙ *Daily 8–sunset.*

The **Wilmington Railroad Museum,** at the corner of Red Cross and Water streets, focuses on the days of the Wilmington and Weldon Railroad (circa 1840) to the present. Children love climbing on the steam locomotive and caboose. ☎ *910/763–2634.* ☛ *$2 adults, $1 children 6–11.* ⊙ *Tues.–Sat. 10–5, Sun. 1–5.*

From the museum, follow Red Cross Street one block toward downtown and turn right on Front Street. On the second block is the **Cotton Exchange,** a shopping-dining complex housed in restored buildings that have flourished as a trading center since the pre–Civil War days. ☎ *910/343–9896.* ⊙ *Mon.–Sat. 10–5:30, some stores open evenings and Sun. 1–5.*

From Front Street, go to Grace Street, head east until you reach Third Street, and then go south to Chestnut Street, to the **New Hanover County Public Library.** The North Carolina Room in the library attracts researchers and genealogists from all over the country. *201 Chestnut St.,* ☎ *910/341–4394.* ☛ *Free.* ⊙ *Mon.–Thurs. 9–9, Fri. 9–6, Sat. 9–5, Sun. 1–5.*

Follow Chestnut Street to 4th Street, then go two blocks to Market Street. On that corner is the **St. James Graveyard,** which contains the headstones of many early settlers. In the next block of South Fourth Street is the **Temple of Israel,** the oldest Jewish place of worship in the state.

Continue several blocks north on Market Street to the **Cape Fear Museum,** which traces the natural, cultural, and social history of Cape Fear

River Country from its beginnings to the present day. *814 Market St.,* ☎ *910/341–7413.* ☛ *$2 adults, $1 students, senior citizens, and children 5–17.* ☉ *Tues.–Sat. 9–5, Sun. 2–5. Closed holidays.*

Several blocks west on Market Street at the corner of Third is the **Burgwin-Wright House,** built in 1770 on the foundations of a jail. This colonial restoration, which includes a period garden, is maintained by the National Society of the Colonial Dames of America and by the state of North Carolina. *224 Market St.,* ☎ *910/762–0570.* ☛ *$3 adults, $1 children.* ☉ *Tues.–Sat. 10–3:30.*

Go two blocks south on Third Street, where you'll find the **Zebulon Latimer House,** built in 1852 in the Italianate style. *126 S. 3rd St.,* ☎ *910/762–0492.* ☛ *$3 adults, $1 children.* ☉ *Tues.–Sat. 10–4.*

Wind up your tour at **Chandler's Wharf** on Water Street. Originally a complex of warehouses, it now contains shops and some good seafood restaurants like Elijah's. This is a great place to conclude your tour of downtown Wilmington.

Cape Fear Coast

Go three blocks east to U.S. 17. On the way out of town, stop at **Greenfield Lake and Gardens,** on South Third Street (U.S. 421). The park offers picnicking and canoe and paddle-boat rentals on a scenic 180-acre lake bordered by cypress trees laden with Spanish moss. ☎ *910/763–9371.* ☛ *Free.* ☉ *Daily.*

Follow U.S. 17 northeast for 9 miles until you reach **Poplar Grove Historic Plantation.** The home of the Foy family for generations, the 1850 Greek Revival plantation was opened to the public in 1980. You can tour the manor house and outbuildings, see craft demonstrations, shop in the country store, and pet the farm animals. *9 mi northeast of Wilmington on U.S. 17,* ☎ *910/686–9989 (restaurant 910/686–9503). Guided tours Feb.–Dec.: $6 adults, $5 senior citizens, $3 students and children 5–16.* ☉ *Mon.–Sat. 9–5, Sun. noon–5. Closed Jan.*

Now head south on U.S. 17 until you reach Military Cut-off Road, which becomes Oleander Drive and leads to **Airlie Gardens** (8 mi east). The gardens are open from March through September. *Airlie Rd. off Rte. 74/76,* ☎ *910/763–4646.* ☛ *$6 adults, $5 senior citizens ($1 less May–Oct.), children under 10 free.*

Take Route 76 west to Route 421 south and follow it to the **Southport–Fort Fisher Ferry** (☎ *910/458–3329*), some 20 miles south of Wilmington. On the way, stop at **Fort Fisher State Historic Park** and the **North Carolina Aquarium** (*see* What to See and Do with Children, *below*). The car-ferry trip is an enjoyable river ride between Old Federal Point at the tip of the spit and the quaint town of Southport. You can see the "Old Baldy" lighthouse en route. *Ferries run every 50 min between 8:50 and 6:50. Fare: $3 per car. The privately owned passenger ferry to Bald Head Island,* ☎ *910/457–5003, runs from Southport on the hour (except noon) 8–6; fare: $15 adults, $8 children.*

After you get off the ferry in Southport, take Route 87 north to the **Carolina Power and Light Company Visitors Center.** Here you can learn about nuclear power through exhibits and movies and then use the picnic area. ☎ *910/457–6041.* ☛ *Free.* ☉ *June–Aug., weekdays 9–4, Sun. and July 4 1–4; Sept.–May, weekdays 9–4.*

Continue north on Route 87/133, and you will arrive at **Orton Plantation Gardens.** The house is not open to the public, but the gardens may be toured anytime. ☎ 910/371–6851. ☛ *$8 adults, $4 children 6–12.* ☉ *Mar.–Aug., daily 8–6, Sept.–Nov., daily 10–5.*

Take a short detour off Route 133 to **Brunswick Town State Historic Site,** where you can explore the excavations of a colonial town, see Fort Anderson, a Civil War earthworks fort, and have a picnic. ☎ 910/371–6613. ☛ *Free.* ☉ *Apr.–Oct., Mon.–Sat. 9–5, Sun. 1–5; Nov.–Mar., Tues.–Sat. 10–4, Sun. 1–4.*

What to See and Do with Children

Fort Fisher State Historic Site was the largest and one of the most important earthwork fortifications in the South during the Civil War. Visitors enjoy the reconstructed battery and Civil War relics and artifacts from sunken blockade-runners. *U.S. 421 at Kure Beach,* ☎ 910/458–5538. ☛ *Free.* ☉ *Apr.–Oct., Mon.–Sat. 9–5, Sun. 1–5; Nov.–Mar., Tues.–Sat. 10–4, Sun. 1–4.*

The **North Carolina Aquarium at Fort Fisher,** one of three state aquariums, has a 20,000-gallon shark tank, a touch pool (where you can handle starfish, sea urchins, and the like), a whale exhibit, and a new alligator exhibit. The park is also a natural area where wildflowers, birds, and small animals thrive. You can also visit the World War II bunker that stood guard against sea attacks from the Atlantic. Field trips and workshops for groups can be arranged. *U.S. 421 at Kure Beach,* ☎ 910/458–8257. ☛ *$3 adults, $2 senior citizens and active military, $1 students 6–17.* ☉ *Mon.–Sat. 9–5, Sun. 1–5. Closed major holidays.*

The **Wilmington Railroad Museum** (*see* Exploring, *above*).

Off the Beaten Path

Military history buffs get a bang out of **Moore's Creek National Battlefield,** where American patriots defeated the Loyalists in 1776. *20 mi northwest of Wilmington on Rte. 210,* ☎ 910/283–5591. ☛ *Free.* ☉ *Daily 8–5.*

★ A visit to **Tryon Palace at New Bern,** about 150 miles from the Outer Banks, 100 miles north of Raleigh, and 80 miles from Wilmington, is an ideal overnight trip. The reconstructed Georgian palace, considered the most elegant government building in the country in its time, was the colonial capitol and the home of Royal Governor William Tryon in the 1770s. It was rebuilt according to architectural drawings of the original palace and furnished in English and American antiques as listed in Governor Tryon's inventory. Costumed interpreters give tours of the house; tours of the 18th-century formal gardens are self-guided. During the summer, actors in period dress give monologues describing a day in the life of Governor Tryon. Special events are held periodically throughout the year, and craft demonstrations are given daily. The stately John Wright Stanly House (circa 1783), Dixon-Stevenson House (circa 1826), and the recently restored New Bern Academy (circa 1809) are a part of the Tryon Palace Complex. An audiovisual orientation is offered in the Visitor Reception Center. *610 Pollock St., New Bern 28560,* ☎ 919/638–1560. ☛ *Palace and gardens only, $8 adults, $4 students 6–17; garden tour only, $4 adults, $2 students; combination tour of all buildings and gardens, $12 adults, $6 students.* ☉ *Mon.–Sat. 9:30–4, Sun. 1–4. Closed major holidays.*

Shopping

Visitors will find it easy to restrict their shopping to Chandler's Wharf, the Cotton Exchange, and the Water Street Market, but the city also offers many unique shops in the Historic District, as well as shopping malls and discount outlets.

Beaches

Three beaches—**Wrightsville, Carolina,** and **Kure**—are within a short drive from Wilmington, and miles and miles of sand stretch northward to the Outer Banks and southward to South Carolina. The beaches offer a full gamut of activities, from fishing to sunbathing to scuba diving, and a choice of accommodations, including weathered cottages, resorts, condos, and motels. There are approximately 100 points of public access along the shoreline. Marked by orange-and-blue signs, these points offer parking, rest rooms, and outdoor showers. Some of the smaller beaches have lifeguards on duty, and many are accessible to people with disabilities. A number of fishing piers are also open to the public.

Wrightsville, about 5 miles east of Wilmington, is a posh and popular beach with a number of outstanding restaurants nearby. **Carolina Beach,** about 12 miles south, caters to families. Camping, fishing, swimming, and picnicking are permitted at **Carolina Beach State Park** (☎ 910/458–8206, marina 910/458–7770). **Kure Beach** is a quiet family enclave with historic sites like Fort Fisher and attractions like the North Carolina Aquarium (*see* What to See and Do With Children, *above*). In some places, twisted live oaks still grow behind the dunes.

Participant Sports

Fishing

Surf fishing is popular on the piers that dot the coast. Charter boats and headboats are available for off-shore fishing. Four major fishing tournaments, for substantial prize money, are held each year—the **Cape Fear Marlin Tournament,** the **Wrightsville Beach King Mackerel Tournament, the East Coast Open King Mackerel Tournament,** and the **U.S. Open King Mackerel Tournament.** For more information on these tournaments, contact the Cape Fear Coast Convention and Visitors Bureau (*see* Visitor Information, *below*).

Golf

There are 10 public and semi-private courses in the Greater Wilmington area, and South Brunswick County is golf heaven, especially the areas around Calabash, Sunset Beach, and Ocean Isle. A few top choices are listed below, but for more information on golf, call the Cape Fear Coast Convention and Visitors Bureau (*see* Visitor Information, *below*) or the South Brunswick Islands Chamber of Commerce (Box 1380, Shalotte, 28459, ☎ 910/754–6644).

Bald Head Island Club (Bald Head Island, ☎ 910/457–5000 or 800/234–1666) is a George Cobb–designed course in a beautiful setting of tropical forest and marsh. **Beau Rivage Plantation Golf Club** (6230 Carolina Beach Rd., Wilmington, 910/392–9022) is an 18-hole course in a natural links setting. The **Cape Golf & Racquet Club** (535 The Cape Blvd., Wilmington, ☎ 910/799–3110) is an 18-hole resort course with driving range. The **Gauntlet at St. James Plantation** (Hwy. 211, Southport, ☎ 910/253–3008 or 800/247–4806) lives up to its name as a challenging course. **Lockwood Folly Golf Links** (100 Club House Dr.,

Holden Beach, ☎ 910/842–5666 or 800/443–7891) is a highly rated resort course. **Marsh Harbour Golf Links** (Hwy. 179, Calabash, ☎ 910/579–3161 or 800/552–2660) was rated one of the best 75 public courses in America by *Golf Digest*. **Oyster Bay Golf Links** (Hwy. 179, Sunset Beach, ☎ 910/579–3528 or 800/552–2660) was selected "best new resort course of 1983" by *Golf Digest* and is known for its oyster shell hazards and gator sightings. **Sea Trail Plantation** (211 Clubhouse Rd., Sunset Beach, ☎ 910/579–4350 or 800/624–6601) features three courses designed by Dan Maples, Rees Jones, and Willard Byrd. These are great courses and a good value.

Scuba Diving
Wrecks such as the World War II tanker *John D. Gill* make for exciting diving off the coast. **Aquatic Safaris** (5751–4 Oleander Dr., Wilmington, ☎ 910/392–4386) rents equipment and leads trips.

Surfing and Board Sailing
These sports are popular at area beaches, and rentals are available at shops in Wilmington, Wrightsville Beach, and Carolina Beach.

Triathlon
Those who enjoy jogging, swimming, and bicycling can join in the annual **Wilmington Triathlon** in the fall. Participants swim across Banks Channel to Wrightsville Beach, then bicycle to Carolina Beach and back to Wilmington, and then run from there back to Wrightsville Beach.

Spectator Sports

College Sports
Local fans support the University of North Carolina at Wilmington's Seahawk basketball, baseball, and swimming teams. The school belongs to the NCAA Division I Colonial Athletic Association. *For tickets, ☎ 910/395–3233.*

Rugby
The **Cape Fear Rugby Tournament** (☎ 910/395–3233) is an annual July 4th event, held at UNC-W.

Dining and Lodging

Dining
Local cuisine is simply seafood. Shrimp (this is where the shrimp boats come in), oysters, Atlantic blue crab, and king mackerel—and lots of it—are prepared in a variety of ways. Homegrown fruits and vegetables, too, are used extensively in local cooking. Barbecued pork is another popular dish. International cuisines—from Mexican to Japanese to German—are also represented. Dress at these restaurants is neat but casual.

CATEGORY	COST*
$$$$	over $25
$$$	$15–$25
$$	$8–$15
$	under $8

*per person for a three-course meal, excluding drinks, service, and 6% sales tax

$$–$$$ **Market Street Casual Dining.** This always-busy eatery offers a wide variety of sandwiches and entrées, including seafood and steaks, served in a casual atmosphere. There's also a bar on the premises. ✕ *6309 Market St.,* ☎ *910/395–2488. No reservations. AE, D, MC, V.*

$$–$$$ **Ocean Terrace Restaurant.** Part of the Blockade Runner Resort (*see* Lodging, *below*), this restaurant attracts large crowds to its Friday lobster night, Saturday seafood buffet, and Sunday brunch. Regular dishes here include grilled New York strip steak with bourbon-shallot butter; sautéed, almond-breaded flounder with shrimp; and sautéed chicken breast with toasted pecans, pears, and apples. ✕ *Blockade Runner Resort Hotel and Conference Center, 275 Waynick Blvd., Wrightsville Beach,* ☎ *910/256–2251 or 800/541–1161. Reservations advised. AE, D, DC, MC, V.*

$$–$$$ **Oceanic Restaurant and Grill.** Its Oceanic Pier location gives patrons the top panoramic view of the Atlantic for miles around—a wonderful backdrop for the fresh seafood, steaks, and chicken served here. ✕ *703 S. Lumina St., Wrightsville Beach,* ☎ *910/256–5551. Reservations advised for large parties. AE, MC, V.*

$$–$$$ **Pilot House.** At this Chandler's Wharf restaurant, known for its seafood, pastas, and fresh vegetables, you can now dine outdoors overlooking the Cape Fear River. The Sunday Brunch (Apr.–Oct.), featuring Low Country Southern food, is the most popular in town. ✕ *2 Ann St.,* ☎ *910/343–0200. Reservations advised. AE, D, MC, V.*

$–$$ **Ken and Art's Studio Café.** This restaurant is where you might spot a star when they're filming on location in Wilmington. The menu features a mixture of California, New York, and Carolinas cuisine, served amid movie memorabilia. ✕ *North Carolina Film Studios, 1223 N. 23rd St.,* ☎ *910/343–3708. Reservations advised. No credit cards. No dinner.*

$ **Water Street Restaurant and Sidewalk Café.** Housed in a restored two-story brick waterfront warehouse that dates to 1835, this outdoor café and restaurant serves up Greek, Mexican, Middle Eastern, and other ethnic cooking. ✕ *5 Water St.,* ☎ *910/343–0042. Reservations not required. MC, V.*

Lodging

Visitors to Wilmington and Cape Fear Coast can choose among 6,000 rooms. The selection includes a variety of chains, condos, and resorts overlooking the ocean, and in-town guest houses. In addition to in-town properties, there are many accommodations at Carolina, Kure, and Wrightsville beaches. A complete list is included in the *Accommodations Guide,* available from the Convention and Visitors Bureau.

CATEGORY	COST*
$$$$	over $100
$$$	$60–$100
$$	$30–$60
$	under $30

*All prices are for a standard double room, excluding 9% tax

$$$$ **Bald Head Island Resort.** Accessible only by ferry (☎ 910/457–5003; fare: $15 adults, $8 children) from Southport, this resort offers privacy in a luxurious isolated setting. Despite the quiet surroundings, there's always something to do on the resort island: Activities include golf, tennis, sailing, and fishing. Other favorite pastimes are watching the loggerhead turtles, and taking a tour led by a naturalist. Accommodations include rental condos, cottages, and bed-and-breakfast inns; a two-night minimum stay is required. ⌧ *Bald Head Island, 28461,* ☎ *910/457–5000 or 800/234–1666,* FAX *910/457–9232. Over 100 rental condos and beach houses. 3 restaurants, pool, boating, shops. AE, DC, MC, V.*

$$$–$$$$ **Blockade Runner Resort Hotel and Conference Center.** This extensive complex is widely known for both its food (*see* Dining, *above*) and lodging. Rooms overlook either the inlet or the ocean. ⌧ *275 Waynick Blvd., Wrightsville Beach 28480,* ☎ *910/256–2251 or 800/541–1161,* FAX *910/256–2251, ext. 404. 150 rooms and suites. Restaurant, pool, health club, boating, bicycles, meeting rooms. AE, D, DC, MC, V.*

$$$–$$$$ **Inn at St. Thomas Court.** Guests are pampered yet enjoy total privacy at this small luxurious apartment-type house, which has one- and two-bedroom suites furnished in a traditional style in keeping with the surrounding historic district. A Continental breakfast is included in the rate. ⌧ *101 S. 2nd St., 28401,* ☎ *910/343–1800 or 800/525–0909,* FAX *910/251–1149. 34 units. AE, DC, MC, V.*

$$$ **Catherine's Inn.** Built in 1883 and in the historic district overlooking the Cape Fear River, this two-story Italianate home, now a B&B, has hardwood floors, a sunken garden, four-poster and canopy beds, and claw-foot tubs—many items collected by the innkeepers over the years. ⌧ *410 S. Front St., 28401,* ☎ *910/251–0863 or 800/476–0723. 3 rooms. AE, MC, V.*

$$$ **Docksider Inn.** In a class of its own, this waterfront hotel in the heart of Kure Beach is nautical both outside and in. Gray with navy shutters, the inn is furnished in light-colored beachy furniture and enhanced with marine art and artifacts, including a set of 1930s British Admiralty signal flags. Each bathroom has an original watercolor. The third floor is being converted into "Captain's Cabins" for those seeking a romantic getaway. ⌧ *202 Fort Fisher Blvd. (U.S. 421), 28449,* ☎ *910/458–4200,* FAX *910/458–6468. 34 rooms. Pool. AE, DC, D, MC, V.*

$$$ **Wilmington Hilton Inn.** Overlooking the Cape Fear River on one side and the city on the other, this is one of the most convenient places to stay in town. The spacious inn has a dining room and lounge. ⌧ *301 N. Water St., Wilmington 28401,* ☎ *910/763–5900 or 800/445–8667,* FAX *910/763–0038. 168 rooms, 10 suites. Pool, meeting rooms, airport shuttle. AE, DC, D, MC, V.*

$$ **Hampton Inn.** This economy chain motel, 3 miles from downtown, is not luxurious but offers such extras as complimentary Continental breakfast, in-room movies, and free local calls. ⌧ *5107 Market St., 28403,* ☎ *910/395–5045 or 800/426–7866,* FAX *910/799–1971. 118 rooms. Facilities: pool. AE, D, DC, MC, V.*

The Arts and Nightlife

The arts are very much a part of Wilmington life. Theatrical productions are staged by the **Thalian Association, Opera House Productions,** and **Tapestry Players.** The city has its own symphony orchestra, oratorio society, civic ballet, and concert association; and the **North Carolina Symphony** makes four appearances here each year. The annual **Wilmington Jazz Festival,** held in February, and the **Blues Festival,** in August, draw big crowds.

The Arts

St. John's Museum of Art is known for its 13 prints by Cassatt, as well as for its works by North Carolina artists. The museum is housed in three buildings, including the 1804 Masonic Lodge Building, the oldest such lodge in the state. There is also a sculpture garden. *114 Orange St., ☎ 910/763–0281. ☛ $2 adults, $1 students under 18, children under 5 free. ۞ Tues.–Sat. 10–5, Sun. noon–4.*

Museum of World Cultures (601 S. College Rd., ☎ 910/395–3411 or 910/350–4007), at the University of North Carolina at Wilmington, exhibits its collections of African art, pre-Columbian textiles, Chinese ceramics, and Middle Eastern artifacts at various locations around the campus.

Thalian Hall, a magnificent opera house built in 1858 and refurbished in 1990 to the tune of $5 million, is the site of theater, dance, and musical performances. *310 Chestnut St., ☎ 910/343–3664 or 800/523–2820. The hall is open for self-guided tours Mon.–Sat. noon–5, as permitted by performance schedules.*

Nightlife

Wilmington nightlife is centered in hotel lounges. The **Ocean Terrace Restaurant** in the Blockade Runner Hotel (*see* Dining and Lodging, *above*) offers live entertainment Thursday through Sunday, with nationally known acts in the **Comedy Zone** March–November. **Ice House Beer Garden** (115 S. Water St., ☎ 910/251–1158 or 910/763–2084) serves food and beer and showcases a different music group nightly. **Johnny Rockit's** (5025 Market St., ☎ 910/791–2001) is known for rock music.

Wilmington and the Cape Fear Coast Essentials

Arriving and Departing, Getting Around

Visitors can get to Wilmington and the Cape Fear Coast via car, plane, bus, or boat. Several cruise lines dock here on their way to Bermuda or the Caribbean.

BY BOAT

Public boat access is offered at Atlantic Marina, Carolina Beach State Park, Masonboro Boat Yard and Marina, Seapath Transient Dock, Wrightsville Gulf Terminal, and Wrightsville Marina. The Wilmington Hilton, Blockade Runner, Harbor Inn, and Summer Sands provide docking facilities for their guests. A river taxi runs (mid-June—Labor Day) across the Cape Fear River between the USS *North Carolina Battleship Memorial* and downtown Wilmington. The fare is $1 roundtrip. A state-run car ferry connects Fort Fisher with Southport on the coast.

BY BUS

Greyhound Lines serves the Union Bus Terminal (201 Harnett St., ☎ 910/762–6625 or 800/231–2222). The **Wilmington Transit Authority** (☎ 910/343–0106) provides service every day except Sunday. There is also taxi service.

BY CAR

U.S. Highways 421, 74, 76, 17, and 117 serve Wilmington. I–40 now links the city with I–95.

BY PLANE

USAir (☎ 800/428–4322) and ASA Delta Connection (to Atlanta; ☎ 800/282–3424) serve the **New Hanover International Airport** (☎ 910/341–4333), ½ mile from downtown Wilmington.

Guided Tours

The **"Guide Map of Historic Wilmington and the Cape Fear Coast"** is available from the Cape Fear Coast Convention and Visitors Bureau in the restored New Hanover County Courthouse and at the Visitor Information Booth at the foot of Market Street (in the summer). The bureau can suggest itineraries and arrange tours of local industries upon advance request.

Wilmington Adventure Walking Tours, run by Bob Jenkins, will guide you around old Wilmington. *Tours operate Apr. 1–Nov. 1.,* ☎ *910/763–1785.* ☛ *$10 adults, $5 children 6–12.*

Walk and Talk Tour, offered by the Lower Cape Fear Historical Society, covers 12 blocks in downtown Wilmington. *Tours operate Feb.–Dec., Wed. only. Depart from Latimer House, 126 S. 3rd St.,* ☎ *910/762–0492.* ☛ *$5 ($6, including Latimer House).*

Sightseeing Tours by Horse Drawn Carriage, given by John and Janet Pucci of Springbrook Farms Tuesday through Sunday during the summer and on weekends off-season, depart from Water & Market streets. ☎ *910/251–8889.* ☛ *$7 adults, $4 children under 12.*

Cape Fear Riverboats, Inc., operated by Capt. Carl Marshburn, offers a variety of cruises aboard a stern-wheel riverboat that departs from Riverfront Park. ☎ *910/343–1611 or 800/676–0162. Sightseeing tours: $9 adults, $4 children. Entertainment/dinner cruises: $29–$32.50 per person. Sunset dinner cruises: $22 adults, $15 children. Moonlight cruises: $9 adults, $5 children (call for boarding times).*

The **Captain J. N. Maffitt Harbor Tour** (☎ 910/343–1611 or 800/676–0162) runs cruises and shuttles passengers between Riverfront Park and the USS *North Carolina Battleship Memorial. Shuttle: every 30 min 10–5 except during tours. Fare: $2. Cruises: $5 adults, $3 children.*

Cape Fear Tours (☎ 910/686–7744) offers walking and driving tours of the Wilmington Historic District, mansions, and the beaches for individuals and groups by reservation. Individual tours are $20 per hour.

Important Addresses and Numbers

EMERGENCIES
Dial 911 for **police** and **ambulance.** For Coast Guard assistance, dial ☎ 910/343–4881. Emergency medical attention is available round the clock at the **Cape Fear Memorial Hospital** (5301 Wrightsville Ave., ☎ 910/452–8100) and the **New Hanover Regional Medical Center** (2131 S. 17th St., ☎ 910/343–7000); both hospitals have 24-hour pharmacies as well.

RADIO STATIONS
AM: WAAV 980, news, talk; WBMS 1340, urban contemporary. **FM:** WHQR 91.3, National Public Radio; WKOO 98.7, oldies; WGNI 102.7, adult contemporary; WWQQ 101.3, country; COAST 97.3, urban contemporary; WSFM 107.5, classic rock.

VISITOR INFORMATION
Cape Fear Coast Convention and Visitors Bureau (24 N. 3rd St., Wilmington 28401, ☎ 910/341–4030 or 800/222–4757).

NORTH CAROLINA HIGH COUNTRY, INCLUDING ASHEVILLE

The majestic peaks, meadows, and valleys of the Appalachian, Blue Ridge, and Smoky mountains characterize the High Country in the western corner of the state. National parks and forests and the Blue Ridge Parkway are the region's main attractions, providing prime opportunities for skiing, hiking, bicycling, camping, fishing, and canoeing, or just taking in the breathtaking views.

The largest and most cosmopolitan city in High Country, Asheville has been a retreat for the wealthy and famous for decades. In recent years this mountain city has been rated, among cities of its size, as America's number-one favorite place to live. It has scenic beauty, low levels of pollution, a good airport and road system, a moderate four-season climate, a variety of hotels and restaurants, and a thriving arts community. Banjo pickers are as revered as violinists, mountain folks mix with city slickers, and everyone loves where they live.

Cities like Boone, Blowing Rock, and Banner Elk have boomed in the 30 years since the introduction of snowmaking equipment. Luxury resorts now dot the valleys and mountaintops. Visitors to the hills take advantage of the many crafts shops, music festivals, theater offerings, and such special events as the Grandfather Mountain Highland Games. The passing of each season is a special visual event here, and autumn is the star.

Exploring

Asheville

Downtown Asheville is noted for its eclectic architecture. The **Battery Park Hotel,** built in 1924, is neo-Georgian; the **Flatiron Building** (1924) is neo-classical; the **Basilica of St. Lawrence** (1912) is Spanish Baroque; **Old Pack Library** (1925) is in Italian Renaissance–style; the **S & W Cafeteria** (1929) is Art Deco. In fact, the city has the largest collection of Art Deco buildings outside of Miami.

Pack Place Education, Arts & Science Center houses the Asheville Art Museum, Colburn Gem & Mineral Museum, Health Adventure, YMI Cultural Center, and the Diana Wortham Theatre. *2 S. Pack Sq.,* ☎ *704/257–4500.* ☛ *Fees vary.* ۝ *June–Oct., Tues.–Sat. 10–5, Sun. 1–5; Nov.–May, Tues.–Sat. 10–5.*

The **Thomas Wolfe Memorial,** built in 1880 in the Queen Anne style, is one of the oldest houses in downtown Asheville. Wolfe's mother ran a boarding house here for years, and he used it as the setting for his novel *Look Homeward, Angel.* Family pictures, clothing, and original furnishings fill the house, now a state historic site. Guided tours are available. *48 Spruce St.,* ☎ *704/253–8304.* ☛ *$1 adults, 50¢ students.* ۝ *Apr.–Oct., Mon.–Sat. 9–5, Sun. 1–5; Nov.–Mar., Tues.–Sat. 10–4, Sun. 1–4.*

From downtown, take U.S. 25 south. The entrance to the architecturally ★ famous **Biltmore Estate** faces Biltmore Village, about three blocks from the interstate. Built as the private home of George Vanderbilt, the 255-room French Renaissance château is America's largest private residence (Vanderbilt's descendants still live in the mansion, but open the bulk of the home and grounds to visitors). Richard Morris Hunt designed it, and Frederick Law Olmsted landscaped the original 125,000-acre estate (now 8,000 acres). It took 1,000 men five years to complete the gargantuan project. On view are the priceless antiques and art collected by the Vanderbilts, and 17 acres of gardens. Visitors can also see the state-of-the-art winery and take Christmas candlelight tours of the house. Allow a full day to tour the house and grounds. ☏ *704/255–1700 or 800/543–2961.* ☛ *$24.95 adults, $18.75 students ages 10–15, accompanied children under 10 free.* ⊙ *Daily 9–5 except Thanksgiving, Dec. 25, and Jan. 1.*

Weaverville

Take U.S. 19–23 Bypass north about 18 miles to Weaverville and the **Zebulon B. Vance Birthplace** state historic site, with a two-story log cabin and several outbuildings, where North Carolina's governor during the Civil War grew up. Crafts and chores typical of his period are often demonstrated. Picnic facilities are available. *Reems Creek Rd. (Rte. 1103),* ☏ *704/645–6706.* ☛ *Free.* ⊙ *Apr.–Oct., Mon.–Sat. 9–5, Sun. 1–5; Nov.–Mar., Tues.–Sat. 10–4, Sun. 1–4.*

Blue Ridge Parkway

★ The most direct route from Asheville to the Boone–Blowing Rock area is the **Blue Ridge Parkway,** a 469-mile stunningly beautiful road that gently winds through mountains and meadows and crosses mountain streams on its way from Cherokee, North Carolina, to Waynesboro, Virginia. To get onto the Parkway from the Vance Birthplace, follow Reems Creek Road west, turn onto Ox Creek Road, and follow it 3 miles to the Parkway entrance. The Parkway is generally open year-round but often closes during heavy snows. Maps and information are available at visitor centers along the highway. *Superintendent, Blue Ridge Pkwy., BB & T Bldg., 1 Pack Sq., Asheville 28801,* ☏ *704/298–0398.*

The **Folk Art Center** (MM 382 on the Blue Ridge Pkwy.) sells authentic mountain crafts made by members of the Southern Highland Handicraft Guild. ☏ *704/298–7928.* ⊙ *Daily except major holidays.*

About 65 miles north of the Folk Art Center, just off the parkway on U.S. 221, is **Linville Caverns,** the only caverns in the Carolinas. They go 2,000 feet underground and have a year-round temperature of 51 degrees. ☏ *704/756–4171.* ☛ *$4 adults, $2.50 children 5–12.* ⊙ *June–Labor Day, daily 9–6; Apr.–May and Sept.–Oct., daily 9–5; Nov. and Mar., daily 9–4:30; Dec.–Feb., weekends only 9–4:30.*

About a mile farther north along the Parkway is **Linville Falls** (MMDM 316.3), one of North Carolina's most frequently photographed waterfalls. An easy trail winds through evergreens and rhododendrons to overlooks where you can get wonderful views of the series of cascades tumbling into Linville Gorge. There's also a visitor center, a campground, and a picnic area.

Just off the parkway at mile marker 305 is **Grandfather Mountain,** famous for its Mile-High Swinging Bridge, a 228-foot-long bridge that sways over a 1,000-foot drop into the Linville Valley. Sweaty-palmed tourists have crossed it since 1952. A Natural History Museum has exhibits on native minerals, flora and fauna, and pioneer life. The annual Singing on the Mountain in June is an opportunity to hear old-time gospel music and preaching, and the Highland Games in July brings together Scottish clans from all over North America for athletic events and Highland dancing. There's also hiking, picnicking, and an environmental habitat. *Blue Ridge Pkwy. and U.S. 221, Linville 28646,* ☏ *704/733–4337.* ☛ *$9 adults, $5 children 4–12.* ⊙ *Apr.–mid-Nov., 8–dusk; mid-Nov.–Mar., 9–4, weather permitting.*

Parks along the parkway include **Julian Price Park** (MM 298–295.1), which offers hiking, canoeing on a mountain lake, trout fishing, and camping, and **Moses H. Cone Park** (MM 292.7–295), which has a turn-of-the-century manor house that's now the **Parkway Craft Center.**

Blowing Rock

Just north of the entrance to Moses H. Cone Park, take U.S. 221/321 to Blowing Rock, a tourist mecca since the 1880s, which has retained the flavor of a quiet mountain village. Only a few hundred people are permanent residents, but the population swells each summer. The **Blowing Rock,** considered the state's oldest tourist attraction, looms 4,000 feet over the Johns River Gorge. If you throw your hat over the sheer precipice, it may come back to you, should the wind gods be playful. The story goes that a Cherokee brave and a Chickasaw maiden fell in love. Torn between his tribe and his love, he jumped from the cliff, but she prayed to the Great Spirit and he was blown safely back to her. It's more or less a gimmick, but the view from the observation tower is nice, and there's a garden landscaped with mountain laurel, rhododendron, and other native plants. *Off U.S. 321,* ☎ *704/295–7111.* ☛ *$4 adults, $1 children 6–11.* ☺ *Summer 8–8, winter 10–5.*

Head north toward Boone on U.S. 321, until you come to **Tweetsie Railroad,** a popular theme park where visitors can ride a train beset by train robbers and Indians. The park also has a petting zoo, country fair (May–Oct.), rides, gold panning, a saloon show, and concessions. ☎ *704/264–9061 or 800/526–5740.* ☛ *$14.95 adults, $12.95 children 4–12 and senior citizens 60 years and older.* ☺ *Late May–Oct. 31, daily 9–6.*

Boone

Boone, named for frontiersman Daniel Boone, is a city of several thousand residents at the convergence of three major highways—U.S. 321, U.S. 421, and NC 105. **"Horn in the West,"** a project of the Southern Highlands Historical Association, is an outdoor drama that traces the story of Boone's life. *Amphitheater off U.S. 321,* ☎ *704/264–2120.* ☛ *$9 (reserved) or $8 (general admission) adults, $4.50 children under 13. Performances nightly at 8:30, except Mon. mid-June–mid-Aug.*

Boone's **Appalachian Cultural Museum** showcases the successes of such mountain residents as stock-car racer Junior Johnson and country singers Lula Belle and Scotty Wiseman, and exhibits a vast collection of antique quilts, fiddles, and handcrafted furniture. *University Hall near Greene's Motel, U.S. 321,* ☎ *704/262–3117.* ☛ *$2 adults, $1.75 senior citizens, $1 children 12–18.* ☺ *Tues.–Sat. 10–5, Sun. 1–5.*

Banner Elk

From Boone, take U.S. 321 west and NC 194 south to Banner Elk, a popular ski resort town surrounded by the lofty peaks of Grandfather, Hanging Rock, Beech, and Sugar mountains.

Ashe County

North of Boone in Ashe County, past Blue Ridge Parkway mile marker 258.6, are the **Blue Ridge Mountain Frescoes.** North Carolina artist Ben Long painted four big-as-life frescoes in two abandoned churches here in the '70s. *The Last Supper* (measuring 17 × 19.5 feet) is in the Glendale Springs Holy Trinity Church. The others are in St. Mary's Episcopal Church at Beaver Creek, including *Mary, Great with Child,* which won the Leonardo da Vinci International Award. Signs from the highway lead to the churches. ☎ 910/982–3076. ☛ *Free.* ⊙ *24 hours a day; staffed 10–4. Guide service available with prior arrangements.*

What to See and Do with Children

Tour an underground mine or dig for gems of your own at **Emerald Village,** an old mine. *McKinney Mine Rd. at Blue Ridge Pkwy., MM 334,* ☎ *704/765–6463.* ☛ *Museum $3.50 adults, $2.50 students, $3 senior citizens, plus cost of gem bucket chosen ($3–$100). A $50 bucket guarantees you a stone, which will be cut free of charge, $100 guarantees two.* ⊙ *June–Labor Day, daily 9–6, May and Sept.–Oct., daily 9–5.*

Sliding Rock. In summer, you can skid 150 feet on a natural water slide in Pisgah National Forest. Wear old jeans and tennis shoes, and bring a towel. *Pisgah National Forest, north of Brevard, off U.S. 276,* ☎ *704/877–3265.* ☛ *Free.* ⊙ *Daily.*

Tweetsie Railroad (*see* Exploring, *above*).

Off the Beaten Path

At **Chimney Rock Park,** about 25 miles southeast of Asheville on U.S. 64/74–A, you can ride an elevator up through a 26-story shaft of rock for a staggering view of Hickory Nut Gorge and the surrounding Blue Ridge Mountains. Trails, open spring–fall, lead to 400-foot Hickory Nut Falls, where *The Last of the Mohicans* was filmed. ☎ *704/625–9611 or 800/277–9611.* ☛ *$9 adults, $4.50 children 6–15.* ⊙ *Mid-Oct.–Apr., daily 8:30–4:30, May–mid-Oct., daily 8:30–5:30.*

About 25 miles south of Asheville via I–26 is **Flat Rock,** the town to which the poet and Lincoln biographer Carl Sandburg moved with his wife, Lilian, in 1945. Guided tours of their house, **Connemara,** where Sandburg's papers still lie scattered on his desk, are given by the National Park Service. In summer, "The World of Carl Sandburg" and "Rootabaga Stories" are presented at the amphitheater. ☎ *704/693–4178.* ☛ *$2 adults, children 16 and under free.* ⊙ *Daily 9–5.*

You'll find everything from ribbons and calico to brogans and overalls in the **Mast General Store,** ten miles northwest of Boone in the tiny town of Valle Crucis. Built in 1882, the store has plank floors worn to a soft sheen and a potbellied stove that's still fired up on chilly mornings. (The company operates a similar store in downtown Boone: Old Boone Mercantile, 104 E. King St., Boone, ☎ 704/262–0000; ⊙ Mon.–Sat. 10–6, Sun. 1–6.) NC 194, Valle Crucis, ☎ 704/963–6511. ⊙ Mon.–Sat. 6:30–6:30, Sun. 1–6.

Shopping

Groovewood Gallery at the Homespun Shops, on the grounds of the Grove Park Inn and established by Mrs. George Vanderbilt, sells woven goods, such as blankets, shawls, and baskets, made on the premises. *111 Groovewood Rd., Asheville,* ☎ *704/253–7651.* ⊙ *Nov.–May, Mon.–Sat. 10–5; June–Oct., Mon.–Sat. 10–5, Sun. 1–5.*

Bolick Pottery sells mountain crafts and pottery, handcrafted on the spot by Glenn and Lula Bolick; Glenn will even throw in a mountain tale, a buck dance, or a tune on his saw free of charge. *Off U.S. 321, Rte. 8, Box 285–A, Lenoir,* ☎ *704/295–3862.* ⊙ *Mon.–Sat. 9–5, Sun. 1–6.*

Goodwin Weavers sell bedspreads, afghans, and other woven goods, as well as home furnishings designed by North Carolina artist Bob Timberlake. *Off U.S. 321 Bypass, Blowing Rock,* ☎ *704/295–3394.* ☉ *June–Dec., daily 9–5, Jan.–May, daily 10–4:30.*

Qualla Arts and Crafts has authentic Cherokee Indian crafts and items from other American tribes. *U.S. 441 and Drama Rd., Cherokee,* ☎ *704/497–3103.* ☉ *June–Aug., Mon.–Sat. 8–8, Sun. 8–5; Sept.–May, weekdays 8–4:30, Sat. 9–4:30.*

Participant Sports

Canoeing and Whitewater Rafting

In the Asheville area, the Chattooga, Nolichucky, French Broad, Nantahala, Ocoee, and Green rivers offer Class I–V rapids. Outfitters include **Carolina Wilderness** (Box 488, Hot Springs 28743, ☎ 704/622–3535 or 800/872–7437) and **Nantahala Outdoor Center** (13077 Hwy. 19W, Box 41, Bryson City 28713, ☎ 704/488–2175 or 800/232–7238).

Near Boone and Blowing Rock, the wild and scenic New River (Class I and II) provides hours of excitement, as do the Nolichucky River, the Watauga River, Wilson Creek, and Toe River. Outfitters include **Edge of the World Outfitters** (Hwy. 184, Box 1137, Banner Elk 28604, ☎ 704/898–9550 or 800/789–3343) and **Wahoo's Adventures** (Box 1915, Boone 28607, ☎ 704/262–5774 or 800/444–7238).

Golf

Western North Carolina offers many challenging courses. For a complete listing of public courses in Asheville, Black Mountain, Brevard, Hendersonville, Lake Lure, Old Fort, and Waynesville, contact Asheville's Visitor Information Center (*see* Visitor Information, *below*). North Carolina High Country Host (*see* Visitor Information, *below*) has information on public courses in Boone, Seven Devils, Newland, and West Jefferson.

Boone Golf Club (Fairway Dr., Boone, ☎ 704/264–8760) is a good 18-hole course for the whole family. **Colony Lake Lure Golf Resort** (201 Blvd. of the Mtns., Lake Lure, ☎ 704/625–2888), located five miles from Asheville, has two 18-hole courses known for their beauty. **Etowah Valley Country Club** (U.S. 64, Etowah, ☎ 704/891–7141 or 800/451–8174), about 20 miles from Asheville, has three very different 9-hole courses with good package deals. **Grove Park Inn** (290 Macon Ave., Asheville, ☎ 704/252–2711 or 800/438–5800) has a beautiful 18-hole course. **Hound Ears Club** (NC 105, Boone, ☎ 704/963–4312) has an 18-hole course with great mountain views. **Linville Golf Club** (Linville, ☎ 704/733–4363), located 17 miles from Boone, has a highly rated Donald Ross course. **Reems Creek Golf Club** (Weaverville, ☎ 704/645–4393), about 12 miles from Asheville, offers what some consider to be perfect mountain golf.

Hiking

More than 100 trails lead off the Blue Ridge Parkway, from easy strolls to strenuous hikes. The **Bluff Mountain Trail** at Doughton Park (MM 238.5) is a moderately strenuous 7.5-mile trail winding through forests, pastures, and valleys, and along the mountainside. Moses H. Cone Memorial Park's (MM 292.7) **Figure 8 Trail** is an easy and beautiful trail that the Cones designed specifically for their morning walks. The half-mile loop winds through a tunnel of rhododendron and a hardwood forest lined with moss-covered rocks, wildflowers, and lush green ferns. Those who tackle the half-mile, strenuous **Waterrock Knob Trail** (MM 451.2), near the southern end of the parkway, will be rewarded with spectacular views from the 6,400-foot-high Waterrock Knob summit. For more information on parkway trails, contact the Blue Ridge Parkway (*see* Exploring, *above*). Another good source is *Walking the Blue Ridge: a Guide to the Trails of the Blue Ridge Parkway* by Leonard Adkins (UNC Press, $11.95), available at most parkway visitor center gift shops.

Trails abound in **Great Smoky Mountains National Park.** For trail maps, contact the Superintendent (Great Smoky Mountains National Park, Gatlinburg, TN 37738, ☎ 615/436–5615). The park maintains an information bulletin board with basic trail information at the entrance at the junction of mile marker 469.1 and U.S. 441.

Serious hikers wishing to explore the **Appalachian Trail,** which runs along the crest of the Appalachian Mountains at the North Carolina–Tennessee border, can pick it up at several points, including at the Newfound Gap Parking Area in Great Smoky Mountains National Park (☎ 615/436–5615) and at Grandfather Mountain (☎ 704/733–4337), where you can get trail maps.

Horseback Riding and Trekking

Trail rides are offered by several Asheville area stables, including **Pisgah View Ranch** (Rte. 1, Candler 28715, ☎ 704/667–9100) and **Cataloochee Ranch** (Rte. 1, Box 500, Maggie Valley 28751, ☎ 704/926–1401 or 800/868–1401). In the Boone–Blowing Rock area, trail rides are offered by **Blowing Rock Stables** (U.S. 221, Blowing Rock, ☎ 704/295–7847), **Elk Creek Stables** (NC 268, Ferguson, ☎ 910/973–8635), and **Banner Elk Riding Stables** (NC 184, Banner Elk, ☎ 704/898–5424). You can hike with llamas carrying your pack into the Pisgah National Forest on day and overnight trips with **Windsong Llama Treks, Ltd.** (120 Ferguson Ridge Rd., Clyde 28721, ☎ 704/627–6111). In Asheville, contact **Avalon Llama Trek** (310 Wilson Cove Rd., Swannanoa, ☎ 704/298–5637).

Rock Climbing

One of the most challenging climbs in the country is the Linville Gorge (MM 317, Blue Ridge Pkwy.). Permits are available from the District Forest Ranger's Office in Marion (☎ 704/652–2144) or from the Linville Falls Texaco Station on U.S. 221. **Edge of the World Outfitters in Banner Elk** (☎ 704/898–9550) provides instruction and guided trips.

Skiing

Ski resorts in the Asheville area include **Cataloochee** (Rte. 1, Box 500, Maggie Valley 28751, ☎ 704/926–0285 or 800/768–0285), **Fairfield–Sapphire Valley** (4000 U.S. 64W, Sapphire Valley 28774, ☎ 704/743–3441 or 800/533–8268), and **Wolf Laurel** (Rte. 3, Mars Hill 28754, ☎ 704/689–4111).

The Boone–Blowing Rock area offers downhill skiing at **Appalachian Ski Mountain** (Box 106, Blowing Rock 28605, ☎ 704/295–7828 or 800/322–2372), **Ski Beech** (Box 1118, Beech Mountain 28604, ☎ 704/387–2011 or 800/438–2093), **Sugar Mountain** (Box 369, Banner Elk 28604, ☎ 704/898–4521), and **Hawksnest Golf and Ski Resort** (1800 Skyland Dr., Seven Devils, 28604, ☎ 704/963–6561 or 800/822–4295). For ski conditions, call 800/962–2322. Cross-country skiing is offered at **Moses H. Cone Park** and at **Linville Falls** on the Blue Ridge Parkway (☎ 704/295–7591), and **Roan Mountain** (☎ 615/772–3303). Tours and equipment are available from **High Country Ski Shop** in Pineola (☎ 704/733–2008).

Dining and Lodging

Dining

Dining choices in Asheville are many: upscale gourmet restaurants, middle-of-the-road country fare, and fast-food eateries. In the past 30 years, High Country towns outside Asheville have seen a tremendous increase in restaurants. Fresh mountain trout, as well as such game meats as pheasant and venison, are regional specialties. Beer, wine, and liquor by the drink are permitted in Blowing Rock, Banner, Elk, and Beech Mountain; beer and wine only in Boone. Dress is usually casual.

CATEGORY	COST*
$$$$	over $25
$$$	$15–$25
$$	$8–$15
$	under $8

per person for a three-course meal, excluding drinks, service, and 6% sales tax

Lodging

Lodging options range from posh resorts to mountain cabins, country inns, and economy chain motels. There's a bed for virtually every pocketbook.

CATEGORY	COST*
$$$$	over $100
$$$	$60–$100
$$	$30–$60
$	under $30

All prices are for a standard double room, excluding 8% tax

Asheville

DINING

$$$$ Market Place on Wall Street. Nouvelle cuisine is served in a relaxed atmosphere. Vegetables and herbs are regionally grown, and bread, pasta, and pastries are made on the premises. The Grill and Patio, a new addition, provides a lower-cost dining alternative, specializing in American and ethnic dishes. ✕ 20 Wall St., ☎ 704/252–4162. Reservations advised. AE, DC, MC, V. No lunch. Closed Sun.

$$ Blue Moon Bakery. Chris and Margaret Kobler offer a variety of pastries and breads made on site, as well as sandwiches and salads for lunch, at their European-style bakery. ✕ 60 Biltmore Ave., ☎ 704/252–6063. No reservations. MC, V.

$$ West Side Grill. Have a country-style meal of meatloaf, turkey, roast beef, or baked chicken, with all the trimmings, at this '50s-style diner. Salads and vegetarian fare are also offered. ✕ 1190 Patton Ave., ☎ 704/252–9605. No reservations. AE, MC, V.

$$ Windmill European Grill/Il Pescatore. As the name implies, the menu is international—this cool, dark, and cozy cellar restaurant even serves Asian dishes. There's also an extensive wine list. ✕ 85 Tunnel Rd., ☎ 704/253–5285. Reservations advised. AE, MC, V. No lunch Tues.–Sat.

DINING AND LODGING

$$$$ **Richmond Hill Inn.** Once a private residence, this elegant Victorian man-
★ sion is on the National Register of Historic Places. Rooms in the mansion feature canopy beds, Victorian sofas and other antiques, while the
more modern cottages have contemporary pine poster beds. Gabrielle's
(reservations advised, jacket required), named for the former mistress
of the house—wife of congressman and ambassador Richmond Pear-
son—is known for innovative cuisine such as grilled medallions of antelope with wild boar sausage; the restaurant is only open to the public
for dinner and Sunday brunch. ☎ *87 Richmond Hill Dr., 28806,* ☎
704/252–7313 or 800/545–9238, FAX *704/252–8726. 12 rooms, 9 cottages. Restaurant, croquet, meeting rooms. AE, MC, V.*

LODGING

$$$$ **Grove Park Inn.** This is Asheville's premier resort, and it's just as beau-
★ tiful and exciting as it was the day it opened in 1913. The guest list
has included Henry Ford, Thomas Edison, Harvey Firestone, and Warren G. Harding. Novelist F. Scott Fitzgerald stayed here while his wife,
Zelda, was in a nearby sanitarium. In the past five years the hotel has
been completely renovated. The two newer wings are in keeping with
the original design. ☎ *290 Macon Ave., 28804,* ☎ *704/252–2711 or
800/438–5800,* FAX *704/253–7053 (guests) or 704/252–6102 (reservations). 486 rooms, 24 suites. 4 restaurants, 2 pools, sauna, hot tub,
18-hole golf course, 12 tennis courts, health club, racquetball, children's
programs, meeting rooms, airport shuttle. AE, D, DC, MC, V.*

$$$$ **Haywood Park Hotel.** Imagine yourself the star in "Are You Being
Served?" at this downtown contemporary hotel that was once a department store. Twenty-Three Page, the hotel's elegant restaurant,
serves seafood and game, and a free Continental breakfast is delivered
to your room. A shopping galleria adjoins the property. ☎ *One Battery Park Ave., 28801,* ☎ *704/252–2522 or 800/228–2522,* FAX
*704/253–0481. 33 rooms, some with refrigerator and whirlpool bath.
2 restaurants, sauna, exercise room. AE, D, DC, MC, V.*

$$$ **Quality Inn Biltmore.** Built on the grounds of the old Biltmore Dairy,
this hotel is especially convenient for Biltmore Estate visitors. It is at-
tached to the Biltmore Dairy Bar, a popular restaurant that offers
sandwiches and ice cream, and adjacent to the Criterion Grill, a full-
service restaurant and lounge. ☎ *115 Hendersonville Rd., 28803,* ☎
704/274–1800 or 800/221–2222, FAX *704/274–5960. 160 rooms.
Pool, meeting rooms. AE, D, DC, MC, V.*

$$–$$$ **Cedar Crest Victorian Inn.** This beautiful cottage was constructed by
Biltmore craftsmen as a private residence around the turn of the cen-
tury. Lovingly restored as a bed-and-breakfast inn, it's filled with Vic-
torian antiques. Guests are treated to afternoon tea; evening coffee or
chocolate; and a breakfast of fruit, pastry, and coffee. ☎ *674 Biltmore
Ave., 28803,* ☎ *704/252–1389 or 800/252–0310,* FAX *704/252–7667.
13 rooms. AE, MC, V.*

$$–$$$ **Hampton Inn.** Guests can swim in the enclosed pool and then relax be-
side the fire in the lobby at this economy motel off I–26 that's conve-
nient to downtown. Some guest rooms have whirlpool baths. ☎ *One
Rocky Ridge Rd., 28806,* ☎ *704/667–2022 or 800/426–7866,* FAX
*704/665–9680. 121 rooms. Pool, sauna, exercise room, airport shut-
tle. AE, D, DC, MC, V.*

Banner Elk

DINING

$$$ Heidi's Swiss Inn. Authentic Swiss-German cuisine is served up at this unique mountain farmhouse-turned-restaurant. ✗ *Rte. 184,* ☎ *704/898–5020. Reservations required. D, MC, V. No lunch. Closed Sun.–Mon.*

$$$ Stonewalls. This contemporary rustic restaurant enjoys one of the best views of Beech Mountain. Fare includes steak, prime rib, fresh seafood, chicken, and homemade desserts. ✗ *Hwy. 194,* ☎ *704/898–5550. No reservations. AE, D, MC, V. No lunch.*

LODGING

$$$ Beech Alpen Inn. Guests have a view of the slopes or the Blue Ridge Mountains at this friendly country inn. Some rooms have fireplaces. A Continental breakfast is included in the rate. ▨ *700 Beech Mountain Pkwy., Banner Elk 28604,* ☎ *704/387–2252. 25 rooms. AE, MC, V.*

Blowing Rock

DINING AND LODGING

$$$$ Hound Ears Club. This Alpine inn, overlooking Grandfather Mountain and a lush golf course, offers comfortable, well-kept rooms dressed in Waverly print fabrics. From April through October, the room rate includes breakfast and dinner. ▨ *Off NC 105, 6 mi from Boone; Box 188, 28605,* ☎ *704/963–4321,* ⬛FAX *704/963–8030. 29 rooms. Restaurant, pool, 18-hole golf course, tennis court. AE, MC, V.*

$$$–$$$$ Chetola Resort. This small resort of about 70 acres grew out of a turn-of-the-century stone-and-wood lodge that overlooks Chetola Lake. The original building now houses the resort's restaurant and meeting rooms and is adjacent to the 1988 lodge, which contains the accommodations. The best rooms have balconies facing the lake, and there are whirlpools in the suites. The property adjoins Moses Cone H. Park, part of the Blue Ridge Parkway system, with hiking trails and riding facilities. ▨ *Box 17, 28605,* ☎ *704/295–9301 or 800/243–8652,* ⬛FAX *704/295–5529. 37 rooms, 5 suites. Restaurant, indoor pool, hot tub, sauna, 2 tennis courts, exercise room, hiking, racquetball, boating, meeting rooms. AE, D, MC, V.*

$$$ Green Park Inn. This 100-year-plus Victorian charmer on the eastern continental divide offers spacious rooms, wide porches with rocking chairs, and large public rooms decorated in greens and maroons. The bilevel restaurant has won high praise for its French-inspired cuisine and extensive walk-through wine cellar. ▨ *U.S. 321, Box 7, 28605,* ☎ ⬛FAX *704/295–3141 or 800/852–2462. 85 rooms. Pool, 18-hole golf course, 4 tennis courts, meeting rooms. AE, D, MC, V.*

Boone

DINING

$$ Mike's Inland Seafood. Calabash-style (lightly battered and fried) or broiled, the seafood here couldn't taste better if it were served at the ocean. (There's another one in Banner Elk.) ✗ *U.S. 321, Boone,* ☎ *704/262–5605. Reservations accepted. AE, DC, MC, V. Closed Mon.*

$$ Shadrack's. Barbecue and seafood are featured at this all-you-can-eat buffet. Patrons also love the live music and square dancing. This is a fun place for a family meal. ✗ *1980 Blowing Rock Rd.,* ☎ *704/264–1737. Reservations advised. D, MC, V.* ◷ *Fri.–Sat. dinner only, Thurs.–Sat. dinner during summer.*

DINING AND LODGING

$$–$$$ **Smoketree Lodge.** Enjoy grand views of Grandfather Mountain, indoor swimming, and great food at this mountain inn near the ski slopes with fully equipped efficiencies. ☎ *Hwy. 105, Box 3407, 28607,* ☎ *704/963–6505 or 800/843–5581 in NC,* FAX *704/963–7815. 40 units. Restaurant, picnic area, indoor pool, hot tub, sauna, exercise room, recreation room, coin laundry. AE, D, MC, V.*

$$ **Broyhill Inn.** Though primarily a conference center, this contemporary hotel on the ASU campus is attractive to individual travelers who enjoy a university atmosphere. The dining room offers a great view of the mountains and hearty Southern cuisine. ☎ *775 Bodenheimer Dr., 28607,* ☎ *704/262–2204 or 800/951–6048,* FAX *704/262–2946. 76 rooms, 7 suites. Restaurant, meeting rooms. AE, MC, V.*

Linville

DINING AND LODGING

$$$$ **Eseeola Lodge and Restaurant.** Built in the 1880s, this lodge is the cornerstone of Linville. Rich chestnut paneling and stonework grace the interior rooms. ☎ *U.S. 221, 28646,* ☎ *704/733–4311,* FAX *704/733–3227. 28 rooms. Restaurant, lounge, pool, 18-hole golf course, 8 tennis courts. MC, V. Closed Labor Day–May.*

Little Switzerland

DINING AND LODGING

$$$–$$$$ **Switzerland Inn and Chalet Restaurant.** This Swiss-style lodge overlooking the mountains offers lodge rooms, parlor-bedroom suites, and a lovely honeymoon cottage with a fireplace. A full breakfast served in the restaurant is included in the room rate. The prime rib and seafood buffet served each Friday night is a big draw. ☎ *MM 334, off Blue Ridge Pkwy., Box 399, 28749,* ☎ *704/765–2153 or 800/654–4026,* FAX *704/765–0049. 66 rooms. Pool, lounge, 2 tennis courts, shuffleboard, 6 shops. AE, D, MC, V. Closed Nov.–Apr. Dining reservations accepted for 5 or more.*

Valle Crucis

DINING AND LODGING

$$$$ **Mast Farm Inn.** You can turn back the clock and still enjoy modern amenities at this charming pastoral inn. Guests have a choice of rooms in the farmhouse or in the log out-buildings. Breakfast and dinner are included in the rate. ☎ *Box 704, 28691,* ☎ *704/963–5857,* FAX *704/963–6404. 12 rooms. Closed early Mar.–late Apr., Dec., and weekdays in Nov. MC, V.*

North Carolina High Country Essentials

Arriving and Departing, Getting Around

BY BUS

Greyhound Lines (☎ 704/253–5353 or 800/231–2222) serves Asheville.

BY CAR

I–40 runs east and west through Asheville. I–26 runs from Charleston, SC, to Asheville. I–240 forms a perimeter around the city. U.S. 23–19A is a major north and west route. The Blue Ridge Parkway runs northeast from Great Smoky Mountains National Park to Shenandoah National Park in Virginia. U.S. 221 runs north from Little Switzerland to the Virginia border through Blowing Rock and Boone and intersects I–40 at Marion. U.S. 321 intersects I–40 at Hickory and heads to Blowing Rock/Boone.

BY PLANE

Asheville Regional Airport (☎ 704/684–2226) is served by American Eagle, Atlantic Southeast Airlines, ComAir, Delta, and USAir. USAir Express (☎ 800/428–4322) serves the **Hickory Airport,** about 40 miles from Blowing Rock.

Guided Tours

Travel Professionals, Inc. (☎ 704/298–3438), **Western Carolina Tours** (☎ 704/254–4603), and **Young Transportation** (☎ 704/258–0084 or 800/622–5444) provide group tours of Asheville.

A brochure entitled **"The Asheville Urban Trail"** (available at the Downtown Welcome Center and many other locations) provides a self-guided walking tour. **Tour Services of Historic Asheville** (☎ 704/255–1093) conducts 2-hour walking tours of downtown, March–December; tours leave from Pack Place. The **Preservation Society of Asheville** has produced a walking tour cassette ($10), available at Pack Place.

Important Addresses and Numbers

EMERGENCIES

Dial 911 for **police** and **ambulance,** or head to **Watauga Medical Center** (☎ 704/262–4100) in Boone or **Cannon Memorial Hospital** (☎ 704/898–5111) in Banner Elk for emergency medical attention.

RADIO STATIONS

AM: WZQR 1350, country; WFGW 1010, Christian; WSKY 1230, talk. **FM:** WCQS 88.1, National Public Radio; WSPA 98.9, easy listening; WMIT 106.9, Christian; WKSF 99.9, country.

VISITOR INFORMATION

The **Visitor Information Center** (151 Haywood St., Asheville 28801, ☎ 704/258–6100) and the **Asheville Travel and Tourism Office** (Box 1010, Asheville 28802, ☎ 800/257–1300). The **Downtown Welcome Center** (14 Battery Park, Asheville, ☎ 704/255–1093) can answer questions and provide maps. **North Carolina High Country Host** (1701 Blowing Rock Rd., Boone 28607, ☎ 704/264–1299 or 800/438–7500).

7 South Carolina

South Carolina's scenic Low Country shoreline is punctuated by the lively port city of Charleston, decked out with fine museums, and the recreational resorts of Myrtle Beach and Hilton Head at each end of the coast. The state capital of Columbia is set in the fertile interior of the state, which stretches toward the Blue Ridge Mountains. Also to the west are the rolling fields of Thoroughbred country and Upcountry South Carolina, at the northwestern tip of the state, noted for incredible mountain scenery and whitewater rafting.

By Edgar and
Patricia
Cheatham

Updated by
Patricia
Cheatham

FROM ITS LOW COUNTRY SHORELINE, with wide sand beaches, spacious bays, and forests of palmettos and moss-strewn live oaks, South Carolina extends into an undulating interior region rich with fertile farmlands, then reaches toward the Blue Ridge Mountains, studded with scenic lakes, forests, and wilderness hideaways. What this smallest of Southern states lacks in land area it makes up for in diversity.

The historic port city of Charleston, lovingly preserved, links past with present. Many of its treasured double-galleried antebellum homes are now authentically furnished house museums. Culturally vibrant, the city nurtures theater, dance, music, and visual arts, showcased each spring during the internationally acclaimed Spoleto Festival USA.

Myrtle Beach is the hub of the Grand Strand, a 60-mile stretch of wide golden-sand beaches and recreational activities (especially golf, a top attraction throughout the state). To the south, tasteful, low-key Hilton Head—a sea island tucked between the Intracoastal Waterway and the ocean and divided into several sophisticated, self-contained resorts—also offers beautiful beaches and wonderful golf and tennis. Nearby is the port city of Beaufort (pronounced *Bew*fort), where the most rewarding activity is wandering the lovely streets dotted with preserved 18th-century homes, live oaks, and palmettos.

Columbia, the state capital, is a lively (and, of course, historic) city cleaved by a rushing river. In addition to several museums and a good minor-league baseball team, the city has one of the country's top zoos. It is also home to the State Museum and the fine new Koger Center for Performing Arts. Nearby lakes and state parks offer abundant outdoor recreation and first-rate fishing.

Thoroughbred Country, centered around the town of Aiken, is a peaceful area of rolling pastures where top race horses are trained. It is also notable for magnificent mansions built by wealthy Northerners who vacationed here at the turn of the century. Upcountry South Carolina, at the northwestern tip of the state, is less visited than the rest of the state but well repays time spent there with dramatic mountain scenery, excellent hiking, and challenging white-water rafting. Scattered along SC 11 are premier parks, some of which offer luxurious accommodations.

Since 1670, when the British established the first permanent European settlement at Charleston, the history of the Palmetto State has been characterized by periods of great prosperity contrasted with eras of dismal depression. This vibrant past is preserved in cherished traditions and an enduring belief in family, which give resonance to the optimism and vitality of today's South Carolina.

CHARLESTON

At first glimpse, Charleston resembles an 18th-century etching come to life. Its low-profile skyline is punctuated with the spires and steeples of 181 churches, representing 25 denominations (Charleston was known for its religious freedom). Parts of the city appear stopped in time because block after block of old downtown structures have been preserved and restored for both residential and commercial use. Charleston has survived three centuries of epidemics, earthquakes, fires, and hurricanes, and it is today one of the South's best-preserved cities.

Along the Battery, on the point of a narrow peninsula bounded by the Ashley and Cooper rivers, handsome mansions in the "Charleston style," surrounded by gardens, face the harbor. Their distinctive look is reminiscent of the West Indies, and for good reason. Before coming to the Carolinas in the late 17th century, many early British colonists had first settled on Barbados and other Caribbean islands where against the warm and humid climate they'd built houses with high ceilings and broad piazzas at each level, to catch the sea breezes. In Charleston, they adapted these designs for other practical reasons. One new type—narrow two- to four-story houses (called single houses) built at right angles to the street—emerged partly because buildings were taxed according to frontage length.

Each year, from mid-March to mid-April, the Historic Charleston Foundation's Festival of Homes and Gardens conducts tours of private homes, gardens, and churches, and celebrates with symphony galas in stately drawing rooms, plantation oyster roasts, and candlelight tours. Each year in May and June, the renowned Spoleto Festival USA and Piccolo Spoleto take place, when hundreds of local and international artists, musicians, and other performers fill the city with sound and spectacle.

Exploring

Numbers in the margin correspond to points of interest on the Charleston map.

If you have just a day to spend in Charleston, you might begin with a carriage tour for the tidbits of history and humor that the driver-guides provide as they take you through the main streets of the historic district. This is the best way to decide where to go on your own. Next, browse through the shops of the Old Market area, where most of the carriage tours begin and end. After that, walk south along East Bay Street, past Rainbow Row (a row of pastel-painted houses near Tradd Street), or along any side streets on your way to your choice of the area's four house museums. Spend the rest of the day wandering the cool, palmetto-shaded streets, discovering all the little surprises that reveal themselves only to those who seek them out.

If you have more time (and you really should), expand your itinerary by adding more sights within the same area; by adding an excursion to the Shops at Charleston Place or along King Street; by including the Marion Square area, which has an excellent art museum and a house museum; or by adding trips to magnificent plantations and gardens west of the Ashley River or to major historic sites east of the Cooper. There are also boat excursions and some very nice beaches.

❶ For a good overview of the city before you begin touring, drop by the **Visitor Information Center,** where there's parking (free for two hours; 50¢ per hour thereafter). Take time to see *Forever Charleston,* a multimedia presentation on the city. *375 Meeting St., ☎ 803/853–8000.* ☛ *$2.50 adults, $2 senior citizens, $1 children 6–12, under 6 free. Shown daily 9–5 on the ½ hour.* ☉ *Mar.–Oct., daily 8:30–5:30; Nov.–Feb., daily 8:30–5.*

The Historic District

★ ❷ On Meeting Street, housed in a $6 million contemporary complex, is the oldest city museum in the United States. The **Charleston Museum,**

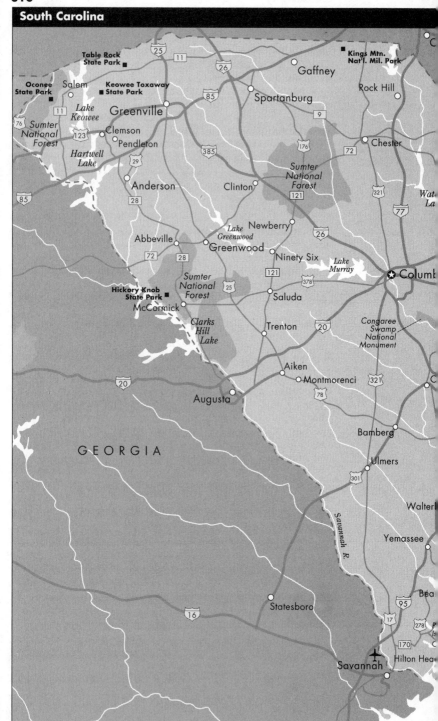

C

25 11
26
Gaffney
■ Kings Mtn.
Nat'l. Mil. Park

Table Rock
State Park ■

85
Spartanburg
Rock Hill

Oconee
State Park ■
Salem
Keowee Toxaway
■ State Park

9

11
Lake
Keowee
Greenville
176
72
Chester

76
Sumter
National
Forest
123
Clemson
Pendleton
385
29
321
Wat
La

Hartwell
Lake

Sumter
National
Forest
121
77

85
Anderson
28
Clinton

Lake
Greenwood
Newberry
26

Abbeville
Greenwood
Ninety Six
Lake
Murray
Columb

72
28
121
378

Sumter
National
Forest
25
Saluda

Hickory Knob
State Park ■
McCormick
Trenton
20
Congaree
Swamp
National
Monument

Clarks
Hill
Lake
Aiken
Montmorenci
321
C

20
78

Augusta

GEORGIA
Bamberg

Ulmers

301
Walter

Savannah R.
Yemassee

Statesboro
Bea
95

16
17
278

170
C

Savannah
Hilton Hea

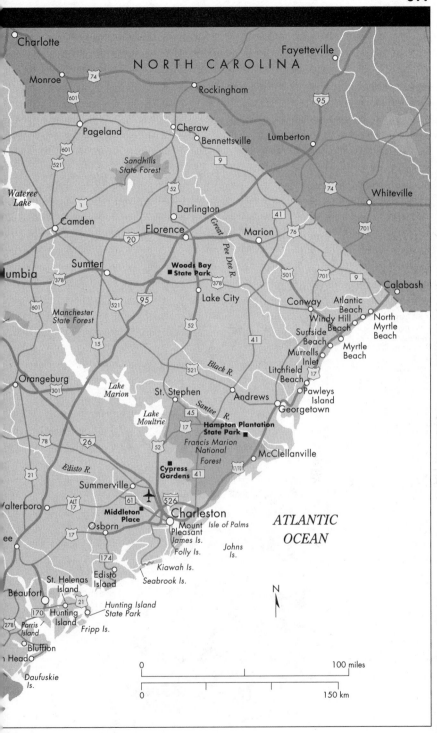

Charlotte

Fayetteville

NORTH CAROLINA

Monroe

601

74

Rockingham

95

Pageland

601

Cheraw

Bennettsville

Lumberton

601

521

Sandhills
State Forest

9

52

Whiteville

74

701

Wateree
Lake

1

Darlington

41

76

501

Camden

Florence

Marion

20

701

9

Calabash

Sumter

umbia

378

601

521

95

Woods Bay
State Park

378

Lake City

Manchester
State Forest

15

52

41

Conway

Atlantic
Beach

Windy Hill
Beach

North
Myrtle
Beach

Surfside
Beach

Myrtle
Beach

521

Black R.

Murrells
Inlet

Orangeburg

301

Lake
Marion

St. Stephen

Andrews

Litchfield
Beach

17

Pawleys
Island

Georgetown

Lake
Moultrie

Santee R.

45

17

Hampton Plantation
State Park

78

26

Francis Marion
National
Forest

52

McClellanville

17/701

21

Edisto R.

Cypress
Gardens

41

Summerville

ALT
17

61

526

alterboro

Middleton
Place

ATLANTIC
OCEAN

Osborn

17

Charleston

Mount
Pleasant

Isle of Palms

174

James Is.

Johns
Is.

Folly Is.

ee

St. Helenas
Island

Edisto
Island

Kiawah Is.

Seabrook Is.

21

Beaufort

170

Hunting
Island

21

Hunting Island
State Park

N

278

Parris
Island

Fripp Is.

Bluffton

n Head

Daufuskie
Is.

0   100 miles

0   150 km

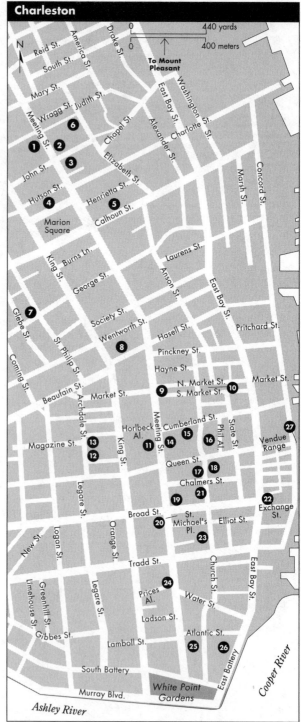

Charleston

founded in 1773, is especially strong on South Carolina decorative arts. The 500,000 items in the collection—in addition to Charleston silver, fashions, toys, snuff boxes, etc.—include objects relating to natural history, archaeology, and ornithology. Three historic homes—the Joseph Manigault Mansion *(see below)*, the Aiken–Rhett House *(see below)*, and the Heyward–Washington House *(see below)*—are part of the museum. *360 Meeting St.,* ☎ *803/722–2996.* ☛ *$6 adults, $3 children 3–12, under 3 free.* ☛ *Combination ticket for museum and houses $15; for just the three houses, $10.* ☉ *Mon.–Sat. 9–5, Sun. 1–5.*

❸ Across John Street is one of Charleston's fine house museums, and a National Historic Landmark, the **Joseph Manigault Mansion.** An outstanding example of Adam-style architecture, it was designed by Charleston architect Gabriel Manigault in 1803 and is noted for its carved-wood mantels and elaborate plasterwork. Furnishings are British, French, and Charleston antiques, including rare tricolor Wedgwood pieces. *350 Meeting St.,* ☎ *803/723–2926.* ☛ *$6 adults, $3 children 3–12, under 3 free (for combination ticket see Charleston Museum, above).* ☉ *Mon.–Sat. 10–5, Sun. 1–5.*

❹ Walk down Meeting Street to Marion Square. Facing the square is the **Old Citadel Building,** built in 1822 to house state troops and arms. Here began the famed South Carolina Military College—the Citadel—now on the Ashley River.

❺ Walk down a block, cross Meeting, and turn east to 110 Calhoun Street to visit **Emanuel African Methodist Episcopal Church,** home of the South's oldest AME congregation, which had its beginnings in 1818. The church was closed in 1822 when authorities learned that Denmark Vesey used the sanctuary to plan his slave insurrection. It was reopened in 1865 at the present site. *Call 803/722–2561 in advance for tour.* ☉ *Daily 9–4.*

❻ Walk north along Elizabeth Street to see the **Aiken–Rhett House,** the newest addition to the Charleston Museum complex. The stately 1819 mansion, residence of South Carolina Governor William Aiken Jr. from 1833–87, was headquarters of Confederate General P.G.T. Beauregard during his 1864 Civil War defense of Charleston. Original wallpapers, paint colors, and some furnishings are displayed. House, kitchen, slave quarters, stable, and outbuildings are maintained much as they were when the Aiken and Rhett families lived there. *48 Elizabeth St.,* ☎ *803/723–1159.* ☛ *$6 adults, $3 children 3–12, under 3 free (for combination ticket, see Charleston Museum, above).* ☉ *Mon.–Sat. 10–5, Sun. 1–5.*

❼ If you've left your car at the visitor center, return now to retrieve it. From here proceed to the lovely **College of Charleston** (founded in 1770), whose graceful main building (1828) was designed by Philadelphia architect William Strickland. The large campus is located at the corner of George and St. Philip's streets. Within the college is the **Avery Research Center for African-American History and Culture,** which traces the heritage of South Carolina Low Country African-Americans. *125 Bull St.,* ☎ *803/727–2009.* ☛ *Free.* ☉ *Reading room/archives weekdays 1–4:30 or by appointment. Group tours weekdays 2–4 or by appointment.*

❽ Next you can make a shopping tour of King Street, or go directly to the market area and head for one of the many parking garages. Now is the time for a carriage tour, many of which leave from here *(see* Guided Tours, *below).* Our tour picks up again at **Congregation Beth Elohim** (90 Hasell St.), considered one of the nation's finest examples of Greek

Revival architecture. It was constructed in 1840 to replace an earlier temple—the birthplace of American Reform Judaism in 1824—that was destroyed by fire. ☏ *803/723–1090.* ⊙ *Weekdays 10–noon.*

❾ Follow Meeting Street south to Market Street, and at the intersection on the left you'll see **Market Hall,** a National Historic Landmark built in 1841 and modeled after the Temple of Nike in Athens. Here you'll find the **Confederate Museum** (88 Meeting St., ☏ 803/723–1541), where the Daughters of the Confederacy preserve and display flags, uniforms, swords, and other memorabilia. The museum is currently closed for renovation and may remain so through 1996; however, costumed guides sometimes stand outside and describe the facility for visitors.

❿ Between Market Hall and East Bay Street is **Old City Market,** a series of low sheds that once housed produce and fish markets. The area now has restaurants and shops, along with vegetable and fruit vendors and local "basket ladies" busy weaving and selling distinctive sweet-grass, pine-straw, and palmetto-leaf baskets—a craft inherited from their West African ancestors. *Usually* ⊙ *Daily 9 AM–sunset.*

TIME OUT This is a great area for some serious time out. Pick up batches of Charleston's famed benne (sesame) seed wafers at **Olde Colony Bakery** (280 King St., ☏ 803/722–2147). Choose from 12 gourmet food stands in the **Gourmetisserie** (☏ 803/722–4455) in the Market Square shopping complex across South Market Street. Or indulge the urge to munch on oysters on the half-shell, steamed mussels, and clams at **A.W. Shucks** (☏ 803/723–1151) in nearby State Street Market.

Across the street is the **Omni Hotel at Charleston Place** (130 Market St.). You might wander over to peer at the lobby or have cocktails or tea in the intimate Lobby Lounge. The city's only world-class hotel is flanked by a four-story complex of upscale boutiques and specialty shops (*see* Shopping, *below*).

⓫ Heading south on Meeting Street, see the **Gibbes Museum of Art.** Its collection of American art includes notable 18th- and 19th-century portraits of Carolinians and an outstanding group of more than 400 miniature portraits. Don't miss the miniature rooms—intricately detailed with fabrics and furnishings and nicely displayed in shadow boxes inset in dark-paneled walls—or the Tiffany-style stained-glass dome in the rotunda. *135 Meeting St.,* ☏ *803/722–2706.* ☛ *$5 adults, $4 senior citizens, $3 children 6–18, children under 6 free.* ⊙ *Tues.–Sat. 10–5, Sun. and Mon. 1–5.*

⓬ For a detour, head south on Meeting Street to Queen Street, then west to Archdale. At no. 8 is the **Unitarian Church,** begun in 1772 and completed in 1787. The building was remodeled in the mid-19th century after plans inspired by the Chapel of Henry VII in Westminster Abbey, including the addition of a Gothic fan-tracery ceiling. *8 Archdale St.,* ☏ *803/723–4617 (weekdays 8:30–2:30). Call ahead for visiting hours.*

⓭ At the corner of Clifford and Archdale streets is the Greek Revival **St. John's Lutheran Church,** built in 1817 for a congregation that celebrated its 250th anniversary in 1992. Notice the fine craftsmanship in the delicate wrought-iron gates and fence. Organ aficionados may be interested in the 1823 Thomas Hall organ case. *5 Clifford St.,* ☏ *803/723–2426.* ⊙ *Weekdays 9:30–3 with advance arrangement.*

⓮ Back at Meeting Street, across from the Gibbes is the unusual Romanesque **Circular Congregational Church,** its corners rounded off, it's said, so the devil would have no place to hide. The church is simple but pretty with a beamed, vaulted ceiling. *150 Meeting St., ☎ 803/577–6400. Tours given Apr.–Oct., weekdays 9–1.*

⑮ On Cumberland Street, one of Charleston's few remaining cobblestone thoroughfares, is the **Old Powder Magazine,** built in 1713, used during the Revolutionary War, and now a museum with costumes, furniture, armor, and other artifacts from 18th-century Charleston. Because the Historic Charleston Foundation is currently restoring the building, visitors should call ahead for information on tours, admission, and opening hours. *79 Cumberland St., ☎ 803/723–1623. ☉ By appointment.*

⑯ Around the corner on Church Street you come to the graceful late-Georgian **St. Philip's Episcopal Church,** the second on the site, built in 1838 and restored in 1994. In its serene graveyard are buried some legendary native sons, including statesman John C. Calhoun and DuBose Heyward, the author of *Porgy. 146 Church St., ☎ 803/722–7734. ☉ By appointment.*

⑰ The **Dock Street Theatre,** across Queen Street, was built on the site of one of the nation's first playhouses. It combines the reconstructed early Georgian playhouse and the preserved Old Planter's Hotel (circa 1809). *135 Church St., ☎ 803/720–3968. ☛ Free tours; call ahead to check ticket prices for performances. ☉ Weekdays 10–4.*

⑱ Across the street is the Gothic-style **French Protestant (Huguenot) Church,** the only one in the country still using the original Huguenot liturgy, which can be heard in a special service held each spring. *110 Church St., ☎ 803/722–4385. Donations accepted. ☉ Weekdays 10–12:30 and 2–4.*

The intersection of Meeting and Broad streets is known as the Four Corners of Law, representing federal, state, city, and religious jurisdiction.
⑲ In the graceful 1801 **City Hall,** on the northeast corner, the second-floor Council Chamber has interesting historical displays and fine portraits, including John Trumbull's 1791 portrait of George Washington and Samuel F. B. Morse's likeness of James Monroe. On the southwest corner, the Old U.S. Post Office building now houses a museum depicting the area's postal history. *80 Broad St., ☎ 803/577–6970. ☛ Free. ☉ Weekdays 10–5.*

⑳ On the last corner is **St. Michael's Episcopal Church,** modeled after London's St. Martin's-in-the-Fields. Completed in 1761, this is Charleston's oldest surviving church. Its steeple clock and bells were imported from England in 1764. *14 St. Michael's Alley, ☎ 803/723–0603. ☉ Weekdays 9–5, Sat. 9–noon.*

From the Four Corners, head east down Broad Street to Church Street.
㉑ The **American Military Museum** displays hundreds of uniforms and artifacts from all branches of service, dating from the Revolutionary War. *40 Pinckney St., ☎ 803/723–9620. ☛ $2 adults, $1 children under 12, uniformed military personnel free. ☉ Mon.–Sat. 10–6, Sun. 1–6.*

㉒ At the corner of East Bay Street stands the **Old Exchange Building/Provost Dungeon,** originally a customs house. The dungeon was used by the British during the Revolutionary War; today, a tableau of lifelike manikins recalls this era. *122 East Bay St., ☎ 803/792–5020. ☛ $4 adults, $3.50 senior citizens, $2.50 children 7–12, children under 7 free.. ☉ Daily 9–5.*

Return to Church Street and continue south to the neighborhood known as Cabbage Row, the home of Dubose Heyward and an area central to Charleston's African-American history. At 87 Church Street

㉓ is the **Heyward–Washington House,** built in 1772 by rice king Daniel Heyward, which was also the setting for Dubose Heyward's *Porgy.* President George Washington stayed here during his 1791 visit. The mansion is full of fine period furnishings by such local craftsmen as Thomas Elfe, and its restored 18th-century kitchen is the only one in Charleston open to visitors. ☎ *803/722–0354.* ☛ *$6 adults, $3 children 3–12, under 3 free (for combination ticket, see Charleston Museum, above.)* ⊙ *Mon.–Sat. 10–5, Sun. 1–5.*

★ ㉔ At 51 Meeting Street is the **Nathaniel Russell House,** headquarters of the Historic Charleston Foundation. Built in 1808, it is one of the nation's finest examples of Adams-style architecture. The interior is notable for its ornate detailing, its lavish period furnishings, and a "flying" circular staircase that spirals three stories with no apparent support. ☎ *803/724–8481.* ☛ *$6 adults, children under 7 free; combination ticket with the Edmonston–Alston House, $10.* ⊙ *Mon.–Sat. 10–5, Sun. 2–5.*

㉕ Continuing south, you'll come into an area where somewhat more lavish mansions reflect the wealth of a later era. The **Calhoun Mansion,** at 16 Meeting Street, is opulent by Charleston standards, an interesting example of Victorian taste. Built in 1876, it's notable for ornate plasterwork, fine wood moldings, and a 75-foot domed ceiling. ☎ *803/722–8205.* ☛ *$10 adults, $5 children 6–16, children under 6 free.* ⊙ *Thurs.–Sun. 10–4. Closed Jan.*

㉖ The imposing **Edmondston–Alston House,** with commanding views of Charleston Harbor, was built in 1825 in the late Federal style and transformed into a Greek Revival structure during the 1840s. It is tastefully furnished with antiques, portraits, Piranesi prints, silver, and fine china. *21 E. Battery,* ☎ *803/722–7171 or 803/556–6020.* ☛ *$6 adults, children under 7 free; combination ticket with Nathaniel Russell House, $10.* ⊙ *Tues.–Sat. 10–5, Sun.–Mon. 1:30–5.*

㉗ After all this serious sightseeing, relax in **White Point Gardens,** on Battery Point, facing the harbor, a tranquil spot shaded by palmettos and graceful oaks. Another option is **Waterfront Park,** on the Cooper River in the historic district. It offers beautiful river views, fountains, landscaped gardens, and a fishing pier. ⊙ *Daily 6 AM–midnight.*

East of the Cooper River

Across the Cooper River Bridges, via U.S. 17, is the town of **Mount Pleasant,** named not for anything in the area resembling so much as a hillock, but for a plantation in England from which a number of the area's settlers hailed. Here, along Shem Creek, where the local fishing fleet brings in the daily catch, seafood restaurants attract visitors and

★ locals alike. **Patriots Point,** the world's largest naval and maritime museum, and now home to the Medal of Honor Society, is also in Mount Pleasant. Berthed here are the aircraft carrier *Yorktown,* the World War II submarine *Clamagore,* the destroyer *Laffey,* the nuclear merchant ship *Savannah,* and the cutter *Ingham,* responsible for sinking a U-boat during World War II. Tours are offered in all vessels, the film *The Fighting Lady* is shown regularly aboard the *Yorktown,* and there is a Vietnam exhibit. *Foot of Cooper River Bridges,* ☎ *803/884–2727.* ☛ *$8 adults, $7 senior citizens and active military personnel, $4 children 6–12.* ⊙ *Labor Day–Mar., daily 9–6:30; Apr.–Labor Day, daily 9–7:30.*

★ Fort Sumter Tours' boats leave from the docks here and from Charleston's Municipal Marina for 2¼-hour cruises that include a stop at **Fort Sumter National Monument,** on a man-made island in the harbor. ☎

803/722–1691. Cost: $9 adults, $4.50 children 6–11, under 6 free. Tours leave from Municipal Marina daily at 9:30, noon, and 2:30. Tours leave from Patriots Point daily at 10:45 and 1:30; Apr.–Labor Day, there is an additional tour at 4 pm.

It was at Fort Sumter that the first shot of the Civil War was fired on April 12, 1861, when Confederate forces at Fort Johnson (now defunct) across the way opened fire. After a 34-hour bombardment Union forces surrendered, and Confederate troops occupied Sumter, which became a symbol of Southern resistance. The Confederacy held the fort—despite almost continual bombardment—for nearly four years, and when it was finally evacuated it was a heap of rubble. Today, National Park Service rangers conduct free guided tours of the restored structure, which includes a museum (☎ 803/883–3123; ☛ Free) with historical displays and dioramas.

Continuing north out of Mount Pleasant along U.S. 17, you'll find "basket ladies" at roadside stands. If you have the heart to bargain, you *may* be able to purchase the baskets at somewhat lower prices than in Charleston. SC 703 will take you to **Sullivan's Island** and **Fort Moultrie,** completed in 1809, the third fort on this site. Here Colonel William Moultrie's South Carolinians repelled a British assault in one of the first Patriot victories of the Revolutionary War. The interior has been restored. A film and slide show tell the history of the fort. *W. Middle St., Sullivan's Island,* ☎ *803/883–3123.* ☛ *Free.* ⊙ *Memorial Day–Labor Day, daily 9–6; Labor Day–Memorial Day, daily 9–5.*

Back on U.S. 17, about 8 miles out of Charleston, is the 1681 **Boone Hall Plantation,** approached via one of the South's most majestic avenues of oaks. The primary attraction is the grounds, with formal azalea and camellia gardens, as well as the original slave quarters—the only "slave street" still intact in the Southeast—and the cotton-gin house used in the made-for-television movies *North and South* and *Queen.* Visitors may also tour the first floor of the classic columned mansion, which was built in 1935 incorporating woodwork and flooring from the original house. ☎ *803/884–4371.* ☛ *$7.50 adults, $6 senior citizens, $3 children 6–12, children under 6 free.* ⊙ *Apr.–Labor Day, Mon.–Sat. 8:30–6:30, Sun. 1–5; Labor Day–Mar., Mon.–Sat. 9–5, Sun. 1–4.*

West of the Ashley River

★ Vestiges of the Old South—and Charleston's beginnings—beckon as you cross the Ashley River Bridge. Take SC 171 north to reach **Charles Towne Landing State Park,** commemorating the site of the original Charleston settlement, begun in 1670. There are a reconstructed village and fortifications, English park gardens with bicycle trails and walkways, and a replica 17th-century vessel moored in the creek. In the animal park species native to the region three centuries ago roam freely. Bicycle and kayak rentals and cassette and tram tours are available. *1500 Old Towne Rd.,* ☎ *803/852–4200.* ☛ *$5 adults, $2.50 senior citizens and children 6–14, children under 6 free.* ⊙ *Memorial Day–Labor Day, daily 9–6; Labor Day–Memorial Day, daily 9–5.*

★ Nine miles west of Charleston via the Ashley River Road (SC 61) is **Drayton Hall,** built between 1738 and 1742. A National Historic Landmark, it is considered the nation's finest example of unspoiled Georgian–Palladian architecture. The mansion is the only plantation house on the Ashley River to have survived the Civil War and serves as an invaluable lesson in history as well as in architecture. It has been left unfurnished to highlight the original plaster moldings, opulent hand-carved woodwork, and other ornamental details. *3380 Ashley River Rd.,* ☎ *803/766–0188.* ☛ *$7 adults, $4 children 6–18, children under 6 free. Guided tours Mar.–Oct., daily 10–4; Nov.–Feb., daily 10–3.*

A mile or so farther north on Ashley River Road (SC 61) is **Magnolia Plantation and Gardens.** The 50-acre informal garden, begun in 1685, has a huge collection of azaleas and camellias and was proclaimed the "most beautiful garden in the world" by John Galsworthy. You can ride a tram for an overall tour with three stops. Nature lovers may canoe through the 125-acre Waterfowl Refuge, explore the 30-acre **Audubon Swamp Garden** along boardwalks and bridges, or walk or bicycle over 500 acres of wildlife trails. Tours of the manor house, built during the Reconstruction period, depict plantation life. You can also see the petting zoo and a mini-horse ranch. ☎ *803/571–1266.* ☛ *$9 adults, $8 senior citizens, $7 children 13–19, $4 children 4–12 (house tour $4 extra; swamp tour $3 extra; tram tour $3 extra; combination tour also available).* ☉ *Daily 8–5:30.*

Middleton Place, 4 miles farther north on SC 61, has the nation's oldest landscaped gardens, dating from 1741. Design highlights of the magnificent gardens—ablaze with camellias, magnolias, azaleas, roses, and flowers of all seasons—are the floral *allées,* terraced lawns, and ornamental lakes. Much of the mansion was destroyed during the Civil War, but the south wing has been restored and houses impressive collections of silver, furniture, paintings, and historic documents. The stableyard is a living outdoor museum: here craftspeople, using authentic tools and equipment, demonstrate spinning, blacksmithing, and other domestic skills from the plantation era. Farm animals, peacocks, and other creatures roam freely. The Middleton Place restaurant serves distinctive Low Country specialties for lunch daily; a gift shop features local arts, crafts, and souvenirs. ☎ *803/556–6020 or 800/782–3608.* ☛ *$10 adults, $5 children 4–12; house tours $6 extra.* ☉ *Daily 9–5; house tours Tues.–Sun. 10–4:30, Mon. 1:30–4:30.*

On the banks of the Old Santee Canal in Moncks Corner is the new **Old Santee Canal State Park,** reached via I–26 and Highway 52. You can explore on foot or take a canoe. There's also an interpretive center. *Rembert C. Dennis Blvd., Moncks Corner,* ☎ *803/899–5200.* ☛ *$3 per car.* ☉ *Daily 9–5, spring and summer until 6.*

The picturesque town of **Summerville,** about 25 miles northwest of Charleston via I–26 (Exit 199), is a pleasant place for a drive or stroll. Built by wealthy planters as an escape from hot-weather malaria, it's a treasure trove of mid-19th-century and Victorian buildings—many of which are listed in the National Register of Historic Places—with colorful gardens of camellias, azaleas, and wisteria. Streets often curve around tall pines, since a local ordinance prohibits cutting them down in this "Flowertown in the Pines." This is a good place for a bit of antiquing in attractive shops. Stop by the **Summerville Chamber of Commerce** (106 E. Doty Ave., Box 670, 29483, ☎ 803/873–2931) to get oriented; they're open weekdays 8:30–12:30 and 1:30–5, Saturday 10–3.

About 24 miles north of Charleston via U.S. 52 is **Cypress Gardens,** a swamp garden created from what was once the freshwater reserve of the vast Dean Hall rice plantation. Explore the inky waters by boat, or walk along paths lined with moss-draped cypress trees, azaleas, camellias, daffodils, wisteria, and dogwood. *3030 Cypress Gardens Rd., Moncks Corner,* ☎ *803/553–0515.* ☛ *$6 adults, $5 senior citizens, $2 children 6–16 (May 1–Feb. 14, $1 less).* ☉ *Daily 9–5.*

What to See and Do with Children

American Military Museum (*see* The Historic District *in* Exploring Charleston, *above*).

Boat Ride to Fort Sumter (*see* East of the Cooper River *in* Exploring Charleston, *above*).

Charles Towne Landing State Park (*see* West of the Ashley River *in* Exploring Charleston, *above*). Birds, alligators, bison, pumas, bears, wolves, and many other animals roam in natural environments. Children's Days are held during the last two weeks of December.

Charleston Museum (*see* The Historic District *in* Exploring Charleston, *above*). The Discover Me Room, designed just for children, has computers and other hands-on exhibits.

Magnolia Plantation and Gardens has a petting zoo and mini-horse ranch (*see* West of the Ashley River *in* Exploring Charleston, *above*).

Middleton Place (*see* West of the Ashley River *in* Exploring Charleston, *above*).

Palmetto Islands County Park. This family-oriented nature park has a Big Toy playground, a two-acre pond, a canoe trail, an observation tower, marsh boardwalks, and a recently added "water island." Bicycles, pedal boats, and canoes can be rented in season. *On U.S. 17N, ½ mi past Snee Farm, turn left onto Long Point Rd.,* ☎ *803/884–0832.* ☛ *$1.* ☉ *Apr., Sept., and Oct., daily 10–6; May–Aug., daily 10–7; Nov.–Mar., daily 10–5.*

Shelling. Kiawah Island has excellent shelling. If you're not staying at the private resort, you can shell at Beachwalker Park, the public beach at the west end of the island. ☎ *803/762–2172. Parking fee: $3.* ☉ *June–Aug., daily 10–7; May and Sept., daily 10–6; Apr. and Oct., weekends 10–6.*

Off the Beaten Path

Angel Oak. Among the continent's oldest and largest oak trees, this 1,500-year-old giant has a 25½-foot circumference and a 151-foot limb spread. *From SC 700 turn left onto Bohicket Rd.; after about ½ mi, turn right at sign and follow dirt road,* ☎ *803/559–3496.* ☛ *Free.* ☉ *Daily 9–5.*

Francis Marion National Forest. About 40 miles north of Charleston via U.S. 52, this site comprises 250,000 acres of swamps, vast oaks and pines, and little lakes thought to have been formed by meteors— a good place for picnicking, camping, boating, and swimming (☎ 803/336–3248). At the park's **Rembert Dennis Wildlife Center** (off U.S. 52 in Bonneau, ☎ 803/825–3387), deer, wild turkey, and striped bass are reared and studied. Admission is free.

At Goose Creek, about 19 miles north of Charleston, is the remarkably well-preserved **St. James United Methodist Church,** built between 1708 and 1719. Not in use since 1808, it retains the original box pews, slave gallery, and pulpit. The British royal arms are still visible above the chancel. The sexton, who lives nearby, will open the church on request. *Off U.S. 78,* ☎ *803/553–3117. Donations accepted.* ☉ *Weekdays 9–noon.*

Shopping

Shopping Districts. Don't miss the colorful produce market in the three-block **Old City Market** at East Bay and Market streets and adjacent to it, the **open-air flea market,** with crafts, antiques, and memorabilia. The **Market** is a complex of specialty shops and restaurants.

Other such complexes in the area are the **Shops at Charleston Place** adjoining the Omni Hotel, **Rainbow Market** (in two interconnected 150-year-old buildings), **Market Square,** and **State Street Market.** Also, some of Charleston's oldest and finest shops are on **King Street.**

Antiques

King Street is the center. **Petterson Antiques** (201 King St., ☎ 803/723–5714) offers books, furniture, porcelain, and glass. **Livingston & Sons Antiques,** dealers in 18th- and 19th-century English and Continental furniture, clocks, and bric-a-brac, has a large shop west of the Ashley (2137 Savannah Hwy., ☎ 803/556–6162) and a smaller one at 163 King Street (☎ 803/723–9697). **Birlant & Co.** (191 King St., ☎ 803/722–3842) offers a fine selection of 18th- and 19th-century English antiques, as well as the famous Charleston Battery bench, identical to those on Charleston Green.

Art and Crafts

The **Birds I View Gallery** (119–A Church St., *n* 803/723–1276) sells bird paintings and prints by Anne Worsham Richardson. At **Birds & Ivy** (235 King St., ☎ 803/853–8534), which sells garden art and accessories of every type, there's a coffee shop in back where you can have a sandwich or a snack. **Charleston Crafts** (38 Queen St., ☎ 803/723–2938) has a fine selection of pottery, quilts, weavings, sculptures, and jewelry fashioned mostly by local artists. The **Elizabeth O'Neill Verner Studio & Museum** (79 Church St., ☎ 803/722–4246), in a 17th-century house, is now open to the public. Prints of Elizabeth O'Neill Verner's pastels and etchings are on sale at adjacent **Tradd Street Press** (38 Tradd St., ☎ 803/722–4246). The **Virginia Fouché Bolton Art Gallery** (127 Meeting St., ☎ 803/577–9351) sells original paintings and limited-edition lithographs of Charleston and Low Country scenes.

Gifts

Charleston Collections (233 King St., ☎ 803/722–7267; at the Straw Market, Kiawah Island Resort, ☎ 803/768–7487; Quadrangle Center, ☎ 803/556–8911) has Charleston chimes, prints, candies, T-shirts, and more. The **Charleston Catalog Company** (139 Market St., ☎ 803/722–6121) also offers merchandise with a Charleston motif. Charleston's and London's own **Ben Silver** (149 King St., ☎ 803/577–4556), premier purveyor of blazer buttons, has over 800 designs, including college and British regimental motifs. He also sells British neckties, embroidered polo shirts, and blazers.

Period Reproductions

Historic Charleston Reproductions (105 Broad St., ☎ 803/723–8292) has superb replicas of Charleston furniture and accessories, all authorized by the Historic Charleston Foundation. Royalties from sales contribute to restoration projects. At the **Old Charleston Joggling Board Co.** (652 King St., ☎ 803/723–4331), these Low Country oddities (on which people bounce) can be purchased.

Sports and the Outdoors

Beaches

The Charleston area's mild climate generally is conducive to swimming from April through October. This is definitely not a "swingles" area; all public and private beaches are family oriented, providing a choice of water sports, sunbathing, shelling, fishing, or a setting for quiet moonlight strolls.

The Charleston County Parks and Recreation Commission operates several public beach facilities. **Beachwalker Park** (☎ 803/762–2172) on the west end of Kiawah Island (which is otherwise a private resort) provides 300 feet of beach frontage, seasonal lifeguard service, rest rooms, outdoor showers, a picnic area, snack bar, and 150-car parking lot. ☛ *$3 per car (up to 8 passengers).* ☉ *June–Aug. daily 10–7; Apr. and Oct., weekends 10–6; May and Sept., daily 10–6.*

Folly Beach County Park (☎ 803/588–2426), located 12 miles from Charleston via U.S. 17 and SC 171 (Folly Rd.), has 4,000 feet of ocean frontage and 2,000 feet of river frontage. Lifeguards are on duty seasonally along a 600-foot section of the beach. Facilities include dressing areas, outdoor showers, rest rooms, picnicking areas, beach chairs, raft and shower rentals, and a 300-vehicle parking lot. Pelican Watch shelter is available year round for group picnics and day or night oyster roasts. ☛ *$3 per car (up to 8 passengers).* ☉ *Aug.–May and Sept.–Oct., daily 10–6; June–Aug., daily 10–7; Nov.–May, daily 10–5.*

Private resorts with extensive beaches and amenities include **Fairfield Ocean Ridge** (☎ 803/869–2561), on Edisto Island; **Kiawah Island** (☎ 903/768–2121 or 800/654–2924); **Seabrook Island** (☎ 803/768–1000 or 800/845–5531); and **Wild Dunes** (☎ 803/886–6000 or 800/845–8880), on the Isle of Palms.

Bicycling
The historic district is ideal for bicycling, and many city parks have biking trails. **Palmetto Islands County Park** also has trails. Bikes can be rented at the **Bicycle Shoppe** (280 Meeting St., ☎ 803/722–8168; on Kiawah Island, ☎ 803/768–9122) and at **Charleston Bicycle Rentals** (26 Cumberland St., ☎ 803/722–7433).

Golf
One of the most appealing aspects of golfing the Charleston area is the relaxing pace. With fewer golfers playing the courses than in destinations that are primarily oriented to golf, golfers find choice starting times and an unhurried atmosphere. For a comprehensive listing of area golf packages, including current rates, contact the Charleston Area Convention and Visitors Bureau (Box 975, Charleston 29402, ☎ 803/853–8000 or 800/868–8118).

Non-guests may play on a space-available basis at private island resorts. The prestigious Pete Dye–designed **Ocean Course at Kiawah Island Resort** (☎ 803/768–7272) was the site of the 1991 Ryder Cup. Other championship Kiawah courses are the Gary Player–designed **Marsh Point** (☎ 803/768–2121); **Osprey Point** (☎ 803/768–2121), by Tom Fazio; and **Turtle Point** (☎ 803/768–2121), a Jack Nicklaus layout. Seabrook Island Resort, a secluded hideaway on Johns Island, offers two more championship courses: **Crooked Oaks** (☎ 803/768–2529) by Robert Trent Jones Sr., and **Ocean Winds** (☎ 803/768–2529), designed by William Byrd. Wild Dunes Resort, on the Isle of Palms, is home to two Tom Fazio designs: the **Links** (☎ 803/886–2180) and **Harbor Course** (☎ 803/886–2301).

Top public courses in the area include **Charleston Municipal** (Charleston, ☎ 803/795–6517), **Charleston National Country Club** (Charleston, ☎ 803/884–7799), the **Dunes West Golf Club** (Mount Pleasant, ☎

803/856–9000), **Links at Stono Ferry** (Hollywood, ☎ 803/763–1817), **Oak Point Golf Course** (Johns Island, ☎ 803/768–7431), **Patriots Point** (Mount Pleasant, ☎ 803/881–0042), and **Shadowmoss Golf Club** (Charleston, ☎ 803/556–8251).

Tennis

Courts are open to the public at **Shadowmoss Plantation** (☎ 803/556–8251), **Kiawah Island** (☎ 803/768–2121), and **Wild Dunes** (☎ 803/886–6000).

Dining

By Eileen Robinson Smith

Updated by Patricia Cheatham

She-crab soup, sautéed shrimp and grits, variations on pecan pie, and other Low Country specialties are served all over the Charleston area, but local chefs whip up some creative contemporary dishes as well. Known for outstanding eateries—ranging from fresh seafood houses to elegant French restaurants—Charleston is a mecca for gastronomes. Across the East Cooper Bridge, in the trendy suburb of Mount Pleasant, there are a number of good restaurants. Dress is casual unless otherwise noted.

CATEGORY	COST*
$$$	over $30
$$	$20–$30
$	under $20

*per person for a three-course meal, excluding drinks, service, and 5% tax

American

$$$ **Anson.** After an afternoon of strolling through the Old City Market, you can walk a couple hundred feet up Anson Street to one of the better, and newer, restaurants in town. The softly lit, gilt-trimmed dining room is framed by about a dozen magnificent French windows; booths are anchored by marble-top tables. Anson's serves up dependable American fare—mainly seafood, chicken, and steak selections—with the occasional foreign twist (like the Thai-influenced, cashew-crusted grouper). Desserts are of the rich, southern variety, so save room. ✗ *12 Anson St., ☎ 803/577–0551. Reservations accepted. AE, D, DC, MC, V. No lunch.*

$$ **82 Queen.** This popular restaurant, part of a complex of pink stucco
★ buildings dating to the mid-1800s, is the unofficial headquarters for many of the city's annual events; during Spoleto, musicians perform in the courtyard garden. Low Country favorites such as crab cakes are served with sweet red-pepper cream sauce. The traditional mingles with such innovations as roast duck with a blueberry-Cointreau glaze and oysters stuffed with Daufuskie crab. For dessert, choose death by chocolate or the healthy cheesecake. ✗ *82 Queen St., ☎ 803/723–7591. Reservations accepted for dinner. AE, MC, V.*

$ **California Dreaming Restaurant & Bar.** The floor-to-ceiling windows of this heavy-volume restaurant, in an impressive stone fort on the Ashley River, look out at night on the lights of the harbor. The crowds come for the great view, low prices, and bountiful platters of food, such as grilled salmon, chicken salads, prime rib, and catch of the day. To make the wait bearable, take to the bar for a frothy piña colada. ✗ *1 Ashley Pointe Dr. (5 min from downtown), ☎ 803/766–1644. No reservations. AE, MC, V.*

$ **Mike Calder's Deli & Pub.** Soups, salads, sandwiches, daily specials, and 12 different draft beers are offered in an "Old World" setting, once a

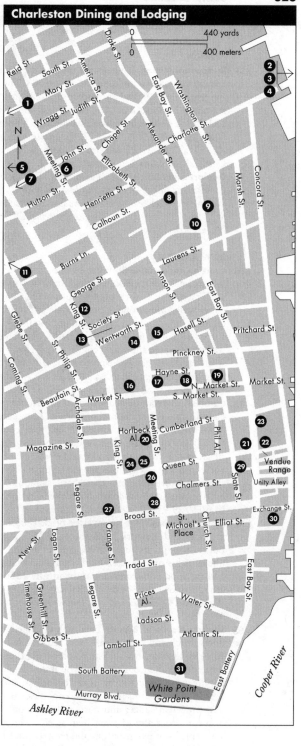

Dining

Anson, **19**
Barbadoes Room, **25**
California Dreaming Restaurant & Bar, **1**
Captain Guilds Cafe, **4**
Carolina's, **30**
82 Queen, **24**
Gaulart and Maliclet Cafe Restaurant, **28**
Louis's Charleston Grill, **16**
Magnolias Uptown/Down South, **21**
Mike Calder's Deli & Pub, **12**
Moultrie Tavern, **22**
Restaurant Million, **29**
Shem Creek Bar & Grill, **2**
Slightly North of Broad, **23**

Lodging

Ansonborough Inn, **15**
Best Western King Charles Inn, **14**
Brasington House Bed & Breakfast, **9**
Cannonboro Inn, **11**
Comfort Inn Riverview, **5**
Days Inn Historic District, **20**
1837 Bed andBreakfast and Tearoom, **13**
Elliott House Inn, **25**
Hampton Inn–Historic District, **6**
Hawthorn Suites Hotel, **18**
Holiday Inn Charleston/Mount Pleasant, **3**
John Rutledge House Inn, **27**
Maison DuPré, **10**
Mills House Hotel, **26**
Omni Hotel at Charleston Place, **16**
Planters Inn, **17**
Quality Inn–Heart of Charleston, **8**
Sheraton Inn Charleston, **7**
Two Meeting Street, **31**

Charleston Dining and Lodging

pharmacy in the historic district. ✕ *288 King St.,* ☎ *803/577–0123. No reservations. D, MC, V. Closed Sun.*

French

$$$ **Restaurant Million.** This restaurant serves French nouvelle cuisine on Limoges china in a building dating to 1788. The rack of lamb and the five-course ($50) and three-course ($28) prix-fixe meals are outstanding. Downstairs at the casual and inexpensive McCrady's (☎ 803/853–8484), soup, salad, sandwiches, and grills are served. ✕ *2 Unity Alley,* ☎ *803/577–7472. Reservations required. Jacket and tie. AE, DC, MC, V. Restaurant Million: No lunch. Closed Sun. McCrady's: No lunch Sat. Closed Sun.*

$$ **Gaulart and Maliclet Cafe Restaurant.** This casual, chic eatery serves Continental dishes—breads and pastries, soups, salads, sandwiches, and evening specials like Seafood Normandy and chicken sesame. ✕ *98 Broad St.,* ☎ *803/577–9797. Reservations accepted. AE, DC, MC, V. No lunch Mon. Closed Sun.*

Low Country

$$$ **Louis's Charleston Grill.** When owner-chef Louis Osteen took over the
★ former Shaftesbury Room in the Omni, he created an elegant low-key ambience, with historic photographs of old Charleston on mahogany-panel walls and wrought-iron chandeliers reflected in gleaming crystal and china. The food is "local, not too fancy," and entrées match a variety of grilled meat and fish fillets with such exotic sauces as pear-walnut conserve and warm cumin vinaigrette. The staff is friendly, not stuffy, and will gladly help you choose from among the wines on its long and distinguished list. ✕ *224 King St. at Charleston Pl.,* ☎ *803/577–4522. Reservations advised. AE, MC, V. No lunch.*

$$ **Carolina's.** European chic with its black lacquer, white, and peach decor, Carolina's is the brainchild of German restaurateurs Franz Meier and Chris Weihs. Many come here for the "appeteasers" and the late-night (until 1 AM) offerings, which include everything from smoked baby back ribs to pasta with crawfish and tasso (spiced ham) in cream sauce. Dinner entrées are selections from the grill: Carolina quail with goat cheese, sun-dried tomatoes, and basil; salmon with cilantro, ginger, and lime butter; and lamb loin with jalapeño chutney. ✕ *10 Exchange St.,* ☎ *803/724–3800. Reservations advised. D, MC, V. No lunch.*

$$ **Moultrie Tavern.** This reconverted brick 1883 warehouse is filled with artifacts and artwork from the Civil War era. Chef/owner Robert Bohrn, who greets guests in a Confederate uniform, is a historian and unearths his own relics. The fife-and-drum music plays continuously and the food and spirits are authentically 1860s. Try an early Southern specialty: baked oyster and sausage pie with puff pastry. ✕ *18 Vendue Range,* ☎ *803/723–1862. Dinner reservations advised. AE, D, DC, MC, V.*

$$ **Slightly North of Broad.** This high-ceilinged haunt with visible air
★ ducts, brick and stucco walls, and red wooden floors opened early in 1994 to a packed house. The best seats are those looking directly into the exposed kitchen. From here you'll see chef Frank Lee laboring over his inventive—but hardly esoteric—dishes: sautéed quail filled with herbed chicken mousse; pad Thai noodles with shrimp, pork, and an authentic fish sauce; and corn-and-crab soup with spinach ravioli. You can order almost every item as either an appetizer or an entrée. The wine list is extensive and moderately priced. ✕ *192 E. Bay St.,* ☎ *803/723–3424. No reservations. AE, MC, V. No lunch Sat. Closed Sun.*

Low Country/Southern

$ **Captain Guilds Cafe.** There are actually two restaurants here: The little downstairs storefront restaurant churns out inexpensive, expertly prepared southern food. The catfish with honey curry butter and the chicken breast breaded with parmesan cornmeal and lemon caper sauce are surprisingly light and tender given the regional tendency to deep fry. For dessert, sample the bread pudding with a brown-sugar cream sauce. Upstairs, formal, prix-fixe, four-course Continental meals ($29) are presented in a grand dining room—the menu changes daily and depends largely on what's fresh that day. ✕ *101 Pitt St., Mount Pleasant,* ☎ *803/884–7009. Reservations required. Jacket and tie. AE, MC, V. Downstairs: No dinner Sun. Closed Mon. Upstairs: No lunch. Closed Sun. and Mon.*

$ **Magnolias Uptown/Down South.** This popular place, in an 1823 ware-
★ house on the site of the old customs house, is cherished by Charlestonians and visitors alike. The magnolia theme is seen throughout, and a custom-built circular bar overlooks the dining room. Specialties include grilled mahimahi fillet topped with succotash of shrimp, butter beans, yellow corn, and fresh spinach. Even the Black Angus strip steak is distinctive, served with fricassee of wild mushrooms, black-eyed peas, and Madeira sauce. Equally innovative appetizers include seared yellow grits cakes with Tasso gravy and yellow corn relish, and the salt-and-pepper fried shrimp with honey mustard–and-horseradish dip. ✕ *185 E. Bay St.,* ☎ *803/577–7771. Reservations advised. AE, MC, V.*

Seafood

$$ **Barbadoes Room.** This large, airy plant- and light-filled space has a sophisticated island look and a view out to a cheery courtyard garden. Entrées include sautéed jumbo shrimp and scallops served with creamy wild mushroom sauce on a bed of fresh spinach; linguini with an assortment of fresh shellfish in a light saffron sauce; and grilled breast of duck served with tarragon pear sauce. There's an elegant and extensive Southern-style breakfast menu and a popular Sunday brunch. ✕ *115 Meeting St., in the Mills House Hotel,* ☎ *803/577–2400. Reservations advised. D, DC, MC, V.*

$ **Shem Creek Bar & Grill.** This pleasant dockside spot is perennially popular for its oyster bar and light fare (until 10 PM Sun.–Thurs., until 1 AM Fri.–Sat.). There's also a wide variety of seafood entrées, including a steam pot—lobsters, clams, oysters, and sausages with melted lemon butter or hot cocktail sauce—big enough for two. ✕ *508 Mill St., Mount Pleasant,* ☎ *803/884–8102. No reservations. AE, D, DC, MC, V.*

Lodging

Rates tend to increase during the Spring Festival of Houses and Spoleto, when reservations are essential. The **Charleston Area Convention and Visitors Bureau** (Box 975, Charleston 29402, ☎ 803/853–8000 or 800/868–8118) distributes a Courtesy Discount Card entitling the bearer to 10%–50% off at many accommodations, restaurants, tours, and shops between mid-November and mid-February. To find rooms in homes, cottages, and carriage houses, try **Charleston East Bed and Breakfast League** (1031 Tall Pine Rd., Mount Pleasant 29464, ☎ 803/884–8208) and **Historic Charleston Bed and Breakfast** (60 Broad St., Charleston 29401, ☎ 803/722–6606). For historic home rentals in Charleston, contact **Charleston Carriage Houses–Oceanfront Realty** (Box 6151, Hilton Head, SC 29938, ☎ 803/785–8161). For condo and house rentals on the Isle of Palms—some with private pools and tennis courts—try **Island Realty** (Box 157, Isle of Palms 29451, ☎ 803/886–8144).

CATEGORY	COST*
$$$$	over $150
$$$	$90–$150
$$	$50–$90
$	under $50

All prices are for a standard double room, excluding 7% tax.

Hotels and Motels

$$$$ **Hawthorn Suites Hotel.** The hotel's spacious suites, all decorated with 18th-century reproductions and canopied beds, include full kitchens or wet bars with microwave ovens and refrigerators. Across from the City Market, the hotel is popular with business people, families, and tour groups. Complimentary full breakfast and afternoon refreshments are included in the rate. ⌧ *181 Church St., 29401, ☎ 803/577–2644 or 800/527–1133, ℻ 803/577–2697. 164 suites. Restaurant, lounge, pool, hot tub, exercise room, business services, meeting rooms. AE, D, DC, MC, V.*

$$$ **Mills House Hotel.** Antique furnishings and period decor give great charm
★ to this luxurious Holiday Inn property, a reconstruction of an old hostelry on its original site in the historic district. There's a lounge with live entertainment, and excellent dining in the Barbadoes Room (*see* Dining, *above*). ⌧ *115 Meeting St., 29401, ☎ 803/577–2400 or 800/874–9600, ℻ 803/722–2712. 214 rooms, 15 suites. Restaurant, 2 lounges, pool. AE, D, DC, MC, V.*

$$$ **Omni Hotel at Charleston Place.** Among the city's most luxurious ho-
★ tels, this graceful, low-rise structure in the historic district is flanked by upscale boutiques and specialty shops. The lobby features a magnificent hand-blown Venetian glass chandelier, an Italian marble floor, and antiques from Sotheby's. Rooms are furnished with period reproductions. ⌧ *130 Market St., 29401, ☎ 803/722–4900 or 800/843–6664, ℻ 803/722–4074. 348 rooms, 46 suites. 2 restaurants, 2 lounges, pool, hot tub, sauna, health club, concierge floor. AE, D, DC, MC, V.*

$$$ **Sheraton Inn Charleston.** Some rooms in this 13-story hotel outside the historic district overlook the Ashley River. Spacious rooms and suites are highlighted with Queen Anne furnishings. There's also concierge service and live entertainment. ⌧ *170 Lockwood Dr., 29403, ☎ 803/723–3000 or 800/968–3569. 334 rooms, 2 suites. Coffee shop, dining room, lounge, pool, exercise room, meeting rooms. AE, D, DC, MC, V.*

$$–$$$ **Holiday Inn Charleston/Mount Pleasant.** This hotel just over the Cooper River Bridge is a 10-minute drive from the downtown historic district. Everything has been gracefully done: brass lamps, crystal chandeliers, Queen Anne–style furniture. The "high-tech suites" offer PC cable hookups, large working areas, glossy ultramodern furniture, and refrigerators. ⌧ *250 U.S. 17, Mount Pleasant 29464, ☎ 803/884–6000 or 800/290–4004, ℻ 803/744–0942. 158 rooms. Restaurant, lounge, raw bar (they mean fruits, veggies, oyster, steamed shrimp, and clams), pool, sauna, exercise room, concierge floor, meeting rooms. AE, D, DC, MC, V.*

$–$$ **Best Western King Charles Inn.** This inn in the historic district has spacious rooms furnished with 18th-century period reproductions. It's location, convenient to the Charleston Convention Center, is the primary attraction. ⌧ *237 Meeting St., 29401, ☎ 803/723–7451 or 800/528–*

1234, FAX 803/723–2041. 91 rooms. Dining room, lounge, pool. AE, D, DC, MC, V.

$–$$ Comfort Inn Riverview. Close to the Ashley River, the historic district, and restaurants, this 7-story contemporary inn offers free parking and complimentary Continental breakfast. ☎ *144 Bee St., 29401,* ☎ *803/577–2224 or 800/228–5150, FAX 803/577–9001. 128 rooms. Pool. AE, DC, MC, V.*

$–$$ Days Inn Historic District. Conveniently located near the Gibbes Museum of Art and other historic district attractions, this modest inn features spacious, quiet rooms with king-size beds. A complimentary breakfast of coffee, juice, and doughnuts is available in the lobby. ☎ *155 Meeting St., 29401,* ☎ *803/722–8411 or 800/325–2525, FAX 803/733–5361. 124 rooms. Dining room, pool. AE, D, DC, MC, V.*

$–$$ Hampton Inn–Historic District. This downtown property has hardwood
★ floors in the lobby, extra-light guest rooms furnished in period reproductions, a courtyard garden, and pool. Guests also get a Continental breakfast. This is a front-runner in the economy category. ☎ *345 Meeting St., 29403,* ☎ *803/723–4000 or 800/426–7866, FAX 803/722–3725. 171 rooms. Pool. AE, DC, MC, V.*

$–$$ Quality Inn–Heart of Charleston. A block from the Gaillard Municipal Auditorium and Exhibition Hall, the inn is clean and run by a friendly staff. It draws loyal repeat visitors because of its convenient courtyard parking and location across from the convention center. Rooms are motel modern, as you would expect from this chain. ☎ *125 Calhoun St., 29401,* ☎ *803/722–3391 or 800/845–2504, FAX 803/577–0361. 126 rooms. Coffee shop, lounge, pool. AE, D, DC, MC, V.*

Inns and Guest Houses

The charms of historic Charleston can be enhanced by a stay at one of its many inns, most in restored structures. Some are reminiscent of European inns; one is tastefully contemporary, tucked away on the grounds of a famous estate.

HISTORIC DISTRICT

$$$$ John Rutledge House Inn. This 1763 house, built by John Rutledge,
★ one of the framers of the U.S. Constitution, is one of Charleston's most luxurious inns. Ornate ironwork on the facade has a palmetto tree and eagle motif, signifying Rutledge's service to both his state and his nation. Wine and tea are served in the ballroom, and Continental breakfast and newspapers are delivered to your room. Two charming period carriage houses also accommodate guests. There are whirlpool tubs in some guest rooms. ☎ *116 Broad St., 29401,* ☎ *803/723–7999 or 800/476–9741, FAX 803720–2615. 11 rooms in mansion, 4 in each carriage house. AE, MC, V.*

$$$ Ansonborough Inn. Formerly a turn-of-the-century stationer's warehouse, this spacious all-suite inn is furnished in antique reproductions. It offers hair dryers, irons, off-street parking, a morning newspaper, message service, wine reception, morning newspaper, and Continental breakfast, but it's best known for its friendly staff. ☎ *21 Hasell St., 29401,* ☎ *803/723–1655 or 800/522–2073, FAX 803/527–6888. 37 suites. Meeting room. AE, MC, V.*

$$$ Brasington House Bed & Breakfast. During afternoon tea or at the Continental breakfast, Dalton and Judy Brasington, educators by profession, will advise you on what to see and do in Charleston. The formal dining room of their restored Greek Revival "single house" in the historic district is filled with antiques and treasures from around the world. ⊠ *328 E. Bay St., 29401,* ☎ *803/722–1274 or 800/722–1274,* ⊠ *803/722–6785. 4 rooms with private baths. MC, V.*

$$$ **Elliott House Inn.** Listen to the chimes of St. Michael's Episcopal Church as you sip wine in the courtyard of this lovely old inn in the heart of the historic district. Then retreat to a cozy room with period furniture, including canopied four-posters and Oriental carpets. A Continental breakfast is included. ⊠ *78 Queen St., 29401,* ☎ *803/723–1855 or 800/729–1855,* ⊠ *803/722–1567. 26 rooms. Hot tub, bicycles. AE, D, MC, V.*

$$$ **Maison DuPré.** A quiet retreat off busy East Bay Street, this 1801 inn was created out of three restored homes and two carriage houses. It is filled with antiques, and each room features an original painting by Lucille Mullholland, who operates the inn with her husband Robert. Enjoy a full Low Country tea (cheeses, finger sandwiches, and cakes, with tea), Continental breakfast, and tickets to the Nathaniel Russell house museum—all complimentary. ⊠ *317 E. Bay St., 29401,* ☎ *803/723–8691 or 800/844–4667. 12 rooms, 3 suites. AE, MC, V.*

$$$ **Planters Inn.** Rooms and suites here are beautifully appointed with opulent furnishings, including mahogany four-poster beds and marble baths. There's a concierge and 24-hour room service. ⊠ *112 N. Market St., 29401,* ☎ *803/722–2345 or 800/845–7082,* ⊠ *803/577–2125. 36 rooms, 5 suites. AE, DC, MC, V.*

$$$ **Two Meeting Street.** As pretty as a wedding cake and just as roman-
★ tic, this turn-of-the-century inn near the Battery features Tiffany windows, carved English oak paneling, and a chandelier from Czechoslovakia. There are two very private honeymoon suites. Guests are treated to afternoon sherry and Continental breakfast. ⊠ *2 Meeting St., 29401,* ☎ *803/723–7322. 7 rooms, 2 suites. No credit cards.*

$$–$$$ **Cannonboro Inn.** One of the most elegant inns in town, this B&B in the historic district has luxurious rooms, tastefully decorated in period furnishings by owners Bud and Sally Allen. Guests are treated to a complimentary full English breakfast, use of the bicycles, and afternoon sherry. ⊠ *184 Ashley Ave., 29403,* ☎ *803/723–8572,* ⊠ *803/723–9080. 6 rooms with private baths. Bicycles. MC, V.*

$$ **1837 Bed and Breakfast and Tea Room.** Though it's not as fancy as some of the B&Bs in town, this inn is long on hospitality. Restored and operated by two artists, the home and carriage house feature rooms filled with antiques (including romantic canopied rice beds). A gourmet breakfast of homemade breads and hot entrées such as sausage pie or eggs Benedict is included in the rate, as is the afternoon tea (which is also open to the public for a nominal price). ⊠ *126 Wentworth St., 29401,* ☎ *803/723–7166. 8 rooms with baths. AE, MC, V.*

Resort Islands

The semitropical islands dotting the South Carolina coast near Charleston are home to several sumptuous resorts. A wide variety of packages is sold. Peak-season rates (during spring and summer vacations) range from $100 to $250 per day, double occupancy. Costs drop considerably off-season.

$$$$ **Kiawah Island Resort.** Choose from 150 inn rooms, 48 suites, and 300 completely equipped one- to four-bedroom villas in two luxurious resort villages on 10,000 wooded acres. The accommodations and much of the property were refurbished in 1994. There are 10 miles of fine broad beaches and an array of recreational options. Dining options are many and varied: Low Country specialties in the Jasmine Porch and Veranda, Indigo House; Continental cuisine in the Charleston Gallery; lagoonside dining at the Park Cafe; casual dining in the Sand Wedge,

Sundancers, Jonah's. ☎ *Kiawah Island, Box 12357, Charleston 29422-2357,* ☎ *803/768-2121 or 800/654-2924,* FAX *803/768-9386. 498 units. Restaurants, 4 18-hole golf courses, 28 tennis courts, boating, fishing, shops, children's programs. AE, DC, MC, V.*

$$$$ **Seabrook Island Resort.** There are 360 completely equipped one- to three-bedroom villas, cottages, and beach houses. Beach Club and Island Club, open to all guests, are centers for dining and leisure activities. ☎ *1002 Landfall Way, Seabrook Island 29455,* ☎ *803/768-1000 or 800/845-2475,* FAX *803/768-4922. 360 units. Restaurants, 4 pools, 2 18-hole golf courses, 13 tennis courts, horseback riding, boating, fishing, bicycles, children's programs. AE, D, MC, V.*

$$$$ **Wild Dunes.** This serene, 1,600-acre resort has 250 one- to three-bedroom villas for rent, each with a kitchen and washer and dryer. There are two widely acclaimed golf courses, a racquet club, a yacht harbor on the Intracoastal Waterway, and a long list of recreational options. Beef specialties are served at the Club House and seafood at the Island House, where all dishes are created by a French master chef. There's a lounge with live entertainment. ☎ *Box 503, Isle of Palms 29451,* ☎ *803/886-6000 or 800/845-8880,* FAX *803/886-2916. 250 units. 2 restaurants, lounge, 2 18-hole golf courses, 16 tennis courts, water sports, boating, fishing, bicycles, children's programs. AE, MC, V.*

The Arts

Pick up the Schedule of Events at the Visitors Center (375 Meeting St.) or at area hotels, inns, and restaurants. Also see "Tips for Tourists" each Saturday in the *News & Courier/The Evening Post.*

Arts Festivals

Spoleto Festival USA. Founded by the composer Gian Carlo Menotti in 1977, Spoleto has become one of the world's greatest celebrations of the arts. For two weeks, from late May to early June, opera, dance, theater, symphonic and chamber music performances, jazz, and the visual arts are showcased in concert halls, theaters, parks, churches, streets, and gardens throughout the city. For information: Spoleto Festival USA (Box 704, Charleston 29402, ☎ 803/722-2764).

Piccolo Spoleto Festival. The spirited companion festival of Spoleto Festival USA showcases the best in local and regional talent from every artistic discipline. There are about 700 events—from jazz performances to puppet shows—held at 60 sites in 17 days, from mid-May through early June, and most performances are free. For a program, contact the Office of Cultural Affairs, Piccolo Spoleto Festival (133 Church St., Charleston 29401, ☎ 803/724-7305).

During the **Festival of Houses and Gardens,** held during March and April each year, more than 100 private homes, gardens, and historic churches are open to the public. (Contact the Historic Charleston Foundation, Box 1120, 29202, ☎ 803/724-8484.)

Moja Arts Festival. Theater, dance, and music performances, art shows, films, lectures, and tours celebrating the rich heritage of the African continent are held at sites throughout the historic district the first two weeks in October. For information: The Office of Cultural Affairs (133 Church St., Charleston 29401, ☎ 803/724-7305).

Southeastern Wildlife Exposition. Held in mid-February, one of Charleston's biggest annual events features art by renowned wildlife artists. *211 Meeting St., 29401,* ☎ *803/723-1748 or 800/221-5273.*

Concerts

The College of Charleston has a **Monday Night Recital Series.** The **Charleston Symphony Orchestra** (☎ 803/723–7528) presents its Classics Concerts Series at Gaillard Municipal Auditorium (77 Calhoun St., ☎ 803/577–4500). Its Brass Quintet plays at the Charleston Museum Auditorium (360 Meeting St., ☎ 803/722–2996) and the Garden Theatre (☎ 803/577–7400) and at other locations around the city.

Dance

The **Charleston Ballet Theatre** (280 Meeting St., ☎ 803/723–7334) performs everything from contemporary to classical dance. The **Charleston Civic Ballet** (☎ 803/722–8779 or 803/577–4502) performs at the Sotille Theater (☎ 803/953–6340). The **Robert Ivey Ballet Company** (☎ 803/556–1343), a student group at the College of Charleston, gives a fall and spring program of jazz, classical, and modern dance at the **Simons Center for the Arts.**

Theater

Several groups, including the **Footlight Players,** perform at the Dock Street Theatre (135 Church St., ☎ 803/723–5648). Performances by the College of Charleston's drama department and guest theatrical groups are presented during the school year at the **Simons Center for the Arts** (☎ 803/953–5600).

Nightlife

Dancing and Music

Windjammer (☎ 803/886–8596), on the Isle of Palms, is an oceanfront spot featuring live rock music. In the market area, there's the **Jukebox** (4 Vendue Range, ☎ 803/723–3431), where a disc jockey spins oldies and contemporary rock. Amid the shops at Charleston Place is **Louis's Jazz Lounge Grill** (☎ 803/722–4900), an intimate, upscale locale featuring live jazz or performances by harpist or pianist.

Dinner Cruise

For an evening of dining and dancing, climb aboard the luxury yacht, *Spirit of Charleston.* ☎ *803/722–2628. Reservations required. Closed Sun. and Mon.*

Film

Stage One Cinema (30 Cumberland St. Courtyard, ☎ 803/722–1900) offers films from around the world in an old livery stable, plus wine, beer, coffee, and pastries.

Hotel and Jazz Bars

The Best Friend Lounge (115 Meeting St., ☎ 803/577–2400), in the Mills House Hotel, has a guitarist playing light tunes Monday–Saturday nights. In the **Lobby Lounge** (130 Market St., ☎ 803/722–4900) in the Omni Charleston, cocktails and appetizers are accompanied by piano. Live jazz is offered Friday and Saturday evenings at **Henry's Restaurant** (54 N. Market St., ☎ 803/723–4363).

Restaurant/Lounges

A.W. Shucks (State Street Market, ☎ 803/723–1151) is a popular spot for relaxed evenings set to taped easy-listening music. **J.B. O'Brien's** (139 Calhoun St., ☎ 803723–1558) is an especially lively late night spot. **East Bay Trading Co.** (161 E. Bay St., ☎ 803/722–0722) has a small dance floor in its lively bar and a DJ playing Top 40s Friday and Saturday nights. You find authentic Irish music at **Tommy Condon's Irish Pub & Restaurant** (160 Church St., ☎ 803/577–3818).

Charleston Essentials

Arriving and Departing

BY BOAT

Boaters traveling the Intracoastal Waterway may dock at the **City Marina** (Lockwood Blvd., ☎ 803/724–7357) in the Charleston Harbor or **Wild Dunes Yacht Harbor** (☎ 803/886–5100) on the Isle of Palms.

BY BUS

Greyhound (3610 Dorchester Rd., N. Charleston, ☎ 800/231–2222).

BY CAR

I–26 traverses the state from northwest to southeast and terminates at Charleston. U.S. 17, the coast road, passes through Charleston.

BY PLANE

Charleston International Airport (☎ 803/767–1100) on I–26, 12 miles west of downtown, is served by American, Continental, Delta, United, and USAir.

Low Country Limousine Service (☎ 803/767–7111 or 800/222–4771) charges $9 per person one-way to downtown Charleston, by reservation. By car, take I–26S into the city.

BY TRAIN

Amtrak (4565 Gaynor Ave., N. Charleston, ☎ 803/744–8264 or 800/872–7245).

Getting Around

BY BUS

Regular buses run in most of Charleston from 5:35 am till 10 pm and to North Charleston until 1 am. The cost is 75¢ exact change (free transfers); at off-peak hours (9:30–3:30), senior citizens and people with disabilities pay 25¢. **DASH** (Downtown Area Shuttle) trolley-style buses provide fast service in the main downtown areas. The fare is 75¢; $1 for an all-day pass. For schedule information for buses or DASH, call 803/747–0922.

BY TAXI

Fares within the city average $2–$3 per trip. Companies include **Yellow Cab** (☎ 803/577–6565), **Safety Cab** (☎ 803/722–4066), and **Low Country Limousine Service** (*see* Arriving and Departing *above*).

Guided Tours

BOAT TOURS

Princess Gray Line Harbor Tours (☎ 803/722–1112 or 800/344–4483) and **Charleston Harbor Tour** (☎ 803/722–1691) ply the harbor. **Fort Sumter Tours** (☎ 803/722–1691) includes a stop at Fort Sumter and also offers Starlight Dinner Cruises aboard a luxury yacht.

CARRIAGE TOURS

Charleston Carriage Co. (☎ 803/577–0042), **Old South Carriage Company** (☎ 803/723–9712), and **Palmetto Carriage Works** (☎ 803/723–8145) run approximately one-hour horse- and mule-drawn carriage tours of the historic district, some conducted by guides in Confederate uniforms.

ORIENTATION

Adventure Sightseeing (☎ 803/762–0088 or 800/722–5394) and **Carolina Lowcountry Tours** (☎ 803/797–1045 or 800/621–7996) offer van or motor-coach tours of the historic district. **Gray Line** (☎ 803/722–4444) offers similar tours, plus seasonal trips to gardens and plantations.

PERSONAL GUIDES

Contact **Associated Guides of Historic Charleston** (☎ 803/724–6419); **Parker Limousine Service** (☎ 803/723–7601), which offers chauffeur-driven luxury limousine tours; or **Charleston Guide Service** (☎ 803/723–4402), the city's oldest guide service.

SPECIAL-INTEREST

Doin' the Charleston (☎ 803/763–1233 or 800/647–4487) combines its narration with audiovisuals and makes a stop at the Battery.

WALKING TOURS

Guided tours are given by **Historic Charleston Walking Tours** (☎ 803/722–6460); **Charleston Strolls** (☎ 803/884–9505); and **Charleston Tea Party Walking Tour** (☎ 803/577–5896 or 803/722–1779), which includes tea in a private garden.

Important Addresses and Numbers

EMERGENCIES

Dial 911 for police and **ambulance** assistance. The emergency rooms are open all night at **Charleston Memorial Hospital** (326 Calhoun St., ☎ 803/577–0600) and **Roper Hospital** (316 Calhoun St., ☎ 803/724–2000).

RADIO STATIONS

AM: WQIZ 810, gospel; WTMA 1250, talk radio; WXTC 1390, sports. **FM:** WAVF 96, alternative rock; WEZL 104, country; WBUB 107.5, country; WJUK 104.5, music from the 70s; WPAL 99, urban contemporary; WSCI 89.3, news, classical, jazz, information line; WSUY 100.7, light adult contemporary; WWWZ 93, urban contemporary; WXLY 102.5, oldies; WXTC 97, music from the 70s; WYBB 98.1, classic rock.

24-HOUR PHARMACIES

Henry's Conway Drug Store (633 King St., ☎ 803/577–5123), **Super E** (572 Meeting St., ☎ 803/722–0176), **Tellis Pharmacy** (125 King St., ☎ 803/723–0682).

VISITOR INFORMATION

Charleston Area Convention & Visitors Bureau (Box 975, Charleston 29402, ☎ 803/853–8000 or 800/868–8118) has information also on Kiawah Island, Seabrook Island, Mount Pleasant, North Charleston, Edisto Island, Summerville, and the Isle of Palms. **Historic Charleston Foundation** (Box 1120, Charleston 29402, ☎ 803/723–1623) has information on house tours.

MYRTLE BEACH AND THE GRAND STRAND

The lively, family-oriented Grand Strand, a booming resort area along the South Carolina coast, is one of the Eastern Seaboard's mega-vacation centers. Myrtle Beach alone accounts for about 40% of the state's tourism revenue. The main attraction, of course, is the broad, beckoning beach—60 miles of it, stretching from the North Carolina border south to Georgetown, with Myrtle Beach at the hub. But the Strand has something for everyone: more than 80 championship golf courses, designed by Arnold Palmer, Robert Trent Jones, Jack Nicklaus, and Tom and George Fazio, among others; excellent seafood restaurants; giant shopping malls and factory outlets; amusement parks, water slides, and arcades; a dozen shipwrecks for divers to explore; fine fishing; campgrounds, most on the beach; plus antique-car and wax museums, the world's largest outdoor sculpture garden, a half dozen country music shows, an antique pipe organ and merry-go-round, and a museum dedicated entirely to rice.

Exploring

Myrtle Beach—whose population of 26,000 explodes to about 350,000 in summer—is the center of activity on the Grand Strand. It is here that you find the amusement parks and other children's activities that make the area so popular with families, as well as most of the nightlife that keeps parents and teenagers happy into the wee hours. If the younger generation can't be amused and entertained here it might as well stay at home! In 1993, the city put up dozens of colorful street-light displays around major intersections, adding yet a few more volts of energy to the already pulsating scene. On the North Strand, there is Little River, with a thriving fishing and charter industry, and the several communities that make up North Myrtle Beach. On the South Strand, the family retreats of Surfside Beach and Garden City offer more summer homes and condominiums. Farther south are Murrells Inlet, once a pirate's haven and now a popular fishing port, and Pawleys Island, one of the East Coast's oldest resorts. Historic Georgetown forms the southern tip.

Our tour begins at the **Myrtle Beach Pavilion Amusement Park**, which underwent a major renovation and expansion in 1994. Here families while away the days enjoying thrill and kiddie rides, the Carolinas' largest flume, video games, a teen nightclub, specialty shops, antique cars, and sidewalk cafés. *Ninth Ave. N and Ocean Blvd., ☎ 803/448–6456. Fees for individual attractions; family discount book available. ☉ Mar.–May and Sept.–Oct., weekdays 6 PM–midnight, weekends 1 PM–midnight; June–Sept., daily 1 PM–midnight.*

More of the unusual awaits at **Ripleys Believe It or Not Museum.** Among the more than 750 exhibits is an 8-foot, 11-inch wax replica of the world's tallest man. *901 N. Ocean Blvd., ☎ 803/448–2331. ☛ $6.50 adults, $3.50 children 6–12. ☉ Daily 10–10.*

Drama, sound, and animation highlight religious, historical, and entertainment sections in the **Myrtle Beach National Wax Museum.** *1000 N. Ocean Blvd., ☎ 803/448–9921. ☛ $5 adults, $3 children 5–12, under 5 free. ☉ Late Feb.–mid-Oct., daily 9 AM–11 PM; in summer months, daily 9 AM–midnight.*

When your family's appetite for more raucous amusements has been sated, it's time to head out of town. Going south on U.S. 17 for about 20 miles brings you to **Murrells Inlet,** a picturesque little fishing village with popular seafood restaurants that's also a great place for chartering a fishing boat or joining a group excursion.

Three miles south, on the grounds of a Colonial rice plantation, is the largest outdoor collection of American sculpture, with works by such artists as Frederic Remington and Daniel Chester French. ★**Brookgreen Gardens** was begun in 1931 by railroad magnate/philanthropist Archer Huntington and his wife, Anna, herself a sculptor. Today, more than

500 works are set amid beautifully landscaped grounds, with avenues of live oaks, reflecting pools, and over 2,000 plant species. Also on the site is a wildlife park, an aviary, a cypress swamp, nature trails, and an education center. *18 mi south of Myrtle Beach off U.S. 17,* ☎ *803/237–4218.* ☛ *$6.50 adults, $3 children 6–12, children under 6 free.* ☉ *Daily 9:30–5:30.*

Across the highway is **Huntington Beach State Park,** the Huntingtons' 2,500-acre former estate. The park's focal point is Atalaya (circa 1933), their Moorish-style, 30-room home, open to visitors in season. In addition to the splendid beach, there are surf fishing, nature trails, an interpretive center, a salt-marsh boardwalk, picnic areas, a playground, concessions, and a campground. ☎ *803/237–4440.* ☛ *Free; parking fee in peak months.* ☉ *Daily dawn to dusk.*

Farther south is **Pawleys Island,** 4 miles long and a half-mile wide, which began as a resort before the Civil War, when wealthy planters and their families summered here. It's mostly made up of weathered old summer cottages nestled in groves of oleander and oak trees. You can watch the famous Pawleys Island hammocks being made here (*see* Shopping, *below*), but there's little else to do.

Bellefield Nature Center Museum, south on U.S. 17 near Georgetown, is at the entrance of Hobcaw Barony, on the vast estate of the late Bernard M. Baruch. Here such guests as Franklin D. Roosevelt and Winston Churchill came to confer with him. The museum, run by the Belle W. Baruch Foundation, is used for teaching and research in forestry and marine biology. There are aquariums, touch tanks, and video presentations. ☎ *803/546–4623.* ☛ *To museum free.* ☉ *Weekdays 10–5, Sat. 1–5. A variety of nature tours and estate tours are given year-round; call at least 1 month in advance for schedules and fees.*

Georgetown, on Winyah Bay, founded in 1729 by a Baptist minister, soon became the center of America's Colonial rice empire. A rich plantation culture took root here and developed on a scale comparable to Charleston's. Today, oceangoing vessels still come to Georgetown's busy port, and the **Harbor Walk,** the restored waterfront, hums with activity. Georgetown's historic district—among the prettiest in the state north of Charleston—encompasses more than 50 homes and other buildings and can be walked in a couple of hours.

The graceful market–meeting building in the heart of town, topped by an 1842 clock and tower, has been converted into the **Rice Museum,** with maps, tools, and dioramas. *Front and Screven Sts.,* ☎ *803/546–7423.* ☛ *$2 adults, children under 18 and students free.* ☉ *Mon.–Sat. 9:30–4:30.*

Nearby, **Prince George Winyah Episcopal Church** (named after King George II) still serves the congregation established in 1721. It was built in 1737 with bricks brought from England. *Broad and Highmarket Sts.,* ☎ *803/546–4358. Donation suggested.* ☉ *Mar.–Oct., weekdays 11:30–4:30.*

Overlooking the Sampit River from a bluff is the **Harold Kaminski House** (circa 1760). It's especially notable for its collections of regional antiques and furnishings, its Chippendale and Duncan Phyfe furniture, Royal Doulton vases, and silver. *1003 Front St.,* ☎ *803/546–7706.* ☛ *$4 adults, $2 children under 13.* ☉ *Mon.–Sat. 10–5, Sun. 1–4.*

Twelve miles south of Georgetown lies **Hopsewee Plantation,** surrounded by moss-draped live oaks, magnolias, and tree-size camellias, overlooking the North Santee River. The mansion has a fine Georgian staircase and hand-carved Adam candlelight moldings. *U.S. 17,* ☎ *803/546–7891.* ☛ *To mansion: $5 adults, $2 children 5–17, under 5 free.* ☛ *To grounds: $2 per car. Mansion open Mar.–Oct., Tues.–Fri. 10–4.* ☉ *Grounds, including nature trail, year-round, daily dawn–dusk.*

Hampton Plantation State Park, at the edge of the Francis Marion National Forest (*see* Off the Beaten Path *in* Charleston section, *above*), preserves the home of Archibald Rutledge, poet laureate of South Carolina for 39 years until his death in 1973. The 18th-century plantation house is a fine example of a Low Country mansion. The exterior has been restored; cutaway sections in the finely crafted interior show the changes made through the centuries. The grounds are landscaped and there are picnic areas. *Off U.S. 17,* ☎ *803/546–9361.* ☛ *Mansion $2 adults.* ☛ *To grounds free.* ☉ *Mansion Apr.–Labor Day, Thurs.–Mon. 1–4; Labor Day–Mar., weekends 1–4.* ☉ *Grounds Thurs.–Mon. 9–6.*

What to See and Do with Children

Brookgreen Gardens (*see* Exploring, *above*).

Myrtle Beach is the minigolf capital of the world, and **Hawaiian Rumble** is its crown jewel, featuring a smoking mountain that erupts fire and rumbles at timed intervals. *3210 33rd Ave. S, U.S. 17, Myrtle Beach,* ☎ *803/272–7812.* ☛ *$4 all day (9–5), $4 per round 5–midnight. Closed Jan.–Feb.*

Huntington Beach State Park (*see* Exploring, *above*).

Myrtle Beach Grand Prix. Auto-mania heaven, it offers Formula 1 race cars, go-carts, bumper boats, mini-go-carts, kiddie cars, and mini-bumper boats for adults and children age 3 and up. *Two locations: 3201 Hwy. 17, Myrtle Beach,* ☎ *803/238–2421; Windy Hill, U.S. 17N, N. Myrtle Beach,* ☎ *803/272–6010. Rides priced individually, $2–$5.50.* ☉ *Mar. 10–Oct. 31, daily 10 AM–11 PM.*

Myrtle Beach Pavilion and Amusement Park (*see* Exploring, *above*).

Myrtle Waves Water Park. There's splashy family fun for all ages in 17 rides and activities. *U.S. 17 Bypass and 10th Ave. N, Myrtle Beach,* ☎ *803/448–1026 or 800/524–9283.* ☛ *$10.95, $8.45 after 3 PM, $5.95 spectators and over 54, children under 3 free.* ☉ *Memorial Day Weekend–Labor Day, daily 10–6 (Tues.–Thurs. until 8); May and Sept., weekends 10–5.*

Shopping

Discount Outlets

Off-price shopping outlets abound in the Grand Strand. At **Waccamaw Pottery and Outlet Park** (U.S. 501 at the Waterway, Myrtle Beach, ☎ 803/236–1100) over 3 miles of shelves in several buildings are stocked with china, glassware, wicker, brass, pewter, and countless other items, and about 50 factory outlets sell clothing, furniture, books, jewelry, and more. **Hathaway/Olga Warner** (☎ 803/236–4200), across from Waccamaw, offers menswear by Chaps, Ralph Lauren, Speedo, and Jack Nicklaus, and women's lingerie.

Malls

Myrtle Square Mall (2501 N. Kings Hwy., Myrtle Beach, ☎ 803/448–2513) has 71 upscale stores and restaurants, and a food court. **Barefoot Landing** in North Myrtle Beach (4898 S. Kings Hwy., ☎

803/272–8349) is a unique complex built over marshland and water. **Briarcliffe Mall** (10177 N. Kings Hwy., Myrtle Beach, ☎ 803/272–4040) has 100 specialty shops. Malls are generally open Monday–Saturday 10–9, Sunday 1–6.

Specialty Stores

The **Hammock Shops at Pawleys Island** (☎ 803/237–8448) is a handsome complex of approximately two-dozen boutiques, gift shops, and restaurants nestled amid moss-draped live oak trees and built with old beams, timber, and ballast brick. Just outside the Original Hammock Shop, in the Hammock Weavers' Pavilion, skilled craftsfolk demonstrate the more than 100-year-old art of weaving the famous cotton-rope Pawleys Island hammocks. In one shop, rope hammocks are being made as they have been since 1880. Others sell jewelry, toys, antiques, and designer fashions.

Beaches

The broad 60-mile-long swath of South Carolina's Atlantic beach known as the **Grand Strand** extends from Little River near the North Carolina line down to Georgetown and its tidelands. All the region's beaches are family oriented, and most are public. The widest expanses are in **North Myrtle Beach,** where, at low tide, the sand stretches up to an eighth of a mile from the dunes to the water. Those who wish to combine their sunning with nightlife and amusement park attractions can enjoy it all at **Myrtle Beach,** the Strand's longtime hub. Vacationers seeking a quieter day in the sun head for the **South Strand** communities of Surfside Beach and Garden City or historic **Pawleys Island.** All along the Strand you can enjoy shell hunting, fishing, swimming, sunbathing, sailing, surfing, jogging, or just strolling.

Participant Sports

Fishing

The Gulf Stream makes fishing usually good from early spring through December. Anglers can fish from 10 piers and jetties for amberjack, sea trout, and king mackerel. Surfcasters may snare bluefish, whiting, flounder, pompano, and channel bass. In the South Strand, salt marshes, inlets, and tidal creeks yield flounder, blues, croakers, spots, shrimp, clams, oysters, and blue crabs. **Capt. Dick's** (U.S. 17 Bus., Murrells Inlet, ☎ 803/651–3676) and **Hague Marina** (Hwy. 707, Myrtle Beach, ☎ 803/293–2141) offer half- and full-day fishing and sightseeing trips. The annual **Grand Strand Fishing Rodeo** (☎ 803/626–7444, Apr.–Oct.) features a "fish of the month" contest, with prizes for the largest catch of a designated species.

Golf

Many of the Grand Strand's 86 courses are championship layouts; most are public. Spring and fall, with off-season rates, are the busiest seasons, and there are many packages (call **Golf Holiday,** ☎ 803/448–5942 or 800/845–4653). Popular courses include: in Myrtle Beach, **Arcadian Shores Golf Club** (☎ 803/449–5217) and **Myrtle Beach National Golf Club** (☎ 803/448–2308 or 800/344–5590); in North Myrtle Beach, **Bay Tree Golf Plantation** (☎ 803/249–1487 or 800/845–6191), **Gator Hole** (☎ 803/249–3543 or 800/447–2668), **Heather Glen Golf Links** (☎ 803/249–9000), and **Robbers Roost Golf Club** (☎ 803/249–2085 or 800/352–2384); near Surfside Beach, **Blackmoor Golf Club** (☎ 803/650–5555); in Cherry Grove Beach, the much touted **Tidewater**

(☎ 803/249–6675); on Pawleys Island, **Litchfield Beach and Golf Resort** (☎ 803/237–3000 or 800/849–1897), **Litchfield Plantation** (☎ 803/237–9121 or 800/869–1410), and **Pawleys Plantation Golf & Country Club** (☎ 803/237–8497 or 800/367–9959).

Scuba Diving
In summer, a wide variety of warm-water tropical fish finds its way to the area from the Gulf Stream. Off the coast of Little River, rock and coral ledges teem with coral, sea fans, sponges, reef fish, anemones, urchins, arrow crabs, and stone crabs. Several outlying shipwrecks are home to schools of spadefish, amberjack, grouper, and barracuda. Instruction and equipment rentals are available from **Scuba Syndrome** (2718 Hwy. 501, Myrtle Beach, ☎ 803/626–6740).

Tennis
There are more than 150 courts on the Grand Strand. Facilities include hotel and resort courts, as well as free municipal courts in Myrtle Beach, North Myrtle Beach, and Surfside Beach. Among tennis clubs offering court time, rental equipment, and instruction are **Myrtle Beach Racquet Club** (☎ 803/449–4031), **Myrtle Beach Tennis and Swim Club** (☎ 803/449–4486), and **Litchfield Country Club** (☎ 803/237–3411).

Water Sports
Surfboards, Hobie Cats, Jet Skis, Windsurfers, and sailboats are available for rent at **Downwind Sails** (Ocean Blvd. at 29th Ave. S, Myrtle Beach, ☎ 803/448–7245) and **Myrtle Beach Yacht Club** (Coquina Harbor, N. Myrtle Beach, ☎ 803/249–5376).

Dining

Coastal South Carolina serves traditionally prepared seafood in lavish portions, garnished with hush puppies, coleslaw, and fresh vegetables. Myrtle Beach's mile-long "Restaurant Row" stretches along U.S. 17 from the city's northernmost limits. Here you'll find every type of cuisine imaginable, but you won't find the gourmet cooking of Charleston and Hilton Head; instead, expect family-style restaurants with predictable, but dependable, menus. Dress is casual unless otherwise noted.

CATEGORY	COST*
$$$$	over $25
$$$	$15–$25
$$	$7–$15
$	under $7

per person for a three-course meal, excluding drinks, service, and 5% sales tax

Georgetown
$$ **Rice Paddy.** This cozy Low Country restaurant is apt to be crowded
★ at lunch, when local solons flock in for homemade vegetable soup, garden-fresh salads, and sandwiches. Dinner is more relaxed, and the menu might have broiled fresh seafood, crabmeat casserole, or veal scaloppine. ✕ 408 Duke St., ☎ 803/546–2021. Reservations accepted. AE, MC, V. Closed Sun.

$$ **River Room.** This restaurant on the Sampit River specializes in chargrilled fish, seafood pastas, and steaks. For lunch you can have shrimp and grits or a variety of sandwiches and salads. It's especially romantic at night when the oil lamps and brass fixtures cast a warm glow on

the dark wood and brick interior of the turn-of-the-century building. ✗ *801 Front St.,* ☎ *803/527–4110. No reservations. AE, MC, V. Closed Sun.*

Murrells Inlet

$$ **Planter's Back Porch.** Sip cool drinks in the spring house of a turn-of-
★ the-century farmhouse, then have dinner in a garden setting. Black wrought-iron chandeliers are suspended from high white beams, and hanging baskets of greenery decorate white latticework archways separating the fireplace-centered main dining room and the airy, glass-enclosed porch. You can't go wrong with baked whole flounder, panned lump crabmeat, or the hearty inlet dinner with several types of fish. ✗ *U.S. 17 and Wachesaw Rd.,* ☎ *803/651–5263. Reservations accepted. AE, D, MC, V. Closed Dec.–mid-Mar.*

Myrtle Beach

$$–$$$ **Crab House.** In this sprawling, two-level dining room with beamed ceil-
★ ings, plank floors, and marine artifacts adorning the walls, the emphasis is on crabs steamed with garlic and other fresh local seafood. There's an extensive all-you-can-eat seafood, salad, and raw bar. The entire top floor is no-smoking. ✗ *Barefoot Landing, 4744 U.S. 17S, N. Myrtle Beach,* ☎ *803/272–1062. Reservations accepted. AE, MC, V.*

$$ **Rice Planters.** Dine on fresh seafood, quail, or steaks grilled to order
★ in a homey setting enhanced by candlelight, Low Country antiques, and rice-plantation tools and artifacts. Shrimp Creole is a house specialty; among the appetizers, don't miss the crab fingers! The bread and the pecan pie are home-baked. ✗ *6707 N. Kings Hwy.,* ☎ *803/449–3456. Reservations accepted. AE, D, MC, V.*

$$ **Sea Captain's House.** At this picturesque restaurant with nautical
★ decor, the best seats are in the windowed porch room, which overlooks the ocean. The fireplace in the wood-paneled dining room inside is warmly welcoming on cool off-season evenings. Menu highlights include she-crab soup, Low Country crab casserole, and avocado-seafood salad. The breads and desserts are baked here. ✗ *3002 N. Ocean Blvd.,* ☎ *803/448–8082. AE, D, MC, V.*

$$ **Southern Suppers.** Here's hearty family dining in a cozy farmhouse filled with country primitive art; handmade quilts line the walls. The menu features an all-you-can-eat seafood buffet and such down-home Southern specialties as fried chicken, country-fried steak, and country ham with red-eye gravy and grits. ✗ *5301 U.S. 17, midway between Myrtle Beach and Surfside Beach,* ☎ *803/238–4557. MC, V. Closed Oct.–Mar.*

North Myrtle Beach

$$–$$$ **Oak Harbor Inn.** Located on a quieter, northern stretch of the beach, this airy, open restaurant overlooks picturesque Vereen's Marina. It's a great local favorite. Specialties include chicken Annie, a boneless breast of chicken in puff pastry laced with ham, Swiss, and blue cheeses, drizzled with Parmesan and Mornay sauce. ✗ *1407 13th Ave. N,* ☎ *803/249–4737. Reservations accepted. AE, D, MC, V.*

$$ **Horst Gausthaus.** Dine on knockwurst, bratwurst, sauerbraten, and other traditional German foods at this Bavarian-style restaurant, where there's oom-pah-pah music every night but Sunday. ✗ *802 37th Ave. S,* ☎ *803/272–3351. Reservations advised. AE, MC, V.*

AFLOAT

Dinner cruises aboard the cruise ship *Hurricane* (☎ 803/249–3571) and yachts of the Neptune's pleasure fleet (☎ 803/280–4100) depart from Vereen's Marina (U.S. 17N and 11th Ave.). The *Barefoot Princess* (☎ 803/272–7743 or 800/685–6601), a replica of a sidewheel riverboat, offers dinner, sunset, and sightseeing cruises along the Intracoastal Waterway from Barefoot Landing (4898 U.S. 17S).

Pawleys Island

$$ Tyler's Cove. This restaurant specializes in such unusual Low Country fare as fried Carolina alligator, seasoned with buttermilk batter, and spicy Cajun chicken tossed in a salad of lettuce, cabbage, and jalapeño honey dressing. Sunday brunch is served. ✗ *Hammock Shops, U.S. 17,* ☎ *803/237–4848. Reservations advised. AE, D, MC, V.*

Lodging

With about 55,000 rooms available along the Grand Strand, it's never difficult to find a place to stay, and discounting is rampant. Package deals are offered year-round, the most attractive of them between Labor Day and spring break. Among other lodgings options, condominiums are popular, combining spaciousness and modern amenities and appealing especially to families. You can choose among cottages, villas, and hotel-style high-rise units. Maid service is frequently available. For the free directories *Grand Hotel and Motel Accommodations* and *Grand Condominium and Cottage Accommodations,* write to the Myrtle Beach Area Convention Bureau (710 21st Ave. N, Suite J, Myrtle Beach, SC 29577, ☎ 803/448–1629 or 800/356–3016).

CATEGORY	COST*
$$$$	over $100
$$$	$65–$100
$$	$45–$65
$	under $45

All prices are for a standard double room, excluding 7% tax.

Georgetown

$$–$$$ 1790 House. This lovely restored house, redecorated in 1993 by new owners Patricia and John Wiley, is in the center of the historic district. Built after the Revolution, when Georgetown's rice culture was at its peak, it contains Colonial furnishings suitable to its age. Guests are treated to gourmet breakfasts, evening refreshments, and the use of bicycles. For a romantic hideaway, request the private carriage house. 🖼 *630 Highmarket St., 29440,* ☎ *803/546–4821. 6 rooms with baths. AE, MC, V.*

McClellanville

$$$ Laurel Hill Plantation. This Low Country plantation bed-and-breakfast house, overlooking the marsh near the Intracoastal Waterway, has been rebuilt after its destruction by Hurricane Hugo (ask to see the scrapbooks of the storm). Owners Lee and Jackie Morrison have furnished it with country antiques. Guests can read a book in the hammock, go fishing or crabbing, take a boat ride, or watch the birds. The Morrisons serve a full breakfast and complimentary afternoon refreshments. 🖼 *8913 N. Hwy. 17, Box 190, 29458,* ☎ *803/887–3708. 4 rooms with bath. No credit cards.*

Myrtle Beach

$$$$ Kingston Plantation: A Radisson Resort. The Grand Strand's most lux-
★ urious property, this 20-story glass-sheathed tower is part of a complex of shops, restaurants, hotels, and condominiums set amid 145 acres of oceanside woodlands. Guest rooms are highlighted by bleached-wood

furnishings and attractive art. The balconied one-bedroom suites have kitchenettes. ☎ *9800 Lake Dr., 29572,* ☎ *803/449–0006 or 800/876– 0010,* FAX *803/497–1110. 614 suites. 2 restaurants, lounge, pool, 2 tennis courts, health club. AE, D, DC, MC, V.*

$$$–$$$$ **Best Western/Landmark.** The rooms in this high-rise oceanfront resort hotel are tastefully decorated in a modern style. Some have balconies and refrigerators. ☎ *1501 S. Ocean Blvd., 29577,* ☎ *803/448–9441 or 800/845–0658,* FAX *803/626–1501. 313 rooms, 14 suites. Restaurant, pub, pool bar, lounges, pool, nightclub, recreation room, children's program. AE, D, DC, MC, V.*

$$$–$$$$ **Breakers Resort Hotel.** The rooms in this recently renovated oceanfront hotel are airy and spacious, with contemporary decor. Many have balconies and refrigerators. ☎ *2006 N. Ocean Blvd., Box 485, 29578- 0485,* ☎ *803/444–4444 or 800/845–0688,* FAX *803/626–5000. 204 rooms, 186 suites. Restaurant, lounge, 3 pools, 2 hot tubs, 3 saunas, exercise room, children's programs, laundry service. AE, D, DC, MC, V.*

$$$–$$$$ **Sheraton Myrtle Beach Resort.** All rooms and suites have a fresh, contemporary look. Oceanfront Lounge, highlighted by tropical colors and rattan furnishings, is a lively evening gathering spot. ☎ *2701 S. Ocean Blvd., 29577,* ☎ *803/448–2518 or 800/992–1055,* FAX *803/449– 1879. 211 rooms, 8 suites. Restaurant, indoor and outdoor pools, health club, arcade. AE, D, DC, MC, V.*

$$$ **Chesterfield Inn.** A remnant from the past, this oceanfront brick inn, hidden beneath the towers of Myrtle Beach's more glitzy hotels, has been in operation for over half a century. The rooms in the old part are simple and plain, but many guests prefer them to the ones in the newer wing. Family-style meals are served on starched white tablecloths in the paneled dining room. ☎ *700 N. Ocean Blvd., 29578,* ☎ *803/448–3177,* FAX *803/626–4736. 57 rooms, 6 kitchenette units. Restaurant, pool, shuffleboard. AE, D, DC, MC V.*

$$$ **Driftwood on the Oceanfront.** Under the same ownership for more than 50 years, this facility is popular with families. Some rooms are oceanfront; all are decorated in sea, sky, or earth tones. ☎ *1600 N. Ocean Blvd., Box 275, 29578,* ☎ *803/448–1544 or 800/942–3456,* FAX *803/448–2917. 90 rooms. 2 pools, exercise room, recreation room. AE, D, DC, MC, V.*

$$$ **Holiday Inn Oceanfront.** This oceanfront inn is right at the heart of the action. The spacious rooms are decorated in cool sea tones. After beach basking, you can prolong the mood in the inn's spacious, plant-bedecked indoor recreation center, which comprises an indoor pool, exercise room, game room, and gift shop. ☎ *415 S. Ocean Blvd., 29577,* ☎ *803/448–4481 or 800/845–0313,* FAX *803/448–0086. 311 rooms. 2 restaurants, 2 lounges, snack bar, outdoor and indoor pools, hot tub, sauna, recreation room. AE, D, DC, MC, V.*

$$–$$$ **Comfort Inn.** This chain motel, 400 yards from the ocean, is clean, predictably furnished, and well maintained. ☎ *2801 S. Kings Hwy., 29577,* ☎ *803/626–4444 or 800/228–5150,* FAX *803/626–0753. 139 rooms, 14 suites. Restaurant, pool, health club. AE, D, DC, MC, V.*

North Myrtle Beach

$ **Days Inn at Waccamaw.** Relax by the pool or in the gazebo after a full day of shopping at the nearby Waccamaw Pottery and Outlet Park. The theaters of the Fantasy Harbour complex are also close at hand. Rooms here are clean and functional, filled with contemporary furnishings, and most are equipped with a refrigerator. ☎ *3650 Hwy. 501,*

29577, ☎ 803/236–1950 or 800/325–2525, FAX 803/236–9415. 160
rooms. Restaurant, lounge, pool, hot tub. AE, D, DC, MC, V.

Pawleys Island

$$$$ Litchfield by the Sea Beach and Golf Resort. Contemporary gray-blue
wood suite units, a short walk from the beach, nestle amid 4,500-acre
gardenlike grounds, which include three private golf clubs and a racquet club open to guests. All suites, tastefully decorated in pastel tones
and light woods, feature marble baths, wet bars, refrigerators, and microwave ovens. Similarly furnished one- and two-bedroom units in the
new five-story Bridgewater complex have private balconies overlooking the pool and Atlantic Ocean. "Country Club" cottages and marsh-
side villas are ideal for families or couples seeking extra privacy. ⊞
U.S. 17, 2 mi north of Pawleys Island, Drawer 320, 29585, ☎ 803/237–
3000 or 800/845–1897, FAX 803/237–4282. 96 hotel suites; 120 condominium, cottage, and villa units. Restaurant, lounge, indoor and
outdoor pools, sauna, hot tub, 3 18-hole golf courses, 19 tennis courts,
exercise room, racquetball, conference center. AE, MC, V.

$$$$ Litchfield Plantation. Period furnishings adorn four spacious suites of
this impeccably restored 1750 rice plantation manor-house-turned-coun-
try-inn fronted by a majestic avenue of live oaks. Guests may also stay
in retreat cottages scattered about the grounds. Golf and tennis privileges at the adjacent country club are part of the package here, as is
a complimentary Continental breakfast. The resort is approximately
2 miles south of Brookgreen Gardens on U.S. 17 (turn right at the Litchfield Country Club entrance and follow the signs to the plantation).
⊞ River Rd., Box 290, 29585, ☎ 803/237–9121 or 800/869–1410.
20 rooms, 6 2-and 3-bedroom cottages. Restaurant, pool, 2 tennis courts,
horseback riding, boating, concierge. AE, MC, V.

$$ Ramada Inn Seagull. This is a very well-maintained inn on a golf
course (excellent golf packages are available). Outfitted with motel-
modern furnishings, the rooms are spacious, bright, and airy. ⊞ U.S.
17S, Box 2217, 29585, ☎ 803/237–4261 or 800/272–6232, FAX
803/237–9708. 99 rooms. Dining room, lounge, pool. AE, DC, MC,
V.

The Arts

Theater productions, concerts, art exhibits, and other cultural events
are regularly offered at the **Myrtle Beach Convention Center** (Oak and
21st Ave. N, Myrtle Beach, ☎ 803/448–7166). The **Atalaya Arts Fes-
tival** at Huntington Beach State Park in the fall is a big draw; phone
803/237–4440 for more information. **Art in the Park,** featuring arts
and crafts, is staged in Myrtle Beach's Chapin Park three times dur-
ing the summer season (call 803/626–7444 for details).

Nightlife

Clubs offer varying fare, including beach music, the Grand Strand's
unique '50s-style sound. During summer, sophisticated live entertain-
ment is featured nightly at some clubs and resorts. Some hotels and
resorts also have piano bars or lounges featuring easy-listening music.

In Myrtle Beach: **Sandals** (500 Shore Dr., ☎ 803/449–6461) is an in-
timate lounge with live entertainment. **Coquina Club,** at the Best West-
ern Landmark Resort Hotel (☎ 803/448–9441), features beach-music
bands. The shag (the state dance) is popular at **Studebaker's** (2000 N.
Kings Hwy., ☎ 803/448–9747 or 803/626–3855) and **Duck's** (229 Main
St., N. Myrtle Beach, ☎ 803/249–3858). At the Breakers Hotel, **At-**

lantis Nightlife (Hwy. 501, ☎ 803/448–4200) is three nightclubs in one: a high-energy dance club, live entertainment and music, and a quiet patio lounge. At the **Afterdeck,** enjoy live bands, dancing, and comedy at an open-air club along the Intracoastal Waterway (Hwy. 17, Restaurant Row, ☎ 803/449–1550).

In Murrells Inlet: **Drunken Jack's** (☎ 803/651–2044 or 803/651–3232) is a popular restaurant with a lounge overlooking the docks and fishing fleets.

Country-western shows and other live acts have added a new dimension to Grand Strand entertainment. Currently, music lovers have 10 family-oriented shows to choose from: the 2,250-seat **Alabama Theater** (Barefoot Landing, 4750 U.S. 17, N. Myrtle Beach, tel 803/272–1111); **Carolina Opry** (82nd Ave. N, Myrtle Beach, ☎ 803/238–8888 or 800/843–6779); **Dolly Parton's Dixie Stampede** (next door to Carolina Opry, 8901-B U.S. 17 Bus., Myrtle Beach, ☎ 803/497–9700); **Dixie Jubilee** (701 Main St., N. Myrtle Beach, ☎ 803/238–8888 or 800/843–6779); **Southern Country Nights** (301 U.S. 17 Bus., Surfside Beach, ☎ 803/238–8888 or 800/843–6779).

The **Fantasy Harbor** complex (Hwy. 51 across from the Waccamaw Outlet Mall) includes five theaters: 200-seat **Gatlin Brothers Theatre** (☎ 803/395–6802 or 800/681–7469); **Euro Circus: The Russian Fantasy** (☎ 803/236–8500 or 800/830–3876); **Magic on Ice** (☎ 803/236–8500 or 800/395–6802); **Medieval Times Dinner & Tournment** (☎ 803/236–8080 or 800/436–4386), which opened early in 1995; and the 2000-seat **Ronnie Milsap Theatre** (☎ 803/236–8500).

Myrtle Beach and the Strand Essentials

Arriving and Departing, Getting Around

BY BOAT

Boaters traveling the Intracoastal Waterway may dock at **Hague Marina** (Hwy. 707, Myrtle Beach, ☎ 803/293–2141).

BY BUS

Greyhound Bus Lines (☎ 800/231–2222) serves Myrtle Beach.

BY CAR

Midway between New York and Miami, the Grand Strand can be reached from all directions via Interstates 20, 26, 40, 77, 85, and 95, which connect with U.S. 17, the major north–south coastal route through the Strand.

BY PLANE

The **Myrtle Beach Jetport** (☎ 803/448–1589) is served by American, American and its American Eagle affiliate, Delta and its Atlantic Southeast Airlines affiliate, and USAir.

BY TAXI

Service is provided by **Coastal Cab Service** in Myrtle Beach (☎ 803/448–3360 or 803/448–4444).

BY TRAIN

Amtrak (☎ 800/872–7245) service for the Grand Strand is available through a terminal in Florence. Buses connect with Amtrak there for the 65-mile drive to Myrtle Beach.

Guided Tours

Palmetto Tour & Travel (☎ 803/626–2660) and **Leisure Time Unlimited/Gray Line** (☎ 803/448–9483), both in Myrtle Beach, offer tour packages, guide services, and charter services. At the **Georgetown County Chamber of Commerce and Information Center** (102 Broad St., ☎ 803/546–8436 or 800/777–7705), you can take tours of historic areas (Mar.–Oct.) by tram, by 1840 horse-drawn carriage, or by boat. You can also rent cassette walking tours and pick up free driving- and walking-tour maps. **Georgetown Tour Company** (627 Front St., ☎ 803/546–9812 or 803/546–6827) offers tram tours of the historic district, a Ghostbusting Tour, and an afternoon Tea 'n Tour.

Important Addresses and Numbers

EMERGENCIES
Dial 911 for emergency assistance. The emergency room is open 24 hours a day at the **Grand Strand General Hospital** (off U.S. 17 at 809 82nd Pkwy., Myrtle Beach, ☎ 803/449–4411).

PHARMACY
The only all-night pharmacy in the area is located at the **Grand Strand General Hospital** (*above*).

RADIO STATIONS
FM: WDAI 98.5, light rock; WJXY 93.9, country; WJYR 92.1, easy listening; WKZQ 101.7, rock and roll; WNMB 105.9, best of the 60's–80's; WRNN 94.5, talk; WSYN 106.5, oldies; WYAK 103.1, country; WYAV 104, classic rock.

VISITOR INFORMATION
Georgetown County Chamber of Commerce and Information Center (*see* Guided Tours, *above*). **Myrtle Beach Area Chamber of Commerce and Information Center** (1301 N. Kings Hwy., Box 2115, Myrtle Beach 29578, ☎ 803/626–7444 or 800/356–3016, for brochures only).

HILTON HEAD AND BEYOND

Anchoring the southern tip of South Carolina's coastline is 42-square-mile Hilton Head Island, named after English sea captain William Hilton, who claimed it for England in 1663. It was settled by planters in the 1700s and flourished until the Civil War. Thereafter, the economy declined and the island languished until Charles E. Fraser, a visionary South Carolina attorney, began developing the Sea Pines resort in 1956. Other developments followed, and today Hilton Head's casual pace, broad beaches, myriad activities, and genteel good life make it one of the East Coast's most popular vacation getaways.

Beaufort (pronounced "Bewfort") is a graceful antebellum town with a compact historic district preserving lavish 18th- and 19th-century homes. Southeast, on the ocean, lies Fripp Island, a self-contained resort with controlled access. And midway between Beaufort and Charleston is Edisto ("ED–is–toh") Island, settled in 1690 and once notable for its silky Sea Island cotton. Some of its elaborate mansions have been restored; others brood in disrepair.

Exploring

Lined by towering pines, wind-sculpted live oaks, and palmettos, Hilton Head's 12 miles of beaches are a major attraction, and the semitropical barrier island also has oak and pine woodlands and meandering lagoons. Choice stretches are occupied by various resorts, or "plantations," among them Sea Pines, Shipyard, Palmetto Dunes, Port Royal, and Hilton Head. In these areas, accommodations range from rental villas and lavish private houses to luxury hotels (except Hilton Head, which has no rentals). The resorts are also private residential communities, although many have public restaurants, marinas, shopping areas, and recreational facilities. All are secured, and visitors cannot tour them unless arrangements are made at the visitor office near the main gate of each plantation.

In the south of the island, at the **Audubon–Newhall Preserve,** you'll find unusual native plant life identified and tagged in a pristine 50-acre site. There are trails, a self-guided tour, and seasonal plant walks. *Palmetto Bay Rd.,* ☎ *803/671–2008.* ☛ *Free.* ☉ *Dawn to dusk.*

Also in the south is the **Sea Pines Forest Preserve,** a 605-acre public wilderness tract with walking trails, a well-stocked fishing pond, a waterfowl pond, and a 3,400-year-old Indian shell ring. Both guided and self-guided tours are available. Sea Pines is located at the southwest tip of the island, accessible via US 278 (also called William Hilton Parkway). ☎ *803/842–1449.* ☛ *To Sea Pines Plantation: $3 per car for nonguests; this allows free access to preserve.* ☉ *Daily 7–4. Closed during the Heritage Golf Classic in Apr.*

The **Museum of Hilton Head Island**'s permanent collection consists of a diorama depicting Indian life on Hilton Head in the 15th century AD; the museum also hosts changing exhibits. Beach walks are conducted on weekdays, and tours of Indian sites, forts, and plantations randomly in season. *100 William Hilton Pkwy.,* ☎ *803/689–6767.* ☛ *Free.* ☉ *Mon.–Sat. 10–5, Sun. noon–4.*

Three miles west of the island, there's the **James M. Waddell Jr. Mariculture Research & Development Center,** where methods of raising seafood commercially are studied. Visitors may tour its 24 ponds and research building to see work in progress. *Sawmill Creek Rd., near the intersection of U.S. 278 and SC 46,* ☎ *803/837–3795.* ☛ *Free. Tours weekdays at 10 AM and by appointment.*

Beaufort

North of here is the waterfront city of **Beaufort,** established in 1710. It achieved immense prosperity toward the close of the 18th century when Sea Island cotton was introduced, and many of its lavish houses—with wide balconies, high ceilings, and luxurious appointments—remain today. Although many private houses in **Old Point,** the historic district, are not usually open to visitors, some may be on the annual Fall House Tour in mid-October, and the Spring Tour of Homes and Gardens, in April or May. The Greater Beaufort Chamber of Commerce (☎ 803/524–3163) can provide more information about house tour schedules. The rest of the year, you'll have to content yourself with appreciating the fine exteriors.

Across the street from the Chamber of Commerce is the **George Elliot House Museum,** which served as a Union hospital during the Civil War. It was built in 1840 in Greek Revival style, with leaded-glass fanlights, pine floors, and rococo ceilings. The furnishings include some fine early Victorian pieces. *1001 Bay St.,* ☎ *803/524–6334.* ☛ *$3 adults, $2 children under 15.* ☉ *Weekdays 11–3. Closed Jan.–early Feb.*

Nearby, the **John Mark Verdier House Museum,** built about 1790 in the Federal style, has been restored and furnished as it would have been between 1790 and the visit of Lafayette in 1825. It was headquarters for Union forces during the Civil War. *801 Bay St.,* ☎ *803/524–6334.* ☛ *$4 adults, $2 children under 15.* ⊘ *Tues.–Sat. 11–4.*

Built in 1795 and remodeled in 1852, the Gothic-style arsenal that was home of the Beaufort Volunteer Artillery now houses the **Beaufort Museum,** with prehistoric relics, Indian pottery, and Revolutionary and Civil War exhibits. *713 Craven St.,* ☎ *803/525–7077.* ☛ *$2 adults, 50¢ students and children 6–18.* ⊘ *Mon.–Tues. and Thurs.–Sat. 10– 5, Sun. 1–5.*

St. Helena's Episcopal Church, dating from 1724, was also touched by the Civil War: It was turned into a hospital and gravestones were brought inside to serve as operating tables. *501 Church St.,* ☎ *803/522– 1712.* ⊘ *Mon.–Sat. 10–4.*

Before setting off to explore outlying areas, pause in the **Henry C. Chambers Waterfront Park** off Bay Street to rest and survey the scene. Barbara Streisand filmed *Prince of Tides* here. Its seven landscaped acres along the Beaufort River, part of the Intracoastal Waterway, include a seawall promenade, a crafts market, gardens, and a marina. Some events of the popular mid-July Beaufort Water Festival, as well as a seasonal farmers'/crafts market, take place here.

On the Coast

Nine miles southeast of Beaufort via U.S. 21 is **St. Helena's Island,** site of the **Penn Center Historic District** and **York W. Bailey Museum.** Penn Center, established in the middle of the Civil War as the South's first school for freed slaves, today provides community services. The museum (formerly Dr. Bailey's clinic) has displays reflecting the heritage of sea island blacks. *Land's End Rd., St. Helena's Island,* ☎ *803/838– 2432. Donation suggested.* ⊘ *Tues.–Fri. 11–4 and by appointment.*

Nine miles farther east via U.S. 21 is **Hunting Island State Park,** a secluded domain of beach, nature trails, and varied fishing. The 1,120-foot fishing pier is among the longest on the East Coast. If you climb the 181 steps of the photogenic 140-foot **Hunting Island Lighthouse** (built in 1859 and abandoned in 1933) you'll be rewarded with sweeping views. ☎ *803/838–2011.* ☛ *$3 per car Mar.–Oct.; free rest of year. For cabin and camping reservations, write to Hunting Island State Park, 1775 Sea Island Pkwy., St. Helena 29920.*

Heading north from Beaufort on U.S. 21 to Gardens Corner, take Routes 17N and S-7-21 to the ruins of the **Sheldon Church,** built in 1753 and burned in 1779 and 1865. Only the brick walls and columns remain beside the old cemetery. Get back on Route 17N and then follow Route 174 to **Edisto Island** (80 miles from Beaufort). Here, magnificent stands of age-old oaks festooned with Spanish moss border quiet streams and side roads; wild turkeys still may be spotted on open grasslands and amid palmetto palms. Many of the island's inhabitants are descendants of former slaves. **Edisto Beach State Park** has 3 miles of beach with excellent shelling, housekeeping cabins by the marsh, and campsites by the ocean. Luxury resort development have also recently begun to encroach upon the scene. For camping reservations, call 803/869–2156 or 803/869–3396.

What to See and Do with Children

On Hilton Head Island, all major hotels offer **summer youth activities,** some have full-scale youth programs. The Island Recreation Center (Wilborn Rd.) runs a summer camp that visiting youngsters can join.

Hilton Head Island Recreation Association, Box 22593, Hilton Head Island 29925, ☎ 803/681–7273. ⊙ Camp mid-June–late Aug., weekdays.

Off the Beaten Path

From Hilton Head, you can go by boat to **Daufuskie Island,** the setting for Pat Conroy's novel *The Water Is Wide,* which was made into the movie *Conrack.* Most inhabitants, descendants of former slaves, live on small farms among remnants of churches, homes, and schools—reminders of prosperous antebellum times. With its unspoiled live oaks, pines, and palmettos, Daufuskie won't remain off the beaten track for long. Excursions to the island are run out of Hilton Head by **Adventure Cruises** (Shelter Cove Marina, ☎ 803/785–4558), **Vagabond Cruises** (Harbour Town Marina, ☎ 803/842–4155), and **Calibogue Cruises** (164-B Palmetto Bay Rd., ☎ 803/785–8242). You can arrange kayak nature trips at Shelter Cove Marina (☎ 803/384–8125) and South Beach Marina (☎ 803/671–2643).

At **Parris Island,** 10 miles south of Beaufort via SC 802, visitors are welcome to observe U.S. Marine Corps recruit training and take a guided tour or drive through in their own vehicles. There's a replica of the Iwo Jima flag-raising monument on the base. The **Parris Island Museum** exhibits vintage uniforms, photographs, and weapons. ☎ *803/525–2951. ☛ Free. ⊙ Fri.–Wed. 10–4:30, Thurs. 10–7.*

Shopping

Malls and Outlets

Major Hilton Head Island shopping sites include the **Mall at Shelter Cove** (Hwy. 278, ½ mi north of Palmetto Dunes Resort, ☎ 803/686–3090), with 55 shops and four restaurants; and **Coligny Plaza** (Coligny Circle, ☎ 803/842–6050), with 60-plus shops, restaurants, a movie theater, and a supermarket. **Shoppes on the Parkway** (Hwy. 278, 1 mi south of Palmetto Dunes Resort, ☎ 803/686–6233) comprises nearly 30 outlets, including Dansk, Gorham, Aileen, and Van Heusen. **Low Country Factory Outlet Village** (Hwy. 278 at the island gateway, ☎ 803/837–4339) has 40 outlets selling clothing, shoes, and housewares.

Antiques

Den of Antiquity (Hwy. 170, Beaufort, ☎ 803/842–6711), the area's largest antiques shop, carries a wide assortment of Low Country and nautical pieces. **Harbour Town Antiques** (Harbour Town, Hilton Head, ☎ 803/671–5999) carries American and English furniture and unusual Oriental and English porcelain.

Art Galleries

In Hilton Head, the **Red Piano Art Gallery** (220 Cordillo Pkwy., ☎ 803/785–2318) showcases works by island artists and craftspeople. In Beaufort, the **Rhett Gallery** (901 Bay St., ☎ 803/524–3339) sells Low Country art by members of the Rhett family and Stephen Webb.

Jewelry

On Hilton Head, the **Bird's Nest** (Coligny Plaza, ☎ 803/785–3737) sells locally made shell and sand-dollar jewelry. The **Goldsmith Shop** (3 Lagoon Rd., ☎ 803/785–2538) features classic jewelry, island charms, custom designs, and repairs. **Touch of Turquoise** (Mall at Shelter Cove, ☎ 803/842–3880) showcases creations in silver and turquoise.

In Beaufort, the **Craftseller** (813 Bay St., ☎ 803/525–6104) showcases jewelry and other items by Southern craftsfolk.

Nature
The **Audubon Nature Store** (The Village at Wexford, ☎ 803/785–4311) and the **Hammock Company** (Coligny Plaza, ☎ 803/686–3636 or 800/344–4264) sell gift items and other things with a nature theme.

Beaches

Although the resort beaches are reserved for guests and residents, there are four public entrances to Hilton Head's 12 miles of ocean beach. Two main parking and changing areas are at Coligny Circle, near the Holiday Inn, and on Folly Field Road, off U.S. 278. Signs along U.S. 278 point the way to Bradley and Singleton beaches, where parking space is limited. **Hunting Island State Park** and **Edisto Beach State Park** each have about 3 miles of public beach.

Sports

Bicycling
There are pathways in several areas of Hilton Head (many in the resorts), and pedaling is popular along the firmly packed beach. Bicycles can be rented at most hotels and resorts and at **Harbour Town Bicycles** (Heritage Plaza, ☎ 803/785–3546), **South Beach Cycles** (Sea Pines Plantation, ☎ 803/671–2453), and **Fish Landing Creek** (Palmetto Dunes, ☎ 803/785–2021).

Fishing
On Hilton Head, you can pick oysters, dig for clams, or cast for shrimp; supplies are available at **Shelter Cove Marina** at Palmetto Dunes (☎ 803/842–7001). Local marinas offer in-shore and deep-sea fishing charters. Each year a billfishing tournament and two king mackerel tournaments attract anglers.

Golf
Many of Hilton Head's 28 championship courses are open to the public, including **Palmetto Dunes** (☎ 803/785–1138), **Sea Pines** (☎ 803/842–8484), **Port Royal and Shipyard** (☎ 803/689–5600), **Island West Golf Course** (Hwy. 278, ☎ 803/689–6660), and **Old South Golf Links** (Hwy. 278, ☎ 803/785–5353). **Harbour Town Golf Links at Sea Pines** hosts the MCI Classic (☎ 803/671–2448) every spring.

Horseback Riding
Many trails wind through woods and nature preserves. Some stables in and near Hilton Head are: **Lawton Stables** (Sea Pines, ☎ 803/671–2586), **Rose Hill Plantation Stables** (Bluffton, ☎ 803/757–3082), and **Sandy Creek Stables** (near Spanish Wells, ☎ 803/689–3423).

Polo
There are matches every other Sunday during spring and fall at **Rose Hill Plantation** (Bluffton, ☎ 803/757–4945).

Tennis
There are more than 300 courts on Hilton Head. **Sea Pines Racquet Club** (☎ 803/842–8484), home of the Family Circle Tournament; **Shipyard** (☎ 803/686–8804); and **Port Royal** (☎ 803/686–8803) are

highly rated. Clubs that welcome guests include **Palmetto Dunes** (☎ 803/785–1152) and **Van der Meer Tennis Center** (☎ 803/785–8388).

Windsurfing

Lessons and rentals are available from **Outside Hilton Head** at Sea Pines Resort's South Beach Marina (☎ 803/671–2643) and at Shelter Cove Plaza (☎ 803/686–6996).

Dining

Hilton Head serves South Carolina seafood, of course, but this cosmopolitan island has restaurants to suit every palate. Dress is casual unless otherwise noted.

CATEGORY	COST*
$$$$	over $25
$$$	$15–$25
$$	$7–$15
$	under $7

per person for a three-course meal, excluding drinks, service, and 5% tax

Beaufort

LOW COUNTRY

$$ New Gadsby Tavern. Dine on fresh seafood and Low Country specials in any of three dining areas overlooking Beaufort's Waterfront Park and bay. The formal dining room and taproom are noted for Italian specialties and great European desserts. On the terrace, you can feast on tapas or selections from a fresh raw bar. ✕ *822 Bay St., ☎ 803/525–1800. Reservations advised. AE, D, MC, V.*

Edisto Island

LOW COUNTRY

$$–$$$ Old Post Office. Try the veal Edistonian, the fussed-over pork chop, or
★ the blue-crab-and-asparagus pie, served with the house salad, vegetables, and freshly baked bread, at this island restaurant on Shore Creek. The house specialty is shrimp and grits. Originally Bailey's General Store and U.S. Post Office, the renovated building contains the original post office boxes and window. ✕ *Hwy. 174, 5 mi from Edisto Beach, ☎ 803/869–2339. Reservations advised. MC, V. Closed Sun. June–Sept., Sun. and Mon. Oct.–May. No lunch.*

Hilton Head

CONTINENTAL

$$$$ Harbourmaster's. With sweeping views of the harbor, this spacious, multilevel dining room offers such dishes as chateaubriand and New Zealand rack of lamb laced with a brandy demiglaze. Service is deft. Prix-fixe early dinners ($16.95) are offered daily except Sunday. ✕ *Shelter Cove Marina, off U.S. 278, ☎ 803/785–3030. Reservations required. Jacket required at dinner. AE, DC, MC, V. No lunch. Closed Sun. and Jan.*

$$$–$$$$ Barony Grill. A series of softly lighted seating areas with upscale coun-
★ try French decor lead off the main dining room, which is centered with a display of drop-dead desserts, marzipan flowers, and exotic cheese and bread. Try an elegant low-calorie dish like chilled coconut-pineapple soup, asparagus salad with quail eggs, poached fillet of Dover sole with seafood mousse, or macédoine of fresh fruit with raspberry sauce.

✕ *Westin Resort, 135 S. Port Royal Dr.,* ☎ *803/681–4000. Reservations required. AE, D, DC, MC, V. No lunch.*

LOW COUNTRY

$$ Old Fort Pub. Tucked away in a quiet site overlooking Skull Creek and beside the Civil War ruins of Fort Mitchell, this rustic restaurant specializes in such dishes as oyster pie, oysters wrapped in Smithfield ham, Savannah chicken-fried steak with onion gravy, and hoppin' john (a Southern concoction of black-eyed peas and rice seasoned with ham hocks and Tabasco). ✕ *Hilton Head Plantation,* ☎ *803/681–2386. Reservations advised. AE, D, DC, MC, V. No lunch Sun.*

SEAFOOD

$$ Crazy Crab. This casual eatery serves seafood as fresh as you can get it—steamed, fried, baked, or broiled—at two locations overlooking the water. They're famous for their steamed seafood pot and Crazy Crab boil. ✕ *U.S. 278,* ☎ *803/681–5021 (no lunch); Harbour Town Yacht Basin,* ☎ *803/363–2722. No reservations. AE, D, MC, V.*

$$ Hemingway's. This oceanfront restaurant serves pompano *en papillote,* trout almandine with herbed lemon-butter sauce, fresh grilled seafoods, and steaks in a relaxed, Key West–type atmosphere. ✕ *Hyatt Regency Hilton Head, Palmetto Dunes Resort,* ☎ *803/785–1234. Reservations advised. AE, D, DC, MC, V. No lunch.*

$$ Hudson's on the Docks and **Carmine's.** Hudson's on the Docks is a huge, airy, family-owned restaurant with its own fishing fleet; freshly caught fish is rushed straight to the kitchens. The dining room seems always to be full, but service is quick and friendly, and diners never feel rushed. There's also an oyster bar. Next door is Carmine's, which specializes in steaks and ribs, as well as serving seafood. A third branch, **Hudson's on the Beach,** nearby at Coligny Place, also emphasizes seafood. ✕ *Hudson's on the Docks and Carmine's: The Landing,* ☎ *803/681–2772. Hudson's on the Beach: Coligny Place,* ☎ *803/842–4888. All three: No reservations. AE, MC, V. Carmine's: No lunch. Closed Sun. Hudson's on the Beach: No lunch Sun.*

Lodging

Sea Pines, the oldest and best-known of Hilton Head's resort developments, or plantations, occupies 4,500 thickly wooded acres with three golf courses, a fine beach, tennis clubs, stables, and shopping plazas. The focus of Sea Pines is **Harbour Town,** built around the charming marina, which has shops, restaurants, some condominiums, and the landmark Hilton Head lighthouse. Accommodations are in luxurious houses and villas facing the ocean or the golf courses.

The Crystal Sands–Crowne Plaza Resort is the oceanfront centerpiece of **Shipyard Plantation,** which also has villa condominiums, three nine-hole courses, a tennis club, and a small beach club. **Palmetto Dunes Resort** has the oceanfront Hyatt Regency Hilton Head, the Hilton Resort and other accommodations, the renowned Rod Laver Tennis Center, a good stretch of beach, three golf courses, and several oceanfront rental villa complexes. At **Port Royal Plantation** there's the posh Westin Resort, which is on the beach and has three golf courses and a tennis club.

Hilton Head Central Reservations (Box 5312, Hilton Head Island 29938, ☎ 803/785–9050 or 800/845–7018, ℻ 803/686-3255) represents almost every hotel, motel, and rental agency on the island. Other options are available through the **Hilton Head Condo Hotline** (☎ 803/785–2939 or 800/258–5852, ext. 53) and **Hilton Head Reserva-**

tions and Golf Line (☏ 803/444–4772). Rates drop appreciably in the off-season (Nov.–Mar.), and package plans are available year-round.

CATEGORY	COST*
$$$$	over $145
$$$	$95–$145
$$	$55–$95
$	under $50

All prices are for a standard double room, excluding 7% tax

Beaufort

$$$ **Rhett House Inn.** True southern hospitality can be had at this story-
★ book inn in the heart of the historic district. Art and antiques fill the rooms, and guests are served breakfast and afternoon tea. The restaurant, which is open to the public by reservation, serves such excellent Continental fare as leek-and-goat cheese tarts, seared veal chops in a green peppercorn sauce, and chicken fricassee with quenelles. ☏ *1009 Craven St., 29902, ☏ 803/524–9030, FAX 803/524–1310. 9 rooms with bath, 1 suite. Bicycles, billiards. MC, V.*

$$$ **Two Suns Inn.** Guests at this B&B, a restored 1917 Neoclassical house overlooking the Beaufort River, enjoy large rooms, afternoon tea-and-toddy hour, and a full breakfast. The inn also has an extensive business center and extremely down-to-earth and friendly hosts, making this a great spot for business travelers after companionship and computer modems. ☏ *1705 Bay St., 29902, ☏ FAX 803/522–1122, ☏ 800/552–4244. 5 rooms with baths. AE, MC, V.*

$$ **Best Western Sea Island Inn.** At this well-maintained resort inn in the downtown historic district, rooms feature period decor. ☏ *1015 Bay St., Box 532, 29902, ☏ 803/524–4121 or 800/528–1234, FAX 803/524–9396. 43 rooms. Restaurant, lounge, pool. AE, DC, MC, V.*

Edisto Island

$$$ **Cassina Point Plantation.** You can live out your fantasies about the antebellum days at this authentically restored plantation house, now a bed-and-breakfast inn, surrounded by fields that used to be planted in Sea Island cotton. Federal troops who occupied the house for three years left their graffiti in the basement. Guests may fish in the creek (watch for the playful porpoises), go crabbing or shrimping, watch birds, or take a stroll. A fruit bowl, beverages, and full breakfast come with the room. ☏ *1642 Clark Rd., Box 535, 29438, ☏ 803/869–2535. 4 rooms with half baths (2 full hall baths). Croquet, boating. No credit cards.*

$$–$$$ **Fairfield Ocean Ridge Resort.** This is a good choice for vacationers seeking to combine all the resort amenities with a get-away-from-it-all setting. There are accommodations in well-furnished two- and three-bedroom villa units tastefully decorated in contemporary style. ☏ *1 King Cotton Rd., Box 27, 29438, ☏ 803/869–2561 or 800/845–8500, FAX 803/869–2384. 100 units. Restaurant, lounge, pool, wading pool, 18-hole golf course, miniature golf, 4 tennis courts, hiking trails, beach, boating, fishing. AE, D, MC, V.*

Fripp Island

$$–$$$ **Fripp Island Resort.** The resort encompasses the entire island, and access is limited to guests only. The two- and three-bedroom villas are contemporary in decor. ☏ *19 mi south of Beaufort via U.S. 21, 1 Tarpon Blvd., 29920, ☏ 803/838–3535 or 800/845–4100, FAX 803/828–2733. 133 units. 3 restaurants, 6 pools, 18-hole golf course, 10 tennis courts, jogging, boating, rental bikes and bike paths. AE, MC, V.*

Hilton Head Island

$$$$ **Hyatt Regency Hilton Head Resort.** Recent renovation added 150 rooms to the island's largest oceanfront resort property. Spacious rooms are in pastel tones; some have balconies. Guests have golf and tennis privileges at the nearby Palmetto Dunes Resort. ⌕ *U.S. 278, Box 6167, 29938,* ☎ *803/785–1234 or 800/233–1234,* 𝔽𝔸𝕏 *803/842–4695. 475 rooms, 30 suites. 3 restaurants, lounge, indoor and outdoor pools (one each), health club, beach, boating, concierge floor, convention facilities. AE, DC, MC, V.*

$$$$ **Westin Resort, Hilton Head Island.** This horseshoe-shaped hotel sprawls
★ in a lushly landscaped oceanfront setting. The expansive guest rooms, most with ocean views, are furnished in a mix of period reproduction and contemporary furnishings. All have comfortable seating areas and desks. Public areas display fine Oriental porcelains, screens, and paintings. ⌕ *2 Grass Lawn Ave., 29928,* ☎ *803/681–4000 or 800/228–3000,* 𝔽𝔸𝕏 *803/681–1087. 415 rooms, 38 suites. 3 restaurants, 3 lounges, pool, health club. AE, DC, MC, V.*

$$$–$$$$ **Crystal Sands–Crowne Plaza Resort.** Holiday Inn Worldwide's first property of this caliber in the United States, this oceanfront resort (formerly Marriott's Hilton Head) opened in 1993. Decorated in a nautical theme and set in a luxuriant garden, it offers all the amenities of Shipyard Plantation. ⌕ *130 Shipyard Dr., 29928,* ☎ *803/842–2400 or 800/465–4329,* 𝔽𝔸𝕏 *803/785–8463. 313 rooms, 25 suites. 2 restaurants, pub, indoor and outdoor pools, spa, 9- and 18-hole golf courses, racquetball, health club, business services, meeting rooms. AE, D, DC, MC, V.*

$$$–$$$$ **Hilton Head Island Resort.** There's a Caribbean feel to this five-story resort hotel. The grounds are beautifully landscaped, and the rooms, all oceanside, are spacious and colorfully decorated in a modern style. ⌕ *23 Ocean La., Box 6165, 29938,* ☎ *803/842–8000 or 800/845–8001,* 𝔽𝔸𝕏 *803/842–4988. 303 rooms, 20 suites. Restaurant, pool, hot tub, sauna, health club, volleyball, boating, fishing, bicycles. AE, DC, MC, V.*

$$$–$$$$ **Marriott's Grande Ocean Resort.** Though built as a time-share property, this beautiful oceanfront condo development, within walking distance of shops and restaurants, offers a limited number of rentals. The fully furnished two-bedroom, two-bath luxurious villas come with kitchens, large whirlpool tubs, and maid service. ⌕ *51 S. Forest Beach Dr., 29929,* ☎ *803/785–2000 or 800/473–6674,* 𝔽𝔸𝕏 *803/842–3413. 140 villas. Deli, lounge, indoor pool, exercise room. AE, MC, V.*

$$$ **Holiday Inn Oceanfront Resort.** This handsome high-rise motor hotel is on a broad, quiet stretch of beach. The rooms are spacious and well furnished in a contemporary style. ⌕ *S. Forest Beach Dr., Box 5728, 29938,* ☎ *803/785–5126 or 800/465–4329,* 𝔽𝔸𝕏 *803/785–6678. 249 rooms. Restaurant, 2 lounges, pool. AE, D, DC, MC, V.*

$–$$ **Red Roof Inn.** This budget-priced, two-story inn is especially popular with families. Clean and functional rooms are just a short drive from the public beaches. ⌕ *5 Regency Pkwy. (U.S. 278), 29928,* ☎ *803/686–6808 or 800/843–7663,* 𝔽𝔸𝕏 *803/842–3352. 112 rooms. AE, D, DC, MC, V.*

The Arts

The **Cultural Council of Hilton Head** (☎ 803/686–3945) has details on Hilton Head arts events. **Community Playhouse** (Arrow Rd., ☎ 803/785–4878) presents up to 10 musicals or plays each year and has a young people's theater program. In warm weather, free outdoor concerts are held at **Harbour Town** and **Shelter Cove.** Concerts, plays, films, art shows, theater, sporting events, food fairs, and minitournaments make up Hilton Head's **SpringFest,** (☎ 803/686–4944), which runs for the month of March.

Nightlife

Dancing

Club Indigo (☎ 803/785–1234), a large cabaret downstairs at the Hyatt Regency Hilton Head, has dancing and two shows nightly Monday through Saturday. **Regatta** (☎ 803/842–8000), a sophisticated oceanfront night spot in the Hilton Resort, features smooth jazz nightly. **Robber's Row** (☎ 803/785–5126), a locally popular lounge in the Holiday Inn Oceanfront Resort, has nightly entertainment, as does **Signals** (☎ 803/842–2400), in the Crystal Sands–Crowne Plaza Resort.

Easy Listening

Cafe Europa (☎ 803/671–3399), at the Lighthouse in Harbour Town, has nightly piano entertainment. **Hemingway's Lounge** (☎ 803/785–1234) at the Hyatt Regency Hilton Head has live entertainment in a casually elegant setting Tuesday through Saturday. The **Pelican Poolside** (☎ 803/681–4000), an oceanfront lounge at the Westin Resort, has informal entertainment every night but Sunday. **Playful Pelican** (☎ 803/681–4000), the pool bar at the same location, has a live calypso band Tuesday through Sunday from 1 to 4 PM.

Hilton Head Essentials

Arriving and Departing, Getting Around

BY BOAT
Hilton Head is accessible via the Intracoastal Waterway, with docking available at **Shelter Cove Marina** (☎ 803/842–7001), **Harbour Town Marina** (☎ 803/671–2704), and **Schilling Boathouse** (☎ 803/681–2628).

BY CAR
The island is 40 miles east of I–95 (Exit 28 off I–95S, Exit 5 off I–95N).

BY PLANE
Hilton Head Island Airport (no ☎) is served by USAir Express. Most travelers use the **Savannah International Airport** (☎ 912/964–0514), about an hour from Hilton Head, which is served by Delta, United, USAir, and ValuJet.

BY TAXI
Yellow Cab (☎ 803/686–6666) and **Low Country Taxi and Limousine Service** (☎ 803/681–8294) provide service in Hilton Head.

Guided Tours

Low Country Adventures (☎ 803/681–8212) offers tours of Hilton Head, Beaufort, and Charleston. **Discover Hilton Head** (☎ 803/842–9217) gives daily historical tours of the island. Hilton Head's **Adventure Cruises** (☎ 803/785–4558) offers dinner, sightseeing, and murder-mystery cruises. Several companies, including **Harbour Town Charters** (☎ 803/363–2628), run dolphin sightseeing and feeding trips. Call the **Greater Beaufort Chamber of Commerce** (☎ 803/524–3163) to find out about self-guided walking or driving tours of Beaufort.

Important Addresses and Numbers

EMERGENCIES
Dial 911 for police, fire, and ambulance assistance. Emergency medical service is available at the **Hilton Head Hospital** (Hospital Center Blvd., ☎ 803/681–6122).

RADIO STATIONS
AM: WFXH 1130, sports talk. **FM:** WFXH 106.1, classic rock; WAEV 97.3, adult contemporary; WLVH 101.1, soft soul; WJCL 96.5, country; WOCW 92.1, oldies; WNCK 99.7, beach, boogie, and blues.

VISITOR INFORMATION
Greater Beaufort Chamber of Commerce (Box 910, 1006 Bay St., Beaufort 29901-0910, ☎ 803/524–3163). In Hilton Head, your best bet for tourist information is to stop by the **Welcome Center and Museum of Hilton Head** (100 William Hilton Pkwy.; calls automatically go to the Hilton Head Island Chamber of Commerce, ☎ 803/785–3673), which opened in 1994. You can also write to the **Hilton Head Island Chamber of Commerce** (Box 5647, Hilton Head 29938, ☎ 803/785–3673). The two **Hilton Head Welcome Centers,** run by a private real estate firm, are on Route 278 next to the bridge to Hilton Head and at 6 Lagoon Road at the south end of the island. In addition to providing tourism information about the island, these centers attempt to entice you into purchasing real estate on Hilton Head.

THE HEARTLAND

South Carolina's Heartland, between the coastal Low Country and the mountains, is a varied region of swamps and flowing rivers, fertile farmland, and vast forests of pines and hardwoods. Lakes Murray, Marion, and Moultrie offer wonderful fishing, and the many state parks are popular for hunting, hiking, swimming, and camping. At the center of the region is the state capital, Columbia, an engaging contemporary city superimposed on cherished historic remnants. It's a city of restored mansions, several museums, a university, a variety of dining, a lively arts scene, and one of the country's best zoos.

In Aiken, the center of South Carolina's Thoroughbred Country, such champions as Kelso and Pleasant Colony were trained. The beautiful scenery is studded with the fine mansions of such wealthy Northerners as the Vanderbilts and Whitneys. Throughout the region, towns like Ninety Six, Sumter, and Camden preserve and interpret the past, with historic re-creations, exhibits, and restorations. Several splendid public gardens provide islands of color during much of the year.

Exploring

Columbia
In 1786, South Carolina's capital was moved from Charleston to Columbia, in the center of the state along the banks of the Congaree River. One of the nation's first planned cities, Columbia's streets are among the widest in America—designed this way because it was then thought that stagnant air fostered the spread of malaria. The city soon grew into a center of political, commercial, cultural, and social activity. But in early 1865 General William Tecumseh Sherman invaded South Carolina with a destructive determination described by a New York newspaper as 50 times worse than the earlier march through Georgia. Two-thirds of Columbia was incinerated, though a few homes and public buildings were spared. Today the city is a sprawling blend of mod-

ern office blocks, suburban neighborhoods, and the occasional ante-bellum home.

Our tour begins at the **State House.** Started in 1855 and completed in 1950, the Capitol is made of native blue granite in the Italian-Renaissance style. Six bronze stars on the outer western wall mark direct hits by Sherman's cannons. The interior is richly appointed with brass, marble, mahogany, and artworks, and a replica of Jean Antoine Houdon's statue of George Washington is on the grounds. The building was closed in 1995 for three years of extensive renovation. *Main and Gervais Sts.,* ☎ *803/734–2430.* ☛ *Free.*

The **Fort Jackson Museum,** on the grounds of the U.S. Army Training Center, displays armaments, heavy equipment from the two world wars, and exhibits on the life of Andrew Jackson. *Bldg. 4442, Jackson Blvd.,* ☎ *803/751–7419.* ☛ *Free.* ☉ *Tues.–Fri. 10–4, weekends 1–4.*

The **Columbia Museum of Art and Gibbes Planetarium** contains the Kress Foundation Collection of Renaissance and Baroque treasures, sculpture, decorative arts, and European and American paintings, with special emphasis on works by Southeastern artists. *1112 Bull St.,* ☎ *803/799–2810.* ☛ *Free; planetarium shows: $2.50 adults, $1.50 children under 18 and senior citizens.* ☉ *Tues.–Fri. 10–5, weekends 12:30–5. Planetarium shows weekends at 2, 3, and 4.*

Exhibits at the **South Carolina State Museum,** in a large, refurbished textile mill, interpret the state's natural history, archaeology, historical development, technological and artistic accomplishments. A permanent exhibit portrays noted black astronauts (dedicated to South Carolina native Dr. Ronald McNair, who died on the *Challenger*), and another focuses on the cotton industry and slavery. An iron gate made for the museum by Phillip Simmons, the "dean of Charleston Blacksmiths," is also on display. *301 Gervais St.,* ☎ *803/737–4921.* ☛ *$4 adults, $3 senior citizens, $1.50 children 6–17.* ☉ *Mon.–Sat. 10–5, Sun. 1–5.*

TIME OUT   For a quick and tasty break, check out the **Gourmet Shop Cafe** (724 Saluda Ave., ☎ 803/799–3705), in the heart of the Five Points Shopping District (*see* Shopping, *below*). You can choose from among dozens of fancy sandwiches and salads here. The Amaretto cheesecake is memorable.

Stop by the Museum Shop at Taylor and Henderson Streets in the historic district to get a map and buy tickets to tour the four Columbia houses that have been restored and opened to the public. The **Hampton–Preston Mansion** (1615 Blanding St., ☎ 803/252–1770), dating from 1818, is filled with lavish furnishings collected by three generations of two influential families. The classic, columned 1823 **Robert Mills House** (1616 Blanding St., ☎ 803/252–1770) was named for its architect who later designed the Washington Monument. It has opulent Regency furniture, marble mantels, silver doorknobs, and spacious grounds. **Mann–Simons Cottage–Museum of African-American Cultures** (1403 Richland St., ☎ 803/252–1770) was the home of Celia Mann, one of only 200 free African-Americans in Columbia in the mid-1800s. The nearby **Woodrow Wilson Boyhood Home** (1705 Hampton St., ☎ 803/252–1770) displays the gaslights, arched doorways, and ornate furnishings of the Victorian period. ☛ *To each house: $3 adults, $1.50 students; combination ticket to all four houses: $10 adults, $5 students.* ☉ *All houses Tues.–Sat. 10:15–3:15, Sun. 1:15–4:15.*

Riverfront Park and Historic Columbia Canal, where the Broad and Saluda rivers meet, is made around the city's original waterworks and hydroelectric plant. Interpretive markers describe the area's plant and animal life and tell the history of the buildings. *312 Laurel St.,* ☎ *803/733–8613.* ☛ *Free.* ⊙ *Daily dawn to dusk.*

★ **Riverbanks Zoological Park and Botanical Gardens** contains more than 2,000 animals and birds, some endangered, in natural habitats. Walk along pathways and through landscaped gardens to see polar bears, Siberian tigers, and American bald eagles. The South American primate collection has won international acclaim, and the park is noted for its success in breeding endangered and fragile species. There's also an aquarium-reptile complex, whose four habitats exhibit South Carolina, desert, tropical, and marine specimens. In June 1995 a new 70-acre Botanical Garden was added on the west bank of the Saluda River, doubling the size of the facility. *I–126 and U.S. 76 at Greystone Riverbanks exit,* ☎ *803/779–8717 or 803/779–8730.* ☛ *$4.75 adults, $3.25 senior citizens, $2.25 children 3–12.* ⊙ *9–4 weekdays, 9–5 summer weekends.*

Camden

From Columbia, drive northeast on I–20 for 32 miles to charming **Camden,** a town with a horsy history and grand Southern Colonial homes. Camden's fanciest roads remain unpaved for the sake of the hooves of the horses who regularly trot over them. A center of textile trade from the late 19th century through the 1940s, Camden attracted Northerners escaping the cold winters; one of its early prominent families, the DuPonts, is today one of Camden's major employers. Because General Sherman spared the town during the War Between the States, most of its antebellum homes still stand. It's South Carolina's oldest inland town, dating to 1732. British General Lord Cornwallis established a garrison here during the Revolutionary War, and burned most of Camden before evacuating it. Today, the **Historic Camden Revolutionary War Site** re-creates the British occupation of 1780 on the site of the early 19th-century village. Several house restorations display period furnishings, including Cornwallis's headquarters, the **Kershaw–Cornwallis House** (circa 1770). Nature trails, fortifications, a powder magazine, a picnic area, and a crafts shop are also here. *U.S. 521, 1.4 mi north of I–20,* ☎ *803/432–9841.* ☛ *$4.50 adults, $4 senior citizens, $1.50 children.* ⊙ *For guided tours Tues.–Sat. 10–4, Sun. 1–4. Museum shop open daily 10–5.*

Sumter

From Camden, drive southeast on U.S. 521 for 30 miles to **Sumter.** Named for the Revolutionary War hero and statesman General Thomas Sumter, the city was settled about 1740 as the center of a cultivated plantation district. Today it is home to varied industries, lumbering, agricultural marketing, and nearby Shaw Air Force Base. The **Sumter County Museum and Archives** (headquarters of the Sumter County Historical Society), in a lovely 1845 Victorian Gothic house, exhibits fine period furnishings, Oriental carpeting, vintage carriages, dolls, and various memorabilia. Archival records are valuable for tracing family roots. *122 N. Washington St.,* ☎ *803/775–0908.* ☛ *Free.* ⊙ *Museum Tues.–Sat. 10–5, Sun. 2–5;* ⊙ *archives Tues.–Sat. 10–5.*

Swan Lake Iris Gardens is like Eden when its 6 million irises are in bloom. Royal-white-mute, black-necked, coscoroba, whooper, trumpeter, and black Australian swans paddle leisurely around the 45-acre lake. The 150-acre park also includes walking trails, picnic areas, tennis courts, a playground, and concessions. *W. Liberty St.,* ☎ *803/775–3304.* ☛ *Free.* ⊘ *Daily 8–sunset.*

Aiken and Beyond

Head south along U.S. 301/601, then west on U.S. 78 to **Aiken,** in Thoroughbred Country, about 64 miles altogether. Aiken's fame began during the 1890s, when wealthy Northerners wintering here built stately mansions and entertained each other with lavish parties, horse shows, and hunts. Many of the mansions—some with up to 90 rooms—remain as testament to this era of opulence. Since those days, the area's horse farms have produced many national champions, which are commemorated at the **Aiken Racing Hall of Fame** with exhibitions of horse-related decorations, paintings, and sculptures, plus racing silks and trophies. The Hall of Fame is on the grounds of the 14-acre **Hopeland Gardens,** with winding paths, quiet terraces, and reflecting pools. There's a Touch and Scent Trail with Braille plaques. Open-air free concerts and plays are presented on Monday evenings mid-July–August. *Corner of Dupree Pl. and Whiskey Rd.,* ☎ *803/642–7630.* ☛ *Free.* ⊘ *Museum fall–spring, Tues.–Sun. 2–5;* ⊘ *grounds daily sunrise–sunset.*

TIME OUT The who's who of Aiken's horsy set can be found most mornings feasting in the **Track Kitchen** (Mead Ave., ☎ 803/641-9628) on the heavy and hearty cooking of Carol and Pockets Curtis. The small dining room is quite unpretentious, with walls of mint-green cinder block and simple formica counters. The best time to people-watch is at about 4 AM.

The **Aiken County Historical Museum,** devoted to early regional culture, has Native American artifacts, firearms, an authentically furnished 1808 log cabin, and a one-room schoolhouse. *433 Newberry St. SW,* ☎ *803/642–2015. Donations accepted.* ⊘ *Tues.–Fri. 9:30–4:30, first Sun. of each month 2–5.*

Aiken surrounds the serene and wild **Hitchcock Woods** (enter from the junction of Clark Road and Whitney Drive, Berrie Road, and Dibble Road), a 2,000-acre tract of southern forest traversed by hiking trails and bridal paths.

About 64 miles northwest of Aiken is **Hickory Knob State Resort Park,** which has everything for a complete vacation. Take SC 19 and U.S. 25 to U.S. 378, drive west to the town of McCormick, then south until you see signs for the park on the shore of Strom Thurmond Lake. There's fishing, waterskiing, sailing, motorboating, a swimming pool, boat slips and a launch, a tackle shop, nature trails, an 18-hole championship golf course, a fully equipped pro shop, tennis courts, and skeet and archery ranges. If none of these is to your liking, bring your favorite canine for a training session on the 4-mile bird-dog field-trial area. An 80-room lodge, nine duplex lakeside cottages, campgrounds, and a restaurant round out Hickory Knob's offerings. *Rte. 1, Box 199B, McCormick 29835,* ☎ *803/391–2450.* ⊘ *Office daily 7 AM–11 PM.*

Abbeville

Return to McCormick via U.S. 378, then drive northwest 30 miles on SC 28 and SC 72 to **Abbeville.** This may well be one of inland South Carolina's most satisfying, though lesser-known, small towns. In Abbeville the "Southern cause" was born and died, for here the first organized secession meeting was held, and here on May 2, 1865, Confederate President Jefferson Davis officially disbanded the defeated armies of the South in the last meeting of his war council. The 1830 house where the council met is the **Burt Stark Mansion** (306 N. Main St., ☎ 803/459–4297 or 803/459–2181). ☛ *$3. ۞ Fri.–Sat. 1–5 or by appointment.*

In the **Abbeville Educational Garden** are the 1837 log cabin home of Marie Cromer Siegler, founder of 4–H clubs, and an old jail housing the Abbeville County Museum. *215 Poplar St., ☎ 803/459–2696.*

The **Abbeville Opera House** faces the historic town square. Built in 1908, it has been renovated to reflect the grandeur of the days when lavish road shows and stellar entertainers came center stage. Current productions range from light, contemporary comedies to Broadway-style musicals. *Town Sq., Abbeville, ☎ 803/459–2157. Reservations taken weekdays 10–5.*

Greenwood
About 14 miles away on SC 72 is **Greenwood.** Founded by Irish settlers in 1802, the city received its name from the gently rolling landscape and dense forests. Andrew Johnson, the 17th U.S. president, operated a tailor shop at Courthouse Square before migrating to eastern Tennessee. The **George W. Park Seed Co.,** one of the nation's largest seed supply houses, maintains colorful experimental gardens and greenhouses here. The flower beds are especially vivid June 15 through July, and seeds and bulbs are for sale in the company's store. The South Carolina Festival of Flowers—with a performing-artists contest, a beauty pageant, private house and garden tours, and live entertainment—is held here annually at the end of June. *On SC 245, 7 mi north of town, ☎ 803/941–4213 or 800/845–3369. ☛ Free. ۞ Gardens daily; ۞ Store Mon.–Sat. 9–6.*

Ninety Six
Drive southeast about 10 miles to the **Ninety Six National Historic Site,** which commemorates two Revolutionary War battles. The visitor center museum has descriptive displays, and there are remnants of the old village, a reconstructed French-and-Indian-War stockade, and Revolutionary-era fortifications. The nearby town of Ninety Six, on an old Indian trade route, is so named for being 96 miles from the Cherokee village of Keowee in the Blue Ridge Mountains. *SC 248, ☎ 803/543–4068. ☛ Free. ۞ Daily 8–5.*

Shopping

Antiques and Flea Markets
Many of Columbia's antiques outlets are in the **Congaree Vista Shopping District** around Huger and Gervais streets, between the State House and the river. A number of shops and cafés are in the **Five Points Shopping District,** which is around the intersection of Blossom and Harden streets. Other antiques shops are across the river on Meeting and State streets in West Columbia. The **Old Mill Antique Mall** (310 State St., W. Columbia, ☎ 803/796–4229) and **Thieves Market Antique Flea Mall** (502 Gadsden St., Columbia, ☎ 803/254–4997) show off the wares of dozens of antiques and collectibles dealers.

Arts and Crafts
Abbeville's Town Square is lined with attractive gift and specialty shops in restored historic buildings dating from the late 1800s. **Historic Camden** also has gifts and crafts for sale. In Walterboro, the South Carolina Artisans Center was recently opened. You can shop for

one-of-a-kind pieces of handcrafted jewelry, pottery, baskets, and other wares while watching top South Carolina artists and craftsfolk ply their crafts. *334 Wickman St.,* ☎ *803/549–0011.* ☛ *Free.* ☉ *Mon.–Sat. 10–8, Sun. 1–6.*

Farmer's Market

The **State Farmer's Market** in Columbia (Bluff Rd., ☎ 803/253–4041) is one of the 10 largest in the country. Seasonal fresh vegetables are sold each weekday, along with flowers, plants, seafood, herbs, and more.

Wineries

Free tours and wine-tastings are offered by **Cruse Vineyards & Winery** (Woods Rd., off SC 72, 4 mi north of Chester, ☎ 803/377–3944) and **Montmorenci Vineyards** (U.S. 78, 2.5 mi east of Aiken, ☎ 803/649–4870; tours by appointment).

Participant Sports

Canoeing

A haunting canoe trail leads into a remote swampy depression at **Woods Bay State Park** (from Sumter, take U.S. 378E to U.S. 301N, ☎ 803/659–4445), where rentals are available for $2 per hour or $10 for a full day. Self-guided canoe trails traverse an alluvial floodplain bordered by high bluffs at the **Congaree Swamp National Monument** (20 mi southeast of Columbia off SC 48, ☎ 803/776–4396). Canoe rentals are available in Columbia at **Adventure Carolina** (☎ 803/796–4505) and the **River Runner Outdoor Center** (☎ 803/771–0353).

Fishing

Lakes Marion and **Moultrie** attract serious anglers after bream, crappie, striped bass, catfish, and large- and small-mouth bass. Supplies, camps, guides, rentals, and accommodations abound. For information, contact Santee Cooper Counties Promotion Commission (Drawer 40, Santee, SC 29142, ☎ 803/854–2131 or, outside SC, 800/227–8510).

Golf

The many fine courses in the area include **Highland Park Country Club** (Aiken, ☎ 803/649–6029), **Sedgewood** (Columbia, ☎ 803/776–2177), and **White Pines Golf Club** (Camden, ☎ 803/432–7442).

Hiking

Congaree Swamp National Monument (*see* Canoeing, *above*) has 22 miles of trails for hikers and nature lovers and a ¾-mile boardwalk for visitors with disabilities. Guided nature walks leave Saturday at 1:30 PM. For information on trails in the **Francis Marion National Forest** and the **Sumter National Forest,** contact the National Forest Service (1835 Assembly St., Columbia 29201, ☎ 803/765–5222).

White-Water Adventures

Rafting, kayaking, and canoeing on the Saluda River near Columbia offer challenging Class-3 and Class-4 rapids. Guided river and swamp excursions are also offered. In the Upcountry, the Chattooga National Wild and Scenic River, on the border of South Carolina and Georgia, provides guided rafting, canoeing, and kayaking. Contact **Wildwater Ltd.** (☎ 800/451–9972) or **Nantahala Outdoor Center** (☎ 800/832–7238).

Spectator Sports

Baseball

The **Columbia Mets** (☎ 803/256–4110), a Class-A affiliate of the New York Mets, play from mid-April through August at Capital City Stadium.

Equestrian Events

In Aiken, polo matches are played at Whitney Field (☎ 803/648–7874) on Sunday afternoons September–November and March–July. Three weekends in late March and early April are set aside for the famed **Triple Crown** (☎ 803/641–1111)—thoroughbred trials of promising yearlings, a steeplechase, and harness races by young horses making their debut. Camden puts on two steeplechase events: the **Carolina Cup** in late March or early April and the **Colonial Cup** in November (☎ 803/432–6513).

Stock-Car Races

Darlington Raceway (SC 34, 2 mi west of Darlington, ☎ 803/393–4041) is the scene of NASCAR's TranSouth 500 (part of the Winston Cup Series) in late March and the exciting Mountain Dew Southern 500 on Labor Day weekend.

Dining

South Carolina Heartland fare ranges from regional specialties like barbecue and country ham with red-eye gravy to unself-conscious Continental cuisine. This is a great place to discover a Southern institution—one of the family-style "fish camps" serving lavish portions of fresh catfish and other catches from fish farms or nearby rivers and lakes. In Columbia, ethnic and specialty restaurants have appeared at a rapid clip in recent years. Costs throughout the region are usually pleasingly moderate. Dress is casual unless otherwise noted.

CATEGORY	COST*
$$$$	over $25
$$$	$15–$25
$$	$7–$15
$	under $7

per person for a three-course meal, excluding drinks, service, and 5% sales tax

Abbeville

$$ Yoder's Dutch Kitchen. In the heart of the Sun Belt, here's authentic Pennsylvania Dutch home cooking in an unassuming redbrick building with a mansard roof. There's a lunch buffet and evening smorgasbord with such choices as fried chicken, stuffed cabbage, Dutch meat loaf, sausage and kraut, breaded veal parmesan, and plenty of vegetables. Shoo-fly pie, Dutch bread, apple butter, homemade salad dressings, and other house specialties can be bought to go. ✕ *U.S. 72,* ☎ *803/459–5556. No reservations. No credit cards. No dinner Wed. Closed Sun.–Tues.*

Aiken

$$$ No. 10 Downing Street. This stately Southern Colonial dates to 1837
★ and serves some of the best—and most diverse—food in town. The menu changes regularly: One month might focus on such Italian fare as *pollo al proscuitto* (chicken wrapped in proscuitto and fresh herbs with

fettucini Alfredo) and baked beef tenderloin with tomatoes, garlic, and oregano; another month may salute country French or regional cuisine. A delicious pâté with french bread is always among the appetizers. A bakery on the premises is open during all meals. ✕ *241 Laurens St.,* ☎ *803/642–9062. Reservations advised. D, DC, MC, V. Closed Sun. and Mon.*

Camden

$$$-$$$$ **1890 McLean's House.** On the first floor of the Victorian Greenleaf Inn, cane-back chairs, fox-hunting prints, elaborately tiled fire places, and hand-painted walls set the tone for an elegant meal. McLean's opened early in 1994 and has quickly become a success with six delicious steak specialties (from Diane to *au poivre*), plus such other options as walnut-crusted chicken with a spicy apricot sauce, and good ole' shrimp and grits. ✕ *1308 Broad St.,* ☎ *803/425–1806. Reservations advised. Jacket and tie. AE, D, MC, V. No lunch Sat. Closed Sun.*

$$$-$$$$ **Mill Pond Restaurant.** In a historic building overlooking a sprawling
★   mill pond, this is one of the state's finest eateries. The creative Low Country cuisine features such starters as grits with andouille sausage, roast peppers, and garlic toast; and marinated quail on mixed greens with Boursin cheese and fried onions. Follow this with blackened mahimahi with crawfish hollandaise or perhaps the mouthwatering crab cakes on shrimp tartar sauce. About a 10-minute drive south of Camden proper, dinner here is worth the drive. ✕ *84 Boykin Mill Rd., Rembert,* ☎ *803/424–0261. Reservations advised. Jacket and tie. MC, V. No lunch. Closed Sun.*

Columbia

$$-$$$ **McCrady's Restaurant.** McCrady's, in the lower level of the AT&T Building, has an extensive menu. It includes fresh seafood, steaks, and egg dishes, plus daily luncheon and dinner specials and nouvelle Southern dishes like speckled grits and tasso. ✕ *1201 Main St.,* ☎ *803/771–2410. Reservations advised. AE, D, DC, MC, V. Closed Sun.*

$$ **Motor Supply Co. Bistro.** Dine on cuisine from around the world at this restaurant in the heart of town. Fresh seafood and homemade desserts are among the many offerings; on Sunday there's a Thai menu. A happy hour is celebrated in the bar. ✕ *920 Gervais St.,* ☎ *803/256–6687. Reservations advised. AE, DC, MC, V.*

$-$$ **California Dreaming.** A splendid example of adaptive use, here's din-
★   ing in an airy, greenery-bedecked space that is the renovated old Union Train Station. Specialties include prime rib, barbecued baby-back ribs, Mexican dishes, and homemade pasta. There's a lounge with a disc jockey. ✕ *401 S. Main St.,* ☎ *803/254–6767. Reservations advised on weekends or for large parties. AE, MC, V.*

$-$$ **Maurice Gourmet Barbecue–Piggie Park.** One of the South's best-
★   known barbecue chefs, Maurice Bessinger has a fervent national following for his mustard sauce–based, pit-cooked ham barbecue. He also serves barbecued chicken, ribs, and baked beans, plus hash over rice, onion rings, hushpuppies, cole slaw, and home-baked desserts. ✕ *1600 Charleston Hwy.,* ☎ *803/796–0220. No reservations. D, MC, V.*

Lodging

In addition to the accommodations listed here, you might seek out chains and bed-and-breakfasts in the area. For a complete list of B&Bs, write to the South Carolina Division of Tourism (Box 71, Columbia, SC 29202, ☎ 803/734–0122) and ask for the pamphlet *Bed & Breakfast of South Carolina.*

CATEGORY	COST*
$$$$	over $100
$$$	$75–$100
$$	$40–$75
$	under $40

All prices are for a standard double room, excluding 7% tax

Abbeville

$$ **Belmont Inn.** Built just after the turn of the century, this restored Spanish-style structure is a popular overnight stop with Opera House visitors. Rooms, which have seen better days, are comfortably furnished rather than opulent. White spreads cover brass beds, and antique quilts decorate some walls. Theater-and-dining package plans are offered at the inn. ⊡ *Court Sq., 29620,* ☎ ℻ *803/459–9625. 24 rooms. Restaurant, lounge, meeting rooms. AE, MC, V.*

Aiken

$$$–$$$$ **Willcox Inn.** Winston Churchill, Franklin D. Roosevelt, and the Astors have slept at this elegant inn, built in grand style in the early 1900s. The lobby is graced with massive stone fireplaces, rosewood pine woodwork, pegged oak floors, and Oriental rugs. The room decor reflects the inn's early days, with floral-print spreads and high four-poster beds. ⊡ *100 Colleton Ave., 29801,* ☎ *803/649–1377 or 800/368–1047,* ℻ *803/643–0971. 30 rooms, 6 suites. Dining room, bar, croquet. AE, DC, MC, V.*

$$ **Briar Patch.** You can learn plenty about both the Old and New South from the knowledgeable innkeepers of this terrific B&B, which was formerly tack rooms in Aiken's stable district. Choose either the frilly room with French Provincial furniture or the less dramatic one with pine antiques and a weathervane. Breakfast here is Continental. ⊡ *544 Magnolia La. SE, 29801,* ☎ *803/649–2010. 2 rooms with bath. Tennis courts. No credit cards.*

Camden

$$–$$$ **Greenleaf Inn.** Alice Boykin, whose name is to Camden what Carnegie's
★ name is to Pittsburgh, opened the Greenleaf in late 1993. The inn comprises three buildings: There are four rooms in the main inn, on the second floor above McLean's Restaurant, seven rooms in a nearby carriage house, and a guest cottage—the latter is particularly good for families. All rooms are done with classic Victorian furniture and wallpaper; they're spacious and have modern baths. You won't find a nicer or more economical lodging in the region. ⊡ *1308 Broad St., 29020,* ☎ *803/425–1806 or 800/437–5874,* ℻ *803/425–5853. 8 rooms with bath, 3 suites, 1 cottage. Restaurant. AE, D, MC, V.*

$$–$$$ **Holiday Inn.** This well-maintained unit of the nationwide chain is three miles west of downtown Camden, in Lugoff. The restaurant is excellent. ⊡ *Box 96, U.S. 1/601S, Lugoff 29078,* ☎ *803/438–9441 or 800/465–4329,* ℻ *803/438–9441. 120 rooms. Restaurant, lounge, pool, whirlpool baths. AE, D, DC, MC, V.*

Columbia

$$$ **Adam's Mark.** This upscale downtown hotel (formerly the Columbia Marriott) is conveniently located near state offices and the University of South Carolina. Public areas and guest rooms are contemporary in feeling. The Palm Terrace Restaurant is in a spectacular atrium with stunning views of decorative details; Veronique's provides an intimate, elegant setting for gourmet dining. ⊡ *1200 Hampton St., 29201,* ☎ *803/771–7000 or 800/228–9290,* ℻ *803/254–2911. 288 rooms, 12* *suites. 2 restaurants, bar, indoor pool, sauna, health club, business services. AE, D, DC, MC, V.*

$$$ **Claussen's Inn.** This welcome retreat from the downtown bustle is a converted bakery warehouse in the attractive Five Points neighborhood. The inn has an open, airy lobby with a Mexican tile floor; the rooms, some two-story, are arranged around the lobby. There are eight loft suites, with downstairs sitting rooms and spiral staircases leading to sleeping areas furnished with period reproductions and four-poster beds. ⌶ *2003 Greene St., 29205,* ☎ *803/765–0440 or 800/622–3382,* ⦰ *803/799–7924. 21 rooms, 8 suites. Hot tub, meeting facilities. AE, MC, V.*

$$$ **Richland Street B&B.** Relax on the front porch or in the spacious com-
★ mon area of this no-smoking inn in the heart of Columbia's Historic District. Each antiques-furnished room has its own personality; the bridal suite includes a whirlpool tub. A Continental breakfast is complimentary. ⌶ *1425 Richland St., 29201,* ☎ *803/779–7001. 7 rooms with bath, 1 suite. AE, MC, V.*

$$–$$$ **Embassy Suites Hotel Columbia.** In the spacious seven-story atrium lobby with skylights, fountains, pools, and live plants, overnight guests enjoy sumptuous breakfasts and an early evening manager's cocktail reception—both complimentary. ⌶ *200 Stoneridge Dr., 29210,* ☎ *803/252–8700 or 800/362–2779,* ⦰ *803/256–8749. 214 housekeeping suites. Indoor pool, health club, gift shop, billiards, dance club. AE, D, DC, MC, V.*

$–$$ **La Quinta Motor Inn.** At this three-story inn on a quiet street near the zoo, the rooms are spacious and well lit, with large working areas and oversize beds. ⌶ *1335 Garner La., 29210,* ☎ *803/798–9590 or 800/531–5900,* ⦰ *803/731–5574. 120 rooms. Pool. AE, D, DC, MC, V.*

Greenwood

$$–$$$ **Inn on the Square.** This elegant inn was fashioned out of a warehouse in the heart of town. Though the rooms suffer from rather unremarkable views, they're bright and spacious with reproduction 18th-century antiques, four-poster beds, writing desks, and such thoughtful touches as turndown service and complimentary morning newspapers. The staff is congenial and attuned to the needs of business travelers and vacationers alike. ⌶ *104 Court Sq., 29648,* ☎ *803/223–4488,* ⦰ *803/223–7067. 48 rooms. Restaurant, lounge, pool. AE, D, DC, MC, V.*

Pendleton

$$ **Liberty Hall Inn.** There's great food and lodging at this country inn in the heart of Historic Pendleton near Clemson University. The inn, which was built in the 1840s and restored in the 1980s, caters to business travelers and vacationers. Rooms are furnished in antiques and family heirlooms; a Continental breakfast comes with the room. ⌶ *621 S. Mechanic St., 29670,* ☎ ⦰ *803/646–7500 or 800/643–7944. 10 rooms with bath. Restaurant. AE, D, DC, MC, V.*

Sumter

$$ **Holiday Inn.** This well-maintained motor inn is 4 miles west of town, near Shaw Air Force Base. Simple, clean rooms are as you would expect from this chain. ⌶ *2390 Broad St. ext., 29150,* ☎ *803/469–9001 or 800/465–4329,* ⦰ *803/469–7001. 124 rooms. Restaurant, pool. AE, D, DC, MC, V.*

$$ Magnolia House. In Sumter's Historic District, this imposing four-columned Greek Revival structure is a nice alternative to the region's generic chain motels. Antiques, many of them French, furnish the rooms; there are also stained-glass windows, inlaid oak floors, and five fireplaces. A full breakfast is included in the rate. ⌘ *230 Church St., 29150,* ☎ *803/775–6694. 3 rooms with bath, 1 suite. AE, MC, V.*

The Arts

Concerts, Opera, and Dance

In Columbia, call the **South Carolina Philharmonic and Chamber Orchestra Association** (☎ 803/771–7937) for information about scheduled concerts of the Philharmonic, the Chamber Orchestra, and the Youth Orchestra. The **Columbia Music Festival Association** (☎ 803/771–6303) can inform callers about events of the **Choral Society,** the **Opera, Opera Guild, Dance Theatre, Brass Band, Caroliers, and Cabaret Company.**

Theater

Columbia's **Town Theatre** (1012 Sumter St., ☎ 803/799–2510), founded in 1919, stages six plays a year from September to late May, plus a special summer show. The **Workshop Theatre of South Carolina** (1136 Bull St., ☎ 803/799–4876) also puts on plays. The **Abbeville Opera House** (Town Square, ☎ 803/459–2157) stages high-caliber productions in an early 20th-century setting.

Nightlife

In Columbia, **Cracker Jacks** (1325 Longcreek Dr., ☎ 803/731–5692) features lively "beach" music for listening and dancing, and occasionally a lusty floor show. **Nitelites Dance Club** (*200 Stoneridge Dr.,* ☎ 803/252–8700) at the Embassy Suites Hotel boasts state-of-the-art lighting and presents a lavish free hors d'oeuvres buffet weekdays 5–7:30. Also try **Dance Factory** (2100 Bush River Rd., ☎ 803/731–0300) at the Sheraton Hotel & Convention Center and the Adams Mark's **Palm Terrace Lounge** (1200 Hampton St., ☎ 803/771–7000).

There's live entertainment at **Jockey's Lounge** in the Holiday Inn Express in Aiken (155 Colony Pkwy., ☎ 803/648–0999). **Plums Restaurant & Lounge** at the Holiday Inns in Lugoff (U.S. 1/601S, ☎ 803/438–9441) and Sumter (2390 Broad St. ext., ☎ 803/469–9001) provides pleasant evening unwinding with live entertainment. Another Camden option is **Paddock Restaurant & Pub** (514 Rutledge St., ☎ 803/432–3222).

Heartland Essentials

Arriving and Departing, Getting Around

BY BUS
Greyhound (☎ 800/231–2222) serves all of South Carolina.

BY CAR
I–77 leads into Columbia from the north. I–26, I–20, and U.S. 1 intersect at Columbia.

BY PLANE
Columbia Metro Airport (☎ 803/822–5000) is served by Air South, American Eagle, Com Air/Delta, and USAir.

BY TRAIN

Amtrak (☎ 800/872–7245) makes stops at Camden, Columbia, Denmark, Dillon, Florence, and Kingstree in the Heartland.

Guided Tours

Richland Country Historic Preservation Commission (☎ 803/252–1770) runs guided tours and rents out historic properties. In Sumter, the charismatic former Mayor **"Bubba" McElveen** (☎ 803/775–2851) gives walking, bus, and auto tours of the area. The **Aiken Chamber of Commerce** runs a 90-minute tour of the historic district and will customize tours to suit individual interests. Customized tours of Camden are also available through either the **Kershaw County Chamber of Commerce** or from **Greenleaf Tours** (contact Louise Burns, ☎ 803/432–1515).

Important Addresses and Numbers

EMERGENCIES

Dial **911** for police, fire, and ambulance assistance. Emergency room services are available at **Richland Memorial Hospital** (5 Richland Medical Park, Columbia, ☎ 803/765–7561).

PHARMACY

Taylor Street Pharmacy (1520 Taylor St. at Pickens in Columbia, ☎ 803/256–1611) is open 7 AM–9 PM weekdays, 9–9 weekends.

RADIO STATIONS

AM: WCOS 1400, country; WOMG 1320, oldies; WVOC 560, news/talk. **FM:** WHKZ 96.7, country; WLTR 91.3, classical; WMFX 102.3, classic rock; WUSC 90.5, alternative (jazz, blues, folk, reggae).

VISITOR INFORMATION

Greater Abbeville Chamber of Commerce (104 Pickens St., Abbeville 29620, ☎ 803/459–4600). **Greater Aiken Chamber of Commerce** (400 Laurens St. NW, Box 892, Aiken 29802, ☎ 803/641–1111). **Greater Columbia Metropolitan Convention and Visitors Bureau** (1200 Main St., Ninth Floor, Box 15, Columbia 29202, ☎ 803/254–0479 or 800/264–4884). **Kershaw County Chamber of Commerce** (724 S. Broad St., Box 605, Camden 29020, ☎ 803/432–2525). **Ninety Six Chamber of Commerce** (Box 8, Ninety Six 29666, ☎ 803/543–2900).

ELSEWHERE IN THE STATE

Those with more time may want to take an excursion into the **Upcountry,** the northwest corner of the state, long a favorite for family vacations. For information, contact: Discover Upcountry Carolina Association (Box 3116, Greenville 29602, ☎ 803/233–2690 or 800/849–4766). The abundant lakes, waterfalls, and several state parks (including **Caesar's Head, Keowee-Toxaway, Oconee, Table Rock,** and the **Chattooga National Wild** and **Scenic River**) provide all manner of recreational activities. Beautiful anytime, the 130-mile **Cherokee Foothills Scenic Highway** (SC 11), through the Blue Ridge Mountains, is especially delightful in spring and autumn. At **Devils Fork State Park** (161 Holcombe Circle, Salem 29676, ☎ 803/944–2639) on beautiful Lake Jocassee, visitors clamor to stay in the luxurious villas at one of the system's newest and most upscale facilities.

The comfortable communities of **Greenville, Spartanburg, Clemson, Pendleton,** and **Anderson** take justifiable pride in their educational institutions, museums, historic preservation, and cultural accomplishments.

Any one of them is worth a day's visit—particularly charming Pendleton, near Clemson University, which has a historic district, interesting architecture, and good restaurants.

Greenville County Museum of Art. Housed in an innovative modern building, the museum displays American art dating from the Colonial era. Exhibited are works by Paul Jenkins, Jamie Wyeth, Jasper Johns, and noted Southern artists along with North American sculpture. *420 College St., Greenville,* ☎ *803/271–7570.* ☛ *Free.* ☉ *Tues.–Sat. 10– 5, Sun. 1–5.*

Kings Mountain National Military Park. The "turning point" Revolutionary War battle on October 7, 1780, was fought on this site. Colonial Tories commanded by British Major Patrick Ferguson were soundly defeated by rag-tag patriot forces from the Southern Appalachians. Visitor Center exhibits, dioramas, and an orientation film describe the action. A paved self-guided trail leads through the battlefield. *20 mi NE of Gaffney off I–85 via a marked side road in North Carolina,* ☎ *803/936–7921.* ☛ *Free.* ☉ *Daily 9–5, until 6 Memorial Day–Labor Day.*

8 Tennessee

Tennessee's dominating characteristics are her music—the blues, which were born in Memphis; rock, which came into popularity with the rise of Elvis Presley (also in Memphis); and country music, which claims Nashville as it's capital—and her scenic geographical features, the Great Smoky Mountains forming the eastern border and the Mississippi River forming the western border. Here, too, are forests, fields, and streams for the nature lover, outlet malls for the die-hard shopper, and an array of entertainment parks to keep the whole family happy.

MOUNTAINS AND MUSIC—these two gifts Tennessee was given in abundance and shares generously with millions of guests each year.

Updated by
Patti Nickell

The Blues were born in Memphis, Tennessee's largest city, which rises out of the flat, cotton-kissed southwest corner of the state, on the banks of the Mississippi River. Beale Street nurtured some of the finest talents of the genre, from blues men W. C. Handy and B. B. King to rockers Elvis Presley and Jerry Lee Lewis. Today, with live music in Handy Park, Beale Street again reverberates with the moody sounds that made it a legend.

Nashville, of course, retains its title as the country music capital of the world. Music City, U.S.A., as it is known, is also the state's capital. Here, amid the heart of Tennessee's green, gently rolling hills, country music is king. In addition to Music Row, stars' homes, and recording studios, the Grand Ole Opry continues to pack its auditorium. The long-running radio-show extravaganza has launched many a singer's and picker's career and is now part of a theme park built around live country music shows. Even the hungriest fan will come away sated.

As for mountains, they don't come any more beautiful than the Great Smokies—site of the nation's most visited national park and part of the Appalachian chain; they're in East Tennessee and are shared by North Carolina. Covered with a dense carpet of wildflowers in spring and ablaze with foliage in autumn, the Smokies—named for the mantle of blue haze that so often blankets them—are a joy to hike or drive through. Spend some time in the little mountain towns and villages dotting the hollows to sample homegrown bluegrass music and traditional cooking and crafts (such as dulcimers fashioned out of wood and dolls out of dried apples), along with the natural warmth of the people.

MEMPHIS

Memphis was founded in 1819, but long before that, the Mississippi River on whose banks it was built exerted a powerful influence on the area. A Native American river culture that existed here from the 11th through the 15th century is documented in archaeological excavations, reconstructions, and exhibits at the Chucalissa Archaeological Museum. The river itself is celebrated with a museum dedicated to its history—part of Mud Island, a unique entertainment-oriented park occupying an island in the river.

The other significant influence on the city has been the music that has flowed through it. W. C. Handy moved from Alabama to Memphis in 1902–03, drawn by the long-thriving music scene, and it was here that he produced most of the songs that made him famous. The recent history of legendary Beale Street reflects that of all modern Memphis. Economic decline in the mid-20th century brought the city to its knees, and the unrest following the assassination in 1968 of Dr. Martin Luther King Jr. at the Lorraine Motel, just south of Beale, dealt a near-fatal blow. Today, thanks to public improvements and an economy built around such distribution giants as Federal Express, Memphis has been brought back to life and Beale Street bursts with clubs and restaurants, as it did in its heyday.

When you mention Memphis to most, one name springs to mind: Elvis, the undisputed King of Rock and Roll. Although he was actu-

Tennessee

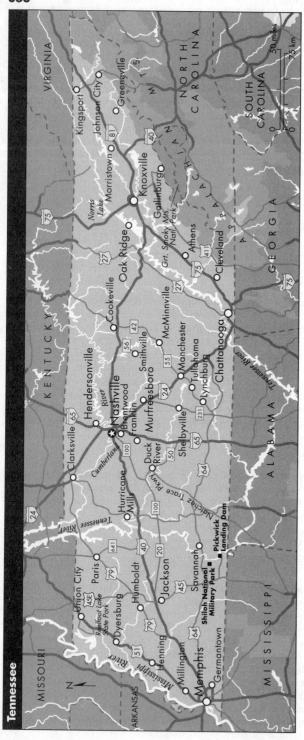

ally born across the state line in Tupelo, Mississippi, Elvis put Memphis on the map, recording his first hits here in Sun Studios. His legacy burns bright at Graceland, the estate where he lived, died, and lies buried. Each year thousands of fans make the pilgrimage to pay homage to the man and his music. Elvis International Tribute Week, held each August at Graceland, has grown to match the myth.

For true Blues fans, a good time to visit is during October's Blues Music Week, when the art form is celebrated with musical performances and other activities throughout the city. The week culminates in the National Blues Music Awards Show, which is attended by luminaries of the music world. For information on a three-day vacation package that includes admission to the awards show as well as to the jam afterward, contact the Blues Foundation (174 Beale St., 38103, ☎ 901/527–2583). Most weekends throughout the year, the Blues emanates from the front porch of the Handy home or in Handy Park.

Many people plan their visit to coincide with the month-long Memphis in May International Festival, at a time when the summer's heat and humidity have not yet begun to set in. Each year the cuisine, crafts, and other cultural offerings of a different country are saluted over four consecutive weekends. The first of these weekends sees the clubs and sidewalks of Beale Street playing host to a rollicking, Blues-based Music Festival, and the second finds hordes of the hungry flocking to the river for the World Championship Barbecue Cooking Contest. A sports weekend featuring races on land and water follows, succeeded by the grand finale of Sunset Symphony, during which the Memphis Symphony plays on the banks of the Mississippi, and a soloist's powerful rendition of "Old Man River" brings the festival to an end and the crowd to its feet.

Exploring

Downtown
Numbers in the margin correspond to points of interest on the Downtown Memphis and Memphis maps.

❶ A good place to start is the **Visitors Information Center** (340 Beale St., ☎ 901/543–5333), where you can pick up free maps, brochures, and other literature about Memphis and the Beale Street Historic District. Parking at the center is free.

❷ At Main and Beale streets is the magnificent 1928 **Orpheum Theatre,** a former vaudeville palace and movie theater, refurbished as a center for the performing arts. Step inside to admire its crystal chandeliers, gilt decorations, and ornate tapestries.

❸ The **Center for Southern Folklore** features exhibits on the people, music, food, crafts, and traditions of the South, focusing in particular on the Mississippi Delta region. The center will also arrange a walking tour of Beale Street (*see* Guided Tours, *below*). At the gift shop, you can purchase regional folk art, handiwork, cassettes, videos, and books pertaining to the region. *130 Beale St., ☎ 901/525–3655. ☛ Free. ☺ Mon.–Thurs. 10–8, Fri.–Sat. 10–10, Sun. 10–8.*

At 163 Beale Street you can step into the past at the highly eccentric, **❹** 114-year-old **A. Schwab's** dry-goods store, where Elvis used to buy some of his glitzy threads, and voodoo potions are still sold (*see* Shopping, **❺** *below*). In **Handy Park,** between Third and Fourth streets, pause to admire the statue of W. C. Handy clutching his famed trumpet.

A. Schwab's, **4**

Center for Southern Folkore, **3**

Chucalissa Archaeological Museum, **20**

Dixon Gallery and Gardens, **18**

Graceland, **19**

Handy Park, **5**

Magevney House, **10**

Mallory-Neeley House, **11**

Memphis Brooks Museum of Art, **16**

Memphis Pink Palace Museum and Planetarium, **17**

Memphis Zoological Gardens and Aquarium, **15**

Mud Island, **8**

National Civil Rights Museum, **13**

National Ornamental Metal Museum, **22**

Old Daisy Theatre, **6**

Orpheum Theatre, **2**

Pyramid, **9**

Sun Studio, **14**

T. O. Fuller State Park, **21**

Visitors Information Center, **1**

W. C. Handy Memphis Home and Museum, **7**

Woodruff-Fontaine House, **12**

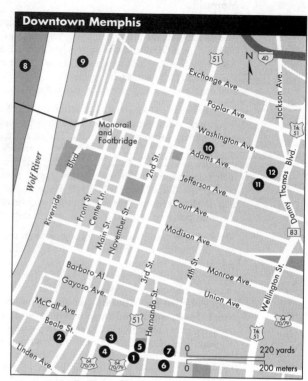

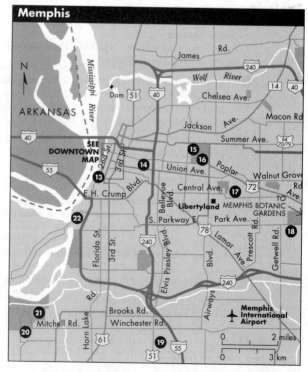

6 At 329 Beale Street the renovated **Old Daisy Theatre** now houses the **Beale Street Blues Museum,** with exhibits tracing the history of Beale Street and the creation of the blues. ☏ *901/527–6008.* ☛ *$5.* ☾ *Apr.–Sept., Mon.–Sat. 10–6, Sun. noon–6; Oct.–Mar., Mon.–Sat. 11– 5.*

7 Diagonally across the street, at 352 Beale Street, is the **W. C. Handy Memphis Home and Museum.** Handy, who wrote some of his most famous music in this house, which has been moved from its original location, is recalled here through photographs, sheet music, and memorabilia. ☏ *901/527–3427.* ☛ *$2.* ☾ *Memorial Day–Labor Day, Tues–Sat. 10–5, Sun. 1–5.*

The next part of the tour is best done by car. Parking on Front Street between Poplar and Adams puts you in a good position to explore both the Victorian Village Historic District and Mud Island.

8 Whether you get there by monorail, pedestrian walkway, or car, **Mud Island** (☏ 901/576–7230), a 52-acre park that explores Memphis's intimate relationship with the river, merits a visit. Here, at the **Mississippi River Museum,** galleries bring the history of the Mississippi to life with exhibits ranging from scale-model boats to life-size, animated river characters (Mark Twain spins his tales anew here) to the Theater of River Disasters. But the most extraordinary exhibit is outside: **River Walk,** a five-block-long scale model of the Mississippi, which replicates its every twist, turn, and sandbar from Cairo, Illinois, to New Orleans, ending in a huge swimming pool bordered by a man-made, sandy beach. Other features include shops, restaurants serving regional foods, and a 5,064-seat amphitheater. The famed World War II B-17 bomber *Memphis Belle,* the first plane of its kind to complete 25 missions, is housed in an open pavilion topped by a gleaming white dome. The plane has been featured in several films. *The footbridge and monorail are at 125 Front St.,* ☏ *901/576–7241.* ☛ *$6 adults, $4 children 4–12 and senior citizens;* ☛ *To grounds only, $2 adults, $1 children 4–12.* ☾ *Most attractions Apr.–Nov., Tues.–Sun., but hours and days of operation vary greatly; call ahead.*

9 One of Memphis's newer landmarks, the **Pyramid** (☏ 901/526–5177), a gleaming, stainless-steel structure and the third largest pyramid in the world, is at Front and Auction, six blocks north of Adams Street. This 32-story arena, covering the equivalent of six football fields, opened in 1991 and is home to the Memphis State University Tigers and a forum for concerts and other events. Guided tours are available.

To leave the 20th century behind, return to Front Street and walk east on Adams Street through the **Victorian Village Historic District,** comprising some 25 blocks on Adams between Front and Manassas. Here, 18 houses ranging from neoclassical to Gothic Revival have been restored to their appearance in the days when cotton was king. Most are privately owned, but the three that follow are open to the public.

10 The charming little white clapboard **Magevney House,** built in the 1830s, is one of Memphis's oldest dwellings and the former home of a pioneer schoolteacher. It's furnished with some of his original possessions. Magevney was an ardent Catholic—the city's first Catholic church service was held in this house, and he later helped build the church next door. *198 Adams Ave.,* ☏ *901/526–4464.* ☛ *Free.* ☾ *June–Labor Day,*

Tues.–Sat. 10–4;Mar.–May and Labor Day–Dec., Tues.–Fri. 10–2 and Sat. 10–4.

⑪ The **Mallory–Neely House** is a 25-room Italianate Victorian home that contains original family furnishings. Note the hand-carved cornices and frescoed ceilings on the first floor, and the double front doors' stained-glass panels. *652 Adams Ave., ☎ 901/523–1484. ☛ $4 adults, $3 students and senior citizens. ☺ Mar.–Dec., Tues.–Sat. 10–4, Sun. 1–4.*

⑫ The **Woodruff–Fontaine House** is an exquisite three-story French Victorian mansion built in 1870. The grand drawing room is graced with the original parquet floors and large mirrors. Antique furnishings include Aubusson carpets, marble mantels, and a Venetian crystal chandelier. Browse through the formal garden with its gingerbread playhouse and chapel, now the museum shop. *680 Adams Ave., ☎ 901/526–1469. ☛ $5 adults, $4 senior citizens, $2 children 6–18. ☺ Mon.–Sat. 10–4, Sun. 1–3:30.*

⑬ The Lorraine Motel on Mulberry Street, where Dr. Martin Luther King Jr. was assassinated in 1968, has been transformed into the **National Civil Rights Museum,** the first in the United States. The $8.8 million complex, opened in the summer of 1991, documents the struggle of African-Americans in this country and the civil rights movement. A Montgomery, Alabama bus, like the one in which Rosa Parks refused to give up her seat, sparking an uprising against segregation; scenes of lunch-counter sit-ins; and audiovisual displays are part of the educational program. *450 Mulberry St., ☎ 901/521–9699. ☛ $5 adults, $4 senior citizens and students, $3 children 6–12; free Mon. 3–5. ☺ Sept.–May, Wed.–Mon. 1–5; June–Aug., Mon. and Wed.–Sat. 10–5, Sun. 1–5.*

Fanning Out

⑭ East of downtown, on Union Avenue, is **Sun Studio,** still housed in the original, albeit modest, building where Elvis himself wandered in one day and recorded two songs—one in honor of his beloved mother—for producer Sam Phillips. Pictures of Elvis and other well-loved rockers from B.B. King to Jerry Lee Lewis to Roy Orbison adorn the walls, and their hits play in the background during tours. At night, recording sessions crank up once again at Sun, with artists hoping that history might repeat itself. *706 Union Ave., ☎ 901/521–0664. ☛ $7 adults, $4 senior citizens, $4 children 5–12. ☺ Daily for tours 10–6.*

⑮ A couple miles east, in **Overton Park,** are the city's zoo and art museum. The **Memphis Zoological Gardens and Aquarium** is one of the South's notable zoos, home to more than 400 species living on 70 well-kept wooded acres. There's a 10,000-gallon aquarium, a large reptile facility, and a natural African veldt setting for larger creatures. For youngsters, there's an animal-contact area and a lake. The 9-acre Cat Country opened in 1993. *2000 Galloway St., ☎ 901/726–4787. ☛ $6 adults, $5 senior citizens, $4 children 2–11. ☺ Daily 9–4:30.*

⑯ The collections of the **Memphis Brooks Museum of Art,** also in the park, span eight centuries and contain 7,000 pieces, including a notable collection of Italian Renaissance works, plus English portraiture, Impressionist and American modernist paintings, decorative arts, prints, photographs, and one of the nation's largest displays of Doughty bird figurines. *☎ 901/722–3500. ☛ $4 adults, $2 senior citizens and students; free on Fri. ☺ Tues.–Sat. 10–5, Sun. 11:30–5.*

⑰ Five miles southeast of the park is the **Memphis Pink Palace Museum and Planetarium,** adjacent to the rambling 1920s pink marble mansion built by Clarence Saunders, whose Piggly Wiggly self-service stores were predecessors of today's supermarkets. Exhibits are eclectic, including natural and cultural history displays, a hand-carved miniature three-ring circus, and displays of African game. *3050 Central Ave.,* ☎ *901/320–6320.* ☛ *To planetarium: $3 adults, $2.50 senior citizens, $2 children 5–13.* ☛ *To museum: $5.50 adults, $5 senior citizens, $4 children.* ☼ *Memorial Day–Labor Day, Mon.–Wed. 10–5, Thur. 10– 8, Fri.–Sat. 10–9, Sun. noon–5; Labor Day–Memorial Day, Mon.–Wed. 9–4, Thurs. 9–8, Fri. 9–9, Sat. 10–9, Sun. noon–5.*

⓲ A different personal statement is made by the **Dixon Gallery and Gardens,** with 17 acres of formal and informal gardens and woodlands— a welcoming bucolic enclave near the heart of the city. The estate and its superb art collections once belonged to the late Margaret and Hugo Dixon, philanthropists and cultural leaders. Included in the intimate museum are French and American Impressionist paintings, British portraiture and landscapes, and the Stout collection of 18th-century German porcelain. The gardens display regional flowering plants and statuary. *4339 Park Ave.,* ☎ *901/761–5250.* ☛ *$5 adults, $4 senior citizens, $3 students.* ☼ *Tues.–Sat. 10–5, Sun. 1–5.*

★ ⓳ Twelve miles southeast of downtown is the attraction that draws millions to Memphis: **Graceland,** a poignant reminder of the many facets of fame. The tour of the Colonial-style mansion once owned by Elvis Presley reveals the spoils of stardom—from his gold records to his glittering show costumes—and a circuit of the grounds (shuttle service is available) leads inevitably to Meditation Garden, where he is buried. Separate tours are available of his car museum and his jet, the *Lisa Marie,* named for his daughter, who now has children of her own. *3764 Elvis Presley Blvd. (off I–55),* ☎ *901/332–3322 or, outside TN, 800/238– 2000.* ☛ *Home tour $9 adults, $4.75 children 5–12.* ☛ *To all attractions: $17 adults, $11 children 5–12. Parking: $2. Reservations suggested in summer.* ☼ *Memorial Day–Labor Day, daily 8–6; Labor Day–Memorial Day, daily 8–5. Mansion closed Tues. Nov.–Feb.*

⓴ At the peaceful, thought-provoking **Chucalissa Archaeological Museum,** about 10 miles southwest of downtown, a simple river culture that existed from AD 1000 to 1500 is immortalized. The four-acre reconstruction is operated by the University of Memphis, and on-site archaeological excavations are often conducted in summer. In the museum, prehistoric tools, pottery, and weapons and a free 15-minute slide presentation describing Chucalissa life and culture offer clues to the workings of that world. Outside, skilled Choctaw craftsfolk fashion jewelry, weapons, and pottery. An annual August powwow is a highlight. *1987 Indian Village Dr.,* ☎ *901/785–3160.* ☛ *$3 adults, $2 senior citizens and children 4–11, children under 4 free.* ☼ *Tues.–Sat. 9–4:30, Sun. 1–4:30.*

㉑ The adjacent **T. O. Fuller State Park** (☎ 901/543–7581) offers camping, golf, and swimming.

㉒ On the way back to downtown Memphis (via I–55N, last exit before bridge) is the **National Ornamental Metal Museum.** On grounds overlooking the Mississippi River sits the nation's only museum preserving the art and the craft of metalworking—from wrought iron to gold. There's also a working blacksmith shop and changing exhibitions and demonstrations. *374 W. California Ave.,* ☎ *901/774–6380.* ☛ *$2 adults, $1 senior citizens and children 5–18.* ☼ *Tues.–Sat. 10–5, Sun. noon–5.*

The Hinterland

From Memphis, the quiet, historic byways seem light-years removed from the busy river city. Driving northward along U.S. 51 through the fertile Mississippi River bottomlands brings you into the heart of King Cotton's domain. About 48 miles along the way, you'll come to **Henning,** a friendly little town remarkably untouched by its world acclaim as the boyhood home and burial place of Alex Haley, Pulitzer Prize–winning author of *Roots.* At the **Alex Haley House Museum,** the only state-owned historic site in West Tennessee, family portraits, mementos, and furnishings are displayed. *200 Church St.,* ☎ *901/738–2240.* ☛ *$2.50 adults, $1 children 6–16.* ☉ *Tues.–Sat. 10–5, Sun. 1–5.*

Reelfoot Lake—about 55 miles farther on (via U.S. 51N and TN 21W), in Tennessee's northwest corner—gains a peculiar and mysterious beauty from a romantic scattering of cypress trees and charred stumps. The 13,000-acre lake was formed when earthquakes in 1811 caused the Mississippi River to flood into the sinking land where a luxuriant forest once stood. From late November through mid-March the lake is a major sanctuary for American bald eagles. At **Reelfoot Lake State Resort Park** (Rtes. 22 and 78, ☎ 901/253–7756), the Tennessee Department of Conservation conducts eagle-spotting tours. For further information, contact the chamber of commerce (Reelfoot Lake 38079, ☎ 901/253–8144).

From Memphis, follow I–40 85 miles northeast to **Jackson** (Jackson/Madison County Convention & Visitors Bureau, 400 S. Highland Ave., Jackson 38301, ☎ 901/425–8333), site of several Civil War battles. A major railroad hub, it was home to Johnathan Luther "Casey" Jones, who was immortalized in the "Ballad of Casey Jones." The famed engineer became a hero by staying aboard his locomotive in a vain attempt to stop his engine from plowing into another train. In Casey Jones Village (at U.S. 45 Bypass), the **Casey Jones Home and Railroad Museum** (☎ 901/668–1223) contains a diverse assortment of railroad memorabilia. On the grounds is a replica of Old No. 382, Casey's steam engine. The Casey Jones Village Old Country Store, also located in the village, features a restaurant; an 1890s-style ice-cream parlor; and gift, souvenir, confectionery, and antiques shops. ☛ *To museum: $3 adults, $2 children 6–12.* ☉ *Mon.–Sat. 9–5, Sun. 1–5.*

One hundred miles east of Memphis via U.S. 64, then 10 miles south on TN 22, is **Shiloh National Military Park,** site of one of the Civil War's grimmest and most important battles. At the visitor center, you'll see a film explaining the battle's strategy, along with a display of Civil War relics. A self-guided auto tour leads past markers explaining monuments and battle sites. Almost 4,000 soldiers, many unidentified, are buried here in the national cemetery. ☎ *901/689–5275.* ☛ *$2 per person, $4 per family, children under 16 free.* ☉ *Visitor center daily 8–5.*

About 10 miles east of Shiloh is scenic **Savannah,** on the east bluff of the Tennessee River. The historic **Cherry Mansion,** built atop a bluff in 1830, served as General Grant's headquarters during the Battle of Shiloh. The house is privately owned, but the owner allows visitors to roam the grounds and take pictures. It's two blocks west of the town square on Main Street. On the square, housed in the same building as the Chamber of Commerce, is the **Tennessee River Museum,** which has exhibits on the Civil War, the river, and fossils from 65 million years ago, when this area was underwater. *507 Main St.,* ☎ *901/925–2363.* ☛ *$2 adults, students free.* ☉ *Mon.–Sat. 9–5, Sun. 1–5.*

Nearby (110 mi east of Memphis on TN 57E) is **Pickwick Landing Dam** (☎ 901/925–4342), one of the Tennessee Valley Authority showcase hydroelectric projects. From the top of the dam, which rises high above the Tennessee River to create Pickwick Lake, there are sweeping views. You're welcome to visit the power plant during daylight hours. **Pickwick Landing State Resort Park** (☎ 901/689–3129) offers a resort inn, a restaurant, playgrounds, swimming beaches, picnic areas, and a par 72, 18-hole golf course.

What to See and Do with Children

Adventure River Water Park. This 25-acre water park has a giant wave pool, water slides, raft and inner-tube rides, a man-made river, a kiddie pool, and more. *6880 Whitten Bend Cove (12 mi east of downtown, off I–40),* ☎ *901/382–9283.* ☛ *$12 adults, $11 children 3–12, $3 senior citizens.* ☉ *Memorial Day–Labor Day, daily 10–8; weekends only in May.*

Meeman–Shelby Forest State Park. Get back to nature at this 12,500-acre park bordering the Mississippi, with hiking and biking. *10 mi north of Memphis, off U.S. 51,* ☎ *901/876–5215.* ☛ *Free.* ☉ *Daily 7 AM–10 PM.*

Shopping

Shopping Districts

More than a dozen shopping centers and malls are scattered about the city. The **Mid-America Mall** (☎ 901/362–9315), on Main Street between Beale and Poplar, is one of the nation's longest pedestrian malls. It was overhauled and turned into a trolley mall in 1993, and is hoped to bring shopping to this heretofore relatively desolate area. **Oak Court Mall** (4465 Poplar Ave., ☎ 901/682–8928), in the busy Poplar/Perkins area of East Memphis, has 70 specialty stores and two department stores. **Overton Square** (24 S. Cooper St., ☎ 901/272–1495)—a three-block midtown shopping, restaurant, and entertainment complex in artfully restored vintage buildings and newer structures—features upscale boutiques and specialty shops.

Discount Outlet

Belz Factory Outlet Mall (3536 Canada Rd., Exit 20 off I–40, 20 mi east of downtown Memphis, Lakeland, ☎ 901/386–3180) includes 50 stores from the Boot Factory to Linens 'n Things to Van Heusen.

Specialty Stores

CLOTHING

The **Woman's Exchange** (88 Racine St., Memphis, ☎ 901/327–5681) specializes in children's wear and handcrafted items. There's a Christmas shop in November and December.

CRAFTS AND COLLECTIBLES

The **Checkerberry Shoppe** (2247 Germantown Rd. S, Germantown, ☎ 901/754–3601) has quilted wall-hangings, country dolls, salt-glazed stoneware, handmade baskets, stained glass, miniatures, and antique reproductions.

ELVIS PRESLEY MEMORABILIA

Six shops at **Graceland** (3717 Elvis Presley Blvd., ☎ 901/332–3322 or 800/238–2000) sell every Elvis-related item imaginable, from cookie jars and T-shirts with his face plastered over them to Elvis records and tapes to collectible vintage items.

One of a Kind

A. Schwab's (163 Beale St., ☎ 901/523–9782) is an old-fashioned dry-goods store whose motto is "If you can't find it at A. Schwab's, you're better off without it!" Elvis shopped here, and you can, too—for top hats, spats, tambourines, bow ties, dresses to size 60, and men's trousers to size 74.

Participant Sports

Boating and Fishing

Boat rentals are available at **Meeman-Shelby Forest State Park** (*see* What to See and Do with Children, *above*), **Pickwick Landing State Resort Park** (*see* The Hinterland *in* Exploring, *above*), and **Reelfoot Lake State Resort Park** (*see* The Hinterland *in* Exploring, *above*). The quiet lakes provide good fishing year-round for bass, crappie, trout, bream, and catfish.

Golf

The Memphis Park Commission (☎ 901/325–5759) operates eight public courses, the most central of which are **Overton Park** (9 holes; ☎ 901/725–9905) and **Galloway** (18 holes; ☎ 901/685–7805).

Hiking

There are trails at **Meeman-Shelby Forest State Park** (*see above*), **Shelby Farms Plough Recreation Area** (☎ 901/382–4250), **Lichterman Nature Center** (☎ 901/767–7322), and **T. O. Fuller State Park** (☎ 901/529–7581).

Ice Skating

The **Ice Capades Chalet,** in the Mall of Memphis (☎ 901/362–8877), is open 7 days a week.

Tennis

The Memphis Park Commission (☎ 901/325–5759) operates nine facilities that offer lessons, tournaments, and league play. **Leftwich** (☎ 901/685–7907), **Ridgeway** (☎ 901/767–2889), and **Whitehaven** (☎ 901/332–0546) have indoor courts. The **International Indoor Tennis Tournament** (☎ 901/765–4400) is played in February at the Racquet Club in East Memphis.

Spectator Sports

Auto Racing

The 600-acre **Memphis Motorsports Park** hosts weekly dirt-track and drag racing. *5500 Taylor Forge Rd., Millington,* ☎ *901/358–7223.* ☛ *Varies.* ☉ *Mar.–Nov.*

Baseball

The **Memphis Chicks,** a class AA team of the Kansas City Royals and member of the Southern League, plays at Tim McCarver Stadium (800 Home Run La., ☎ 901/272–1687).

Football

Each December a top Southern collegiate event—the **Liberty Bowl Football Classic**—is held at the Liberty Memorial Stadium (☎ 901/795–7700), which hosts the Memphis State University Tigers and other football teams.

Golf

In June the Tournament Players Club at Southwind Country Club (3325 Club at Southwind) hosts the **Federal Express–St. Jude Classic,** featuring top pros. The 1995 tournament (☏ 901/748–0534) is the last week of June.

Hockey

The **Memphis Riverkings** (☏ 901/278–9009, Nov.–Mar.), a minor league club, plays at the Mid-South Coliseum.

Tennis

The **International Indoor Tennis Championship** (☏ 901/765–4400) brings top pros from around the world to the Racquet Club in February.

Dining

Not so long ago, Memphis offered little more than various neighborhood restaurants featuring "home cooking," several Chinese chop-suey houses, a handful of Italian spaghetti-and-lasagna spots, and numerous establishments serving pork barbecue. Even the city's few higher-priced restaurants served only the ordinary.

Happily, the dining choices have not only expanded greatly but improved dramatically in quality during the past 15 years. In addition to a number of restaurants serving imaginative American cuisine, Memphis now boasts many competent and attractive international dining rooms. Hotel dining in Memphis (which used to mean tired menus and lifeless cooking) has been revitalized, and today the city's most inspired dishes are often served in its finer hotels.

Memphis's top culinary attraction, however, remains barbecue, and a visit to one of the 70-odd barbecue restaurants is recommended for anyone wanting to savor local color as well as tasty ribs. Locals still debate which is better: wet or dry ribs—a reference to the cooking style, not how moist the meat is. True fanciers may want to schedule their visit around the International Barbecue Cooking Contest, held during the annual Memphis in May International Festival. This cook-off draws 300 teams from around the world (as well as more than 100,000 spectators) for its three-day run on the banks of the Mississippi. Dress is casual unless otherwise noted.

CATEGORY	COST*
$$$$	over $50
$$$	$40–$50
$$	$20–$40
$	under $20

per person for a three-course meal, excluding drinks, service, and 7.75% sales tax

American

$$$$ **Folk's Folly Prime Steak House.** Folk's is a Memphis favorite for one simple reason: You can dig into the juiciest sizzling-hot steaks in town. The generous vegetable side dishes, such as stuffed baked potatoes and fresh asparagus, are also delicious. Heaping portions of fresh seafood and whole lobster are always available. The "steak house" name is a bit misleading—this restaurant resembles a suburban home, with a lounge and five separate dining rooms plus eight private rooms for small parties. It's in East Memphis, in close proximity to some of the city's nicest

Dining

Automatic Slim's Tonga Club, **4**
Blues City Cafe, **6**
Cafe Olé , **8**
Cafe Society, **10**
Charlie Vergos' Rendezvous, **2**
Chez Philippe, **3**
Corky's, **20**
Dux, **3**
Folk's Folly Prime Steak House, **19**
John Wills's Memphis Bar & Grill, **14**
Justine's, **7**
La Tourelle, **13**
Landry's Seafood House, **5**
Marena's, **9**
Owen Brennan's Restaurant, **22**
Paulette's, **11**
Restaurant Raji, **18**

Lodging

Adam's Mark Hotel, **21**
Days Inn Graceland, **16**
French Quarter Suites Hotel, **12**
Hampton Inn Airport, **17**
Holiday Inn Crowne Plaza, **1**
Peabody Hotel, **3**
Wilson World Hotel, **15**

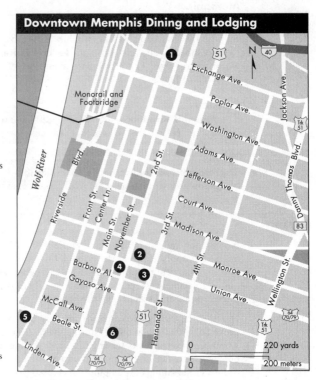

Downtown Memphis Dining and Lodging

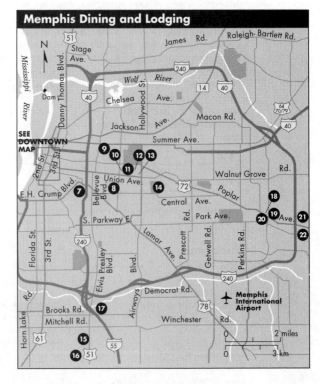

Memphis Dining and Lodging

residential areas. ✗ *551 S. Mendenhall St., ☎ 901/762–8200. Reservations accepted. AE, MC, V. No lunch.*

$$ Blues City Cafe. This downtown restaurant specializes in huge steaks and ribs, hamburgers, and hot tamales in a diner setting. ✗ *138 Beale St., ☎ 901/526–3637. ☉ Daily; hours vary, so call ahead. AE, MC, V.*

Barbecue

$ Charlie Vergos' Rendezvous. Charlie Vergos has become something of
★ a Memphis ambassador of barbecued ribs: Not only does his downtown basement restaurant draw thousands of tourists each year, but he also ships his ribs by air express all over the country. The decor here is museumlike: The walls are filled with memorabilia and bric-a-brac, from old newspaper cartoons to Essolene gas signs. But what packs in the crowds are the delicious pork loin plate and the barbecued pork ribs. ✗ *52 S. Second St., ☎ 901/523–2746. No reservations. AE, MC, V. Closed Sun. and Mon.*

$ Corky's. Expect to wait in line at this no-frills East Memphis barbeque joint. One taste of the ribs or pork platter explains why. Letters from customers and articles on Corky's cover the walls. ✗ *5259 Poplar Ave., ☎ 901/685–9744. No reservations. AE, D, DC, MC, V.*

$ John Wills's Memphis Bar & Grill. John Wills parlayed his two victo-
★ ries in the International Pork Barbecue Cooking Contest into this successful restaurant, open since 1983. Attractive, with green tables, natural-wood booths, and cute photos of pigs adorning the walls, the busy establishment offers a wide selection of well-prepared barbecued meats, including pork ribs, pork shoulder, beef brisket, and sausage. The barbecued beans are nicely spiced, and the coleslaw has a tart mustard seasoning. ✗ *5101 Sanderlin St., ☎ 901/761–5101. No reservations. AE, MC, V.*

Cajun

$$$ Owen Brennan's Restaurant. This New Orleans–style eatery in an upscale Memphis shopping center specializes in those fine Cajun and Creole dishes that usually require a jaunt to the French Quarter. Favorite dishes include blackened chicken or fish and seafood gumbo. The lavish Sunday brunch is attended religiously, and easy banter, champagne, and jazz flow freely. Best of all, an outdoor patio under towering shade trees offers cool respite from Memphis's sizzling summer sun. ✗ *6150 Poplar Ave., ☎ 901/761–0990. Reservations accepted. AE, DC, MC, V.*

Continental

$$$$ Justine's. Fresh roses from the restaurant's gardens adorn each table, and soothing piano music flows through the six dining rooms of this restored Victorian mansion, built in 1843. In Midtown more than 30 years, Justine's is a gracious reminder of the style of the Old South. The New Orleans–influenced menu is hardly innovative, but it is reliable, especially the fresh and well-prepared seafood. Excellent specialties are crabs Justine, a crabmeat casserole with buttery sauce; broiled pompano with chives, parsley, and lemon; and beef tenderloin with artichoke hearts and béarnaise sauce. ✗ *919 Coward Pl., ☎ 901/527–9973. Reservations required. Jacket and tie. AE, DC, MC, V. Closed Sun. and Mon.*

$$ **Paulette's.** This Overton Square restaurant was serving bistro-style cooking before it became popular in Memphis; for more than two decades, Paulette's has retained its vitality. With a crisp, fresh house salad and airy popovers with strawberry butter, Paulette's packs them in at lunch and dinner. Entrées include several crêpe dishes, along with grilled salmon, swordfish, and chicken, baked scallops, and brochettes of shrimp or beef. Save room for the hot chocolate crêpes. On weekends a pianist plays requests ranging from Gershwin to Beale Street Blues. ✕ *2110 Madison Ave.,* ☎ *901/726–5128. Reservations accepted. AE, MC, V.*

French

$$$ **Cafe Society.** This sidewalk café in Midtown brings imagination and a fresh range of choices to its lunch and dinner menu. Outdoor tables, across the street from a small park, are popular with the happy-hour crowd. Expect to find treats like coconut-fried shrimp with pineapple chutney, grilled salmon with sesame and poppyseed crust and shrimp biscayne sauce, and veal and pasta dishes. The best dessert is the Italian cheesecake. ✕ *212 N. Evergreen,* ☎ *901/722–2177. Reservations accepted. AE, MC, V. No lunch Sat.*

$$$ **La Tourelle.** This quiet, turn-of-the-century bungalow is reminiscent of
★ a small country restaurant in France, with fine lace curtains and wood floors. Three- and five-course prix-fixe meals are served nightly, or you can order à la carte. The restaurant features a wonderful changing menu that emphasizes fresh seafood prepared with a French or Italian slant, interesting side dishes, and beautiful presentations. The Queen Mother cake is a triple chocolate knockout. ✕ *Overton Sq., 2146 Monroe Ave.,* ☎ *901/726–5771. Reservations recommended. MC, V. No lunch Sat. Closed Mon.*

Indian

$$$$ **Restaurant Raji.** Chef-owner Raji Jallepalli blends nouvelle styles and Indian seasonings in a cuisine as subtle and refined as can be found. Her creations range from fragrant Indian consommé with white peppercorns and coriander to supreme of duck with curry masala sauce or grilled scallops and lobster in lentil pastry with a ginger-flavored beurre blanc. Several intimate dining rooms in a former residence have elegant and refined decor. ✕ *712 W. Brookhaven Circle,* ☎ *901/685–8723. Reservations required. AE, MC, V. Closed Sun. and Mon. No lunch.*

Mediterranean

$$ **Marena's.** This midtown restaurant opened in 1991 to rave reviews.
★ The decor features colorful hand-painted furniture and paneling. The food is just as artistic, with Mediterranean specialties from North Africa to the middle east to the south of France, Italy, and Spain. The menus change monthly and are always full of surprises, but repeated favorites like the grilled tuna in *chermoula* (a Moroccan sauce of olive oil, spices, and hot peppers) and creme caramel are not to be missed. ✕ *1545 Overton Park,* ☎ *901/278–9774. Reservations recommended. AE, MC, V. Closed Sun. No lunch.*

Mexican

$ **Cafe Olé.** If Mexican with a healthy twist sounds intriguing, this popular midtown hangout is for you. Specialties—sans the animal fats that make most Mexican fare so fattening—include spinach enchiladas and chili rellenos. The exposed brick walls are decorated with Mexican paintings and ceremonial masks. ✕ *959 S. Cooper St.,* ☎ *901/274–1504. Reservations accepted for dinner. AE, D, DC, MC, V.*

New American

$$$ **Dux.** Done up in black, white, and maroon, this stylish hotel restau-
★ rant serves innovative nouvelle American cuisine complemented by an American wine list. Steaks are a specialty, but the aromatic pastas and overstuffed sandwiches are popular as well. The restaurant's entrance is decorated with beautiful glass and ceramic ducks in honor of the legendary live ones you'll see regularly parading through the hotel's famous and newly renovated lobby. ✕ *Peabody Hotel, 149 Union Ave.,* ☎ *901/529–4199. Reservations accepted. AE, DC, MC, V.*

Nouvelle French

$$$$ **Chez Philippe.** The decor—high ceilings, *faux* marble columns, huge
★ murals depicting a masked ball—is wonderfully lavish. The service, by waiters in white tie, is impeccable. Most important, the cuisine—Memphis's most innovative and sophisticated—lives up to its regal setting. Chef José Gutierrez is recognized as one of the country's outstanding young chefs, and his talent is evident in a menu that ranges from delicate terrines to lamb tenderloin in puff pastry to hot soufflés. The restaurant has been voted Memphis' best for the past 9 years in the *Memphis Magazine* readers poll. ✕ *Peabody Hotel, 149 Union Ave.,* ☎ *901/529–4188. Reservations advised. AE, DC, MC, V. No lunch. Closed Sun.*

Seafood

$$ **Landry's Seafood House.** This newly remodeled riverfront place is one of Memphis's busiest restaurants, teeming with tourists and locals, too. Though it seats more than 300, the waiting list often exceeds one hour. Patio dining is especially refreshing, if you can get a table. The fare—seafood, steaks, and Cajun dishes—is simple but consistently good. Among the better offerings are shrimp in a brown-butter sauce, flounder stuffed with shrimp and crabmeat, and fried oysters and shrimp. ✕ *263 Wagner Pl.,* ☎ *901/526–1966. Reservations for 8 or more. AE, MC, V.*

Southwestern

$$ **Automatic Slim's Tonga Club.** This popular, hip new restaurant is downtown across from the Peabody hotel. The split-level dining room is usually crowded on weekends and many weeknights, too. The restaurant specializes in Southwestern and Caribbean fare served in thick and spicy sauces; signature dishes include deep fried red snapper with tomato and jalepeño relish and Jamaican jerk duck. ✕ *83 S. 2nd St.,* ☎ *901/525–7948. Reservations accepted. AE, MC, V. No lunch Sat.*

Lodging

Memphis hotels are especially busy in the spring, when the Memphis in May International Festival and June's Cotton Carnival Memphis are in progress; in mid-August, when pilgrims observe Elvis Presley's death; and between Christmas and New Year's during the Liberty Bowl Football Classic. Be sure to reserve well in advance during those times. To find out about B&Bs in Memphis, contact the **Bed & Breakfast in Memphis Reservation Service** (Box 41621, Memphis 38174, ☎ 901/726–5920 or 800/336–2087, FAX 901/725–0194).

CATEGORY	COST*
$$$$	over $125
$$$	$70–$125
$$	$50–$70
$	under $50

All prices are for a standard double room, excluding 11.75% tax.

$$$$ **Adam's Mark Hotel.** This luxury property, a 27-story circular glass tower, is in the flourishing eastern suburbs near I–240. From your glass-walled aerie, you'll have sweeping vistas of Memphis and its outskirts. ⌑ *939 Ridge Lake Blvd., 38120,* ☎ *901/684–6664 or 800/444–2326,* ⅏ *901/762–7411. 376 rooms, 13 suites. Restaurant, lounge, pool, health club. AE, D, DC, MC, V.*

$$$$ **Peabody Hotel.** This 12-story Italianate Renaissance hostelry, a down-
★   town landmark since 1925, was restored impeccably and reopened in 1981 after being closed for a time in the mid-'70s. A full renovation in 1994 spruced up the decor and added a concierge floor. Rooms have been lightened with bright yellows and pastels, and the luxurious bathrooms are done in peach marble. The lobby preserves its original stained-glass skylights and ornate travertine marble fountain—home to the hotel's famed resident ducks, who waddle down each morning from their penthouse apartment and parade across a red carpet to the stirring sounds of Sousa's "King Cotton March"; the show is repeated each afternoon. ⌑ *149 Union Ave., 38103,* ☎ *901/529–4000 or 800/732–2639,* ⅏ *901/529–3600. 453 rooms, 15 suites. 4 restaurants, bar, indoor pool, health club. AE, DC, MC, V.*

$$$ **French Quarter Suites Hotel.** With its mellow rose-brick exterior and
★   classic architectural lines, this pleasant New Overton Square hostelry is reminiscent of an older, New Orleans–style inn. All the one-bedroom suites have living rooms and whirlpool baths that accommodate two, and some are balconied. ⌑ *2144 Madison Ave., 38104,* ☎ *901/728–4000 or 800/843–0353,* ⅏ *901/278–1262. 104 suites. Pool, exercise room. AE, DC, MC, V.*

$$$ **Holiday Inn Crowne Plaza.** Memphis was the birthplace of Holiday Inns, and this is the flagship of the area's seven-inn fleet. Adjacent to the downtown Convention Center, this sleek high-rise (18 floors) offers a concierge floor and sizable meeting facilities, plus ample work space and lighting in the spacious guest rooms and suites. The lobby lounge, a tasteful, greenery-filled retreat, is a pleasant spot to relax and listen to music from the grand piano. ⌑ *250 N. Main St., 38103,* ☎ *901/527–7300 or 800/465–4329,* ⅏ *901/526–1561. 396 rooms, 7 suites. Restaurant, lounge, indoor pool, hot tub, sauna, health club. AE, DC, MC, V.*

$$ **Hampton Inn Airport.** This is a member of the economy-priced system
★   that was spun off from the Holiday Inn chain. The building has a pleasing contemporary design. Spacious, well-lighted rooms have Scandinavian-style teakwood furnishings. With a good location for families, this is a front runner in the moderate category. ⌑ *2979 Millbranch Rd., 38116,* ☎ *901/396–2200 or 800/426–7866,* ⅏ *901/396–7034. 128 rooms. Pool. AE, DC, MC, V.*

$$ **Wilson World Graceland.** This new kid on the block, across the street from Graceland, has caught Memphis's infectious case of Elvismania. Two life-size portraits of the King grace the lobby. You can take free popcorn back to your mauve-colored room and munch away to free movies on the Elvis channel. Rooms are equipped with microwaves and fridges. ⌑ *3677 Elvis Presley Blvd., 38116,* ☎ *901/332–2107 or 800/945–7667,* ⅏ *901/366–6361. 134 rooms. Meeting rooms, airport shuttle. AE, DC, MC, V.*

$ **Day's Inn Graceland.** This modest hotel's claim to fame is its close prox-
★ imity to Graceland, and it makes the most of that with a guitar shaped
swimming pool and free Elvis Movies 'round the clock. ☎ *3839 Elvis
Presley Blvd.,* ☎ *901/346–3839,* FAX *901/794–5412. 60 rooms. Pool.
AE, DC, MC, V.*

The Arts

For a complete listing of weekly events, check the Playbook section in
the Friday *Memphis Commercial Appeal,* or *The Memphis Flyer,* distributed free at newsstands around the city. The Visitor Information
Center will also provide an up-to-date rundown of events.

Concerts
Big-name entertainers and musical groups appear at the **Mud Island
Amphitheatre** (☎ 901/576–7241) from April through October. Among
the offerings at the **Orpheum Theatre** (203 S. Main St., ☎ 901/525–
3000) are easy listening and jazz concerts.

Dance
The Orpheum Theatre is also the scene of performances by two dance
companies: **Memphis Concert Ballet** (☎ 901/763–0139) features professional dancers and celebrity guest artists.

Opera
Opera Memphis performs at the Orpheum Theatre (☎ 901/678–2706
for tickets).

Theater
Playhouse on the Square (☎ 901/726–4656, Sept.–July) features the
city's only professional repertory company. The **Orpheum Theatre** (☎
901/525–3000 for tickets), an impeccably restored former vaudeville
palace, is the site of Broadway-style shows and other productions. **Center Stage,** at the Jewish Community Center (☎ 901/761–0810), and
the **Circuit Playhouse** (☎ 901/726–4656, Sept.–June) offer a wide variety of performances. At **Ewing's Children's Theatre** (☎ 901/452–3968),
performances are directed, designed, and acted entirely by children. Community theaters include **Theatre Memphis** (☎ 901/682–8323), acclaimed as one of the best in the United States, and **Germantown
Community Theatre** (☎ 901/754–2680), in a restored schoolhouse. Memphis State's **University Theatre** (☎ 901/678–2350) and Rhodes College's **McCoy Theatre** (☎ 901/726–3839, Sept.–May) present dramatic
and musical productions starring students, faculty, and guest performers.

Nightlife

Blues
At **B. B. King's Blues Club** (147 Beale St., ☎ 901/524–5464), live blues
nightly is accompanied by southern food specialties. At the **New Daisy
Theatre** (330 Beale St., ☎ 901/525–8979)—a 900-seat venue where
B.B. King got his start—blues, jazz, and (predominantly) rock bands
perform. There's live blues and dancing nightly at the **Rum Boogie Cafe**
(182 Beale St., ☎ 901/528–0150).

Nightclubs
Alfred's on Beale (197 Beale St., ☎ 901/525–3711), one of the city's
hottest dance clubs, also serves great food. Rock bands perform

Wednesday through Saturday, and a DJ spins popular dance tunes during the week.

Memphis Essentials

Arriving and Departing

BY BOAT

The paddle-wheel steamers *Delta Queen* and *Mississippi Queen* (Robin St. Wharf, New Orleans, LA 70130, ☎ 800/543–1949) stop at Memphis on excursions between New Orleans, St. Louis, Cincinnati, and St. Paul.

BY BUS

Greyhound Bus Lines (203 Union Ave., ☎ 800/231–2222) offers service throughout the region.

BY CAR

From Memphis, I–55 leads north to St. Louis and south to Jackson, Mississippi; I–40, east to Nashville and Knoxville. I–240 encircles the city.

BY PLANE

Memphis International Airport (☎ 901/544–3495), served by American, Delta, Northwest, and Northwest Airlink, is 9½ miles south of downtown.

Taxi fare downtown is about $17. Try Yellow Cab (☎ 901/577–7700). By **car,** take I–240 to downtown.

BY TRAIN

Amtrak (545 S. Main St., ☎ 901/526–0052 or 800/872–7245) operates the *City of New Orleans,* which stops in Memphis on the trip between New Orleans and Chicago.

Getting Around

BY BUS

Memphis Area Transit Authority (☎ 901/274–6282) buses cover the city and immediate suburbs (weekdays 4:30 AM–11:15 PM, Sat. 5 AM–6:15 PM, Sun. 9–6:15; fare $1, transfers 10¢). There is short-hop service on designated buses between Front, Third, and Exchange streets from 9 AM to 3 PM and between downtown and the Medical Center complex from 7 AM to 6 PM (35¢). A trolley runs between the north and south ends of downtown (50¢).

BY TAXI

The fare is $1.25 for the first 1/11 mile, $1.10 for each additional mile. There are stands at the airport and bus station.

Guided Tours

BOAT TOURS

Memphis Queen Line Riverboats (☎ 901/527–5694 or 800/221–6197) offers 1½-hour sightseeing and 2-hour dinner cruises. Sightseeing cruises run daily throughout the year, dinner cruises run Wednesday–Sunday from May–September.

CARRIAGE TOURS

Carriage Tours of Memphis (☎ 901/527–7542) offers horse-drawn carriage rides.

ORIENTATION
Blues City Tours (☎ 901/522–9229) and **Gray Line** (☎ 901/948–8687) offer three-hour motor-coach tours that include downtown highlights as well as Graceland.

SPECIAL-INTEREST
Gray Line (*see above*) offers nightlife and Mud Island tours. **Unique Tours** (☎ 901/527–8876 or 800/235–1984) has three-day, two-night tours of Graceland, the National Civil Rights Museum, Mud Island, and other attractions. **Blues City Tours** (*see above*) offers tours of Memphis and attractions, including Mud Island and Beale Street; riverboat rides; and nightly tours that include dinner and a show. The **Center for Southern Folklore** (☎ 901/525–3655) gives tours of Beale Street, a farm on the Delta, and prominent areas of musical interest. **Heritage Tours** (☎ 901/527–3427) explores the area's rich African-American cultural heritage.

Important Addresses and Numbers

EMERGENCIES
Dial 911 for **police** and **ambulance** in an emergency. Near-downtown hospitals with 24-hour emergency service include **Baptist Memorial Hospital Medical Center** (899 Madison Ave., ☎ 901/227–2727) and **Methodist Hospitals of Memphis** (1265 Union Ave., ☎ 901/726–7000).

PHARMACY
Walgreen's (3476 Poplar Plaza, ☎ 901/458–9233).

RADIO STATIONS
AM: WMC 79, news and talk. **FM:** WEGR 103, adult contemporary and easy listening; WHRK 97, rhythm and blues.

VISITOR INFORMATION
Visitors Information Center (340 Beale St., 38103, ☎ 901/543–5333; ☉ Weekdays 9–5, Sat. 9–6, Sun. noon–5). **Memphis Convention & Visitors Bureau** (47 Union Ave., 38103, ☎ 901/543–5300 or 800/873–6282; ☉ Weekdays 8:30–5).

NASHVILLE

Heralded as Music City, U.S.A. and the country music capital of the world, Tennessee's fast-growing capital city also shines as a leading center of higher education, appropriately known as the Athens of the South. Both labels fit. Nashville has prospered from them both, emerging as one of the South's most vibrant cities in the process.

Nashville's "Grand Ole Opry" radio program, which began as station WSM's "Barn Dance" in 1925 and thrived throughout the Great Depression right into today's MTV years, established the town as a music center. The Opry, which has added such popular newcomers as Vince Gill and Emmylou Harris to its cast, now performs in a sleek $15 million Opry House at Opryland. The infusion of talent is attracting a new generation of fans. The Opry is still as gleeful and down-home informal as it was when ticket holders used to jam into the old Ryman Auditorium with hand-held fans for battling the sweltering heat. Bolstering Nashville's reputation as a music town are dozens of clubs, performance stages, and television tapings open to the public, as well as memorials—some kitschy, some moving—to many country music stars. And, of course, legendary Music Row continues to beckon aspiring singers, musicians, and songwriters with stars in their eyes and lyrics tucked in their back pockets.

Much of Nashville's role as a cultural leader, enhanced by the presence of the new performing arts center, derives from the presence of 16 colleges and universities, two medical schools, two law schools, and six graduate business schools. Several, including Vanderbilt University, have national or international reputations, and many have private art galleries. As ancient Athens was the "School of Hellas," so Nashville, where a full-size replica of the Parthenon graces Centennial Park, fills this role in the contemporary South. The historic sites throughout the city add another dimension. Belle Meade Plantation, Belmont Mansion, Fort Nashborough, Travellers Rest, and President Andrew Jackson's Hermitage demonstrate vividly Nashville's growth from a military outpost to a land of genteel plantations.

The surrounding Tennessee Heartland, a pocket of gently rolling Cumberland Mountain foothills and bluegrass meadows, is one of the state's richest farming areas. Such small nearby towns as Franklin, which historian Shelby Foote calls one of the nation's top Civil War sites, offer wonderful antiques shops and crafts boutiques, as well as the welcoming hospitality for which the South is known.

Exploring

Numbers in the margin correspond to points of interest on the Downtown Nashville and Nashville maps.

Nashville sprawls. The river horizontally bisects the central city. Numbered avenues, running north–south, are west of and parallel to the river; numbered streets are east of the river and parallel to it.

Downtown

Though considerably smaller, the Cumberland River has been as important to Nashville as the Mississippi has been to Memphis. **Riverfront Park** at First Avenue and Broadway, a welcoming green enclave on the west bank of the Cumberland, has an expansive view of the busy barge traffic on the muddy river. The park serves as a popular venue for free summer concerts, block parties, and picnics, as well as a docking spot for riverboat excursions (*see* Guided Tours, *below*). Opryland's new, 57-foot Opryland USA Water Taxis link the park with Opryland USA (☎ 615/889–6611; $5.95 one-way, $9.95 round-trip adults; $3 one-way, $6 round-trip children) across the river.

North on First Avenue is **Fort Nashborough.** High on the limestone bluffs overlooking the river that brought settlers here, a crude log fort, built in 1779 for protection and shelter, overlooks Nashville. Today it has been painstakingly re-created to serve as a monument to the city founders' courage, and, in five log cabins, costumed interpreters evoke the indomitable spirit of the American age of settlement. *170 First Ave. N,* ☎ *615/862–8400.* ☛ *Free.* ☉ *Daily 9–5.*

By the early 19th century, logs had given way to brick and marble. Downtown was thriving, and today it thrives anew, thanks to an extensive preservation program begun in the early 1980s. From Fort Nashborough, turn left onto Church Street to reach the heart of the **Historic Second Avenue Business District** (a.k.a. "The District"), where 19th-century redbrick warehouses and storefronts have been handsomely restored to house clubs, restaurants, and funky specialty shops. On Thursday (June–Sept.), an after-work street party, Dancin' in the District, assembles with live music from jazz to alternative rock. The 1994 additions of the Wildhorse Saloon, a huge country music dance hall, and the Hard Rock Cafe have only increased the festive atmosphere.

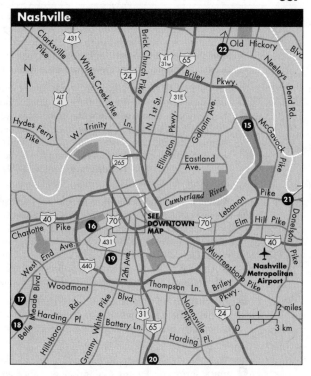

Nashville

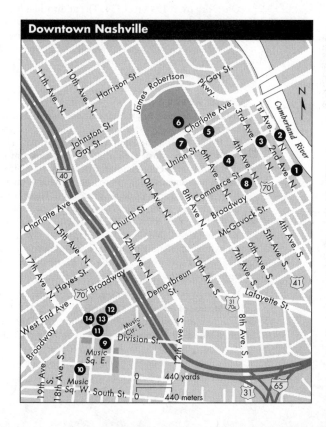

Downtown Nashville

Continue west on Church Street, which between Fourth and Eighth avenues is cobblestoned and tree-lined, retaining a picturesque quality reminiscent of a European town. At the corner of Fifth is the **Downtown Presbyterian Church,** an Egyptian Revival tabernacle (circa 1851) designed by noted Philadelphia architect William Strickland.

Strolling north on Fifth Avenue, you'll come to one of the city's finest contemporary structures: the James K. Polk Office Building, home to the impressive **Tennessee State Museum.** Here over 6,000 artifacts are displayed in settings that explore life in Tennessee. Included are a log cabin, an exhibition of Native American life, and changing art and history exhibitions. Also part of the complex is the Tennessee Performing Arts Center. *505 Deaderick St., ☎ 615/741–2692. ☛ Free. ☉ Tues.–Sat. 10–5, Sun. 1–5.*

Walking west along Charlotte Avenue between Sixth and Seventh avenues, you'll come to the Greek Revival **State Capitol,** also designed by Strickland, who was so impressed with his creation that he requested—and received—entombment behind one of the building's walls. On the grounds—guarded by statues of such Tennessee heroes as Andrew Jackson—the 11th U.S. president, James K. Polk, and his wife are buried. *☎ 615/741–1621. ☉ For free tours weekdays, 9–4.*

On the corner of Seventh and Union is the **War Memorial Building,** built to honor the state's World War I dead and now housing a collection of military memorabilia. *☎ 615/726–0518. ☛ Free. ☉ Mon.–Sat. 10–5, Sun. 1–5.*

Walk two blocks east and two and a half blocks south to a country music shrine: the **Ryman Auditorium and Museum,** home of the Grand Ole Opry from 1943 to 1974. The auditorium has undergone an $8.5 million restoration and now seats 2,000 for live performances from classical, jazz, pop, and gospel fields, and, of course, country. *116 Opry Pl. (5th Ave. N, between Broadway and Commerce Sts.), ☎ 615/254–1445. ☛ $4 adults, $2 children 6–12. ☉ Daily 8:30–4. Call for show schedules and ticket prices.*

Music Row
By car, take the Demonbreun exit off I–40 to Music Row, the heart of the city's dreamscapes, where songwriters have come for decades, hoping to get someone to listen to their demo tapes. The free parking next to the **Country Music Hall of Fame and Museum** is convenient to all the country attractions clustered nearby and has moving displays—costumes, instruments, film, photos, and insights—on well-loved stars from Roy Acuff to Patsy Cline to Vince Gill. The museum will be moving downtown in 1996. A ticket for the Hall of Fame includes admission to the legendary RCA **Studio B** two blocks away. Elvis, Dolly Parton, and countless others once recorded here; now the studio is a hands-on exhibit area showing how records are produced. *4 Music Sq. E, ☎ 615/256–1639. ☛ $7.50 adults, $2 children 5–12. ☉ June–Aug., daily 8–7; rest of year, 9–5.*

If inspired by your visit to Studio B, consider stopping by the **Recording Studios of America** (1510 Division St., ☎ 615/254–1282) to record, at a nominal cost, a demo tape of your own. The studio is part of **Barbara Mandrell Country,** an intimate look at the career and family life of that superstar (including a replica of her bedroom). This attraction also has the Music Row area's best gift shop. ☎ *615/242–7800.* ☛ *$3.25 adults, under 11 free.* ☉ *Sept.–May, daily 9–5; June–Aug., daily 9–7.*

Music Row itself is along Sixteenth Avenue, where glitzy new record company offices surround the Hall of Fame. Stretching toward Belmont are several blocks of unassuming houses that have been turned into music publishing companies and recording studios. Avoid this area at night.

TIME OUT Mix and mingle with the lunchtime Music Row crowd at **Jamaica** (1901 Broadway, ☎ 615/321–5191). Besides serving heaping portions of spicy seafood, jerk chicken, and pork ($5–$16 entrées), this restaurant offers a respite from the hordes of tourists milling about the nearby gift shops. Eleven saltwater aquariums, hand-painted murals of Jamaican scenery and folks, and live entertainment at the back bar make for a relaxing break.

Hard-core country music fans will get a kick out of the area's other museums. At the **Hank Williams Jr. Museum,** family memorabilia includes Hank Sr.'s '52 Cadillac and Hank Jr.'s '58 pink Cadillac. *1524 Demonbreun St.,* ☎ *615/242–8313.* ☛ *$4 adults, children under 16 free.* ☉ *Mar.–Sept., Mon–Sat. 8–9:30, Sun. 8–7:30; Oct.–Feb., daily 8–5.*

A few doors away, the **Car Collectors Hall of Fame** displays one of Elvis's Cadillacs, Webb Pierce's "silver dollar car," Marty Robbins's Packard, and 50 other flashy vehicles with country provenances. *1534 Demonbreun St.,* ☎ *615/255–6804.* ☛ *$4.95 adults, $3.25 children 6–11.* ☉ *Sept.–May, daily 9–5; June–Aug., daily 8AM–9PM.*

On the same block, the **Country Music Wax Museum and Mall** lionizes more than 60 country stars, with wax figures complete with original stage costumes and musical instruments. *118 16th Ave. S,* ☎ *615/256–2490.* ☛ *$5 adults, $2 children 6–12, under 6 free.* ☉ *June–Aug., daily 9–8; Sept.–May, daily 9–5.*

Opryland

★ ⑮ **Opryland USA,** a 120-acre entertainment theme park just 15 minutes from downtown via the Briley Parkway, is almost twice as large as Disneyland and is Nashville's most popular attraction. The emphasis here is on good old-fashioned family entertainment—with a heavy dose of country—featuring 70 live shows and almost 30 rides, ranging from Chaos, a $7 million indoor thriller combining a roller-coaster ride with spectacular audiovisual effects, to tame mini-ferris wheels perfect for tykes. The shows, especially *Country Music USA,* are toe-tapping good fun, and music rings throughout the park. Wannabes might test their singing talent at Opryplace Recording Studios. *9 mi northeast of downtown, Exit 11, off Briley Pkwy., between I–40 and I–65.* ☎ *615/889–6611.* ☛ *$26.95 adults, $16.95 children 4–11.* ☉ *Late-Mar.–May, Sept., Oct., weekends 10–9; May–early Oct., daily 10–9.*

The theme park was created in part because the enormously popular **Grand Ole Opry**—having recently celebrated its 70th birthday—had outgrown its old stomping grounds, the Ryman. Each weekend, top stars perform at the nation's oldest continuous radio show, in the world's largest broadcast studio (seating 4,424). The Opry has overhauled its image as the home of fading stars by adding current favorites Garth Brooks, Emmylou Harris, Vince Gill, Travis Tritt, and Marty

Stuart, among others. Special matinees in summer are your best chance for last-minute tickets. *Buy tickets well in advance from the Grand Ole Opry, 2808 Opryland Dr., Nashville 37214,* ☎ *615/889–3060. For park information,* ☎ *615/889–6611.* ☛ *Reserved seats $16 evenings, $14 matinees; upper balcony $14 evenings, $12 matinees.*

The **Roy Acuff Museum** (☎ 615/889–6611) contains memorabilia, including many guns and fiddles, belonging to the late "king of country music." Acuff was a fixture at the Grand Ole Opry. **Minnie Pearl's Museum,** relocated to the same building in 1989, provides a nostalgic tour of the performer's life. Admission to the museums in Opryland Plaza is free; hours vary widely, so call first. The **General Jackson,** Opryland's $12 million, four-deck paddlewheeler, offers several two-hour cruises daily; a musical revue is presented in its Victorian Theater (☎ 615/889–6611; lunch cruise $16.95; dinner $44.95).

Another addition to the entertainment happenings at Opryland USA is **Nashville on Stage** (☎ 615/889–6611), where hot-as-a-fresh-biscuit country acts from Tanya Tucker to Marty Stuart perform three shows a night at three theaters at Opryland from May to early October. Prices range from $14.95 to $21.95.

Just down the road from Opryland, early risers can catch Grand Ole Opry star Del Reeves and the Early Times Breakfast Band, made up of session musicians from around town, at **Nashville's Breakfast Theater.** The 225-seat theater is open 7:45 to 10 AM, and a breakfast buffet is served. *2620 Music Valley Dr.,* ☎ *615/329–2091.* ☛ *$17.85 adults, $10 children 5–12.*

Farther Afield

16 Centennial Park features the **Parthenon,** constructed to commemorate Nashville's 1897 centennial. It's an exact copy of the Athenian original. Across the street from Vanderbilt University's campus, it's a magnificent sight, perched on a gentle green slope beside a duck pond. The newly renovated structure houses the Cowan Collection, featuring 63 works of art by American artists, traveling exhibits, and such exquisite statuary as the 42-foot *Athena Parthenos,* the tallest indoor sculpture in the Western world. *West End and 25th Aves.,* ☎ *615/862–8431.* ☛ *$2.50 adults, $1.25 senior citizens and children 4–17.* ☉ *Oct.–Mar., Tues.–Sat. 9–4:30; Apr.–Sept., Tues.–Sat. 9–4:30, Sun. 12:30–4:30.*

17 Known as the "Queen of the Tennessee plantations," **Belle Meade Mansion,** a stunning Greek Revival house that sports Civil War bullet holes in its columns, is the centerpiece of a 5,300-acre estate that was one of the nation's first and finest thoroughbred breeding farms. It was also once the site of the famous Iroquois, the oldest amateur steeplechase in America, a society event now run each May in nearby Percy Warner Park. A Victorian carriage museum with an impressive collection continues the equine theme. *5025 Harding Rd.,* ☎ *615/356–0501.* ☛ *$6 adults, $5.50 senior citizens and children 6–12, $2 children ages 7–12.* ☉ *Mon.–Sat. 9–5, Sun. 1–5.*

The 1920s Georgian-style mansion at nearby **Cheekwood** (take Harding Rd. east, turn right onto Belle Meade Blvd., and look for the sign; **18** it's adjacent to Percy Warner Park) is now the **Tennessee Botanical Gardens & Museum.** Fifty-five acres showcase herbs, roses, irises, daffodils, and area wildflowers. Greenhouses, orchid hothouses, a Japanese garden, streams, and pools make this a delightful spot for a picnic. The art museum contains a permanent collection of 19th- and 20th-century American art. A traditional southern lunch is available at the mansion's Pineapple Room and the gift shop has elegant choices. *1200 Forrest Park Dr.,* ☎ *615/356–8000.* ☛ *$5 adults, $4 senior citizens, $2 children 7–18.* ⊙ *Mon.–Sat. 9–5, Sun. noon–5.*

⑲ Belmont Mansion, on Belmont College's campus, was the home of Adelicia Acklen, Nashville's answer to Scarlett O'Hara, who married "once for money, once for love, and once for the hell of it." This outstanding Italianate villa of the 1850s is a gem right down to its sweeping staircase designed for grand entrances and cast-iron gazebos perfect for romance. *1900 Belmont Blvd.,* ☎ *615/386–4459.* ☛ *$5 adults, $2 children 6–12.* ⊙ *Tues.–Sat. 10–4.*

From here, take I–65 south to the first of two Harding Place exits to **⑳ Travellers' Rest,** the early 19th-century clapboard home of pioneer landowner and Judge John Overton. Following the fortunes of Overton, the law partner, mentor, campaign manager, and lifelong friend of Andrew Jackson, whose own home is nearby, the house metamorphosed from a 1799 four-room cottage to a 12-room mansion with Federal-influenced and Greek Revival additions. Also on the grounds are a restored smokehouse, kitchen house, and formal gardens. *636 Farrell Pkwy.,* ☎ *615/832–2962.* ☛ *$5 adults, $3 children 6–11.* ⊙ *Tues.–Sat. 10–5, Sun. 1–5.*

㉑ Forming the eastern end of this semicircle of homes is the **Hermitage,** 12 miles east of Nashville (I–40E to Old Hickory Blvd. exit), where the life and times of Andrew Jackson, known as "Old Hickory," are reflected with great care. Jackson, our seventh president, built this mansion on 600 acres for his wife, Rachel, for whose honor he fought and won a duel. Both are buried in the family graveyard. The **Andrew Jackson Center,** a 28,000-square-foot museum, visitor, and education center, contains many Jackson artifacts never before exhibited. An 18-minute film, *Old Hickory,* is shown in its auditorium; the structure also includes Rachel's Garden Cafe and a museum store. Knowledgeable guides take you through the mansion, furnished with many original pieces. Note the guitar-shaped driveway. Across the road stands **Tulip Grove,** built by Mrs. Jackson's nephew, and the **Hermitage Church,** fondly known as "Rachel's Church." *4580 Rachel's La., Hermitage,* ☎ *615/889–2941.* ☛ *(includes Tulip Grove and church): $7.50 adults, $6.50 senior citizens, $4 children 6–12.* ⊙ *Daily 9–5.*

In Hendersonville, 20 miles northeast of downtown Nashville (8 miles from the Hermitage), are yet more shrines to country music notables. **㉒** The **House of Cash** displays possessions and memorabilia of country legend Johnny Cash, the "Man in Black," including some superb Frederic Remington bronzes. Cash, a collector himself, also displays such valuable pieces as John Wayne's Colt Peacemaker and Buddy Holly's motorcycle. *700 Johnny Cash Pkwy.,* ☎ *615/824–5110.* ☛ *$6 adults, $4 senior citizens, $1 children 6–12.* ⊙ *Apr.–Nov., Mon.–Sat. 9–4:30.*

What to See and Do with Children

Children's Discovery House. This is a youngster's dream, with bubble blowers on the front lawn, colored chalk by the sidewalks, dress-up clothes, a play store and play hospital, a nature collection, and more. *503 N. Maple St., Murfreesboro,* ☎ *615/890–2300.* ☛ *$3 adults, $2 children, under 2 free.* ⊙ *Tues.–Sat. 10–5, Sun. 1–5 (closes 1 hr. earlier in summer).*

Cumberland Museum and Science Center. Children are invited to look, touch, smell, climb, listen, and explore. The planetarium has star and laser shows. *800 Ft. Negley Blvd., Nashville,* ☎ *615/862–5160.* ☛ *$6 adults, $4.50 senior citizens and children 3–12; planetarium $1.* ☉ *June–Aug., Mon.–Sat. 9:30–5, Sun. 12:30–5:30; Sept.–May, Tues.–Sat. 9:30–5, Sun. 12:30–5:30.*

Grassmere Wildlife Park. The smaller of Nashville's two zoos, which are both of the "open-spaces" variety, Grassmere is five miles south of downtown in suburban Brentwood. Sadly, at press time it was closed due to budget cuts, but was expected to reopen by 1996; call ahead to be sure. The 10-acre walk-through park features animals native to the area, such as cougar, black bear, bison, elk, and river otter. The Croft Center features an aviary and an exhibit of fish and reptiles. *3777 Nolensville Rd., 5 mi south of Nashville,* ☎ *615/401–5089.* ☛ *$5.50 adults, $3.50 senior citizens and children 3–12.* ☉ *Daily 9:30–5.*

Nashville Academy Theatre. This professional children's theater troupe performs September–May. *724 Second Ave. S,* ☎ *615/254–9103.*

Nashville Zoo. Larger than Grassmere, this zoo features lions, clouded leopards, white tigers, lemurs, and more than 800 other animals. It's on 50 acres in Joelton, which is about 15 miles north of Nashville. *1710 Ridge Rd. Cir.,* ☎ *615/370–3333.* ☛ *$5.50 adults, $3.50 children 3–12.* ☉ *Memorial Day–Labor Day, daily 9–6; Labor Day–Memorial Day, daily 10–5.*

Nashville Toy Museum. Toy trains, dolls, and models of ships and soldiers are contained within this collection, spanning 150 years. *2613 McGavock Pike,* ☎ *615/883–8870.* ☛ *$3.50 adults, $3 senior citizens, $1.50 children 6–12.* ☉ *Summer, daily 9–9; rest of year, daily 9–5.*

Opryland USA (*see* Opryland *in* Exploring Nashville, *above*). The petting zoo, especially, delights the younger ones.

Picnicking. Get away for a day outdoors, picnicking, horseback riding, hiking, and walking through the nature preserves at 14,200-acre **J. Percy Priest Lake** or 22,500-acre **Old Hickory Reservoir** (*see* Boating and Fishing, *below*).

Wave Country. This water park, a mile from Opryland, has a large wave pool and a three-flume water slide. *Two Rivers Pkwy., off Briley Pkwy.,* ☎ *615/885–1052.* ☛ *$5 adults, $4 children 5–12, ½ price after 4 PM.* ☉ *Memorial Day–Labor Day, daily 10–8.*

Off the Beaten Path

Lynchburg is home to the **Jack Daniels Distillery,** the oldest registered distillery in the country, where you can observe every step of the sour-mash-whiskey-making art. *75 mi north of Nashville, ½ mi northeast of Lynchburg on TN 55,* ☎ *615/759–6180.* ☛ *Free. Guided tours daily 8–4.*

Miss Mary Bobo's Boarding House is a Tennessee institution. Diners flock to the big two-story 1867 white frame house with a white picket fence to feast family-style at tables groaning with fried chicken, roast beef, fried catfish, stuffed vegetables and sliced tomatoes fresh from the gardens out back, corn on the cob, homemade biscuits, cornbread, pecan pie, lemon icebox pie, fruit cobblers, and strawberry shortcake. *½ block from the Public Sq., Lynchburg,* ☎ *615/759–7394. Reservations required, at least 2 weeks in advance in summer. One meal served daily, promptly at 1 PM, Mon.–Sat. Fixed price: $10.25 adults, $5 children under 10.*

The little town of **Franklin** (Williamson County Tourism, City Hall, Franklin 37065, ☎ 615/794–1225, ext. 50, or 800/356–3445, ext. 50), which is 18 miles south of Nashville, rivals Natchez, Mississippi, in charm and Civil War history. A self-guided walking tour begins at the town square and takes in several antebellum homes and the meticulously restored downtown business district, which has more than 50 shops, including several antiques shops and art galleries. Stop at **H.R.H. Dumplin's** (428 Main St.) old-fashioned tea room for a salad or dessert. The **Carnton Plantation,** where some of the Civil War's bloodiest battles were fought, and **Confederate Cemetery** are nearby. So is the entrance to the Natchez Trace Parkway (off I–40), which wends its way through three states of gorgeous scenery.

At **Loretta Lynn's Ranch,** in Hurricane Mills, the singer's personal museum is housed in an old restored gristmill. Tours are of the downstairs of the coal miner's daughter's stately antebellum home, a simulated coal mine, and re-creation of her childhood home. Camping, canoeing, paddle boats, trout fishing, and swimming are among the many activities available here. *North of I–40W to TN 13N (Exit 143),* ☎ *615/296–7700.* ☛ *Tour $10.50 adults, children under 6 free. Camping: $13–$18 per night for 2 people.* ☉ *Mar.–Dec. for tours; Apr.–Oct. for camping.*

Back in Nashville, Alfred Stieglitz rewarded Fisk University's progressive arts program with a bequest from his collection of 20th-century paintings and his own superb photographs. These are now on display in the **Van Vechten Art Gallery.** Stieglitz's wife, Georgia O'Keeffe, helped install the collection, highlighted by her own paintings, as well as works by Picasso and Renoir. The gallery also features African sculpture. *Fisk University at 18th Ave. N,* ☎ *615/329–8543.* ☛ *$4 adults, children free.* ☉ *Tues.–Fri. 10–5, weekends 1–5.*

Shopping

Shopping Districts

Tri-level **Church Street Centre** (☎ 615/254–4260) is the major downtown shopping area and has department stores, smaller chain stores, and numerous boutiques. Present your hotel room key at the service desk and get a coupon book with $200 worth of discounts. **Bellevue Center** (7620 Hwy. 70S, off the Bellevue Exit of I–40W, ☎ 615/646–8690) is Nashville's premiere mall, with more than 125 stores including the Disney Store, Abercrombie & Fitch, and Country Road Australia. The **Mall at Green Hills** (Hillsboro and Abbott Martin Rd., ☎ 615/298–5478), about 15 minutes from Music Row, is another good choice.

Specialty Stores

ANTIQUES

Murfreesboro, about 30 miles southeast of Nashville, calls itself the Antique Center of the South. Pick up a free antiques shopping guide at **Cannonsburgh Pioneer Village** (Front St., ☎ 615/890–0355), a living museum of 19th-century life in the South. Browse for distinctive 18th- and 19th-century English antiques and objets d'art east of downtown at **Madison Antique Mall** (320 Gallatin Rd. S, ☎ 615/865–4677), close to Music Row at **Nashville Antique Mall** (657 Wedgewood Ave., ☎ 615/256–1465), or in Andrew Jackson's stomping grounds at **Smorgasbord Antique Mall** (4144-B Lebanon Rd., Hermitage, ☎ 615/883–5789).

ARTS AND CRAFTS

Major regional artists' works are at **Cumberland Gallery** (4107 Hillsboro Circle, ☎ 615/297–0296). For pottery and ceramics, seek out **Forrest Valley Pottery** (325 Forrest Valley Dr., ☎ 615/356–5136), a working studio.

BOOKS

Bibliophiles appreciate the three-story **Davis–Kidd Booksellers** (Grace's Plaza in Green Hills, 407 Hillsboro Rd., ☎ 615/385–2645), open late on the weekends. Curl up in a chair with a glass of wine and the latest *New York Times* bestsellers.

COUNTRY-AND-WESTERN WEAR

Geared to the latest look in country clothing is the **Nashville Cowboy** (118 16th Ave. S, ☎ 615/242–9497; 1516 Demonbreun St., ☎ 615/256–2429). **Boot Country** (2412 Music Valley Dr., ☎ 615/883–2661) carries every size and skin for the boot wearer as well as other accessories and apparel.

RECORDS AND TAPES

Country fans can find good selections of compact discs and tapes at **Conway's Twitty Bird Record Shop** (1530 Demonbreun St., ☎ 615/242–2466). **Ernest Tubb Record Shops** (2414 Music Valley Dr., ☎ 615/889–2474; 417 Broadway, ☎ 615/255–7503) carry a full line of classic and new artist country music on CD, cassette, 45s and video as well as song books and a variety of souvenirs.

Farmer's Market

Every day from late spring through early autumn, farmers and gardeners set up stands in a downtown area behind the state capitol.

Flea Market

From treasures to just plain "junque"—the **Nashville Flea Market** at the Tennessee State Fairgrounds has it all. Usually, 1,000 traders, craftsfolk, and antiques dealers ply their wares the fourth weekend of every month (except Dec.). Arrive early for the best finds; stay late for the best deals. ☎ *615/862–5016.* ☞ *Free.* ☉ *Sat. 6–6, Sun. 7–5.*

Participant Sports

Boating and Fishing

You'll find boat rentals at **J. Percy Priest Lake** (11 mi east of Nashville, off I–40, ☎ 615/883–2351) and **Old Hickory Reservoir** (15 mi northeast of Nashville via U.S. 31E, ☎ 615/824–7766).

Golf

Among courses open to the public year-round are the 18-hole **Harpeth Hills** (2424 Old Hickory Blvd., ☎ 615/862–8493) and **Hermitage Golf Course** (3939 Old Hickory Blvd., ☎ 615/847–4001), and the nine-hole **Rhodes Golf Course** (1901 Ed Temple Blvd., ☎ 615/862–8463). Hermitage is the site each April of the LPGA Sara Lee Classic.

Horseback Riding

You can jog or canter on gentle steeds at **Riverwood Recreation Plantation and Riding Academy** (Cooper La., off McGavock Pike, 5 mi from Opryland, ☎ 615/262–1794), and **Ramblin' Breeze Ranch** (3665 Knight Rd., White's Creek, ☎ 615/876–1029).

Ice Skating

Indoor skating is available at **Sportsplex** in Centennial Park. *25th Ave. N, at Brandau Ave.,* ☏ *615/862–8490.* ☛ *$4 adults, $3 children under 12.*

Jogging

Favorite sites include **Centennial Park,** the **Vanderbilt University running track, J. Percy Priest Lake,** and **Percy Warner Park.** The 1,700-plus-member running club Nashville Striders (☏ 615/833–4124) can recommend choice spots and will provide information on many summer races.

Miniature Golf

Enjoy this uniquely American family sport at **Grand Old Golf** (☏ 615/871–4701), across the street from the Opryland Hotel.

Tennis

Several municipal tennis facilities offer good play. **Centennial Sportsplex Tennis Center** (☏ 615/862–8490) has outdoor courts plus indoor courts.

Spectator Sports

Auto Racing

Top drivers compete at the **Nashville Motor Raceway** (State Fairgrounds, ☏ 615/726–1818), from April through October.

Baseball

You can root for the **Nashville Sounds,** the AAA affiliate of the Chicago White Sox, from April through mid-September at 17,000-seat Herschel Greer Stadium (☏ 615/242–4371).

Hockey

The **Nashville Knights** (☏ 615/255–7825), a farm club of the Atlanta Knights and Tampa Bay Lightning, are the city's minor league hockey team.

Horse Show

For 10 days from late August to early September, Shelbyville hums as visitors, horses, and riders come from all over the land for the **Tennessee Walking Horse National Celebration** (Box 1010, Shelbyville 37160, ☏ 615/684–5915), the world's greatest walking horse show.

Dining

If you expect Nashville dining to be all cornbread, turnip greens, and grits, you're in for a staggering surprise. Here you will find sophisticated restaurants with service that is as polished as any you'll find in cities twice its size. Patrons are often casual in dress and prone to linger over meals. The mix of politics, country music, conventions, and business (several major companies are headquartered here) means deal-making at every meal, lending prosperity and longevity to some of the city's best places. Don't be surprised to find waiters, captains, and chefs who have worked in the same place for a decade. Such tenure translates into quality dining. On the other hand, Nashville is notorious for flashes in the pan: restaurants that open with a splash and close with a fizzle—often just a year later. Dress is casual unless otherwise noted. .

CATEGORY	COST*
$$$	over $30
$$	$12–$30
$	under $12

per person for a three-course meal, excluding drinks, service, and 7.75% sales tax

American

$$$ Belle Meade Brasserie. In 1988 Mark Rubin and Robert Siegel created a comfortable suburban restaurant in Nashville's poshest neighborhood. The menu is filled with surprises—an appetizer of corn fritters and pepper jelly, New York strip cowboy-style, San Francisco–style crabcakes, and shrimp and scallops served on a bed of black linguine. Desserts are just as compelling, including a knockout Russian raspberry gratin. ✗ *101 Page Rd., ☎ 615/356–5450. Reservations recommended. AE, DC, MC, V. No lunch. Closed Sun.*

$$$ Merchants. A $3.2 million renovation of a historic property in downtown Nashville, this former hotel provides three levels of dining and an appealing outdoor patio. Specialties include California-style pizzas, the freshest seafoods, and meats grilled over native hardwoods. The menu changes to lighter fare in summer and all rolls, pastas, and pastries are made fresh daily. Save room for the Key lime pie. ✗ *401 Broadway, ☎ 615/254–1892. Reservations recommended. AE, DC, MC, V. No lunch weekends.*

$$ F. Scott's. At this elegant art deco–inspired café and wine bar patrons enjoy the owners' private collection of impressionist-style art. A new chef has changed the emphasis from gourmet fare to nouveau American, adding dishes such as hickory-smoked venison with fresh corn cakes, seared black pepper–crusted yellow-fin tuna, and roasted rack of lamb with Dijon and herbs. F. Scott's 32-page wine list is one of Nashville's most extensive, with many fine wines available by the glass. ✗ *2210 Crestmoor, ☎ 615/269–5861. Reservations advised. AE, D, DC, MC, V. No lunch Sat.*

$$ Mad Platter. This local favorite in historic downtown Nashville blends traditional gourmet with California cuisine, using locally available ingredients from the nearby Farmer's Market. The baked salmon with red grapes and feta cheese, rack of lamb, and bananas Foster are favorites here. It's a popular spot for power lunches by day. Jazz music transforms the cozy 18th-century brownstone into a romantic nook at night. ✗ *1239 Sixth Ave. N, ☎ 615/242–2563. Reservations required for dinner. AE, D, MC, V. No lunch weekends.*

$$ 106 Club. A black baby grand and a bar of shiny black enamel and glass brick set the atmosphere in this intimate, art deco–style dining room in suburban Belle Meade. The cuisine is a mix of California nouvelle and international favorites such as Bahamian sailfish. The free-range chicken with pasta primavera is one of the best dishes in town. Relax with one of 106's rich desserts and listen to old and new melodies on the baby grand. ✗ *106 Harding Pl., ☎ 615/356–1300. Reservations advised. AE, DC, MC, V.*

$$ Sunset Grill. The works of artist Paul Harmon, who divides his time
★ between Nashville and Paris, decorate this hip, postmodern hangout, frequented by country glitterati like Tanya Tucker. The hickory-smoked, Tennessee trout is terrific. The outside courtyard is popular in summer. Tip: Food prices are slashed by 50% after 10 PM (midnight on weekends). ✗ *2001A Belcourt Ave., ☎ 615/386–3663. AE, D, DC, MC, V. No lunch Sat. Closed Sun.*

Dining

Arthur's, **6**

Belle Meade Brasserie, **12**

Cakewalk Restaurant, **17**

F. Scott's, **13**

Loveless, **9**

Mad Platter, **20**

Mario's Ristorante Italiano, **2**

Merchants, **7**

Mère Bulles, the Wine Bar and Restaurant, **8**

106 Club, **11**

Pancake Pantry, **15**

Sunset Grill, **16**

Sylvan Park, **10**

Wild Boar, **3**

Lodging

Comfort Inn Hermitage, **24**

Courtyard by Marriott–Airport, **23**

Hampton Inn Vanderbilt, **1**

Holiday Inn Crowne Plaza, **4**

Loew's Vanderbilt Plaza, **18**

Lyric Springs Country Inn, **14**

Opryland Hotel, **22**

Ramada Inn Across from Opryland, **21**

Shoney's Inn on Music Row, **19**

Stouffer Nashville Hotel, **5**

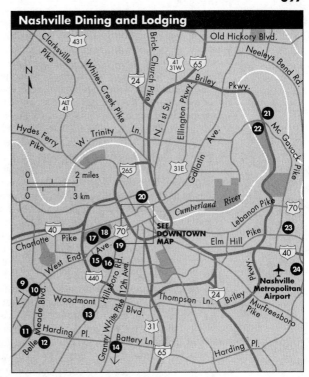

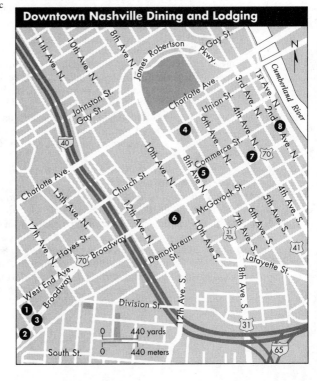

Continental

$$$ **Arthur's.** This restaurant is in the stylishly renovated Union Station, where an upscale hotel has taken the place of the train terminal. The seven-course meals are dazzling (à la carte is also available) and the ambience romantic. The menu changes daily but specialties include rainbow trout, duck, and lamb. Save room for dessert; the bananas Foster is especially filling. The decor is lush, with lace curtains, velveteen-upholstered chairs, white linen, and fine silver service. ✕ *Union Station, 1001 Broadway,* ☎ *615/255–1494. Jacket and tie. AE, DC, MC, V. No lunch.*

$$$ **Mère Bulles, the Wine Bar and Restaurant.** An aura of casual elegance greets patrons of this locally popular restaurant (chosen Nashville's most romantic in a *Tennessean Magazine* readers poll) with a brass-trimmed mahogany bar and changing art decorating exposed brick walls. Romantics especially will enjoy tapas and drinks in the cozy lounge, before moving into one of three intimate dining areas with views of the river. A specialty is pesto Mère Bulles—shrimp and scallops with walnut-pesto sauce served on a bed of shell pasta. There is an extensive wine list. In the heart of the District, there's live entertainment downstairs nightly, usually jazz or folk music. ✕ *152 2nd Ave. N,* ☎ *615/256–1946. Reservations advised. Jacket and tie. AE, DC, MC, V.*

$$$ **Wild Boar.** Chef David Poulton and local restaurateur Mario Ferrari
★   have pooled their enormous talents to create the Wild Boar. Decorated like an English hunting lodge with $2.5 million in original art, this restaurant yields culinary treasures for those on the hunt. Rack of venison with seared foie gras is a specialty. The American menu emphasizes game, trout, lobster, duck, and beef dishes, with several that are prepared at tableside. The atmosphere is casual. The Wild Boar, with 15,000 bottles in its wine cellar, has one of the top wine lists in the world. ✕ *2014 Broadway,* ☎ *615/329–1313. Reservations recommended. AE, D, DC, MC, V. No lunch Sat. Closed Sun. and Mon.*

Mixed Menu

$$ **Cakewalk Restaurant.** The first things to catch your eye at this cozy bistro are the intriguing paintings on the turquoise walls by local artists. The eclectic cuisine is equally imaginative, blending the best of nouvelle California, a bit of Southwestern, a dash of Cajun and Creole, and some down-home American specialties thrown in for fun. Desserts are outstanding—especially the Kahlua cake, a four-layer chocolate cake laced with the liqueur. ✕ *3001 West End Ave.,* ☎ *615/320–7778. Reservations recommended for dinner. DC, MC, V. No lunch Sat.*

Northern Italian

$$$ **Mario's Ristorante Italiano.** Owner Mario Ferrari is the genius behind this Nashville institution. Country music stars, visiting celebrities, and local society come here to see and be seen. The atmosphere is elegant but never stuffy, with lots of brass and an impressive wine collection on view. The seafood and veal—such as the *saltimbocca,* veal medallions with mozzarella, prosciutto, mushrooms, and fresh sage—are equally palate-pleasing. ✕ *2005 Broadway,* ☎ *615/327–3232. Reservations required, 2–3 days in advance for Fri. and Sat. Jacket required. AE, D, DC, MC, V. Closed Sun.*

Southern

$ **Loveless.** An experience in true down-home Southern cooking. Don't
★ come for the decor—decidedly lax, with red-and-white-checked table-
cloths—but, rather, for the feather-light homemade biscuits and preserves, country ham and red-eye gravy, and fried chicken. The waitresses
are extra friendly and swift. ✕ *8400 Hwy. 100,* ☎ *615/646–9700. Reservations advised. MC, V.*

$ **Pancake Pantry.** This institution half a mile from Music Row is well
worth the wait—and you will wait. A favorite haunt of Garth Brooks
and Faith Hill, this crowded diner stylizes pancakes 24 ways and
makes its own syrups to boot. Though it's open until 7:30 PM, breakfast is its raison d'etre. ✕ *1724 21st Ave. S,* ☎ *615/383–9333. No reservations. AE, D, DC, MC, V.*

Lodging

With 125 hotels and motels, Nashville offers an impressive selection
of accommodations in all price categories and levels of luxury. Although
some establishments increase rates slightly during the peak summer travel
season, most maintain the same rates year-round. Some downtown luxury hotels offer lower rates on weekends. **Bed & Breakfast Adventures**
(Box 150586, Nashville, TN 37215, ☎ 615/383–6611 or 800/947–
7404) and **Bed & Breakfast Host Homes of Tennessee** (Box 110227,
Nashville, TN 37222, ☎ 615/331–5244 or 800/458–2421) have listings for homes here and throughout the state.

CATEGORY	COST*
$$$$	over $130
$$$	$80–$130
$$	$50–$80
$	under $50

All prices are for a standard double room, excluding 11.75% tax.

$$$$ **Holiday Inn Crowne Plaza.** Downtown near the State Capitol, this 28-
story tower has a vast, skylighted atrium lobby awash with greenery
and overseen by glassed-in elevators. Rooms are extra spacious and
contemporary in decor with great views of the growing Nashville skyline. The hotel is topped by the Pinnacle, Nashville's only revolving
rooftop restaurant. ▦ *623 Union St., 37219,* ☎ *615/259–2000 or
800/447–9825,* FAX *615/742–6096. 464 rooms, 14 suites. 2 restaurants,
coffee shop, lounge, no-smoking rooms. AE, DC, MC, V.*

$$$$ **Loew's Vanderbilt Plaza Hotel.** Celebrities and business travelers grav-
★ itate to this quiet, recently renovated, European-style luxury hotel
known for top-notch service. Convenient to Music Row and downtown, the grand pristine white lobby makes a big impression. Musicians play nightly in the piano bar. Gracious guest rooms, some with
skyline views, are done with dark cherry furniture. Plaza suites are individually decorated and the club level rooms have luxurious baths and
extra phone and fax lines. ▦ *2100 West End Ave., 37203,* ☎ *615/320–
1700 or 800/235–6397,* FAX *615/320–5019. 325 rooms, 13 suites. 3
restaurants, piano bar, health club. AE, DC, MC, V.*

$$$$ **Opryland Hotel.** This massive hostelry—one of the 25 largest in the
★ world—is adjacent to Opryland and has almost doubled in size recently.
Even if you don't stay here, take a look—it's an attraction in its own
right. The two-acre glass-walled conservatory is a lush enclave of tropical vegetation, streams, waterfalls, statuary, and fountains. At the revolving bar at the Cascades, another skylighted interior space with
streams, waterfalls, and a half-acre lake, you can listen to harp music
in the early evenings. Rooms, fairly standard in size, feature Victorian

floral decor in beige and rose tones; request one overlooking the gardens. The hotel claims to have more meeting space than any other in the nation. The culinary staff is directed by a member of the U.S. Culinary Olympics Team. ☎ *2800 Opryland Dr., 37214,* ☎ *615/889–1000,* FAX *615/871–5728. 1,771 rooms, 120 suites. 4 restaurants, pool, wading pool, 22 shops. AE, D, DC, MC, V.*

$$$$ **Stouffer Nashville Hotel.** This luxurious, ultracontemporary high-rise hotel adjoins the Nashville Convention Center and is also connected to Church Street Centre Mall (*see* Shopping, *above*). Spacious rooms are highlighted by period reproduction furnishings. Executive Club concierge floors offer extra privacy and personal services. ☎ *611 Commerce St., 37203,* ☎ *615/255–8400,* FAX *615/255–8163. 649 rooms, 24 suites. Restaurant, coffee shop, lounge, indoor pool, hot tub, sauna, health club, concierge floors. AE, DC, MC, V.*

$$$ **Courtyard by Marriott–Airport.** This handsome, low-rise motor inn with a sunny, gardenlike courtyard offers some amenities you'd expect in higher-priced hotels: spacious rooms, king-size beds, oversized work desks, and hot-water dispensers for in-room coffee. ☎ *2508 Elm Hill Pike, 37214,* ☎ *615/883–9500 or 800/321–2211,* FAX *615/883–0172. 133 rooms, 12 suites. Restaurant, lounge, no-smoking rooms, indoor hot tub. AE, D, DC, MC, V.*

$$$ **Lyric Springs Country Inn.** Nestled in the green, rolling hills of nearby
★ Franklin—a renowned Civil War site—the Lyric Springs is a real find. This small bed-and-breakfast inn strikes the right notes with its bright and cheerful decor of 1940s Americana and uptown country antiques. Talent agent and owner Patsy Bruce—who penned "Mammas Don't Let Your Babies Grow Up to Be Cowboys"—is the perennial Nashville insider. A full gourmet breakfast is included, and dinner reservations are accepted. ☎ *7306 S. Harpeth Rd., Franklin 37064,* ☎ *615/329–3385 or 800/621–7824,* FAX *615/329–3381. 4 rooms with bath. MC, V.*

$$$ **Ramada Inn Across from Opryland.** This contemporary-style, well-maintained low-rise motor inn has the closest location to the theme park other than the Opryland Hotel. ☎ *2401 Music Valley Dr., 37214,* ☎ *615/889–0800,* FAX *615/883–1230. 300 rooms, 7 suites. Restaurant, lounge, indoor pool, hot tub, sauna. AE, DC, MC, V.*

$$ **Comfort Inn Hermitage.** Near the Hermitage, this inn offers reasonably priced accommodations, some with water beds or whirlpool baths. ☎ *5768 Old Hickory Blvd., 37076,* ☎ *615/889–5060,* FAX *615/871–4137. 99 rooms, 7 suites. No-smoking rooms, pool. AE, D, DC, MC, V.*

$$ **Hampton Inn Vanderbilt.** Near the Vanderbilt University campus and Music Row, this six-story, newly renovated inn is clean and contemporary and especially popular with visiting music executives and musicians. Rooms, done in shades of maroon, green, and cream, are spacious. A multipurpose hospitality suite has a conference table, chairs, and an audiovisual unit for meeting and business groups, making this a popular corporate choice. ☎ *1919 West End Ave., 37203,* ☎ *615/329–1144 or 800/426–7866,* FAX *615/320–7112. 171 rooms. Pool, meeting rooms. AE, D, DC, MC, V.*

$$ **Shoney's Inn on Music Row.** Located on the Trolley Line and a guitar strum away from the Country Music Hall of Fame and other Music Row attractions, this is a typical, clean chain motel. The inn's namesake restaurant has a good, low-cost, all-you-can-eat breakfast bar. ☎ *1521 Demonbreun St., 37203,* ☎ *615/255–9977,* FAX *615/242–6127. 134 rooms, 13 suites. Restaurant. AE, DC, MC, V.*

The Arts

For a complete listing of weekly events, consult the Visitor Information Center or the local newspapers. For information on concerts and special events, call **WSM Radio's entertainment line** (☎ 615/737–9595). **TicketMaster** (☎ 615/737–4849) has information on events at various Nashville venues.

Ballet and Theater

James K. Polk Theater (*see* Concerts, *above*) hosts touring Broadway shows and local theatrical performances. **Chaffin's Barn** (8204 Hwy. 100, ☎ 615/646–9977 or 800/282–2276) offers dinner theater year-round, and a live country show is staged here daily Memorial Day–Labor Day. The **Nashville Ballet** (2976 Sidco Dr. ☎ 615/244–7233 or 800/333–4849), a company of 25 dancers, performs works accompanied by the Nashville Symphony Orchestra.

Concerts

Country music takes center stage at the 4,424-seat **Grand Ole Opry Auditorium** (☎ 615/889–3060). The Nashville Symphony Orchestra's classical and pops series and concerts by out-of-town groups are staged at **Andrew Jackson Hall** (TicketMaster, ☎ 615/741–2787), part of the Tennessee Performing Arts Center (TPAC). Chamber concerts take place at TPAC's **James K. Polk Theater** (☎ 615/741–7975). Some rock and country events are held at the **Nashville Municipal Auditorium** (☎ 615/862–6395). The **Starwood Amphitheatre** (☎ 615/641–5800) is the site of rock, pop, country, and jazz concerts, musicals, and special events; it's also the summer home of the Nashville Symphony. Vanderbilt University stages music, dance, and drama productions (many free) at its **Blair School of Music** (☎ 615/322–7651).

Festivals

Summer Lights Music City Festival. The first weekend in June, more than half a million visitors attend Nashville's unique music and arts festival, showcasing almost 200 top names and newcomers in pop, rock, jazz, country, classical, and reggae on five outdoor stages downtown, at the legislative plaza near Deaderick Street. The work of 50 Tennessee visual artists are exhibited in warehouses and storefronts along First and Second avenues. Local cuisine is available from street vendors or sidewalk cafés, and clowns and other street entertainers fill the Family Arts Arcade. *Summer Lights Office, 201 Church Street Centre,* ☎ *615/259–0900. ☛ $7 adults, $2 children.*

International Country Music Fan Fair. Held annually by the Grand Ole Opry and the Country Music Association on the second week in June at the Tennessee State Fairgrounds, Fan Fair is country music's premiere event. This week-long celebration lets fans rub elbows with their favorite stars. The Fair delivers more than 35 hours worth of shows sponsored by local record labels, picture and autograph sessions with stars, and the Grand Masters Fiddling Championship. Many tour companies offer packages, but plan ahead; tickets sell out months in advance. *Fan Fair, 2804 Opryland Dr., 37214,* ☎ *615/889–7503.*

Radio and TV Tapings

The **Ernest Tubb Record Shop Midnight Jamboree,** a live radio show, features performances by new talent as well as Opry stars, sometimes including Justin Tubb, son of the late Ernest Tubb. *2414 Music Valley Dr.,* ☎ *615/889–2474. Show Sat. midnight–1 AM (arrive by 11:30 PM).*

Several television shows produced at Opryland USA and other Nashville sites—including *Nashville Now, Crook and Chase,* and TNN cable programs—are open to visitors, and most are free. *Call TNN Viewer Services at 615/883–7000 for schedules and information.*

Nightlife

Ace of Clubs (114 2nd Ave. S, ☎ 615/254–2237) in the District is a soulful joint with a mix of DJs and live bands. The **Bluebird Cafe** (4104 Hillsboro Rd., 615/383–1461) is the stomping ground for Grammy Award–winning talent and Music City's up-and-coming stars. Songwriters often try out their latest material here, and this club is a favorite with locals and music biz executives. Get an earful of country's latest and greatest at this small, unassuming club, where Garth Brooks was discovered, in the posh Green Hills neighborhood.

Boot scoot over to the **Wildhorse Saloon** (120 Second Ave. N, ☎ 615/251–1000), a spanking new, $7.5 million dance hall with a 3,300-foot dance floor and seating for 1,600. The Nashville Network tapes live on the dance floor.

Douglas Corner Cafe (2106A Eighth Ave. S, ☎ 615/298–1688) is a well-known place for everything from blues to country. For giggles, go across the street to **Zanies Comedy Showplace** (2025 Eighth Ave. S, ☎ 615/269–0221).

A Nashville tradition, the **Stock Yard Bull Pen Lounge** (901 Second Ave. N and Stock Yard, ☎ 615/255–6464) has nightly live country performers—heavyweights do drop in—and dancing. However, the steak-and-seafood restaurant is unexceptional.

Nashville Essentials

Arriving and Departing

BY BOAT
The **Delta Queen Steamboat Co.** (☎ 504/586–0631) offers four-night paddle wheeler cruises on the Mississippi, Ohio, and Cumberland rivers between St. Louis and Nashville, with stops along the way.

BY BUS
The **Greyhound Bus Lines** (☎ 800/231–2222) terminal is at 200 8th Avenue South and McGavock Street.

BY CAR
From Nashville, I–65 leads north into Kentucky and south into Alabama, and I–24 leads northwest into Kentucky and Illinois and southeast into Chattanooga and Georgia. I–40 traverses the state east–west, connecting Knoxville with Nashville and Memphis. I–440 connects I–40, I–65, and I–24, and helps circumvent clogged major arteries during rush hour. I–840, which will skirt Nashville's northside and connect I–40 with I–24N and I–65N, is under construction.

BY PLANE
Metropolitan Nashville Airport (☎ 615/275–1675), approximately 8 miles from downtown, is served by American—for which it is a hub—American Eagle, Atlantic Southeast, ComAir, Delta, Northwest, Southwest, TWA, United, USAir, USAir Express, and Valujet. Daily service to London's Gatwick Airport began May 1994 via American.

Shuttle service downtown (☎ 615/275–1180) costs $8–$10 per person. A cab costs about $16. To reach downtown by car, take I–40W.

Getting Around

BY BUS

Metropolitan Transit Authority (MTA) buses (☏ 615/242–4433; run 4 AM–11:15 PM; fare: $1.15, exact change) serve the entire county. For travelers with disabilities, a van is available for the same fare for downtown transport (☏ 615/242–4433).

BY TAXI

The fare is $1.50, plus 10¢ for each ¼ mile. Try **Allied Taxi** (☏ 615/244–7433), **Music City Taxi** (☏ 615/262–0451 or 800/359–9692), or **Madison Rivergate Taxi** (☏ 615/865–4100).

BY TROLLEY

Nashville Trolley Co. (☏ 615/242–4433; fare: 75¢, exact change) runs regularly scheduled trolleys through downtown and along Music Row.

Guided Tours

EXCURSION-BOAT TOURS

Belle Carol Riverboat Co. (106 1st Ave. S, Riverfront Park 37201, ☏ 615/244–3430 or 800/342–2355) offers Cumberland River sightseeing, luncheon, and dinner cruises from the Nashville Old Steamboat Dock at Riverfront Park. From its dock, **Opryland USA** (☏ 615/889–6611) offers 1½-hour daytime cruises with Opryland-style entertainment and two-hour evening dinner cruises aboard its four-deck *General Jackson* showboat (*see* Opryland in Exploring, *above*).

ORIENTATION

Gray Line (☏ 615/227–2270 or 800/251–1864) and **Grand Ole Opry Tours** (☏ 615/889–9490) offer tours that include drives past stars' homes and visits to the Grand Ole Opry, Music Row, and The District (historic downtown).

SPECIAL-INTEREST

Johnny Walker Tours (☏ 615/834–8585 or 800/722–1524) has 3-hour sightseeing tours, Grand Ole Opry, Opryland and special concert tours.

WALKING TOURS

At the Nashville Convention and Visitors Bureau (*see* Visitor Information, *below*), pick up a self-guided tour map of downtown.

Important Addresses and Numbers

EMERGENCIES

Dial 911 for **police** and **ambulance.** Emergency rooms are open all night at centrally located **Baptist Hospital** (2000 Church St., ☏ 615/329–5555) and **Vanderbilt University Medical Center** (1211 22nd Ave. S, ☏ 615/322–7311).

PHARMACY

Revco (303 E. Thomspon La., ☏ 615/361–3636).

RADIO STATIONS

AM: WLAC 1510, news and talk. **FM:** WPLN 90.3, classical and jazz; WSIX 97.9, country; WSM 95, country.

VISITOR INFORMATION

Nashville Convention & Visitors Bureau (161 4th Ave. N, ☏ 615/259–4700; ☉ Weekdays 8–4:30). **Visitor Information Center** (I–65 and James Robertson Pkwy., Exit 85, ☏ 615/259–4747; ☉ Labor Day–Memorial Day, daily 9–5; rest of year, 8–8).

EAST TENNESSEE

East Tennessee combines wholesome vacation ingredients much in the way a skilled mountain cook creates a sumptuous down-home feast, with bounty from forests, fields, ice-cold streams, and the family farm. From the misty heights of the Great Smoky Mountains to the Holston, French Broad, Nolichucky, and Tennessee rivers, this exquisitely beautiful part of the state beckons with a cornucopia of scenic grandeur and recreational possibilities from hiking to white-water rafting.

The highest and most rugged elevations are in the Great Smoky Mountains National Park, a cool and scenic retreat for those seeking relief from the humidity of summer. The gateway city to the nation's most heavily visited park (500,000 acres of protected forests in Tennessee and North Carolina) is Gatlinburg. This tourist town, popular with honeymooners and families, has steadily sprouted from a remote little place with a sprinkling of hotels, chalets, and mountain crafts shops to the sprawling network of tourist come-ons—minigolf courses and homemade-candy "shoppes"—it is today. During the summer, the town is clogged with visitors, complete with the annoyances of traffic jams and packed restaurants. Nonetheless, the majesty of the mist-shrouded Smokies eases away these irritations. Fall brings an unparalleled fiesta of colors to these mountains, and in the early springtime wild azaleas and rhododendron lace the mountainsides with delicate pinks, lavenders, and whites. No wonder hikers, campers, and boaters flock to this park. And when you wander among the rhododendrons surrounding Cade's Cove, a grist mill and farm preserved in its 19th-century state, you can easily forget the sometimes maddening crowds.

Neighboring Pigeon Forge, home of mountain native Dolly Parton's namesake theme park, Dollywood, has enough heavy-duty outlet shopping and kids' entertainment to keep families busy for a few days. But the intentionally corn-pone image can become wearing and fails to reflect the quiet folksiness of the Appalachian communities scattered throughout these parts.

East Tennessee's largest cities are Knoxville and Chattanooga. The former is a lively college town, convenient to the Great Smoky Mountains; the latter is an up-and-coming river and railroad town with an intriguing past. Chattanooga's Tennessee Aquarium, the world's largest freshwater aquarium, is a must-see.

Exploring

Numbers in the margin correspond to points of interest on the East Tennessee map.

The tour outlined on the following pages requires about three to five days and takes you through cities and towns clustered in valleys, sprawled on upland plateaus, and tucked away in hidden reaches of high mountains. Here and there you'll encounter poverty-ridden hardscrabble places, but many communities have respectable economies and some have achieved enviable prosperity. Notably, Chattanooga has transformed itself in less than a decade from a polluted city struggling to clean up its outmoded industries to a bright, revitalized community that's a model for any small city looking to reinvent itself.

Knoxville

In 1786, Patriot General James White and a few pioneer settlers built a fort beside the Tennessee River. A few years later, territorial Governor William Blount selected White's fort as capital of the newly formed Territory of the United States South of the River Ohio and renamed the settlement **Knoxville** after his long-time friend, Secretary of War Henry Knox. It flourished from its beginning, and became the first state capital when Tennessee was admitted to the Union in 1796.

In the 20th century, Knoxville has been synonymous with energy: The headquarters of the Tennessee Valley Authority, with its vast complex of hydroelectric dams and impounded recreational lakes, is here, and during World War II, atomic energy was secretly developed at nearby Oak Ridge. Today the University of Tennessee adds its own energy—intellectual and cultural—to this dynamic city.

Knoxville's history has been preserved. At the **Governor William Blount Mansion,** a modest white-frame structure dating from 1792, the governor and his associates planned the admission of Tennessee as the 16th state in the Union. The home is furnished with original and period antiques, along with memorabilia of Blount's checkered career. A visitor center in the adjacent Craighead-Jackson House, built in 1818, presents an introductory slide program, museum exhibits, and a glass collection. *200 W. Hill Ave.,* ☎ *615/525–2375.* ☞ *$4 adults, $3 senior citizens, $1.50 children 6–12.* ☉ *Tues.–Sat. 9:30–4:30, Sun. 2–4:30.*

Other eras of local history are celebrated at **James White Fort** (205 E. Hill Ave., ☎ 615/525–6514), a series of seven log cabins with authentic furnishings and pioneer artifacts; the **John Sevier Historical Site** (1220 John Sevier Hwy., ☎ 615/573–5508), where Tennessee's first governor built his summer home, Marble Springs; and the **Armstrong–Lockett House** (2728 Kingston Pike, ☎ 615/637–3163), an eloquent farm mansion dating from 1834, now a showcase of American and British furniture, silver, and ornate appointments, along with terraces and fountains in Italianate gardens.

Mabry–Hazen House. This antebellum home served as headquarters for both Confederate and Union forces during the Civil War. It was built by a prominent Knoxvillian, Joseph A. Mabry Jr., in 1858 and is now on the National Historic Register. *1711 Dandridge Ave.,* ☎ *615/522–8661.* ☞ *$3 adults and children, $2.50 senior citizens.* ☉ *Weekdays 10–3, weekends by appointment.*

The McClung Museum, on the University of Tennessee campus, has diverse collections of anthropology, natural history, geology, science, and fine arts. *1327 Circle Park Dr.,* ☎ *615/974–2144.* ☞ *Free.* ☉ *Weekdays 9–5, Sat. 10–3, Sun. 2–5.*

The Knoxville Museum of Art is housed in a handsome $10.5 million, 52,000-square-foot structure at World's Fair Park. Designed by renowned museum architect Edward Larrabee Barnes, the four-level concrete-and-steel building is faced in Tennessee pink marble. The museum includes four exhibition galleries, an exploratory gallery for children, a great hall, an auditorium, a museum store, and outdoor sculpture and educational program gardens. *World's Fair Park Dr.,* ☎ *615/525–6101.* ☞ *Free, except for special exhibits.* ☉ *Tues. 10–9, Wed.–Sat. 10–5, Sun. noon–5.*

The **East Tennessee Discovery Center and Akima Planetarium** contain displays of pioneer tools and clothes, mounted animals, and fresh- and saltwater aquariums. Youngsters especially like the hands-on and audiovisual exhibits. *516 Beaman St., in Chilhowee Park,* ☎ *615/637–1121.* ☞ *$3 adults, $2 senior citizens, $1 children 2–5. Museum open Tues.–Fri. 9–5, Sat. 1–5. Planetarium show Sat. 2:30 PM.*

East Tennessee

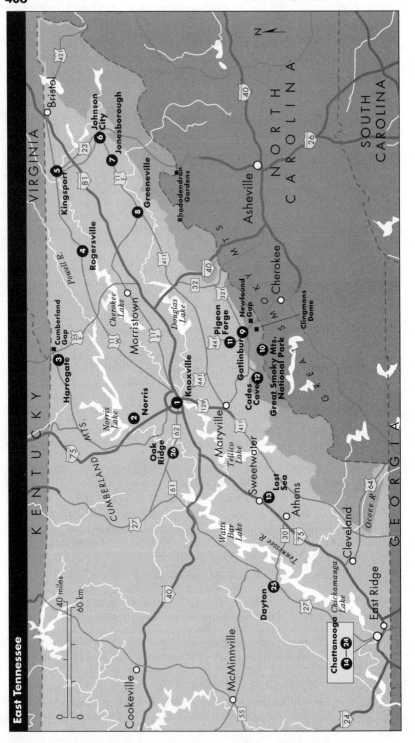

Plan on a full day at the **Knoxville Zoological Park,** famous for breeding large cat species and African elephants. The 1,100 animals include rare red pandas, wild creatures native to the African plains, polar bears, seals, and penguins. There are rides on a miniature steam train or an elephant, as well as a petting zoo. New exhibits include Gorilla Valley, Cheetah Savanna, Chimpanzee Ridge, and a North American River Otter exhibit. *In Chilhowee Park on Rutledge Pike S, 4 1/2 mi east of I–40 Exit 392,* ☏ *615/637–5331.* ☛ *$6.50 adults, $4 children 3–12 and senior citizens.* ☉ *Memorial Day–Labor Day, daily 9:30–6; Labor Day–Memorial Day, daily 10–4:30.*

For relaxed enjoyment and views of an especially scenic portion of the Tennessee River, step aboard the *Star of Knoxville* (Neyland Dr., ☏ 615/522–4630). One-and-a-half-hour sightseeing excursions as well as lunch and dinner cruises are offered daily April–December.

To the North and East
From Knoxville, scenic U.S. 441 leads northwest to **Norris,** a distance of 25 miles. This delightful planned town was built in 1933 as a workers' community during construction of the **Norris Dam,** TVA's first. The dam, which spans the Clinch River and impounds a 72-mile-long lake, has a visitor lobby and two overlooks. Some of the best views, though, are from **Norris Dam State Park** (1261 Norris Fwy., Lake City 37769, ☏ 615/426–7461), which has cabins and campsites. Here also is the **Lenoir Museum,** where Native American, pioneer, Civil War, and regional historical artifacts are displayed. A restored country store and an 18th-century gristmill where you can purchase stone-ground cornmeal are on the grounds.

Norris's prime attraction is the **Museum of Appalachia,** where about 35 log structures—among them a molasses mill powered by mules—have been restored to reflect the hardscrabble life of the early mountaineers. More than 250,000 period furnishings and implements are found in the buildings, and there is a working farm. Locals sometimes bring their musical instruments for an old-time hoedown. *On TN 61, 1 mi east of I–75 Exit 122,* ☏ *615/494–7680.* ☛ *$6 adults, $5 senior citizens, $4 children 6–15; family rates available.* ☉ *Daily 8–5; summer hours vary.*

A 50-mile drive northeast of Norris along I–75, U.S. 25W, and TN 63 leads to **Harrogate,** by the Virginia border. Here, at **Lincoln Memorial University,** founded in 1896, the Great Emancipator's principles and philosophies prevail. **Lincoln Memorial Museum** contains the world's third-largest collection of Lincolniana. One of the most poignant exhibits is the ebony-and-silver cane Lincoln carried to Ford's Theatre. *On campus, off U.S. 25E,* ☏ *615/869–6237.* ☛ *$2 adults, $1.50 senior citizens, $1 children 6–12.* ☉ *Weekdays 9–4, Sat. 11–4, Sun. 1–4.*

From Harrogate, drive about 50 miles along U.S. 25E and 11W to **Rogersville** (Chamber of Commerce, 415 S. Depot, Rogersville 37857, ☏ 615/272–2186), a little hideaway East Tennessee town established in 1786. All of downtown is on the National Register of Historic Places, and it has both the oldest courthouse and inn in the state.

A 28-mile drive along U.S. 11W through rolling hills, meadows, and woodlands brings you to thriving **Kingsport,** founded in 1761. At **Exchange Place, Gaines-Preston Farm,** a restored pioneer homestead, craftspeople demonstrate their skills in commodious log houses. Their handmade quilts, baskets, wood carvings, ceramics, and stuffed dolls are sold in nearby shops. *4812 Orebank Rd.,* ☎ *615/288–6071.* ☛ *Free. Limited hours; call first.*

The Netherland Inn Historic House Museum, built in 1802, overlooking the Holston River, was for 150 years a stop on the Great Stage Road. Now restored as a museum, it features 1818 furnishings, a flatboat, a garden, and a log cabin with displays for children. *2144 Netherland Inn Rd.,* ☎ *615/247–3211.* ☛ *$3 adults, $1 students.* ☉ *May–Oct., Sat.–Mon. 2–4:30; or by appointment.*

Bays Mountain Park and Planetarium on Route 4 (853 Bays Mountain Park Rd., ☎ 615/229–9447) is a 3,000-acre sanctuary for native plants and animals, including a recently opened wolf habitat. Explore the 25 miles of hiking trails after a visit to the interpretive center. You can also take barge rides on the 44-acre lake.

Heading South

❻ A 21-mile drive southeast along U.S. 23 brings you to **Johnson City,** an important center for agriculture, manufacturing, and education—it is home to Washington College, the oldest institution of higher education in the state, and East Tennessee State University, with more than 9,000 students.

At Tipton-Haynes Historic Site, the 19th-century main house, granary, horse barn, and law office have been authentically restored. *4 mi south of U.S. 23, Exit 31, via University Pkwy. and S. Roan St.,* ☎ *615/926– 3631.* ☛ *$3 adults, $2 senior citizens, $1.50 students accompanied by adults.* ☉ *Apr.–Oct., weekdays 10–5, weekends 2–5; Nov.–Mar., weekdays 10–4:30.*

Rocky Mount, a two-story log mansion completed in 1772, was Governor William Blount's territorial capitol from 1790 until he moved to Knoxville two years later. Faithful restoration and careful selection of authentic furnishings testify to a simple yet eloquent pioneer lifestyle. Guides decked in period costumes take you through the kitchen, slave quarters, blacksmith shop, and a flax house where weaving is demonstrated. *4 mi northeast on U.S. 11E at Piney Flats, 200 Hyder Hill Rd.,* ☎ *615/538–7396.* ☛ *$5 adults, $2.50 students.* ☉ *Mon.–Sat. 10–5, Sun. 2–6. Closed Dec. 21–Jan. 5, weekends Jan.–Feb.*

❼ About 8 miles south via U.S. 11E/321, you'll drive into a veritable time warp: **Jonesborough,** the state's oldest town. Visitors admire a trio of antebellum churches, lovely vintage houses, brick and wooden fretwork shops, and the period Court House, all dating from the late 1700s. Of the many special events held here, the most famous is October's National Storytelling Festival, when professional and amateur storytellers from throughout the world come for a weekend to enchant visitors with tall tales. At the **Visitor Center and History Museum** (just off U.S. 11E on Boone St., ☎ 615/753–1010), a slide show and local art exhibit describe the town's history.

❽ After a 25-mile drive southwest along U.S. 11E/411, you'll come to the pleasant town of **Greeneville,** founded in 1783. Young Andrew Johnson settled here in 1826 after an arduous trek over the mountains from North Carolina, opened a tailor shop, and married. **Andrew Johnson National Historic Site** preserves his primitive tailor shop, the homestead where he lived from 1851 until his death in 1875, and his hilltop gravesite, marked by an elaborate monument. Displays in the visitor center include notes he made at his impeachment trial. *Depot and Col-*

lege Sts., ☎ 615/638–3551. ☛ To Homestead: $2 adults, children under 17 and senior citizens free. ⊙ Daily 9–5.

Sixty-one miles south via U.S. 411/321 and set in the narrow valley of the Little Pigeon River—actually a turbulent mountain stream—is **❾ Gatlinburg,** Tennessee's premier mountain resort town. With more than 400 specialty shops, it's also a browsing mecca. Family attractions include a number of local trout farms, the **Gatlinburg Sky Lift** (☎ 615/436–4307) to the top of Crockett Mountain, the **Guinness World Record Museum** (☎ 615/436–9100), and the **Ober Gatlinburg Tramway** (☎ 615/436–5423) to a mountaintop amusement park, ski center, and shopping mall/crafts market. **Arrowmont School of Arts & Crafts** (556 Parkway St., ☎ 615/436–5860) is a nationally known visual arts complex. The town is at the heart of numerous festivals, with the latest being Smoky Mountain Lights—when the town is decorated with more than 2 million lights from November to February. Call the **Gatlinburg Convention and Visitors Bureau** (☎ 800/822–1998) for more information.

★ ❿ At the **Great Smoky Mountains National Park** (107 Park Headquarters Rd., ☎ 615/436–1200), the southern Appalachians reach their ultimate grandeur as 16 peaks soar more than 6,000 feet. From Gatlinburg, the northern gateway to the park, drive south along the scenic Newfound Gap Road (U.S. 441) to the Sugarlands Visitor Center at park headquarters. Here are informative films, exhibits, maps, and brochures about the park. Driving along on the Newfound Gap Road, stop often at scenic overlooks, perhaps taking time to explore one or more of the nature trails that lead off from many of them. The road ascends to **Newfound Gap** on the Tennessee–North Carolina border, a haunting viewpoint. From here, a 7-mile spur road leads to **Clingmans Dome**—at 6,643 feet, the highest point in Tennessee—where you can walk up a spiral pathway to the top of an observation tower for panoramic views of the Smokies. Autumn is the favorite season for the spectacular foliage. *☎ 615/436–5615 for recorded information. ⊙ Apr.–May and Sept.–Oct., daily 8–6; June–Aug., daily 8–7; Nov.–Mar., daily 8–4:30. For the fall foliage hotline, ☎ 615/741–4862.*

From Gatlinburg, follow the crowds half a dozen miles or so along U.S. **⓫** 321/441 to **Pigeon Forge** (Visitor's Center, ☎ 615/453–8574 or 800/251–9100), where 200 outlet specialty stores, crafts shops, country hoedown emporiums, and kid-friendly attractions line the main thoroughfare for several miles. Among family favorites are **Magic World** and **Ogle's Water Park** (*see* What to See and Do with Children, *below*), and **Carbo's Smoky Mountain Police Museum** (☎ 615/453–1358).

A dinner theater, **Dixie Stampede** (☎ 615/453–4400 or 800/356–1676), offers a hearty chicken-and-ribs dinner March through December in a 1,000-seat arena; it's accompanied by a colorful, western-themed musical show and rodeo.

The 1830s-era **Old Mill** (☎ 615/453–4628; ⊙ Mon.–Sat. 8:30–6:30), beside the Little Pigeon River, still grinds corn, wheat, and rye on water-powered stone wheels. Here you can purchase flour, meal, grits, and buckwheat. Across the road is Pigeon Forge Pottery (*see* Shopping, *below*).

★ **Dollywood,** Dolly Parton's popular theme park, embodies the country superstar's own flamboyance—plenty of Hollywood flash mixed with simple country charm that you either love or hate. This endeavor brings to life the folklore, fun, food, and music of the Great Smokies, which inspired many of Parton's early songs. In a re-created 1880 mountain village, scores of talented and friendly craftspeople demonstrate their artistry. Museum exhibits trace Parton's rise to stardom from her backwoods upbringing. The many amusement rides include a thrilling river raft trip and "Thunder Express," a twisting, turning coaster ride through a dense backwoods setting. Of course, music is the park's underpinning: Live shows are performed on the park's seven stages. Throughout the season, some of the nation's best known entertainers lead a line-up of more than 200 performances in "Showcase of Stars." Occasionally Dolly shows up for a surprise appearance. The gala National Crafts Festival is a romp, in an old-fashioned harvest setting from late September to early November. When hunger strikes, try Aunt Fanny's Dixie Fixin's Restaurant for down-home mountain cookery. *1020 Dollywood La.,* ☎ *615/428–9488 or 800/365–5996.* ☛ *$22.10 adults, $15.45 children 4–11, under 3 free;* ☛ *Free next day on tickets purchased after 3.* ☉ *Last weekend Apr.–first weekend Nov., daily 9–6; extended hours mid-June–Labor Day and, rest of year, most weekends; closed Thurs. May, Sept., Oct.*

To the West

From Pigeon Forge, drive west on U.S. 321, a lovely scenic route, for about 20 miles to the junction of TN 73, which becomes Laurel Creek Road to the left, leading to **Cades Cove in the Great Smoky Mountains National Park.** This isolated mountain valley, with its 19th-century farmhouses, barns, churches, and an old gristmill still in operation, is one of the regions' best attractions. You can drive through on the loop road, but walking the grounds gives you a better feel for the area. From spring through autumn, special park ranger programs and demonstrations describe the pioneer agriculture, crafts, and folkways in the Cove. **The Visitor Center** (☎ 615/436–5615) has exhibits and provides information and literature. At the old gristmill (☉ Apr. 5–Oct., daily 9:30–5) you can take a tour and purchase stone-ground cornmeal that produces the feather-light cornbread found in country restaurants. For a deep-forest drive, take Parson Branch Road, a quiet, one-way trek out of the park to U.S. 129. The Foothills Parkway will get you back into the park.

Drive southwest for 54 miles along U.S. 321, U.S. 411, and TN 68 for a visit to the **Lost Sea,** outside Sweetwater, where you can explore a 4½-acre underground lake by glass-bottom boat. ☎ *615/337–6616.* ☛ *$7.50 adults, $3.75 children 6–12.* ☉ *Nov.–Feb., daily 9–5; Sept.–Oct., daily 9–6; Mar.–Apr., daily 9–6; May, June, and Aug., daily 9–7; July, 9–8.*

Continue on TN 68 to I–75; take this south for 70 miles to **Chattanooga,** a city that only 10 years ago ranked among the nation's worst in air pollution. Civic pride and unity (as well as a $850 million downtown revitalization effort) have transformed the ragged downtown area into one of the southeast's most vibrant communities. A rich Civil War history, a verdant mountainous countryside, and the presence of such unabashedly hokey, but popular, tourist attractions as Rock City and Ruby Falls, laid the promising foundation for the city's comeback. City leaders set forth an ambitious program in the mid-1980s to take back Chattanooga: Industry was told to shape up or ship out, and indeed, many factories left—the jobs they took with them were gradually replaced with more service-oriented positions. The 1996 summer Olympics in Atlanta, just two hours away, will undoubtedly continue to bolster Chattanooga's progress—the nearby Ocoee River is to host the canoe and kayaking events. A free downtown shuttle transports visitors between the Chattanooga Choo-Choo Hotel and the Tennessee Aquarium with stops at all points in between.

Numbers in the margin correspond with the numbered points of interest on the Chattanooga map.

★ ⑮ In 1992 the opening of the $45 million **Tennessee Aquarium,** the largest freshwater facility of its kind, capped the city's miraculous recovery, drawing more than a million visitors within its first six months. Chattanooga *is* river country, and this 130,000-square-foot monument to the Tennessee River tells the story. You'll see the 60-pound catfish that prowl the Tennessee and the small, mysterious fish inhabiting Japan's Shimanto River. This world-class aquarium lets visitors view the inhabitants behind glass in a spectacular 60-foot canyon with two living forests and 22 tanks. "Rivers of the World" presents for examination the flora and fauna of six freshwater rivers, from the St. Lawrence to the Zaire. You'll also walk inside a replica of a hardwood forest, explore several levels of the Tennessee River, and understand the formation of the Mississippi River. Designed by the Cambridge Seven Associates, who created Baltimore's National Aquarium, this contemporary riverside structure, crowned with four glass rooftop pyramids, looms oddly above Chattanooga's low, sprawling skyline. Expect a long wait during the summer months. Go in the late afternoon to avoid the crowds. *1 Broad St.,* ☎ *615/265–0695.* ☛ *$9.75 adults, $5.25 children.* ☉ *Daily 10–6, until 8 on summer weekends.*

Surrounding the aquarium is the new $10 million Ross's Landing Park and Plaza, a collaborative effort among world-class architects, artists, and landscape designers to provide an open-air retrospective of Chattanooga's long history as the starting point for the infamous Trail of Tears, the site of key Civil War battles, as well as its role as a major railroad town. A promenade connects Ross's Landing to the restored
⑯ **Walnut Street Bridge,** the longest pedestrian bridge in the world. In 1978, the bridge was closed to traffic, slated for eventual demolition. But a 15-year struggle to save the bridge by Chattanooga's tenacious preservationists culminated happily with its reopening, as a pedestrian bridge, on May 1, 1993. Thousands gathered to see the completely renovated structure, which, in 1991, was added to the National Register of Historic Places. Built in 1891, this 2,370-foot truss bridge eloquently spans the murky Tennessee River. Architect Garnet Chapin, who hails from Chattanooga and oversaw the restoration of the Statue of Liberty and Ellis Island, managed the project.

A couple of blocks east is the Bluffview Arts district. In a restored Classical Revival mansion overlooking the river, the **Hunter Museum of Art**
⑰ houses an eclectic collection of mostly American painting, photography, and sculpture. *10 Bluff View,* ☎ *615/267–0968. Donation: $5 adults, $2.50 children.* ☉ *Tues.–Sat. 10–4:30, Sun. 1–4:30.*

Along this block are a couple of interesting galleries and the **Houston Museum of Decorative Art,** a Victorian home packed to the rafters with American decorative arts. The emphasis is on glassware; of particular note are the museum's displays of blue Staffordshire and English lustreware china. *201 High St.,* ☎ *615/267–7176.* ☛ *$2.50 adults, $2.25 senior citizens and children.* ☉ *Tues.–Sat. 10–4, Sun. 1–4.*

⑱ Chattanooga's turn-of-the-century Terminal Station, a.k.a. the **Chattanooga Choo Choo** (1400 Market St., ☎ 615/266–5000), is now a **Holiday Inn** (*see* Lodging, *below*). Immortalized in Glenn Miller's song, it's one of the area's best-loved attractions. Stop by if only to see the elegant lobby, under its original 85-foot free-standing dome, which

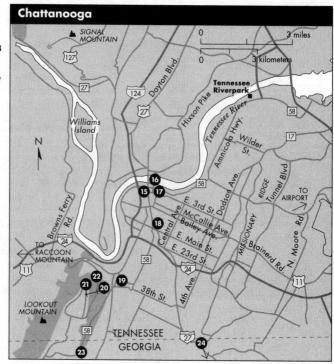

appears much as it did before trains stopped chugging into the terminal in 1973. The grand, light-drenched dining room is pretty; unfortunately, the food is the standard grub that gives hotels a bad name. Save your appetite, and explore the renovated train cars and a small but fascinating model railroad.

⑲ Continue south on Broad Street, bearing left onto Route 58. On your left you'll see the **Battles for Chattanooga Museum** (once called the **Confederama**), a kitschy dioramic rendering of Chattanooga's Civil War history. *3742 Tennessee Ave.,* ☎ *615/821–2812.* ☛ *$4 adults, $2 children 3–12.* ☉ *June–Labor Day, daily 8:30–8:30; Labor Day–May, daily 9–5.*

⑳ Just down the street is the **Incline Railway,** the steepest passenger railway in the world, at a grade of 72.7 degrees. The tracks appear to defy
★ gravity as they cut a swath straight up **Lookout Mountain.** The view is spectacular, but the faint of heart may opt to drive to the top instead. *827 E. Brow Rd., Lookout Mountain,* ☎ *615/821–4224.* ☛ *$6 adults, $3 children.* ☉ *Labor Day–Memorial Day, daily 8:30 AM–9:40 PM; trains run about every 15–20 min.*

㉑ Once there, you can walk around the neighborhood and admire Chattanooga's poshest homes, stop by a small museum and bookshop on Lookout Mountain's history, and walk through **Point Park,** a breezy, wooded promontory overlooking the region. A few markers relate the fact that one of the Civil War's most remarkable battles was fought in this area, with Confederate troops firing on Union soldiers attempting to scramble up the craggy mountainside. The subtle reminders of war are at odds with the dramatic beauty that surrounds this park.

㉒ From the top of the mountain, take Highway 148 down to **Ruby Falls,** which, in addition to nearby Rock City, is one of the area's most hyped attractions. There are two elements to these falls: Above ground is a restaurant, souvenir shops, lookout tower, and children's playground all predictably contained within one castlelike structure. Inside, an elevator whisks groups of visitors several hundred feet below to a natural cave that leads ½ mile to the deepest and highest underground waterfall (145 ft) in America. *Lookout Mountain Scenic Hwy.,* ☎ *615/821–2544.* ☛ *$7.50 adults, $3.50 children.* ☾ *Memorial Day–Labor Day, daily 8 AM–9 PM; Sept.–Oct. and Apr.–May, daily 8–8; Nov.–Mar., daily 8–6.*

At one time, more than 900 barns throughout the southeastern United States were emblazoned with the immortal words: "See Rock City." ★ **㉓** Only a few remain, but visitors still flock here year-round to **Rock City Gardens.** This craggy tribute to fairy tales and geology, just over the Tennessee state line in Georgia, was begun in 1932 as a small network of paths and trails. The garden's position high atop Lookout Mountain allows views for hundreds of miles. The project grew through the years, and hand-painted exhibits depicting the tales of Mother Goose and Little Red Riding Hood were added gradually. Walt Disney even consulted with Rock City's founders before designing his own magical kingdom. Of all the sites in the Lookout Mountain area, this one seems to offer the broadest appeal. *1400 Patten Rd., Lookout Mountain, GA,* ☎ *706/820–2531.* ☛ *$7.95 adults, $3.95 children.* ☾ *Daily 8:30–sunset.*

★ **㉔** **Chickamauga/Chattanooga National Military Park** documents the region's important role during the Civil War. The 1863 battles for Chattanooga were some of the most violent ever fought—and they were a major turning point in the war. At this battlefield, apart from taking advantage of miles of hiking trails and acres of scenic beauty, you can explore an extensive gun museum and watch an ingenious audiovisual presentation on the battles. *U.S. 27, Fort Oglethorpe, GA,* ☎ *706/866–9241.* ☛ *Free.* ☾ *Memorial Day–Labor Day, daily sunrise–sunset; rest of year, daily 8–4:45.*

Tennessee River

Numbers in the margin correspond to points of interest on the East Tennessee map.

㉕ A 36-mile drive north along U.S. 27 will bring you to **Dayton,** where the famous Scopes "Monkey Trial" was held in 1925. At the **Rhea County Courthouse,** the room where the trial took place has been preserved. There is also a small museum with displays about the trial. *1475 New Market St.,* ☎ *615/775–7801.* ☛ *Free.* ☾ *Mon.–Thurs. 8–4, Fri. 8–5:30.*

㉖ Sixty-two miles north along U.S. 27, I–40E, and TN 58 is **Oak Ridge,** the famous "atomic city," established secretly during World War II. Some of the original installations here include the **Oak Ridge National Laboratory,** still involved in programs of nuclear fission and magnetic fusion energy; the **Graphite Reactor,** 10 miles southwest, now a National Historic Landmark, with a display area open to the public; and the **K-25 Visitors Overlook** for views of the **Oak Ridge Gaseous Diffusion Plant,** where uranium is enriched for use in nuclear reactors.

The **American Museum of Science and Energy** focuses upon uses of nuclear, solar, and geothermal energy, mainly for peaceful purposes. Exhibits include hands-on experiments, demonstrations, and computer games. A slide show furnishes valuable background on Oak Ridge and the museum. *300 S. Tulane Ave.,* ☎ *615/576–3200.* ☛ *Free.* ⊙ *June–Aug., daily 9–6; Sept.–May, daily 9–5.*

What to See and Do with Children

American Museum of Science and Energy, Oak Ridge (*see* Tennessee River *in* Exploring, *above*).

Dollywood, Pigeon Forge (*see* Heading South *in* Exploring, *above*).

Knoxville Zoological Park (*see* Knoxville *in* Exploring, *above*).

Lost Sea, Sweetwater (*see* To the West *in* Exploring, *above*).

Magic World. This theme park centered on a magic show also offers rides and a haunted castle. *3034 Pkwy., Pigeon Forge,* ☎ *615/453–7941.* ☛ *$10.95, children under 3 free; season pass $15.95.* ⊙ *Apr.–Oct. Hours vary; call ahead.*

Ogle's Water Park. This is a family park with a giant wave pool, a kiddie play area, 10 water slides, and miniature golf. *2530 Pkwy., Pigeon Forge,* ☎ *615/453–8044.* ☛ *$13.12 adults, $12.02 children 4–11, under 4 free.* ⊙ *June–July, daily 10–8; Aug., daily 11–6; May and early Sept., weekends 11–6.*

Tennessee Valley Railroad. This is the largest historic railroad operating in the South. Children can ride the rails aboard a steam locomotive or diesel trains dating from World War II and explore the train museum. *4119 Cromwell Rd., Chattanooga,* ☎ *615/894–8028.* ☛ *$8 adults, $4 children 3–12.* ⊙ *May–Labor Day, Mon.–Sat. 10–5, Sun. noon–5; Apr., Sept.–Nov., Sat. 10–5.*

Tennessee Aquarium (*see* Chattanooga *in* Exploring, *above*).

Off the Beaten Path

Rhododendron Gardens. Atop 6,285-foot Roan Mountain on the border of Tennessee and North Carolina is the world's largest natural display of the multihued flowering shrub. Quiet pathways wend among the 600 acres of plants, which generally reach peak bloom in mid-June. So numerous are the varieties of plants and wildlife that naturalists from throughout the world come to observe and study. At nearby **Roan Mountain State Park,** there's a museum, a picnic area, a campground, a swimming pool, rental cabins, and a restaurant. *U.S. 19E to TN 143,* ☎ *615/772–3303.* ☛ *Free to garden and state park.*

Shopping

Crafts

The mountain towns of East Tennessee are known for Appalachian folk crafts, especially wood carvings, corn-husk dolls, pottery, dulcimers, and beautiful handmade quilts. These crafts can be found in shops throughout the state, but a major concentration of them is at the **Great Smoky Arts and Crafts Community,** a collection of 80 shops and craftsperson's studios along 8 miles of rambling country road. Begun in 1937, the community includes workers in leather, pottery, weaving, hand-wrought pewter, stained glass, quiltmaking, handcarving, marquetry, and more. Everything sold here is made on the premises by the community members. Also here are two restaurants and the popular Wild Plum Tearoom. *Off U.S. 321, 3 mi east of Gatlinburg,* ☎

615/430–5925. For more information, write Box 807, Gatlinburg 37738.

Other area shops selling mountain crafts are **Pigeon Forge Pottery** (2919 Middle Creek Rd., Pigeon Forge, ☎ 615/453–3883), where internationally esteemed tableware, vases, and bird and animal figurines are handmade and sold.

Iron Mountain Stoneware Plant. Hidden away in the northeastern corner of Tennessee and entirely surrounded by the Cherokee National Forest is the tiny village of Laurel Bloomery, the only place where the high-fired stoneware is made. It is also available through numerous retail outlets in the Appalachian Mountains. *TN 91, about 8 mi north of jct with U.S. 421,* ☎ *615/727–8888.* ☉ *Daily 8–5.*

Factory Outlets

Warehouse Row (12th and Market Sts., Chattanooga, ☎ 615/267–1111) yields some of the best buys in the region (*Woman's Day* named it one of the top five outlet malls in the nation). More than 45 shops, from Adrienne Vittadini to Perry Ellis to Van Heusen, are handsomely ensconced in several restored, redbrick buildings in the heart of the town's historic district.

Participant Sports

Canoeing and Rafting

The Ocoee River, site of the 1996 Olympic kayaking events, has very difficult, powerful rapids in the Class III and IV categories. **Cripple Creek Expeditions** (☎ 615/338–8441; Apr.–Oct.) offers canoe rentals and guided raft trips down the Ocoee's wild waters. The Sequatchie River is a gentler river suitable for year-round floating; try **Canoe the Sequatchie** (☎ 615/949–4400; Apr.–Oct.) for equipment. **Hiwassee Outfitters** in Reliance (☎ 615/338–8115; mid-Mar.–early Nov.) has canoes, rafts, tubes, and funyaks for beginners and intermediates; the nearby Hiwassee has occasional rapids. The mountain streams of the Smokies are exciting, too. **Rafting in the Smokies** in Gatlinburg (☎ 615/436–5008; Apr.–Oct.) offers guided white-water raft trips.

Fishing

At Norris Lake, there's seasonal angling for striped bass, walleye, white bass, and muskie, as well as boat launch ramps (but no rentals) at **Norris Dam State Resort Park** (125 Village Green Circle, Lake City, ☎ 615/426–7461). Other good spots for largemouth and white bass are Cherokee, Douglas, and Fort Loudon Lake. Trout lovers do best at Tellico-Chilhowee Lakes, especially at night in April and May. Fly fishing is popular in the Smokies' many streams.

Golf

East Tennessee courses open to the public include **Brainerd Golf Course** in Chattanooga (☎ 615/855–2692), **Whittle Springs Municipal Golf Course** in Knoxville (☎ 615/525–1022), **Bent Creek Mountain Inn and Country Club** in Gatlinburg (☎ 615/436–3947), **South Hills Golf Club** in Oak Ridge (☎ 615/483–5747), and **Warrior's Path State Park Golf Course** in Kingsport (☎ 615/323–4990).

Hiking

An unusually elevated and scenic portion of the **Appalachian Trail** runs along high ridges in the Great Smoky Mountains National Park.

The Trail can be easily reached at Newfound Gap from U.S. 441 (Gatlinburg, ☎ 615/436–5615).

Horseback Riding

McCarter's Riding Stables (Gatlinburg, ☎ 615/436–5354) arranges guided horseback riding in the Great Smoky Mountains National Park from March through October.

Skiing

Ober Gatlinburg Ski Resort (☎ 615/436–5423 or, Nov.–mid-Mar. only, 800/251–9202) can make its own snow. Its slopes on Mount Harrison—reached by double and quad chair lifts—are fun and the views are breathtaking.

Dining

Mountain cooks have long been noted for preparing fresh ingredients many different ways. Corn remains the old standby, used in the making of grits, luscious muffins, cornbread, and savory spoonbread. At historic water-powered gristmills you can stock up on flour and cornmeal ground between massive antique limestone wheels. The limestone residue blends with the flour and meal, adding nutrients and flavor.

Barbecued ribs, thick pork chops, and generous slices of country ham with red-eye gravy rank as local favorites. Freshwater fish, such as varieties of trout, walleye, crappie, muskie, and catfish, will also be found in varied and delicious preparations (but remember to save room for home-baked pies and cobblers). Dress is casual unless otherwise noted.

CATEGORY	COST*
$$$$	over $25
$$$	$15–$25
$$	$10–$15
$	under $10

per person for a three-course meal, excluding drinks, service, and 7.75% sales tax

Chattanooga

$$$–$$$$ **Southside Grill.** This downtown neighborhood restaurant reinterprets the food of the region with a gourmet touch. The restaurant has hardwood floors and dark panelled walls hung with fine art. Grilled portobello mushroom with lobster relish and creamy grits, and grilled ribeye with crawfish cakes and chilled leek soup, are just two of the many grilled selections. ✗ *1400 Cowart St.,* ☎ *615/266–9211. Reservations required. Jacket and tie. AE, D, DC, MC, V.*

$$–$$$ **212 Market.** This terrific restaurant near the Tennessee Aquarium
★ serves New American cuisine, with an emphasis on healthy fare; the Taylor River enchilada has fresh spinach, black beans, cheeses, and salsa, and the poached salmon is in a tart ginger-lime sauce. For an excellent starter, try the vegetable terrine, served with a sauce *verte* (a green concoction of parsley or basil). The cavernous, contemporary dining room is bright and unpretentious—food is served on colorful Fiestaware. ✗ *212 Market St.,* ☎ *615/265–1212. Reservations accepted. AE, MC, V. No dinner Sun.*

$ **Big River Grille & Brewing Works.** You can watch the brewing process through a soaring glass wall beside the bar of this restored trolley warehouse, handsomely appointed with high ceilings, exposed brick walls, and hardwood floors. Order the sampler for a taste of this new microbrewery's four different concoctions. The sandwiches and salads are generous and tasty. ✗ *222 Broad St.,* ☎ *615/267–2739. No reservations. AE, D, DC, MC, V.*

Gatlinburg

$$–$$$ **Burning Bush Restaurant.** Reproduction antique furnishings and ac-
★ cessories evoke a Colonial atmosphere; the menu is Continental. Broiled Tennessee quail and beef Rossini—an 8-ounce fillet served on an English muffin with Madeira sauce—are house specialties. Bountiful breakfasts are also featured. ✗ *1151 Parkway,* ☎ *615/436–4669. Reservations advised, especially on weekends. AE, D, MC, V.*

$$–$$$ **Smoky Mountain Trout House.** Of the eight distinctive trout preparations to choose from at this cozy restaurant, an old favorite is trout Eisenhower: pan-fried, using cornmeal breading and bacon flavorings, and served with bacon-and-butter sauce and a side dish of mushrooms. Prime rib, country ham, and fried chicken are also available. ✗ *410 N. Parkway,* ☎ *615/436–5416. No reservations. AE, DC, MC, V. No lunch. Closed Dec.–Mar.*

$ **Ogle's Restaurant.** Indulge in bountiful feasting, either in the green-
★ and-beige dining room or on the patio, which extends over a turbulent mountain river. The buffet tables offer five choices of country-style meat, such as fried chicken, prime rib, country ham; five vegetables fresh from the farm; and 70 fixins for your salad. Don't miss the sourwood honey. ✗ *516 Parkway,* ☎ *615/436–4157. No reservations. MC, V.*

$ **Pancake Pantry.** This is a family favorite of repeat guests to the Smokies. A house specialty is Austrian apple-walnut pancakes covered with apple cider compote, black walnuts, apple slices, sweet spices, powdered sugar, and whipped cream. Other selections include waffles, omelets, sandwiches, soups, and fresh salads. Century-old brick, polished-oak paneling, rustic copper accessories, and spacious windows create a delightful ambience. Box lunches are available for mountain picnics. ✗ *628 Parkway,* ☎ *615/436–4724. No reservations. No credit cards. No dinner.*

Knoxville

$$–$$$ **Regas Restaurant.** This cozy Knoxville classic, with fireplaces and
★ original art, has been around for 76 years. The specialty, prime rib, is carefully aged on the premises, baked very slowly all day, then sliced to order and served with creamy horseradish sauce. ✗ *318 N. Gay St.,* ☎ *615/637–9805. Reservations advised. AE, MC, V. No lunch Sat., no dinner Sun.*

$–$$$ **Copper Cellar/Cumberland Grill.** A favorite of the college crowd and young professionals, the original downstairs Copper Cellar has an intimate atmosphere with friendly service. Upstairs, the Cumberland Grill features aged Colorado beef, fresh seafood, salads, sandwiches, and award-winning desserts. There's a children's menu and a lavish Sunday brunch. ✗ *1807 Cumberland Ave., across from Univ. of Tenn. campus,* ☎ *615/673–3411. Reservations advised for downstairs. AE, D, DC, MC, V.*

$ **Calhoun's.** Serving delicious barbecued ribs in a riverside setting is a specialty at this sprawling rib-house across the street from the site of one of Knoxville's original hotspots, the long-gone Chisholm's Tavern of pioneer days. Calhoun's barbecued ribs are famous throughout the South, having taken more than one first-place cookoff ribbon. ✗ *400 Neyland Dr.,* ☎ *615/673–3355. No reservations. AE, D, DC, MC, V.*

Pigeon Forge

$ **Apple Tree Inn Restaurant.** A traditional East Tennessee menu is of-
★   fered here, including fried chicken and a special spoonbread: a regal
soufflé of cornmeal, flour, eggs, buttermilk, and seasonings, served hot
from the baking dish. Order family-style or individually in this very
relaxed dining room. ✗ *3215 Parkway,* ☎ *615/453–4961. No reservations. AE, MC, V. Closed Dec.–Feb.*

Lodging

Some restored historic hotels in larger cities offer lodging in settings
reminiscent of earlier times. The major resort areas of Gatlinburg and
Pigeon Forge have abundant choices. For reservations at hotels, motels, chalets, and condominiums throughout the area, contact **Smoky
Mountain Accommodations Reservation Service** (526 E. Parkway, Suite
1, Gatlinburg 37738, ☎ 615/436–9700 or 800/231–2230). For B&B
reservations, contact the **Tennessee Bed & Breakfast Innkeepers' Association** (Box 120428, Nashville 37212, ☎ 615/321–5482 or 800/820–
8144). In the categories below, the high-season summer and autumn
rates are given; these drop considerably at other times of the year.

CATEGORY	COST*
$$$$	over $100
$$$	$75–$100
$$	$50–$75
$	under $50

All prices are for a standard double room, excluding 11.75% tax

Chattanooga

$$–$$$ **Bluff View Inn.** This restored Colonial Revival mansion was built in
★   1928 on a bluff overlooking the Tennessee River. It's been painstakingly restored and tastefully decorated with 18th-century English antiques and art. Located on the new Riverwalk promenade, the River
Gallery Outdoor Sculpture Garden is beside the inn, and the Tennessee Aquarium is within easy walking distance. Some bedrooms
have fireplaces, and all have private baths and phones; a complimentary gourmet breakfast is made to order. ☎ *412 E. 2nd St., 37403,* ☎
615/265–5033, ☏ *615/265–5944. 7 rooms, 2 suites. Restaurant,
café. D, MC, V.*

$$–$$$ **Chattanooga Choo-Choo Holiday Inn.** This landmark hotel adjoins the
showcase 1905 Southern Railway Terminal, one of the first to be sal-
vaged in the South. It's been renewed with restaurants, lounges, shops,
exhibits, well-groomed gardens, and an operating trolley. Children delight in exploring the trains parked on the tracks. Guest rooms are nicely
appointed, especially the restored Victorian parlor cars—replete with
the heavy brocade and red upholstery ubiquitous in the late 1800s—
converted to overnight aeries. The parlor cars are big with honeymooners
and those who miss the time when train travel was the only way to
cross the country. ☎ *1400 Market St., 37402,* ☎ *615/266–5000 or
800/465–4329,* ☏ *615/265–4635. 303 rooms, 10 suites, 48 rail cars.
5 restaurants, lounge, indoor and outdoor pools, 2 hot tubs, 3 tennis
courts. AE, D, DC, MC, V.*

$$–$$$ **Marriott at the Convention Center.** This 16-floor convention hotel, the
town's largest, is clean, newly renovated, and convenient to such
downtown attractions as the Tennessee Aquarium and the tony Warehouse outlet shops. Rooms are spacious, and those on the higher floors
have a great view of either the Tennessee River or Lookout Mountain.
Adjacent to the city's convention center, this hotel is the choice of many

business travelers, but families will appreciate its baby-sitting service and well-appointed health club. ☎ *2 Carter Plaza, 37402,* ☎ *615/756–0002 or 800/841–1674,* FAX *615/266–2254. 327 rooms, 16 suites. 2 restaurants, 2 lounges, indoor and outdoor pools, health club, laundry service, airport shuttle. AE, D, DC, MC, V.*

$$–$$$ **Radisson Read House—A Plaza Hotel.** A traditional favorite in the mid-
★   South, the Georgian-style Read House dates from the 1920s and has been restored to the original grandeur that drew heads of state to lodge here in its heyday. The lobby, listed on the National Register of Historic Places, is highlighted by a large archway, stately columns, and highly polished walnut panels. Mailboxes from the days when guests stayed for months still neatly line one passageway. Formal portraits of soldiers from the Civil War add to the hotel's stately appeal and recall Chattanooga's military past. Guest rooms in the main hotel continue the Georgian motif; rooms in the annex are more contemporary. ☎ *827 Broad St., 37402,* ☎ *615/266–4121 or 800/333–3333,* FAX *615/267–6447. 140 rooms, 100 suites. Restaurant, coffee shop, dining room, lounge, pool, sauna, hot tub. AE, DC, MC, V.*

$ **Econo Lodge East Ridge.** Rooms are spacious, contemporary in style, clean, and well maintained. ☎ *1417 St. Thomas St., 37412,* ☎ *615/894–1417 or 800/446–6900. 89 rooms. Restaurant, pool. AE, D, DC, MC, V.*

Gatlinburg

$$$$ **Buckhorn Inn.** This small inn run by John and Connie Burns is set on
★   40 acres of remote woodlands about 6 miles outside Gatlinburg. Guests—including seclusion-seeking diplomats, government officials, and celebrities—have been coming here for more than 40 years. The views of Mt. LeConte and the Great Smokies are spectacular, and the Great Smoky Arts and Crafts Community is convenient to the inn. Inside, the country-inn atmosphere is reinforced by wicker rockers, paintings by local artists, a huge stone fireplace, and French doors that open onto a large stone porch. All rooms are spacious and some have king-size beds. Outstanding gourmet breakfasts and dinners are included in the rates; savor the home-baked breads, creamed soups, marinated beef tenderloin, and fruit tortes. A six-course gourmet dinner is available, too. ☎ *Off U.S. 321, 2140 Tudor Mountain Rd., 37738,* ☎ *615/436–4668. 6 rooms, 4 cottages with private bath. Restaurant, hiking, fishing. MC, V.*

$$$ **Holiday Inn Resort Complex.** The hotel is near the Convention Center
★   and the aerial tramway, which in winter whisks ski addicts to the snowy slopes at Ober Gatlinburg. The adjacent Holidome Indoor Recreation Center is attractive and cheerful, with lavish plantings, a pool, and a spacious atrium. ☎ *520 Airport Rd., 37738,* ☎ *615/436–9201 or 800/465–4329,* FAX *615/436–7974. 395 rooms, 7 suites. Coffee shop, dining room, lounge, 2 indoor pools, outdoor pool, hot tub, 2 saunas, putting green, nightclub, meeting rooms. AE, D, DC, MC, V.*

$$–$$$ **Best Western Twin Islands Motel.** In the center of Gatlinburg, beside the surging Little Pigeon River, this motel is notable for its low-key contemporary architectural style. All rooms have balconies overlooking the river. Kitchenette units are also available. ☎ *U.S. 441, Box 648, 37738,* ☎ *615/436–5121 or 800/223–9299,* FAX *615/436–6208. 97 rooms, 10 suites. Restaurant, pool, fishing, playground. AE, DC, MC, V.*

$$–$$$ **Park Vista Hotel.** This large hotel on a mountain ledge has modern, lavishly decorated public areas and large, elegantly appointed guest rooms, each with a balcony overlooking colorful gardens, the town of

Gatlinburg, the Little Pigeon River, and the mountains beyond. Nonetheless, this white, semicircular contemporary tower, though handsome, is a jarring sight in the Great Smoky Mountains. ⊞ *Airport Rd. at Cherokee Orchard Rd., Box 30, 37738,* ☎ *615/436–9211 or 800/421–7275,* ℻ *615/436–5141. 306 rooms, 6 suites. Restaurant, lounge, piano bar, indoor pool, wading pool, hot tub, 2 saunas, meeting rooms. AE, DC, MC, V.*

$$–$$$ **Rainbow Motel.** Here is a small, neat, well-maintained lodging, a pleasant choice for budget-minded vacationers. ⊞ *390 E. Parkway (3 blocks east of U.S. 441), Box 1397, 37738,* ☎ *615/436–5887 or 800/422–8922. 41 rooms, 1 efficiency, 2 2-bedroom units. Pool. D, MC, V.*

Knoxville

$$$$ **Hyatt Regency Knoxville.** This is a handsome, contemporary adapta-
★ tion of an Aztec pyramid atop a hill overlooking the Tennessee River, the city, and mountainous hinterlands. The eight-story sky-lit atrium lobby blends modern furnishings and art in Mesoamerican motifs with abundant flora and colorful accessories. Rooms, done in light woods and peach and blue pastels, have either windows or balconies that open to fresh breezes. ⊞ *500 Hill Ave. SE, Box 88, 37901,* ☎ *615/637–1234 or 800/233–1234,* ℻ *615/522–5911. 361 rooms, 26 suites. Coffee shop, dining room, sports bar, pool, exercise room, volleyball. AE, D, DC, MC, V.*

$$ **La Quinta Motor Inn.** Recently renovated, the rooms here are spacious and well lighted, with convenient working areas. ⊞ *258 Peters Rd. N, 37923,* ☎ *615/690–9777 or 800/531–5900,* ℻ *615/531–8304. 130 rooms. Pool. AE, D, DC, MC, V.*

Pigeon Forge

$$$ **Best Western Plaza Inn.** Within easy reach of shops, restaurants, and family attractions, the inn offers amenities for the entire family. Rooms are spacious and well furnished, and some have refrigerators; some overlook mountain scenery, others an indoor swimming pool. ⊞ *3755 Parkway, Box 926, 37868,* ☎ *615/453–5538 or 800/232–5656,* ℻ *615/453–2619. 198 rooms, 2 suites. 1 indoor and 2 outdoor pools, wading pool, 2 hot tubs, 2 saunas, recreation room. AE, DC, MC, V.*

$$$ **Grand Hotel.** Central and near major attractions, this five-story inn features some ultramodern rooms with water beds and fireplaces. There are even a few rooms with large whirlpool tubs. ⊞ *3171 Parkway, 37863,* ☎ *615/453–1000 or 800/362–1188,* ℻ *615/453–0056. 415 rooms, 10 suites. Restaurant, pool, hot tub. AE, DC, MC, V.*

$$$ **Holiday Inn.** This inn is in the middle of the action. Its vast Holidome Indoor Recreation Center features lush greenery and activities for the entire family. Especially pleasant rooms and extra services are available on the concierge floor. ⊞ *3230 Parkway, 37863,* ☎ *615/428–2700 or 800/782–3119,* ℻ *615/428–2700. 204 rooms, 4 suites. Restaurant, indoor pool, sauna, hot tub, health club. AE, DC, MC, V.*

The Arts

Concerts, Dance, and Opera

The **Knoxville Opera Company** (☎ 615/523–8712) sponsors New York Metropolitan Opera competitions each year, along with two locally produced operatic performances. The **Knoxville Symphony Orchestra** (☎ 615/523–1178) presents seven concerts a year, often with esteemed guest artists. **Lamar House Bijou Theater** in Knoxville (☎ 615/522–0832) offers seasonal ballet, concerts, and plays.

In Chattanooga, events at the **Tivoli Theater** (☎ 615/757–5042) include concerts and operas. Throughout the summer free concerts from blues to Irish bands play on **Miller Plaza** (☎ 615/265–0771).

Theater

Sweet Fanny Adams Theatre and Music Hall in Gatlinburg (☎ 615/436–4038) offers original musical comedies, Gay '90s revues, and old-fashioned sing-alongs. The **Music Mansion** (☎ 615/428–7469) features an electrifying country music variety show featuring Dollywood's award-winning James Rogers. The **Carousel Theatre,** at the University of Tennessee in Knoxville (☎ 615/974–5161), presents professional and student players at a theater-in-the-round.

In Chattanooga, the **Market Street Performance Hall** (☎ 615/267–2498), in a renovated trolley car barn, has great nightly entertainment. The **Chattanooga Little Theatre** (☎ 615/267–8534) stages 32 productions a year. The **Backstage Playhouse** (☎ 615/629–1565) is a weekend dinner theater.

Nightlife

Chattanooga

Try **Coyote's** (3617 Brainerd Rd., ☎ 615/698–5982) for everything from live blues to ballroom dancing, Wednesday–Sunday.

Gatlinburg

At Ober Gatlinburg's **Old Heidelberg Restaurant** (take the aerial tramway from downtown; ☎ 615/430–3094), there's dancing to DJ-selected rock and roll. The lounge at **Sade and Dora's** (☎ 615/436–9201) at the Holiday Inn Resort Complex features live entertainment and dancing. Spirits' Lounge at the **Edgewater Hotel** (☎ 615/436–4151) features live country and easy-listening.

Knoxville

The Old City, on the north side of downtown, is the site of Knoxville's most varied nightlife, with restaurants and clubs sharing space with the industries that have been in the warehouse district for decades. There is **Manhattan's** (☎ 615/525–4463) for music and honest bar food, **Amigo's** (☎ 615/546–9505) for authentic Tex-Mex, **Patrick Sullivan's** for saloon shenanigans (☎ 615/522–4511), and **Hooray's** (☎ 615/546–6729) for more of the same. Providing an exotic aromatic background are the smells of roasting coffee at the **JFG plant** around the corner. If it's quiet, Old World elegance you're after, try the lounge at the **Orangery Restaurant** (☎ 615/588–2964) in west Knoxville.

East Tennessee Essentials

Arriving and Departing, Getting Around

BY BUS

There are **Greyhound Bus Lines** (☎ 800/231–2222) stations in Chattanooga and Knoxville.

BY CAR

I–75 runs north–south from Kentucky through Knoxville, then to Chattanooga, where it enters Georgia. I–81 enters East Tennessee from Virginia at Bristol and continues southwest until it ends at the junction with I–40 northeast of Knoxville. I–40 enters from North Car-

olina, traces a northwesterly course to Knoxville, then heads west. U.S.
11 joins Chattanooga with Knoxville.

BY PLANE

Knoxville Airport (☎ 615/970–2773), 12 miles from downtown, is served
by American Eagle, ComAir, Delta, Northwest, Trans World Express,
United/United Express, and USAir.

The **Chattanooga Airport** (☎ 615/855–2200), 8 miles from downtown,
is served by American Eagle, ASA, ComAir, Delta, Northwest Airlink,
and USAir.

Guided Tours

In Knoxville, **Knoxville Tours, Inc.** (☎ 615/688–6232) offers local and
area tours, with pickup at Knoxville Quality Inn West, 7621 Kingston
Pike. **Smoky Mountain Tour Connection** (☎ 615/436–2108) in Gatlinburg has native guides for tours in the Smokies. Self-guided-tour maps
and brochures are available at many local visitor information centers.
In Pigeon Forge, **Smoky Mountain Tours and Pigeon River Bus Line** (☎
615/453–0864) offers guided tours to Cades Cove, Cherokee (NC),
Roaring Fork Motor Nature Trail, and out-of-the-way places in the
Great Smoky Mountains.

Important Addresses and Numbers

EMERGENCIES

Dial 911 for **police** and **ambulance** in an emergency. Medical assistance
is available in Chattanooga at **Erlanger Medical Center** (975 E. Third
St., ☎ 615/778–7000) and in Knoxville at **Baptist Hospital** (137 Blount
Ave., ☎ 615/632–5011).

PHARMACIES

In Chattanooga, try **Eckerds** (3532 Brainerd Rd., ☎ 615/629–7323).
The **Kroger Pharmacy** in Knoxville (2217 N. Broadway, ☎ 615/525–
4629) is open 24 hours.

RADIO STATIONS

FM: WDEF 92.3, contemporary easy listening; WUSY 101.7, country;
WIVK 107.7, country; WMYU 102.1, adult contemporary.

VISITOR INFORMATION

Chattanooga Area Convention and Visitors Bureau (2 Broad St. at
Ross's Landing, 37402, ☎ 615/756–8687, 800/322–3344 in TN) is
open daily 8:30–5:30. **Gatlinburg Convention and Visitors Bureau**
(Box 527, Gatlinburg 37738, ☎ 800/822–1998). **Knoxville Area Convention and Visitors Bureau** (810 Clinch Ave., Box 15012, Knoxville
37901, ☎ 615/523–7263 or 800/727–8045) is open weekdays 8:30–
5. **Northeast Tennessee Tourism Association** (Box 415, Jonesborough
37659, ☎ 615/753–4188) is open weekdays 8–5.

INDEX

Escape to ancient cities and

journey to *exotic islands with*

CNN Travel Guide, a wealth of valuable advice. Host

Valerie Voss will take you to

all of your favorite destinations,

including those off the beaten

path. Tune-in to your passport to the world.

CNN TRAVEL GUIDE
SATURDAY 12:30 PMet   SUNDAY 4:30 PMet

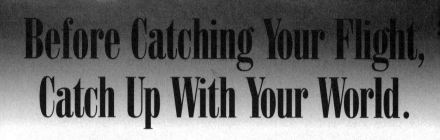

Before Catching Your Flight,
Catch Up With Your World.

Fueled by the global resources of CNN and available in major airports across America, CNN Airport Network provides a live source

of current domestic and international news,

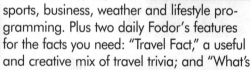

sports, business, weather and lifestyle programming. Plus two daily Fodor's features for the facts you need: "Travel Fact," a useful and creative mix of travel trivia; and "What's Happening," a comprehensive round-up of upcoming events in major cities around the world.

With CNN Airport Network, you'll never be out of the loop.

HERE'S YOUR OWN PERSONAL VIEW OF THE WORLD.

Here's the easiest way to get up-to-the-minute, objective, personalized information about what's going on in the city you'll be visiting—before you leave on your trip! Unique information you could get only if you knew someone personally in each of 160 destinations around the world. Everything from special places to dine to local events only a local would know about.

It's all yours—in your Travel Update from Worldview, the leading provider of time-sensitive destination information.

Review the following order form and fill it out by indicating your destination(s) and travel dates and by checking off up to eight interest categories. Then mail or fax your order form to us, or call your order in. (We're here to help you 24 hours a day.)

Within 48 hours of receiving your order, we'll mail your convenient, pocket-sized custom guide to you, packed with information to make your travel more fun and interesting. And if you're in a hurry, we can even fax it.

Have a great trip with your Fodor's Worldview Travel Update!

Fodor's WORLDVIEW TRAVEL UPDATE

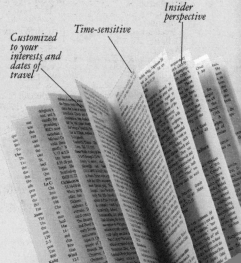

Customized to your interests and dates of travel

Time-sensitive

Insider perspective

DESTINATIONS

Worldview covers more than 160 destinations worldwide. Choose the destination(s) that match your itinerary from the list below:

Europe
Amsterdam
Athens
Barcelona
Berlin
Brussels
Budapest
Copenhagen
Dublin
Edinburgh
Florence
Frankfurt
French Riviera
Geneva
Glasgow
Lausanne
Lisbon
London
Madrid
Milan
Moscow
Munich
Oslo
Paris
Prague
Provence
Rome
Salzburg
Seville
St. Petersburg
Stockholm
Venice
Vienna
Zurich

United States (Mainland)
Albuquerque
Atlanta
Atlantic City
Baltimore
Boston
Branson, MO
Charleston, SC
Chicago
Cincinnati
Cleveland
Dallas/Ft. Worth
Denver
Detroit
Houston
Indianapolis
Kansas City
Las Vegas
Los Angeles
Memphis
Miami
Milwaukee
Minneapolis/St. Paul
Nashville
New Orleans
New York City
Orlando
Palm Springs
Philadelphia
Phoenix
Pittsburgh
Portland
Reno/Lake Tahoe
St. Louis
Salt Lake City
San Antonio
San Diego
San Francisco
Santa Fe
Seattle
Tampa
Washington, DC

Alaska
Alaskan Destinations

Hawaii
Honolulu
Island of Hawaii
Kauai
Maui

Canada
Quebec City
Montreal
Ottawa
Toronto
Vancouver

Bahamas
Abaco
Eleuthera/
  Harbour Island
Exuma
Freeport
Nassau &
  Paradise Island

Bermuda
Bermuda Countryside
Hamilton

British Leeward Islands
Anguilla
Antigua & Barbuda
St. Kitts & Nevis

British Virgin Islands
Tortola & Virgin
Gorda

British Windward Islands
Barbados
Dominica
Grenada
St. Lucia
St. Vincent
Trinidad & Tobago

Cayman Islands
The Caymans

Dominican Republic
Santo Domingo

Dutch Leeward Islands
Aruba
Bonaire
Curacao

Dutch Windward Island
St. Maarten/St. Martin

French West Indies
Guadeloupe
Martinique
St. Barthelemy

Jamaica
Kingston
Montego Bay
Negril
Ocho Rios

Puerto Rico
Ponce
San Juan

Turks & Caicos
Grand Turk/
  Providenciales

U.S. Virgin Islands
St. Croix
St. John
St. Thomas

Mexico
Acapulco
Cancun & Isla Mujeres
Cozumel
Guadalajara
Ixtapa & Zihuatanejo
Los Cabos
Mazatlan
Mexico City
Monterrey
Oaxaca
Puerto Vallarta

South/Central America
Buenos Aires
Caracas
Rio de Janeiro
San Jose, Costa Rica
Sao Paulo

Middle East
Istanbul
Jerusalem

Australia & New Zealand
Auckland
Melbourne
South Island
Sydney

China
Beijing
Guangzhou
Shanghai

Japan
Kyoto
Nagoya
Osaka
Tokyo
Yokohama

Pacific Rim/Other
Bali
Bangkok
Hong Kong & Macau
Manila
Seoul
Singapore
Taipei

INTERESTS

For your personalized Travel Update, choose the eight (8) categories you're most interested in from the following list:

1.	**Business Services**	Fax & Overnight Mail, Computer Rentals, Protocol, Secretarial, Messenger, Translation Services

Dining

2.	**All-Day Dining**	Breakfast & Brunch, Cafes & Tea Rooms, Late-Night Dining
3.	**Local Cuisine**	Every Price Range — from Budget Restaurants to the Special Splurge
4.	**European Cuisine**	Continental, French, Italian
5.	**Asian Cuisine**	Chinese, Far Eastern, Japanese, Other
6.	**Americas Cuisine**	American, Mexican & Latin
7.	**Nightlife**	Bars, Dance Clubs, Casinos, Comedy Clubs, Ethnic, Pubs & Beer Halls
8.	**Entertainment**	Theater – Comedy, Drama, Musicals, Dance, Ticket Agencies
9.	**Music**	Classical, Opera, Traditional & Ethnic, Jazz & Blues, Pop, Rock
10.	**Children's Activites**	Events, Attractions
11.	**Tours**	Local Tours, Day Trips, Overnight Excursions
12.	**Exhibitions, Festivals & Shows**	Antiques & Flower, History & Cultural, Art Exhibitions, Fairs & Craft Shows, Music & Art Festivals
13.	**Shopping**	Districts & Malls, Markets, Regional Specialties
14.	**Fitness**	Bicycling, Health Clubs, Hiking, Jogging
15.	**Recreational Sports**	Boating/Sailing, Fishing, Golf, Skiing, Snorkeling/Scuba, Tennis/Racket
16.	**Spectator Sports**	Auto Racing, Baseball, Basketball, Golf, Football, Horse Racing, Ice Hockey, Soccer
17.	**Event Highlights**	The best of what's happening during the dates of your trip.
18.	**Sightseeing**	Sights, Buildings, Monuments
19.	**Museums**	Art, Cultural
20.	**Transportation**	Taxis, Car Rentals, Airports, Public Transportation
21.	**General Info**	Overview, Holidays, Currency, Tourist Info

Please note that content will vary by season, destination, and length of stay.

Name

Address

City   **State**   **Country**   **ZIP**

Tel # (   )   -   **Fax #** (   )   -

Title of this Fodor's guide:

Store and location where guide was purchased:

INDICATE YOUR DESTINATIONS/DATES: You can order up to three (3) destinations from the previous page. Fill in your arrival and departure dates for each destination. **Your Travel Update itinerary (all destinations selected) cannot exceed 30 days from beginning to end.**

		Month	Day	Month	Day
(Sample) **LONDON**	From:	6 /	21	To: 6 /	30
1	From:	/		To:	/
2	From:	/		To:	/
3	From:	/		To:	/

CHOOSE YOUR INTERESTS: Select up to eight (8) categories from the list of interest categories shown on the previous page and circle the numbers below:

1 2 3 4 5 6 7 8 9 10 11 12 13 14 15 16 17 18 19 20 21

CHOOSE WHEN YOU WANT YOUR TRAVEL UPDATE DELIVERED (Check one):
❑ Please send my Travel Update immediately.
❑ Please hold my order until a few weeks before my trip to include the most up-to-date information.
Completed orders will be sent within 48 hours. Allow 7–10 days for U.S. mail delivery.

ADD UP YOUR ORDER HERE. SPECIAL OFFER FOR FODOR'S PURCHASERS ONLY!

	Suggested Retail Price	Your Price	This Order
First destination ordered	$ 9.95	$ 7.95	$ 7.95
Second destination (if applicable)	$ 6.95	$ 4.95	+
Third destination (if applicable)	$ 6.95	$ 4.95	+

DELIVERY CHARGE (Check one and enter amount below)

	Within U.S. & Canada	Outside U.S. & Canada
First Class Mail	❑ $2.50	❑ $5.00
FAX	❑ $5.00	❑ $10.00
Priority Delivery	❑ $15.00	❑ $27.00

ENTER DELIVERY CHARGE FROM ABOVE: +

TOTAL: $

METHOD OF PAYMENT IN U.S. FUNDS ONLY (Check one):
❑ AmEx ❑ MC ❑ Visa ❑ Discover ❑ Personal Check (U. S. & Canada only)
❑ Money Order/International Money Order

Make check or money order payable to: Fodor's Worldview Travel Update

Credit Card __/__/__/__/__/__/__/__/__/__/__/__/__/__/__/__/ **Expiration Date:** __/__

Authorized Signature

SEND THIS COMPLETED FORM WITH PAYMENT TO:
Fodor's Worldview Travel Update, 114 Sansome Street, Suite 700, San Francisco, CA 94104

OR CALL OR FAX US 24-HOURS A DAY.
Telephone **1-800-799-9609** • Fax **1-800-799-9619** (From within the U.S. & Canada)
(Outside the U.S. & Canada: Telephone 415-616-9988 • Fax 415-616-9989)

(Please have this guide in front of you when you call so we can verify purchase.)
Code: FTG   Offer valid until 12/31/97